Musical Theater
An Appreciation

Alyson McLamore
Cal Poly San Luis Obispo

PEARSON

Prentice
Hall

Upper Saddle River, NJ 07458

Library of Congress Cataloging-in-Publication Data

McLamore, Alyson
 Musical theater : an appreciation /Alyson McLamore.—1st ed.
  p. cm.
 Includes bibliographical references (p.) and index.
 ISBN 0-13-048583-7
 1. Musicals—United States—History and criticism. 2. Musical theater—History. I. Title.
ML2054.M35 2004
792.6'09—dc22

                                                    2004040075

for Terry —
who knows all the words

VP, Editorial Director: Charlyce Jones Owen
Executive Editor: Charles Cavaliere
Associate Editor: Emsal Hasan
Editorial Assistant: Shannon Corliss
Executive Marketing Manager: Heather Shelstaad
Marketing Assistant: Cherron Gardner
Managing Editor (Production): Joanne Riker
Production Editor: Jan H. Schwartz
Permissions Supervisor: Ron Fox
Permissions Research: Licensing Associates
Manufacturing Buyer: Tricia Kenny/Ben Smith
Cover Design: Bruce Kenselaar
Cover Illustration/Photo: © Rachel Royse/CORBIS
Photo Researcher: Kathy Ringrose
Image Permission Coordinator: Robert Farrell
Manager, Print Production: Prema Ramalingam
Composition: Integra
Printer/Binder: Phoenix Color Corporation

Credits and acknowledgments borrowed from other sources and reproduced, with permission, in this textbook appear on appropriate page within text.

Pearson Prentice Hall™ is a trademark of Pearson Education, Inc.
Pearson® is a registered trademark of Pearson plc
Prentice Hall® is a registered trademark of Pearson Education, Inc.

Pearson Education LTD.
Pearson Education Singapore, Pte. Ltd
Pearson Education, Canada, Ltd
Pearson Education—Japan

Pearson Education Australia PTY, Limited
Pearson Education North Asia Ltd
Pearson Educación de Mexico, S.A. de C.V.
Pearson Education Malaysia, Pte. Ltd

10 9 8 7 6 5 4 3 2 1
ISBN 0-13-048583-7

CONTENTS

Introduction vii

Acknowledgments viii

PART ONE   THE ANTECEDENTS TO THE GENRE
                      OF "MUSICAL THEATER" 1

1   **The Birth of "Staged" Music 1**
Sidebar: The Florentine Camerata, *Le nuove musiche*, and Opera **3**
Sidebar: Opera and the Castrati **3**
Musical Example 1: *The Coronation of Poppea*, Act I, Scenes 3 and 4 **4**

2   **Developing Genres in the Eighteenth Century: Ballad Opera and Singspiel 6**
Musical Example 2: *The Beggar's Opera*, Act I, Scene 1, "Our Polly Is a Sad Slut" **10**
Musical Example 3: *Bastien und Bastienne*, No. 10, "Diggi Daggi" **10**

3   **Developing Genres in the Eighteenth Century: Opera Buffa
and Dramma Giocoso 11**
Musical Example 4: *Don Giovanni*, Act I, Scene 2, "The Catalogue Aria" **14**

4   **The Musical Stage in the American Colonies 16**
Musical Example 5: *Tammany; or The Indian Chief*, "Alkmoonac" **18**

PART TWO   THE MUSICAL STAGE IN THE NINETEENTH CENTURY 19

5   **France and Spain in the Nineteenth Century 19**
Sidebar: Jacques Offenbach, the Mozart of the Champs-Élysées **22**
Musical Example 6: *Orphée aux enfers*, "Galop infernal" **23**

6   **The Serious and Not-so-Serious: Italy, Germany,
and Austria in the Nineteenth Century 24**
Sidebar: The Strauss Family and the Waltz **27**
Musical Example 7: *Die Fledermaus*, "The Watch Duet" **28**

7   **England in the Nineteenth Century: Gilbert and Sullivan 31**
Musical Example 8: *The Pirates of Penzance*, "I Am the Very Model of a Modern Major-General" **36**

8   **The United States in the Early Nineteenth Century 38**
Musical Example 9: "Camptown Races" **41**

9   **New American Genres of the Later Nineteenth Century 42**
Behind-the-Scenes: Buster Keaton in Vaudeville **47**
Musical Example 10: *The Black Crook*, "Amazons' March" **48**
Musical Example 11: *Evangeline*, "My Heart" **48**

10   **Operetta in America, 1880–1903 49**
Sidebar: The Wizard of Oz—1903 versus 1939 **51**
Behind-the-Scenes: The Integrity of the Score **52**

Musical Example 12: *Robin Hood,* "Brown October Ale" **53**
Musical Example 13: *Babes in Toyland,* "I Can't Do the Sum" **54**

PART THREE   DIVERGING PATHS IN THE TWENTIETH CENTURY   55

11   **The Continuing Dominance of Operetta 55**
Sidebar: Women in the Creative Credits **58**
Sidebar: Victor Herbert and ASCAP **59**
Musical Example 14: *Naughty Marietta,* "Italian Street Song" **60**

12   **Challenges to Operetta 61**
Sidebar: Tin Pan Alley **66**
Musical Example 15: *In Dahomey,* "(I Wants to Be) A Actor Lady" **67**
Musical Example 16: *Little Johnny Jones,* "Yankee Doodle Boy" **68**

13   **The Princess Shows 69**
Sidebar: Jerome Kern and a Musical Chain **73**
Sidebar: The "Princess Shows" **73**
Musical Example 17: *Leave It to Jane,* "Cleopatterer" **74**

14   **Increasing Drama on the Stage 75**
Musical Example 18: *Rose-Marie,* "Indian Love Call" **78**
Musical Example 19: *The Vagabond King,* "Song of the Vagabonds" **78**

15   **Musical Theater of the Lighter Kind 80**
Sidebar: Youmahs and Gershwin **80**
Musical Example 20: *No, No, Nanette,* "Tea for Two" **83**

PART FOUR   BEGINNINGS OF A GOLDEN AGE: SYNTHESIS OF STYLE AND SUBSTANCE   84

16   **Great Partnerships of the Early Book Musical: Kern and Hammerstein 84**
Behind-the-Scenes: Helen Morgan and Prohibition **88**
Musical Example 21: *Show Boat,* "Ol' Man River" **89**

17   **Great Partnerships of the Early Book Musical: Rodgers and Hart 90**
Sidebar: Musicals and the Classics **91**
Sidebar: The Great Mr. Abbott **92**
Musical Example 22: *On Your Toes,* "The Three B's" **95**

18   **Great Partnerships of the Early Book Musical: The Gershwins (1) 97**
Sidebar: All Jazzed Up—New Sounds on the Musical Stage **99**
Sidebar: The Role of the Book **102**

19   **Great Partnerships of the Early Book Musical: The Gershwins (2) 104**
Sidebar: Opera versus Musical—The *Porgy and Bess* Debate **105**

20   **Great Solo Acts: Irving Berlin 109**
Musical Example 23: *As Thousands Cheer,* "Supper Time" **113**

21   **Great Solo Acts: Cole Porter and Other Efforts in the 1930s 114**
Musical Example 24: *Anything Goes,* "Anything Goes" **117**

PART FIVE   A GREATER MATURITY   119

22   **New Achievements from Familiar Names: Rodgers and Hart, Irving Berlin 119**
Musical Example 25: *Pal Joey,* "Bewitched, Bothered, and Bewildered" **126**
Musical Example 26: *Annie Get Your Gun,* "Anything You Can Do" **127**

23 **A Cole Porter Renaissance and the Rise of Recognition 129**
Sidebar: Shakespeare on Broadway **130**
Musical Example 27: *Kiss Me, Kate,* "I Hate Men" **134**

24 **Politics and Social Commentary 136**
Musical Example 28: *The Threepenny Opera,* "The Ballad of Mack the Knife" **139**

PART SIX **NEW PARTNERSHIPS 140**

25 **Rodgers and Hammerstein: *Oklahoma!* 140**
Sidebar: The Rise of the Broadway Choreographer **141**
Behind-the-Scenes: Oscar Hammerstein Has the Last Word **143**
Musical Example 29: *Oklahoma!,* "The Surrey with the Fringe on Top" **145**

26 **Rodgers and Hammerstein: *Carousel* and *South Pacific* 146**
Musical Example 30: *Carousel,* "What's the Use of Wond'rin'?" **152**
Musical Example 31: *South Pacific,* "Bali Ha'i" **153**

27 **Rodgers and Hammerstein: *The King and I***
     and *The Sound of Music* 154
Sidebar: Rodgers and Hammerstein as a Legacy **158**
Behind-the-Scenes: Bessie Mae Sue Ella Yaeger **158**
Musical Example 32: *The King and I,* "Hello, Young Lovers" **160**
Musical Example 33: *The Sound of Music,* "Do-Re-Mi" **161**

28 **Lerner and Loewe 164**
Sidebar: The Functions of Dance **165**
Behind-the-Scenes: A Theatrical Façade? **168**
Musical Example 34: *Brigadoon,* "Almost Like Being in Love" **170**
Musical Example 35: *My Fair Lady,* "Just You Wait" **171**

PART SEVEN **NEW FACES OF THE 1940s AND 1950s 172**

29 **Leonard Bernstein 172**
Sidebar: The Role of the Theater Lyric **175**
Behind-the-Scenes: Getting Your Money's Worth **177**
Musical Example 36: *West Side Story,* "America" **178**
Musical Example 37: *West Side Story,* "Tonight (Quintet)" **179**

30 **Jule Styne and Frank Loesser 181**
Sidebar: The Role of the Overture **183**
Behind-the-Scenes: Think Before You Punch **186**
Musical Example 38: *Gypsy,* "Everything's Coming Up Roses" **188**
Musical Example 39: *Guys and Dolls,* "Fugue for Tinhorns" **188**

31 **Meredith Willson and Other Faces of the 1950s 190**
Musical Example 40: *The Music Man,* "Goodnight, My Someone" **196**
Musical Example 41: *Once Upon a Mattress,* "Shy" **196**

PART EIGHT **NEW FACES OF THE 1960s AND 1970s 198**

32 **New Names in Lights in the 1960s 198**
Musical Example 42: *1776,* "Momma, Look Sharp" **203**

33 **Sondheim in the 1960s: Flash in the Pan? 205**
Musical Example 43: *A Funny Thing Happened on the Way to the Forum,* "Comedy Tonight" **211**

34   **New Partnerships: Bock and Harnick 213**
Musical Example 44: *She Loves Me*, "A Trip to the Library" **217**
Musical Example 45: *Fiddler on the Roof*, "Do You Love Me" **218**

35   **New Partnerships: Kander and Ebb 219**
Musical Example 46: *Cabaret*, "Tomorrow Belongs to Me" **225**
Musical Example 47: *Chicago*, "The Cell Block Tango" **225**

36   **New Partnerships: Andrew Lloyd Webber and Tim Rice 228**
Musical Example 48: *Jesus Christ Superstar*, "Pilate's Dream" **234**
Musical Example 49: *Evita*, "Another Suitcase in Another Hall" **234**

37   **Wunderkinder of the 1970s 236**
Sidebar: Superstition and the Gypsy Robe **238**
Musical Example 50: *A Chorus Line*, "I Can Do That" **241**

38   **Sondheim in the 1970s: The Endless Experiments 242**
Behind-the-Scenes: Good Electronics Make Good Neighbors **247**
Musical Example 51: *Company*, "Getting Married Today" **249**
Musical Example 52: *Sweeney Todd*, "A Little Priest" **250**

PART NINE   **THE LATE TWENTIETH CENTURY AND BEYOND 253**

39   **Andrew Lloyd Webber without Tim Rice: *Cats* and *Starlight Express* 253**
Musical Example 53: *Cats*, "Mungojerrie and Rumpleteazer" **258**
Musical Example 54: *Starlight Express*, "Poppa's Blues" **258**

40   **The Luxuriant Lloyd Webber 260**
Sidebar: The Frank Rich Fan Club **264**
Musical Example 55: *The Phantom of the Opera*, "The Phantom of the Opera" **267**
Musical Example 56: *Sunset Boulevard*, "With One Look" **267**

41   **The New Team in Town: Schönberg and Boublil 269**
Musical Example 57: *Les Misérables*, "Castle on a Cloud" **276**
Musical Example 58: *Miss Saigon*, "I Still Believe" **276**

42   **Somewhat in the Shadows 277**
Sidebar: "If I Can Make It There . . . " **279**
Musical Example 59: *Chess*, "One Night in Bangkok" **283**

43   **Stephen Sondheim: Never a Formula 285**
Musical Example 60: *Into the Woods*, "Agony" **291**
Musical Example 61: *Assassins*, "The Ballad of Booth" **292**

44   **New Names of the 1990s and Beyond 295**
Musical Example 62: *Rent*, "Santa Fe" **300**

45   **Whither Musical Theater? 302**

Glossary 305

Index 315

INTRODUCTION

For many years, the process of cultural assimilation that took place in America (and elsewhere) was called a "melting pot." Although many sociologists now prefer a "salad bowl" metaphor, the melting pot remains a valid image for many musical products. Many artistic works have resulted from the synthesis of various ingredients. Jazz is certainly the best-known example, incorporating aspects of European art music with elements drawn from Africa and Latin America. Another fusion took place on the stage, when long-standing operatic traditions merged with various kinds of popular song and dance. One resulting mixture was the musical.

Because of jazz's origins in the speakeasies and brothels of New Orleans's red-light district, it took many years for it to shake loose its immoral reputation. Similarly, a musical is frequently condemned as "low-brow" thanks to the parts of its lineage that come from vaudeville, minstrel shows, and music hall antecedents. Nevertheless, musicals also hold fast to much of their operatic ancestry—and thus are valuable bridges to this more rarefied past for audiences unfamiliar with "high art" stage conventions.

The musical's reputation as a form of popular entertainment rather than as an elite manifestation of art music makes it a valuable tool in music education. Thanks to the proliferation of movie musicals, community theaters, and school productions, most people know what a musical *is*. Far more people have seen a performance of a musical than have ever attended an opera. This familiarity makes the musical an effective tool for illustrating musical elements, techniques, history, and artistic values.

This text therefore combines an overview of the development of the musical with an exposure to the vocabulary used to talk about and understand music in general. As in a music appreciation textbook, specific song excerpts function on several levels: they illustrate particular musical elements (tempo, form, texture, and so forth); they reflect individual artistry (of a composer, lyricist, librettist, and/or choreographer); and they demonstrate the *changes* in style and technique from one era to the next. Learning to understand the interaction of these multiple artistic considerations helps students to appreciate and value not only musicals, but also music as a whole.

ACKNOWLEDGMENTS

A book is never a solo endeavor, and this project is indebted to the assistance of many institutions and individuals. I appreciate the support of Cal Poly San Luis Obispo, which awarded me sabbatical release time to conduct much of the research for this text. I also appreciate the support of my colleagues in the Music Department, who had to cover my classes and committees; they are genuine troopers. I thank the British Library, the University of London Senate House Library, the New York Public Library, and Cal Poly's Kennedy Library for the use of their materials. Like many scholars working outside of urban areas, I am enormously indebted to the Interlibrary Loan system and to the California State University's Link + system; my thanks to all those who keep these invaluable tools functioning.

I appreciate the many guides at Prentice Hall who led me through the somewhat dark jungles of this undertaking, especially Chris Johnson, Evette Dickerson, and the ever-stalwart Jan Schwartz. I am also grateful to Kathleen Karcher of Licensing Associates for tackling the formidable permissions needed for this book, and to Kathy Ringrose for helping to find illustrations that are much richer than any thousand words.

It was astonishing to me that busy artists such as Stephen Sondheim and Sheldon Harnick could find the time to share their knowledge on behalf of this book. My thanks also go to Bert Fink and Amy Asch of the Rodgers and Hammerstein Organization for their careful scrutiny. Anyone who aspires to publish anything would be lucky to work with a person like Kara Darling, the Williamson Music publishing coordinator.

I appreciate the comments and suggestions of colleagues who have read (and in some cases, used) portions of this text: my thanks in particular to Clifton Swanson, Colleen Reardon, William T. Spiller, and Jennifer Judkins. Special thanks go to the reviewers who gave early support to this project: Dennis Davenport, Otterbein College; Candace Ellman, University of Colorado; George French, University of Minnesota; Paul Laird, University of Kansas; Michael Schwartzkopf, Indiana University; Charlotte Shields, College of St. Mary; and David Warner, Hagerstown Community College. My students, too, have helped shape the dimensions of this text with their questions and their curiosity.

My parents launched my own interest in musicals long, long ago by always buying the soundtracks; I thank them as well as the many friends who endured endless hours of musicals on the car stereo during road trips. Most of all, I am so very, very grateful to all the producers, directors, writers, performers, and stage crews of musical theater productions, who labor so hard to entertain and enrich us. Truly, this book is an expression of appreciation for their continual creativity.

The Antecedents to the Genre of "Musical Theater"

Part One

Chapter 1
The Birth of "Staged" Music

Where should we begin a study of musical theater?—with ancient Greek plays, medieval dramas, Renaissance *intermedi*? If we journeyed to Florence in the late sixteenth century, we would find two groups of people cultivating new ideas about music-making and their concepts can be traced forward through time to the modern musical. The first of these groups became known as the **Florentine Camerata**; like the second group, it was an assembly of artists, writers, and musicians. (See the *Sidebar*: The Florentine Camerata, *Le nuove musiche*, and Opera.) These Florentines advocated a simpler, more expressive approach to making music, and believed that they were reviving the singing and theatrical practices of the ancient Greeks. By applying this "new" singing style to contemporary dramas, the participants created **opera**. The birth of opera coincided with what many historians now call the **Baroque** period—an era beginning around 1600 and lasting until the early eighteenth century. The first of the Florentine operas was *Dafne*, although scholars disagree about the year of *Dafne*'s first performance; it may have been as early as 1594 or as late as 1598.

In 1600, operas began to be printed, and the impact of this new operatic approach quickly spread outside of Florence, where other composers soon tried their hands at this new **genre**. (Musicians use the French word genre to mean "category" or "type.") A **composer's** contribution to an opera is the **score**—the "music." The first operatic masterpiece, *L'Orfeo*, debuted in 1607 in the ducal palace in Mantua with a score by **Claudio Monteverdi** (1567–1643). The **librettist** (poet) Alessandro Striggio wrote the **libretto** (the opera's poetry or text), basing his story on the ancient Greek myth of Orpheus. Striggio's libretto related the sad tale: Orpheus's bride Eurydice dies after being bitten by a snake, so Orpheus (a wonderful singer) travels to the underworld to charm the gods into releasing her. The gods agree—but on the condition that Orpheus not look at Eurydice until they have returned to the living world. Alas! En route, Orpheus looks back at his wife, and thus she dies a second time. Although, according to legend, Orpheus starts to hate all women,

Striggio changed the ending so that Orpheus is taken to heaven and Eurydice's image appears in the stars.

Like theatergoers today, the Mantuans felt preperformance electricity before the debut of *L'Orfeo*. One man wrote to his brother in Rome, announcing, "Tomorrow evening the Most Serene Lord the Prince is to sponsor a performance. . . . It should be most unusual, as all the actors are to sing their parts." Monteverdi used a large **orchestra**—in this instance, some 40 instruments—to create distinctive **accompanimental** background sounds for different situations: He employed the

Claudio Monteverdi.
Bernardo Strozzi, (1581–1644) Claudio Monteverdi, composer (1567–1643), Oil on canvas/Landesmuseum Ferdinandeum, Innsbruck, Austria/©Photograph by Erich Lessing/ Art Resource, NY.

louder instruments (including trombones) for scenes set in the underworld, while quieter instruments usually supported Orpheus and his friends. A group of singers known as the **chorus** also appeared in many scenes.

L'Orfeo was not the first opera, but it was a masterful demonstration of the expressiveness that opera could achieve. Although **musical theater** might seem far removed from these early Baroque origins, *L'Orfeo* and its kindred works laid an important foundation. Not only did opera demonstrate that it was possible for audiences to suspend disbelief and allow actors to sing their roles, but it proved that a musical setting could intensify and enhance the emotional reactions evoked by the story.

From Florence, opera spread to a number of Italian cities; it was known as "the delight of princes," since early opera was the exclusive privilege of the nobility and the very wealthy. The powerful Barberini family built a private theater that could hold more than 3,000 people. The first opera in their new theater, *Sant' Alessio* (1632), included some unexpected comic scenes. Comedy had not played any part in the very earliest operas; Italians laughed instead at the antics of the **commedia dell'arte**—skits enacted by traveling troupes of actors portraying stock characters who behave in amusing ways. As humor found its way into opera plots, however, the popularity of the commedia dell'arte waned. Eventually the troupes vanished, but the storylines lived on. (A twentieth-century musical, *Pippin*, incorporated aspects of the old commedia dell'arte tradition in its costuming and, in part, in its antics.)

It was not long until operas began to spread outside the borders of Italy. Interestingly, one of the first Italian operas to be performed outside of Italy was composed by a woman, Francesca Caccini. She was the daughter of Giulio Caccini, a member of the original Florentine Camerata. Her opera, *La liberazione di Ruggiero dall'isola d'Alcina* (*Ruggiero's Liberation from the Island of Alcina*), had been written in 1625 to honor Prince Władisław of Poland; it was performed in Warsaw in 1628.

Another exciting change took place in Venice, where the first *public* **opera house** opened in 1637. Suddenly, a person did not have to be a guest of a wealthy aristocrat in order to hear opera; he or she needed only to have the price of a ticket. Soon, rival public **theaters** were built, and between 1637 and 1700, 388 operas were performed in Venice. During the 1680s, the Venetians—some 50,000 inhabitants—would support six opera troupes continuously. By the turn of the eighteenth century, opera houses were as common as movie theaters are today.

When wealthy aristocrats supported private operas, performances were often lavish. In Venice, however, public theater owners looked for ways to keep costs down. The size of the **cast**—the vocal performers—was reduced, with six or eight singers becoming the norm. (By eliminating the chorus, composers were leaving the Florentine Camerata's "ancient Greek" models far behind.) The orchestras grew smaller as well. Much of this economy was offset by the expense of **machinery** because the Venetians loved elaborate stage effects: Clouds or other objects transported the singers from location to location, storms were created on stage, and magical transformations took place. In one seventeenth-century

opera, a scene ends with a fountain mutating into an eagle and flying away. There are clear precedents for *The Phantom of the Opera*'s collapsing chandelier!

The music written for mid-seventeenth-century operas was changing; it was beginning to take on particular functions within the story. Monteverdi's last opera, **L'Incoronazione di Poppea** (**The Coronation of Poppea**), reflects how operatic style had evolved by 1642. Monteverdi had left Mantua and was now the choirmaster at the prestigious St. Mark's Cathedral in Venice. He composed several operas for the burgeoning Venetian opera houses, writing *The Coronation of Poppea* at the age of 75 (perhaps with some assistance).

The Coronation of Poppea is somewhat unusual, for the librettist **Giovanni Francesco Busenello** (1598–1659) based the plot on history rather than on myth (although Busenello did incorporate a healthy dose of mythical additions; see the **Plot Summary**). There is humor, such as the chattering guards who are trying to keep awake outside Poppea's house, and the "disguise" scene in which Ottone wears Drusilla's garments. Curiously, Nero and Poppea are clearly not virtuous characters who are worthy of the earthly rewards they receive. (A Roman historian tells us that Nero later kicked Poppea to death "in a fit of pique," but the opera stops short of that unsavory ending to the lovers' story.)

During "Tornerai" (**Musical Example 1**) in Act I, the **primo uomo** ("leading man") Nero is rather languorously saying goodbye to the **prima donna** ("leading woman") Poppea after a romantic night together. Interestingly, both roles were originally written for **sopranos**, since Monteverdi could draw upon the singing powers of **castrati**; see the *Sidebar*: Opera and the Castrati. The scene illustrates three kinds of singing, reflecting different kinds of dramatic needs. The opening of this scene (1) uses a singing style called **recitative**. Recitative imitates the rhythms (and speed) of speech in a fairly dry, businesslike way, without memorable melodies. In the background, a couple of instruments play **chords** (groups of **notes** or **pitches** played simultaneously) to support the singers during the recitative passages, so Nero and Poppea can sing through their lines as quickly or slowly as they wish. Recitative is often

Poppea (Marie Angel) caresses Nero (Nigel Robson) in *The Coronation of Poppea*.
Corbis/Bettmann.

Sidebar: The Florentine Camerata, *Le nuove musiche*, and Opera

Beginning around 1573, Count Giovanni Bardi di Vernio began to host gatherings of several Florentine scholars, poets, and artists, including Giulio Caccini and Vincenzo Galilei (father of the famous astronomer Galileo). The group became known as the **Florentine Camerata** because *camerata*—meaning "chamber" or "salon"—described the type of room in which the group assembled. Gradually, after corresponding with other people elsewhere in Italy, they conceived the idea for a new melodic style. The vocal music of the earlier sixteenth century had become very complicated, sometimes with several melodies occurring simultaneously; the words often were obscured and hard to understand. In the Camerata's new style, the melody imitated the rhythm of speech, and the accompaniment was designed to be simple and unobtrusive. The resulting **singing style** was called *stile rappresentativo* ("dramatic style") because of its expressive qualities. Using the new style, Caccini published a collection of short pieces in 1602, which he called *Le nuove musiche* ("the new music"); the phrase caught on quickly as a nickname for the Camerata's efforts.

Bardi left Florence in 1592, and another nobleman, Jacopo Corsi, established a similar group. Like the earlier Camerata, Corsi's group wanted to make vocal music more dramatic, modeling their efforts on what they knew (or thought they knew) of ancient Greek plays. When the technique of *stile rappresentativo* was applied to longer dramatic works, not just poems, **opera** was born.

---

used for dialogue and narrative portions within operas, since the quick pace can seem very lifelike.

In contrast, section **2**, labeled **arioso**, has some tuneful, melodic qualities. Arioso seems more like singing than speaking, while recitative seems more like speaking than singing. During this arioso passage, some words or phrases are repeated in a songlike fashion, and you may occasionally feel a slight background **pulse** in the **accompaniment** (the background musical support). Why does Nero switch to arioso singing at **2**? His dialogue is a bit more dramatic at this point; he's trying to prove his devotion by proclaiming—in a more flowery, arioso fashion—that he cannot live without her. Poppea is not too impressed by Nero's arioso declaration, and she persistently repeats the same question—"Tornerai?"—yet again at **3**.

Another distinctive singing style, labeled **aria**, appears in this excerpt at **5**. The aria stands in marked contrast to the previous recitative; the aria is *much* more tuneful and memorable, and the accompaniment is provided by the whole orchestra. Also, a steady background pulsation, or **beat**, has begun—it is easy to clap and even sing along as Poppea performs section **5**. Monteverdi uses this different singing style because the poetry of section **5** is different. In general, an aria is used to express a character's feelings; a composer tries to enhance the mood by using suitable **text expression** in the musical setting. A sad song might be set to a slow speed; an angry song might be particularly loud. Since Nero has just departed, Poppea is now singing to herself about her nervous excitement at the idea her schemes might work. The faster singing reflects her tension. Moreover, when Poppea reminds herself that she has the goddesses of Love and Fortune fighting on her behalf, the musical setting resembles a military fanfare.

Characterization—helping an audience to understand a character's personality—is also at work here. The first four times Poppea is heard in this scene, she persistently asks the same thing ("Will you return?"), a bit higher each time, until she at last gets Nero to promise that he *will* return (although she instantly responds by asking "when?"!). This repetition reveals her stubborn tenacity; she keeps asking until she gets her way. Nero, in contrast, has a changeable, almost neurotic nature—he is quick to rage and cruelty, and also quick to show Poppea generosity. His responses to Poppea reflect how he jumps from idea to idea (and from recitative to arioso). Characterization is an important technique for bringing the characters in an opera (or musical) "to life."

The singers also make occasional use of **ornamentation**. Ornamentation is the technique of "decorating" or embellishing the music. A common type of ornamentation is the **trill**, in which the singer wavers very rapidly between two pitches. The skillful use of ornamentation is a sign of a **virtuoso** (or, if the singer is female, a **virtuosa**)—a very adept (and usually star) performer. The performers playing the roles of Nero and Poppea often take the opportunity to embellish the repeated "Addio" in section **4**. Ornamentation has proven to be a bone of contention for composers and performers; composers feel that too much ornamentation overshadows the original melody and text, while singers want to seize every opportunity they can to show off their abilities. The battle continues.

Sidebar: Opera and the Castrati

There are thousands of compositions that call for instruments that have fallen into obscurity, such as the basset horn or the hurdy-gurdy. Many recent musicians have developed an interest in **performance practice**—the study of how earlier music was performed—and it is not uncommon now to hear concerts and recordings that feature "forgotten" instruments. Some singers have studied the vocal techniques of the past—but one area of vocal performance practice has been difficult to recreate, and that is the once-widespread use of high-pitched male singers known as **castrati**.

Castrati were produced by castrating boys before they reached puberty, so that they would not develop secondary sexual characteristics and would retain the high voices of their childhood, but coupled with adult strength. As an adult, a castrato voice would span the same range as an adult woman's voice, settling into either a **soprano** range

Continued

(a high-pitched woman's voice) or an **alto** range (a low-pitched woman's voice). For about 200 years, from the mid-sixteenth century to the mid-eighteenth, castrati were in great demand. The castrato voice was powerful and its higher range allowed it to ring out clearly over accompanying orchestras and other singers. Hundreds of opera roles were designed to be sung by castrati, such as the role of Nero in *The Coronation of Poppea*. The greatest castrati were able to command huge salaries and were treated much as rock stars are today.

For the Catholic church, however, a castrato presented a moral dilemma. The church forbade women singers in many chapels, and so castrati would sing the higher parts in choral compositions—but the process of castration rendered the boy infertile, and such procedures were against the teachings of the church. Gradually, demand dropped for this peculiar voice type, and in 1903, Pope Pius X banned castrati from the papal chapel; opera composers had long since stopped writing for the voice type.

The question remains: what to do with the roles that were designed for castrati? Opera directors generally choose one of three alternatives: they cast a woman in the role; they use a "countertenor" (a male singer who uses a **falsetto** voice, an artificial boylike sound that is not as powerful as the castrato voice); or they rewrite the castrato part for a **tenor** (the highest "normal" male voice). No solution is ideal—but all are considered preferable to forcing male singers to readopt the original practice!

FURTHER READING

Fenlon, Iain. *The Story of the Soul: Understanding* Poppea. Royal Musical Association Monographs, David Fallows, ed. No. 5. London: Royal Musical Association, 1992.

Sternfeld, F. W. *The Birth of Opera.* Oxford: Clarendon Press, 1993.

Whenham, John, ed. *Claudio Monteverdi*: Orfeo. Cambridge Opera Handbooks. Cambridge: Cambridge University Press, 1986.

PLOT SUMMARY: *THE CORONATION OF POPPEA*

Giovanni Francesco Busenello turned to the Roman historian Tacitus for the plot of *The Coronation of Poppea*, but the opera's opening "Prologue" is entirely imaginary. In the Heavens, the Goddesses of Virtue, Fortune, and Love are quarreling because Love claims to have the most power over mankind and history. The rest of the opera is, in a sense, the "proof" of Love's claim, for indeed virtue does *not* win in this tale. The virtuous characters—the Empress Ottavia, the wise advisor Seneca—are utterly defeated by the end, while the adulterous Emperor Nero and his mistress Poppea are triumphant throughout.

The story is set in Rome in A.D. 65, and Poppea's objective is clear: she wants to become Empress of Rome. She abandons her former lover Ottone and seduces Nero. As the dawn breaks, Poppea extracts a promise from Nero that he will return soon (see **Musical Example 1**). Poppea is almost giddy with excitement because her scheme is working so well, but her servant Amalta cautions her to be wary of the Empress. Indeed, Ottavia begs the gods for vengeance. Seneca counsels Ottavia to bear her misfortunes with dignity, and he also advises Nero to honor his wife rather than divorce her; Seneca's advice falls on deaf ears in both cases. Moreover, Nero, egged on by Poppea, orders Seneca's execution. Ottone seeks romantic consolation with Drusilla, yet the act ends with him still murmuring Poppea's name.

Act II begins with the god Mercury forewarning Seneca of his death sentence. Seneca's stoic acceptance of death stands in marked contrast to Nero and Poppea's gleeful celebration of Seneca's forced suicide. In the meantime, Ottavia orders Ottone to murder Poppea. Ottone, disguised in Drusilla's clothes, sneaks up on Poppea while she is napping in her garden—but the Goddess of Love intervenes, and Poppea awakens just in time to see "Drusilla" escaping.

The real Drusilla is arrested in Act III for the attempted murder; she makes a false confession in an effort to save Ottone. Ottone, conscience-smitten, then confesses that *he* made the murder attempt, dressed as Drusilla. Nero strips Ottone of his property and orders him into exile; Drusilla begs (and is allowed) to go with Ottone. Nero then directs his rage at Ottavia; she, too, must be banished. He orders that she be placed in a boat; she must go wherever the winds carry her. Ottavia sings a lovely lament as she prepares to leave her family and country, and the opera ends—as foretold in the title—with the coronation of Poppea.

MUSICAL EXAMPLE 1

THE CORONATION OF POPPEA
CLAUDIO MONTEVERDI/GIOVANNI FRANCESCO BUSENELLO, 1642
EXCERPT FROM ACT I, SCENES 3 AND 4

Recitative: (*text in italics is repeated*)

Poppea

1

Tornerai? Will you return?

Nero

Se ben io vò, *pur teco io stò* . . .   Though I am leaving you, *I am really staying* . . .

Poppea
Tornerai?   Will you return?

Nero
Il cor dalle tue stelle mai mai non si divelle . . .   My heart can never be torn away from your eyes . . .

Poppea
Tornerai?   Will you return?

Arioso:

Nero

2   *Io non posso da te*, viver disgiunto   *I cannot* live separated from you
Se non si smembra l'unita del punto . . .   Unless unity itself can be divided . . .

Recitative:

Poppea
3   Tornerai?   Will you return?

Nero
Tornerò.   I will return.

Poppea
Quando?   When?

Nero
Ben tosto.   Soon.

Poppea
Ben tosto, me'l prometti?   Very soon—you promise me?

Nero
Te'l giuro.   I swear it to you!

Poppea
E me l'osserverai?   *And will you keep your promise to me?*

Nero
E s'a te non verrò, tu a me verrai!   *If I do not come to you, you'll come to me!*

Poppea
4   Addio.   Farewell.

Nero
Addio.   Farewell.

Poppea
Nerone, Nerone, addio.   Nero, Nero, farewell.

Nero
Poppea, Poppea, addio.   Poppea, Poppea, farewell.

Poppea
Addio, Nerone, addio.   Farewell, Nero, farewell.

Nero
Addio, Poppea, ben mio.   Poppea, Poppea, my beloved. *(Nero exits)*

Aria:

Poppea (to herself)
5   Speranza, tu mi vai il core accarezzando;   O hope, you caress my heart;
Speranza, tu mi vai il genio lusingando;   *O hope, you* encourage my talents;
E mi circondi intanto   And meanwhile you drape around me
Di regio sì, ma immaginario manto.   A robe that is royal, yet remains imaginary.
No, no, non temo, di noia alcuna: *No, no, I will not be afraid* of any troubles:
Per me guerreggia, guerreggia,   *I have, fighting on my behalf,*
Amor, guerregia Amor e la Fortuna, e la Fortuna.   Fighting on my behalf, the gods of Love and Fortune!

Chapter 2
Developing Genres in the Eighteenth Century: Ballad Opera and Singspiel

Italian opera continued to be a dominant artistic force in Europe over the next 150 years, but it wasn't long until other European countries developed native versions of this new type of entertainment. Some of these eighteenth-century productions hold significant places in the twentieth-century musical theater's "family tree"; among these are the English **ballad opera** and the German (and Austrian) **Singspiel**.

Both the ballad opera and the Singspiel owe a debt to France. France had cultivated stage genres such as *opéra* and *comédie-ballet*, but the entertainment at various fairs was also important. The legal maneuvering to present these shows was almost as amusing as the entertainments themselves. Initially, the fairs featured dancing animals, but when humans began to replace the animals, the theaters viewed this as a threat to their monopoly and a court battle began. When the fairs were forbidden to present "any spectacle where there is dialogue," the fair players switched to a *monologue* format in which one actor spoke and the other actors responded by miming gestures. When forbidden to employ *any* speaking, the fair performers resorted to singing. Eventually, they were not allowed to make any sound at all, so they put the words of songs on placards and had the orchestra play the melodies so that the *audience* could sing. This resulting **opéra-comique** genre was remarkably popular. Two subtypes developed: the *pièces* (or *comédies*) *en vaudevilles* used well-known folk and popular songs, while the *pièces à ariettes* used Italian arias with French words. Gradually, spoken dialogue was used to link the songs together, resulting in a format almost identical to the English ballad opera that would follow.

Did **John Gay** (1685–1732)—the "father" of the ballad opera—ever see a production of a French *comédie en vaudeville*? Gay made two trips to France during the height of the French genre's popularity. Also, touring French companies brought productions to London in the 1720s, so it is hard to believe that Gay was completely unaware of the French innovation. In any event, in 1728, Gay revolutionized the English stage with his production of ***The Beggar's Opera***, a work in the new ballad opera genre: a play in English with spoken dialogue (instead of recitative) and songs that were created by putting new words to familiar (often anonymous) ballads. These **ballads** were simple songs in which the same tune was used for stanza after stanza.

England had already heard two of these elements—prose dialogue and new poetry sung to preexisting songs—in an older genre called the **masque**. A few English composers had then tried merging the masque with features of Italian opera (such as aria and recitative), resulting in works like Henry Purcell's *Dido and Aeneas* (c. 1689). Italian works, however, still dominated the English stage; some were imported and some were written by immigrants such as George Frideric Handel.

The Beggar's Opera capitalized on the audience's familiarity with Italian opera, and it parodied the foreign genre unmercifully. Moreover, *The Beggar's Opera* satirized the government, official corruption, fashionable morals, and many other features of English society—which was undoubtedly one of the reasons for its resounding success. At one point, when Peachum is reading through a list of criminals, he comes upon "Robin of Bagshot, alias Gorgon, alias Bluff Bob, alias Carbuncle, alias Bob Booty." To the audience, this was hilarious, for these were all nicknames for the current Prime Minister, Sir Robert Walpole. *The Beggar's Opera* also drew (sometimes uncomfortable) parallels between the poorest and richest classes. As the principles of the Age of Enlightenment swept Europe, the traditionally exalted—even divine—position of the aristocracy was questioned. Without a doubt, productions like *The Beggar's Opera* forced people to re-examine certain societal values.

The Beggar's Opera opened in 1728 in London; the theater manager, John Rich, had been reluctant to stage the work. Rich rejoiced, however, after *The Beggar's Opera* played a record-breaking 62 performances (the norm at the time was often a mere handful). Today, we would call such a successful show a **hit** (whereas an unsuccessful production is a **flop**). Not only was *The Beggar's Opera* said to have "made Gay rich and Rich gay," but it was also the most popular English production of the century.

As would be the case with some nineteenth-century works by Gilbert and Sullivan, and even with occasional twentieth-century shows like *Hello, Dolly!*, various "theme" presentations of *The Beggar's Opera* followed: Lilliputian companies, all-female productions, and "reversed gender" settings (men in women's roles and vice versa). The show traveled widely; the American colonies saw a production in 1750. This ballad opera appeared repeatedly over the next three centuries, often updated to mock contemporary society; a London adaptation in 2000 made reference to American gangsterism and fondness for guns. The story also inspired Kurt Weill's *The Threepenny Opera* (1933), a biting commentary on the rise of Nazism, which is examined in Chapter 24, "Politics and Social Commentary."

The somewhat unsavory characters who star in *The Beggar's Opera* (see the **Plot Summary**) were not entirely Gay's idea; he had been encouraged by his literary friends Alexander Pope and Jonathan Swift. Moreover, earlier English plays had featured characters drawn from the lowest orders of society—thieves, rogues, and highwaymen—while the notorious Newgate prison had also been featured in several previous stories. Although Gay wrote new poetry for *The Beggar's Opera*, most of the music comes from folk melodies; therefore, the composer is anonymous for most of the 69 songs. Only a few pieces have known composers, such as the "March" from Handel's opera *Rinaldo* (1711), used while Macheath's band of followers march away from the tavern in the second act.

Originally, Gay planned for the actors to sing the tunes without any accompaniment; musicians call this type of performance **monophony**. It doesn't matter how *many* singers or instrumentalists perform a melody at the same time; if they all sing the *same* melody simultaneously, then the texture is **monophonic**—such as when a group of friends sing "Happy Birthday" together. (We sometimes call this "singing in **unison**"—only "one sound" or melody is heard at any given moment.) It was suggested to Gay that the actors would sing more confidently *with* accompaniment, so Gay hired Johann Christoph Pepusch (a German composer then residing in London) to devise accompaniments for the songs and to write an **overture**. (An overture is an introductory piece of music for the orchestra alone; it generally sets the tone for the upcoming stage presentation and indicates to the audience that it's time to sit down and listen!) Since the songs now had accompaniment, Pepusch had changed the musical texture from monophony to **homophony**; **homophonic texture** describes music consisting of a melody partnered by some sort of subordinate accompaniment. (Although we generally think of accompaniment as being instrumental, such as when a singer is supported by a guitar, piano, or orchestra, it is possible that the accompaniment could be performed by other *voices*, such as the backup singers used in many popular recordings.) Homophony is the most prevalent texture used in vocal music, because the accompaniment helps singers to sing the correct pitches.

The score for Pepusch's overture still exists today, but the majority of his accompaniments for the songs have vanished; in most cases, we have only the words and a little of the music. Modern performers must make their own arrangements of the songs, speculating about the ways in which Pepusch might have arranged the music. This sort of modern arrangement is another form of performance practice, a concern that was introduced in Chapter 1.

Musical Example 2, "Our Polly Is a Sad Slut!," is the seventh tune heard in *The Beggar's Opera* and its original melody was "Oh, London Is a Fine Town." In this song, a modern arranger, Frederic Austin, has divided the text between Polly's parents. In Austin's arrangement, Mrs. Peachum sings the first half of the melody and Mr. Peachum sings the second half. At **2**, the melody is repeated, with new words; again, the two Peachums alternate. During **1** and **2**, a small orchestra accompanies them,

The Peachums argue with their daughter Polly in *The Beggar's Opera.*
Harvard Theatre Collection.

so their texture is homophonic. Austin made an interesting arranging choice at **3**; here, the Peachums sing the same tune yet again—but now they overlap each other, in the manner of a **canon**. In a canon, or **round**, multiple performers present the same melody—but each performer enters a few pulses *after* the previous performer has started, while the earlier performer is still singing or playing. (A well-known canon is "Row, Row, Row Your Boat"; a canon is also heard in the "Fugue for Tinhorns" in Chapter 30, "Jule Styne and Frank Loesser.") This treatment of a melody so that it overlaps with itself is called **imitative polyphony**. You may notice that the words are not as easy to understand during the polyphonic section, which is one reason why this texture is not used as much as homophony. Also notice that the song is *very* short, which demonstrates how it was possible for Gay to include 68 other tunes in the course of the show.

The Beggar's Opera was soon viewed as dangerous, even immoral. The Archbishop of Canterbury preached a sermon against it, while the head of London's police force begged Rich not to let the ballad opera play on Saturday nights, reasoning that Saturday was the "night off" for apprentices, and if they saw the show, they might be inspired to imitate the thievery. One of the targets of *The Beggar's Opera*, Prime Minister Walpole, avenged himself by persuading the Lord Chamberlain to forbid any performances of *Polly*, the sequel to *The Beggar's Opera*.

Despite these official and unofficial sanctions, Londoners heartily embraced this novel presentation, written in their native language, using tunes they knew well. A host of imitators quickly appeared, such as *The Quaker's Opera, The Cobler's Opera, The Beggar's Wedding, The Lover's Opera, The Sailor's Opera*, and so forth; none achieved the success of the original, but they demonstrated the great impact of *The Beggar's Opera*. The new genre of ballad opera lasted only about 50 years, but its influence on later approaches to musical theater has continued to the present day.

A fairly direct line of continuity can be drawn between ballad opera and **Singspiel**, a popular eighteenth-century genre in German-speaking lands. Like the English, German listeners liked the ballad opera's mixture of spoken dialogue with simple, unpretentious songs; they, too, were a bit tired of Italian opera. German composers soon began writing original works modeled on ballad operas, calling their version Singspiel (literally "sung-play"). Besides the language difference, a Singspiel differed from a ballad opera in that its score was usually newly written, rather than borrowing pre-existing folksongs.

In the 1750s and 1760s, German and Austrian composers produced a host of *Singspielen.* Young **Wolfgang Amadeus Mozart** (1756–1791), who traveled through Europe with his family, tried his hand at most musical genres he encountered. It was no wonder then, that in 1768, the 12-year-old Mozart was happy to accept a **commission** for a short Singspiel. (A commission is a promise to pay for a work before it has been created.) The commission came from Dr. Franz Anton Mesmer, whose name—in the form of the verb *mesmerize*—remains in the English language. Dr. Mesmer wanted young Mozart to set *Bastien und Bastienne*, a simple story of two estranged lovers (see the **Plot Summary**), which had originated with the philosopher Jean Jacques Rousseau. Satires of Rousseau's play soon appeared all over Europe; a friend of the Mozart family, **Johann Andreas Schachtner** (1731–1795), may have helped adapt a German version in preparation for Mozart's musical setting.

It is believed that *Bastien und Bastienne* was performed at Dr. Mesmer's estate in September or October of 1768. No comments survive about the audience's reaction, but the surviving score reveals that Mozart did an outstanding job of capturing the story's charm. **Musical Example 3**, "Diggi, Daggi," illustrates the young Mozart's compositional command in several ways. In this aria, the tenth vocal number of the Singspiel, Colas is accompanied by an orchestra, and so the texture is homophonic. However, the orchestra does contribute to the text expression: the rapid downward lines played at the opening (and when Colas starts to sing) might well represent lightning bolts—a suitably stormy backdrop for the casting of a magical spell.

Musicians often use the term **medium** (or sometimes **performance medium** or **performing forces**) to describe the performers needed for a particular work, and so the medium for "Diggi, Daggi" is voice and orchestra. Even more specifically, Colas's voice type is **bass,** the term for male singers who can reach the lowest pitches. To the eighteenth-century ear, still familiar with the high-pitched castrati, the bass voice seemed to have an inherently humorous quality. In Mozart's day, the bass voice simply "sounded funny"; it made people laugh. So, Mozart is consciously undermining the spooky effect of Colas's sorcery at the same time the orchestra is working to create an aural storm.

In the Musical Example, you'll see that the original text of "Diggi, Daggi" and the English translation are generally identical. This is because the words are just nonsense—along the lines of "hocus pocus"—to make Bastien believe that magic is happening. You'll also notice that the words of

Wolfgang Amadeus Mozart as a child.
Art Resource, New York.

section **1** are repeated at **2**. However, you'll hear that they are *not* sung to the same melody; Mozart has devised a very different tune for **2**. This differentiation gives us the sense that the aria has two halves, which we might label *a* and *b*. When a piece of music conveys a sense of distinct sections, we say it has **form**; in this case, we would call the form **binary** or **two-part** form. In a binary form, each half is different, and the melody of *a* is no longer heard once we have proceeded into the *b* portion of the song.

One aesthetic concern of late eighteenth-century music was the **principle of increasing animation**—in other words, as the piece progresses, the music starts to sound busier and busier and the notes start to follow each other more rapidly. The two sections of "Diggi, Daggi" illustrate this principle nicely: in **1** (or *a*), Colas sings each syllable clearly and distinctly, in a slow, measured manner. At **2** (the *b* section), as the excitement of the spell has intensified, Colas presents the same words much faster. In fact, you may feel that the **tempo**, or speed of the music, has increased. However, this is Mozart's aural equivalent to an optical illusion; if you clap the beat during section **1**, you will find that you can keep clapping at the *same* pace during **2**, and your clapped pulses will still coordinate with the melody. However, you may also find that you can clap twice as fast during **2** and still feel "coordinated" with the melody. This is because Mozart has squeezed twice as many notes into the same amount of time during the second half of the aria. The listener's perception, therefore, is that the tempo changes after the *a* section. At the start of the aria, Mozart indicates that the tempo should be **Andante** *maestoso* (a "majestic walking speed"); there is no change of tempo marking at the start of **2**, but because of the "aural illusion" of the increased animation, our ears might hear this *b* section as now being in an **allegro** (fast) tempo.

As you can perhaps tell from the translations of these tempo terms, the literal speed—by the clock—is subjective; one person's walking speed might be a bit faster or slower than the next person's. However, musicians usually agree on an appropriate "ballpark" speed for most of the common tempo labels. Even after the invention of the **metronome** in the nineteenth century (the clock-like pendulum device that "ticks" to give a performer a more objective measurement of musical speed), composers continued to use the traditional subjective tempo terms to add a certain nuance of feeling to their works.

Like a multilayered novel or film, Mozart's works often reveal more each time you listen to them. As your musical perceptions and vocabulary increase, you will hear even more in this not-so-simple work. In particular, you may want to compare the *b* portion of "Diggi, Daggi" to later examples of **patter song**, such as Gilbert and Sullivan's "I Am the Very Model of a Modern Major-General," heard in Chapter 7, "England in the Nineteenth Century," or Stephen Sondheim's "Getting Married Today" in Chapter 38, "Sondheim in the 1970s." In a patter song, the singer presents the words almost as quickly as humanly possible, usually for comic effect. The 12-year-old Mozart demonstrates that many of the catchy or impressive features of present-day "musicals" were already part of his personal bag of compositional tricks more than 200 years ago. Although he would try his hand at many of the other stage genres of the Classic period, he would return to Singspiel in 1791 to write his masterpiece in that genre, *The Magic Flute.*

FURTHER READING

Fiske, Roger. *English Theatre Music in the Eighteenth Century.* London: Oxford University Press, 1973.

Gagey, Edmond McAdoo. *Ballad Opera.* New York: Columbia University Press, 1937. Reissued 1965 by Benjamin Blom, Inc.

Gutman, Robert W. *Mozart: A Cultural Biography.* San Diego: Harcourt, 1999.

Osborne, Charles. *The Complete Operas of Mozart.* New York: Da Capo, 1978.

Schultz, William Eben. *Gay's* Beggar's Opera: *Its Content, History and Influence.* New York: Russell & Russell, 1967.

PLOT SUMMARY: *THE BEGGAR'S OPERA*

Like a good farce, the plot of *The Beggar's Opera* is a mass of threads that intertwine, forming at last the rope by which the master criminal Captain Macheath is (almost) hanged. Macheath is a receiver of stolen property (a "fence"). Before the story opens, he has secretly wed Polly Peachum. Mr. and Mrs. Peachum, two thieves, are irate when they discover the surreptitious marriage—for they had groomed

and polished their daughter to become the mistress of a wealthy and influential patron. By marrying, Polly has thwarted her parents' hopes for her career as a successful prostitute! "Our Polly Is a Sad Slut!" (**Musical Example 2**) is the scene in which Polly's parents berate her for her foolishness. (In one of Gay's "digs" at high society, he has Mrs. Peachum tell her daughter in exasperation, "Why, thou foolish jade, thou wilt be as ill us'd [used], and as much neglected, as if thou hadst married a Lord"—implying that aristocrats were no strangers to spousal abuse.) Mr. Peachum worries that Macheath knows too much about the Peachums and might betray his father-in-law for financial gain. Soon, Mr. and Mrs. Peachum hit upon the perfect solution: Polly should turn Macheath in to the authorities, thus earning the reward for *his* arrest—but instead Polly warns Macheath about his danger.

In the second act, opening in a tavern, Macheath tells his gang that he must lie low for a while—and then he begins to entertain a group of "women of the town" (prostitutes) who have arrived at the tavern. One of the "ladies" signals the constables, who enter to arrest Macheath. The next scene is set in Newgate prison, run by the jailer Lockit, where Lockit and Peachum are arguing about reward payments. Soon, the jailer's pregnant daughter Lucy enters Macheath's jail cell; Macheath is the father of her child. Lucy is understandably outraged to hear that he has married Polly—and is even more irate when Polly arrives at the jail to visit her husband. A violent quarrel ensues, mimicking a famous real-life argument between two operatic sopranos that had taken place on stage some years earlier. After Polly is dragged away by her father, Macheath manages to calm Lucy down by claiming that Polly has invented the marriage. When Macheath promises to marry Lucy, she helps him escape.

Macheath is not free for long in the third act; Lockit and Peachum find out where Macheath is hiding. Meanwhile, Polly visits Lucy in order to apologize and Lucy presents Polly with a glass of poisoned wine. Before Polly can sip from the glass, however, she drops it in horror upon seeing Macheath enter in chains, having been recaptured. Both women plead with their fathers for mercy toward Macheath, but to no avail: Macheath is carried off to trial and is sentenced to hang. But before he goes to the gallows, a Beggar and a Player appear. The Player exclaims that the Beggar (ostensibly the author of this story) can't allow Macheath to die, since that would be a tragic finish, and operas are supposed to end happily. The Beggar agrees to change the ending, illogical as such a last-minute reprieve might be, and at last Macheath admits that his marriage to Polly was entirely legal.

PLOT SUMMARY: *BASTIEN UND BASTIENNE*

Although only three cast members are required for this short pastoral tale, they are more than sufficient to reveal quite a bit about human nature. The one-act story begins with an unhappy shepherdess, Bastienne, who laments that the shepherd Bastien no longer loves her. Bastien has been beguiled by a noblewoman from the nearby palace. Bastienne asks Colas, the village wise man, for help. Colas tells her that in order to win Bastien back, she must pretend that *she* no longer cares for *him*. Bastien soon believes that Bastienne has found someone else to love, and he in turn begs Colas for help; Colas utters the magic spell "Diggi, Daggi" (**Musical Example 3**). Bastien is overjoyed at having his shepherdess returned to him, but is stunned to find that not only does she still not seem to care for him, but also she seems not even to recognize him. At last he convinces her that he has no interest in other women and she relents; they are happily reunited and they end by praising Colas and his "magic."

MUSICAL EXAMPLE 2

THE BEGGAR'S OPERA
(ARRANGED BY JOHANN CHRISTOPH PEPUSCH)/JOHN GAY, 1728
"Our Polly Is a Sad Slut!"
ACT I, SCENE 1

Mrs. Peachum

1   Our Polly is a sad Slut! Nor heeds what we have taught her.

Mr. Peachum

I wonder any Man alive will ever rear a Daughter!

Mrs. Peachum

2   For she must have both Hoods and Gowns, and Hoops to swell her Pride,

Mr. Peachum

With Scarfs and Stays, and Gloves and Lace; and she will have Men beside;

	Mr. Peachum	**Mrs. Peachum**
3	And when she's drest	And when she's drest
	with Care and Cost,	with Care and Cost,
	all tempting, fine and gay,	all tempting, fine and gay,
	As Men should serve a Cucumber,	As Men should serve a Cucumber,
	she flings herself away.	she flings herself away.

MUSICAL EXAMPLE 3

BASTIEN UND BASTIENNE
WOLFGANG AMADEUS MOZART/JOHANN ANDREAS SCHACHTNER? (K6. 46b), 1768
No. 10: "Diggi, Daggi"

Colas

1	Diggi, daggi, schurry, murry,	Diggi, daggi, schurry, murry,
	horum, harum, lirum, larum,	horum, harum, lirum, larum,
	raudi, maudi, giri, gari, posito,	raudi, maudi, giri, gari, posito,
	besti, basti, saron froh,	besti, basti, saron froh,
	fatto, matto, quid pro quo.	fatto, matto, this for that.
2	Diggi, daggi, schurry, murry,	Diggi, daggi, schurry, murry,
	horum, harum, lirum, larum,	horum, harum, lirum, larum,
	raudi, maudi, giri, gari, posito,	raudi, maudi, giri, gari, posito,
	besti, basti, saron froh,	besti, basti, saron froh,
	fatto, matto, quid pro quo.	fatto, matto, this for that.

Bastien

Ah, ist die Hexerei zu Ende?   Ah, has your spell come to an end?

Colas

Ja, tritt nur näher! Tröste dich   Yes, come closer! Take comfort in this:
du wirst deine Schäferin wieder sehen.   You will see your shepherdess again.

Chapter 3
Developing Genres in the Eighteenth Century: Opera Buffa and Dramma Giocoso

Italian opera changed quite a bit during Monteverdi's lifetime and it continued to evolve as the seventeenth and eighteenth centuries progressed. Many operas eliminated comic scenes, believing that they were detrimental to the majestic and heroic qualities that could be expressed in a well-written opera. The resulting genre was called **opera seria** (serious opera). For much of the eighteenth century, opera seria—with its emphasis on vocal virtuosity—was the queen of the Italian genres.

Like a stubborn weed, however, humor was impossible to abolish from the Italian musical stage completely. One manifestation was in a genre called the **intermezzo**. An intermezzo was a comic interlude presented between the acts of an opera seria. In time, the comic episodes began to have a connected storyline. The effect was of two alternating plots—the opera seria story and the comic intermezzo story—and the intermezzi occasionally surpassed the serious operas in popularity. It was not long before some intermezzi "broke free" and were performed independently. The term **opera buffa** (comic opera) was soon coined to distinguish them from their serious counterparts.

One Neapolitan intermezzo eventually became an enormous hit; this was Giovanni Battista Pergolesi's *La serva padrona (The Maid as Mistress)* of 1733. It uses a tiny cast of three characters (only two of whom sing). In order to escape his bossy maid Serpina, the old bachelor Uberto decides to take a bride—but is at last tricked into marrying (not *too* unwillingly) Serpina herself. As in many artworks of the Age of Enlightenment, "real" people—not gods or noblemen—were the characters. The music is lively and engaging, and Pergolesi set Uberto as a bass voice with the same comic effect that Mozart later cultivated in *Bastien und Bastienne*.

La serva padrona did not make too large a splash until an Italian touring company presented it in Paris in 1752, sparking a debate known as the **Querelle des Bouffons ("The War of the Buffoons")**. This argument pitted supporters of traditional French opera (similar in its lofty character to opera seria) against the fans of the new Italian opera buffa. Although there was never any real chance that the French would abandon their national style and switch to creating comic works in Italian, the debate was valuable because it articulated the merits of both approaches.

As Italian opera divided into separate strands of *seria* and *buffa* in the early eighteenth century, it paralleled—and perhaps influenced—other changes in music. We now describe these changes as a transition from the Baroque era to the **Classic** period. Baroque works tended to sustain a single emotional mood throughout a composition. In Classical works, emotions *could* change in the course of a piece. The music could reflect the character's shifting moods, perhaps by varying the **dynamic level**—the volume. Also, as orchestras grew in size, composers could draw upon a bigger variety of **timbres** to alter the emotional atmosphere. (Timbre, or **tone color**, is the distinct sound that each voice and instrument has—allowing us to tell, with our eyes closed, whether a trumpet or a flute is playing.)

Armed with these changes—variable emotions, more flexibility in dynamics, a greater number of available instruments—Classical opera composers had many ways to make their music expressive. Twelve-year-old Mozart had already shown his capability in *Bastien und Bastienne*; he continued to make his mark as an adult, especially in opera buffa and a hybrid genre, *dramma giocoso*. This term seems to have originated with the playwright Carlo Goldoni. Around 1750, Goldoni began combining serious roles, such as a pair of noble lovers, with comic servants, peasants, and so forth. Sometimes, he wrote parts that fell between the two extremes; these roles were half-serious, half-comic. Goldoni called the resultant genre *dramma giocoso*, or "lighthearted drama"; historian Daniel Heartz suggests "a frolic with serious elements" as a possible paraphrase.

Mozart's only work in the *dramma giocoso* genre was **Don Giovanni** of 1787; its full title is *Il dissoluto punito, ossia Il Don Giovanni (The Dissolute One Punished, or Don Juan)*. Mozart's librettist was **Lorenzo da Ponte** (1749–1838), and this was their second collaboration after triumphing in 1786 with an opera buffa titled *The Marriage of Figaro*. The National Theater in Prague commissioned the work (after a successful production of *Figaro*). For the plot, da Ponte turned to the notorious Don Juan legend (see the **Plot Summary**). Mozart wrote *Don Giovanni* during a difficult period; his father died and his finances were growing exceedingly precarious. Mozart did not finish the overture until the last minute, so the orchestra had to **sight-read**—perform with no rehearsal—the overture at the premiere.

Fortunately, *Don Giovanni* was very well received in Prague, thanks in large part to Mozart's score. Mozart used music to help distinguish each of his three sopranos. He gave a serious part to Donna Anna, who sings in dramatic, virtuosic fashion. At the other end of the spectrum is the servant Zerlina, a comic character. Donna Elvira plays a mixed role: We pity her for believing the Don's lies, but her pursuit of him becomes almost comical in its single-mindedness (and it's not entirely clear—probably even to her—if she would kill him or embrace him if she ever caught up with him again). Don Giovanni is also a mixed role his voice type is **baritone**, which falls halfway between the tenor and the bass voices. His voice type hints that Don Giovanni can mix with people of either station in life. (Don Ottavio is a serious role—but he is cast as a tenor, not a male soprano; the fad for castrati had lost its grip by 1787.)

Although there are magical aspects to the story (such as the "living" statue), *Don Giovanni* seems realistic in several regards. It is rare in *Don Giovanni* for characters to stand and sing their thoughts aloud, in the manner of a **soliloquy**; instead, nearly all the singing communicates with other characters. In **Musical Example 4**—known as the "Catalogue Aria"—Leporello horrifies Donna Elvira with a detailed list of the Don's sexual conquests. For the audience, the "Catalogue Aria" grows funnier and funnier, and it is a direct antecedent to the twentieth-century musical's **list song**.

Operas had quickly adopted the same formal "sectional" labels that were used in stage plays, so the large divisions of the story were called **acts**, and the subsections within an act (usually determined by the entrances and exits of characters) were called **scenes**. The total number of arias allotted to each singer in each act was carefully negotiated in their contracts (as is still the case today); the composer usually had numerous requirements to meet before he had written a note of music. Mozart thrived under this system; he loved the challenge of "writing to order" because, as he wrote in 1778, "I like an aria to fit a singer as perfectly as a well-tailored suit of clothes." In the case of Leporello, Mozart knew the comic bass who would perform the role, and he wrote to suit the singer's vocal and acting abilities.

The "Catalogue Aria" opens at an Allegro tempo, with the orchestra establishing a rapid pulsation in the background, rather like a counting machine. At **1**, after Leporello sings *leggete con me* ("read along with me") the second time, the string instruments (echoed by the wind instruments) play a little downward **scale** (a series of step-wise notes) that sounds like orchestral laughter. The "laughter" repeats after each of Leporello's statements at **2**. At **3**, when Leporello reaches the line *ma in Ispagna* ("but in Spain"), the steady tempo halts. Some of the syllables are stretched out, by means of a **fermata** (a sustained note), focusing our attention on Leporello's claim of "1003" conquests in Spain. The allegro tempo resumes at **4**, while at **5**, his delivery becomes very rapid, in the manner of a patter song. The words of **2** repeat at **6**, but they are sung to a different melody this time; Mozart creates continuity by using the same "laughing" scales in the orchestral background. Mozart uses fermatas again at **7** so that Leporello can once more highlight Spain in his list. The next portion of text (**8**) is the same as **4**, but here the words are sung to a new melody, set in another rapid-fire patter style. (You may notice that Leporello is singing scales similar to the orchestral laughter heard during **2**.)

It sounds as if we have reached the end of the aria at the end of **8**, but after a tiny pause, Mozart indicates at **9** that the tempo should drop to **Andante con moto** (walking speed, with motion). This slower speed allows Leporello to imitate the gentle, seductive way in which his master delivers his many "pick-up lines." Briefly, Leporello sings a patter passage at **10**, but the lyrical mood returns at **11**, which repeats the melody heard at **9**. Because of these repeated tunes, it might seem that Mozart was following some pre-existing form—but the "Catalogue Aria" does not follow any standard pattern and can therefore be called **non-standard**. (Because of its contrasting speeds, some historians call this type of piece a **two-tempo aria**.) There *are* repeated passages, but these don't adhere to any "stock" scheme. If there had been no repetition at all, we would call the piece **through-composed**, meaning that there was no clear repetition of melodies through the course of the aria. However, non-standard form is a better term for a piece with recurring melodies that do not conform to a predictable pattern.

Don Giovanni did not do as well in Vienna as it had done in Prague, and Emperor Joseph II was of the opinion that the music was too hard for the singers. Nevertheless, the emperor commissioned another opera from Mozart in 1789. Mozart turned again to Lorenzo da Ponte for the libretto, and the result was an opera buffa titled *Così fan tutte, ossia La scuola degli amanti*. The second half of the title is easy to translate—*The School for Lovers*—but the first half is more of a challenge. Literally, it is *Thus Do All*, but the pronoun is feminine, so translators have tried phrases like *Thus Do All Women* or *All Women Do It*.

"Dammi un bacio" from *Così fan tutte*.
Lebrecht Collection/NL.

Da Ponte's story depicted the stratagems when two soldiers—Ferrando and Guglielmo, engaged to Fiordiligi and Dorabella (who are sisters)—make a bet with an old cynic, Don Alfonso. Each soldier believes that *his* fiancée will be faithful to him no matter what. The soldiers put on disguises and each man proceeds to woo the other's girlfriend. The sisters' maid Despina, as cynical as Don Alfonso, also tries to manipulate the girls. The sisters hold fast for quite a while, but at last they yield to the very flattering devotion of the two strangers. When the men reveal the truth, the sisters beg for forgiveness. The couples have learned that they should trust reason, not the ups and downs of emotional excess.

The fact that the women are duped has made *Così fan tutte* a little unpalatable to some viewers. (It will not be the last show whose subject matter made some audiences uncomfortable!) One writer described *Così* as "a miserable thing, which lowers all women, cannot possibly please female spectators, and will therefore not make its fortune." Even Beethoven condemned the story as immoral (although this didn't keep him from using an aria from *Così fan tutte* as a model). However, the downfall of the women is engineered by a rather sordid intrigue; in other words, we don't admire the men very much, either.

Così fan tutte takes place in simple settings—a modest home and garden—without any need for spectacle. Even the small cast reflects the opera's tight economy of means. Andrew Steptoe uses the diagram shown in **Figure 3–1** to illustrate the interrelationships between the characters of *Così fan tutte*; this balance and symmetry was a hallmark of the Classical style.

Although much attention has been given to the great **solo** arias in opera (featuring only one singer), the **ensemble numbers** for two or more singers are also an extremely important component of operatic writing. Many ensemble groupings have familiar names, such as the **duet** (or **duo**) for two performers, the **trio** for three, the **quartet** for four, and the **quintet** for five. Musicians continue the terminology upwards to as many as nine performers: **sextet** (6), **septet** (7), **octet** (8), and **nonet** (9). Since Mozart had six singers at his disposal in *Così fan tutte*, all sorts of combinations were possible. *Così fan tutte* is sometimes called an **ensemble opera** due to its many groupings of singers into coherent musical partnerships, a task that is far more difficult than Mozart makes it seem.

An exciting musical moment of the plot comes in the sextet "Dammi un bacio," when the sisters believe that the strangers have taken poison and require a kiss to be cured. Mozart gives each character a slightly different melodic line, performed simultaneously—in a texture called **non-imitative polyphony**. What makes this passage comprehensible is that the characters are each repeating melodies they had sung previously, so the audience has a general idea what each singer is contributing to the mix.

Non-imitative polyphony is a powerful tool in the hands of a skilled composer, but one that is easy to misuse. Individual lines become hard to hear when multiple melodies and texts are sung simultaneously. Yet, there are certainly noisy real-life situations in which people talk (and repeat themselves) at the same time. We will see in Chapter 29—almost two centuries later—that Leonard Bernstein handles his "Tonight" (Quintet) in *West Side Story* in a manner almost identical to Mozart: Bernstein has the various groups of characters introduce their ideas one at a time, and then he begins to layer the various melodies one on top of another for an exhilarating, dramatic number that prepares us for the fight to come. Mozart was not truly an innovator in any theatrical genre, but he used the ideas of his predecessors to create outstandingly expressive works that are still influential—and regularly performed—to this day.

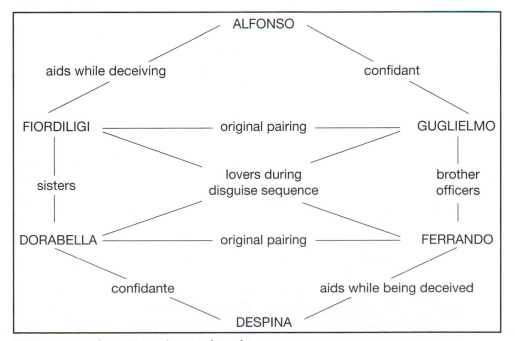

Figure 3–1 Andrew Steptoe's diagram of *Così fan tutte*.

From Steptoe, Andrew. "The Mozart-Da Ponte Operas: The Cultural and Musical Background to Le nozze di Figaro, Don Giovanni and Così fan tutte." Copyright © 1990 Oxford University Press. Reprinted by permission of Oxford University Press.

FURTHER READING

Dent, Edward J. *Mozart's Operas: A Critical Study*. London: Chatto and Windus, 1913. Reprinted Oxford: Clarendon Press, 1947.

Heartz, Daniel. *Mozart's Operas*. Berkeley: University of California Press, 1990.

Orrey, Leslie. *A Concise History of Opera*. New York: Charles Scribner's Sons, 1972.

Osborne, Charles. *The Complete Operas of Mozart*. New York: Da Capo, 1978.

Rushton, Julian, ed. *W. A. Mozart: Don Giovanni*. Cambridge: Cambridge University Press, 1981.

Steptoe, Andrew. *The Mozart–Da Ponte Operas: The Cultural and Musical Background to* Le nozze di Figaro, Don Giovanni, *and* Così fan tutte. Oxford: Clarendon Press, 1988.

PLOT SUMMARY: *DON GIOVANNI*

Don Juan—the legendary Spanish lover—began appearing in literature as early as the late sixteenth century. In essence, his story is a simple one: after seducing hundreds (or thousands?) of women, Don Juan (or, in Italian, Don Giovanni) refuses to repent and is at last punished for his many sins.

As the opera begins, Don Giovanni's servant Leporello waits in a street in Seville while his master tries to seduce Donna Anna. (We are never sure whether Don Giovanni had been successful in this seduction.) When Donna Anna's father, the aged Commendatore, comes to her rescue, he is killed by Don Giovanni. Donna Anna and her fiancé Don Ottavio swear vengeance.

Later, Don Giovanni and Leporello run into Donna Elvira, who had been searching for the Don since he seduced her. Don Giovanni orders Leporello to tell her about his other conquests (in "The Catalogue Aria"; see **Musical Example 4**) so the Don can escape while Donna Elvira listens to the overwhelming list. Don Giovanni's attention is soon drawn to Zerlina, a peasant who is celebrating her marriage. Leporello distracts the groom Masetto while the Don "entertains" Zerlina. Zerlina has almost yielded to the Don when Donna Elvira interrupts them. The Don then pretends to help Donna Anna and Don Ottavio search for the Commendatore's murderer. The first act ends with a brilliant party at the Don's palace, during which he tries to seduce Zerlina once again—and, once again, he manages to elude the pursuing Donna Anna, Don Ottavio, and Donna Elvira.

The second act is filled with narrow escapes for the Don. While chattering next to the cemetery, Don Giovanni hears a voice warning him to leave the dead in peace. The Don realizes that a statue of Donna Anna's father is addressing him, so the Don cockily invites the statue to dinner; Leporello is horrified when the statue bows to his master and says, "Yes." It is not long until an ominous knock is heard; when the Don answers the door and shakes the statue's hand, he finds he cannot escape the stone guest's icy grip. Repeatedly, the statue asks Don Giovanni to repent, but the Don steadfastly refuses until flames swallow him up. The other characters reappear to warn the audience, "As one has lived, so shall he die."

MUSICAL EXAMPLE 4

DON GIOVANNI
WOLFGANG AMADEUS MOZART/LORENZO DA PONTE (K. 527), 1787
"The Catalogue Aria"
ACT I, SCENE 2, NO. 4

Leporello

1	Madamina, il catalogo è questo	My lady, this is a list
	Delle belle che amò il padron mio;	Of the beauties whom my master has loved;
	Un catalogo egli è che ho fatt'io;	A list which I have made myself;
	Osservate, leggete con me.	*Observe, read with me.*
2	In Italia seicento e quaranta;	In Italy, six hundred and forty;
	In Allemagna duecento e trent'una;	In Germany, two hundred and thirty-one;
	Cento in Francia; in Turchia novant'una;	A hundred in France; in Turkey, ninety-one;
3	Ma in Ispagna, ma in Ispagna,	But in Spain, but in Spain,
	son già mille e tre, mille e tre, mille e tre.	Already there've been one thousand and three, 1003, 1003.
4	V'han fra queste contadine,	Among these are peasants,
	Cameriere, cittadine,	Maidservants, city girls,
	V'han contesse, baronesse,	Among these are countesses, baronesses,
5	Marchesane, principesse,	Machionesses, princesses,
	E v'han donne d'ogni grado,	Ladies of every rank,
	D'ogni forma, d'ogni età.	*Every shape, every age.*
6	In Italia seicento e quaranta;	In Italy, six hundred and forty;
	In Allemagna duecento e trent'una;	In Germany, two hundred and thirty-one;
	Cento in Francia; in Turchia novant'una;	A hundred in France; in Turkey, ninety-one;

7   Ma, ma, ma in Ispagna, ma in Ispagna   But, but, but in Spain, but in Spain
    son già mille e tre, mille e tre, mille e tre.   Already there've been one thousand and three, 1003, 1003.
8   V'han fra queste contadine,   Among these are peasant girls,
    Cameriere, cittadine,   Maidservants, city girls,
    V'han contesse, baronesse,   Among these are countesses, baronesses,
    Marchesane, principesse,   Machionesses, princesses,
    E v'han donne d'ogni grado,   Ladies of every rank,
    D'ogni forma, d'ogni età.   *Every shape, every age.*
9   Nella bionda egli ha l'usanza   With blondes it is his habit
    Di lodar la gentilezza,   To praise their kindness,
    Nella bruna la costanza,   In brunettes, their loyalty,
    Nella bianca la dolcezza.   In the white-haired, their sweetness.
    Vuol d'inverno la grassotta,   In winter he likes plump ones,
    Vuol d'estate la magrotta;   In summer he likes lean ones,
    È la grande maestosa,   And the big ones are majestic,
10 *La piccina è ognor vezzosa.*   *The little ones are always graceful.*
11 Delle vecchie fa conquista   He seduces the old ones
    Del piacer di porle in lista;   For the pleasure of adding them to the list;
    Sua passion predominante   His primary passion
    È la giovin principiante.   Is the young beginner.
    Non si picca se sia ricca,   It doesn't matter if she is rich,
    Se sia brutta, se sia bella;   Ugly, or beautiful;
    Se sia ricca, brutta, se sia bella;   Rich, ugly, or beautiful;
    Purchè porti la gonnella,   *If she wears a skirt,*
    Voi sapete quel che fa, voi sapete quel che fa.   *You know what he does, you know what he does.*

Chapter 4
The Musical Stage in the American Colonies

When did musical theater begin to appear in the colonies? Opera was performed in the Spanish colonies in Mexico as early as 1711 (and in Peru in 1701), but no news of these achievements trickled northward; they had little direct influence on the development of the twentieth-century American musical. In the northern English-speaking colonies, the earliest performance that has come to light was a ballad opera called *Flora; or Hob in the Well*, which appeared in South Carolina in 1735. Like most pieces presented in the northern colonies, this ballad opera was a foreign import, as was the venerable *The Beggar's Opera*, performed in 1746 by amateurs in Rhode Island and then by professionals in New York in 1750.

We know that music played a role from the earliest days of colonial history. The first book printed in the New England colonies was *The Whole Booke of Psalmes Faithfully Translated into English Metre* of 1640, better known as the "Bay Psalm Book." In it, the texts of the Biblical psalms had been rewritten so that they could be sung easily. Moreover, household inventories from the seventeenth century reveal that people from all walks of life owned musical instruments. Eighteenth-century newspapers advertised instruments and music lessons. People also enjoyed singing the newest ballads, to the dismay of some ministers. A Harvard College instructor published an essay on the skill of reading music in 1720, and the New England colonies developed a widespread collection of "singing schools" and societies.

Theatrical presentations also figured in the lives of the colonists. The first theater in the English-speaking colonies was built in Williamsburg, Virginia, in 1716; a "New Theatre" was advertised in New York late in 1732. It may well be the case that some stage production before *Flora* should actually be credited as the northern colonies' first musical theater presentation, for the distinction was becoming quite blurred between "spoken plays with added songs" and ballad operas with their spoken dialogue between songs. You may recall that *The Beggar's Opera* contained 69 tunes, while Mozart's *Bastien und Bastienne* had only 15. How do these two works compare with a 1756 production of Shakespeare's play *The Tempest* that incorporated 32 inserted songs and duets? It was difficult for an eighteenth-century American audience to see a play *without* a substantial amount of vocal music.

Not only were works from England the most commonly performed pieces in America, but England sent the colonies an important theatrical company. A **troupe** (group of performers) called the London Company of Comedians arrived in 1752 and toured widely up and down the Atlantic seaboard. After disbanding briefly, it reformed and was rechristened the American Company, and it continued to be a regular visitor to many East coast cities.

The American Company *almost* performed the first "made-in-America" (non-imported) musical theater work in 1767, but the show was cancelled before its first performance. It was to have been a ballad opera with the rather inauspicious title *The Disappointment; or The Force of Cruelty*. Like other ballad operas, most of the melodies in *The Disappointment* were pre-existing folk tunes, but *The Disappointment* is interesting to American historians because the fourth song—according to the libretto—was to be sung to the tune of "Yankee Doodle." This is the earliest known reference in print to what was obviously already a well-known melody. Like the first ballad opera, *The Beggar's Opera*, *The Disappointment* was a pointed satire. Apparently, it was *too* pointed for some prominent Philadelphia citizens, who saw to it that the show was cancelled.

All efforts to create a "homegrown" musical stage work came to a halt in 1774, when the First Continental Congress decreed, "We will . . . discourage every species of extravagance and dissipation, especially all horse-racing, and all kinds of gaming, cock-fighting, exhibition of shews (shows), plays, and

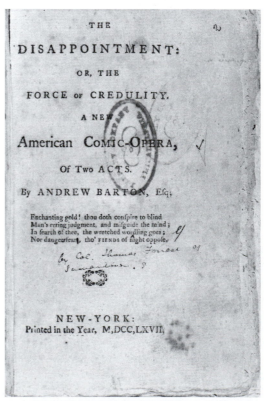

The cover page from the libretto of the cancelled *The Disappointment*.
The Library Company of Philadelphia.

other expensive diversions and entertainments." Not needing to be told twice, the American Company took itself into exile in Jamaica. Soon, theater was legal only in Maryland and New York. Most of the only notable efforts at drama during the years of the Revolutionary War were ballad operas performed by British soldiers stationed in New York and Philadelphia.

The American Company was not completely defeated, however. In 1784, it began to present a series of "lectures," "entertainments," and "concerts," which all carried designations carefully selected to circumvent the anti-theater laws. (We know that when George Washington bought some "lecture" tickets in 1784, he wrote in his diary that he had "purchased four Play Tickets"—clearly, audiences understood the "code" words for theatrical presentations.) Even more daringly, the American Company presented *The Poor Soldier*—an imported English **comic opera**—in 1785. Comic opera, like ballad opera, had spoken dialogue, but most of the songs were newly composed; the stories taught a moral lesson of some sort. *The Poor Soldier* enjoyed an unprecedented popularity and was performed 18 times at New York's John Street Theatre (a *very* long **run**—series of performances—for America at the time).

During the summer of 1788, the American Constitution was finally ratified—and a different mood swept the new nation. In 1789, the Pennsylvania Assembly repealed the anti-theater act; other states soon followed (although Boston waited until 1793). Hallam renamed his troupe the "Old American Company" and established a steady **circuit** through several of the new states. (A circuit is a series of regular stops in various cities that are visited year after year.) French immigrants fleeing the French Revolution brought a variety of French pantomimes, ballets, and operas; the works of German playwrights were also often performed. English imports, however, still dominated the American stage.

The English works avoided sung recitative and elaborate vocal ornamentation, which suited American taste and explains why there were relatively few performances of full-fledged operatic works from other countries. No less a figure than Benjamin Franklin complained about vocal music that contained elaborate ornamentation or "graces," telling his brother in a letter: "A modern song ... neglects all the proprieties and beauties of common speech, and in their place introduces its *defects* and *absurdities* as so many graces." A Boston writer made a similar complaint in 1792 when he argued that "banished forever ... should be all unintelligible Italian airs, trills, affected squeaks and quavers."

Despite developing American musical preferences, there was quite a gap between the abortive attempt at presenting *The Disappointment* in 1767 and the next group of candidates for the title of "the first American musical theater work." At one point it was believed that *The Temple of Minerva* deserved the honor. However, this 1781 composition was not staged but was instead a vocal work for concert performance. In 1782, *The Blockheads; or Fortunate Contractor* was published in London, with the assertion that it had been written and previously performed in New York—but scholars have found no documentation to substantiate this claim. In 1789, two more works were published in America—*The Better Sort; or the Girl of Spirit* and *Darby's Return*. Only *Darby's Return* was

performed—but it contained only two musical numbers, making its claim as the first American "musical" stage work a bit tenuous. A 1790 piece called *The Reconciliation; or The Triumph of Nature* suffered the same fate as *The Disappointment*: it was rehearsed but never performed. Another competitor, *Edwin and Angelina; or The Banditti*, was written in 1791—but this comic opera did not actually debut until 1796 (and was performed only once). Nevertheless, the authors certainly wanted audiences to recognize that *Edwin and Angelina* was a candidate for the record books; in advertisements they billed it as "the first opera of which all parts are known to have been created in America, and which then came to production."

The first American work to appear on stage was ***Tammany, or The Indian Chief***, a ballad opera produced in 1794 by the Old American Company. The libretto was by a woman, **Anne Julia Hatton**—wife of a New York musical instrument builder—while the music was arranged (although not composed) by **James Hewitt**, conductor of the Old American Company's orchestra. Billed as a "Serious Opera," the subject matter was ostensibly about Native Americans (see the **Plot Summary**), but it was actually highly political, representing the right of mankind to be free from aristocratic tyranny.

Mrs. Hatton's plot was intended to support the views of the Tammany Society (the ancestor of the notorious nineteenth-century political organization later based at Tammany Hall). The Tammany Society, founded in 1789, was a group of anti-Federalists who wanted the United States to support the French Revolution. Federalists, on the other hand, wanted America to remain neutral. Members of both factions crowded into the theatre on the night of the premiere, and emotions ran high. Hewitt was slow (or reluctant) to respond when the audience called for **encores** (repetitions) of its favorite tunes (most of which had political associations), and the atmosphere grew so heated that Hewitt was actually physically attacked. The production was delayed while he recovered from the shock of his blows. Despite the tumult of the opening performance, the work was performed seven more times in three different cities.

As with most ballad opera tunes, the composer of **Musical Example 5**, "Alkmoonac, or the Death Song of the Cherokee Indians," is unknown. A printed version in England claimed that the melody had been brought from America by "a gentleman who was conversant with the Indian tribes." The poet Anne Home Hunter wrote the words for the tune, and Mrs. Hatton modified the words for "*Alkmoonac*," creating the duet version. The melody later evolved into a religious **hymn-tune** called "Morality."

It is unlikely that the tune for "Alkmoonac" truly came from an Indian tribe, since it is much more characteristic of colonial popular songs. "Alkmoonac" illustrates **strophic form**, which is a pattern that can be diagrammed as *a-a-a* (etc.) Each of the three **verses**, or **strophes** (labeled as **1**, **2**, and **3**) of "Alkmoonac" is sung to the same melody (*a*), even though the words are different for each verse. This pattern of repetition is extremely common in folk music, Christmas carols, church hymns, and children's songs, but *not* in Native American music. By varying the medium in the song—letting Tammany sing one verse, giving Manana the second verse, and having the lovers join together to sing the last verse—Hatton and Hewitt created variety in what is a very repetitive structure. Nevertheless, the uncomplicated repetition scheme allows the listener to concentrate on the message of the singer's words.

What about America's influence on the rest of the world? The first work to be performed in America and *then* performed overseas was an 1808 "Operatic MeloDrame" called *The Indian Princess, or La Belle Sauvage.* However, *The Indian Princess* did not travel across the Atlantic to London until 1820. Although many Americans like to think of musical theater as an American phenomenon, it would be a long, slow process before American works for the musical stage began to have any noticeable impact.

FURTHER READING

Chase, Gilbert. *America's Music from the Pilgrims to the Present.* Revised Third Edition. Urbana and Chicago: University of Illinois Press, 1992.

Hamm, Charles. *Music in the New World.* New York: W. W. Norton, 1983.

Lowens, Irving. *Music and Musicians in Early America.* New York: W. W. Norton, 1964.

Mates, Julian. *America's Musical Stage: Two Hundred Years of Musical Theatre.* New York: Praeger, 1985. Paperback edition, 1987.

Porter, Susan L. *With an Air Debonair: Musical Theatre in America, 1785–1815.* Washington and London: Smithsonian Institution Press, 1991.

Sonneck, O. G. "Early American Operas," in *Miscellaneous Studies in the History of Music.* New York: Macmillan Co., 1921. Reprinted New York: Da Capo Press, 1968.

Virga, Patricia H. *The American Opera to 1790.* Ann Arbor, Michigan: UMI Research Press, 1982.

PLOT SUMMARY: *TAMMANY; OR THE INDIAN CHIEF*

Not much of *Tammany* was preserved for posterity—the score and the libretto were never published, so we have only scattered bits of information and the words to the songs to use in piecing together a sense of the story. *Tammany* opened with a prologue (written by Richard Bingham Davis) that lamented the destruction of the Native American way of life once the European colonists began to arrive.

Tammany focuses on the Cherokee Tammany, son of Alkmoonac, who loves Manana. Their happiness is threatened, however, for Spaniards have invaded the Cherokee homeland, and Ferdinand is also attracted to Manana. Ferdinand captures Manana and carries her off. There is a brief comic interlude while Wegaw, another Indian, sings a song in praise of "firewater," but then Tammany sings of his anguish over Manana's abduction and vows revenge. Tammany rescues Manana, and they flee to his cabin—but the pursuing Spaniards set the cabin on fire. The lovers—realizing they are about to die—sing a duet of determination and defiance (**Musical Example 5**). The story ends with the chorus singing the praises of "valiant, good and brave" Tammany and "chaste" Manana.

MUSICAL EXAMPLE 5

TAMMANY; OR THE INDIAN CHIEF
ANONYMOUS (ARRANGED BY JAMES HEWITT)/ANNE JULIA HATTON, 1794
"Alkmoonac, or The Death Song of the Cherokee Indians"

ACT III

Tammany

1
The sun sets [at] night and the stars shun the day
But glory unfading can never decay,
You white men deceivers your smiles are in vain;
The son of Alkmoonac, shall ne'er wear your chain.

Manana

2
To the land where our fathers are gone we will go,
Where grief never enters but pleasures still flow,
Death comes like a friend: he relieves us from pain,
Thy children, Alkmoonac, shall ne'er wear their chain.

Both

3
Farewell then ye woods which have witness'd our flame,
Let time on his wings bear our record of fame,
Together we die for our spirits disdain,
Ye white children of Europe your rankling chain.

The Musical Stage in the Nineteenth Century

Part Two

Chapter 5
France and Spain in the Nineteenth Century

In the late seventeenth and early eighteenth centuries, the French opéra-comique and its derivatives had anticipated many of the comic procedures that the English ballad opera *The Beggar's Opera* would later use to such advantage. Again, in the nineteenth century, France developed a new comic theatrical genre—the **opéra-bouffe**—that would again open the door to an English imitation, the **operetta**, and to the famous team of Gilbert and Sullivan. What was it about this new opéra-bouffe genre that gave it such appeal and impact? Its zany humor was one important factor; its emphasis on dancing was another.

Opéra-bouffe was offbeat right from the start. In our modern society, the celebrities who are known by a single name—Cher, Brandy, Madonna, Prince, Eminem—still excite comment, so the name Hervé, adopted by one of opéra-bouffe's chief cultivators, seemed especially novel in the nineteenth century. Moreover, Hervé had honed his skills writing musical stage works for the inmates of an insane asylum.

Even before Hervé, France had delighted in humorous stage presentations. Two major Parisian theaters carried on a lively rivalry, thereby supporting the careers of composers such as Adolphe Adam, who aspired to write music that "is easy to understand and amusing to the public." Italian-born Gaetano Donizetti was commissioned to write *La Fille du Régiment* (*The Daughter of the Regiment*) for one of the theaters in 1840, and the opera was a hit (to the chagrin of many native French composers).

However, it was outside these theaters that opéra-bouffe developed. In 1839, a 14-year-old Florimond Ronger was such an impressive church organist that he was invited to create a music class for the mental patients at an asylum. After seeing the patients perform a work composed by Ronger, members of the medical community were sufficiently impressed that they published scholarly papers about the asylum's "*musicothérapie*."

Ronger began living a sort of "double life," completing his church duties during the day and working at suburban Parisian theaters in the evenings. Perhaps in an effort to placate his religious employers, Ronger began to use the alias Hervé for his theatrical activities.

Hervé's works were short (one-act) sketches performed in small theaters with tiny casts of no more than four characters, with spoken dialogue and plots that were parodies of Parisian society. The government mandated most of these characteristics; French theaters were strictly licensed, and only the "big" theaters could present multi-act, large-scale musical works. In fact, when Hervé made a move to present one of his shows at a larger theater, his rivals were successful in having the production banned. But Hervé, it seems, had some friends in high places. In 1854 he was given a license to open his own small theater. The theater quickly became a popular Parisian destination, and the theater presented not only works by Hervé himself, but also an early work by a young man known as **Jacques Offenbach** (see the *Sidebar: Jacques Offenbach, the Mozart of the Champs-Élysées*).

Encouraged by his success at Hervé's theater, Offenbach rented a tiny theater on the Champs-Élysées and renamed it the *Bouffes-Parisiens*; his brother Jules conducted the orchestra. The timing was good, since in 1855 Paris was hosting an international Exhibition and there was an extra surge of potential theatergoers in the city. By the time the Exhibition closed, Offenbach had built a substantial audience and was able to transfer the *Bouffes-Parisiens* productions (and the theater name) to a larger theater in the heart of Paris. Besides writing a series of hits for the new venue, Offenbach also sponsored a competition in 1857 for composers. The winners were Georges Bizet, who would later compose the famous opera *Carmen*, and Charles LeCocq, who would also become a leading theatrical composer.

The legal restrictions governing productions were at last struck down in 1858, and Offenbach immediately created ***Orphée aux enfers*** (*Orpheus in the Underworld*), the first true opéra-bouffe (see the **Plot Summary**). It was initially a two-act work (expanded to four acts in 1874), and its librettists were **Hector Crémieux** (1828–1892) and **Ludovic Halévy** (1834–1908). Halévy asked that his name be left off the **bills**, or advertisements, since he didn't want to jeopardize his job in the diplomatic service. *Orphée* got off to a slow start, and early in 1859, Offenbach provoked an extremely negative review from a critic who claimed *Orphée* was "a profanation of holy and glorious antiquity." However, the critic, Jules Janin, was most offended by a ridiculous speech delivered by Pluton—it was borrowed directly from some of Janin's own writing—and Offenbach had publicly revealed the source. Janin's attempt to condemn the work backfired; Parisians flocked to see the show that had produced such verbal fireworks, and *Orphée* proceeded to run 228 performances and began touring outside of France as well.

Parisian audiences were titillated to find the gods dancing the **can-can** at the end of *Orpheus in the Underworld*, for this naughty dance had previously been associated only with rather lewd locales—certainly not the (somewhat) more respectable theater stage. Certainly, the high spirits of the dance helped to propel the opéra-bouffe to a rambunctious conclusion. The dance occurs as the second half of **Musical Example 6**, the opéra-bouffe's Number 28; the first half (beginning at **2**) is a tongue-in-cheek *menuet* (a courtly dance of the eighteenth century, spelled *minuet* in English). The elegance of the minuet (even with exceedingly silly words) contrasts with the high-energy "*galop infernal*"—the can-can, at **5**. (In a can-can, the dancers perform high kicks while lifting up the front of their ruffled skirts.)

Tempo certainly distinguishes the two halves of **Musical Example 6**. However, a contrast in **meter** also sets the two dances apart. Whenever a piece has a steady pulse or **beat**, the beats usually occur in repetitive groupings—and meter is a term to describe how those beats are grouped together. Sometimes your feet want to move "left-right-left-right," in the manner of a march, and this "strong-weak-strong-weak" alternation of beats is called **duple meter**. If the pattern has a waltzlike feeling—a strong beat followed by *two* weaker beats—the meter is **triple**. **Quadruple meter** describes a pattern of a strong beat succeeded by three weaker beats. **Figure 5–1** presents some familiar melodies that illustrate these beat groupings.

The meter changes more than once during **Musical Example 6**. The orchestral introduction (**1**) is in duple meter, while Jupiter's entrance at **2** and the choral minuet at **4** are in triple meter. During the orchestral interlude at **5**, the meter shifts to a lively duple meter. You may find that it helps you to "feel" the beats if you try to count out loud. Try using a *1-2-3-1-2-3* counting system during section **4**—coordinating your counts with the places you would move your hands or feet if you were clapping or marching or dancing along—and a *1-2-1-2-1-2* counting pattern during sections **6** through **8**. Once you start to feel comfortable with these two counting systems, try reversing them! When you count *1-2-1-2* during the *menuet* and *1-2-3-1-2-3* during the *galop infernal*, you will probably find it hard to keep counting—since the numbers no longer seem to "fit" with the music.

Orphée aux enfers was only the first of many opéra-bouffe successes for Offenbach. *La Grande-Duchesse de Gérolstein* (*The Grand Duchess of Gérolstein*), written for the Paris Exposition of 1866, became a particularly hot item because of Offenbach's battles with the censors; the political parody in this new work nearly led to its closure. The notoriety made tickets sell all the faster and the show traveled widely; it reached the United States the following year.

Although Offenbach had begun his career by imitating Hervé, Offenbach's success with the new genre of opéra-bouffe meant that Hervé was soon imitating *him*. Although Hervé's plots generally possessed a great deal of humor and invention, Offenbach's stage works often displayed greater musical sophistication. Although the two men rivaled each other for the attention of Parisian audiences, they were not personal enemies. In 1878, Hervé was invited to play the role of Jupiter in a **revival** of *Orphée aux enfers*. (A revival is a subsequent production of a show, after the original production has closed.) Hervé agreed to perform—but only if Offenbach would conduct.

The French opéra-bouffe thrived for a number of years, both in France and elsewhere in the world. One of the

Duple Meter										
	Row,	row,	**row** your boat,	**Gently**	down the **stream** ------			**Merrily,**	merrily ...
beats:	**1**	**2**	**1** **2**	**1**	**2** **1**	**2**	**1**	**2** ...

Triple Meter									
	My	coun- try	**Tis**-----of	thee **Sweet**	land of	**Lib**-----er- ty	**Of**	thee I	**sing** ...
beats:	**1**	**2** **3**	**1** **2** **3** **1**	**2** **3**	**1** **2** **3**	**1** **2** **3**	**1** **2** ...

Quadruple Meter								
	Are	you	sleep- ing,	**Are**	you	sleep- ing,	**Bro-**	ther	John-----	**Bro-**	ther	John----- ...
beats:	**1**	**2**	**3** **4**	**1**	**2**	**3** **4**	**1**	**2**	**3** **4**	**1**	**2**	**3** **4** ...

Figure 5–1

An advertisement for *Orpheus in the Underworld*, 1858.
Lebrecht Collection/NL.

winners of Offenbach's 1857 competition, Charles LeCocq, had found it difficult to get his career going despite the early recognition. His efforts were at last rewarded by the overwhelming reception given to *La Fille de Madame Angot* (*Mrs. Angot's Daughter*), which soon became the biggest hit of the 1870s. In England, it was such a success that three productions ran simultaneously in three London theaters. Another French composer created *Les Cloches de Corneville* (*The Bells of Corneville*, better known in English as *The Chimes of Normandy*), a show that broke nearly as many records as *La Fille de Madame Angot*. Perhaps the surest measure of the opéra-bouffe's influence, however, was the success of its direct descendent, the **operetta**—a genre that would rise to international fame in various countries, but particularly in the hands of two Englishmen, Gilbert and Sullivan.

Spain, meanwhile, had developed its own national genre of stage music, the **zarzuela**. Like several European genres, the *zarzuela* mixed spoken dialogue with sung numbers; it may have taken its name from the *zarza*, which a 1611 Spanish lexicon defined as "a spiny mat . . . a thing that is all linked together and intertwined in itself." On the other hand, many early works were performed at a royal palace near Madrid called La Zarzuela, which undoubtedly influenced the genre's name as well. *Zarzuelas* varied quite a bit, but in general they used Spanish folk music and dances in addition to a healthy mixture of solo and choral singing; the accompanying "orchestra" was usually a large band of harps and guitars.

The *zarzuela* moved from the court to the public theaters in the early eighteenth century. At the same time, certain changes occurred in its format; the War of the Spanish Succession had brought the Bourbon kings to the Spanish throne, and with the Bourbons came Italian opera. (The internationally famous Farinelli, one of the great Italian castrati, came to Madrid, and his beautiful singing was soon credited with helping to cure King Philip V's depression.) More and more, the *zarzuela* began to mix typically Spanish numbers with forms drawn from Italian opera seria.

During the last quarter of the eighteenth century, however, attention shifted from the *zarzuela* to other works. Italian opera still predominated, but shorter, comic Spanish shows also arose in the late eighteenth century, such as **sainetes** and **tonadillas**. These shorter productions also borrowed the typical groupings of singers from Italian opera, featuring comic arias, duets, and larger ensembles. The plots were very topical and the shows usually ran for less than a week. By the nineteenth century, these ephemeral works had flooded the popular theaters, pushing the *zarzuela* aside until it was only a memory, while Italian opera—using the Italian language—almost completely dominated the "high-art" Spanish cultural scene.

Things did not change until the middle of the nineteenth century when a few composers began to revive works written in Spanish, using—once again—spoken dialogue. (Ironically, one of the pioneers in the *zarzuela*'s rebirth was Basilio Basili, an Italian.) The first "modern" *zarzuela* is hard to pin down, but *Colegiales y soldados* (*Students and Soldiers*) in 1849 was particularly successful. That same year, a number of Spanish composers banded together to form a *Sociedad Artística* ("Artistic Society"); their goal was to create an entire theatrical season each year of *zarzuelas*. After some initial faltering, the society hit its stride with a show called *Jugar con fuego* (*Playing with Fire*). The society's subsequent works were a fascinating blend of Italian musical characteristics and Spanish topics placed within the structure of the French opéra-comique. Several of the works were direct adaptations of French plots.

In 1856 the entrepreneurs began to build the *Teatro de la Zarzuela* (a theater that exists to this day). Not all of the productions kept the theater in good financial shape, and bankruptcy loomed more than once, but time after time,

---

Sidebar: Jacques Offenbach, the Mozart of the Champs-Élysées

Like his professional rival Hervé, Jacques Offenbach (1819–1880) also worked under a pseudonym, but for very different reasons. Offenbach's father left his native town of Offenbach am Main and moved to the German city of Cologne. There, he was nicknamed Der Offenbacher—a name he passed down to his sons Jacob and Julius. The boys were so musically talented that their father took them to Paris and persuaded the elderly director of the Paris Conservatory, Luigi Cherubini, to admit 14-year-old Jacob as a student—no mean feat considering that Cherubini didn't like to enroll young or foreign-born pupils, and had already rejected a 12-year-old Franz Liszt for those very reasons. Jacob's name was soon "Frenchified" into Jacques, the name he would use for the rest of his life. His reputation as a virtuoso on the cello grew and he toured widely as a soloist.

Although his success as a cellist was considerable, what Offenbach *really* wanted to do was compose. After one of his works made a successful debut at Hervé's *Folies-Nouvelles* theater in 1854, however, Offenbach never looked back. He wrote more than 90 operatic works in his lifetime, as well as numerous pieces in many other genres; Gioachino Rossini once dubbed him "the Mozart of the Champs-Élysées," and Richard Wagner also grudgingly admitted that Offenbach "writes like the divine Mozart." He died with perhaps his greatest work not quite finished, *The Tales of Hoffmann*, but it was completed by Ernest Guirard. To some extent, it reflects a change of direction for Offenbach; certainly, it remains in the repertory of opera companies to this day.

---

a long-running show seemed to come at the right moment to rescue the theater from financial ruin. In the 1860s, the society experimented with works in the style of Offenbach. These **buffo zarzuelas** proved to be enormous hits. More and more, the triumphs of the French comic stage—such as LeCocq's *La Fille de Madame Angot*—began appearing in Spanish translation and almost overran the older *zarzuelas* once again.

After the Spanish Revolution of 1868, a new genre made an appearance: the **género chico**. Pieces written in this new format featured a lot of dialogue and not a lot of music; much of the music that was incorporated was drawn from Spanish folklore. (Stylistically, the *género chico* had much in common with American vaudeville, a genre to be examined in Chapter 9, "New American Genres of the Later Nineteenth Century".) Even more than the adapted comic works from France, the *género chico* rang the death knell for the traditional *zarzuela*. The *género chico* was so popular at the end of the nineteenth century that 11 theaters in Madrid performed these works exclusively. Only a few composers continued to support the venerable *zarzuela*, and by the early twentieth century, the older genre appeared only in an occasional revival; very few new works appeared.

All through the history of the *zarzuela*, Spain was very much aware of changing trends outside its borders. Unlike many other countries, however, Spain was never very successful in exporting its own native productions to non-Spanish-speaking lands. For the Spanish, the outpouring of works coming first from Italy, then from France, was a difficult flood to stem, and soon even France's dominance would be challenged by a new genre: the host of operettas beginning to emerge from Austria and England.

FURTHER READING

Chase, Gilbert. *The Music of Spain*. Second revised edition. New York: Dover Publications, 1959.

Faris, Alexander. *Jacques Offenbach*. New York: Charles Scribner's Sons, 1980.

Kracauer, S. *Orpheus in Paris: Offenbach and the Paris of His Time*. Translated by Gwenda David and Eric Mosbacher. New York: Alfred A. Knopf, 1938.

Sturman, Janet L. *Zarzuela: Spanish Operetta, American Stage*. Urbana and Chicago: University of Illinois Press, 2000.

Traubner, Richard. *Operetta: A Theatrical History*. Garden City, New York: Doubleday & Company, 1983.

PLOT SUMMARY: *ORPHÉE AUX ENFERS*

In this updated retelling of the Orpheus legend, Orphée (Orpheus) is an atrociously bad musician who plays the violin incessantly, boring his wife Eurydice to tears. To enliven her days (and nights), she has embarked on an affair with a shepherd/honey-manufacturer, Aristée (Aristeus). The opéra-bouffe opens with Eurydice picking flowers. Sneaking up on her, Orphée begins a serenade—for he has mistaken Eurydice for a shepherdess he has wanted to seduce. Each soon realizes that the other is being unfaithful and a violent quarrel ensues; each of them stomps away in a fury. Eurydice is soon bitten by a snake, but Aristée reveals that he is actually the god Pluton (Pluto), and he offers to take her away to the Underworld. Eurydice is delighted to leave. When Orphée gets word of Eurydice's disappearance, he is euphoric—but his exultation is cut short by L'Opinion publique (Public Opinion)—a character feared by gods and mortals alike. L'Opinion publique bluntly informs him that he *must* go to Jupiter and demand the return of his wife. With enormous reluctance, Orphée obeys the order.

Act II is set in Olympus, where the gods and goddesses gossip about Pluton's "abduction" of Eurydice. Jupiter scolds Pluton, who angrily reminds Jupiter about *his* many affairs with mortal women (could Jupiter represent Napoleon III, a known womanizer?). Jupiter's wife Junon (Juno) takes umbrage, and Vénus encourages the inevitable riot. The uproar is interrupted at last by the entrance of Orphée, led by L'Opinion publique. Despite the halfheartedness of Orphée's pleas, Jupiter agrees that Eurydice should be returned to Orphée, even though he himself has developed an interest in Eurydice.

In the third and fourth acts, Eurydice is kept in seclusion, but this is no challenge for Jupiter; he merely turns himself into a fly and enters Eurydice's chamber through the keyhole. She and Jupiter hit it off immediately. Eventually, though, Orphée (still dogged by L'Opinion publique) reminds Jupiter of his promise. Jupiter tells Orphée that Eurydice will follow him back to his boat, but he must not turn to look at her. Obediently, Orphée heads back to the river—and Jupiter hurls a thunderbolt at Orphée to make *sure* he turns. Orphée is thrilled by this development, since he can now rejoin his shepherdess. L'Opinion publique is disgusted, but the gods are delighted to welcome Eurydice back to the Underworld. They perform a series of wild dances, including the frantic Galop infernal (**Musical Example 6**), better known as the can-can.

MUSICAL EXAMPLE 6

ORPHÉE AUX ENFERS (ORPHEUS IN THE UNDERWORLD)
JACQUES OFFENBACH/HECTOR CRÉMIEUX AND LUDOVIC HALÉVY, 1858
"Galop infernal"
ACT IV, NO. 28

1   [orchestral introduction]

Jupiter

2
Maintenant je veux, moi?	Now, what I want,
Qui suis mince et fluet,	(since I'm slim and slight)
Comme au temps du grand roi,	—as in the time of the great king–
danser un menuet.	is to dance a minuet.

Soloists and Chorus

3
| Ah! Ah! Ah! Ah! Ah! | Ah! Ah! Ah! Ah! Ah! |
| La la la la | La la la la |

4
Le Menuet n'est vraiment si charmant	*The minuet is never so charming*
Qhe lorsque Jupin le danse.	*As when Jupie dances it.*
Comme il tend d'un air coquet le jarret,	How flirtatiously he flexes his leg,
Comme il s'élance en cadence!	How rhythmically he moves.
Le Menuet n'est vraiment si charmant	The minuet is never so charming
Qhe lorsque Jupin le danse.	As when Jupie dances it.
Terpsichore dans ses pas n'a pas plus d'appas;	*Terpsichore does not have more charm in her steps*
Le Menuet n'est vraiment si charmant	*The minuet is never so charming*
Qhe lorsque Jupin le danse.	*As when Jupie dances it.*

5   [orchestral interlude]

Soloists and Chorus

6
Ce bal est original,	This dance is peculiar.
D'un galop infernal donnons tous le signal,	For the hellish gallop let's give the signal,
Vive le galop infernal!	Long live the infernal gallop!
Donnons tous le signal d'un galop infernal!	Let's give the signal for the hellish gallop!
Amis, *vive le bal!*	Friends, *long live the dance!*

7   [orchestral interlude]

Soloists and Chorus

8
| *La la la la la la la . . .* | *La la la la la la la . . .* |

Chapter 6
The Serious and the Not-So-Serious: Italy, Germany, and Austria in the Nineteenth Century

Just as the opera seria and intermezzo had coexisted in eighteenth-century Italy, a clear-cut division between "serious" and "comic" works continued to be the European norm over the next hundred years. Both kinds of stage works continued to evolve in the nineteenth century. France and Spain primarily cultivated comic genres in the nineteenth century, and the comic approach was also enormously successful in England, as we will see in the next chapter. Austria produced successful stage works of both types, but in nineteenth-century Italy and Germany, the focus was largely on serious compositions. The endeavors of Verdi, Wagner, and Puccini, among others, have wielded a direct influence on composers of "popular" stage music clear up to the present day.

One of the stylistic shifts of the early nineteenth century was toward what we now call **Romanticism** in music. Mozart wrote in the Classical era; his music emphasized balance and reason. (You may recall the symmetry of relationships in the plot of *Così fan tutte*, or that Colas's "magic" in *Bastien und Bastienne* was little more than good old common sense.) In the Romantic era, artists made emotion and individuality their priorities, and music was often used to convey feelings. This was the age when Sigmund Freud would begin studying human psychology, and through music, composers could explore the dreams and fears of the subconscious mind. Tales of the supernatural fascinated society; one of the great German operas of the early Romantic era, *Der Freischütz*, centered around forces of good and evil and the selling of souls to the Devil. Audiences were equally interested in exotic cultures.

Music was also used to express national pride; both Verdi and Wagner were seen as symbols of **nationalism** for their respective countries. Audiences began to lionize composers, treating them like the rock stars of today (and, similarly, turning a blind eye to most of their foibles). The day was long gone that musicians were merely servants of the aristocracy. Italian music and musicians exemplify a number of these Romantic trends.

Italy—the birthplace of opera—continued to believe that the **sung-through** approach (in which *all* words were set to music) was the way to go, even though many other countries had abandoned sung recitative for spoken dialogue. To the Italians, nothing was as important as the singing voice, and this focus led to *bel canto opera*. *Bel canto*, quite literally, means "beautiful singing," and this had been the centermost concern of nearly all Italian vocal music. Composers working in Italy turned to dramatic stories, since it was felt that beautiful singing was even more effective when linked to serious texts.

When the emotion of the operatic story was linked to the feelings of the audience itself, the result was explosive. The 1842 opera *Nabucco* launched Giuseppe Verdi's career in a particularly spectacular fashion; it included a poignant depiction of exiled Israelites, which Italians took to represent their own plight as a downtrodden people struggling to free themselves from the hated rule of the Austrian Hapsburgs. One choral number became a patriotic anthem in the Italian struggle for independence. Moreover, Verdi's name itself became a rallying cry for the liberation of Italy. Italians believed that their best hope lay in unification under King Vittorio Emanuele. The Hapsburgs forbade the Italians to show support for this proposed ruler, but who could object to "Viva Verdi!"—the enthusiastic endorsement of a composer? The nation soon recognized the code, however, as illustrated in **Figure 6–1**.

Certainly, opera lies at the heart of much of the nationalistic Italian spirit. When the newly unified country formed its first parliament in 1861, Verdi was made an honorary deputy—an astonishing recognition for a composer. Moreover, when Verdi died, the Italian schools were closed and many of the thousands who marched in his funeral procession sang the same Israelite hymn from *Nabucco* that had galvanized the revolutionary effort in the first place. The Italians' fervor for Verdi's works demonstrated that it had become possible to take opera very, very seriously. (In the next century, much musical theater would undergo a similar metamorphosis, mutating from lighthearted song-and-dance musical comedies to dark stories like *Les Misérables*.)

Given the charged atmosphere in which they were written, it is not surprising that nearly all of Verdi's operas are serious.

Viva	**Viva**	Long live
V	Vittorio	Vittorio
E	Emanuele,	Emanuele,
R	**Rè**	King
D	**d'**	of
I!	Italia!	Italy!

Figure 6–1 "Viva Verdi!" code

Characters "sang" their emotions almost continuously, and Verdi took care to select librettos that gave his singers plenty of emotional—and sometimes violent—situations to sing about. This approach took even firmer root in the **verismo** operas of the next generation of Italian composers. The adjective means "realism" or "true-to-life" and it was applied to works that focused on raw emotions in sometimes seamy environments.

The composer who achieved the greatest degree of fame after Verdi was Giacomo Puccini. Puccini adopted certain techniques he had observed in the works of Germany's Richard Wagner—especially the use of evocative melodies, which reflected specific characters in the story—and merged these methods with the customary glorification of the singing voice. Puccini wielded a lot of power in shaping the storyline of his works, which was particularly true in *La Bohème* (*The Bohemian*, 1896).

Although *La Bohème* is not a *verismo* opera, some of its brilliance is due to the same desire for realism. In the party scenes, for instance, we move from one group of chattering guests to the next in a seamless flow, much as a filmmaker might depict the event today. During the later scenes, the music often repeats short snippets of melody, or **motifs**, that the audience remembers having heard at earlier intense moments in the opera. In this way, the musical score can at times function like memory, intensifying the audience's understanding of how the characters *feel* in the story.

Like a number of other composers, Puccini helped to demonstrate the power of melody to elevate and underscore our understanding of character and psychology. Moreover, at least two of Puccini's operas would later serve as the basis for modern stage pieces: *Madama Butterfly* contributed to the plot of *Miss Saigon* (1989), while *La Bohème* found itself recast in *Rent* (1996). Puccini's use of sometimes gritty realism coupled with soaring melodic lines pointed the way to a particularly effective kind of music for the stage—shocking and beautiful at the same time.

Stage music in Germany in the early Romantic era had featured international imports more than native efforts. Many prominent German composers—such as Beethoven and Schumann—tried their hand at opera only once or not at all (as was the case with Brahms, Bruckner, and Mahler). It took the work of Richard Wagner to change things—but change them he did, in ways that were far-reaching and inescapable. Wagner was born the same year as Verdi but took a very different path through life, and he left behind a personal legacy that proved far more divisive.

Wagner was full of innovative ideas, such as linking certain melodies and even **keys** to certain characters or objects (a key is a set of pitches belonging to a scale). Wagner believed in an "Artwork of the Future," which would be free from capitalistic pressures; he argued that all the arts should be unified into a **Gesamtkunstwerk** ("total art work"). In the *Gesamtkunstwerk*, no aspect of artistic endeavor could be neglected; music, dance, poetry, scenery, and stage design should all aspire to the highest level of achievement, and the whole would prove to be greater than the sum of the parts. Wagner promptly applied this principle to his subsequent works, producing the genre now called **music drama**.

The most famous product of Wagner's *Gesamtkunstwerk* efforts is his massive "Ring" cycle of four music dramas known as *Der Ring des Nibelungen* (*The Ring of the Nibelungs*). A **cycle** is a set of pieces connected by common ideas or motifs. Two things made Wagner's enormous music dramas coherent and cohesive: the first was Wagner's own fervent nationalism, for the plots presented mythic stories drawn in part from ancient German legends, interweaving the Teutonic gods with brave mortals, duplicitous dwarves, and various other magical and supernatural beings.

The second unifying device was an elaborate system of musical **leitmotifs**. A *leitmotif* ("leading motive") was a melodic fragment linked to a particular character, object, or even an idea. In truth, Wagner never used the actual term himself, nor was Wagner the first to use the idea—but Wagner did create a vast universe of *leitmotifs* that interwove and supported each other in overwhelming complexity; they foreshadowed characters yet to appear, indicated what a particular character was thinking, or even contradicted what a certain character might be saying.

Although the *leitmotifs* are occasionally sung by the characters in the music dramas, these evocative melodies are usually played by instruments, giving the orchestra a much more significant role in the drama of stage music than it had ever had before. A particularly powerful example occurs in a passage nicknamed "Wotan's Farewell," which depicts the sorrowful parting when Wotan, king of the Teutonic gods, must punish his daughter Brünnhilde by putting her into an enchanted slumber. The orchestra presents a whole series of *leitmotifs* representing the "Renunciation of Love," "Magic Sleep," "Slumber," the "Farewell Song," "Fate," "Law," and the "Magic Fire"; some of the *leitmotifs* are even played simultaneously. The singing stops several minutes before the orchestra finishes "telling the story."

The psychological understanding that *leitmotifs* can contribute to a scene is a powerful device, one that is heard in theatrical works by many later composers (and in film scores as well). Rudolf Friml adopts certain *leitmotifs* in *Rose-Marie*; Kurt Weill lets Mack the Knife's "Moritat" reappear at telling moments in the course of *The Threepenny Opera*; Mama Rose's "I had a dream" runs all through Jule Styne's *Gypsy*, while Andrew Lloyd Webber and Stephen Sondheim each experiment with *leitmotif*-like associations in various shows, including *Evita* and *Sweeney Todd*. Not only does Jerome Kern's "river theme" ("Ol' Man River") wind its way throughout *Show Boat*, but even Kern's lighthearted Princess Shows echo the basic concerns of *Gesamtkunstwerk*.

Wagner's legacy to music is somewhat tarnished by his anti-Semitic views and his advocacy for a "pure" Aryan race. In the twentieth century, Adolf Hitler (and Nazi Germany) would become a proponent of Wagner's music, and thus negative associations with Wagner's music still overwhelm some listeners. Certainly, Wagner would not be the last theatrical composer whose personal views would affect the public perception of his works—and undoubtedly there have been composers who learned, from Wagner's example, that it is sometimes wiser to keep their nonmusical opinions to themselves!

Vienna had been a magnet for composers since the Classic era, when the city was so awash in talent that even a genius like Mozart did not particularly stand out from the crowd. The Viennese were anxious for fresh (usually imported) repertory, so Italian opera—both serious and comic—was all the rage for a time. By the mid-nineteenth century, Vienna began to host performances of operas by both Wagner and Verdi (despite the Austrian empire's slipping grip on its rule over Italy). At the same time, not only were comic works by Offenbach imported and imitated, but Offenbach himself also came to Vienna.

Although the public adored Offenbach's works, rival theater managers weren't as happy with the situation. The composer Franz von Suppé was asked to create something to compete with the all-too-successful Offenbach productions. Suppé's results became known as **Viennese operetta**, consisting of silly, childlike stories—sometimes even fairy tales—masking witty satires of local social or political events. A quirk of these pieces is that they were generally in three acts rather than in the more typical two—since it was the habit of Viennese theater owners to pay librettists "by the act"!

One of the new genre's most beloved characteristics, however, was its emphasis on dance. Today, a singer might sing a hit song from a particular show in a concert or on a CD; in the nineteenth century, the Viennese wanted their operettas to contain tunes they could dance to at parties and balls. Suppé certainly obliged them, but he was superseded by **Johann Strauss** the Younger (1825–1899)—in the same way that the French composer Hervé had been overshadowed by his younger rival Offenbach.

The name Johann Strauss was already very familiar to the Viennese public, for it was the name of the operetta composer's father as well. (See the *Sidebar:* The Strauss Family and the Waltz.) Both father and son were prominent orchestra leaders, and known for their well-trained ensembles. Both men had written hundreds of dances; in fact, the younger Strauss was nicknamed "the Waltz King" by critics of the day, and he was recognized as Europe's leading composer of dance music by the mid–1860s.

Strauss's first two works met with mixed success; tickets sold well, but the critics were divided. A week after one of his works opened, Vienna suffered its "Black Friday," a stock market crash with repercussions all through Europe. The economy was still rocky in 1874 when Strauss's next operetta, *Die Fledermaus* (*The Bat*), made its debut. In fact, the show ran for only 68 performances initially—a very disappointing run for the time. But *Die Fledermaus* triumphed when it was taken to Berlin, Hamburg, and even Paris (in what must have been a particularly gratifying achievement, since this success took place on Offenbach's "home turf"), and the authors decided to launch it a second time in Vienna. More than one historian has joked that *Die Fledermaus* "never stopped playing" after that point.

The storyline (see the **Plot Summary**) was based on an 1872 French play by Henri Meilhac and Ludovic Halévy (Halévy had been one of the librettists of *Orphée aux enfers*), although their play had been inspired in turn by an earlier German comedy. The text for Strauss's version was adapted by **Karl Haffner** (1804–1876) and **Richard Genée** (1823–1895). Inspired by their libretto, Strauss needed only 43 days to complete the score. Like the Suppé operettas and Strauss's earlier works, *Die Fledermaus* is crammed full of dance music and ensemble numbers as the characters flirt with, tease, and entertain each other. There are a number of musical highlights, including Adele's "Laughing Song." The "Watch Duet" (**Musical Example 7**) is another delightful moment in the show.

The tempo, meter, and texture all change several times during the course of this duet as the battle of wits unfolds between Eisenstein and Rosalinde. Eisenstein begins at **2** with homophony, but some brief exchanges of imitative polyphony begin at **3**. At **5**, the two voices create homophony; the couple does not sing the *same* melody, but they harmonize with each other, singing the same words in essentially the same rhythm. (You'll notice that the meter is a very clear duple at **6**, mimicking the "tick-tock" of Eisenstein's pocket watch.) The texture gradually changes to non-imitative polyphony at **7**, as it dawns on Eisenstein that this mysterious Hungarian countess is *not* cooperating with his little hypnotism trick—instead, she's stealing his watch! The tempo steadily increases as well, to reflect the nervous energy, in a process called **accelerando**. (The term for a gradual slowing of the tempo is **ritardando**.)

Rosalinde's amused *Ach!* at **9** is only a single syllable, but she sustains this one syllable over many, many, many notes. Musicians use the term **text setting** to describe how the syllables of the poetry correspond to the notes of the melody; when there is a one-to-one relationship of syllables to notes, as is the case in most vocal music, the text setting is called **syllabic**. (The children's tune "Are You Sleeping?" is an example of syllabic text setting.) It is possible, however, for a singer to stretch a single syllable of text over a long series of changing notes, as Rosalinde does at **9**; this technique is called **melismatic** text setting. (Another example of a **melisma** occurs in the Christmas carol "Angels We Have Heard on High"; the syllable *Glo-* of the word *Gloria*—near the end of the tune—is extended over a long series of descending notes.) For many listeners, melismatic singing is a stereotypical hallmark of opera, since melismas are an ideal opportunity for a singer to show off the agility of the voice without having to worry about enunciating poetry. Certainly, a long melisma like Rosalinde's requires a great deal of vocal control and flexibility, for the technique is nowhere near as easy to do as it might seem.

Despite the eventual triumph of *Die Fledermaus*, few of Strauss's other stage works achieved similar levels of success. Nevertheless, other composers produced a host of Viennese operettas, and the era has become known in Viennese history as the Golden Age—ending with Strauss's death in 1899. Although new Austrian composers would come to the fore during the "Silver Age" that would follow, the Viennese of the late nineteenth century continued to be interested in the best foreign imports that came their way—particularly the works of a new British team known as Gilbert and Sullivan.

FURTHER READING

Budden, Julian. *The Operas of Verdi*. New York: Oxford University Press, 1973.

Newman, Ernest. *The Wagner Operas*. New York: Alfred A. Knopf, 1949.

Pastene, Jerome. *Three-Quarter Time: The Life and Music of the Strauss Family of Vienna*. New York: Abelard Press, 1951. Reprinted Westport, Connecticut: Greenwood Press, 1971.

Traubner, Richard. *Operetta: A Theatrical History*. Garden City, New York: Doubleday, 1983.

Wechsberg, Joseph. *The Waltz Emperors: The Life and Times and Music of the Strauss Family*. New York: Putnam, 1973.

PLOT SUMMARY: *DIE FLEDERMAUS*

If your friend Gabriel von Eisenstein had stranded you at a masquerade party, forcing you to walk home by yourself in broad daylight while dressed in a bat costume, what would you do? Well, if you were Dr. Falke, you'd seek your revenge by making a fool of Eisenstein in return. Falke's elaborate scheme is the plot to *Die Fledermaus*, set in Vienna in the second half of the nineteenth century.

Falke has enlisted the help of Prince Orlofsky, who plans to host another masquerade ball. Falke distributes a number of invitations to the ball, but he keeps the guest list a secret—so Rosalinde, for instance, doesn't know that her husband Eisenstein is going to this party, and neither of them know about their maid Adele's invitation. What they

---

Sidebar: The Strauss Family and the Waltz

Many early nineteenth-century observers feared that a new threat to public morality had arisen in, of all places, the ballroom. The menace was the **waltz**—a "revolving dance" in triple meter—and it was viewed as "an incitement to sinful passion" as well as "demoralizing and lewd" because the partners held each other in a close embrace, arms wrapped around each other's torso. To generations accustomed to public contact limited to the fingertips at most, the waltz facilitated a horrifying display of intimacy. One German writer published a "medical" pamphlet titled *Proof That the Waltz is a Main Cause of the Weakness of Body and Mind of Our Generation*. Nevertheless, despite the public outcry (and perhaps in part because of it), waltzing became all the rage in Vienna. At one point, public ballrooms could accommodate 50,000 dancers—approximately one-fourth of the Viennese adult population.

Many orchestras were needed to fill these ballrooms and new music was always in demand. The senior Johann Strauss adopted the technique of writing "topical" dances—galops, polkas, quadrilles, and of course waltzes—as well as marches. Strauss soon became the toast of Vienna—so much so that he hired enough musicians to staff several orchestras so that he could have ensembles performing in different venues simultaneously. He dashed from place to place, leading each orchestra himself in a few tunes, and then leaving a deputy in charge of the performers for the rest of the evening. He organized his personal life along similar lines, but after several years of dividing his time between two households, he left his wife and five children in 1846 and moved in full-time with his long-time mistress and *their* seven children. (He died three years later of scarlet fever, contracted from one of his illegitimate offspring.)

Strauss's oldest son, also named Johann, grew up imitating his father's musical style, but was not actually taught by his father. In fact, the older Strauss was opposed to a musical career for any of his sons; he told his ex-wife (through his lawyer) that she would receive no more financial support if any of the boys studied music, so the young Johann Strauss's musical training took place in secret. However, he would develop

into an even bigger star than his father; no less a composer than Verdi stated, "I honour him as one of my most gifted colleagues." Even if Johann Strauss, Jr, had not turned his pen to operetta in his forties, he would have been remembered to this day for his most beloved waltzes: *Wine, Women, and Song!*, *Tales from the Vienna Woods*, and of course *The Blue Danube*.

212
JOHANN STRAUSS
1825-1899

Johann Strauss, Jr.
Lebrecht Collection/NL.

do know is this: a short time earlier, Eisenstein had been convicted of a minor offense, and Eisenstein is due to report for his short prison sentence on the same night as Orlofsky's ball. Falke convinces Eisenstein that they have time to go to the ball briefly before Eisenstein goes to jail, so Eisenstein dresses up; Rosalinde, thinking he's on his way to the prison, is a bit surprised by his attire. However, she's distracted by the approaching secret visit of a former boyfriend, Alfred, who is planning to arrive after her husband has left the house. The maid Adele has also been excused for the night, so Rosalinde and Alfred are all set for a private evening together.

Their rendezvous is interrupted when the prison governor Colonel Frank arrives at the house to escort Eisenstein to prison. Alfred (prodded by Rosalinde) makes a quick decision: he pretends to be Eisenstein, since it would ruin Rosalinde's reputation for her to be home alone with a man who is *not* her husband. After Alfred and the warden have left, Rosalinde receives a note from Falke, telling her that her husband has gone to a party and she should come and see what he's up to.

Rosalinde disguises herself as a Hungarian countess and heads off to Prince Orlofsky's ball.

At the party, Eisenstein's having a bad night: he flirted with a lovely lady who turned out to be his own parlor maid, Adele; her "Laughing Song" was a merry reaction to his mistake. He then tries to impress a beautiful Hungarian countess by showing her a trick he can perform with his pocket watch (the **Musical Example 7** "The Watch Duet")—but the countess is of course Rosalinde, who recognizes the trick *and* her husband. She manages to trick *him* by stealing the watch away.

The party continues until Eisenstein realizes he'd better make his way to the prison. He is unnerved to hear that the jail already has a prisoner named "Eisenstein," but then he figures out what must have happened. When Rosalinde arrives, he starts to berate her for her infidelity. But *she* has the watch—and by producing it, reminds Eisenstein that he had not behaved too well himself while at the masquerade party. All the other guests arrive at the prison and blame the whole affair on—too much champagne!

MUSICAL EXAMPLE 7

Die Fledermaus (The Bat)
Johann Strauss II/Karl Haffner and Richard Genée, 1874
"The Watch Duet"
Act II, No. 9

1   *[orchestral introduction]*

Eisenstein *(to himself)*

2
Dieser Anstand, so manierlich,	This graciousness so mannerly,
Diese Taille fein und zierlich	This waist petite and dainty,
Und ein Füsschen, das mit Küsschen	And a tiny foot that with burning kisses
Glühend man bedecken sollt'	Should be covered
Wenn sie's nur erlauben wollt!	If only she'd allow it!

Rosalinde *(to herself)*

Statt zu schmachten im Arreste,	Instead of languishing in jail,
Amüsiert er sich auf's Beste	He's having a wonderful time,
Denkt ans Küssen, Statt ans Büssen;	Thinking of kisses, instead of atonement;
Warte nur, du Bösewicht,	You'll not escape
Du entgehst der Strafe nicht.	*your punishment.*

Eisenstein

Ach, wie leicht könnt' es entschweben,	Oh, how easily it could disappear,
Dies holde Zauberbild!	This gracious enchanted mask!
Willst du nicht die Maske heben	Will you not raise the mask
Die dein Antlitz mir verhüllt?	That hides your face from me?

Rosalinde

Ei, mein schöner Herr, ich bitte,	Really, dear Sir, no, no!
Nicht verwegen, nichts berührt!	Do not dare, do not touch!
Denn es heischt die gute Sitte,	For custom demands
Dass man Masken respektiert!	That masks be respected.

3
Rosalinde *(to herself)*		**Eisenstein** *(to himself)*	
Wie er gieret,	How he yearns	Halb verwirret,	Half confused,
kokettieret	and flirts,	halb gerühret,	half moved,
Wie er schmachtend	How languishingly	Retirieret	She withdraws

Rosalinde		**Eisenstein**	
mich fixieret!	he stares.	sie vor mir.	from me.
Keine Mahnung,	No warning,	Lass doch seh'n,	Let us see
keine Ahnung	no inkling	ob es geht,	if it works,
Kündet ihm, wer vor ihm steht.	Tells him who's before him.	Ob sie widersteht?	Or if she'll resist.
Ja, bald werd' ich	Yes, soon I	Ja, bald werd' ich	Yes, soon I
reüssieren,	will succeed,	reüssieren,	will succeed,
Will den Frevler	I'll convict him,	Ich will doch seh'n,	I'll see
überführen,	the rogue:	Ob sie mir	if she
Will's probieren,	I'll try it and see	widersteht,	resists me,
ob er in die Falle geht!	if he falls in the trap!	Ob sie die Falle geht!	If she'll fall into the trap!

(Eisenstein's watch strikes)

Rosalinde *(weak of voice; staggers hand on heart to the sofa)*

4
Ach, wie wird mein Auge trübe,   Oh, my eyes are dimmed,
Wie das Herz so bang mir Schlägt.   And uneasily beats my heart!

Eisenstein *(watching her in triumph)*

Ha, schon meldet sich die Liebe,   Ha! Already love appears
die das Herz ihr bang bewegt!   and moves her heart uneasily!

Rosalinde

Leider ist's ein altes Übel, doch vorübergehend nur.   I fear it's an old ailment, but a quickly passing one.
Stimmen meines Herzens Schläge mit dem Tiktak einer Uhr?   Does my heart beat time to the ticking of a watch?

Eisenstein

Ei, das können wir gleich seh'n!   Ah, we'll soon find out!

Rosalinde

Zählen wir, ich bitte schön!   Please, let's count.

Rosalinde & Eisenstein

5
Ja, zählen wir.   Yes, let's count.

Eisenstein

6
Eins, zwei, drei, vier,   One, two, three, four,

Rosalinde

Fünf, sechs, sieb'n, neun,   Five, six, seven, nine,

Eisenstein

Nein, das kann nicht sein,   No, that cannot be,
Denn nach der Sieb'n kommt erst die Acht.   For after seven first comes eight.

Rosalinde

Sie hab'n mich ganz verwirrt gemacht,   You have quite confused me.
Wir wollen wechseln.   Let us change.

Eisenstein

Wechseln? Wie?   Change? How?

Rosalinde

Den Schlag des Herzens zählen Sie   You count my heartbeats
Und ich das Tiktak Ihrer Uhr,   And I the ticking of your watch,
Ich bitt auf fünf Minuten nur.   for just five minutes please.

(She takes the watch, which Eisenstein hands her, together with the chain)

Jetzt zählen Sie, mein Herr Marquis!   Now count, dear Marquis!

Eisenstein

Bin schon dabei!   I'm ready!

Rosalinde & Eisenstein

Eins, zwei, drei, vier, Fünf, sechs, sieb'n, acht,   One, two, three, four, Five, six, seven, eight,

Rosalinde		**Eisenstein**	
7			
Neun, zehn, elf, zwölf,	Nine, ten, eleven, twelve,	Hopp, hopp, hopp, hopp,	Clip, clop, clip, clop,
Dreizehn, vierzehn, fünfzehn,	Thirteen, fourteen, fifteen,	Das geht im Galopp!	That's quite a gallop!
Sechzehn, siebzehn, achtzehn,	Sixteen, seventeen, eighteen,	Sechs, sieben, acht,	Six, seven, eight,
Neunzehn, zwanzig, dreissig, vierzig,	Nineteen, twenty, thirty, forty,	Neun, zehn, elf, zwölf,	Nine, ten, eleven, twelve,
Fünfzig, sechzig,	Fifty, sixty,	Hopp, hopp, hopp, hopp,	Clip, clop, clip, clop,

Rosalinde

achtzig, hundert!   eighty, one hundred!

So weit können wir noch nicht sein!   We cannot be so far already!
Nein, nein, nein!   No, no, no!

Eisenstein

im Galopp;   at the gallop,
Sechshundert und neun!   Six hundred and nine!
O, ich bin weiter schon!   Oh, I'm further still!
Eine halbe Million!   A half million!

Eisenstein

8   Ja, eine halbe million!   Yes, a half million!

Rosalinde

Wie kann man gar so grob nur fehlen!   How can anyone go wrong so badly?

Eisenstein

Da mag der Teufel richtig zählen!   The very devil couldn't count correctly!

Rosalinde

Heut wirst du nimmer repetieren!   You'll not strike again today!

Eisenstein

Sie will die Uhr sich annexieren! Meine Uhr!   She's going to keep my watch! My watch!

Rosalinde

Ich danke von Herzen!   I thank you kindly!

Eisenstein

Ich wollte nur. . .   I only wanted. . .

Rosalinde

Belieben zu scherzen!   You choose to jest!

Rosalinde *(laughing)*

9   *Ach!   Ah!*

Eisenstein

Sie ist nicht ins Netz gegangen,   She has not entered my net,
Hat die Uhr mir abgefangen;   But has taken my watch.
Dieser Spass ist etwas teuer,   This prank is rather expensive,
hab' blamiert mich ungeheuer!   I've made a dreadful fool of myself.
(snatches at the watch)
Ach, meine Uhr, ich bitte sehr,   Oh, my watch, please,
Ich wollte nur . . .   I only wanted. . . .
Sie ist nichts ins Netz gegangen,   She has not entered my net,
Ach, meine Uhr,   oh, my watch,
Hätte ich sie wieder nur!   If I only had it back!
O weh, o weh!   Oh dear, oh dear,
Dieser Spass ist etwas teuer,   This prank is rather expensive,
hab' blamiert mich ungeheuer!   I've made a dreadful fool of myself!
Meine Uhr ist annexiert!   My watch has gone!
Ach, ich bin blamiert! Weh mir!   I've been fooled! Woe is me!

Chapter 7
England in the Nineteenth Century: Gilbert and Sullivan

After the rage for *The Beggar's Opera* and other ballad operas had passed, eighteenth-century English theaters turned instead to comic opera. Not everyone admired these works; one writer, George Hogarth, dismissed them as "unmeaning sing-song." It would take a new genre—English operetta—and a new team of writers—Gilbert and Sullivan—for England to be able to regain a strong position in the international market for musical theater.

Comic opera had already been challenged by other genres, such as **burlesque**. Although the term would become more unsavory in the early twentieth century, the nineteenth-century burlesque was, quite simply, an amusing *travesty*, or satire, of some other kind of familiar work, such as a play, a fairy tale, or a literary creation. (The Italian verb *burlarsi* means "to make fun of" or "to laugh at.") Grand opera was a favorite target for burlesque adaptation. These travesties employed every means they could to generate humor—roles might be given to the "wrong" sex, logic was abandoned, and no opportunity for silly puns was overlooked. Costumes for the actresses grew skimpier and skimpier. These creations were profitable enough that John Hollingshead built a new theatre in London, the Gaiety, to feature burlesque productions; he commissioned shows such as *Aladdin II* and *Cinderella the Younger* (although initially he turned to French composers, including Hervé, for the musical scores). Hollingshead billed himself as a "licensed dealer in legs, short skirts, French adaptations, Shakespeare, Taste, and the musical glasses."

Hollingshead's "French adaptations" reflected the growing competition that came from across the English Channel. French opéra-bouffe productions soon found their way onto the English stage, as did Viennese operettas. **William Schwenk Gilbert** (1836–1911) helped to translate and adapt several of the French works. At the same time, English theaters were fighting against a negative social stereotype. The Victorian mindset generally viewed plays as immoral (and the actors in plays were held in even greater disdain); musical theater productions fared even worse. Presentations that were "educational" were more acceptable, so many plays were billed as "illustrations," and the actors' roles were called "assumptions." Sacred music depicting religious stories was acceptable, since generally these works were **unstaged**—meaning that the performers merely stood and sang their roles. A young composer named **Arthur Sullivan** (1842–1900) built his early reputation on works in this sacred style.

A family called the German Reeds worked hard to remove the stigma of theatrical presentations. They kept their presentations free from vulgarity, which allowed middle-class audiences to enjoy the shows without guilt. The German Reeds also presented short satiric works by Sullivan (who was working with the writer Francis Burnand). Sullivan and Burnand's efforts reflected a more elevated musical comedy that would become acceptable to Victorian audiences, and could well be viewed as the birth of **English operetta**. (The label operetta was by no means universally applied, however; these types of pieces were also frequently advertised as "comic operas," "light operas," as well as opéra-bouffes, despite being written in English.)

Interestingly, in 1869, *Cox and Box*—by Sullivan and Burnand—shared the program for a time with *No Cards*, with music by Thomas German Reed and lyrics by Gilbert. Moreover, Gilbert reviewed *Cox and Box* for *Fun* magazine, declaring that Sullivan's music was "too good" for the play. (This comment might not have been a straightforward compliment, since, in later years, Gilbert sometimes maintained that Sullivan's music was again "too good"—that is, too "classical"—for their joint endeavors.)

Although Sullivan and Gilbert finally met in 1869, it was not until 1871 that the two men first collaborated. Hollingshead commissioned them for a burlesque at his Gaiety Theatre. The result was *Thespis, or The Gods Grown Old*, and it owed a great deal to Offenbach's *Orpheus in the Underworld* with its satiric view of the gods' (mis)behavior. The short work was only moderately successful, but it ran 63 performances, thereby outlasting several other seasonal productions.

Despite their eventual fame as a team, Gilbert and Sullivan never actually "clicked" on a personal level—Gilbert was much more formal and rigid (but outspoken) in his views than the more easygoing and bohemian Sullivan. Perhaps nothing more would have come of their partnership had it not been for Richard D'Oyly Carte, the manager of the Royalty Theatre in London. It was customary to precede major stage works with short one-act presentations (rather like the opening bands at rock concerts). D'Oyly Carte suggested that Gilbert take his script for *Trial by Jury* to Sullivan. Sullivan later recalled that Gilbert read the script to him

. . . in a gradual crescendo of indignation, in the manner of a man considerably disappointed with what he had written. As soon as he came to the last word, he closed up the manuscript violently, apparently unconscious of the fact that he had achieved his purpose as far as I was concerned, inasmuch as I was screaming with laughter the whole time.

A caricature of Gilbert and Sullivan.
Lebrecht Collection/NL.

Sullivan was so energized by the story that he was able to compose the score in only a few weeks.

Despite their differing personalities, the partners were in agreement on several fundamental artistic philosophies. As Gilbert later related,

> *We resolved that our plots, however ridiculous, should be coherent, that our dialogue should be void of offence; on artistic principles, no man should play a woman's part and no woman a man's. Finally, we agreed that no lady of the company should be required to wear a dress that she could not wear with absolute propriety at a private fancy ball.*

With these principles in place, Gilbert and Sullivan developed a formula that worked almost unfailingly for them. *Trial by Jury* opened at the Royalty Theatre in 1875 and became an immediate hit. The one-act operetta ran 200 performances, prompting D'Oyly Carte to establish the Comedy Opera Company, which would be devoted to works by English writers. (He found an oddball collection of investors to support the endeavor, including Sullivan's music publisher, a piano manufacturer, and the owner of a street-sprinkler monopoly.)

By 1877, however, Gilbert and Sullivan were ready to present *The Sorcerer.* This spoof of the British clergy put D'Oyly Carte's new Comedy Opera Company on a healthy footing. Moreover, the operetta's **company**—the theatrical troupe—became the nucleus of actors and actresses who would continue to perform Gilbert and Sullivan's future works. The team had looked long and hard for singers who could act, and this carefully selected ensemble helped their show to run for 175 performances.

Scarcely six weeks after *The Sorcerer* opened, Gilbert sent Sullivan a draft of *H. M. S. Pinafore, or The Lass That Loved a Sailor.* Gilbert had always been fascinated with the sea; his

father had been a naval surgeon, and Gilbert believed he was related to an Elizabethan explorer, Sir Humphrey Gilbert, who had traversed Newfoundland in 1583 and had established the first English colony in North America. Sullivan set to work, despite suffering from an excruciating kidney stone. He reminisced,

> *It is, perhaps, rather a strange fact that the music of* Pinafore, *which is thought to be so merry and spontaneous, was written while I was suffering agonies from a cruel illness. I would compose a few bars, and then be almost insensible from pain. When the paroxysm was passed, I would write a little more, until the pain overwhelmed me again.*

Gilbert and Sullivan traveled to the naval harbor at Portsmouth to inspect the deck and riggings of H. M. S. *Victory,* and they contracted with a naval supplier for absolutely authentic costumes. Sullivan, knowing many of the singers who would perform, wrote music suitable for specific voices (in much the same way that Mozart had "tailored" roles). He and Gilbert directed the actors to perform utterly seriously, regardless of how silly or ridiculous the situation, which only enhanced the humor.

After the operetta's debut in 1878, a June heat wave—in the days before air-conditioning—almost proved its undoing. By July, the nightly **take**—money taken in from ticket sales—was less than £40 and the cast agreed to take a one-third cut in salary. Six times, the nervous investors in the show posted closing notices, which D'Oyly Carte hurriedly removed. Finally, it looked as though the show *would* have to close, but Sullivan had an idea. He was directing summer Promenade Concerts at the Royal Opera House in Covent Garden, so he assembled a medley of operetta excerpts for the Promenade performances—and ticket sales for *Pinafore* shot sky-high (while cooler August weather didn't hurt, either). The vocal score sold like hotcakes in London music shops; at one point, 10,000 copies were purchased on a single day. London had never seen such a hit. The show ran some 571 performances, not including 46 performances of *The Children's Pinafore,* featuring a cast comprised entirely of children. *Pinafore* would not be the last musical show to be rescued by a clever advertising campaign.

Even though the receipts jumped up to some £500 a week, the show's investors weren't satisfied. They decided to open their own production of *Pinafore* at a nearby theater, so they stormed the backstage of the Opera Comique Theatre in an attempt to wrest the **props** (portable objects used in a play) and scenery from the original production. The "authentic" *Pinafore's* **stagehands** (the people who handle the curtain and move the scenery from place to place) gave battle, eventually triumphing over the interlopers. The whole situation ended up in court, where the judge eventually delivered a decision in favor of D'Oyly Carte and *Pinafore's* authors.

A different kind of problem was developing in the United States, where *Pinafore* mania was running rampant. More than 50 companies were performing the operetta across the nation, while in New York there were eight different productions staged within five blocks of each other. *Pinafore* appeared in "theme" productions with all-Black or all-Catholic casts;

it played on canal boats and paddle steamers. The problem was that all these productions were **pirated**—meaning that none of them were **authorized** (sanctioned by the authors), and perhaps more importantly, none of them paid the authors any **royalties** (the percentage of the profits that are delivered to those holding the copyright of a work). Part of the issue was that international copyright agreements had not yet come into being. When the first law was written in 1887 at the Berne Convention, the United States was not one of the 14 participating countries.

The partners were determined not to yield their rights without a fight, so Gilbert, Sullivan, and D'Oyly Carte sailed to New York in 1879 to present the first "authorized" U.S. production of *Pinafore*, which was enthusiastically received when it opened on December 1. Moreover, they had decided to protect their copyright interest in their *next* show by remaining on hand in the United States for its premiere. This next operetta was **The Pirates of Penzance, or The Slave of Duty**. They had made arrangements for an English premiere of the operetta to take place just before the New York premiere, since even a single presentation would protect their British copyright privileges.

Arriving in New York, Sullivan was horrified to find that he had left the score for the entire first act of *The Pirates of Penzance* back in England. In those pre-email, pre-fax-machine days, he had no recourse but to re-compose the missing music. New York visitors can now find a plaque at No. 45 East 20th Street that reads, "On this site Sir Arthur Sullivan composed *The Pirates of Penzance* during 1879."

Moreover, the New York orchestral musicians were threatening to strike; they claimed that the new work was more complex than a "mere" operetta and thus merited the higher pay awarded to members of opera orchestras. Sullivan retorted that the orchestra of the Covent Garden opera house would be glad to come overseas and that he and a friend would accompany the singers with a piano and a harmonium (a small organ-like instrument) until the opera orchestra arrived. The New York musicians, afraid to call Sullivan's bluff, decided to

cancel the strike. Afterwards, Sullivan admitted how very relieved he was, explaining, "The idea of getting the Covent Garden band over was hardly less absurd than the ludicrous idea of using the pianoforte and harmonium in a big theatre." (Almost 60 years later, however, composer Marc Blitzstein would indeed have to use a piano to accompany *The Cradle Will Rock* when—because of political pressure—the musicians' union forbade the orchestra to take part in his musical.)

Despite these early obstacles, audiences loved the frenzied storyline (see the **Plot Summary**), and D'Oyly Carte soon organized performances in Boston and Philadelphia, while two other companies toured the nation. The London production ran 363 performances, closing a day short of its one-year anniversary. *The Pirates of Penzance* was the first operetta in which D'Oyly Carte, Gilbert, and Sullivan split the profits three ways, and its success cemented their partnership for many years to come.

Musical Example 8 features Major-General Stanley in "I Am the Very Model of a Modern Major-General." The excerpt begins with a passage written in recitative (**1**), reminiscent of the traditional Italian approach to opera. A clearer sense of beat develops at **2**, and the beats fall into a duple meter, as shown in **Figure 7–1**.

However, there's a bit of a sing-song feeling to this passage, and this "swaying" sensation comes from the grouping of pulses *between* each of these beats. From **2** until **3**, each beat is subdivided into *three* equal parts; this type of **subdivision** is called **compound**. **Figure 7–2** uses the symbols "&" and "a" to depict the second and third segments, or subdivisions, of each beat:

At **3**, however, the meter is still duple, but each beat is now subdivided into *two* equal pulsations. The term for this effect is **simple subdivision**. **Figure 7–3** illustrates the duple meter's main beats, while **Figure 7–4** demonstrates how the same syllables coordinate with the simple subdivision.

Any meter can have simple or compound subdivision (simple triple, compound duple), but the two-part subdivision of a beat is the most common in popular music. "I Am the

(And it) is,		it	is	a	glo- ri-	ous thing		to	be	a	Ma-		jor	Ge- ne- ral! . . .
1		**2**			**1**	**2**		**1**		**2**			**1**	**2**

Figure 7–1 Duple meter.

(And it) is,		it	is	a	glo- ri-	ous thing		to	be	a	Ma-		jor	Ge- ne- ral! . . .
1 & a	**2** & a	**1** & a	**2** & a	**1** & a	**2** & a	**1** & a	**2**

Figure 7–2 Duple meter with compound subdivision.

(I)	am the	ver-y	mod-el	of a	mod-ern	ma-jor	gen-er-	al, I've . . .
	1	**2**	**1**	**2**	**1**	**2**	**1**	**2**

Figure 7–3 Duple meter.

(I)	am	the	ver-	y	mod-	el	of	a	mod-	ern	ma-	jor	gem-	er-	al,	I've
	1	&	**2**	&	**1**	&	**2**	&	**1**	&	**2**	&	**1**	&	**2**	&

Figure 7–4 Duple meter with simple subdivision.

Very Model" provides a good opportunity to compare the sensations of compound duple and simple duple back to back.

Musical Example 8 is a **character song**, since it reveals much of Major-General Stanley's personality. (It is also a frequently parodied song; the comedian Tom Lehrer is celebrated for his delivery of the entire periodic table of the elements to this melody!) "I Am the Very Model" is in strophic form (starting at **3**), with the chorus echoing the last lines of each verse. Moreover, this number is also a very famous **patter song**, for at **5**, the singer delivers the 16-syllable lines almost as fast as humanly possible. The tempo drops a bit at **4**, allowing the last section (**5**) to sound even faster in comparison. In this performance, Major-General Stanley's spoken request at **5** to the conductor—*Presto agitato, s'il vous plaît, Maestro*—means "Very fast with agitation, if you please, Sir." The subsequent frenetic delivery is an illustration of vocal virtuosity!

There is some textual ingenuity at work as well; Gilbert had a remarkable facility for rhyming unexpected words: "lot o' news" / "hypotenuse," "differential calculus" / "beings animalculous," and so forth. The audience, delighting in the accumulation of these rhymes, waits expectantly at the end of the eighth line of **4**, when the Major-General needs a rhyme for "strategy." In desperation, he produces "sat a gee." This made-up word is a **neologism**, and its unexpectedness adds to the humor.

While the team worked on its next endeavor, D'Oyly Carte began building a new theater, calling it the Savoy Theatre since it was built on the site of a medieval palace of one of the princes of Savoy. (The Savoy was the first London theater to be illuminated by electricity rather than the customary gas lights.) The operettas of Gilbert and Sullivan became known as the **Savoy Operas**—a term that has generally been applied retroactively to *all* the Gilbert and Sullivan collaborations—while the performers were often known as the **Savoyards**. (When works by other authors began to be performed at the theatre, these also became known as Savoy Operas, so the situation grew to be a bit confusing at times.)

The next Gilbert and Sullivan operetta, *Iolanthe, or The Peer and the Peri* (1882), premiered at the new Savoy Theatre. D'Oyly Carte decided to borrow an idea from French theaters. The waiting patrons were asked to form an orderly line and then allowed into the theater in the same order in which they stood in line. The previous London custom had been to let the audience into the theater *en masse*, with people shoving and pushing to reach the unallocated seats. The production also contained some musical novelties; Sullivan had become fascinated by Wagner's *leitmotif* concept, and Gilbert and Sullivan parodied a number of elements from Wagner's "Ring" cycle in the staging of *Iolanthe*.

By 1884, after *Princess Ida, or Castle Adamant* had opened, cracks were beginning to show in the partnership. Sullivan wanted to attempt works in a grand opera style, emphasizing the music; he felt that there was too much focus on Gilbert's poetry. Meanwhile, Gilbert was pushing for a story with supernatural elements in it, to which Sullivan was adamantly opposed. The impasse was broken when Gilbert, inspired by the current Japanese Exhibition in London, suggested a plot with a loose Japanese theme. The result was *The Mikado, or The Town of Titipu*, which proved to be the most popular of

all the Savoy Operas despite the growing discord between the authors.

The Mikado opened in March 1885, starting a run that would last 672 performances. D'Oyly Carte also pulled off a publicity coup by sending an incognito company to the United States in August (the members of the cast sailed under aliases) so that the New York opening of the "authorized" production came as a total surprise. Again, American audiences embraced the Gilbert and Sullivan creation wholeheartedly; not only did it run 430 nights in New York, but it played at 170 locations in the United States, and the city of Mikado, Michigan, was christened in the operetta's honor.

As they had done in *Pinafore*, Gilbert and Sullivan made sure the costuming was authentic, and they hired Japanese women from the Japanese Exhibition to coach the actors in proper gestures, bowing, and handling fans. There are a few nods to Japanese music in Sullivan's score, such as the use of a five-pitch scale in the opening chorus, evoking the scale system used in much Asian music. A more explicit Japanese musical reference occurs in Act II, when Sullivan quotes a genuine Imperial Army marching song called "Miya sama, miya sama."

The remainder of the score abandons any pretense at eastern exoticism, however, and reflects the customary Gilbert and Sullivan operetta exuberance. One of the operetta's most popular ensembles, "Three Little Maids from School," was written primarily as a **sight gag**—the visual humor of the song was that it was performed by the three tiniest female stars of the company.

"Three Little Maids" from *The Mikado*.
Lebrecht Collection/NL.

The Mikado was an undeniable success, but it did not manage to heal the fractures that had developed in Gilbert and Sullivan's partnership. Having signed a contract with D'Oyly Carte, they were obligated to continue their association, but the results sometimes reflected their internal difficulties. *Ruddigore, or The Witch's Curse* (1887) actually encountered some "boos" on its opening night. Another uncomfortable period became known as the Carpet Quarrel. Gilbert was appalled at a £500 expenditure for new carpeting in the Savoy Theatre, and there was disagreement whether this should be a production expense, which the three partners customarily divided, or a theater maintenance expense, which was D'Oyly Carte's sole responsibility. When Sullivan took D'Oyly Carte's side in the matter, Gilbert took it so far as to sue them both in court. (Gilbert won the case.) At last, D'Oyly Carte's wife Helen managed to smooth the ruffled feathers, but it took three more years for Gilbert and Sullivan to complete their next work. The legacy of their string of masterpieces remained, however, and Gilbert and Sullivan's operettas have survived in the permanent repertory of musical theater to this day.

For a time, it seemed that D'Oyly Carte might have found a successor to Sullivan in Edward ("Teddy") Solomon, but although Solomon's works enjoyed satisfactory runs, they are now forgotten. (He is better remembered for his bigamous marriage to American actress Lillian Russell.) Gradually, operettas began to lose their grip on England and other types of theater began to enjoy a resurgence. Hollingshead's Gaiety Theatre was still in operation, presenting burlesques, and a new theater, Daly's, was attracting ever-larger audiences for the same kinds of productions. An entrepreneur named George Edwardes took over the management of both theaters as well as the Prince of Wales Theatre.

Over the last years of the century, Edwardes presented a variety of works—burlesques, operettas, and a new hybrid, which would be the genesis of British **musical comedy**—works in modern costume, with believable, witty dialogue and catchy, popular tunes. These new productions had various labels, such as musical farce or farcical musical comedy, while some were known as Gaiety shows because of their links to the Gaiety Theatre. The first of Edwardes's musical comedy shows actually to play *at* the Gaiety Theatre was *The Shop Girl* (1894). Although operettas would continue to appear in British theatres for many years to come, the Gaiety works foreshadowed the new style of show that would dominate the first half of the twentieth century—both in England and in America.

FURTHER READING

Baily, Leslie. *Gilbert and Sullivan: Their Lives and Times*. New York: Viking Press, 1973.
Bradley, Ian, ed. *The Annotated Gilbert and Sullivan*. New York: Penguin Books, 1982.
Hardwick, Michael. *The Drake Guide to Gilbert and Sullivan*. New York: Drake Publishers, 1973.
Hayton, Charles. *Gilbert and Sullivan*. (Modern Dramatists.) New York: St. Martin's, 1987.
Jefferson, Alan. *The Complete Gilbert & Sullivan Opera Guide*. New York: Facts on File, 1984.
Moore, Frank Ledlie. *The Handbook of Gilbert and Sullivan*. London: Arthur Barker, Ltd., 1962.
Traubner, Richard. *Operetta: A Theatrical History*. Garden City, New York: Doubleday, 1983.

PLOT SUMMARY: *THE PIRATES OF PENZANCE, OR THE SLAVE OF DUTY*

Gilbert and Sullivan's fourth collaboration began with the working title of *The Robbers*, and so the incorporation of policemen made perfectly good sense. When, midway through the show's creation, Gilbert and Sullivan converted the robbers into pirates, the policemen were harder to explain—but their continued presence helped support the crazy illogic of the overall story. But there is logic as well, if you accept the premise that "doing one's duty" is the most important responsibility that one has.

The story opens along the coast of Cornwall, where the pirates are celebrating: their apprentice Frederick has just turned 21 and has ended his indenture. Frederick is not so happy, however, for his nursemaid Ruth has just informed him that she—being a bit hard of hearing—made a small mistake in his apprenticeship: Frederick's father wanted his son to be trained as a pilot, but Ruth misheard him, so Frederick ended up as a *pirate*. Frederick is now torn: he loves his comrades, but he feels his duty to society compels him to shun the dishonest life of piracy. Duty wins out; in fact, he informs the pirates that he feels duty-bound to make every effort to destroy them. But because they are his friends, he does warn them that their tenderhearted ways are affecting their success as pirates; word has gone out up and down the coast that since the pirates are orphans themselves, anyone they attack who claims to be an orphan is able to escape unmolested. Amazingly, all of Cornwall seems to be populated by orphans!

Frederick has a second mission as well. Although Ruth assures him that she is beautiful and would make a suitable bride, he hasn't seen any other woman since the age of eight and he wants to make a comparison first. By coincidence, a group of sisters have come to the beach where Frederick has left the pirate ship. One sister, Mabel, agrees to help redeem him from his previous life of crime by marrying him. Just then, the pirates discover the maidens, and they decide to force the young women into matrimony. Frederick cannot defend the sisters single-handedly, but their father—Major-General Stanley—makes his appearance (see **Musical Example 8**). It appears the Major-General is himself an orphan, so the pirates unwillingly agree to release him and his daughters.

Now the Major-General is overcome by guilt: he is *not* an orphan after all. Frederick talks him out of confessing, however, and tells his future father-in-law that policemen plan to arrest the pirates. But there is bad news for Frederick: it turns out he was born on February 29, so he is still only a little past five years old—his indenture won't end for 51 more years. Again, Frederick struggles with his sense of duty, but since he is now once again a pirate, he decides he must tell the Pirate King that the Major-General is no orphan. Learning of this deception, the Pirate King vows to attack that very night.

The Major-General's home is protected by policemen, but they are no match for the pirates. The Pirate King warns them not to claim to be orphans, but the Sergeant has a better idea: he appeals to the pirates as loyal Englishmen to

yield in the name of Queen Victoria. The pirates, who also recognize *their* duty when they hear it, are immediately vanquished. But before they are led off to jail, Ruth announces that these aren't *real* pirates, but are merely noblemen gone wrong. As (repentant) peers who have renounced their evil profession, they are now entirely suitable as sons-in-law, so all ends happily.

MUSICAL EXAMPLE 8
THE PIRATES OF PENZANCE
SIR ARTHUR SULLIVAN/SIR WILLIAM GILBERT, 1879
"I Am the Very Model of a Modern Major-General"

Mabel

1 Hold, monsters! Ere your pirate caravanserai proceed, against our will, to wed us all,
Just bear in mind that we are Wards in Chancery, and father is a Major-General!

Sam

We'd better pause, or danger may befall, their father is a Major-General.

Girls

Yes, yes; he is a Major-General!

Major-General

Yes, yes—I am a Major-General!

Sam

2 For he is a Major-General!

All

He is! Hurrah for the Major-General!

Major-General

And it is—it is a glorious thing to be a Major-General!

All

It is! *Hurrah for the Major-General!*

Major-General

3 I am the very model of a modern Major-General,
I've information vegetable, animal, and mineral;
I know the kings of England, and I quote the fights historical,
From Marathon to Waterloo, in order categorical;
I'm very well acquainted, too, with matters mathematical,
I understand equations, both the simple and quadratical,
About binomial theorem I'm teeming with a lot of news
With many cheerful facts about the square of the hypotenuse

All

With many cheerful facts, *etc.*

Major-General

I'm very good at integral and differential calculus,
I know the scientific names of beings animalculous;
In short, in matters vegetable, animal and mineral, I am the very model of a modern Major-General.

All

In short, in matters vegetable, animal and mineral, he is the very model of a modern Major-General.

Major-General

I know our mythic history, King Arthur's and Sir Caradoc's,
I answer hard acrostics, I've a pretty taste for paradox.
I quote in elegiacs all the crimes of Heliogabalus, in conics I can floor peculiarities parabolus.
I can tell undoubted Raphaels from Gerard Dows and Zoffanies,
I know the croaking chorus from the "Frogs" of Aristophanes,
Then I can hum a fugue of which I've heard the music's din afore,
And whistle all the airs from that infernal nonsense "Pinafore."

All

And whistle all the airs, *etc.*

Major-General
Then I can write a washing bill in Babylonic cuneiform,
And tell you every detail of Caractacus's uniform;
In short, in matters vegetable, animal and mineral, I am the very model of a modern Major-General.
All
In short, in matters vegetable, animal and mineral, he is the very model of a modern Major-General.
Major-General

4

In fact, when I know what is meant by "mamelon" and "ravelin,"
When I can tell at sight a Mauser rifle from a javelin,
When such affairs as sorties and surprises I'm more wary at,
And when I know precisely what is meant by commissariat,
When I have learnt what progress has been made in modern gunnery,
When I know more of tactics than a novice in a nunnery;
In short, when I've a smattering of elemental strategy,
You'll say a better Major-General has never—sat a gee!
All
You'll say a better, *etc.*
Major-General
For all my military knowledge, though I'm plucky and adventury,
Has only been brought down to the beginning of the century;
But still, in matters vegetable, animal and mineral, I am the very model of a modern Major-General.
All
But still, in matters vegetable, animal and mineral, he is the very model of a modern Major-General.
Major-General
[*"Presto agitato, s'il vous plaît, Maestro"*]

5

In fact, when I know what is meant by "mamelon" and "ravelin,"
When I can tell at sight a Mauser rifle from a javelin,
When such affairs as sorties and surprises I'm more wary at,
And when I know precisely what is meant by commissariat,
When I have learnt what progress has been made in modern gunnery,
When I know more of tactics than a novice in a nunnery;
In short, when I've a smattering of elemental strategy,
You'll say a better Major-General has never—rode a horse!
All
You'll say a better, *etc.*
Major-General
For all my military knowledge, though I'm plucky and adventury,
Has only been brought down to the beginning of the century;
But still, in matters vegetable, animal and mineral, I am the very model of a modern Major-General.
All
But still, in matters vegetable, animal and mineral, he is the very model of a modern Major-General.

Chapter 8
The United States in the Early Nineteenth Century

The mixture of musical entertainments presented to Americans during their first century as a nation was as richly diversified as the people living within the country's ever-expanding borders. Immigrants and visitors to the United States brought many genres. At the same time, Americans began to develop new musical and theatrical traditions; as might be expected, these new forms of entertainment generally reflected the attitudes and habits of the people who created them. For this reason, the storylines and depictions of the nineteenth-century American stage reveal now-uncomfortable strains of racism, sexism, and at times a distinct cultural divide between social classes. Yet, these characterizations also reflect humor, enterprise, pathos, and ingenuity, and like many cultural artifacts, they need—at least in part—to be examined by the standards of their day.

Levels of education varied wildly among American citizens, which might account for the ways European works were adapted when they were performed in the United States. Italian operas were usually translated into English, and the recitatives were often replaced by spoken dialogue (in the manner of ballad operas, Singspiels, and many other genres). Moreover, the more complex polyphonic ensembles of Italian opera were often omitted entirely and replaced by simpler pieces in strophic form. These "Englished" operas were a very popular entertainment in the first half of the nineteenth century.

Not all imported works were modified, however; Manuel García toured with his opera company in the 1820s, performing works in Italian and giving many famous European works their American premiere. The García troupe (which included several members of the García family) did not limit its performances to the eastern states; it traveled through many parts of the nation and ventured as far south as Mexico City. Even after the Garcías' visit, a certain enthusiasm for opera remained; in 1833, New York built the Italian Opera House (although the enterprise failed after two years).

Certain other European genres developed an American following. Among them was the **burletta**, a three-act comic opera that spoofed historical or legendary stories, as well as the **pantomimes**, which were ballets depicting mythological stories or sometimes outright fantasy. Americans also enjoyed the novelty of **shadow shows**, in which puppets were operated behind a semitransparent screen in front of a bright light. Even the old English **masque**, described in Chapter 2, "Developing Genres in the Eighteenth Century," made an occasional appearance.

Meanwhile, Americans were increasingly entertained by ethnic portrayals, especially the depiction of African Americans. It is difficult to find the earliest instance of this sort of characterization; some historians point to ancient Greek plays as well as certain stock characters of the commedia dell'arte as precedents. However, Charles Matthews, an English actor visiting the United States in 1822, made it his mission to learn all he could about the mannerisms and behavior of African Americans; he then imitated what he had observed while performing in **blackface**—that is, with the skin of his face made up in an exaggerated mimicry of African American facial features. A number of other white performers soon followed Matthews's lead, calling themselves "Ethiopian Delineators"; they performed short skits as diversions during larger works, such as between the acts of a play. One of these actors was Thomas Dartmouth Rice, who, in 1828, watched an aged African American dance and decided he could make a humorous song-and-dance act out of the gnarled old man's clumsy movements. Rice advertised the blackface characterization as "Jim Crow," a term that would grow to have increasingly unpleasant associations in the next century, when it would be used to describe laws and practices that discriminated against African Americans. However, Jim Crow's rapid absorption into the nation's vocabulary is evidence of how popular Rice's act quickly became, earning him the title "Father of Minstrelsy."

It was another 15 years before a group of individual "Delineators" banded together in 1843 to present an entire evening's show in blackface. The four men—Dan Emmett, Billy Whitlock, Frank Pelham, and Frank Brower—called themselves the Virginia Minstrels, and billed their presentation as a "novel, grotesque, original, and surprisingly melodious Ethiopian Band." (They adopted the term *minstrels* because of the recent success of a touring group called the Tyrolese Minstrel Family.) Their **minstrel show** was an instant success and sparked immediate imitators, including a rival group headed by Edwin Christy called the Christy Minstrels. Although the Virginia Minstrels established a characteristic minstrel show attire of long blue coats, striped shirts, and white trousers, Ed Christy developed the majority of the typical minstrel show's performance conventions. Christy's performers (who varied in number from 4 or 5 up to 17 or 18) sat in a semicircle on the stage, with "end-men": "Mr. Tambo" (who played the tambourine) and "Mr. Bones" (who performed on the "rattle-bones," a percussion instrument). Mr. Tambo and Mr. Bones would swap jokes back and forth, while "Mr. Interlocutor" sat in the center of the semicircle and served as the master of ceremonies (and was often the target of Mr. Bones's and Mr. Tambo's jokes). The accompanying instrumentalists would be seated either behind the semicircle or in the pit. A measure of the success of the Christy Minstrels' "formula" can be seen in the income for one season: charging 25 cents admission, they reportedly grossed $317,598.

Minstrel shows were divided into three acts. The first act was often a whirlwind of entertainment; besides the jokes, members of the troupe presented song-and-dance acts, and sometimes the entire cast would sing in chorus. The act would end with a **walk-around**, a choral number that allowed each person a brief featured moment at the center of the semicircle, competing for the audience's approval. (Walk-arounds grew to be so popular that they were frequently performed at the end of the minstrel show as the highlight of the evening.) Sometimes, the walk-arounds featured a **cakewalk**, a popular "challenge-dance" that had originated among the slaves on southern plantations. In a cakewalk, black dancers strutted and posed in imitation of the perceived mannerisms of white couples at fancy balls. The prize for the best mimicry was a cake (which led to the expression "to take the cake"), and the cakewalk was a highlight of many minstrel shows.

The second act was known as the **olio**, or sometimes the **fantasia**. Here, the individuals performed more extended specialties—performances on odd instruments, female impersonations (no women performed in the early minstrel troupes), and peculiar dances. The third act customarily "burlesqued" some other kind of piece; Italian operas were favorite targets, but plays, political figures, personalities, and current events were also mimicked. Shakespeare's *Macbeth* (The Thane of Cawdor), for instance, was rechristened as *Bad Breath, the Crane of Chowder*.

A host of imitators soon flooded the American stages and traveled from town to town, making an impressive splash in England as well. Scarcely a year after the Virginia Minstrels made their debut, another troupe was invited to perform at the White House. The minstrel shows were sometimes the only theater that small towns would ever see, and the shows were enormously influential in developing shared experiences and attitudes (as well as stereotypes).

Minstrel shows emphasized humor, although occasional sentimental numbers were included. Much of the humor was the exaggerated "tall-tale" boasting typical of the American frontier, such as the stories about the legendary Paul Bunyon. By and large, black slaves were stigmatized as ignorant and gullible, although some skits depicted clever slaves who outwitted their masters (like Serpina in the eighteenth-century intermezzo *La Serva Padrona*). It's been argued that the minstrel shows subtly educated their audiences; by presenting slaves who are confounded by use of language, new inventions, and new ideas, the audience members themselves learned about these novelties in a painless second hand fashion. The overwhelming majority of minstrel shows portrayed plantation life as happy and satisfying for the slaves—and the African Americans as lighthearted, playful children. Only occasionally did more serious topics appear, such as the vulnerability of slave families and the cruelty of sadistic masters.

Much of the early material for the minstrel shows was adapted from authentic songs and dances of African American

An advertisement for the Virginia Serenaders, Boston, 1844.
Harvard Theatre Collection.

slaves, but there was an increasing demand for new music to fill out the programs and to make the minstrel shows more appealing and competitive. A few composers rose specifically to fill this niche; in 1858, Dan Emmett was hired by Bryant's Minstrels not only to play various instruments—banjo, fiddle, fife, and drum—but to write new numbers for the walk-around segment of their show. Emmett's most famous walk-around tune was "Dixie's Land," better known as "Dixie." Like Jim Crow, "Dixie" would eventually become a symbol of oppression to many listeners—but for many years it was one of the most popular tunes to derive from the minstrel shows. It contains hints of the **call-and-response** singing pattern typical of many black work songs, for the original tune specifies for the chorus to respond to the soloist with "Look away" and "Hooray." Emmett is also remembered for "Old Dan Tucker" and "De Blue Tail Fly" (better known as "Jimmy Crack Corn").

Stephen Foster (1826–1864) was another songwriter who built his career by providing music for minstrel shows; in fact, Foster was the first composer to make a living in the United States solely through sales of his music. (Like Gilbert and Sullivan, however, Foster struggled against unscrupulous pirate publishers and the shaky state of U.S. copyright law.) It was Foster's ambition to be America's best "Ethiopian song writer," and, although only 23 of his songs address life in the American South, sales of these provided as much as 90 percent of his income. Foster's early songs fell into two main categories: **minstrel songs** and **parlor songs**. The minstrel songs tended to be snappy, upbeat numbers, such as his first big success, "Oh! Susanna" (1848), while the parlor songs—not intended for minstrel shows—were sentimental tunes designed to be sung at home (in the parlor); one of Foster's most famous examples is "(I Dream of) Jeanie with the Light Brown Hair" (1854).

During Foster's career, his minstrel songs began to change—they grew more nostalgic about southern life and they used less **dialect**. (Dialect, in this context, was the spelling of words to reflect how many black slaves pronounced them; i.e., *they* would be printed as "dey.") Foster's greatest hit, "Old Folks at Home," frequently called "Swanee River" (1851), belongs to this new style, and Foster labeled these new kinds of pieces **plantation songs**. An example is "My Old Kentucky Home," which was published in 1853 without *any* dialect. Foster wrote many of his best plantation songs for the Christy Minstrels, and he advised the troupe to perform them "in a pathetic, not a comic style."

Foster's "Camptown Races" (1850), **Musical Example 9**, illustrates many characteristics of the earlier minstrel song approach. Its form label, **verse-chorus**, reflects the performance procedures initially used when singing songs of this type. A verse-chorus song consists of a series of verses with differing words (sung by a soloist), performed in alternation with a repetitive **refrain** that uses the same text each time (at **9, 12, 14,** and **16**). The reason the refrain is often called the **chorus** is because in works such as "Camptown Races," the refrain was performed *by* a four-part chorus of singers. (The choral parts are designated soprano, alto, tenor, and bass, which are frequently abbreviated as an **SATB chorus**.) After each refrain, a short instrumental interlude provided an opportunity for dancing.

As Emmett would do in "Dixie," Foster adapted the African American **call-and-response** technique for the verses of "Camptown Races." Each narrative statement of the soloist (**1, 3, 5,** and **7**), describing the exciting events of the horse race, is met by brief commentary from the chorus (**2, 4, 6,** and **8**). The choral responses at **2** and **6** make use of a "short-long" rhythmic pattern; because the emphasized "long" note (the -*dah!* of *Doodah!*) occurs just *after* the main beat, we call this a **syncopated** rhythm. (**Syncopation** describes stressed, or **accented**, notes that appear on weak beats—or between the beats—of the established meter. Syncopation would later be an important feature of many ragtime and jazz tunes.) The snappy effect of the syncopation adds to the energy and excitement of the dialogue.

Any minstrel song may be criticized for its perpetuation of unfair stereotypes, but Stephen Foster's works also conveyed relatively positive messages. Foster's gradual departure from the minstrel song's conventional use of dialect may or may not have reflected an increasing respect for African Americans. The covers of his printed sheet music avoided the exaggerated, cartoon-like depictions of slaves that were common among other published minstrel songs, and he customarily elevated the black female subjects of his songs to the status of "ladies" rather than "women." Unlike the songs of many competitors, he depicted African American couples as loving and faithful. Certainly, the sheer commercial success of Foster's music made him an enormously influential American composer of the mid-nineteenth century, and his legacy continues to this day: "My Old Kentucky Home" is the state song of Kentucky, while "Old Folks at Home" is Florida's state song.

For more than 20 years, the minstrel show was the province of white performers disguised in blackface. However, in 1865, after the end of the Civil War, Charles Hicks organized the first minstrel show comprised of African American performers. (His company is said to have originated the "Why did the chicken cross the road?" gag.) Other all-black troupes soon followed, and almost universally, the African American minstrel shows perpetuated the format of the older versions: singing, dancing, humor, and a generally nostalgic view of plantation life. Oddly, the African American companies used blackface make-up as well. The all-black companies were accepted by black and white audiences alike, and a few black composers also enjoyed brisk sales. James A. Bland was particularly successful, writing—among his reputed 600 works—the popular walk-around tune, "O, Dem Golden Slippers" (1879). Virginia adopted Bland's "Carry Me Back to Old Virginny" (1878) as its state song in 1940.

Gradually, the minstrel show began changing. Sam T. Jack, an African American theater owner, presented *The Creole Show* in 1890; its main attractions were not the established stars but the 16 beautiful girls. The **advance man** (who traveled ahead of the company from town to town, making arrangements for upcoming performances) for *The Creole Show* was John William Isham; in 1895, he produced his own entertainment titled *Octaroons*, featuring 16 men and 17 women. *Octaroons* still contained many minstrel show features, but a vague plotline began to connect the specialty acts together.

Isham's 1896 show, *Oriental America*, dropped many of the more slapstick minstrel show routines. Moreover, rather than ending with the usual items such as a cakewalk, a "hoe-down" (a popular rural square dance), or a walk-around, *Oriental America* closed with a medley of legitimate operatic selections. This production was the first all-black presentation to play (albeit briefly) in a Broadway theater, proving that paying audiences would attend non-minstrel-show performances of African Americans. Encouraged by this commercial success, a few black entrepreneurs would, over time, tackle more ambitious stage productions—and, in Chapter 12, "Challenges to Operetta," we examine the first of the African American musical comedies to reach Broadway.

FURTHER READING

Austin, William W. *"Susanna," "Jeanie," and "The Old Folks at Home": The Songs of Stephen C. Foster from His Time to Ours*. New York: Macmillan, 1975.

Dizikes, John. *Opera in America: A Cultural History*. New Haven and London: Yale University Press, 1993.

Kislan, Richard. *Hoofing on Broadway: A History of Show Dancing*. New York: Prentice Hall Press, 1987.

Nathan, Hans. *Dan Emmett and the Rise of Early Negro Minstrelsy*. Norman: University of Oklahoma Press, 1962.

Riis, Thomas L. *Just Before Jazz: Black Musical Theater in New York, 1890–1915*. Washington and London: Smithsonian Institution Press, 1989.

Sampson, Henry T. *Blacks in Blackface: A Source Book on Early Black Musical Shows*. Metuchen, New Jersey: The Scarecrow Press, 1980.

Toll, Robert C. *Blacking Up: The Minstrel Show in Nineteenth-Century America*. New York: Oxford University Press, 1974.

MUSICAL EXAMPLE 9

"CAMPTOWN RACES"
STEPHEN FOSTER/STEPHEN FOSTER, 1850

Solo
1 De Camptown ladies sing dis song
Chorus
2 Doodah! Doodah!
Solo
3 De Camptown racetrack five miles long
Chorus
4 Oh! doodah day!
Solo
5 I come down deh wid my hat caved in
Chorus
6 Doohdah! Doodah!
Solo
7 I go back home wid a pocket full of tin
Chorus
8 Oh! doodah day!
9 Gwine to run all night! Gwine to run all day!
I'll bet my money on de bobtail nag. Somebody bet on de bay.

10 *[interlude]*

Solo **Chorus**
11 De long tail filly and de big black hoss Doodah! Doodah!
Dey fly de track and dey both cut across Oh! doodah day!
De blind hoss sticken in a big mud hole Doohdah! Doodah!
Can't touch bottom wid a ten foot pole Oh! doodah day!
Chorus
12 Gwine to run all night! Gwine to run all day!
I'll bet my money on de bobtail nag. Somebody bet on de bay.

[interlude]

Solo **Chorus**
13 Old muley cow come on to de track Doodah! Doodah!
De bob-tail fling her ober his back Oh! doodah day!
Den fly along like a railroad car Doohdah! Doodah!
Runnin' a race wid a shootin' star Oh! doodah day!
Chorus
14 Gwine to run all night! Gwine to run all day!
I'll bet my money on de bobtail nag. Somebody bet on de bay.

[interlude]

Solo **Chorus**
15 See dem flyin' on a ten mile heat Doodah! Doodah!
Round de race track, den repeat Oh! doodah day!
I win my money on de bob-tail nag Doohdah! Doodah!
I keep my money in an old tow-bag Oh! doodah day!
Chorus
16 Gwine to run all night! Gwine to run all day!
I'll bet my money on de bobtail nag. Somebody bet on de bay.

Chapter 9
New American Genres of the Later Nineteenth Century

As the nineteenth century progressed, America was changing as well, and its tastes in stage entertainment shifted to embrace new genres. Some of the most popular works, such as **melodrama**, **extravaganza**, and burlesque, were constructed around a connected storyline, while **variety**, later called **vaudeville**, was similar to the minstrel show in that it consisted of various, unconnected skits. Despite the varied characteristics of these genres, they had one feature in common: they each had an influence on the subsequent development of "musical theater."

When most people today hear the term **melodrama**, they think of overacted gothic plays in which the heroine is placed in a dangerous situation by a villain—such as being tied to railroad tracks—from which she is dramatically rescued at the last possible second by a romantic hero. In fact, the term melodrama carries several meanings, and in the history of musical theater, melodrama has a somewhat more specific definition: it refers to a drama in which the characters speak either during pauses in the accompanying music or *while* that music is playing; sometimes the characters do not speak at all, but silently act out exaggerated gestures in **pantomime**. As in the gothic plays, however, stock situations are used; the stories tend to be sentimental, and, by the end, evil is punished and virtue is always triumphant. In a melodrama, the music is essential in creating the full emotional effect; without it, the stage depiction would fall flat.

It was the French who were truly expert in what they called *mélodrame*; one composer, René Charles Guilbert de Pixérécourt, wrote almost 60 plays in this style, and he is sometimes called the "Father of Melodrama." One of the earliest melodramas performed in America (in 1797) was composed by a French immigrant. However, a German dramatist introduced another feature into melodramas that made them particularly appealing to Americans living on the frontier. August von Kotzebue had written a number of stories with the same message: that education was not necessary for the man whose heart was pure. Many pioneer Americans were suspicious of "book-learning," and, set as melodramas, Kotzebue's stories circulated repeatedly through the United States, long past his assassination in 1819.

Arguably, pantomimed melodramas continued to be presented into the twentieth century, then in the new guise of silent movies. In both the melodrama and silent films the musical score was integral in conveying emotion and expression; the music helped to explain the meaning of the story—an approach that continues to be used in television and movie soundtracks to this day.

In the middle of the nineteenth century, another genre—known variously as **extravaganza** or **spectacle**—began to make a splash in the United States. Like the elaborate laser shows that enhance many rock concerts today, extravaganzas put stagecraft foremost. Audiences marveled at the elaborate stage sets and lighting, the seemingly miraculous transformations between sets, and the huge casts of performers.

Theater historian George P. Oliver classified at least five types of spectacles that were popular from the 1850s through the 1870s: one was the *equestrian spectacle*, featuring performers on horseback; a second was the *military-nautical spectacle*, with large numbers of performers and stage machinery depicting military endeavors, often set in foreign locales. Oliver's third type was the *burlesque spectacle*, which was—like English burlesques—a satiric retelling of some familiar story, with the added attraction of women in scanty costumes, many dances, and transformation scenes. (A transformation scene involved a rapid transition between backdrops, costumes, and stage sets; thanks to the ingenious use of trapdoors and stage machinery, the alteration could appear almost instantaneously.) A fourth type was the *fairy spectacle*, with "magical" transformations of various people and animals, and the fifth type, the *romantic spectacle*, often featured natural disasters—flood, fire, and so forth—with increasingly lavish costumes, complex machinery, and musical scores drawn from operas and orchestral works.

A work that featured elements of several of these spectacle types was ***The Black Crook***, an extravaganza that made its debut at Niblo's Garden in New York City in 1866, just after the end of the Civil War. Several studies of American musical theater use this show as their starting point, for it might well be considered the first "blockbuster" hit in the history of the United States—the show ran for 474 performances and earned more than a million dollars. Various legends have arisen about the genesis of *The Black Crook*. One engaging myth is that a French ballet corps was left stranded without a place to perform when its New York theater—the Academy of Music—burned down, but the manager at Niblo's Garden quickly figured out a way to incorporate them into the "flop" play then struggling to survive at his theater—and this was therefore the birth of the "song-and-dance" musical. This is not quite how things happened, however; the Academy of Music *did* burn down—but many months before the ballet troupe was due to arrive from Paris. Moreover, there would have been dancing in *The Black Crook* no matter what, since audiences had long since grown to expect a group of attractive female dancers—known as **chorus girls** or the **chorus line**—in this type of entertainment. In fact, there was very little about *The Black Crook* that was truly innovative; its place in the history books stems primarily from its commercial success.

There were several factors contributing to *The Black Crook*'s triumph—but, in general, these did *not* include either the music *or* Charles M. Barras's plot (see the **Plot Summary**). Thomas Baker was credited with the score, but he drew heavily upon pre-existing popular numbers by other composers. (An Italian term for this type of compilation score is **pasticcio**.) The most popular song in *The Black Crook* was the slightly suggestive number "You Naughty, Naughty Men," with text by T. Kennick and music by G. Bickwell. Subsequent revivals and touring productions of *The Black Crook* introduced new and newly borrowed pieces as well, generally assembled by someone new each time; **Giuseppe Operti** seems to have overseen most of the music for the 1871 production. Most of the musical numbers have little to do with the story; rather, they were simply an opportunity to feature the singers or dancers. To be fair, it would have been difficult for the music to have done much to support the plot, for the storyline is sketchy and, at times, barely coherent.

What *The Black Crook* did have going for itself was visual appeal. Part of this appeal stemmed from the fantastic **stage sets**, including Queen Stalacta's glittering cave and the enormous chorus line (with more than a hundred dancers): at various points, they appeared as fairies on silver couches, angels in chariots, and marching Amazons. A highlight of *The Black Crook* was its "hurricane in the Harz mountains," achieved by clever **lighting** effects. It was reported that the production cost between $25,000 and $55,000; even the lower figure was an enormous amount for the time.

Costuming also contributed to the show's visual impact; the chorus was dressed as dancing gemstones in one ballet, as demons in another, and as elaborate sea creatures in yet another. Even more important, however, was the *lack of* costumes—in several numbers, the chorus appeared *without* skirts, wearing flesh-colored tights that made their legs appear nude. Reviewers for the several New York newspapers alluded to the ballet corps' attire (or absence thereof) with various euphemisms; the *Evening Post* reported that the dancers were "perhaps less concealed than would be deemed proper by those of stout views as to where dresses should begin and end."

For 1866 audiences, the daring nature of this risqué presentation quickly produced a public uproar. Women who attended the performances wore heavy veils so they could not be recognized. Preachers denounced the notorious show from their pulpits, and of course ticket sales shot way up. A host of imitative productions opened, such as *The Black Crook, Jr., The White Crook, The Red Crook, The Black Rook,* and so forth. Moreover, pirated productions of *The Black Crook* were mounted all over the United States, paying no royalties, thanks to a judge who ruled that the work was "corrupt" and "not even subject to copyright since it cannot be denied that this spectacle of *The Black Crook* merely panders to the

The scandalous "lower limbs" of *The Black Crook*'s chorus line. *Culver Pictures, Inc.*

pernicious curiosity of very questionable exhibitions of the female person."

The origins of the "Amazons' March" are not completely clear. "March of the Amazons" is listed in the 1866 production, arranged by Emil Stigler. However, Operti may have newly composed our **Musical Example 10** for the 1871 production; the text may or may not have been by Barras. No matter who created the work, it stands as a good example of a **production number**—a piece designed to feature the majority of the cast in a song-and-dance presentation.

Like *Bastien und Bastienne's* "Diggi Daggi," the "Amazons' March" is in binary form—section *a* begins at **2**, and section *b* starts at **4**. The melodies of these two sections are quite different from one another; the melody at **2** starts at a fairly high pitch and makes a downward descent, while the new tune at **4** begins on a much lower pitch and proceeds to work its way upward. What might strike us as unexpected is the significant amount of instrumental music during this number. The orchestral **introduction** (**1**) seems to continue quite a bit longer than we might anticipate, and there is a substantial **interlude** (**3**) for the orchestra in between the two vocal sections as well. After section *b* has ended, the orchestra is again featured at **5**, in a sizable concluding passage that is sometimes called a **postlude** or **coda**. (A coda, from the Italian word for "tail," is an ending section that sounds like it is wrapping up the work.) The presence of so much orchestral music is not hard to explain; the lengthy instrumental passages allow the chorus line to perform their **choreography**—the dance steps and patterns—without having to conserve breath for singing. Since this is a march, it is set, logically enough, in duple meter, but we know little about the actual choreography except that most contemporary reports regarded the ensemble numbers as the highlights of the show. Moreover, one theatrical commentator recalled that the dancers wore small electric lights during some later productions of *The Black Crook*, which may well have been some of the first uses of electricity in American theaters.

The Black Crook enjoyed numerous revivals throughout the remainder of the nineteenth century and on into the twentieth. Collectively, the revivals serve as a mini-history of theatrical dance, for the ballet numbers were gradually replaced each time with contemporary dance fashions and fads. In 1892, four French dancers scandalized audiences with their high kicks and, even more astonishing, their performance of the split. Agnes de Mille, who would later design an innovative dream ballet for *Oklahoma!* (Chapter 25, "Rogers and Hammerstein: *Oklahoma!*"), made her debut as a choreographer for a 1929 revival of *The Black Crook*. Sigmund Romberg composed his last score for *The Girl in Pink Tights*; this musical was a slightly fictionalized version of the circumstances leading up to the initial 1866 production of *The Black Crook*. Certainly, the notoriety of *The Black Crook* focused attention on the musical stage (and the chorus line) in a way that had seldom been seen before.

Other shows featured their own innovations; *The White Fawn* (1868), for instance, was the first American work to feature the can-can, that naughty dance that had figured so prominently in Offenbach's *Orpheus in the Underworld* (Chapter 5, "France and Spain in the Nineteenth Century"). In more and more productions, the songs and dance supported the plot—unlike the singing and dancing in *The Black Crook*. However, the music continued to be borrowed; the innovation of a newly composed score for an American musical theater work was left to an 1874 burlesque called *Evangeline*.

Like its English counterpart, an American burlesque was a satirical version of a familiar work. (In the early twentieth century, burlesque shows began to put much more emphasis on sexual innuendo and even smut, but in the nineteenth century, burlesque still described reasonably innocent parodies.) Some scholars place the origin of American burlesque in the 1860s, when various dance ensembles such as "Lydia Thompson and her British Blondes" began touring the United States. Under the pretense that the dancers needed to play male characters, they were dressed in extremely revealing tights. Productions of this nature were sometimes called *leg dramas*.

Two friends, **Edward Everett Rice** (1848–1924) and **John Cheever Goodwin** (1850–1912), both members of Boston's Papyrus Club (a literary and dramatic society), attended one of Lydia Thompson's leg dramas around 1873. Disgusted with the vulgarity of Thompson's burlesque, they believed they could create a better one—and proceeded to sit up until 4 A.M. drafting an outline. They chose to satirize the narrative poem *Evangeline, a Tale of Acadie*, published by

Henry Wadsworth Longfellow in 1847. *Evangeline* took more than a year to complete because Rice was not a trained musician (he was a publicist for the Cunard Steamship Line); he picked out the tunes on the piano and had an assistant write them down in conventional musical notation. The partners tried out the songs for their fellow Papyrus Club members and tossed out the tunes the other members didn't like. Rice estimated that he wrote some 500 songs for *Evangeline* in this manner.

At last *Evangeline* opened in 1874 at Niblo's Garden, the same theater that had housed *The Black Crook*. However, *Evangeline* did not repeat the success of its predecessor; it was inserted as a two-week interim booking between other productions, and so it closed after 16 performances. Negative reviews in the newspapers, however, indicated that the show probably would not have been able to survive much longer. Goodwin later acknowledged that the "production was awful, and deserved all the hard things the critics said of it." After *Evangeline*'s short run ended, the partners sat back down and revised it. Two subsequent productions in Boston did better, so Rice and Goodwin at last reintroduced *Evangeline* to New York in 1877. Their perseverance paid off, for the revised *Evangeline* took the town by storm.

During its 1874 appearance, Rice called *Evangeline* both a "musical comedy" and an "extravaganza," but he later turned to another genre label, calling it an "American opera bouffe." In truth, this burlesque contained aspects of all these genres—Goodwin's script was laden with outrageous puns and humorous **asides** (comments made directly to the audience), while the show featured a spouting whale, a dancing cow, and even a balloon ascension (see the **Plot Summary**). The overriding principle behind Rice and Goodwin's *Evangeline* was their desire "to concoct a burlesque diversion to which an entire family might be taken, in lieu of the imported entertainment at which only the black sheep from every fold were expected."

Despite Rice's inexperience as a composer, he produced a wide variety of pieces for *Evangeline*, including ballads, comic songs, duets, trios, and choruses, plus many types of dance music, particularly marches, polkas, and waltzes. "My Heart" (**Musical Example 11**) exemplifies his ability to write graceful melodies that suit the text. In this instance, Rice uses a flowing compound subdivision to evoke an aural image of the spinning wheel at work. (Rice did not innovate this particular technique; **spinning-wheel songs** had become almost a cliché in the nineteenth century.) Rice also referred to "My Heart" as a **romanza**, and as the label suggests, Rice allows the romantic vocal melody to rise and fall in fluid waves, evoking the "turbulent tides of the ocean" mentioned in the lyrics. The poetry is a bit florid and hard to follow, but the elegant lyrics stand in marked contrast to some of the dreadful, slangy puns and "in" jokes of *Evangeline*'s spoken dialogue. (LeBlanc, explaining the crumpled condition of the will, tells us that it's "somewhat *jammed* but that's 'cause I *preserved* it," and later he asks Catherine, "Do you take me for a Chinaman because I work for *Rice*?").

"My Heart" illustrates a common musical pattern known as **ternary form**, a three-part form that can be diagrammed as *a-b-a*. The first *a* section consists of two identical phrases

(**1** and **2**). The *b* melody at **3**, in contrast, uses repeated notes in a lower range and shifts to the **minor mode**. Western music customarily makes use of two kinds of mode, **major** and **minor**. A scale in the **major mode**, called a major scale, or a major key, consists of the familiar "do-re-mi" pitches; a slightly different choice of pitches comprises the minor scale (also called the minor key or **minor mode**). A great many simple melodies are written in the major mode, such as "Row, Row, Row Your Boat," "Mary Had a Little Lamb," and so forth; the minor mode is less common, but is exemplified by "When Johnny Comes Marching Home" and the Christmas carol "We Three Kings of Orient Are." Composers often use the major mode to create a more cheerful effect in music, while the minor mode sometimes enhances a more serious or solemn atmosphere. The change in mode in "My Heart" occurs while Evangeline asks herself questions: What is causing her cheeks to glow? What rapture makes the world seem fairer? The major mode *a* melody returns while she answers her own questions at **4** and **5**. By varying his techniques in unexpected ways, Rice maintains interest in what is, after all, a fairly simple little tune.

Although few people would call "My Heart" a masterpiece of composition, its simple charm captures the uncomplicated nature of Evangeline's feelings for Gabriel. By writing a completely **original score**—creating new tunes to fit the varied situations of their story—Rice and Goodwin ushered in a quiet revolution: a new level of artistic expectation was introduced to the musical stage. Both men went on to contribute to theater in various other ways; Goodwin is regarded by many as the first important American librettist, while Rice was a shrewd businessman who soon realized the advantages of maintaining control over his materials. In addition to running a publishing company, he built theaters and became a notable producer who helped to introduce performers such as Lillian Russell, Fay Templeton, and female impersonator Julian Eltinge; as Chapter 12, "Challenges to Operetta" explains, Rice was unwittingly instrumental in launching the career of Will Marion Cook.

Although none of Rice's works are familiar to theatergoers today, many of his theatrical innovations had a lasting impact on subsequent generations. His *Adonis* (1884) was the first show—musical *or* straight play—to run more than 500 performances on Broadway. Rice introduced electric lighting to Broadway in 1888; Thomas Edison personally supervised the installation. And, later, Rice's support of a young Jerome Kern helped launch the Broadway career of one of the most important composers during musical theater's "Golden Age."

It is almost impossible to pinpoint the origins of the **variety show**, or **vaudeville**, since so many of its features had been seen before. Certainly its short skits, songs, and dances have much in common with the "olio" portion of minstrel shows (see Chapter 8, "The United States in the Early Nineteenth Century"), but even in the eighteenth century, English theater managers had allowed specialized performers (singers, dancers, rope-dancers, and so forth) to entertain audiences in between the acts of plays and operas. As the nineteenth century progressed, the entertainments developed into full-fledged productions known as **music halls**. The music halls presented all sorts of music—ballads, folk songs, patriotic tunes, even opera excerpts—and made constant reference to current events. Entrepreneurs such as the German Reed Family (see Chapter 7, "England in the Nineteenth Century") made the entertainments "respectable," thereby appealing to an increasingly large middle-class audience.

The American equivalent to music hall performances went by other names. There is debate as to when the term *vaudeville* came into common usage, but it is often attributed to John W. Ransome who used the term at his theater during the 1880s. The leading theater managers were mixed in their reaction to the change of label; Tony (Antonio) Pastor detested the new term, calling it a "sissy" label for what he viewed as the "correct" term, variety. On the other hand, B. F. Keith, who oversaw a large network of East Coast theaters (known as the Keith Circuit), embraced the new designation.

Despite their differences of opinion, both Pastor and Keith agreed on the need for vaudeville to "clean up its act." Pastor took the drinking bar out of his theater, censored anything suggestive or objectionable from the stage material, and tried to make all his performances appealing to women and children. He didn't allow his performers to smoke, drink, or swear, and he had a system of fines to punish those who broke his rules. Similar strict guidelines were posted backstage at the Keith theaters (known among performers as the "Sunday School Circuit"). The following is a typical backstage notice to vaudeville actors:

NOTICE TO PERFORMERS

You are hereby warned that your act must be free from all vulgarity and suggestiveness in words, action, and costume, while playing in any of Mr. ———'s houses, and all vulgar, double-meaning and profane words and songs must be cut out of your act before the first performance. If you are in doubt as to what is right or wrong, submit it to the resident manager at rehearsal.

Such words as Liar, Slob, Son-of-a-Gun, Devil, Sucker, Damn, and all other words unfit for the ears of ladies and children, also any reference to questionable streets, resorts, localities, and barrooms, are prohibited under fire of instant discharge.

The "clean" reputation of vaudeville meant that audiences could attend performances without fear of offense, and by the early twentieth century some two thousand theaters offered vaudeville shows. Each show, or **bill**, consisted of between 8 and 15 separate short routines. Sometimes—as in the minstrel shows—a longer play would comprise a substantial portion of the vaudeville program.

A host of performers built or sustained their reputations via vaudeville: legitimate actresses performed heart-wrenching numbers; comedy teams presented ethnic portrayals and slapstick physical humor. Dozens of **specialty acts**, or **turns**, made the rounds: besides song-and-dance performers, vaudeville audiences witnessed excerpts from grand opera, circus acts (featuring acrobats, aerialists, and wire walkers), banjo players, blackface comics, trick cyclists, magicians, rope spinners, whip snappers, jugglers, monologists, ventriloquists, novelty musical acts, sister teams, dog acts, and piano teams. Specialty dances included not only venerable ballet (or "toe"), but tap, "eccentric," comic, and acrobatic routines. The **Behind-the-Scenes** example includes Buster Keaton's auto-biographical account of typical (if somewhat brutal!) vaudeville comedy turns. Rather like today's celebrities making talk show appearances, people then "in the news" took their turns on the vaudeville stages: Carrie Nation appeared in sketches that depicted her destroying saloons as she had during her temperance crusade; afterwards, she handed out souvenir axes to the audience. Both Babe Ruth and Helen Keller appeared in vaudeville, while Charles Lindbergh turned *down* an offer of $100,000 per week to tour the vaudeville circuit.

Orchestral musicians benefited from vaudeville because—in a manner similar to melodrama—the stage performers often depended on music to underscore and enhance the drama, pathos, or humor of the stage action. Orchestras varied from a single performer (usually a pianist or a banjo player) to some eight or nine instrumentalists. However, the orchestra members usually worked for a specific house, while the stage performers traveled from theater to theater. The actors seldom carried sheet music for their performances, so this meant that the orchestral players had to develop a vast system of **cues**—brief musical numbers that established various moods—that they could play to suit the requirements of each actor's stage routine. A typical **cue sheet**—a listing of the music the orchestra needed to play when particular lines were delivered on stage—is shown in **Figure 9–1**.

In most vaudeville shows, the individual routines were completely unrelated to each other. In the 1870s, however, Nate Salisbury tried an experiment: he designed a loose storyline to connect the skits and assigned a character to each performer so that the overall show had, in essence, a plot. This hybrid genre became known as a **farce-comedy**. Although the heyday of farce-comedies lasted only five years or so, they demonstrated how vaudeville routines could be merged into the more dramatically coherent musical comedies, and they would influence the revue as well.

Some aspects of vaudeville may well make us feel uncomfortable today: the dialect comedians did not stop at imitating the accents of various ethnic groups, but also perpetuated (and even created) many stereotypes about ethnic behavior. Gender roles were constrained into equally predictable and narrow patterns. On the other hand, vaudeville producers were the first to employ African American performers in theaters that had been limited exclusively to whites. Although the first roles were meager (and stereotyped), they were an important step toward the eventual integration of musical theater stages.

Although vaudeville was a dominant form of American entertainment on into the first three decades of the twentieth century, it was no match for the triple threats of radio, moving pictures, and the Great Depression. The last of the great vaudeville houses, the Palace Theatre in New York, had switched by 1935 to being a movie house in order to keep its doors open. However, the premise of "a variety of entertainments" would influence future stage (and television) genres such as the **revue**, and even some conventional musicals of the later twentieth century—particularly Sondheim's show *Company* (Chapter 38, "Sondheim in the 1970s") and Kander and Ebb's 1975 *Chicago* (Chapter 34, "New Partnerships")—owe a great deal to the vaudeville format.

FURTHER READING

Corio, Ann. *This Was Burlesque*. New York: Madison Square Press, 1968.

Gilbert, Douglas. *American Vaudeville, Its Life and Times*. New York: Whitlesey House, 1940.

Jackson, Allan S. "Evangeline: The Forgotten American Musical." *Players: The Magazine of American Theatre* 44, no. 1 (October/November 1968): 20–25.

Figure 9–1 Musical Cue Sheet

At rise of curtain		Orchestra (lively music)
Cue	It is good Squire Beasley	" (jolly music for squire's entrance)
Cue	(When comic falls down)	" (Drum crash)
Cue	I feel like dancing	" (Specialty)
Cue	The villagers are coming	" (Lively 6–8 time)
Cue	(Old man sits down suddenly)	" (Clarinet squeal)
Cue	While the villagers make merry	" (Country dance)
Cue	I spurn you	" (Chord in D)
Cue	I am poor, and alone	" (plaintive music)
Cue	Try to forget my troubles	" (hornpipe by soubrette)
Cue	It contains dynamite	" (G chord—fortissimo)
Cue	(When burglars enter)	" (Sneaky music)
Cue	(For knife combat)	" (Allegro)
Cue	Will tell my sad story	" (Adagio with muted violin)
Cue	(For change of scene)	" (Waltz)
Cue	It is the cavalry	" (Bugle call)
Cue	The mill is on fire	" (Hurry music)
Cue	We must save her	" (Frenzied music)
Cue	Saved	" (Joyous music until curtain)

Jackson, Richard, ed. *Evangeline (1877).* Early Burlesque in America, Vol. 13. New York: Garland Publishing, Inc., 1994.

Kislan, Richard. *Hoofing on Broadway: A History of Show Dancing.* New York: Prentice Hall Press, 1987.

Loney, Glenn, ed. *Musical Theatre in America: Papers and Proceedings of the Conference on the Musical Theatre in America.* (Contributions in Drama and Theatre Studies, Number 8). Westport, Connecticut: Greenwood Press, 1984.

Mates, Julian. *America's Musical Stage: Two Hundred Years of Musical Theatre.* New York: Praeger, 1985. Paperback edition 1987.

Matlaw, Myron, ed. *The Black Crook and Other Nineteenth-Century American Plays.* New York: E. P. Dutton & Co., 1967.

Root, Deane L. *American Popular Stage Music, 1860–1880.* Ann Arbor, Michigan: UMI Research Press, 1981.

Spitzer, Marian. *The Palace.* New York: Atheneum, 1969.

Stein, Charles W., ed. *American Vaudeville As Seen by Its Contemporaries.* New York: Alfred A. Knopf, 1984.

BEHIND-THE-SCENES: BUSTER KEATON IN VAUDEVILLE

Pop made me the featured performer of our act when I was five. There were dozens of other popular family acts in vaudeville at the turn of the century, but none of the children in them was featured as early as that. . . . The reason managers approved of my being featured was because I was unique, being at that time the only little hell-raising Huck Finn type boy in vaudeville. The parents of the others presented their boys as cute and charming Little Lord Fauntleroys. The girls were Dolly Dimples types with long, golden curls. . . .

The act started with Pop coming out alone and announcing that he would recite. Sometimes he said he would sing a beautiful song. He had hardly started on "Maud Muller" or "Where Is My Wandering Boy Tonight?" when I'd come out and fastidiously select one of the thirteen or fourteen old brooms that were on the end of the battered kitchen table we used in our act.

Ignoring him, I would carefully sweep off the table, then appear to see something that wasn't there. Picking up this imaginary object with my cupped hand, I examined it and then put it down on another part of the table. This distressed Pop. Stopping his singing or reciting, he moved the invisible thing back to the place where I'd picked it up. I'd move it to where I wanted it, he'd move it back. That went on with our rage mounting until we were fighting wildly, blasting, kicking, punching, and throwing one another across the table and all over the stage.

PLOT SUMMARY: *THE BLACK CROOK*

The playwright Charles M. Barras copyrighted the script of *The Black Crook* in 1863, but its central premise is an old and familiar one: a man makes a bargain with the devil that his life will be extended in exchange for delivering other human souls. The main villain of *The Black Crook* is Hertzog, who has struck a deal with the devil Zamiel: Hertzog will get an additional year of life for each human soul he can damn during the coming year. (Hertzog has the title role, for he is a hunchback, or "crook" back.) Another villainous character is the Count Wolfenstein, who has designs on the beautiful maiden Amina. Amina's foster mother, Dame Barbara, agrees to send Amina to the count's castle in the Harz mountains, where she will be educated in the ways of the nobility so that she can eventually become his bride. Amina is not happy at the prospect, for she loves the impoverished painter Rodolphe. Secretly, the count gives orders for Rodolphe to be captured and thrown into a dungeon of his castle.

In Act II, Hertzog and his comic servant Greppo visit Rodolphe in his cell. Hertzog tells Rodolphe about riches in the mountains; with this wealth Rodolphe could claim Amina's hand. With Greppo's help, Rodolphe wants to go search for the treasure; Hertzog gloats, knowing that he is sending Rodolphe straight into Zamiel's clutches. (Meanwhile, Dame Barbara has begun flirting with Von Puffengruntz, the count's steward.) During Rodolphe's journey, he drives a serpent away from a small bird, and he thus unwittingly rescues the disguised Stalacta, Queen of the Golden Realm, from Zamiel. Stalacta rewards Rodolphe with various gifts, including a magic ring.

The third act opens six months later, when a grand masquerade ball is in progress in honor of the count's birthday. A group costumed as Amazons performs as part of the revels (**Musical Example 10**). A mysterious "prince" has arrived at the ball, but the count orders the guests to unmask—and the prince and his servant prove to be Rodolphe and Greppo. Rodolphe kisses his magic ring and the fairies instantly come to his aid. In the confusion, Rodolphe escapes with Amina (and Greppo persuades one of Amina's attractive handmaidens, Carline, to come along as well). During the fourth act, Hertzog and the count pursue the runaways, chasing them through the forest of Bohemia, a forest fire, and a cave with glittering stalactites. At last Rodolphe defeats the count in a duel; Hertzog runs away, only to be forced to forfeit his life in Zamiel's demonic underworld. The extravaganza ends with a series of astonishing transformations depicting the wonders of Stalacta's magical kingdom.

PLOT SUMMARY: *EVANGELINE*

By refusing to present "sex" on stage (in the form of scantily clad chorus girls), Rice and Goodwin needed to hold their audience by other means. Their silly but engaging plot presented a number of "cliff-hanger" moments as the two lovers Gabriel and Evangeline (Eva) struggle to join in marriage. The story opens in the village of Acadia in Nova Scotia. A Lone Fisherman appears from time to time, never speaking but entertaining the audience with his various adventures (silently wrestling an eel, a lobster, and so forth); he also unwittingly contributes to an important plot twist.

As the show begins, Gabriel (played by a woman) toasts Eva, the woman he loves. We soon learn that Eva is harboring two sailors who have deserted their ship. Moreover, her deceased uncle, who hated marriage, has bequeathed her his fortune on the condition that she *not* wed; if she does marry, she forfeits the inheritance and it goes to LeBlanc. However, Eva knows nothing of this bequest, for LeBlanc has hidden the will and is trying to facilitate her wedding to Gabriel. Meanwhile, Catherine, Gabriel's aunt (played by a man), has *her* heart set on marrying LeBlanc. One dramatic moment occurs when a whale pursues Eva until Gabriel rescues her. Also, a stammering corporal comes to search for the missing sailors, but he fails to find them.

While sitting at her spinning wheel, Eva takes time to reflect on Gabriel's wonderful qualities in "My Heart" (**Musical Example 11**). However, she and Gabriel quarrel over her pet heifer, since Eva wants the cow to accompany them on their honeymoon. Eva's father Ben breaks up the argument, and LeBlanc has a wedding contract all ready to sign. After Gabriel has written his name, Evangeline starts to sign hers. She is interrupted when a military captain leads in a group of soldiers. The sailors are discovered, so Eva is arrested

for concealing them. She will be taken to England to be tried for her crime; all the other characters go along as chaperones.

Shipwrecked, the travelers come to a mysterious country where diamonds litter the ground. Of course they pick some up, and native policemen arrive to arrest them. The local king orders that these diamond thieves must be executed. However, the prisoners display masonic signals (Freemasons were members of a secret society)—and the native king turns out to be a mason as well! The marriage ceremony resumes, and Eva again starts to sign the contract—but once more, soldiers are heard in the distance. However, the captain is no longer interested in prosecuting Eva, so she finishes her signature at last. LeBlanc is ecstatic—until it turns out that the Lone Fisherman had used the will to light his pipe. Catherine promises to share all she has with him when they are married, but the joke is on LeBlanc; her fortune proves to be a handful of change. The story ends with the dazzling balloon ascent, with at least Eva and Gabriel living happily ever after.

MUSICAL EXAMPLE 10

THE BLACK CROOK
GIUSEPPE OPERTI/CHARLES M. BARRAS, 1866
"Amazons' March" (1871 Production)

1   *[introduction]*

Chorus
2   Gaily we come from deep and dark blue sea, and lightly we march through the world.
We're midnight fairies roaming to music of the waves, and gaily wander 'til morning.

3   *[interlude]*

4   Then let us sing while gaily marching and merrily enjoy earth while we may;
Yes, let us revel in the moonlight, and merrily march until the morning.

MUSICAL EXAMPLE 11

EVANGELINE
EDWARD E. RICE/J. CHEEVER GOODWIN, 1874
"My Heart"

Evangeline
1   My heart feels a newborn emotion it has never known before,
The turbulent tides of the ocean seem thrilling it to the core.
2   Since Gabriel's arms were around me, no peace in my mind I've known:
Some spell in its fetters hath bound me, its magical power I own.
3   What can it be that unbidden causes my cheek to glow?
What is the rapture that, hidden, makes the world fairer below?
4   Blushes defying repression, joy that is almost pain.
Force me to make the confession vainly I seek to restrain.
5   Love in my heart has its dwelling, leaving its home in the skies,
And rapture that passes all telling laughs out from my love-lit eyes.

Chapter 10
Operetta in America, 1880—1903

Despite the flowering of "native" minstrel shows, vaudeville, melodramas, extravaganzas, and burlesques, foreign imports—such as the Gilbert and Sullivan operettas—continued to hold a prominent position on the nineteenth-century American stage. It was not long, however, before American composers began to try their hands at "homegrown" operettas (also known as comic operas). Early attempts began to appear after midcentury, but these were sporadic. However, a work from Boston, *The Doctor of Alcantara* (1862), toured widely and for many years.

A rash of new American operettas began to appear during the 1880s, although several of the initial efforts met with failure. The composer **Reginald De Koven** (1859–1920) and the lyricist **Harry Bache Smith** (1860–1936) teamed up for the first time in 1887. Their initial collaboration, *The Begum*—a "Hindoo comic opera" inspired by *The Mikado*—sought (unsuccessfully) to cash in on the fad for exotic Asian settings. (Smith explained, "[We] were enthusiastic admirers of the early Gilbert and Sullivan operas and when we started to work on our first piece we decided to bestow on the distinguished collaborators the sincere flattery of imitation.") Their second attempt also did poorly, but their third try was the charm; *Robin Hood* (see the **Plot Summary**) was perhaps the most celebrated American operetta of the nineteenth century.

Even though much of the operetta uses somewhat archaic English, Smith's lyrics were greatly admired, and later he was the first American lyricist to have his best librettos printed as a book. Several features familiar from earlier types of stage works were present in *Robin Hood*: not only did the plot abound with people in disguise, but the male character Allan-a-Dale was sung by a woman in what is often called a **breeches role**. This casting gave the directors the chance to dress the actress in tights, thereby revealing her legs in the same alluring manner that had attracted audiences to *The Black Crook* and *Evangeline*. The actress playing the Lady Marian also wore a masculine costume at various points; interestingly, audiences seemed to have no difficulty in understanding that Allan-a-Dale, played by a woman, was a "man," while Lady Marian—even when disguised as a male—was a "woman."

Given the fairly dismal track record of the two collaborators, not too much faith was placed in *Robin Hood* before its premiere in Chicago in 1890. In rehearsals, the cast displayed little enthusiasm for the new work. According to Smith,

They were not particularly pleased with the result of our labors. . . . Barnabee, however, liked his character, the Sheriff of Nottingham, and Will MacDonald [as Little John] felt that

"Brown October Ale" gave him a good chance. . . . Jessie Davis [playing Allan-a-Dale] was particularly recalcitrant, complaining with some justice that she had no solo till the last act. . . . The rehearsals were not encouraging. At one of them when "The Tinker's Song" was first tried, the musical director declared that he would not conduct such poor stuff. . . .

Owing to lack of confidence in the pieces, no money was spent on costumes, and the curtain rose on the opening night disclosing a production that had cost $109.50. The tenor sang Robin Hood in his "Il Trovatore" costume, and the dresses of all the principals had seen service in "Martha," "The Bohemian Girl" and other operas of their repertoire.

Despite the cast's reservations, *Robin Hood* opened to resounding applause, although the biggest hit, "Oh, Promise Me," was initially not part of the show. After Davis's complaints, De Koven offered her "Oh, Promise Me," staged as a marriage proposal from Allan-a-Dale to Annabel. It proved to be so overwhelmingly popular that Davis was often forced to **encore** (repeat) the number two or three times each evening. When Davis estimated she had sung the song about 5,000 times in approximately 2,000 performances, she once tried to replace it with a new song. The audience hooted her off the stage soon after she had started singing her new tune; they forgave her only after she came back and sang the old favorite. (The tune was also a perennial feature at American weddings for many years.)

Robin Hood opened in New York in 1891, and like the first production of *Evangeline*, played a fairly short initial run because of a previously scheduled booking in its theater. Unlike *Evangeline*, though, *Robin Hood* did well in New York from the very start, and it was revived almost constantly over the next 50 years. After "Oh, Promise Me," the second biggest hit of *Robin Hood* was "Brown October Ale" (**Musical Example 12**). In this rollicking number, Little John and the Merry Men encourage Allan-a-Dale to drown his sorrows, and so it functions a bit differently from many of the previous songs we've studied. In this situation, it truly makes *sense* for the actors to sing, because "real" people do indeed sing drinking songs in taverns. Usually, the audience must "suspend disbelief," because the performers are singing in situations in which we would use speech to communicate in real life. However, when it is truly believable to have the characters sing—during a church service, or while rocking a baby to sleep—the singing can be called **source music**, a **diegetic song**, or a **prop song**. Similar terms can describe the music of a film: if you *see* someone playing a piano in the movie, and you "hear" piano music on the soundtrack, the piano performance is diegetic. In this way, "Brown October

Allan-a-Dale (Jessie Bartlett Davis) identifies the Sheriff of Nottingham (Henry Clay Barnabee) in *Robin Hood.*
Museum of the City of New York.

Ale" is a prop song, since it makes perfect sense for the chorus to be singing at this point of the story.

Admittedly, De Koven's score for "Brown October Ale" is more complicated than the kind of song that would usually result from the carousings of a bunch of drunken men! The tune is structured as a straightforward verse-chorus form (*a-B-a-B*), with Little John featured during the two verses (**1** and **3**). When Allan and the Merry Men are added to the *B* sections (**2** and **4**), they sing in **harmony** (in the same manner as the minstrel show singers performing "Camptown Races"). During these harmonized portions, the texture is still homophonic, since Little John and Allan sing the main melody while the chorus *supports* that melody in the manner of an accompaniment. The harmony presents the same words in the same basic rhythm as the melody, so it is never hard to distinguish the main tune (or the words).

The rhythm of "Brown October Ale" is also more sophisticated than the typical drinking song. The score is sprinkled with a number of fermatas (indicated in the Musical Example the by underlining), as was the case in Mozart's "The Catalogue Aria" in *Don Giovanni.* It is a bit hard to imagine that inebriated singers could sustain certain notes and then—in perfect coordination—resume a steady beat. Nevertheless, despite this artistic license, this prop song seems "genuine" in a way that many theater songs do not.

With the triumph of *Robin Hood,* operetta began to dominate America's theaters, pushing vaudeville, farce-comedies, and other genres aside. Not only did a number of European composers take up residence in the United States to capitalize on the genre's increasing popularity, but several American composers tried their hands at operetta as well (including the "March King," John Philip Sousa). Moreover, New York had begun to assume its position as the center of theatrical activity in the United States. Producers would "try out" new productions in other cities before bringing them to New York, since a success in New York was so important.

By 1900, New York had more major theaters—41—than any other city in the world. Most of these theaters were located on or near Broadway Boulevard in Manhattan, in an area 12 blocks long and two blocks wide, which is why productions that play in these theaters are called **Broadway shows.** Shows that appear in smaller New York theaters outside of this concentrated district are said to be **off-Broadway.** In recent years the term **off-off-Broadway** has been used to describe venues that are *very* far afield (and often *very* small); these frequently include informal spaces such as lofts, churches, and so forth. In 1901, O. J. Gude coined the phrase "the **Great White Way**" to describe the new electric lights that were replacing the gas and arc lights of earlier years, and the term quickly became a slang label for the Broadway theater district itself.

Even as Broadway theaters switched over to electrical power, producers adopted new twists in their shows in order to make them "electrifying" as well. One successful approach was the merger of operetta with the older genre of extravaganza, with its elaborate, fantastic sets; the result was sometimes known as a **scenery show.** The first major success of this combined strategy was *The Wizard of Oz* (1903). Like the 1939 film (see the **Sidebar:** *The Wizard of Oz*—1903 versus 1939), the operetta put much of its emphasis on various spectacle effects. At one point, the chorus girls (wearing enormous hats) depicted a field of bright poppies. After the magical effect of a snowstorm, the poor poppies lay dead in the snow. Audiences were dazzled by the scenery and were able to disregard the rather meaningless songs.

Like any big success to this day, *The Wizard of Oz* inspired many imitations. One of the most successful copycats was rushed into production the same year, opening in October 1903. This new operetta-extravaganza was ***Babes in Toyland,*** and it firmly established **Victor Herbert** (1859–1924) as a leading name in American musical theater. His earliest endeavors had been in art music, both as a performer and a composer, but he had started writing operettas in 1894.

Victor Herbert.
Culver Pictures, Inc.

Babes in Toyland—unlike the forgettable score of *The Wizard of Oz*—would rise to the level of the visual spectacle. The imaginative story (see the **Plot Summary**) by **Glen MacDonough** (1870–1924) lent itself to fantastic sets; after the opening storm, audiences witnessed the frightening Spider's Forest and the magical country of Toyland itself. Other wonderful stage sets included Uncle Barnaby's farm, Mary's garden, the Moth Queen's floral palace, Christmas Tree Grove, a Toyland street, the Toymaker's workshop, and the Toyland Palace of Justice.

Herbert's charming music for *Babes in Toyland* matched the appeal of the grandiose stage sets. Interestingly, singers did not get *all* the great music of the score; the orchestra presented one of the operetta's big hits, "The March of the Toys." There were vocal hits as well, of course, including the lyrical "Toyland" and "I Can't Do the Sum" (**Musical Example 13**). "I Can't Do the Sum" featured the complexities of "new math," Toyland-style. The chorus members were seated along a wall behind Jane and Alan, much in the manner of Humpty Dumpty. Because Jane is a child (played by an adult actress), Herbert wrote a very simple accompaniment to the melody. Jane's text setting is almost entirely syllabic, except when she reaches the repeated phrase "Oh! Oh! Oh!" The switch to a melismatic text setting at this point adds to the effect of Jane's despairing wails over her calculations.

The form of this tune, like "Brown October Ale," is verse-chorus in an *a-B-a-B* (etc.) pattern. In each of the song's five verses (heard at **1**, **3**, **5**, **6**, and **7**), Jane puzzles over an absurd word problem. The chorus of Mother Goose characters joins in for the chorus, or *B* section, of the song (**2**, **4**, and **8**), and they add to the charm by using the chalk to tap a short echoing rhythm on their hand-held slates.

Although *Babes in Toyland* was Herbert's first big success, it was by no means his last triumph. However, he did not repeat the formula of "operetta-plus-extravaganza"; unlike some of his colleagues, he constantly sought to keep up with changing tastes and musical styles. However, even while Herbert and other operetta composers were rising to stardom, new theatrical genres began to develop that were a conscious reaction *against* their most successful operetta endeavors.

He also began to lead the Pittsburgh Symphony Orchestra in 1898, elevating it to the level of Boston's and New York's fine orchestras. Herbert resigned the conducting position in 1904 after disagreements with the management—and after the overwhelming success of *Babes in Toyland*. (Herbert would be involved in other disputes; see **Behind-the-Scenes**.)

Babes in Toyland quickly achieved the same popularity as its predecessor, *The Wizard of Oz*. Julian Mitchell had directed both scenery shows, but by hiring Herbert to create the second operetta's score, Mitchell was determined that the music for

---

Sidebar: *The Wizard of Oz*—1903 versus 1939

Although author L. Frank Baum was directly involved with the 1903 operetta version of *The Wizard of Oz*, the operetta is in some ways further from his children's book than the 1939 MGM movie of the same story, filmed some 20 years after Baum's death. In the operetta, Dorothy is accompanied by her *cow*, Imogene, rather than her little dog, Toto. (The cow was a clear attempt to cash in on the continued popularity of dancing bovines inaugurated by *Evangeline*.) Because David Montgomery and Fred Stone were already a successful comedy team, their roles as the Tin Woodman and Scarecrow in the operetta were far bigger than the small part given to the Cowardly Lion. The operetta's plot was considerably different from both the book and movie as well: Dorothy becomes involved in trying to help the deposed King of Oz regain his throne, and she is assisted by various allies—her friend Trixie, General Riskitt, the poet Dashemoff Dailey—none of whom figure in the original novel (or the film).

Although both the operetta and the movie contained songs, all the music for the 1939 film was newly written; no songs from the operetta were repeated. In fact, the only significant thing that the operetta and the film had in common was an emphasis on fabulous special effects, such as the cyclone that whisks Dorothy off to the Land of Oz in the first place. However, all three works—the novel, the operetta, and the film—enjoyed outstanding success in their time, and Baum's engaging story would inspire still more adaptations in the years to come, including the musicals *The Wiz* in 1975 and *Wicked* in 2003.

FURTHER READING

Bordman, Gerald. *American Operetta from* H.M.S Pinafore *to* Sweeney Todd. New York: Oxford University Press, 1981.

Fields, Armond, and L. Marc Fields. *From the Bowery to Broadway*. New York and Oxford: Oxford University Press, 1993.

Root, Deane L. *American Popular Stage Music, 1860–1880*. Ann Arbor, Michigan: UMI Research Press, 1981.

Schoenfeld, Gerald. "The Broadway Theatre circa 1983." [n.p.] The League of New York Theatres and Producers, 1983.

Smith, Cecil. *Musical Comedy in America*. New York: Theatre Arts Books (Robert M. MacGregor), 1950.

Smith, Harry B. *First Nights and First Editions*. Boston: Little, Brown, and Company, 1931.

———. *Stage Lyrics*. New York: R. H. Russell, 1900.

Traubner, Richard. *Operetta: A Theatrical History*. Garden City, New York: Doubleday, 1983.

BEHIND-THE-SCENES: THE INTEGRITY OF THE SCORE

Although, by the turn of the century, most Broadway productions featured new scores devised by a single composer, it was not at all uncommon for the director or producer to interpolate songs by someone else into a show. These **interpolations** often had little to do with the show's plot; usually they were added merely to "freshen up" a show that had been running for some time. The added song might allude to current events or a recent fad, or it might simply feature a particular performer. Composers of the original score usually had little say about the decision to add interpolated songs, but by the early twentieth century, Victor Herbert had earned enough prestige that he flatly refused to conduct the orchestra during interpolated songs he had not written. He would hand the baton to the orchestra's concertmaster (the principal violinist), who would lead the orchestra during the interpolated numbers.

In 1904, Marie Cahill was hired to star in Herbert's *It Happened in Nordland*. After some time, Cahill added two new interpolations and was aggravating the instrumentalists and conductor by occasionally singing extra verses without warning the orchestra beforehand. She, in turn, was aggravated by Herbert; she felt that he was being too ostentatious as he turned over the baton to his assistant. During one performance, she had reached the second verse of a song when she stopped, stamped her foot, started to cry, then excused herself to the audience and left the stage. Hearing the eerie silence, the show's producer, Lew Fields, persuaded the sobbing Cahill to resume her performance.

Cahill came back on stage to audience applause and told them, "I will try to sing without the orchestra, it is so intentionally bad." The orchestra took offense at this snub, and began to hiss; the audience scolded the orchestra by shouting "Shame! Shame!" After finishing the song, Cahill proceeded to give a speech about her feelings of persecution; the audience cheered. She was encouraged by their support to give Fields an ultimatum; she would sing only if Herbert were banned from the theater. She clearly believed that she was essential to the show's success, and she was shocked when Fields elected to support Herbert's position. Fields believed that the show itself was stronger than any particular actress; it didn't need Cahill to succeed. With this step, the "freedom to interpolate" suffered its first notable blow. Although the practice would survive for many years, composers fought for increasing legal control over their scores so that changes could *not* be made without their consent—which is largely how things stand today.

PLOT SUMMARY: *ROBIN HOOD*

Since the Middle Ages, people have retold the legend of Robin Hood in song, and de Koven and Smith's 1890 operetta adhered to most (but not all) of the conventions of this long tradition. Set in England at the time of King Richard I's reign, the operetta opens in the town of Nottingham. Friar Tuck, the spiritual guide to a band of outlaws of Sherwood Forest, auctions stolen booty to the poor, while one outlaw, Allan-a-Dale, flirts with Annabel, daughter of the innkeeper Dame Durden. Annabel's father has been fighting in the Crusades with the king for the past decade, and Dame Durden is troubled that she has received no reply to her annual letter and gift of a homespun suit; has she become a widow?

Many people have come to Nottingham for an archery contest, including young Robert of Huntingdon. He's ready to claim his father's title and legacy from the Sheriff of Nottingham, who had been guardian of the estate until Robert came of age. The Sheriff is also guardian of Lady Marian Fitzwalter, who has just received King Richard's decree that she is to marry the new Earl of Huntingdon. Lady Marian dresses herself as a page so that she can go to the fair and judge the young man for herself, but she quickly abandons her disguise after meeting and falling in love with Robert (who wins the archery competition). However, the Sheriff has other plans: he has forged documents giving the Huntingdon earldom to Sir Guy of Gisborne. Sir Guy will get the title *and* Lady Marian; the Sheriff will keep Huntingdon's riches for himself. After the Sheriff announces the substitution, the dispossessed Robert takes refuge with the Merry Men of Sherwood Forest.

Robert, or "Robin," thinks Lady Marian is a willing bride and tries to distract himself with Annabel. Allan-a-Dale is outraged, but Little John advises him to drown his sorrows with "Brown October Ale" (**Musical Example 12**). The Sheriff and Sir Guy have come to Dame Durden's inn in disguise—but the Sheriff's tinker's costume leads to problems: Dame Durden recognizes it as the last homespun suit she had sent to her spouse. She thinks that her husband has returned (even if he's grown unrecognizable), and the Sheriff—who had bought his outfit from Friar Tuck—doesn't dare explain her mistake. If he reveals where he got the clothes, he would have to arrest himself for receiving stolen property, so he goes along with the pretense for the time being.

Lady Marian has escaped from Nottingham in order to join the outlaws of Sherwood Forest. She is dismayed to learn that Robin is pursuing Annabel, but decides to wait at Annabel's window herself in order to confront Robin when he comes to sing a serenade. The couple soon straighten out the confusion, and Lady Marian happily agrees to marry Robin. However, in the dark, Allan-a-Dale thinks it is *Annabel* who is promising to wed Robin, so, in anger, Allan reveals Robin's presence to the Sheriff and Sir Guy; Robin is promptly arrested.

In the third act, the situation looks dire: not only is Robin to be executed, but Annabel has been carried off to Nottingham to wed the Sheriff in a double ceremony with Lady Marian and Sir Guy. Friar Tuck and Little John, wearing monks' robes, arrive at Robin's cell to hear his confession, and Robin is able to escape by swapping clothes. Robin disguises himself as the bishop who will conduct the wedding, and at the crucial moment, not only does Robin reveal himself, but so does King Richard, who has unexpectedly returned from the Crusades. The King pardons the true Earl of Huntingdon for his illegal activities as Robin Hood, and all ends happily (except, of course, for the Sheriff and Sir Guy).

PLOT SUMMARY: *BABES IN TOYLAND*

Although it is an original story, *Babes in Toyland* draws heavily from Mother Goose for its familiar nursery-rhyme characters. Jane and Alan, two orphaned siblings, are deliberately shipwrecked by their wicked Uncle Barnaby, who wants to seize control of their fortune. Barnaby also has designs on Contrary Mary, the girl Alan loves, and Barnaby pressures Mary's mother, the Widow Piper, into agreeing that her daughter should marry Barnaby now that Alan is lost in the shipwreck.

Contrary Mary, true to form, runs as far away as she can manage—which means she flees to Toyland. The Widow Piper's son Tom-Tom—Jane's fiancé—goes in pursuit of his sister, fearing she won't be safe. To Barnaby's further chagrin, his niece and nephew survived the shipwreck and have returned. Improvising quickly, he tells Jane and Alan that their home has burned down while they were gone, but that they have a new house. They are led into the Spiders' Forest, but they realize that they're in danger, so they struggle to find a way out of the woods. However, they take time to free a beautiful white moth caught in a web. The moth transforms into the Moth Queen, and her butterfly subjects lead Jane and Alan safely through the forest to the magical country of Toyland (where math problems, as Jane discovers in **Musical Example 13**, don't always work out as expected).

Jane and Alan joyfully encounter Contrary Mary and her brother Tom-Tom. The two couples soon realize that although Toyland seems to be a wonderful place, full of every imaginable childish delight, something is wrong—it turns out that the evil Toymaker holds sway over the land. He hates children and is secretly crafting toys that kill! Uncle Barnaby and the Toymaker soon join forces, but some of the Toymaker's dangerous toys end up killing their creator. Poor Alan tried to rescue the Toymaker, and has been accused of murder. Even though Contrary Mary marries Barnaby to save Alan, Barnaby breaks his word and hands Alan over to the Toyland authorities. Alan is quickly convicted and is sentenced to die, unless he can plead "the benefit of widow." This obscure Toyland custom allows a widow to marry a condemned man and thereby save him from execution. Unfortunately for Alan, though, Toyland currently has only one widow, an opera singer, and she regards Alan's singing as inadequate. Alan's executioners decide to make the job simple by poisoning his wine—but Barnaby, scolded endlessly by Mary—grabs for the wine-glass to fortify himself, and he immediately drops dead. It takes Mary only a moment to realize that now *she* is a widow and can save her beloved by marrying him. Moreover, Alan has found a vial of the Toymaker's magic dust and is able to remove the evil from the murderous toys. The story ends with the toys all coming to life and rejoicing over the happy ending.

MUSICAL EXAMPLE 12

ROBIN HOOD
REGINALD DE KOVEN/HARRY B. SMITH, 1891
"Brown October Ale"

[Underlining indicates fermatas]

Little John

1 And it's will ye quaff with me, my <u>lads</u>, and it's will ye quaff with me?
It is a draught of nut-brown ale I offer unto ye.
All humming in the tankard, lads, it cheers the heart forlorn.
Oh! Here's a friend to everyone, 'tis stout John Barleycorn.

2 So laugh, lads, and quaff, lads, 'twill make you stout and hale.
Through all my days I'll sing the praise of brown October ale.

Chorus

<u>Yes</u>, laugh, lads, and quaff, lads, 'twill make you stout and hale. <u>Ah</u>!

Little John

Through all my days I'll sing the praise of brown October <u>ale</u>.

Chorus

Of brown Octo<u>ber</u> ale.

Little John

3 And it's will ye love me true, my <u>lass</u>, and it's will ye love me true?

If not, I'll drink one flagon more, and so farewell to you.

If Jean or Moll, or Nan or Doll, should make your heart to mourn,

Fill up the pail with nut-brown ale and toast John Barleycorn.

4 So laugh, lads, and quaff, lads, 'twill make you stout and hale.

Through all my days I'll sing the praise of brown October ale.

Chorus

<u>Yes</u>, laugh, lads, and quaff, lads, 'twill make you stout and hale. <u>Ah</u>!

Little John

Through all my days I'll sing the praise of brown October <u>ale</u>.

Chorus

Of brown Octo<u>ber</u> ale.

MUSICAL EXAMPLE 13

Babes in Toyland
Victor Herbert/Glen MacDonough, 1903

"I Can't Do the Sum"

Jane

1 If a steamship weighed ten thousand tons, and sailed five thousand miles

With a cargo large of overshoes, and carving knives and files,

If the mates were almost six feet high, and the bos'n near the same,

Would you subtract or multiply to find the captain's name? Oh! Oh! Oh!

2 Put down six and carry two. [Click, click, click. Click, click, click]

Gee! but this is hard to do. [Click, click, click. Click, click, click]

You can think and think and think till your brains are numb, [Click, click]

I don't care what teacher says, I can't do the sum.

3 If Clarence took fair Gwendolin out for an auto ride,

And if at sixty miles an hour one kiss to capture tried,

And quite forgot the steering gear on her honeyed lips to sup,

How soon would twenty men with brooms sweep Clare and Gwennie up? Oh! Oh! Oh!

4 Put down six and carry two. [Click, click, click. Click, click, click]

Gee! but this is hard to do. [Click, click, click. Click, click, click]

You can think and think and think till your brains are numb, [Click, click]

I don't care what teacher says, I can't do the sum.

5 If Harold took sweet Imogene with him one eve to dine,

And ordered half the bill of fare with cataracts of wine,

If the bill of fare were thirteen ninety-five and poor Harold had but four,

How many things would Harold strike before he struck the floor? Oh! Oh! Oh!

6 If a woman had an English pug, ten children, and a cat,

And she tried in seven hours to find a forty-dollar flat,

With naught but sunny outside rooms in a neighborhood of tone,

How old would those ten children be before they found a home? Oh! Oh! Oh!

7 If a pound of prunes cost thirteen cents at half-past-one today,

And the grocer is so bald he wears a dollar-five toupee

And if with every pound of tea he will give two cut-glass plates,

How soon would Willie break his face on his new roller skates? Oh! Oh! Oh!

8 Put down six and carry two. [Click, click, click. Click, click, click]

Gee! but this is hard to do. [Click, click, click. Click, click, click]

You can think and think and think till your brains are numb, [Click, click]

I don't care what teacher says, I can't do the sum.

Diverging Paths in the Twentieth Century

Part Three

Chapter 11
The Continuing Dominance of Operetta

Although by the turn of the century, homegrown American operettas were seizing a large portion of performance profits, European composers continued to demonstrate their own expertise in the genre. One of the most celebrated operettas in America in the early twentieth century came from the pen of an Austrian, Franz Lehár (1870–1948), perhaps the leading operetta composer of Vienna's "Silver Age." Lehár's operetta *The Merry Widow* debuted in New York in 1907, two years after its Viennese premiere. Not only was its score an instant hit, with countless couples dancing to "The Merry Widow Waltz," but women all across the United States soon wore "Merry Widow" hats, gowns, perfume, and corsets; men and women ate "Merry Widow" chocolates," drank "Merry Widow" liqueurs, and even smoked "Merry Widow" cigarettes. The trend for **merchandizing** in conjunction with a Broadway production was off to a flying start.

Victor Léon and Leo Stein wrote the libretto for *The Merry Widow*; their idea came from an earlier French play. They gave their libretto to composer Richard Heuberger. At this point, the old saying "what goes around comes around" was proven once again: several years earlier, Lehár had auditioned as a conductor for the Vienna Concert Society (in an **audition**, a job applicant demonstrates his or her skills). Heuberger, one of the judges, argued that Lehár knew nothing about waltzes, thereby costing Lehár the job. Now, Heuberger brought back the first act of *The Merry Widow* and played his score for the librettists. Their dismayed reaction was that Heuberger's music was feeble and uninspired—especially his waltzes!

A theatrical associate pressured Léon and Stein into letting Lehár compose a trial aria. Léhar telephoned Léon the following day and, over the phone, played his setting of "Silly, Silly Cavalier." Léon was instantly sold. The theater director was not as confident, so he staged the production as cheaply as

A cartoon satirizing the *Merry Widow* craze, c.1908.
Lebrecht Collection/NL.

he could (much like *Robin Hood*'s inaugural performance); he even used paper lanterns in one glamorous party scene. *The Merry Widow* opened in 1905 to generally positive reviews (although one critic condemned the show as "the most distasteful I have ever seen in a theatre"). For a while, ticket sales were slow, and the management resorted to **papering the house**—distributing a large number of free tickets so that *The Merry Widow* would reach its 50th performance (a point of pride). Instead of tapering off, however, demand for tickets gradually grew. Better costumes and sets were purchased—but superstition kept the paper lanterns in the show! *The Merry Widow* later repeatedly included a young Adolf Hitler in its audience (ironically, since both lyricists and the composer's wife were Jewish).

It was not long after *The Merry Widow* had become a sensation that it began to open in other European cities. George Edwardes brought an English translation of *The Merry Widow* to London in 1907. Unlike the Viennese premiere, *The Merry Widow* was a hit from the very start in London. Edwardes told Lehár that tickets were selling for performances during Christmas 1908—18 months in the future! *The Merry Widow* ran 778 performances in London, with some patrons attending more than 100 times. Even King Edward VII was in the audience on four occasions. *The Merry Widow* came to the United States some four months after its London debut, opening in New York on October 21, 1907. The delighted response to the Broadway production—which ran for 416 performances—led not only to the quick and widespread merchandizing, but to a burlesque version by comedians Joe Weber and Lew Fields, which itself ran for 156 performances.

Lehár was not the only foreign composer to triumph on the American stage in the early twentieth century. Works such as Oscar Straus's *The Chocolate Soldier* and Ivan Caryll's *The Pink Lady* were enormous hits. Gustave Kerker's *The Belle of New York* (1897) deserves special mention, not because it was a success in New York—it wasn't—but because it went on to be a smash hit overseas despite its earlier American failure. *The Belle of New York* was the most popular American musical show of its time—just not in America. It is an irony that the first real step toward an era when America would dominate musical theater worldwide was taken by a show that Americans didn't like.

Operetta in New York was still dominated by another emigré, Victor Herbert, composer of the extravaganza *Babes in Toyland*. Herbert cemented his reputation with the American public with a 1910 production called **Naughty Marietta**. In his "creole comic opera," Herbert had a pair of particularly fine singers to use, because the operetta was the brainchild of Oscar Hammerstein (grandfather to the future lyricist) who was the **impresario** of the Manhattan Opera Company. (An impresario is an operatic equivalent to the modern-day **producer** of movies, television programs, and Broadway shows; he raises the money, often hires the composer, writers, and performers, and may even come up with the initial idea for a show.) The opera company had some sizable debts, so Hammerstein decided to feature his stars—especially the soprano Emma Trentini—in a more popularly oriented production than their usual operas. Operetta seemed the perfect vehicle and Herbert the perfect composer.

Herbert's librettist was **Rida Johnson Young** (1869–1926), one of the few women active as a writer or composer on

Broadway (see the *Sidebar*: Women in the Creative Credits). Her romantic libretto (see the **Plot Summary**) was a suitable backdrop for Herbert's soaring melodies. The period of the play's setting was unclear, and Young explained, "We don't know ourselves. You see, we selected one date, and then the costumer decided that another would give him more latitude in the designing of his costumes, so it is all a little indefinite, but it is some time during the eighteenth century." The story did not allow itself to be interrupted by stock comedians, and much of the music was diegetic, appearing naturally as part of the plot. The opening of the operetta was especially unusual; Herbert wrote an atmospheric evocation of dawn for the chorus, full of the cries of street vendors and the chatter of street sweepers and convent girls on their way to school. Herbert deserves credit for making the opening of his shows "meaningful," thereby encouraging American theatergoers not to be late!

Since Herbert composed *Naughty Marietta* with "star" soprano Trentini in mind, the operetta is a **star vehicle**—a production that is specifically designed to showcase an individual's talents. The "Italian Street Song" (**Musical Example 14**) is a good illustration of why many amateur companies still have trouble performing *Naughty Marietta*. The singer in the role of Marietta needs to be a **coloratura soprano**, who not only can sing quite high, but whose voice must be supple, capable of singing rapid scales, leaps, and trills with ease.

The "Italian Street Song," after a brief orchestral introduction, opens with a passage for Marietta alone (accompanied by the orchestra), in which she reminisces about life in Naples (**1**). This triple-meter opening has a sing-song feeling. However, it is harder to sing this graceful tune than it might seem, for the deceptively fluid melody is **disjunct**, meaning that it is filled with quick leaps between high and low pitches. A completely different effect starts at **2**, when Marietta sings an energetic refrain. The meter changes to a march-like duple pulsation with simple subdivision. The melody becomes much more **conjunct**, which means that her pitches move up and down mostly by step; she also sings many repeated notes, in which the pitch does not change at all. Moreover, her many nonsense syllables are an example of **onomatopoeia**; she is imitating the sounds of the mandolins described in the poetry.

Marietta, now supported by the chorus, repeats the entire refrain of **2** again at **3**. Things change quite a bit at **4**, when the chorus takes over and the mode shifts temporarily to minor. Although the mode returns to major at **5**, Marietta is not heard until the chorus's last note at **7**, when she soars above them with an impressive high C, a very high pitch. At **8**, while the chorus resumes the same refrain that had appeared earlier at **2** and **3**, Marietta sustains the C, and then starts to perform rapid scales and leaps while singing the single syllable "ah"—like Rosalinde in *Die Fledermaus*, she is singing melismatically. Her melismas and high range create a **countermelody**, a theme that contrasts with the syllabic refrain being sung by the chorus, thereby producing a passage of non-imitative polyphony.

In retrospect, the opening passage at **1** stands completely apart from the remainder of the song—no aspect of its music returns later. Some analysts call this type of passage a "verse," considering it to be a vestige of the verse-chorus form seen in "Camptown Races." However, it is hard to explain the interlude

1		Vocal Introduction (triple meter, disjunct melody)
2	*A*	Marietta alone (duple meter, conjunct melody)
3	*A'*	Marietta in harmony with chorus
4–7	*B*	chorus alone; minor mode and different text
8	*A''*	simultaneous melismatic and syllabic singing
9	*A''*	simultaneous melismatic and syllabic singing

Figure 11–1

that occurs at **4** through **7**, since it has nothing in common with the opening verse. It might be preferable to consider the opening passage to be a **vocal introduction**, since this is a better description of its actual function in the structure of the song. If this label is adopted, then it is easier to regard the remainder of the "Italian Street Song" as a ternary form. As seen in **Figure 11–1**, the paired presentations of *A* (**2–3** and **8–9**) surround the choral interlude, which acts as the *B* section of the form.

No matter what form label is used, however, the "Italian Street Song" is an impressive opportunity for virtuosic vocal display, and a rousing number in the course of the story. *Musical America* published a review of *Naughty Marietta*'s opening night in 1910:

> *Mr. Herbert himself wielded the baton on the first night with the result that everything went for its full value. At the close of the first act the enthusiasm was positively riotous and the principals were showered with flowers. Victor Herbert received a stormy welcome when dragged on the stage by Miss Trentini, but the audience would not calm down until Mr. Hammerstein had risen in his box to bow four or five times. . . .*

Despite this auspicious start, the relationship of Herbert and Trentini went the way of his earlier dealings with Marie Cahill. Trentini took a vacation, and when she returned to the show, she started living up to the worst of the stereotypes about prima donnas: she would refuse to give encores, or sometimes she wouldn't even sing a song all the way through. On occasion, managers had to go to her hotel and drag her to the theater half an hour before the performance, and they had to pay all her tips, despite her rather spectacular salary of $1,000 per week. George Blumenthal, a theater employee, later wrote—in something of an understatement—"I surely did have a terrible time with this woman." (In Trentini's defense, the role of Marietta *was* quite physically demanding.)

During a special gala performance of *Naughty Marietta*, Herbert heard thunderous applause after the "Italian Street Song," so he gave Trentini the signal for an encore—but she ignored him and continued to bow to the audience. At last, he simply started conducting, whereupon Trentini put her nose in the air and marched off the stage. Not one to swallow an insult, Herbert handed the baton to his assistant and marched out of the orchestra pit. His revenge didn't stop there; he had been commissioned by Arthur Hammerstein, Oscar's nephew, to write a second star vehicle for Trentini. Telling Hammerstein that he had never been so insulted in his entire

Emma Trentini
Culver Pictures, Inc.

career, Herbert refused to write a note of the new score. (Composer Rudolf Friml got the job instead, and Friml got along much better with Trentini. In fact, Friml's wife later sued him for divorce because of adultery, naming Trentini as the "other woman"!) Herbert, meanwhile, helped establish **ASCAP**, a new organization to protect creative artists and publishers from pirated performances of their music (see the *Sidebar*: Victor Herbert and ASCAP).

The Merry Widow and *Naughty Marietta*'s rousing success showed that glamorous operetta—whether imported or homegrown—still held a solid place in Broadway theaters; it would hold that position until the late 1920s. Nevertheless, a variety of newer genres were rising to the fore, and in some ways they rejected the flowery settings and stringent vocal requirements of operetta. Audiences were beginning to appreciate the splash and energy of other approaches that put less focus on the singing voice and more emphasis on comedy, modern settings, and the latest popular music and dance. The time was ripe for "musical comedy" to make its mark.

FURTHER READING

Alpert, Hollis. *Broadway: 125 Years of American Musical Theatre.* New York: Little, Brown, 1991.

Grun, Bernard. *Gold and Silver: The Life and Times of Franz Lehár.* London: W. H. Allen, 1970.

Although women composers like Francesca Caccini had written operas as early as the seventeenth century, it was not at all common to find women as part of the creative team for Broadway musical theater. One of the first women to have any impact was Rida Johnson Young (1869–1926), a native of Baltimore, who seems to have met Victor Herbert through his publishing house, Witmark. Her creative career began as a playwright, but her reputation as an effective librettist wasn't firmly established until the success of *Naughty Marietta*. Young's subsequent theatrical road did not proceed completely smoothly; she had a couple of flops, one of which, *The Red Petticoat*, had a score by a Broadway novice, Jerome Kern. *Sometime*, a 1914 collaboration with Rudolf Friml, however, was one of the biggest hits of the season; audiences seem to have been intrigued with the unexpected use of "flashback" scenes, a novelty for the day. Young also enjoyed considerable success with her 1917 show *Maytime*, with a score by Sigmund Romberg. Young's career ended with her contributions to the libretto for Victor Herbert's last work, *The Dream Girl*, which was presented in 1924 after Herbert's death.

Only a few other women participated as librettists, lyricists, or composers in early twentieth-century Broadway; among them were Anne Caldwell (1867–1936), Clare Kummer (1886–1958), and Dorothy Donnelly (1880–1928). Caldwell—married to lyricist James O'Dea—was the composer of some songs interpolated in *The Social Whirl*, a 1906 show. After limited success as a playwright, Caldwell wrote lyrics for Victor Herbert and Ivan Caryll. She also collaborated with Jerome Kern, Vincent Youmans, and a handful of other composers; several of her librettos were designed to feature the members of the famous Montgomery and Stone comedy team who had starred in *The Wizard of Oz*.

Like Caldwell, Clare Kummer doubled as a composer as well as a writer; like Young, she was a successful playwright of "straight" (spoken) plays. She was not a prolific contributor to musical theater, but she co-wrote an English libretto for a Viennese import in 1912. Kummer also transformed one of her own plays into a musical theater libretto in 1924; the result was *Annie Dear*. She wrote some of the tunes herself, but other songs came from Sigmund Romberg and Harry Tierney. She struggled with producer Florenz Ziegfeld over the direction of *Annie Dear*, and he, in exasperation, closed the show after 103 performances. Even so, it ran longer than a second effort by Kummer of that same year, *Mme. Pompadour*, which was another adaptation of a Viennese original. These frustrations marked the end of Kummer's Broadway musical output.

Dorothy Donnelly, formerly a noted Broadway actress, made a bit of a splash with the libretto for the bittersweet operetta *The Student Prince* in 1924. The score is often regarded as Sigmund Romberg's finest achievement, and the show ran for 608 performances in New York; it toured for some 25 years. Her collaborations with other composers were disappointing in comparison, but her last work was another operetta with Romberg, *My Maryland* (1927), which broke Philadelphia records during its **tryout tour**, the out-of-town trial run. Donnelly did not live to see its New York success; she died shortly after it opened. New female faces would appear with the next generation of musical theater, but it would be a long time before any woman would match the triumph enjoyed—at least on occasion—by these pioneers.

MacQueen-Pope, W., and D. L. Murray. *Fortune's Favourite: The Life and Times of Franz Lehár*. London: Hutchinson, 1953.

Mordden, Ethan. *Better Foot Forward: The History of American Musical Theatre*. New York: Grossman Publishers (A Division of the Viking Press), 1976.

Traubner, Richard. *Operetta: A Theatrical History*. Garden City, New York: Doubleday, 1983.

Waters, Edward N. *Victor Herbert: A Life in Music*. New York: Macmillan, 1955.

PLOT SUMMARY: *NAUGHTY MARIETTA*

In the eighteenth-century French colony of New Orleans, Étienne Grandet, son of the acting governor, has returned from a trip to France. Or has he? Actually, Étienne is living a double life: he is also the pirate Bras Priqué, who has been terrorizing the Louisiana coast. Moreover, as part of a scheme to seize control of Louisiana, he has secretly imprisoned the true governor of New Orleans. Only a couple of people know the pirate's real identity: his father (a cowardly man who is willing enough to share in the pirate's plunder) and Étienne's mistress, the slave Adah. The citizens of New Orleans are frightened not only by Bras Priqué but also by the "ghost" of one of his supposed victims: a disembodied voice has been heard to sing an incomplete melody—"Ah, Sweet Mystery of Life"—in the town fountain.

A ragtag group of men march into New Orleans, led by Captain Dick Warrington, singing one of *Naughty Marietta*'s big hits, "Tramp, Tramp, Tramp." Since their supply ships have been suffering from Bras Priqué's attacks, they have come to New Orleans to get an arrest warrant for the pirate as well as to meet a ship bearing *casquette* girls—the eighteenth-century equivalent of mail-order brides. In hopes of winning the brides for themselves, they want to be present as the unusual cargo debarks.

After the excitement of the *casquette* girls' arrival fades and the town square empties, the ghostly melody is again heard wafting from the fountain—but then a very human singer emerges from a large urn. It is Marietta, an Italian runaway who has fled an unwelcome marriage. She is spotted by Captain Dick, but she regards him as a friend—she'd met him and his troop earlier—so she asks him to help her hide.

Sidebar: Victor Herbert and ASCAP

Sweeping changes can sometimes result from an act as simple as dining at a particular restaurant. In 1910, the Italian opera composer Puccini was visiting the United States. He repeatedly heard melodies from his operas being played by restaurant orchestras to entertain the diners, and was appalled to find that he was earning no financial benefit from these performances. He criticized the United States for not defending composers' rights in the same way that composers were protected in Europe. Puccini's criticism fell on fertile ground, and a Midwestern composer, Raymond Hubbell, was determined to do something about the situation.

Hubbell wanted Victor Herbert on his side. Herbert was one of America's most admired composers, and in 1909, when the U.S. government was formulating America's first sweeping copyright law, Herbert's testimony before Congress had helped to ensure that composers would receive royalties from sales in the fledgling industry of sound recordings. Hubbell soon convinced Herbert that a battle was needed to guarantee that composers were paid for *live* performances of their music.

Herbert, Hubbell, and some seven other colleagues held a meeting in 1913 that led, in 1914, to the founding of the American Society of Composers, Authors, and Publishers (**ASCAP**). ASCAP was to be a "collecting agency" for the royalties due to the artists and publishers whenever their copyrighted works were performed. Naturally, there was a lot of resistance at first; many performers had no intention of paying for what they'd been able to do for free. In 1915, Herbert heard that the Shanley's Restaurant orchestra was entertaining the diners with the title song from Herbert's operetta *Sweethearts* (1913). Herbert therefore launched ASCAP's test case. He sued the restaurant, arguing that he should be paid when his work was played. The court decision went against Herbert. Herbert appealed, and the Circuit Court of Appeals again ruled against Herbert. Herbert continued to appeal, and the case at last went to the Supreme Court, where, on January 22, 1917, Justice Oliver Wendell Holmes ruled in Herbert's favor. From that point forward, all hotels, theaters, dance halls, cabarets, and restaurants would need to purchase a license from ASCAP before they could legally perform pieces written or published by ASCAP members. ASCAP's triumph held even more importance in the coming years as radio (and later, television) became popular. Although ASCAP's monopoly would be challenged in the 1940s, and a rival organization—Broadcast Music Incorporated (BMI)—was established as an alternative, American writers and composers have continued to benefit from the protections inaugurated by Herbert's activism.

Reluctantly, he arranges for her to pose as the son of Rudolfo, who operates a marionette theater. Teasingly, before she leaves, she asks Dick if he can finish her incomplete melody; she dreamed that the man who can complete the tune will prove to be the man she loves. Dick refuses to try and is irritated when he finds himself whistling the tune a short time later.

Marietta performs the "Italian Street Song" in the town square (**Musical Example 14**), just before the news arrives that the King of France is offering a large reward for the Contessa d'Altena, who was known to have traveled with the *casquette* girls after fleeing her aristocratic family. The Contessa can be identified by a partial melody she is in the habit of singing. Étienne, reading the dispatch, sings a portion of the melody, and the townspeople realize that it's the same tune they've been hearing in the fountain. Unfortunately for Marietta, Captain Dick's lieutenant spots her and identifies her as a *casquette* girl in disguise. She is pulled forward, and she admits she's a boy but denies that she's the Contessa. In the resulting confusion, she manages to escape with Rudolfo.

In the second act, Captain Dick advises Marietta not to go to the annual Quadroon Ball, so of course she does attend! Marietta thinks Dick is interested in Adah, so she encourages Étienne's attentions. Étienne, in the meantime, is convinced that Marietta is indeed the Contessa, and he wants her as his wife, since he can use her fortune to support his plans to take over the colony. He proposes, and she asks what he will do about Adah; carelessly, he says that he will sell her off. He is as good as his word; in the middle of the ball, he announces the auction. Adah, terrified that she will be sold to someone even more hateful, begs Captain Dick for help, so he bids until he has topped all other offers. Jealous, Marietta announces her engagement to Étienne—and he decides that speed is of the essence; he orders that the wedding should take place immediately. Adah approaches her new master, Dick—but he tells her that she is free. Adah wants to thank him, so she tells him that she knows how he can stop the wedding. All Dick needs to do is tear open Étienne's right sleeve, for he has his pirate alias tattooed upon his arm.

Delighted, Dick does what Adah has suggested—but when the pirate is exposed, it turns out that Dick cannot arrest him, for the Grandet family have an official "whipping boy," Simon, who is the one who must be punished for any of their wrongdoing; poor Simon is dragged off to jail. When Marietta returns in her bridal gown and discovers the truth about Étienne, she refuses to marry him, so he imprisons her. Soon, however, she hears a voice singing—and completing—the song from her dream. It is Dick, come to her rescue, and now she knows him to be the man she truly loves. Étienne is vanquished, and the lovers join together in a happy duet of "Ah! Sweet Mystery of Life." The operetta ends with the chorus joining in for one last repetition of the "Italian Street Song."

MUSICAL EXAMPLE 14

Naughty Marietta
Victor Herbert/Rida Johnson Young, 1910
"Italian Street Song"

Marietta

1   Ah! my heart is back in Napoli, dear Napoli, dear Napoli,
And I seem to hear again in dreams her revelry, her sweet revelry.
The mandolinas playing sweet, the pleasant fall of dancing feet.
Oh! could I return, oh! joy complete! Napoli, Napoli, Napoli!

2   Zing, zing, zizzy, zizzy, zing, zing, boom, boom, aye.
Zing, zing, zizzy, zizzy, zing, zing, mandolinas gay.
Zing, zing, zizzy, zizzy, zing, zing, boom, boom, aye.
La, la, la, ha, ha, ha, zing, boom, aye. La, la, la, la, ha, ha, ha, zing, boom, aye.

Marietta and Chorus

3   Zing, zing, zizzy, zizzy, zing, zing, boom, boom, aye.
Zing, zing, zizzy, zizzy, zing, zing, mandolinas gay.
Zing, zing, zizzy, zizzy, zing, zing, boom, boom, aye.
La, la, la, ha, ha, ha, zing, boom, aye. La, la, la, la, ha, ha, ha, zing, boom, aye.

Chorus

4   La, la, la, la. La, la, la, la. Zing, la, la, ha, ha!

Men	**Women**
5 Mandolinas gay dancing as we play. Boom! Boom!	Zizzy, zizzy, zing, zing, zing. La, la! Ha, ha!

Chorus

6   Zing, zing, zing, zing, zing, zing, boom,

Chorus	**Marietta**
7 Aye!	Ah!
8 Zing, zing, zizzy, zizzy, zing, zing, boom, boom, aye!	Ah! ah
Zing, zing, zizzy, zizzy, zing, zing, mandolinas gay.	Ah!
Zing, zing, zizzy, zizzy, zing, zing, boom, boom, aye.	Ah, ah, ah
La, la, la, ha, ha, ha, zing, boom, aye.	Ah, ah, ah, ah, ah, ah, ah
La, la, la, la, ha, ha, ha, zing, boom, aye!	Ah, ah, ah, ha, ha, ha, ah
9 Zing, zing, zizzy, zizzy, zing, zing, boom, boom, aye!	Ah! ah
Zing, zing, zizzy, zizzy, zing, zing, mandolinas gay.	Ah!
Zing, zing, zizzy, zizzy, zing, zing, boom, boom, aye.	Ah, ah, ah, ah, ah, ah
La, la, la, ha, ha, ha, zing, boom, aye.	Ah, ah, ah, ah, ah, ah, ah
La, la, la,	

Marietta and Chorus

10   La, ha, ha, ha! zing, boom, aye!

Chapter 12
Challenges to Operetta

Even though operetta retained its firm grip on the American stage at the start of the twentieth century, several alternatives—especially revues and musical comedies—were developing loyal followers. Moreover, the increasing clout of the popular song-publishing industry meant that the new revues and musical comedies were an increasingly important showcase for popular music and dance.

The idea for the **revue** came from Paris, where audiences enjoyed annual performances that satirized the preceding year's main events in a series of scenes. England began to experiment with the format as early as 1825, but the first attempt at an American presentation was not until 1869; it did not catch on. In 1894, though, *The Passing Show* was presented in New York, where it launched a host of imitators. Unlike earlier revues, this production did not focus merely on events from the previous year, but was a **mixed bill**—a composite of various types of entertainment, much like vaudeville.

Nevertheless, the revue differed from vaudeville; in a vaudeville show, each separate specialty act had different performers. In a revue, the same performers appeared throughout the evening in the various skits. Revues incorporated some of the satire (and limited clothing on females) of the burlesque, and also borrowed **bits** from burlesque shows; bits were short, unrelated comic sketches, which revues retitled as **blackouts**. (At the end of the sketch, the stagelights were turned off instantly—the more common use of the term "blackout"—in order to accentuate the comic punchline.) Moreover, the revue adopted the sumptuous settings and emphasis on physical beauty of the extravaganza. Although there was no clear-cut plot in a revue, there might be a general theme linking the separate sketches—much like the farce-comedy of the late nineteenth century, except that the revue often employed a greater number of performers and was able to be more ambitious in its productions.

The revue's producer determined its tone, and no producer earned more fame for his revues than Florenz Ziegfeld. Ziegfeld produced his first *Follies* in 1907; he proceeded to direct 21 *Follies*, with each edition seeming to outdo the previous year. The first edition cost $13,000; by 1919, Ziegfeld was spending $150,000 in his proclaimed effort to "glorify the American girl." Ziegfeld's emphasis on feminine beauty led to the term **showgirl** as a description for members of his chorus lines. Initially, the first show was to be called the *Follies of the Year*, a title coined by Harry B. Smith (librettist of *Robin Hood*), indicating that it had returned to the French concept of satirizing recent current events, but Ziegfeld retitled it the *Follies of 1907*; in 1911, he began to call the productions the *Ziegfeld Follies*.

Many of Ziegfeld's innovations had a lasting impact; in 1908, "Shine On, Harvest Moon" was one of the first hit songs to come from a revue. Indeed, **Tin Pan Alley**'s success (see the *Sidebar*) stemmed in part from revues. In 1910, Ziegfeld also hired the African American performer Bert Williams. This significant hiring racially integrated the Broadway revue for the first time—but not all of the other performers welcomed the change; Ziegfeld had to cajole some members of the company into performing with Williams, and he had to fire others who absolutely refused to share the stage. The increasingly elaborate stage sets also contributed to Ziegfeld's reputation; in 1915, Ziegfeld hired Joseph Urban, an architect from Austria who would become one of the most important scenic designers in America.

Ziegfeld was not alone in producing a famous series of revues; John Murray Anderson started a series of *Greenwich Village Follies* in 1919, moving the productions from Greenwich Village to Broadway two years later. Earl Carroll produced nine years of *Vanities*. Even Irving Berlin produced four years of *Music Box Revues* starting in 1921. Berlin also contributed to *Cocoanuts* in 1925, featuring the talents of the Marx Brothers. More intimate revues included *The Garrick Gaieties*, which helped to launch the new writing team of Richard Rodgers and Lorenz Hart. In later years, African American revues also took the stage, including several versions of *Shuffle Along*, as well as *Blackbirds of 1928*.

Two other important revue producers had a significant impact on dance: J. J. Shubert began a series of *Passing Shows* in 1912, and George White presented 13 years of *Scandals*. For the third edition of *The Passing Show*, Shubert hired Marilynn Miller, who would go on to become America's highest paid musical theater star. Miller almost single-handedly shifted the American taste in chorus girls from the hearty, buxom curves of the *Black Crook* era to a slender, modern silhouette. The *George White's Scandals*, on the other hand, popularized fast, upbeat jazz dances—numbers like the Charleston and the Black Bottom. George Gershwin contributed dozens of jazz-tinged songs to the *George White's Scandals*.

It is somewhat astonishing to see how many important names in dance history were involved in revue productions: the great ballerina Anna Pavlova, the dancer and choreographers Martha Graham, George Balanchine, and Michel Fokine (in American revues), Massine and Frederick Ashton (in England). Some of the most important contributors to theatrical dance found their way into the revue, including Robert Alton, Jack Cole, Busby Berkeley, and Helen Tamiris; later stars such as Ray Bolger and the Astaires danced their way through revue productions. The husband-and-wife team of Ruth St. Denis and

Ted Shawn did much to legitimize and popularize "serious" dance on the musical theater stage, and they trained future generations of dancers to their high standards by founding Denishawn, a school for dancers. Ted Shawn's efforts were particularly important in encouraging men to undertake careers in dance and raising them to the status enjoyed by female dancers; Shawn founded a "Men Dancers" company in 1933, and years later, Gene Kelly attributed the company's performance at his high school in Pittsburgh as the impetus that launched his own dancing career.

The surge of popularity enjoyed by the revue began to ebb after the first 30 years of the twentieth century, although isolated revues continued to appear up until the 1950s. Many of the revue's characteristics had been absorbed into various types of musical theater, but even more elements found their way to the new medium of the television variety show. In recent years, however, there has been an increasing trend to offer the hit tunes of a particular songwriter in a loosely themed retrospective production (known variously as **compilation** or **catalog** shows) that has much in common with the old-time revues; for example, *Ain't Misbehavin'* features the music of Fats Waller, while the songs of Jerry Leiber and Mike Stoller are featured in *Smokey Joe's Café*.

At the same time that revues were coming to the fore, new **musical comedy** productions were entertaining audiences on both sides of the Atlantic. One of George Edwardes's shows, *A Gaiety Girl*, came to New York in 1894, and viewers were delighted by the modern, realistic settings; six more English productions were imported to New York the following year. Jerome Kern later credited the Gaiety shows with shaping his desire for a show to have grace, charm, and—perhaps most important—cohesion, qualities which were evident in Kern's "Princess Shows," discussed in Chapter 13. The chorus lines of the Gaiety productions—known as the Gaiety Girls—also helped to elevate the dignity and reputation of the young women who danced in the company; costuming was much more elegant and modest than the revealing tights and skimpy outfits worn by earlier generations of dancers.

It was not long before American writers began to create their own versions, and one of the early musical comedies was the product of African Americans. Although *In Dahomey* was not a tremendous success when it opened in New York in 1903, it was an important milestone in the history of Broadway. Earlier, 1897 had also been a significant year, for Bob Cole had organized the first New York-based black theater company that provided theatrical training for African American performers. The following year, he produced *A Trip to Coontown* (1898), known as the "first Negro musical comedy." Although *A Trip to Coontown* did not attain the blockbuster status of the show whose title it mimicked (*A Trip to Chinatown*), it certainly did well, playing off-Broadway until 1900; it even enjoyed a brief Broadway run. It was the first full-length production created by black writers, directors, performers, and producers, but its plot was very loose, and—much like the typical revue—the storyline was merely a general framework for an array of specialty acts, and little of the music was newly composed.

The musical score for another show, *Clorindy, the Origin of the Cakewalk* (1898), was given much more emphasis by the African American composer Will Marion Cook (1869–1944). Cook was classically trained, and it was an enormous disappointment to his mother that he didn't proceed to challenge white composers in "art music" genres—symphonies, sonatas, and so on—but was turning instead to **coon songs**, the now-distasteful label that was routinely applied at the turn of the century to songs written in African American dialect and style.

After finishing *Clorindy* in 1898, Cook started to search for a producer. Hearing that Edward E. Rice (composer of *Evangeline*) was looking for a new act, Cook later recalled his stratagem:

I went to see Ed Rice . . . every day for a month. Regularly, after interviewing a room full of people, he would say to me (I was always the last): "Who are you, and what do you want?" On the thirty-first day—and by now I am so discouraged that this is my last try—I heard him tell a knockabout act: "Come up next Monday to rehearsal, do a show, and if you make good, I'll keep you on all week."

I was desperate. . . . On leaving Rice's office, I went at once . . . to find a few members of my ensemble. I told them a most wonderful and welcome story: we were booked at the Casino Roof! . . . That was probably the most beautiful lie I ever told.

On Monday morning, every man and woman, boy and girl that I had taught to sing my music was at the Casino Roof. . . . Luckily for us, John Braham, the English conductor of the Casino orchestra, was a brick. And, still more luckily for us, Ed Rice did not appear at rehearsal until very late that morning. . . . I had twenty-six of the finest Negro voices in America. . . . Like a mighty anthem in rhythm, these voices rang out. . . .

At the opening, Rice's manager made the simple announcement that the Negro operetta, Clorindy, the Origin of the Cakewalk, *would now be produced for the first time on any stage. . . . When I entered the orchestra pit, there were only about fifty people on the Roof. When we finished the opening chorus, the house was packed to suffocation. What had happened was that the show downstairs in the Casino Theatre was just letting out. The big audience heard those heavenly Negro voices and took to the elevators. . . .*

My chorus sang like Russians, dancing meanwhile like Negroes, and cakewalking like angels, black angels! When the last note was sounded, the audience stood and cheered for at least ten minutes. . . .

Although *Clorindy* was not a full-length show (it was about an hour long), the appreciative audience response made Cook's confidence soar. For his next project, Cook wanted to feature the talents of Bert Williams (1876–1922) and George Walker (1873–1911), one of America's finest African American comedy teams, who had recently come to New York to play vaudeville after leaving the West Coast where they had starred in minstrel shows.

The show that Cook devised for Williams and Walker was **In Dahomey**. Cook worked with Paul Laurence Dunbar (1872–1906), as well as with Jesse Shipp, who apparently got many of *In Dahomey*'s plot ideas—and even a song title or two—from a work called *The Cannibal King*, written by their competitors Bob Cole and James Weldon Johnson. *In Dahomey* opened in the New York Theatre in 1903 and ran for 53 performances—not too impressive a run by Broadway standards, but still the best run ever enjoyed by an African American production in a major Broadway theater. Moreover, the critics enjoyed the show as well. A number of writers had expressed fears that there would be racial incidents, but after the show opened without problems, the critics found it to be an infectious, comic presentation.

Despite Cook's greater care with the music for *In Dahomey*, several of the songs had little to do with the plot, although this was certainly the norm for early musical comedies (see the **Plot Summary**). Moreover, quite a few songs by other writers were interpolated into the show, as is the case with "(I Wants to Be) A Actor Lady" (**Musical Example 15**), written by a non-African American, **Harry von Tilzer** (1872–1946), with lyrics by **Vincent Bryan** (1883–1937). Von Tilzer also ran a successful Tin Pan Alley publishing business and would later employ Irving Berlin.

Von Tilzer and Bryan wrote "(I Wants to Be) A Actor Lady" to spotlight the talents of George Walker's wife, Aida Overton Walker. This type of featured number was a **star turn**—a small-scale equivalent of the star vehicle. During *In Dahomey*'s run, this song did not always occur in the same place in the story, although it was usually incorporated somewhere in the second act of the show. Since the song's text had nothing to do with *In Dahomey*'s plot, it didn't really matter where "A Actor Lady" occurred! The song is rather like a brief play-within-a-play, because Rosetta Lightfoot (Aida Overton Walker) depicts the stage aspirations of a mythical performer, Carrie Brown, as entertainment for her fellow colonists.

The song incorporates several then-current catchphrases as well as references to well-known writers of the time. Clyde Fitch, for instance, was a familiar playwright, while Laura Jean Libby wrote heartthrob romances. In a sly bit of self-promotion, von Tilzer included a reference to Leslie Carter being unable to sing "Good Morning, Carrie"—a song that he himself had published.

Although von Tilzer was not a black composer, he captured much of the musical style that had been characteristic of minstrel show compositions. Von Tilzer and Bryan did not employ black dialect in the text, but they did make deliberate use of poor grammar. Like "Camptown Races," "(I Wants to Be) A Actor Lady" incorporates snappy syncopated rhythms. These syncopations are prominent in the instrumental introduction and then in the choruses (**2** and **4**) of this verse-chorus form. In fact, the rhythm of these sections reflects the growing rage for **ragtime**, a popular musical style pioneered by Scott Joplin and other African American composers. Although there is debate about the actual origin of the term, the "ragged rhythms" of the syncopations seem a likely explanation for the label. The verses (**1** and **3**) of this song—sung in a slower tempo—are not syncopated, and certain words of the last line in each verse (*lunch, bunch, -ton* of Wellington, and *done*) are elongated by means of fermatas. Throughout the verses and the chorus, the accompaniment plays a steady "boom-chick" rhythm (a clear simple subdivision!), giving the impression of the ragtime pieces played on upright pianos in cheap nightclubs known as honky-tonks; this rhythm itself is sometimes called a **honky-tonk** accompaniment.

Encouraged by the positive comments of Broadway critics, the creators of *In Dahomey* took a gamble and transported the company to England. *In Dahomey* ran for 251 performances during its seven months in London and even enjoyed a command performance at Buckingham Palace for the Prince of Wales's ninth birthday. Walker was impressed by their reception:

> *We were treated royally. That is the only word for it. We had champagne from the Royal cellar and strawberries and cream from the Royal garden. The Queen was perfectly lovely, and the King was as jolly as he could be and the little princes and princesses were as nice as they could be, just like little fairies.*

Williams, too, appreciated how England accepted him as a talented artist without regard for his race; some years later, he commented, "I have never been able to discover that there was anything disgraceful in being a colored man. But I have often found it inconvenient—in America."

After the English production closed, *In Dahomey* ran in New York City once again, earning a 400 percent profit. Despite the promising results of this production, successful African American stage shows on Broadway were to remain a rarity clear through the remainder of the century.

One of the most appealing aspects of *In Dahomey* for English audiences was its extreme energy. This quality was not limited to African American productions, however; another young former vaudevillian was also making a mark on the Broadway stage. The performer was **George M. Cohan** (1878–1942), and in addition to starring in his new shows, he was their composer, lyricist, choreographer, director, and producer.

George Walker, Aida Overton Walker, and Bert Williams, in *In Dahomey*.
Museum of the City of New York.

Cohan's Broadway aspirations led him to expand one of his family's vaudeville sketches into a musical comedy. On the show's opening night, he gave his actors a "pep talk," articulating the theatrical philosophy that would drive his successive works. He told the performers,

Don't wait for laughs. Side-step encores. Crash right through this show to-night. Speed! Speed! and lots of it; that's my idea of the thing. Perpetual motion. Laugh your heads off; have a good time; keep happy. Remember now, happy, happy, happy.

Cohan was driven to create shows as different from the somewhat static operettas as he could manage. Cohan's role models for his new, more energetic approach were the comedians Edward Harrigan and Tony Hart, whose rapid-fire vaudeville routines had lampooned the growing tides of urban immigrants, especially the Irish. Instead of targeting a particular ethnic group, however, Cohan (who may or may not have been born on the Fourth of July), chose to display a fervent patriotism in his productions. This enthusiasm was warmly embraced by a nation proud of its accomplishments; audiences were delighted by Cohan's unabashed flag waving. (Cohan's shows did not do as well overseas, due at least in part to their blatant American nationalism.)

Cohan did not delude himself about his level of talent, but he wasn't overly humble either. In tongue-in-cheek fashion, he once defended his abilities by claiming, "I can write better plays than any living dancer, and dance better than any living playwright." As an untrained composer, he was limited to the four chords that he could play using only the black keys of the piano, but he had a genuine gift for developing catchy melodies out of that limited array of notes. He composed his biggest hit, "Over There," after America entered World War I, and, inspired by a veteran who called the American flag a "grand old rag," he wrote "You're a Grand Old Flag." Oscar Hammerstein II once remarked, "Cohan's genius was to say simply what everyone else was subconsciously feeling."

For his second Broadway musical comedy, Cohan again expanded a family vaudeville skit. Cohan's third musical comedy, however, was developed from an original idea—and, according to Cohan's reminiscences, a rather hastily conceived idea at that:

After a short consultation with [the theater manager] A. L. Erlanger, it was understood that I was to open in a Broadway theater the following September.
    "What's the name of the piece?" asked Erlanger.
    "'Little Johnny Jones,'" I replied.
    "What's it all about?" he inquired.
    "Wait till you see it. It's the best thing I've ever done." As a matter of fact, I hadn't done it at all. All I'd thought of so far was the title, and that struck me as being a hundred per cent "box office."
    . . . I'd been to London the summer before and had conceived the idea of using the Cecil Hotel courtyard for one scene and the Southampton pier for another, but beyond that I had given no thought to story, situations, or musical numbers, and

was far too busy to get down to actual writing until about ten days before the rehearsal call.

Despite its last-minute conception, ***Little Johnny Jones*** opened on schedule in 1904, starring Cohan in the title role. This was also the first time that Cohan collaborated with co-producer Sam H. Harris, who would be Cohan's partner until 1920. Harris was not involved in the creative aspects of the show—Cohan was again responsible for the songs, the lyrics, the plot, the dances, and the direction—but Cohan listed Harris as the lyricist because Cohan thought it might look better.

Despite the show's burlesque of current public figures (see the **Plot Summary**), the critics and audiences were only slightly more enthusiastic than they had been for Cohan's earlier two works, and *Little Johnny Jones* closed after 52 performances. Not all critics panned the production; one writer felt that the show was "a new departure in musical comedy." The critic felt that *Little Johnny Jones* was

a musical comedy with all the customary insanity eliminated. The characters act and speak and move like really and truly human beings, and while there is no pretense at seriousness, there is no lapse into horse play or imbecility in straining after fun, as there is in so many of the rival attractions.

In fact, Cohan had made a conscious effort to distinguish *Little Johnny Jones* from other musical comedies of the day by calling it a **musical play** in its advertising—this certainly could be understood as a subtle indication that the songs related to the storyline of the show. Today we think of *Little Johnny Jones* as being an archetypal musical comedy of its time, but Cohan was certainly aware that he was breaking somewhat new ground in his approach to the genre. Perhaps encouraged by the *Daily News* critic's remarks, Cohan continued to tinker with the story and the songs until he was more satisfied with the work. Cohan and Harris then brought *Little Johnny Jones* back to New York, where it at last became a hit. In all, *Little Johnny Jones* played more than 200 performances, firmly establishing Cohan's name as a Broadway force.

Like *In Dahomey*—and very much unlike the current operettas—*Little Johnny Jones* made use of American characters and vernacular, slangy speech that had much more in common with much of its audience than the elegant language of the operetta librettos. (Cohan clearly violated Charles K. Harris's strictures against slang; see the ***Sidebar***!) In "Yankee Doodle Boy" (**Musical Example 16**), Cohan also makes frequent use of **musical quotation**, incorporating snippets of well-known tunes into the song. Audiences delighted in hearing the references to "Yankee Doodle" at **1, 2, 7, 8, 9,** and **14**; phrases from "Dixie" at **3** and **10**; and "The Star-Spangled Banner" at **5** and **12**. Cohan's audiences would have also recognized the quotation from "The Girl I Left Behind Me" at **4** and **11**, although this tune is unfamiliar to most listeners today.

"Yankee Doodle Boy" is a straightforward verse-chorus form in duple meter, but unlike "A Actor Lady," it has no distinction in tempo between the verses (starting at **1** and **8**)

George M. Cohan sings "Yankee Doodle Boy" in *Little Johnny Jones.*
Museum of the City of New York.

and the chorus (which begins at **6** and **13**). In fact, the steady, driven quality to the tune leads some theater historians to classify it as a **rhythm song**—a tune with a prominent beat that provokes unconscious toe-tapping or other body movement in the listener. In Cohan's day, rhythm songs were known as **jump tunes**, and every musical comedy production was expected to present at least one of these exuberant numbers.

The success of *Little Johnny Jones* paved the way for Cohan's subsequent hits. During his energetic career, in which he wrote some 500 songs, Cohan had always been careful to treat his performers with integrity and to pay them fairly. Proud of this reputation, he was understandably resistant to the idea that actors might need a union—a bargaining agency that would represent its members. In 1919, when the fledgling **Actor's Equity Association** called a general strike among its members in order to force theater members to recognize it as a bargaining representative, Cohan was outraged when his actor friends did not line up with him against Equity. He swore that he'd abandon the theater and become an elevator operator if the actors won. A strike leader retorted, "Somebody better tell Mr. Cohan that to run an elevator he'd *have* to join a union." Equity added fuel to the conflict by posting a sign in its office window that read, "WANTED—ELEVATOR OPERATOR—GEORGE M. COHAN PREFERRED." Cohan felt betrayed, and he regarded Equity's ultimate triumph as a personal defeat. Embittered, he pulled his name from membership in the Friars and the Lambs (two theatrical clubs), and he broke up his long-standing partnership with Harris.

Cohan performed on and wrote for Broadway only intermittently over the years until his death in 1942, refusing to the end to join Equity. Cohan's shows proved not to have much "staying power"; they reflected the spirit of their day and didn't speak to later generations of theatergoers. When *Little Johnny Jones* was revived in 1982 (starring Donny Osmond in the role of Johnny), the production closed after one night. However, a more lasting tribute to Cohan came in 1959, thanks to a campaign organized by Oscar Hammerstein II. Hammerstein collected donations to erect a statue in Cohan's memory in Times Square (the heart of Broadway's theater district), and it is the only statue on Broadway that commemorates any of Broadway's creative artists; nevertheless, there were those who were still bitter over Cohan's resistance to Equity and refused to donate toward the cost of the tribute. Despite the mixed reaction to Cohan and his politics, the "Yankee Doodle Boy" played an indisputably important part in merging the verve and energy of vaudeville with the Broadway theater in a way that audiences found fresh, exciting, and, most of all, "American."

FURTHER READING

Cohan, George M. *Twenty Years on Broadway and the Years It Took to Get There: The True Story of a Trouper's Life from the Cradle to the "Closed Shop."* New York: Harper & Brothers, 1925.

Everett, William A., and Paul R. Laird, eds. *The Cambridge Companion to the Musical*. Cambridge: Cambridge University Press, 2002.

Harris, Charles K. *After the Ball, Forty Years of Melody: An Autobiography*. New York: Frank-Maurice, Inc., 1926.

Jasen, David A. *Tin Pan Alley: The Composers, the Songs, the Performers and their Times*. New York: Donald I. Fine, 1988.

Kahn, E. J., Jr. *The Merry Partners: The Age and Stage of Harrigan and Hart*. New York: Random House, 1955.

Loney, Glenn, ed. *Musical Theatre in America: Papers and Proceedings of the Conference on the Musical Theatre in America*. (Contributions in Drama and Theatre Studies, Number 8). Westport, Connecticut: Greenwood Press, 1984. See: Helen Armstead-Johnson, "Themes and Values in Afro-American Librettos and Book Musicals, 1898–1930," 133–142; Jane Sherman, "Denishawn in Vaudeville and Beyond," 179–185; and Stephen M. Vallillo, "George M. Cohan's *Little Johnny Jones*," 233–234.

Mates, Julian. *America's Musical Stage: Two Hundred Years of Musical Theatre*. New York: Praeger, 1985.

McCabe, John. *George M. Cohan: The Man Who Owned Broadway*. Garden City, New York: Doubleday, 1973.

Riis, Thomas L. *Just Before Jazz: Black Musical Theater in New York, 1890–1915*. Washington and London: Smithsonian Institution Press, 1989.

————. *More than Just Minstrel Shows: The Rise of Black Musical Theatre at the Turn of the Century.* (I.S.A.M. Monographs: Number 33.) Brooklyn: Institute for Studies in American Music, 1992.

————, ed. *The Music and Scripts of* In Dahomey. (Recent Researches in American Music, Volume 25) (Music of the United States of America, Volume 5). Madison: A-R Editions, 1996.

Sampson, Henry T. *Blacks in Blackface: A Source Book on Early Black Musical Shows.* Metuchen, New Jersey: The Scarecrow Press, 1980.

Woll, Allen. *Black Musical Theatre From* Coontown *to* Dreamgirls. Baton Rouge: Louisiana State University Press, 1989.

PLOT SUMMARY: *IN DAHOMEY*

Although the basic premise of *In Dahomey* generally remained the same—African American scam artists search for a lost heirloom while preying on "reverse colonists" who are hoping to return to Africa—the songs and dances performed in the course of the story changed dramatically between productions of *In Dahomey* and even during the course of a single production. The focus was almost exclusively on entertainment; in fact, a reviewer commenting on the London production warned prospective audience members to "forget purpose, plot, reason, and coherence, simply look and listen."

In Dahomey's lost heirloom is a small, engraved silver box, and its owner is Cicero Lightfoot, a resident of Gatorville,

---

Sidebar: Tin Pan Alley

A tourist consulting a map of New York City will search in vain for Tin Pan Alley—it's not an actual place, but rather a nickname. The nickname has at least two meanings: for a time, it referred to 28th Street and its environs, where a large percentage of the early sheet music publishers were clustered, and the term also describes the *type* of music they published—the catchy parade of hits that *were* America's popular music from the 1880s until around the 1950s.

Before phonographs (the stereo systems of yesteryear) became standard household equipment, the only way you could enjoy a favorite song on your own schedule was to play it yourself at your own piano. Therefore, you'd have to purchase the **sheet music**—the printed score—of the song, and this is where the publishing houses came in. They cranked out a seemingly endless supply of all the latest hit tunes and maintained a **backlist** of older favorites. Publishers were always looking for new songwriters and new songs they could add to their **catalog**—the collection of music they had for sale.

How would you know if you wanted to buy a new tune? You would have heard it performed: perhaps in a Broadway show, or in a vaudeville act, or at a restaurant or cabaret, or maybe you heard the song played by a **song-plugger**—a publishing firm's employee who would hammer out the tune for you on a beat-up old piano in the publisher's office or perhaps in the music section of a department store. At the turn of the last century, Monroe Rosenfelt wrote several articles about the rise of this new publishing industry. While researching his stories, he visited Harry von Tilzer's office, then located at 42 West 28th Street, at the heart of the publishing district. From up and down the street Rosenfelt could hear a barrage of song-pluggers riotously pounding away at the same time. He commented that the din from all these demonstrations sounded like a bunch of tin pans clanging; he called the street "the Alley."

Tin Pan Alley song-pluggers also worked very hard to "place" tunes, persuading singers to add them to their night-club shows, vaudeville skits, Broadway shows, or revues. Conductors of orchestras with weekly radio broadcasts were prime targets. Initially, a performer would be given a free copy of the song as persuasion to sing it; soon, additional incentives included free drinks, gifts, and cash.

A number of musical theater composers worked as song-pluggers early in their careers; Irving Berlin got his start by "plugging" for Harry von Tilzer, while George Gershwin worked for Jerome H. Remick (and got in trouble for playing his own compositions when he was supposed to be playing tunes from the Remick catalog). Many other composers became "known" by hits that were promoted in the Tin Pan Alley system. After 40 years in the business, the publisher and songwriter Charles K. Harris shared some tips with aspiring Tin Pan Alley composers, saying

Watch your competitors. Note their successes and failures; analyze the cause of either and profit thereby. Take note of public demand. If you do not feel competent to write or compose a certain kind of song, stick to the kind you are sure of, and gradually adapt yourself to the other, if possible, before publicly presenting your work.

Avoid slang and vulgarism; they never succeed.

Many-syllabled words and those containing harsh consonants, wherever possible, must be avoided.

In writing lyrics be concise; get to your point quickly, and then make the point as strong as possible.

Simplicity in melody is one of the great secrets of success.

Let your melody musically convey the character and sentiments of the lyrics.

In another publication called *How to Write a Popular Song,* Harris suggested that composers look to the newspapers for ideas. Harris also warned the neophyte composer, "Know the copyright laws"!

Even though Harris had never learned to read or write music, he knew what he was talking about. His "After the Ball", plugged by John Philip Sousa at the Chicago World's Fair, sold over five million copies. For some 70 years, Tin Pan Alley functioned as a sort of "lottery" for composers and publishers, making winners out of many hopeful writers, until it was at last overwhelmed by changes in lifestyle, musical tastes, and the advent of a strong recording industry.

Florida, who happens to be the president of the Dahoman Colonization Society. Anxious to retrieve his treasure, Lightfoot writes to an intelligence agent in Boston and asks him to send two detectives. The intelligence man suspects that the casket is just misplaced, not lost, so he decides to offer the job to two out-of-work con men, Shylock Homestead and Rareback Pinkerton (played by the famous comedy team of Bert Williams and George Walker). The two friends are startled to hear the details of the case, for they know that casket! They had just sailed upriver from the South, and they had sold the casket to a fellow passenger after buying it from another stranger on the boat. They also learn that their friend Hustling Charlie has managed to get hired to escort the southern colonists to Africa; Charlie will get a percentage from the doctor who treats the travelers for seasickness, and if a colonist fails to survive the journey, Charlie even has a deal worked out with an undertaker. Charlie agrees to cut Homestead and Pinkerton in on his scam. They all travel to Florida so the pseudo-detectives can "search" for the casket before the party sails. In Act II, set in Gatorville, the con men meet various members of the colonization society, including Lightfoot's daughter, Rosetta. In several versions of *In Dahomey*, Rosetta performs "A Actor Lady" (**Musical Example 15**) during this act. Of course, Homestead and Pinkerton fail to locate the casket in Florida, so they travel with the colonists to Dahomey, the setting of Act III.

Inadvertently, by giving the King of Dahomey a gift of whisky (from the colonists' supplies), Homestead and Pinkerton have performed a special Dahoman gesture of appreciation, so the king appoints them as Caboceers—a sort of councilor or governor—in return. The colonists don't fare so well; they manage to offend the king, so are put in jail to be executed on the next festival day, known as a Customs Day. The new Caboceers present the king with yet another gift of whisky, and the king agrees, in exchange, to allow the prisoners to be released. In fact, to show that he bears no ill will, the king presents the colonists with a silver box obtained from a sailor who had been shipwrecked along Dahomey's shore—it is Lightfoot's heirloom, miraculously returned to him. Moreover, the king wishes to present his Caboceers with a special honor: he wants them to carry a message to his great-grandfather who has been dead for some hundred years. Homestead and Pinkerton are not slow to figure out what this "honor" entails, and they quickly decide that their best course of action is

to join with the colonists in their plans to return to the United States.

PLOT SUMMARY: *LITTLE JOHNNY JONES*

Corny, sentimental, patriotic, naïve—*Little Johnny Jones* has been called all these things, and merits them all (as does Cohan himself). A brash young jockey named Johnny Jones (modeled after the real jockey Tod Sloan, who rode a horse for the King of England in the 1903 Derby) has come to England to ride a horse named Yankee Doodle in the Derby races. Johnny advises his fellow Americans gathered in the lobby of the Hotel Cecil to bet on the "Yankee Doodle Boy" (**Musical Example 16**). After winning the race, Johnny plans to retire and marry his girlfriend Goldie Gates. A manipulative gambler, Anthony Anstey, tries to persuade Johnny to lose, since, from a gambling perspective, that would be more profitable. Johnny angrily refuses to get involved in anything dishonest—but then, when Johnny really does lose the race, Anstey, in revenge, spreads a rumor that Johnny *had* "thrown" the race—had lost deliberately—and Johnny's reputation is in tatters.

At an English port, Johnny prepares to board a U.S.-bound ship, but he meets a large crowd of angry race-goers who had bet on Yankee Doodle. Johnny decides that he must stay in England and clear his name. His detective friend "The Unknown" (based on a New York sheriff, Big Tom Foley) stays on the ship to continue investigating the source of the rumor. While the ship pulls away, Johnny waves and asks the passengers to "Give My Regards to Broadway." As the ship reaches the horizon (in an impressive transformation scene), Johnny sees some fireworks launched from its deck—the Unknown's signal to Johnny that he's discovered some useful evidence on board. Johnny cheers up enormously.

Matters grow more complicated when the villain Anstey kidnaps Goldie Gates and takes her—where else?—to San Francisco, where Anstey has a gambling establishment. Johnny pursues them through exotic Chinatown, but pauses to deliver his famous soliloquy "Life's a Funny Proposition After All." Although Johnny has no answers to his soliloquy's rhetorical questions, he is at last able to defeat Anstey's schemes and regain his good name *and* fiancée.

MUSICAL EXAMPLE 15

IN DAHOMEY
WILL MARION COOK/PAUL DUNBAR, 1902
INTERPOLATION BY HARRY VON TILZER/VINCENT BRYAN

"(I Wants to Be) A Actor Lady"
Rosetta Lightfoot

1   Crazy for the stage was Carrie Brown, she worked in a dry-goods store uptown.
Ev'ry time a play opened on Broadway, in the gall'ry Carrie could be found.
Carrie could recite the Maiden's Prayer; she could sing 'most any ragtime air.
Each day just after lunch she would entertain the bunch,
And when they'd all applaud her she'd declare:

2   I wants to be a actor lady, star in the play, up on Broadway,
Spotlight for me, no back-row shady, I'm the real thing, I dance and sing.
Miss Carter she may play "Du Barry," but she can't sing "Good Morning, Carrie."
I wants to be a actor lady, too, indeed I do!

3   Carrie said that Shakespeare was a shine, Clyde Fitch may be good, but not for mine.
There is Laura Jean Libby, she's a queen; if she wrote a play I'd act it fine.
"Ha! the child's in London," then you say; them's the kind of parts I wants to play.
"Troskeena Wellington, you can't square what you have done!"
With lines like these I'd knock them on Broadway.

4   I wants to be a actor lady, star in the play, up on Broadway,
Spotlight for me, no back-row shady, I'm the real thing, I dance and sing.
Miss Carter she may play "Du Barry," but she can't sing "Good Morning, Carrie."
I wants to be a actor lady, too, indeed I do!

MUSICAL EXAMPLE 16

LITTLE JOHNNY JONES
GEORGE M. COHAN/"HARRIS" (COHAN), 1904
"Yankee Doodle Boy"

Johnny
1   I'm the kid that's all the candy, I'm a Yankee Doodle Dandy.
I'm glad I am.

Chorus
So's Uncle Sam.

Johnny
2   I'm a real life Yankee doodle, made my name and fame and boodle
Just like Mister Doodle did, by riding on a pony.

3   I love to listen to the Dixey strain,
4   I long to see the girl I left behind me;
And that ain't a josh, she's a Yankee, by gosh!

Chorus
5   Oh, say can you see anything about a Yankee that's a phoney?

Johnny
6   I'm a Yankee Doodle Dandy, a Yankee Doodle do or die;
A real live nephew of my Uncle Sam's, born on the Fourth of July.
I've got a Yankee Doodle sweetheart, she's my Yankee Doodle joy,
7   Yankee Doodle came to London just to ride the ponies—I am a Yankee Doodle boy.
8   Father's name was Hezekiah, Mother's name was Ann Maria,
Yanks through and through.

Chorus
Red, White and Blue!

Johnny
9   Father was so Yankee hearted, when the Spanish War was started,
He slipped on his uniform and hopped up on a pony.
10   My mother's mother was a Yankee true,
11   My father's father was a Yankee, too
And that's going some, for the Yankee, by gum.

Chorus
12   Oh, say, can you see any thing about my pedigree that's phoney?

Johnny
13   I'm a Yankee Doodle Dandy, a Yankee Doodle do or die,
A real live nephew of my Uncle Sam's, born on the Fourth of July.
I've got a Yankee Doodle sweetheart, she's my Yankee Doodle joy,
14   Yankee Doodle came to London just to ride the ponies—I am a Yankee Doodle boy.

Chapter 13
The Princess Shows

Operettas and Cohan-style musical comedies continued to dominate Broadway theaters well into the second decade of the twentieth century, but each had its followers as well as its detractors. The far-fetched settings and operatic characteristics of operetta were off-putting to some audiences, while the mindlessness of many musical comedies offended others. One reviewer complained, "I would defy even Sherlock Holmes himself to discover anything more utterly banal, pointless, devoid of humor, boring, silly, un-melodious and generally calculated to make one tired than the average musical comedy." In 1915, however, a new kind of show made a quiet debut in the Princess Theatre, a small venue located at 39th Street and 6th Avenue in New York. The show was *Nobody Home*, and the composer was a 30-year-old **Jerome Kern** (1885–1945) (see the *Sidebar*: Jerome Kern and a Musical Chain).

The Princess Theatre itself was quite new, having opened in 1913. It seated 299 people—a carefully chosen number, since most theater laws were written for houses seating 300 or more. Most of the seating was on the orchestra level, the "ground floor" of the theater (hence the term **orchestra seating**); the tiny balcony had only two rows. The stage itself was the smallest of any Broadway house, and the backstage facilities were very limited. Plans for the theater wavered; at one point it was going to feature children's classics, but it was also announced that the theater would stage gothic horror shows in the **Grand Guignol** tradition (the Grand Guignol was a small theater in Paris, which specialized in gruesome stage productions).

When the theater finally opened, it featured a series of experimental one-act plays by unknown authors, which, not surprisingly, failed to draw much of an audience. Elisabeth "Bessie" Marbury, a literary agent, suggested to her partner, producer F. Ray Comstock, that they should present a small-scale musical to make the theater profitable. (Marbury's ideas were often good ones; she is credited with convincing writers to ask for a percentage of the gross profits rather than settling for a flat fee.) Marbury even chose the **property** (a novel, drama, short story, or so forth that inspires the plot of a musical), deciding that the play *Mr. Popple of Ippleton* could be a charming production. All she needed was Victor Herbert to make the musical adaptation.

Herbert, however, proved to be unavailable for the small fee Marbury and Comstock offered, so Marbury turned to Kern and **Guy Bolton** (1882–1979). Kern had become a hot item after one of his songs, "They Didn't Believe Me," became a runaway hit, selling more than 2 million copies of the sheet music. Marbury was Bolton's agent, and she had introduced him to Kern. Their first collaboration did poorly—there were weaknesses in the storyline and a temperamental star to contend with—but Kern's score was praised, so Marbury hired them again to turn *Mr. Popple* into *Nobody Home*.

A third partner was needed—a lyricist—because Bolton specialized in **book** writing. The division of labor had begun to change, and the old term *libretto* began to refer to the spoken dialogue only (as well as the overall plot), and it was often replaced by the English term *book*. The poems in the songs were called the **lyrics**—and more and more often, a specialist would write these song lyrics, not the same author who had written the book. The lyricist hired to work on *Nobody Home* was Schuyler Greene.

Kern, Bolton, and Greene were given quite a few stipulations for *Nobody Home*, which was billed as a "Farce Comedy in Two Acts with Music." (A **farce** is a story with broad humor—often satirical—and an improbable plot.) There could be only two sets (one for each act), costume changes were to be kept to a minimum, and the cast should number no more than 30—including the chorus. The orchestra would encompass 11 players. The show's budget was a mere $7,500—tiny even by 1915 standards. The storyline would not be interrupted by **guying**—an all-too-common practice in which comedians would break the storyline to address the audience directly and tell in-jokes and gags.

At the same time, Kern had his own stipulations based on his growing belief that the songs should be **integrated** into the storyline. He argued, "It is my opinion that the musical numbers should carry the action of the play and should be representative of the personalities of the characters who sing them. Songs must be suited to the action and the mood of the play." Later in life, Kern said, "I am just a musical clothier. I can only write music to fit a given situation, character, or lyric within a play or motion picture the way a good tailor fits a garment to a mannequin." (Did Kern know Mozart's views about "fitting arias to singers like a tailor fits a suit of clothes"? It's interesting that the two composers, 150 years apart, chose the same analogy.) Kern had seen too many interpolations of songs that made absolutely no sense in the context of the story, and he felt the practice should stop. Kern went a long way toward achieving his conviction with the successive Princess productions, which is why the **Princess Shows** are often called "integrated"—this does not refer to any racial balance in the cast, but describes the interconnections between songs and plot. By no means were these the *first* musically integrated shows, as is sometimes claimed, but they reminded Broadway—which had wandered far away from single-composer shows—how effective an integrated conception could be.

The focus on integration was not limited to the book and score. In a faint and probably unconscious echo of Wagner's *Gesamtkunstwerk*, Marbury believed that people looked at the sets and costumes as much as they listened to the performers and the music. She imported fashionable—even cutting-edge—costumes from Paris and made sure that the stage designs presented elegant and appealing settings. Marbury marketed the show with a brochure that emphasized the "newness" of their approach.

Comstock and Marbury's gamble paid off; *Nobody Home* was a hit. After two months, the producers moved *Nobody Home* to a larger theater, since the bigger capacity would mean more ticket sales; the show ran 135 performances. It also spawned three separate **road companies**; these touring ensembles, which carried the show to theaters all over the country, were another measure of a show's success.

The producers soon turned to the same creative team for another show, and *Very Good Eddie*, billed as the "annual Princess Theatre production," appeared in the same calendar year (1915). However, it belonged to the following theatrical **season** (measured from the beginning of June to the end of May). *Very Good Eddie* built on the strengths of *Nobody Home*, using contemporary language in an American setting, proceeding at a lightning pace, and creating a story in which the situations were comic but believable. The humor grew out of the characters and the dilemmas in which they found themselves instead of relying on irrelevant jokes or vaudevillian puns. (Vaudeville did have an influence on the title of the show; a ventriloquist's dummy was called an "eddie" by vaudevillians, and a "very good eddie" was a cooperative, compliant dummy.) Rather than wearing skimpy, revealing costumes, the chorus girls were dressed in tasteful, ankle-length gowns, and the chorus was "individualized." A newspaper columnist explained what this meant: "Each girl has a dress of her own. No, that's not exactly what we mean. What we intend to convey is that each girl is costumed differently, as suits her style." Like *Nobody Home*, *Very Good Eddie* soon transferred to a larger theater for a run of 341 performances.

One member of the audience on *Very Good Eddie*'s opening night was **Pelham Grenville "Plum" Wodehouse** (1881–1975), a prolific author. (His most famous literary creation was Jeeves, the archetypal English butler who would later inspire a musical by Andrew Lloyd Webber.) Wodehouse attended the post-show party at Kern's apartment and, during the evening, agreed to start working with Bolton and Kern. Years later, Bolton and Wodehouse—humorists to the end—published their individual tongue-in-cheek diary accounts of that evening.

The Bolton diary of this date has the following entry:

Eddie opened. Excellent reception. All say hit. To Kerns for supper. Talked with P. G. Wodehouse, apparently known as Plum. Never heard of him, but Jerry says he writes lyrics, so, being slightly tight, suggested we team up. W. so overcome couldn't answer for a minute, then grabbed my hand and stammered out his thanks.

Turning to the Wodehouse diary, we find:

Went to opening of Very Good Eddie. *Enjoyed it in spite of lamentable lyrics. Bolton, evidently conscious of this weakness,*

offered partnership. Tried to hold back and weigh the suggestion, but his eagerness so pathetic that consented. Mem: Am I too impulsive? Fight against this tendency.

In a highly embellished account of their history in the theater, the two humorists also perpetuated the myth that Kern had been booked to sail on the ill-fated voyage of the *Lusitania*, which was sunk by a German U-boat—but that Kern had overslept and missed the sailing. Sadly, the sinking of the *Lusitania* did in truth take the life of Kern's former mentor Charles K. Frohman.

The first product of the new collaborators did not play in the Princess Theatre, nor did their second work, *Have a Heart* (1917), which was produced by Colonel Henry Savage. Marbury had introduced the team to Savage, and Comstock was so infuriated by what he saw as her disloyalty that he fired her as coproducer at the Princess. Stylistically, *Have a Heart* might be considered a Princess Show (see the **Sidebar** for a list of all the possible candidates), since it displayed many "Princess" characteristics.

Despite his anger, Comstock welcomed the next musical produced by the trio. *Oh, Boy!* opened at the Princess on February 20, 1917 (a little over a month after *Have a Heart*'s premiere). With *Oh, Boy!*, the Princess Shows were back in their groove. It was a more expensive show to mount—costing $29,000—so Comstock raised ticket prices to a then-staggering $3.50. Despite this expense (and partly because of it), the show enjoyed the largest **box office advance** (income from tickets sold before the show has opened) that any theater had seen. Part of the attraction was the presence of two stars from the *Ziegfeld Follies*, but the growing reputation of Kern, Bolton, and Wodehouse was part of the draw. The following anonymous verse encapsulates the partners' growing stature in the theater world:

This is the trio of musical fame,
Bolton and Wodehouse and Kern;
Better than anyone else you can name,
Bolton and Wodehouse and Kern,
Nobody knows what on earth they've been bitten by,
All I can say is I mean to get lit and buy
Orchestra seats for the next one that's written by
Bolton and Wodehouse and Kern.

Not surprisingly, *Oh, Boy!* ran for an impressive 463 performances.

The next Princess Show did not actually play at the Princess Theatre. **Leave It to Jane** (1917) was scheduled to follow *Oh, Boy!*, but by the time *Leave It to Jane* was ready to open, *Oh, Boy!* was still running so well that Comstock decided to open the new show at the Longacre Theatre. Daringly, *Leave It to Jane* opened on August 28, when most theaters—in this era before air conditioning—were closed for the summer. At 167 performances, it had a shorter run than *Oh, Boy!*, but *Leave It to Jane* did send out three road companies. Moreover, when the show was revived off-Broadway in 1959, the production was seen 928 times.

Part of *Leave It to Jane*'s success can be attributed to its **comedy songs**, and one of the finest is "Cleopatterer"

The "Trio of Musical Fame": Guy Bolton, P. G. Wodehouse, and Jerome Kern, c. 1915.
Museum of the City of New York.

(**Musical Example 17**), sung by Flora, who has her own perspective on ancient history (see the **Plot Summary**). The first comedienne to play the role, Georgia O'Ramey, incorporated a comic pseudo-Egyptian dance into her performance. The combination of dance and song made "Cleopatterer" a **showstopper**, meaning the audience reaction was so enthusiastic after this number that their applause stopped the momentum of the show for a significant time. Showstoppers often needed to be encored before an audience was satisfied and would allow the play to continue.

The best form label for "Cleopatterer" is an interesting question. There are two distinct units used in its structure, much like the verse-chorus format seen in "I Can't Do the Sum," "(I Wants to Be) A Actor Lady," and "Yankee Doodle Boy." However, those earlier tunes all used an *a-B-a-B* format; you'll recall that the *B* is capitalized because both the music *and* the words repeat during the chorus. "Cleopatterer," on the other hand, would have to be diagrammed as *a-b-a-b-a-b*, since the words of its chorus are *not* the same each time. In a situation like this, a better label might be **alternation form** to emphasize the equal importance of the verse and chorus. (Robert Russell Bennett, an orchestrator who often worked with Kern, later recalled, "Kern would play pieces for me, and I'd say, 'Is that the verse or the chorus?' And Jerry used to die because I couldn't tell which was which.") In a traditional verse-chorus form, a performer may choose to eliminate one or more of the choruses, because after one or two repetitions, the audience knows exactly what the chorus will be. But, to eliminate any of the choruses—the *b* sections—from "Cleopatterer" would force us to miss some of the jokes. In a subtle way, "Cleopatterer" points

the direction that a number of songs will take. The balance between verse and chorus will change dramatically in many instances, necessitating new form labels altogether.

No matter what term is used to describe the form of "Cleopatterer," the contrast between the alternating sections is distinctive. Kern creates a brief atmospheric opening (which may owe more to the tango than to any Egyptian source!); he then uses the minor mode and a repetitive "long–short–short" rhythmic pattern in the accompaniment to evoke an Egyptian ambiance. (It's very much a "Hollywood" Egyptian sound, although this show predates the rise of film scores.) This exotic mood is sustained at **1** during the verse (or *a*). Then, unexpectedly, the chorus (or *b*) at **2** switches to the major mode and a bouncy, Tin Pan Alley-style setting. It is easy to imagine a flapper singing and dancing during this portion. The first line in each chorus is fairly disjunct (creating that bouncy quality), while there is also a hint of the patter song style in the second line.

The slangy, contemporary feel of *Leave It to Jane* is very evident in the lyrics of "Cleopatterer." As in "(I Wants to Be) A Actor Lady," there are occasional contemporary references—Theda Bara, for instance, with her large, kohl-ringed eyes, was a seductive star of the early silent films. She played an alluring vampire in her first film, thus giving the term *vamp* to American slang. Moreover, Bara played Cleopatra in a 1917 film of the same name, making her a very immediate reference for this song. Another catchphrase in "Cleopatterer"—*Oh, you kid*—had been around even longer. In 1904, a Tin Pan Alley song appeared, titled "I Love My Wife; But, Oh, You Kid." By assigning this phrase to Cleopatterer's admirers, Wodehouse subtly underscores the moral danger they faced when contemplating a relationship with her. The combination of these catchy allusions, the sheer humor in the poetry itself, and the exaggerated pseudo-Egyptian dance made this song a high point of the production. The production itself was very well received; one reviewer wrote,

> *The old timers will soon begin to grieve sorely . . . as they view the new form of rational musical comedy "getting over." . . . No more are we asked to laugh at the bottle-nosed comedian as he falls down stairs; no longer is the heroine a lovely princess masquerading as the serving maid, and no more is the scene Ruritania or Monte Carlo. Today is rationally American and the musical show has taken on a new lease on life.*

The next project for Kern, Bolton, and Wodehouse was a revue, *Miss 1917*. Perhaps its one distinguishing feature was that it employed a 19-year-old rehearsal pianist named George Gershwin. However, the triumvirate returned to the Princess Theatre with *Oh, Lady! Lady!!* in 1918. A historical footnote was the song "Bill," which was *dropped* from the show, but later would receive great acclaim in Kern's *Show Boat* (1927). Shortly after *Oh, Lady! Lady!!* opened, Bolton was interviewed about the "Improvement in Musical Comedy Standards." He advocated the same sort of story-music integration that Kern had promoted, albeit from the book writer's perspective. He pointed out how his books "deal with subjects and peoples near to the audiences." He believed the success of their shows was due to the "plot and the development of their characters" as much as to the music, but emphasized that "if the songs are going to count at all in any plot, the plot has to build more or less around, or at least, with them." He explained, "We endeavor to make everything count. Every line, funny or serious, is supposed to help the plot continue to hold."

Despite these shared objectives, *Oh, Lady! Lady!!* was the last Princess Show to be composed by the Kern–Bolton–Wodehouse team for several years. Tensions had begun to develop as early as *Oh, Boy!*, when Bolton and Wodehouse learned that Kern had negotiated a larger percentage of the profits for himself than for either of them. Even though the unity of the partnership was wavering, the ramifications of their collaboration were beginning to be felt in shows by other writers, such as *Irene* (1918). *Irene* was, as the writer Gerald Bordman puts it, "a believable plot told about believable people who sang lovely songs brought naturally into the story." (*Irene* was also the first of a rash of "Cinderella" musicals in which a poor girl makes good.) The show's smash hit was "Alice Blue Gown," a reference to the daughter of President Theodore Roosevelt. Alice Roosevelt was noted for favoring a special shade of blue—nicknamed Alice blue—and thus, like the Princess Shows, *Irene* kept itself firmly grounded in the cultural world of its viewers through topical references.

The trio was reunited briefly for *Sally*, another Cinderella story, although P. G. Wodehouse soon withdrew from the project because of other commitments. The show featured the dancer Marilyn Miller (before she began spelling her first name with two *n*'s), and *Sally* broke away from the dazzling **star entrance** that had been the norm for musical comedy. Instead of coming onstage to great fanfare, Bolton's book called for Miller to appear at the end of a line of ragged orphans. Producer Florenz Ziegfeld was opposed to the idea, wanting to give the audience every opportunity to applaud the star, but Miller sided with Bolton; again, more emphasis was being given to the *story*.

Kern, Bolton, and Wodehouse worked together once more, on what many scholars call the "last" Princess Show: *Sitting Pretty*. (Irving Berlin had originally been slated to compose the score, but pulled out when the original stars dropped out of the project.) Produced by Comstock, the show opened at the Fulton Theatre on April 8, 1924. Kern's style had changed to some degree from the earlier Princess Shows; while the majority of his earlier tunes had been potential dance numbers, Kern put greater emphasis on songs with more romantic (and fewer choreographic) characteristics. A particularly unusual feature was *Sitting Pretty*'s overture. By this time, an overture generally was a compilation of melodies from the show, meant to "whet the audience's appetite" for the tunes to come. In the case of *Sitting Pretty*'s overture, however, Kern composed an independent orchestral piece that he called "A Journey Southward." This overture was **programmatic**, meaning the instrumental music illustrated a story that had no words or visual depiction; the "events" took place solely in the audience's imaginations, as prompted by the music played by the orchestra. In this case, the story, or **program**, was a train journey from New York to Florida,

since the musical's first act was set in New Jersey, and the second in Florida.

Sitting Pretty received excellent reviews, but Kern made a decision that probably limited the run: he withheld permission for the show's tunes to be recorded. His point was that the songs would *not* be reproduced exactly as he wrote them (the practice of making recordings of the original cast had not yet begun in the United States); instead, the customary practice was to rearrange show tunes in a jazz style that sometimes made the original songs almost unrecognizable. (A more modern comparison might be the "Muzak" arrangements of popular tunes heard so often on elevators and in dentists' offices: these arrangements often leave the character of the original tune far behind.) By forbidding the customary recordings of this show, Kern limited the **dissemination**, or circulation, of the melodies. Not knowing anything about the music, many potential audience members stayed away—and *Sitting Pretty* closed early. Clearly, recordings—whether good or bad—were not only a source of revenue for a show's creators, but also an increasingly important form of advertising for Broadway productions.

FURTHER READING

Bordman, Gerald. *Jerome Kern: His Life and Music.* New York: Oxford University Press, 1980.

Davis, Lee. *Bolton and Wodehouse and Kern: The Men Who Made Musical Comedy*. New York: James H. Heineman, 1993.

Freedland, Michael. *Jerome Kern*. New York: Stein & Day, 1978.

Wilk, Max. *They're Playing Our Song: From Jerome Kern to Stephen Sondheim—The Stories Behind the Words and Music of Two Generations*. New York: Atheneum, 1973; London: W. H. Allen, 1974.

Wodehouse, P. G., and Guy Bolton. *Bring on the Girls!: The Improbable Story of Our Life in Musical Comedy, with Pictures to Prove It*. New York: Simon & Schuster, 1953.

PLOT SUMMARY: *LEAVE IT TO JANE*

One of the novelties of *Leave It to Jane* was that it was a "football" musical—one of the first shows to acknowledge the growing American mania for the sport. By using a collegiate setting, Bolton and Wodehouse could incorporate campus romance (and parental interference), undergraduate hijinks, and loose references to history and literature.

The initial premise of the story, taken from a 1904 play, is not so far-fetched: Hiram Bolton, an alumnus of Bingham College, is delighted with his son Billy's football prowess, so he sends Billy—an all-American halfback—to his alma mater so that Bingham can defeat its archrival, Atwater College (and thereby win a large bet for Hiram). But, the very day that Billy arrives at Bingham, he meets Jane Witherspoon, and *her* father just happens to be the president of Atwater. Billy, along with "Stub" Talmadge and most other males in the cast, finds Jane enchanting. Jane sings "A Siren's Song" to Billy (a literary

Sidebar: *Jerome Kern and a Musical Chain*

Composers writing for Broadway or the West End do not operate in a vacuum—they are fully aware of and often dependent upon their predecessors. Often, older composers take an active interest in the next generation, and this was certainly the case with Victor Herbert, who was very supportive of the younger Jerome Kern; Herbert once exclaimed that Kern "will one day inherit my own mantle." Edward E. Rice, composer of *Evangeline*, had allowed the young Kern to interpolate songs into some pre-existing shows. These interpolations were important in establishing Kern's name, and he was finally given the chance to write an entire show score in 1912.

Despite Kern's almost exclusive interest in music all through school, his father did not think that composition was a viable career, so he put Jerome to work in his merchandizing business. The younger Kern nearly bankrupted his father when he was sent to the Bronx to buy two pianos; succumbing to a glib sales pitch, he bought 200 pianos instead. Kern's father decided music study *was* safer for his son (and his business), and agreed to let Jerome study abroad.

Kern wrote songs for a number of English shows, which convinced him that his future lay in popular rather than classical music. Back in the United States, before contributing to Rice's shows, he worked as a song plugger as well as a **rehearsal pianist** (the full orchestra does not attend the early rehearsals of a new show, so a rehearsal pianist plays the accompanying parts to support the singers as they learn the score). After the Princess Shows, Kern went on to write the classic *Show Boat* (see Chapter 16, "Great Partnerships of the Early Book Musical: Kern and Hammerstein") and many other musicals and film scores. He had composed over 1,000 songs before his death in 1945.

But what of the musical chain? In 1914, a young George Gershwin, aged 16, heard an orchestra play a Kern song at his aunt's wedding and was inspired to try modeling his own compositions on Kern's style. Vincent Youmans idolized Kern's music, and a 14-year-old Richard Rodgers spent his allowance on at least a half dozen performances of *Very Good Eddie* in an attempt to figure out Kern's musical techniques. Rodgers reminisced, "The sound of a Jerome Kern tune was not ragtime, nor did it have any of the Middle European inflections of Victor Herbert. It was all his own—the first truly American theatre music—and it pointed the way I wanted to be led."

The number of composers who were later influenced by Gershwin and Rodgers is incalculable, but certainly we can look to Rodgers's own family for a sense of dynasty: he was followed by his daughter Mary Rodgers Guettel, and her son, Adam Guettel, who is active today as a musical theater composer. It will be interesting to see what links may be added to this musical chain in the future.

reference to the legend of the Lorelei) and, in so doing, persuades him to transfer to Atwater College and play for *its* football team under an assumed name.

Comedy enters the show through mistaken identity (Billy is pretending to be a visiting botanist) and through the "education" of a country boy, Bub Hicks, who learns, among other things, how to get engaged to (and later "dis"-engaged from) Flora Wiggins, a local waitress with idiosyncratic views about history, as we learn in "Cleopatterer" (**Musical Example 17**). Romance appears during the Big Game on Thanksgiving Day, when Jane confesses to Billy that she initially had gotten him to come to Atwater merely to beat Bingham—but now she's grown to love him for himself. Inspired, Billy leads the Atwater team to victory, thus winning the game and Jane as well.

Sidebar: The "Princess Shows"

Year		Title	Producer	Authors	Theater
1915		*Nobody Home*	Comstock	Kern, Bolton, Greene	Princess Theatre
1915		*Very Good Eddie*	Comstock	Kern, Bolton, Bartholomae, Greene, Reynolds	Princess Theatre
1916		*Miss Springtime*	Klaw/Erlanger	Kern, Bolton, Wodehouse	New Amsterdam Theatre
1916		*Go To It!*	Comstock	Golden, Hazzard, Caldwell	Princess Theatre
1917		*Have a Heart*	Savage	Kern, Bolton, Wodehouse	Liberty Theatre
1917	*	*Oh, Boy!*	Comstock	Kern, Bolton, Wodehouse	Princess Theatre
1917	•	*Leave It to Jane*	Comstock	Kern, Bolton, Wodehouse	Longacre Theatre
1918	*	*Oh, Lady! Lady!!*	Comstock	Kern, Bolton, Wodehouse	Princess Theatre
1918		*Oh, My Dear!*	Comstock	Hirsch, Bolton, Wodehouse	Princess Theatre
1924	•	*Sitting Pretty*	Comstock	Kern, Bolton, Wodehouse	Fulton Theatre

*The "full team"—Kern, Bolton, Wodehouse, and Comstock—in the Princess Theatre
•The "full team," but in a different venue

MUSICAL EXAMPLE 17

LEAVE IT TO JANE
JEROME KERN/GUY BOLTON AND P. G. WODEHOUSE, 1917
"Cleopatterer"

Flora

1   In days of old beside the Nile a famous Queen there dwelt;
Her clothes were few, but full of style; her figure slim and svelte;
On ev'ry man that wandered by she pulled the Theda Bara eye:
And ev'ry one observed with awe that her work was swift, but never raw.

2   I'd be like Cleopatterer, if I could have my way,
Each man she met she went and kissed. And she'd dozens on her waiting list.
I wish that I had lived there. Beside the Pyramid;
For a girl today don't get the scope that Cleopatterer did.

3   And when she tired as girls will do, of Bill or Jack or Jim,
The time had come, his friends all knew, to say goodbye to him.
She couldn't stand by any means, reproachful, stormy farewell scenes;
To such coarse stuff she would not stoop; so she just put poison in his soup.

4   When out with Cleopatterer, men always made their wills,
They knew there was no time to waste when the gumbo had that funny taste.
They'd take her hand and squeeze it: they'd murmur "Oh, you kid!"
But they never liked to start to feed till Cleopatterer did.

5   She danced new dances now and then, the sort that make you blush.
Each time she did them, scores of men got injured in the rush.
They'd stand there, gaping, in a line and watch her agitate her spine;
It simply used to knock them flat, when she went like <u>this</u> and then like <u>that</u>.

6   At dancing Cleopatterer was always on the spot.
She gave these poor Egyptian ginks something else to watch besides the sphinx.
Mark Antony admitted that what first made him skid
Was the wibbly, wobbly, wiggly dance that Cleopatterer did.

Chapter 14
Increasing Drama on the Stage

In the centuries following the birth of opera, an increasingly clear division between serious and comic musical stage works had come into being. Operas, particularly the *verismo* productions of Italy and the music dramas of Germany, had grown very serious. Most of the musical stage works produced in the United States had followed the humorous path, resulting—at the beginning of the twentieth century—in operettas, featuring nothing worse than lovers' tiffs, or in musical comedies, whose genre reflected their lighthearted approach. Drama in operettas or musical comedies tended to feature exaggerated villains (who blustered and leered but never quite followed through with their threats), or spooky, magical elements that never seemed too threatening. "Good" characters triumphed, "bad" people were punished, while scalawags managed to find ingenious solutions to the tangles they created for themselves.

A gradual shift in emphasis began to appear in many Broadway shows of the 1920s. Although the endings were by and large still "happy" for most of the characters, some of life's harsher realities were addressed on occasion, often in realistic, believable ways. Moreover, the plots of some shows dealt with unexpected topics, such as *Dearest Enemy* (1925), which addressed colonial American history, and *Peggy-Ann*, which incorporated the fledgling field of dream psychology.

As America explored these new avenues, its interest in foreign works diminished, and *Bitter-Sweet* (1929) was the only **book musical** (a show organized around a coherent storyline, as opposed to a revue) to be sent from England to the United States during the 1920s. Some 25 American productions were exported to London during the same time period, however—the American reputation as "the" source for musicals was beginning to blossom.

As operettas and musical comedies began to incorporate serious threads, the question arose: what do you call this new hybrid genre? The creative team for **Rose-Marie** (1924) wrestled with this question for some time. They advertised it as a "musical play"—the same term Cohan had applied to *Little Johnny Jones*—but *Rose-Marie* was considerably different from Cohan's peppy, patriotic musical comedy. A year later, **Oscar Hammerstein II** (1895–1960), one of *Rose-Marie*'s co-lyricists, explained that the show "was a carefully directed attack at the Cinderella show in favor of operatic musical comedy." However, in the same article, he noted, "the type [of show] that persists, that shows the signs of ultimate victory, is the operetta—the musical play with music and plot welded together in skillful cohesion." "Operetta" *is* probably the most accurate designation for *Rose-Marie*, since the vocal demands of the score are more sizable than typical musical comedy songs; the title role was given to soprano Mary Ellis, a featured member of the Metropolitan Opera Company who was making her Broadway debut. No matter what the nomenclature, however, *Rose-Marie* proved to be the biggest international hit of the 1920s, running 557 performances in New York, and 851 performances in London. Hammerstein was a very wealthy man within a few months.

The impetus for *Rose-Marie* came from Arthur Hammerstein, uncle of Oscar Hammerstein II. Arthur had heard of a Canadian winter festival that featured ice sculptures and a huge melting palace as a climax. He sent two lyricists, Hammerstein and **Otto Harbach** (1873–1963), to Canada to research the ice show. Unfortunately for Hammerstein and Harbach, when they reached Canada, no one seemed to know anything about the festival they sought. Arthur was unfazed at the news of their failure; he still wanted a show set in Canada, so Hammerstein and Harbach proceeded to create a story from scratch (see the **Plot Summary**). It shares a few characteristics with *Naughty Marietta*, including a villain who has to be unmasked and a tune that is shared between the lovers of the story.

Dennis King and Mary Ellis sing the title song in *Rose-Marie*.
Culver Pictures, Inc.

One of the co-composers of *Rose-Marie* was **Rudolf Friml** (1879–1972), whose Broadway career had begun with *The Firefly*, the operetta written for Emma Trentini after Victor Herbert had refused to write a sequel to *Naughty Marietta*. Like Herbert, Friml was an emigré; he was born in Czechoslovakia, where he published a "Barcarolle" for piano at the tender age of ten. Friml shared the responsibility for *Rose-Marie*'s score with Herbert Stothart (1885–1949), but the biggest hits from *Rose-Marie*—the title song "Rose-Marie," "Indian Love Call," and "Totem Tom-Tom"—were all written by Friml.

Rose-Marie clearly had ambitions to be different from earlier operettas. In the printed **program**, the audience did not find the customary list of songs to be performed; instead, there was a note that read, "The musical numbers of this play are such an integral part of the action that we do not think we should list them as separate episodes." As had been the case with the Princess shows, *Rose-Marie*'s creative team was striving for integration. It is hard to defend songs like "Totem Tom-Tom" as being integral to the plot, however; this production number was far more effective as sheer entertainment for the eyes, as it featured an enormous number of chorus girls dressed in totem pole outfits. The costumes for this one number cost $2,400—an extraordinary expense for the time. In fact, Robert Benchley, writing for *Life* magazine, called this "one of the most effective chorus numbers we have ever seen."

On the other hand, several of the songs did push the action forward—a jumble of vocal and instrumental music accompanies the opening barroom scene, and even the shocking murder scene was depicted as a pantomime with the orchestra creating shifting moods to support the dramatic action. Also, perhaps in a nod to the innovations of Richard Wagner and his music dramas, certain musical themes—like Wagner's *leitmotifs*—are heard whenever the Mounties make their appearance or to enhance romantic moments. Whether or not the authors of *Rose-Marie* truly succeeded in integrating the songs is a matter of debate, but certainly they had taken a large step away from the type of show in which irrelevant interpolations could be thrown in at will.

The recurring "Indian Love Call" (**Musical Example 18**), rather like "Ah! Sweet Mystery of Life" in *Naughty Marietta*, helps to establish musical continuity during *Rose-Marie*, and it also plays an important part in the story, since Rose-Marie uses it to signal Jim to stay away for safety. Moreover, instead of ending with the whole cast onstage, *Rose-Marie* uses "Indian Love Call" as a tender final duet between the reunited lovers in what is sometimes known as a **recognition scene**. Like "Brown October Ale" in *Robin Hood*, "Indian Love Call" is diegetic; it functions as believable source music. In other words, it makes sense that Rose-Marie and Jim would have to *sing* this "traditional Indian melody."

In its initial presentation in Act I, sung by Rose-Marie as she plans their musical signal, the entire structure of the song is heard. Unlike "Yankee Doodle Boy," in which a verse-chorus form is heard, "Indian Love Call" is reduced to one introductory verse (**1**) and one main statement of the chorus (**2** through **5**). The song opens with the instantly recognizable melismatic "oohs!" that figure prominently in the chorus as well, dropping slowly through a series of **chromatic** pitches in a conjunct fashion. Chromatic notes are additional pitches that don't belong to the major or minor scale used in a song; by sprinkling these unexpected notes amid the melody, Friml enhances the exotic "Indian" atmosphere (although this song has nothing to do with genuine Native American music of any sort). The verse grows gradually more disjunct as it progresses, but it is written in a free-flowing style that seems to pause and continue at will, shifting between major and minor mode as well. In fact, the flexible rhythmic pace of this verse has much in common with operatic recitative.

Unlike the verse, which grows more disjunct as it proceeds, the chorus becomes more conjunct. The beat is steadier during the chorus as well—but Friml's continued use of chromaticism during the chorus obscures the major mode somewhat. Friml uses a pattern of repetition for the song's phrases that will become increasingly common in musical theater tunes. The eight lines of text are divided up so that **2** and **4** are sung to essentially the same melody (*a*), while **3** and **5** are each independent themes (*b* and *c*). This pattern, *a-b-a-c*, is often called **show tune form**.

Despite the form's simplicity, the melody contains considerable vocal demands. Most untrained singers have difficulty singing beyond a complete **octave**—the span of eight notes that measure from the bottom to the top of major and minor scales. "Indian Love Call" calls for almost *two* octaves in **range**—the span from its lowest note to its highest; clearly, Friml had an operatic voice in mind. When the melody reappears in the Act 1 finale, Friml requires Mary Ellis to sing higher still at some of the song's climactic moments. (Unexpectedly, the singer friendly syllables presented some challenges as well; Hammerstein recalled that when they were auditioning vocalists for the London production of *Rose-Marie*, one aspiring soprano came out on stage and, following the sheet music carefully, sang, "When I'm calling you, double o, double o . . . !")

Ellis's co-star in *Rose-Marie* was Dennis King, a fine singer and actor whose good looks enhanced his performance as Jim. King was also cast as the star of Friml's next operetta, ***The Vagabond King*** (1925), and the actor's swashbuckling personality suited the role perfectly. King and Friml were the main points of continuity between *The Vagabond King* and the preceding *Rose-Marie*, however; the producer was now Russell Janney (1884–1963), rather than Arthur Hammerstein, and **Brian Hooker** (1880–1946) wrote the lyrics. The book was credited to Janney and Hooker, with additional dialogue contributed by W. H. Post. *The Vagabond King*, based on a 1901 play by Justin Huntly McCarthy, might have been a different show altogether if Janney had been successful in his initial plans. Richard Rodgers and Lorenz Hart had already created an amateur musical version of McCarthy's play, and Janney thought they could polish their score up as a Broadway production. Rodgers and Hart were still relative newcomers to Broadway, however, and Janney wasn't able to find financial backers who would support the team. Janney had to turn to Friml and his proven track record.

Although the show was once again labeled a musical play, it was quite different in style from *Rose-Marie*; it had more in common with the lush romanticism of European operettas like *The Merry Widow* (see the **Plot Summary**). *The Vagabond*

King is considered by many to be Friml's finest score, although its initial run of 511 performances made it slightly less successful than *Rose-Marie*. Its run seems more impressive, however, when we consider that *The Vagabond King* opened the same week as *Dearest Enemy*, *Sunny*, and *No, No, Nanette*.

"Song of the Vagabonds" (**Musical Example 19**) is one of the most exciting numbers in a diverse and effective score. Friml, during an interview, once remarked, "I can't write music unless there are romance, glamour, and heroes"; he had all these factors available in *The Vagabond King*. The numbers for Huguette—"Love for Sale" and her "Waltz"—are heart-breaking and poignant. The rousing "Song of the Vagabonds" quickly became a favorite number for choral societies, and it is **reprised** several times during the course of the operetta. A reprise returns to a melody introduced earlier in a show, sometimes with the same words or sometimes with modified text. A reprise can reveal how characters have changed or how they have stayed the same; it can return the audience to the same emotional state produced when the tune was first heard. The reprises of "Song of the Vagabonds" function primarily in this latter way; the shouts of "to Hell with Burgundy!" rally Villon's ragtag army to renewed energy.

The "Song of the Vagabonds" is integrated into the plot of *The Vagabond King*, and this integration is reflected in the tune's structure. The song opens with Villon singing alone; he is grabbing the attention of the rabble, so he sustains his second word—*all*—in a fanfare-like fashion—a sort of "ta-daaaah" effect. The chorus of vagabonds begins to echo some of his phrases as they are drawn into his enthusiasm. Villon builds into a steady duple pace at **2**, rallying the vagabonds with a syncopated, catchy melody in a dramatic minor mode (contrasting with the major mode heard at **1**). Then, just like a crowd caught up by an inspirational speaker, the beggars repeat what Villon has just sung, except that **3** has some passages of harmony for the rabble, giving this repetition a richer, fuller effect.

The opening passage of the song (**1**) has the same type of flexible, recitative-like rhythm that had introduced the "Indian Love Call." Although **1** would usually be called the song's verse, it never returns, even though there are two repetitions of the song's refrain at **2** and at **3**. It might be preferable to view **1** as a vocal introduction to a strophic tune. Regardless of its label, the song produces a stirring theatrical effect, and it is impressive to see how easily the plot is advanced in the course of this simple structure.

Rose-Marie and *The Vagabond King* contained many elements that clearly reflected their heightened interest in dramatic effects. Both operettas incorporate an on-stage death—Wanda's murder of Blackeagle and Huguette's self-sacrificing suicide—and both of these deaths are pivotal moments in their stories. Both these works underscored the effectiveness of integrated musical numbers, but *The Vagabond King* demonstrated that audiences did not have to laugh their way through an entire evening in order to find an entertainment satisfying. Although neither of these works completely revolutionized musical theater—silly comedy was by no means vanquished, and interpolations were still quite feasible in many musical scores—the door to more serious and ambitious works was slowly beginning to open.

FURTHER READING

Bordman, Gerald. *American Operetta from H.M.S. Pinafore to Sweeney Todd*. New York: Oxford University Press, 1981.

Fordin, Hugh. *Getting to Know Him: A Biography of Oscar Hammerstein II*. New York: Random House, 1977.

Mordden, Ethan. *Make Believe: The Broadway Musical in the 1920s*. New York: Oxford University Press, 1997.

Traubner, Richard. *Operetta: A Theatrical History*. Garden City, New York: Doubleday, 1983.

PLOT SUMMARY: *ROSE-MARIE*

Although *Rose-Marie* is not a melodrama, it has many of the features you might associate with old-time melodrama: a heroine threatened with an unwanted marriage to a villain in order to protect the man she loves, as well as a dose of heroism from a Canadian Mountie. In this story, however, the Canadian Mountie is not the main hero; several of the characters work together to expose the evildoers.

The Canadian setting of *Rose-Marie* features natural scenery, far removed from the European ballrooms so prevalent in conventional operettas. The story opens in the bar at Lady Jane's rustic hotel in Fond du Lac, Saskatchewan, with a raucous gathering of mountain men and local residents. Two of the leading characters of the show—Rose-Marie La Flamme (half Indian, half French-Canadian) and the miner she hopes to marry, Jim Kenyon—are out taking a moonlit walk. Rose-Marie's brother Émile and the unctuous Ed Hawley from Quebec have other schemes, however; regardless of her wishes, they plan to marry her to Hawley. They agree that Émile should take Rose-Marie away from Fond du Lac to the trapping grounds at Kootenay Pass, so she'll be out of Jim's reach. Jim is no fool, however, and arranges to meet Rose-Marie at a deserted mountain cabin near a legendary "lover's stone," high above a valley. It is said that the Indians used to sing the "Indian Love Call" (**Musical Example 18**) next to the stone, sending the melody down through the echoing valley in order to win maidens in marriage.

Before leaving Fond du Lac, Jim goes with some maps to Blackeagle's cabin in order to settle an argument over the rights to a gold mine Jim is excavating with his partner, Hard-Boiled Herman. Unwittingly, Jim interrupts a rendezvous between Hawley and the duplicitous Wanda, who has been carrying on an affair with Hawley even though she is Blackeagle's lover. Hawley hides while Wanda gets rid of Jim; Jim leaves the maps behind to prove his case. Wanda and Hawley then pick up where they left off—Hawley is "buying off" Wanda so he'll be free to marry Rose-Marie—but the lovers are caught in a final amorous embrace by Blackeagle. Enraged, the Indian begins choking Hawley, but Wanda snatches up a knife and stabs Blackeagle in the back. When Sergeant Malone of the Royal Canadian Mounted Police investigates, Wanda shows Malone the maps and blames Jim for the murder.

Meanwhile, Jim has been offered a mining job in Brazil. If Rose-Marie decides to travel with Jim, she will meet him that evening at their hidden cabin; if she decides to stay, she will sing the "Indian Love Call" up the valley to him as a signal that he should journey alone. Although Rose-Marie wants to go with Jim, she changes her plan when Sgt. Malone arrives with a warrant for Jim's arrest. She promises to marry Hawley if Émile swears not to reveal where Jim is, and then she sings the "Indian Love Call," sending it echoing up the valley so that Jim will leave for South America without her.

The second act opens in Québec, where Rose-Marie is slowly starting to believe Wanda's tales that Jim *is* a murderer. Jim risks arrest by sneaking into Québec to see Rose-Marie, but when Rose-Marie sees Wanda in Jim's company, she refuses to believe he is innocent. Meanwhile, Herman wheedles the truth out of Wanda by implying that Hawley is blaming the murder on *her*. As the marriage ceremony begins, Wanda interrupts by announcing to all the guests that she had murdered Blackeagle in order to protect Hawley, the man she loves. Rose-Marie races back to the Kootenay Pass, where she joins Jim in one last echoing performance across the valley of the "Indian Love Call," ending the story in his arms.

PLOT SUMMARY: *THE VAGABOND KING*

The Vagabond King is set in medieval France during the reign of Louis XI. The fictional story centers around a real historical figure: François Villon, a vagabond poet. He has fallen in love with a haughty lady of the court, Katherine de Vaucelles, and has written to her. Intrigued, Katherine meets Villon at a Parisian tavern, where Villon claims he would lay the whole world at her feet "if he were king." The jaded King Louis is in disguise at the same tavern, where he not only overhears Villon's pursuit of Katherine, but also hears himself sneeringly condemned by Villon as a "do-nothing, dare-nothing" king. Outraged over being mocked, Louis decides to force Villon to take Louis's throne for a day; moreover, in order to chastise Katherine, Louis orders Villon to woo her, and if Villon is not successful in winning her by the end of the day, he will be executed. During Villon's day as ruler, Paris is besieged by the army of the Duke of Burgundy—an enemy that King Louis has been unable to defeat. Villon turns to the beggars and thieves of Paris—the "lousy rabble of low degree"—and rouses them into taking up arms to defend their city in the stirring "Song of the Vagabonds" (**Musical Example 19**). The vagabonds are successful in protecting their kingdom, and Villon is equally successful in his pursuit of Katherine—much to the heartbreak of Huguette de Hamel, a Parisian prostitute who loves Villon and had hoped to marry him. In a striking act of self-sacrifice, Huguette allows herself to be killed when she realizes that she stands in the way of Villon's courtship of Katherine. The ungrateful Louis had still planned to execute Villon, regardless of Villon's successes, but he is stunned by Huguette's selflessness. Louis realizes that he knows of no citizen who would do the same for him, and he decides to allow the aristocratic Katherine and the low-born Villon to marry, thus sparing Villon at the last moment.

MUSICAL EXAMPLE 18

ROSE-MARIE
RUDOLF FRIML /OTTO HARBACH AND OSCAR HAMMERSTEIN II, 1924

"Indian Love Call"

Rose-Marie

1 Ooh! [*echo*] Ooh! So echoes of sweet love-notes gently fall
Thru the forest stillness, as fond waiting Indian lovers call!
When the lone lagoon stirs in the spring, welcoming home some swany white wing,
When the maiden moon, riding the sky, gathers her star-eyed dream children nigh:
That is the time of the moon and the year when love-dreams to Indian maidens appear.
And this is the song that they hear:
2 When I'm calling you oo-oo oo-oo-oo! Will you answer too oo-oo oo-oo-oo?
3 That means I offer my love to you, to be your own.
If you refuse me, I will be blue and waiting all alone;
4 But if when you hear my love call ringing clear, and I hear your answering echo, so dear,
5 Then I will know our love will come true, you'll belong to me, I'll belong to you!

MUSICAL EXAMPLE 19

THE VAGABOND KING
RUDOLF FRIML /BRIAN HOOKER AND W. H. POST, 1925

"Song of the Vagabonds"

François

1 Come all, ye beggars of Paris-town, you lousy rabble of low degree

Chorus

You rabble of low degree

François
We'll spare King Louis to keep his crown and save our city from Burgundy.
Chorus
Our city from Burgundy.
François
You and I are good for nothing but to die, we can die for Liberty!
2   Sons of toil and danger, will you serve a stranger, and bow down to Burgundy?
Sons of shame and sorrow, will you cheer tomorrow for the crown of Burgundy?
Onward! Onward! Swords against the Foe! Forward! Forward the lily banners go!
Sons of France around us, break the chain that bound us, and to Hell with Burgundy!
Chorus
3   Sons of toil and danger, will you serve a stranger, and bow down to Burgundy?
Sons of shame and sorrow, will you cheer tomorrow for the crown of Burgundy?
Onward! Onward! Swords against the Foe! Forward! Forward the lily banners go!
Sons of France around us, break the chain that bound us, and to Hell with Burgundy!

Chapter 15
Musical Theater of the Lighter Kind

Kern's "Princess Shows" showed how musical comedy could be less "silly," while Friml's operettas demonstrated how operettas could address more serious issues. Their ideas did not usher in overnight changes, however. Many operettas, such as *The Desert Song* (1926), continued to dizzy audiences simply with the sheer beauty of their lush romanticism; their plots were negligible, and the emphasis instead was on exotic, far-off worlds. At the opposite extreme of the theatrical spectrum were musical comedies that were so up-to-date that they created current fashion, such as *No, No, Nanette* (1925).

No, No, Nanette was an adaptation of a 1919 play based, in turn, on a 1914 novel. An entrepreneur, Harry Frazee, wanted to produce a full-fledged musical on the subject, and Frazee's neighbor, **Vincent Youmans** (1898–1946), begged Frazee to let him write the score. Frazee wasn't impressed by Youmans's minimal track record, but Youmans's mother came to the rescue by offering to back the new show to the tune of $9,000 or $10,000. In thanks, Youmans assigned his mother one-half of his royalties.

Youmans worked on *No, No, Nanette* with librettists Otto Harbach and Frank Mandel (1884–1958), a coauthor of the original play. Harbach was initially assigned to write the lyrics as well, but he stepped aside for **Irving Caesar** (1895–1996), since Youmans and Caesar had an established working relationship. For many observers, *No, No, Nanette* represents American musical comedies of the 1920s better than any other show, and the historian Andrew Lamb suggests that "Tea for Two" "may epitomize the spirit of the decade." It is curious, however, that even with the notable success of *No,*

No, Nanette, Youmans's name has almost vanished into obscurity, while that of his exact contemporary, George Gershwin, is still known virtually around the world (see the **Sidebar:** *Youmans and Gershwin*).

It wasn't clear at first that *No, No, Nanette* would ever reach "hit" status. The tryout tour began in Detroit in April 1924, receiving only moderately favorable reviews; a week later, in Cincinnati, the critics were even more lukewarm. Frantically, Frazee fired some performers, took over the direction of the production himself, and told Youmans and Caesar that the show needed some new songs, pronto.

One of the four replacement songs had actually been written some weeks before. One evening, Caesar had barely fallen asleep when Youmans called, saying he had just come up with a great melody and wanted some lyrics. After listening to what he privately thought was a monotonous tune, the sleepy Caesar begged Youmans to wait for the words until the next morning, but Youmans insisted. Caesar began spouting out a **dummy lyric** (a poem that is nonsensical, but has the right rhythm and rhyme scheme), saying apologetically, "It stinks—but I'll write you a good lyric in the morning." Youmans disagreed, saying that the poetry was perfect. The result was "Tea for Two" (**Musical Example 20**).

"Tea For Two" and "I Want to Be Happy" were inserted into the show by the time it reached Chicago. These additions proved so popular that instead of traveling on to New York, *No, No, Nanette* stayed in Chicago for an entire year. These added tunes quickly grew to be popular songs on their own account; they were heard on the radio and played by

---

Sidebar: Youmans and Gershwin

Two future musical theater composers were born within 24 hours of each other in 1898: George Gershwin on September 26 and Vincent Youmans on September 27. When they discovered this fact, Youmans started calling Gershwin "Old Man" and Gershwin retaliated by dubbing Youmans "Junior." Although the two men shared many musical characteristics and even personal histories, their success took dramatically different paths; Gershwin's name is known virtually round the world, while Youmans's is largely forgotten by all but the most dedicated theater buffs.

Most likely, the men met at one of the Tin Pan Alley publishers. They each worked for the publisher Max Dreyfus, and apparently Gershwin helped Youmans get his first Broadway assignment by plugging some of Youmans's songs to producer Alex Aarons (who had given Gershwin *his*

first opportunity to write for Broadway). Both composers were inspired by Jerome Kern, and both men were intrigued by the syncopated rhythms of jazz and the complexities of art music. In the late 1920s, their experiences began to diverge sharply; while Gershwin's "experimental" shows were interspersed with enough hit productions to sustain his career comfortably, Youmans began to suffer failure after failure.

Like Gershwin's, Youmans's Broadway career ended at a relatively young age. In Youmans's case, however, the end of the career was due to illness; because of tuberculosis, he was forced to give up composing for the stage at age 35 after producing 12 shows in the preceding 12 years. It took another 12 years for the disease to take his life and his last months were sad and bitter—a lasting irony for the man who wrote "I Want to Be Happy."

virtually every restaurant and club orchestra in the nation and in England too. When *No, No, Nanette* at last opened in New York in 1925, it was viewed almost as old hat. The *New York Daily News* opened its review rather pointedly: "Boston saw it. Philadelphia saw it. Chicago saw it. London saw it, and Guatemala, Medicine Bend and the Canary islands have probably seen it as well." Perhaps because the show *was* so familiar by the time it arrived in New York, the run was a slightly disappointing 321 performances.

The catchy tunes were only one factor leading to the success of *No, No, Nanette*; as in the case of *The Merry Widow* almost 20 years earlier, dance also helped the show's popularity. *No, No, Nanette* featured the jazz-oriented dances of the Roaring Twenties: one-steps, two-steps, snake steps, skip steps, slide steps, tap-dance, and soft-shoe. At certain points, dance was even integrated into the storyline itself, such as the "challenge" dance that takes place during "Fight Over Me" (see the **Plot Summary**). All this enthusiastic physical display gave *No, No, Nanette* tremendous visual appeal.

Nearly all of the hit tunes from *No, No, Nanette* are immediately followed by a dance set to the preceding song's melody, and "Tea for Two" is no exception. The song itself is set in a verse-chorus form, and the chorus (**2** and **4**) uses a persistent "soft-shoe" dance rhythm. Youmans created this soft-shoe effect by writing **dotted notes**—a notational device that produces a long–short, long–short, long–short pattern. This characteristic motif makes easy both to dance and to sing the song. The motif can be called an **ostinato**, a term for a repetitive pattern in music. Youmans's use of the long–short rhythm is not quite as pervasive as some writers have indicated, but it certainly is a mainstay of the chorus, occurring steadily for two or three measures at a time.

The text itself of "Tea for Two" describes a cozy, honeymoon environment; songs of this type were enough of a 1920s fad that some people called them **love-nest ballads**. The rhyme scheme is simple, frequently featuring an alternation between *ee* and *oo* sounds in alternation. (Caesar created occasional breaks in the anticipated rhyme in much the same way that Youmans broke the repetitive rhythmic pattern.) Certainly, "Tea for Two" has assumed a life of its own; not only has it been used in new settings by numerous jazz musicians over the years, but it has been rearranged by classical composers. "Tea for Two" is undoubtedly the most recognizable tune that Youmans ever wrote.

If *No, No, Nanette* captured the energy and pizzazz of the Flapper Era, *The Desert Song* (1926) demonstrated that traditional operetta could still pack in audiences as well. In its own way, *The Desert Song* was as up-to-date and fashionable as *No, No, Nanette*—musical theater scholar Ethan Mordden calls it "Headline Operetta." Not only were moviegoers stirred up by the cinematic adventures of Rudolf Valentino as "The Sheik" (who had brought his fans to a peak of hysteria by dying some three months before *The Desert Song* premiered), but the public was also fascinated by the real-life exploits of Lawrence of Arabia, the French Foreign Legion, and the Riff uprising in Morocco. The show demonstrated that a strong score and exotic Middle East stage sets could easily counterbalance a weak book—for despite the harsh critical comments directed toward the plot, *The Desert Song* ran 465 times in New York. (It would be by no means the last time that critical and popular opinion diverged sharply!)

In retrospect, the storyline seems no worse than many others of its day, but it may well be that expectations were heightened after some of the more dramatic shows of the early 1920s. Richard Watts, Jr., opened his review for the *Herald Tribune* by saying, "The question of how simple-minded the book of a musical comedy can be was debated last night, and the verdict arrived at was 'no end'." Watts also disliked the

A tearful scene in *No, No, Nanette*.
Harvard Theatre Collection.

Emotions run high in *The Desert Song.*
Culver Pictures, Inc.

clearly absorbed many of the lessons of the Princess Shows and other integrated productions. He explained,

> *I have been endeavoring to have singing, dancing, comedy and a good cohesive story in one production, and to blend all these elements into one compact presentation which will not only please the ears and eyes, but also appeal to the intelligence of the playgoer. The book must be so arranged that neither dancing, music, nor comedy must appear foreign to the action of the story.*

The efforts of Romberg and others led to changing theatrical music overseas. European theaters presented American shows with increasing frequency, and even works by European composers reflected American music; jazz numbers as well as popular dances (the fox-trot, the tango, the shimmy, and so forth) found their way into the score alongside waltzes and marches. One of the most successful productions in England was a sweetly sentimental operetta called *Bitter-Sweet* (1929). Although it played for more than 700 performances, it was the *only* British show during the 1920s to be exported to the United States. Moreover, it failed to outrun the American operetta *Rose-Marie* in London; clearly, the balance of power in the theatrical world was beginning to shift to an American domination.

FURTHER READING

Bordman, Gerald. *American Operetta from* H.M.S. Pinafore *to* Sweeney Todd. New York: Oxford University Press, 1981.

———. *Days to Be Happy, Years to Be Sad: The Life and Music of Vincent Youmans.* New York: Oxford University Press, 1982.

Kislan, Richard. *The Musical: A Look at the American Musical Theater.* New, revised, expanded edition. New York and London: Applause Books, 1995.

Mordden, Ethan. *Make Believe: The Broadway Musical in the 1920s.* New York: Oxford University Press, 1997.

Snelson, John, and Andrew Lamb. "Musical" in *The New Grove Dictionary of Music and Musicians,* 2nd ed., edited by Stanley Sadie. Vol. 17, 453–465, London: Macmillan, 2001.

Traubner, Richard. *Operetta: A Theatrical History.* Garden City, New York: Doubleday, 1983.

Wilk, Max. *They're Playing Our Song: From Jerome Kern to Stephen Sondheim—The Stories Behind the Words and Music of Two Generations.* New York: Atheneum, 1973; London: W. H. Allen, 1974.

PLOT SUMMARY: *NO, NO, NANETTE*

Nanette is a young woman who longs to misbehave a bit. Her guardians are Jimmy and Sue Smith, and Jimmy is as generous a man as Sue is tight-fisted. Jimmy—a Bible publisher—has been generous too often during his travels, and now three women (Betty, Winnie, and Flora) are depending on him. Therefore, he turns to his lawyer Billy Early for help. Billy has troubles of his own; his wife Lucille is an extravagant spender, so Billy is glad to get the fee Jimmy will pay. Billy's assistant,

song lyrics, complaining, "With so many pleasant people in the cast and so much music, color, and romance, I am perhaps ungrateful in regretting that, with the exception of one song called 'It,' the lyrics gave indication that W. S. Gilbert lived and died in vain."

The targets of this criticism were the same lyricists responsible for *Rose-Marie,* Otto Harbach and Oscar Hammerstein II. They shared the responsibility (or blame) for the book with Frank Mandel, an author of *No, No, Nanette.* Collectively, it was their first collaboration with Sigmund Romberg (1887–1951), and Hammerstein felt he learned a lot from the experienced composer:

> *Sigmund Romberg got me into the habit of working hard. . . . I remember one day bringing up a finished lyric to him. He played it over and said, "It fits." Then he turned to me and asked me, "What else have you got?" I said that I didn't have anything more, but I would go away and set another melody. He persuaded me to stay right there and write it while he was working on something else. He put me in another room with a pad and pencil. Afraid to come out empty-handed, I finished another refrain that afternoon.*

Romberg's own career in music had been launched when he discovered that he could earn more than twice the salary entertaining restaurant diners on the piano than he could working in a pencil factory. As a composer, Romberg had

Tom Trainor, loves Nanette but finds Nanette's desire to kick up her heels a bit shocking, and they end up quarreling.

When Flora telephones and says she's coming to see Jimmy, he flees to his seaside cottage; he secretly invites Nanette to come along, since Sue had earlier refused permission for Nanette to go to the beach with her friends, and Jimmy wants to cheer up Nanette. Meanwhile, Jimmy and Billy's whispered plans spark the suspicions of Lucille and Sue, who start wondering what their husbands are up to.

Gradually, all Jimmy's "friends" arrive at the cottage; they think that Jimmy is cutting off his financial support because they have *not* had affairs with him—so a dance competition results while the astonished Jimmy sings "Fight Over Me." Billy and Tom arrive, and Tom is appalled that Nanette could have spent the night alone with a married man, even if he is her guardian. Nanette manages to placate Tom, and they start dreaming with her about the future in "Tea for Two" (**Musical Example 20**). After Flora and Lucille also arrive, Billy hits on the idea of telling Jimmy's three "charities" that Jimmy is offering them a severance package because he's handing all his money over to his wife.

When Sue appears, she believes that *Billy* is the one carrying on a triple affair. Sue takes the side of the three women, since she thinks Billy should be punished for his misbehavior, and Sue eggs the women on into demanding a higher and higher settlement. Lucille, meanwhile, is distraught until she realizes that Billy *couldn't* have been supporting these women—he doesn't have any money! It doesn't take long for Sue and Lucille to straighten things out, and even Nanette starts telling the truth—and only the truth—to Tom, allowing everyone to sing one last chorus of "I Want to Be Happy."

MUSICAL EXAMPLE 20

No, No, Nanette
VINCENT YOUMANS/IRVING CAESAR, 1925
"Tea for Two"

Tom

1   I'm discontented with homes that are rented so I have invented my own.
Darling, this place is a lovers' oasis where life's weary chase is unknown.
Far from the cry of the city, where flowers pretty caress the streams.
Cozy to hide in, to live side by side in; don't let it abide in my dreams.

2   Picture you upon my knee, just tea for two, and two for tea,
Just me for you and you for me alone. Nobody near us to see us or hear us,
No friends or relations on weekend vacations.
We won't have it known, dear, that we own a telephone, dear.
Day will break and you'll awake and start to bake a sugar cake
For me to take for all the boys to see.
We will raise a family, a boy for you, a girl for me.
Can't you see how happy we would be.

Nanette

You are revealing a scene so appealing I can't help but feeling for you.
3   I know you've planned it, and I understand it, it's yours to command it, please do!
All that you say I'm admiring, it's worth desiring, But can't you see?
I'd like to wait, dear, for some future date, dear; it won't be too late, dear, for me.
Picture me upon your knee, just tea for two, and two for tea,
Just me for you and you for me alone. Nobody near us to see us or hear us,
No friends or relations on weekend vacations.
We won't have it known, dear, that we own a telephone, dear.
Day will break and I'll awake and start to bake a sugar cake
For you to take for all the boys to see.
We will raise a family, a girl for you, a boy for me.
Can't you see how happy we would be.

Beginnings of a Golden Age: Synthesis of Style and Substance

Part Four

Chapter 16
Great Partnerships of the Early Book Musical: Kern and Hammerstein

By the mid-1920s, there were several figures in American musical theater who took an explicit stand in favor of integrated shows. Chapter 13, "The Princess Shows," presented Jerome Kern's stipulations that "the musical numbers should carry the action of the play and should be representative of the personalities of the characters who sing them." Oscar Hammerstein II explained, as noted in Chapter 14, "Increasing Drama on the Stage," that he had omitted the customary song listing in *Rose-Marie*'s printed program because "the musical numbers of this play are such an integral part of the action that we do not think we should list them as separate episodes." It seemed inevitable that these two men should meet—and one of their collaborations, **Show Boat** (1927), may well be the "flagship" of American musical theater's Golden Age.

Nevertheless, Kern's and Hammerstein's first joint effort, *Sunny*, was as far removed in character from *Show Boat* as one could imagine. Not only did producer Charles Dillingham want *Sunny* to be a star vehicle for Marilynn Miller, but also, as Hammerstein ruefully reminisced,

> *Our job was to tell a story with a cast that had been assembled as if for a revue. . . . [Dillingham] had signed Cliff Edwards, who sang songs and played the ukulele and was known as Ukulele Ike. His contract required that he do his specialty between ten o'clock and ten fifteen! So we had to construct our story in such a way that Ukulele Ike could come out and perform during that time and still not interfere with the continuity. . . . [There] was Jack Donahue, a famous dancing comedian, and . . . Clifton Webb and Mary Hay, who were a leading dance team of the time. Joseph Cawthorn, a star comedian, Esther Howard, another, Paul Frawley, the leading juvenile. . . . We had also to take care of*

> *George Olson's Dance Band on the stage. Well, we put it all together and it was a hit.*

To top it off, Hammerstein (and Otto Harbach) needed to write a libretto that could encompass a circus, a foxhunt, an ocean liner, and a grand ball. They made it work, but, curiously, the story ended with Sunny in the arms of one of the men in the New York production—while she chose the *other* man in the London version! *Sunny* was not particularly noteworthy except for the fact that Miller reputedly was paid the highest salary ever given to a musical theater star up to that time—said to be $3,000 a week.

Show Boat, on the other hand, was an entirely different matter. The "book" was terribly important this time around—Kern telephoned Hammerstein one evening to say that he thought Edna Ferber's 1926 novel *Show Boat* was the property they needed. Ferber, on the other hand, was horrified to think that her sprawling story might be presented as "musical comedy." Only after Kern swore to Ferber that his work would maintain the highest standards did she reluctantly agree to sign over the rights.

In her autobiography, Edna Ferber described what made her sure she had made the right decision:

> *Jerome Kern appeared in my apartment late one afternoon with a strange look of quiet exultation in his eyes. He sat down at the piano . . . and sang "Ol' Man River." The music mounted, mounted, and I give you my word my hair stood on end, the tears came to my eyes, I breathed like a heroine in a melodrama. This was great music. This was music that would outlast Jerome Kern's day and mine.*

Kern and Hammerstein labored for an entire year on *Show Boat*, in an era when it was not uncommon to throw together a show in a couple of weeks. They visited a genuine show boat to ensure that what they created would seem authentic. Hammerstein adapted the novel himself, and he painstakingly crafted a two-hour story, struggling to bring Ferber's wide-ranging story within bounds.

There was a brief tug-of-war over who would produce the show. Kern and Hammerstein knew that Oscar's uncle Arthur wanted to handle the production, but he was very conservative. They wanted to work with Florenz Ziegfeld, and this choice contributed to the show's eventual enormous visual appeal, since few producers had a more lavish touch than Ziegfeld. They signed their contracts in late 1926, promising to deliver a script by January 1, 1927, so that the play would be ready to open by April 1.

Ziegfeld contracted several performers for the lead roles, expecting that the show would launch his own new theater, currently under construction and due to open in April 1927. Since Kern and Hammerstein did not finish the script and score until November 1927, Ziegfeld had had to release three of the performers from their contracts; one singer was Paul Robeson, for whom the role of Joe (and the song "Ol' Man River") was intended. Robeson later joined the cast for the 1928 London production, and he appeared in the 1936 film version of *Show Boat* as well.

As it turned out, *Show Boat* was well worth the wait. During its tryout tour, it needed to be trimmed by an hour and a half, but the production made a successful Broadway debut on December 27, 1927, at the Ziegfeld Theatre. Despite a slight scare (see **Behind-the-Scenes**), *Show Boat* settled in for a 572-performance run. It has been revived every decade since its premiere, undergoing revisions in each revival; in fact, there really isn't a definitive version of *Show Boat*. Some modifications resulted from evolving production standards—as better mechanisms and motorized sets became available, some of the **scene change songs** (sung in front of the curtain to distract the audience) could be eliminated. Also, some songs were added to the various film versions and were then added to later stage productions.

Some of the show's modifications resulted from changes in public attitudes about depictions of race on (and off) stage. One of Hammerstein's challenges in adapting the expansive novel was the book's treatment of miscegenation—the controversial issue of marriage between members of different races (see the **Plot Summary**). As Ziegfeld knew from his earlier revues, there were those who were opposed to white and black actors appearing on the same stage—especially simultaneously, as called for in many of *Show Boat*'s scenes. (Not all of *Show Boat*'s "black" performers *were* African American; the woman playing Queenie was Tess Gardella, a white performer who had become famous through vaudeville for her blackface depiction of an "Aunt Jemima" character.) By and large, however, Kern, Hammerstein, and Ziegfeld were successful in casting the show the way they wanted.

One of the stickiest aspects for later productions was that the original *Show Boat* (and Ferber's novel) frequently used the objectionable term "nigger"—heard as the very first word of the show's opening choral work song. Although the word was still in widespread usage during the era in which the show is set, changes in social attitudes soon made the term unacceptable on stage. Hammerstein himself switched to "coloured folks" for the 1928 London production. Directors of subsequent revivals have sought various solutions that allow the rhythms of the song to "work." The 1966 revival at Lincoln Center avoided the issue altogether by cutting the

Joe (Paul Robeson) sings "Ol' Man River" in the 1936 film *Show Boat*.
Corbis/Bettmann.

Figure 16–1

1	Verse (repeated from opening of show)	Verse
2–5	Chorus (*a-a-b-a'*) ("song form")	Chorus
6	Verse	Verse
7	*b* (release/bridge of the song form)	Abbreviated Chorus
8	Verse	Verse
9–14	Chorus (*a-a-b-a'*)	Chorus

Figure 16–2

Long	*Long*	*Short*	*Long*	*Long*	*Long*	*Short*	*Long*
			-er		Cot-	-ton	
		Riv-					Blos-
Ol'	Man						-som

first **chorus number**. To his credit, Hammerstein *did* create a remarkably sensitive and honest expression of the African American sense of frustration and helplessness. His careful craftsmanship earned *Show Boat* the right to be taken seriously as "theater."

The genre of *Show Boat* has been rather hotly debated among musical theater historians—Richard Traubner and Gerald Bordman unabashedly include it in their studies of operettas, while Ethan Mordden flatly maintains, "*Show Boat* isn't an operetta." Although Kern and Hammerstein originally billed *Show Boat* as an "All American Musical Comedy," it wasn't long until they changed the designation to "All American Musical Play." In recent years, *Show Boat* has been performed both in Broadway theaters and in opera houses. Many of the songs are catchy, memorable tunes that do not require enormous vocal expertise (although others sound deceptively simple, but have musical challenges).

No matter what the genre label, music plays an incredibly important role in *Show Boat*. Not only did the songs suit their performers, but also Kern deliberately used pre-existing tunes at several points to enhance the "historical" mood: for example, when Ellie and Frank perform at the Trocadero, they sing an old vaudeville song. When Magnolia makes her own hesitant debut at the Trocadero, she sings "After the Ball"—the huge hit from *A Trip to Chinatown* (1891). This prop song "works" for Magnolia's stage audience partly because it is nostalgic for them; it was also genuinely nostalgic for the real 1927 audience. Kern also found a satisfactory place for a **trunk song** (an earlier, unused tune of his own); he had written "Bill" for one of the Princess Shows, but it had been cut. In *Show Boat*, however, "Bill" at last perfectly suited the philosophical, resigned affection that Julie expresses for the man she loves.

Kern used a substantial portion of **underscoring** in *Show Boat*. This technique—playing instrumental music while the actors recite their dialogue—is now absolutely conventional in television and in films, but it was uncommon in musical theater. However, underscoring helps to merge the musical song into the spoken story, so it's rather surprising that the technique is used so seldom.

Kern's tightly knit score for *Show Boat* uses a number of recurring motifs, subtly underscoring psychological peaks of the drama. "Ol' Man River" (**Musical Example 21**) demonstrates the many layers of "musical meaning" that Kern's music adds to Hammerstein's (and Ferber's) prose. In other words, studying "Ol' Man River" is a bit like peeling an onion: there are dimensions to the song that aren't apparent at first glance. For instance, "Ol' Man River," as it is sung on stage in *Show Boat*, is actually part of a longer musical scene. However, a concert singer performs only sections **1** through **5**, or even merely **2** through **5**. This portion of "Ol' Man River" is in **song form**, or *a-a-b-a*, since sections **2**, **3**, and **5** use essentially the same *a* melody, while section **4** is a contrasting theme, or *b* (sometimes called the **release** or the **bridge**). Many Tin Pan Alley songs and show tunes—such as the refrain of "Song of the Vagabonds"—began using this pattern in the mid-1920s. (Song form was originally called *popular song form*, and was sometimes abbreviated as **pop song form**; it is also occasionally known as **32-bar form**.) The first section of "Ol' Man River" (**1**) can therefore be regarded as the verse that precedes the chorus, while the chorus itself is a song form.

Careful listeners will recognize section **1**'s verse (and **6** and **8**) as the same "work song" melody heard at the very opening of *Show Boat* (the choral number with the problematic text discussed above). The verse is a motivic "symbol" of the inescapable hard work allotted to African Americans. Similarly, the *b* theme (**4**) repeats an earlier melody sung by the "Gals" during *Show Boat*'s opening choral number. In this subtle way, Joe's melody—and therefore Joe himself—is very much a part of the people who populate Natchez, Mississippi. In the lyrics, Hammerstein also echoes the images of slavery by using imperative verbs in both **4** and **7** to represent the orders directed at the workers: "Tote dat barge! Lift dat bail!" and "Don't look up an' don't look down."

The structure of the "Ol' Man River" scene at first might seem fairly random, but Kern put the scene together with perhaps more clarity than we realize, as shown in **Figure 16–1**. Since **7** is simply a truncated version of the entire chorus, one could argue that the overall scene follows an almost conventional verse-chorus pattern.

The song form refrain of **2** through **5** is often called the "river" motif, since it evokes the river each time it is heard, much in the manner of Wagner's use of *leitmotifs*. The *Cotton Blossom* also has a repetitive motif. What is *not* immediately evident is that the "river" motif and the "*Cotton Blossom*" motif are **inversions** of each other—they follow the same basic rhythm (long–long–short–long), but while the pitches of one motif ascend, the other motif's pitches descend, as **Figure 16–2** illustrates. This musical relationship produces a

Figure 16–3

Long	Long	Short	Long	Short	[Very Long]
Ol'	Man	Riv-	-er,	Dat	
Ol'	man	riv-	-er,	He	
Mus'	know	sum-	-pin'	But	
Don't	say	nuth-	-in',	He	
Jes'	keeps	rol-	-lin',	He	
Keeps	on	rol-	-lin'	A-	-long . . .

subconscious link between the boat and the river on which it depends. The inversion creates a psychological association that is both important and entirely logical.

Kern plays with psychology in other ways. During the first section of the chorus (**2**), he takes the long–long–short–long rhythm discussed above and adds one more short note to it; **Figure 16–3** shows how Kern then repeats that rhythm— exactly, without variation—six times in a row. (It seems that Kern was indulging in a bit of **word-painting**—letting music illustrate the meaning of a word or phrase—by setting the syllable "-long" to a sustained pitch!) This same rhythmic ostinato returns for the second and third repetitions of *a* of the song form (**3** and **5**). It is entirely possible that this repetitive rhythm represents the unchanging nature of the river itself—or even the continually downtrodden role of African Americans.

Because there is so much rhythmic repetition, Hammerstein could afford to go for long stretches without any rhymes in the text. The resulting free-flowing quality of the lyrics, which are not overtly "poetical," suits the uneducated Joe admirably. In an interview, Hammerstein explained,

> I wanted to keep the spirit of Edna's book and the one focal influence I could find was the Mississippi River, because she had quite consciously brought the river into every important turn in the story. So I decided to write a theme, a river theme. I put the song into the throat of a character who is a rugged and untutored philosopher. It's a song of resignation with an implied protest. . . . There are no rhymes at all for a long part of the song's refrain, and when you imagine the refrain with rhymes you realize how much weaker it might be.

Hammerstein is undoubtedly right: too much poetry might overwhelm this simple song. Yet the song is not as simple as it appears. Written for a bass voice, the song spans an octave and a sixth (a sixth is three-fourths of an octave), and it ends with a sustained and very high pitch for the singer. Perhaps more importantly, the song treats Joe with respect—unlike most earlier stage depictions of African Americans—he is never a figure of fun or a simpleton.

Despite the remarkably intricate interworkings of "Ol' Man River," the song doesn't sound like a "composed" tune. In an unconscious compliment, several African American members of the chorus told Kern that they were *sure* they remembered the song from their childhood. Kern himself grew superstitious about "Ol' Man River," feeling that he needed to play through it before every new venture to

ensure good luck. In 1945, he and his wife Eva boarded a train from California to New York because Kern had been hired to write *Annie Get Your Gun.* A day or two into the journey, Kern realized that he had forgotten to play "Ol' Man River" before they left. He fretted about it repeatedly during the trip, to the extent that Eva grew worried about it as well. Shortly after their arrival in New York, Kern collapsed on a street corner and died a few days later without regaining consciousness.

"Ol' Man River" is an excellent representative of the care and craftsmanship expended by both Kern and Hammerstein. *Show Boat* is rich in integrated **book songs**—numbers that were tied into the plot and often carried the plot further along. It would become increasingly hard for subsequent artists to do any less—but like many innovations, it took time for *Show Boat*'s achievements to be fully recognized, much less emulated. It stands apart from the majority of pieces from the 1920s and 1930s. Even subsequent collaborations of Kern and Hammerstein never came close to the power of this one great work.

One of Kern's most promising post-*Show Boat* works, *Sweet Adeline* (1929), was also his next collaboration with Hammerstein. It got off to an excellent start—but then came the enormous stock market crash of October 1929. (*Variety*— an important magazine devoted to theatrical affairs—referred to the devastating financial collapse as if it were a flop production; *Variety*'s headline read "Wall Street Lays an Egg.") Although Kern lost the $2 million he had invested in the stock market, he was protected financially by his collection of antique silver and of course by his creative talent—for, despite the onset of the Great Depression that resulted in part from the crash, there was still a healthy market for Broadway shows as well as a place in Hollywood for composers.

After various other projects, Kern resumed a partnership with Harbach for *Roberta* in 1933. Kern had hoped to work with Hammerstein again, but Hammerstein had prior commitments in London. Although *Roberta*'s plot is not very complex, one song—"Smoke Gets in Your Eyes"—became an enormous hit and a social catchphrase as well. The tune also answered a question that the composer Charles K. Harris had posed some seven years earlier: "The burning question of today is how the radio will affect the composers of the future. Will it help to popularize or will it destroy a song? Time alone can tell." Radio proved to be *Roberta*'s salvation. "Smoke Gets in Your Eyes" got heavy airplay, leading to tremendous sheet music and ticket sales.

Given the song's popularity, the structure of "Smoke Gets in Your Eyes" is surprisingly simple; like "Ol' Man River," it is in song form. What, then, makes this song "work"? It is probably a combination of factors: the song's bittersweet quality, the disjunct melody that makes it hard to predict all the twists and turns of the theme, and possibly even its surprising harmonic change, or **modulation**. Kern makes an unexpected shift at the bridge, moving to another key that is *six* steps away, not the usual five. Although most listeners would not consciously perceive this **key change**, they probably *do* notice the rather surprising sense of "lift" that occurs at the bridge. For composers and others who read music, Kern's startling modulation is a fascinating compositional device to analyze.

After bringing *Roberta* to the stage for 295 performances, Kern's career turned largely to Hollywood. He worked with Hammerstein on a Broadway show in 1939, but except for an additional song for the 1946 revival of *Show Boat*, Kern would not write for Broadway again. Nevertheless, he left behind an important legacy: he was one of America's most prolific songwriters (composing some thousand songs), he composed one of the finest works of the 1920s, *Show Boat*, and he was an enormous influence on two of musical theater's next generation of compositional stars, George Gershwin and Richard Rodgers.

FURTHER READING

Bordman, Gerald. *American Operetta from* H. M. S. Pinafore *to* Sweeney Todd. New York: Oxford University Press, 1981.

Fordin, Hugh. *Getting to Know Him: A Biography of Oscar Hammerstein II*. New York: Random House, 1977.

Freedland, Michael. *Jerome Kern*. New York: Stein & Day, 1978.

Furia, Philip. *The Poets of Tin Pan Alley*. New York: Oxford University Press, 1990.

Hammerstein, Oscar, II. *Lyrics*. Reprinted Milwaukee, Wisconsin: Hal Leonard Books, 1985.

Higham, Charles. *Ziegfeld*. Chicago: Regnery, 1972; London: W. H. Allen, 1973.

Kreuger, Miles. *Show Boat*. New York: Oxford University Press, 1977.

Mordden, Ethan. *Make Believe: The Broadway Musical in the 1920s*. New York: Oxford University Press, 1997.

Traubner, Richard. *Operetta: A Theatrical History*. Garden City, New York: Doubleday, 1983.

Wilder, Alec. *American Popular Song: The Great Innovators, 1900–1950*. London: Oxford University Press, 1972.

BEHIND-THE-SCENES: HELEN MORGAN AND PROHIBITION

Show Boat almost had to close shortly after it opened, thanks to Helen Morgan, who was playing the role of Julie. Kern had "discovered" Morgan as she sang in a small revue; she also supported herself by singing in Billy Rose's New York speakeasy. Speakeasies were clubs, usually with entertainment, where patrons could buy illegal alcohol. These clubs had burgeoned after the Eighteenth Amendment to the U.S. Constitution had been ratified in 1920; this amendment, (un)popularly known as Prohibition, forbade the purchase,

manufacture, and importation of alcoholic beverages. Morgan—who later died of cirrhosis of the liver—probably valued her access to alcohol at the speakeasy as much as she liked performing. Despite Ziegfeld's objections, she kept singing at Billy Rose's after *Show Boat* premiered, heading over to the speakeasy each evening after the Broadway show ended.

The fourth night of *Show Boat*'s run was New Year's Eve and disaster struck. While Morgan was perched on top of the piano, a group of 25 federal agents burst through the door of the speakeasy, led by Maurice Campbell. They conducted a typical "bust"; they smashed the liquor bottles, tore down the luxurious draperies, shot the lights out of the chandeliers—and took the personnel, including Morgan, into custody. Ziegfeld promptly bailed out his star, but knew that it would be difficult to defend her presence at the illegal speakeasy. Then Ziegfeld was struck by a thought. He telephoned Campbell and asked him, "Did you have a warrant?" When Campbell admitted that he did not, the case against Morgan collapsed, and she was free to return to *Show Boat*, much to the relief of all concerned (although Prohibition itself would not be repealed until 1933).

PLOT SUMMARY: *SHOW BOAT*

In the first of *Show Boat*'s many unexpected moments, the curtain rises, not to parade a chorus line of leggy showgirls, but to reveal a group of African American dockworkers, complaining in song about their back-breaking labor. Soon, though, they and the townspeople of Natchez, Mississippi, are thrilled to see the *Cotton Blossom* arrive, one of the "show boats" that were floating theaters, offering entertainment to audiences along the river. Andy Hawkes is its captain; he introduces Frank and Ellie, the comedy team, as well as Julie LaVerne, the sultry star. Her husband and costar, Steve, gets into a fistfight with Pete, a deckhand, just as Cap'n Andy is describing the cast on the show boat as "one big happy family."

Andy and his wife Parthy Ann have a daughter, Magnolia, who has just met a charming gambler, Gaylord Ravenal; their attraction is instant *and* mutual. The sheriff declares that men like Gaylord aren't welcome in Natchez; he should move along. Regardless, Magnolia asks Joe, an African American stevedore, for information about Gaylord. Joe shrugs and tells her she'd be better off asking "Ol' Man River" (**Musical Example 21**).

When Julie sings "Can't Help Lovin' Dat Man" about Steve, Queenie, the cook, wonders how a white woman would know that African American song. Soon afterwards, the mystery is explained. Pete has revealed to the sheriff that Julie is half black. The sheriff threatens to arrest Julie and Steve—who is white—for miscegenation. Steve has cut Julie's hand and sucked blood from the wound so that he, too, has Negro blood in him. Undaunted, the sheriff warns Cap'n Andy that it's against the law in Mississippi for black and white performers to appear on the same stage. Julie and Steve pack their belongings, leaving Cap'n Andy in a bit of a lurch: he has a show to put on! Cap'n Andy promotes Magnolia into the starring role (over Parthy Ann's strenuous objections). Gaylord Ravenal, who has asked for a lift downriver, appears to be the easy solution for a replacement leading man.

In time, Magnolia and Gaylord marry and leave the *Cotton Blossom*. But Gaylord hasn't been able to stop gambling, and eventually he deserts Magnolia and their young daughter Kim. The coincidences come fast and furious for a while: Frank and Ellie run into Magnolia, and they suggest that she seek a job at the Trocadero. At the Trocadero, the headliner turns out to be Julie, now an alcoholic, who is rehearsing "Bill" for the upcoming New Year's Eve show.

Magnolia arrives for an audition, and Julie eavesdrops from her dressing room. Hearing how much Magnolia needs a job, Julie abruptly resigns. (Julie vanishes at this point, although in Ferber's novel, she is later glimpsed in a house of prostitution. Clearly, though, Julie's inexorable descent gives American musical theater what the writer Ethan Mordden calls "its first tragic heroine.")

Magnolia's parents have come for a surprise New Year's visit, unaware of Gaylord's recent desertion. While Parthy Ann sleeps, Cap'n Andy finds himself at the Trocadero, just as Magnolia makes her shaky debut. He urges her on, and she wins over the crowd with the nostalgic "After the Ball."

After a stellar career, Magnolia retires to the *Cotton Blossom*. One day, an old man appears at the showboat. He is of course Gaylord, and despite the hurts of the past, he and Magnolia are still in love—so they, with most of the other main characters, are reunited for the final scene.

MUSICAL EXAMPLE 21

Show Boat
Jerome Kern/Oscar Hammerstein II, 1927
"Ol' Man River"

Joe

1   Dere's an ol' man called de Mississippi, dat's de ol' man dat I'd like to be.
What does he care if de world's got troubles? What does he care if de land ain't free?

2   Ol' Man River, dat ol' man river, he mus' know sumpin' but don't say nuthin',
He jes' keeps rollin', he keeps on rollin' along.

3   He don't plant taters, he don't plant cotton an' dem dat plants 'em
Is soon forgotten, but ol' man river, he jes' keeps rollin' along.

4   You an' me, we sweat an' strain, body all achin' an' racked wid' pain.
Tote dat barge! Lift dat bale! Git a little drunk an' you land in jail.

5   I git weary an' sick of tryin', I'm tired of livin' an' skeered of dyin';
But ol' man river, he jes' keeps rollin' along!

6   Colored folks work on de Mississippi, colored folks work while de white folks play.
Pullin' dem boats from de dawn to sunset, gittin' no rest till de Judgment Day.

Men

7   Don't look up an' don't look down, you don't dast make de white boss frown;
Bend yo' knees an' bow yo' head, an' pull dat rope until yo're dead.

Joe

8   Let me go 'way from de Mississippi, let me go 'way from de white man boss.
Show me dat stream called de river Jordan, dat's de ol' stream I longs to cross!

Men

9   Ol' Man River, dat ol' man river, he mus' know sumpin' but don't say nuthin',
He jes' keeps rollin', he keeps on rollin' along.

Joe

10   Long ol' river forever keeps rollin' on.

Men

11   He don't plant taters, he don't plant cotton an' dem dat plants 'em
Is soon forgotten, but ol' man river, he jes' keeps on rollin' along.

Joe

12   Long ol' river keeps hearin' dat song.

13   You an' me, we sweat an' strain, body all achin' an' wracked wid' pain.
Tote dat barge! Lift dat bale! Git a little drunk an' you land in jail.

Joe and Men

14   I git weary an' sick of tryin', I'm tired of livin' an' skeered of dyin';
But ol' man river, he jes' keeps rollin' along!

Chapter 17
Great Partnerships of the Early Book Musical: Rodgers and Hart

Even after his death, Jerome Kern cast a long shadow over younger musical theater composers. The 14-year-old **Richard Rodgers** (1902–1979) "researched" Kern's style by seeing *Very Good Eddie* (1915) over and over again, carefully scrutinizing his own work to see if he met Kern's standards. In his autobiography, Rodgers commented, "No matter what I myself accomplished, I always felt I was continuing to build the same kind of musical theatre that Kern had helped to create." In actuality, Rodgers helped to expand musical theater even further. Some of these changes took place in the storylines and in the treatment of dance, while other modifications occurred behind the scenes. Like Kern, Rodgers later wielded enormous influence upon the next generation of composers. Lionel Trilling, describing Rodgers, remarked, "Few men have given so much pleasure to so many people."

One of the most astonishing aspects of Rodgers's career is that it was actually *two* careers. After a 24-year partnership with **Lorenz ("Larry") Hart** (1895–1943), when many people would be considering a well-deserved retirement, Rodgers started a second long-term collaboration, this time with Oscar Hammerstein II, which lasted from 1943 until Hammerstein's death in 1960. The achievements of either partnership would have ensured Rodgers his lasting place in theatrical history—and, curiously, these were two very *different* careers, since the two teams created markedly different products.

Rodgers's initial meeting with Hart in 1919 didn't seem too auspicious; Hart came to the door in a pair of tuxedo trousers, an undershirt, and a frayed pair of slippers. They had been introduced through one of Rodgers's brother's classmates at Columbia, Philip Leavitt (when Hart was 23 and Rodgers merely 16). After the initial shock of Hart's disheveled appearance, Rodgers and Hart spent the afternoon chatting, playing through tunes, and discussing their theatrical philosophies. Rodgers recalled,

Larry talked about a lot of things that afternoon, including arcane matters of his trade, such as interior rhymes and feminine endings, that I had never heard of before. But what really brought us together was our mutual conviction that the musical theatre, as demonstrated by the pioneering efforts of Bolton, Wodehouse and Kern, was capable of achieving a far greater degree of artistic merit in every area than was apparent at the time. We had no idea exactly how it could be done, but we both knew that we had to try.

Rodgers summed up the meeting, saying, "I left Hart's house having acquired in one afternoon a career, a partner, a best friend, and a source of permanent irritation."

Rodgers and Hart soon felt ready to show off their portfolio. Through Leavitt, they met Lew Fields, who had risen to fame in vaudeville in the comedy team of (Joe) Weber and Fields; Fields was now a Broadway producer. Fields's children Herbert and Dorothy were present when Rodgers demonstrated the team's songs, but Hart was not; he had developed a "blinding headache," which Rodgers learned was a common reaction (or ploy) of Hart's whenever business was to be discussed. Nevertheless, Fields decided to purchase a song and interpolate it into a show of his that had been running for some months.

The new team got its first chance to write a complete show in 1920, thanks to a commission from the Akron Club, a group of amateurs. The result was proudly labeled "an atrocious musical comedy." The same year, Rodgers and Hart also had a musical chosen as the Columbia Varsity Show, an annual theatrical presentation at Columbia University. The chance to compete was the main reason that Rodgers had just enrolled at Columbia as a freshman. (Hammerstein, a Columbia alumnus himself, had been a judge.) Herbert Fields choreographed the show's dances, so his father Lew attended one of the performances—and again, he liked what he heard. The older Fields decided to hire the team to write a score for his next Broadway production, *Poor Little Ritz Girl*. It is a bit flabbergasting that a college freshman could be tapped to write a professional Broadway score, but this is part of the Richard Rodgers legend. Admittedly, when the show failed to win over audiences in Boston, Fields made major changes—including replacing eight songs with pieces by Sigmund Romberg. Nevertheless, Rodgers and Hart once again had their work (or at least a portion of it) performed professionally on Broadway.

Although they continued to collaborate on Varsity shows, Rodgers dropped out of Columbia and enrolled at the Institute of Musical Art (now known as the Juilliard School of Music). He and Hart were soon writing songs for the Institute's end-of-year musical revue. Their first effort was such a hit that Rodgers feared his scholarships were awarded just to ensure that he would be around to write future revues! The Institute musicians appreciated the inside jokes of the show, for it reworked an opera by a Russian composer, Rimsky-Korsakov. Rodgers and Hart were not alone; a number of other shows used "art music" as their basis (see the *Sidebar: Musicals and the Classics*).

It was several years before Rodgers and Hart were able to take another stab at Broadway. One chance slipped away when producer Russell Janney couldn't get backers to support the unknown team. (Janney gave the job to Rudolf Friml, resulting in *The Vagabond King*.) With Herbert Fields, Rodgers and Hart tried writing a play (not a musical), which they did manage to bring to Broadway; a reviewer, George Jean Nathan, dryly commented, "The plot is not only enough to ruin the play; it is enough—and I feel that I may say it without fear of contradiction—to ruin even *Hamlet*."

At last, by 1925, Rodgers was ready to quit show business and take a job as a traveling salesman for babies' underwear—but a last-minute phone call offered the team another revue. The performers would be the "Theatre Guild Junior Players," part of the Theatre Guild (a prestigious production corporation). The Junior Players wanted to raise money for tapestries for the Guild's new theater, and the producers would be the Guild impresarios, Theresa Helburn and Lawrence Langner. A production under their guidance was a wonderful opportunity.

Rodgers and Hart set to work on *The Garrick Gaieties*, named for the Guild's theater. Only two performances were planned, but the audience reaction showed that they had a hit on their hands. Initially, Helburn let them use the Garrick Theatre on afternoons when there wasn't a matinee scheduled, but after a couple of weeks, Helburn closed the current show and let *The Garrick Gaieties* take over the theater full-time for a regular run. The revue ran from May until late November, and the Rodgers and Hart Broadway career was finally, truly launched. According to Rodgers,

> A few years later Larry and I happened to attend an opening-night performance at the Guild Theatre. Larry looked at the two huge tapestries hanging from the side walls and nudged me. "See those tapestries?" he said. "We're responsible for them."
>
> "No, Larry," I corrected him. "They're responsible for us."

One of the most unusual aspects of their partnership was that it was exclusive. Most composers and lyricists changed pairings from show to show, often at the whim of the producer. Rodgers and Hart were the first American stage writers to become a recognizable "team"—and one in which both partners received equal billing. In contrast, in shows by the Gershwins, composer George Gershwin got top billing, often in a larger font than his lyricist (and brother) Ira Gershwin. It was also unusual that Rodgers and Hart had not made their rise to fame via the "Tin Pan Alley" route.

Sidebar: Musicals and the Classics

Long before Rodgers and Hart came on the scene, musical theater had quoted classical music. Many productions were burlesques, or spoofs—but gradually more serious treatments began to appear. Two main approaches were used: Some shows were a popularized version or an adaptation of an earlier opera, whereas other shows used melodies by serious composers, appended to some completely new storyline.

Rodgers and Hart's spoof of a Rimsky-Korsakov opera was an example of the first approach. In 1943, Oscar Hammerstein wrote new words for Georges Bizet's opera *Carmen*; the result was *Carmen Jones*. Sometimes, an older opera's plot was used, but with new words *and* music. This process led to Claude-Michel Schönberg and Alain Boublil's *Miss Saigon* (1989) (discussed in Chapter 41, "The New Team in Town"), which borrowed ideas from Puccini's *Madama Butterfly*, while Puccini's *La Bohème* was the inspiration for Jonathan Larson's *Rent* (1996), a depiction of modern-day New York "Bohemians" (Chapter 44, "New Names for the 1990s and Beyond").

The second approach has been widely used as well; Rodgers and Hart borrowed themes from classical composers for "The Three B's," and Rodgers inserted a bit of Tchaikovsky's *Nutcracker Suite* into another of his musical theater scores. Tchaikovsky's music was heard in numerous shows, and Chopin's works were particularly popular melodic sources. In a show titled *Polonaise* (1945), the score consisted solely of Chopin polonaises (a type of Polish dance). Music by Alexander Borodin found its way into *Kismet* (1953), while Rachmaninoff's works were heard in *Anya* (1965). The music of Jacques Offenbach was used for years, ranging from a 1917 operetta to a 1961 musical comedy.

Sigmund Romberg's *Blossom Time* (1921) straddles the two types; it used Franz Schubert's songs to present a fictionalized biography of the Austrian composer, but it was also based on an earlier Viennese operetta. Using a composer's music to depict a fanciful biographical account of his life was a fairly common ploy; Edvard Grieg's life (and music) was the subject of *The Song of Norway* (1944). *White Lilacs* (1928) was a fictionalized account of Chopin's life, while Tchaikovsky was the subject of *Music in My Heart* (1947). Jacques Offenbach was featured as the subject of *The Love Song* (1925). *The Great Waltz* (1934) and its London equivalent, *Waltzes from Vienna* (1931), were fictionalized biographies of Johann Strauss Junior and Senior, based of course on their greatest waltz melodies.

The use of all this older music served a twofold purpose: in some instances, it demonstrated the increasingly high expectations that could be held of musical theater audiences. Just as turn-of-the-century audiences responded to George M. Cohan's flag-waving quotations of patriotic songs, the listeners in succeeding generations would react to the "highbrow" musical literature featured in these shows. A second benefit to using older musical material was that if a tune was in the public domain, no royalty payments needed to be paid for its use (which is why classical music is often heard on television and in film scores). Producers, like anyone, are happy to save money wherever they can.

"Rodgers and Hart" shows quickly became a commodity, and they maintained a pace of at least two shows every year, not to mention five musicals in 1926. They tried many different experiments: In *The Girl Friend* (1926), the humor was adult, and its tunes upbeat; critics were impressed with songs such as "Blue Room," in which poetic rhymes (blue / new / two) were reinforced in the ear by being set to the same musical pitch. *Peggy-Ann* (1926), which began and ended with the stage in almost total darkness, presented no songs until 15 minutes into the story—an unprecedented wait in musicals of the day.

Rodgers, Hart, and Herbert Fields used a Mark Twain novel as the basis for *A Connecticut Yankee* (1927). They had written it long before their *Garrick Gaieties* success but no producer had wanted it. Now, however, Lew Fields was happy to present the show, and it was their longest running hit of the 1920s. Their next show, *Chee-Chee* (1928), is sometimes jokingly called the "castration musical," since it features a Grand Eunuch's son who tries to remain "unqualified" for his father's post. As in Friml and Hammerstein's *Rose-Marie*, the collaborators did not list the songs in the program, announcing, "The musical numbers, some of them very short, are so interwoven with the story that it would be confusing for the audience to peruse a complete list." Truly, many of the numbers *were* short—some were only four bars long. They hoped this brevity would keep the show moving; the reality was that there was no time for the melodies to take hold in the audience's ears. *Chee-Chee* closed after four weeks.

In subsequent shows, Rodgers and Hart each displayed his personal craftsmanship. Rodgers wrote some astonishingly complex harmonies in *Spring Is Here* (1929), while Hart's lyrics in *Heads Up* (1929) included a number in Pig Latin. After spending several years in Hollywood, they returned to New York for a circus musical, *Jumbo* (1935). Staged by producer Billy Rose in the Hippodrome, a vast, barn-like theater, *Jumbo* cost $340,000. A seven-month run was sufficient to recoup only about half of its costs. (The show was hurt by Rose's refusal to allow any tunes from *Jumbo* to be broadcast on the radio.) Nevertheless, *Jumbo* was the first time that **George Abbott** (1887–1995) directed a musical, and it was Abbott's first collaboration with Rodgers and Hart (see the *Sidebar*: The Great Mr. Abbott).

Rodgers and Hart then asked George Abbott for some help with the book (which they had written themselves) for **On Your Toes**. Abbott also agreed to direct the production, but he grew impatient over various delays, and he abruptly quit. Rodgers and Hart hired another director, but after a disastrous Boston opening, Rodgers and Hart desperately telegraphed Abbott, begging him to come "fix" the show. Abbott soon arrived, watched that evening's performance—and described his reaction in his memoirs:

The book . . . was a mess; the story line had been destroyed by experimenting, and the actors were out of hand. I behaved ruthlessly to the cast to force them to play parts instead of fighting for

---

Sidebar: The Great Mr. Abbott

George Abbott was born in 1887 and died in 1995—at the age of 107. In fact, he was halfway to his 108th birthday when he passed away. The day before he died, he was still busy, working on revisions for a revival of *The Pajama Game*. In 1993, while Abbott was updating *Damn Yankees*, the writer Mark Steyn asked what the new script was like. Abbott hedged at first, and then said, "But it's better than what most 106-year-old writers are doing." Another perspective on Abbott's historical position came from director Hal Prince, who quipped, "Always remember, George was too old for World War One."

Abbott's longevity is mind-boggling, but the depth and breadth of his career during those 107 years was his truly remarkable achievement. Abbott started as an actor, but he got his first chance to be a **show doctor**—a person who is brought in to "save" (or "fix") a troubled production—in 1918, when his rescue of the play *Lightnin'* led to Broadway's longest run for seven years. From there Abbott turned to writing and directing for stage *and* film; his *All Quiet on the Western Front* won the Best Picture Oscar in 1930.

Abbott was already 48 when he presented his first musical, *Jumbo*. This genre lit a fire under him; over the next 27 years he staged 26 shows—and 22 of them were hits. During those years, there was only one two-week stretch in which he had *no* shows on Broadway. He established records that may never be broken: he had three simultaneous hits on Broadway at the age of 75; his 1983 revival of *On Your Toes* at age 96 made him the oldest director to stage a hit on Broadway, while the same show in London two years later (aged 98) earned him the equivalent record on the West End.

Abbott was clearly very, very good at what he did. As a show doctor (or **fixer**), he insisted on a strong book—a story that could stand alone without songs or dances. Like George M. Cohan's earlier thirst for "Speed! Speed!," Abbott had a horror of sequences that slowed down the pacing. Moreover, he wasn't afraid of innovation, as seen in three shows he created with Rodgers and Hart: the first truly integrated ballets (in *On Your Toes*, 1936); the first American musical based on Shakespeare (*The Boys from Syracuse*, 1938); and the first musical to feature a slimeball as the lead character (*Pal Joey*, 1940).

Abbott fostered Broadway careers for many others, including Leonard Bernstein, Frank Loesser, the team of Richard Adler and Jerry Ross, and Stephen Sondheim. Abbott was strong-willed and opinionated; not everyone agreed with all his decisions, but there was no one who did not respect his values and his theatrical intuition. As a tacit acknowledgment of his significant position, even as modes of address grew more relaxed in the last part of the twentieth century, he was always known as Mister Abbott. His contributions to the development of the twentieth-century musical are immeasurable.

material, and I straightened the book out by the simple device of putting it back the way I had written it in the first place.

Immediately, the show started to work, and it was soon ready to transfer to New York.

Rodgers and Hart had written the original story (see the **Plot Summary**) as a movie script with Fred Astaire in mind. Astaire declined the part of Junior Dolan, however, because he wouldn't be able to wear his trademark top hat and tails. The role went to Ray Bolger, who would go on to greater fame as the Scarecrow in the 1939 film version of *The Wizard of Oz*. Initially, Marilynn Miller was announced as playing the role of Vera Baronova, but Miller turned it down, and the ballerina Tamara Geva took over. Choreographer **George Balanchine** (1904–1983) was participating in a book musical for the first time. Balanchine had recently founded the American Ballet Company after emigrating from Europe, and Rodgers was a bit uncertain about how to work with a serious choreographer:

I didn't know a thing about choreography and told Balanchine that I was unsure how we should go about it. Did he devise his steps first and expect me to alter tempos wherever necessary, or did he fit his steps to the music as written? Balanchine smiled and with that wonderful Russian accent of his said simply, "You write. I put on."

Balanchine requested that his credit line in the program read, "Choreography by George Balanchine," rather than the more usual designations of "Dances by" or "Dance Director." Thus, the program made it clear that dance would be taken seriously. Dance had already played an important part in the dramas of earlier shows, while ballet had also begun to be featured in selected revues. Nevertheless, *On Your Toes* incorporated dance into the plot in one of the most coherent ways Broadway had yet seen.

Rodgers and Hart took the score and lyrics equally seriously, even while aspiring to write an entertaining musical comedy. For instance, "The Three B's" (**Musical Example 22**) is set in a music classroom, where students confuse classical works with the latest popular songs. Rodgers's score interweaves the classical themes Junior is trying to teach to his students. Junior gives his class an informal "listening identification" quiz, beginning with César Franck's *Symphony in D minor* at **1**, followed by an excerpt from *Les Préludes*, a programmatic orchestral work by Franz Liszt (**2**). The students bat about 50 percent on the listening quiz; although they identify the Franck symphony correctly, they mispronounce his name, and they completely confuse *Les Préludes* with a drinking song.

Sections **1** and **2** act as a vocal introduction to the remainder of the number, which is roughly in verse-chorus form and which presents a series of questions and confused answers. Sidney's response at **6**—that Shostakovich wrote *Lady Macbeth from Minsky*—is a typical error. The title of Shostakovich's opera (recently banned by the Soviet government) was *Lady Macbeth from the Mtsensk District*—not "Minksy's," an infamous New York burlesque house. At **8**, Sidney volunteers the misinformation that Puccini wrote "Poor Butterfly." Again, Sidney is wrong, but not entirely. Puccini's opera was *Madama*

Butterfly, but a popular song, "Poor Butterfly," was based on the same story. Like many "real" students, Sidney confused the original work with a derivative.

In the 1936 production, Junior asks an extended question (with plenty of clever "–inity" rhymes) at **9**. In the 1983 revival, Junior merely speaks his main question: "Who are the Three B's of Music?," while the orchestra plays the transitional music leading to the first chorus, or refrain, at **10**. The students all know the proper response here—the Three B's are Bach, Beethoven, and Brahms—but they also claim that these composers, with their "charms of Orpheus," have a somnolent effect that throws them "right into the arms of Morpheus" (the god of sleep)! The students maintain the stereotypes of musical class distinction here; classical music may be "good," but it's boring. (At **11**, in the middle of the refrain, Junior sneaks in another musical quotation: the loud chords that open Beethoven's Fifth Symphony.)

At **13**, the students are seeking a composer whose name ends in "-vitch," and "Borrah Minevitch" is promptly suggested—a comedy player who was currently a featured Hollywood performer along with his "Harmonica Rascals." (Lorenz Hart slipped up a bit here; "The Three B's" earlier made reference to ShostakoVICH, but this much more famous composer is overlooked at this point.) The song concludes with another lively repetition of the refrain at **14** (with the Beethoven symphony quotation again appearing at **15**). After this scene, it's not so hard to understand why Junior is willing to spend so much time with the ballet company instead of his lackluster students!

Tamara Geva and Ray Bolger dance "Slaughter on Tenth Avenue" in *On Your Toes*.
Museum of the City of New York.

"The Three B's" (which was rechristened "Questions and Answers" in the 1983 revival), is a song in which "the more you know, the funnier it seems." The text depends on various topical references for some of its humor. It also depends on an awareness of classical music for other laughs—for instance, the audience will enjoy the introductory section more if it knows the correct pronunciation of "Franck" or recognizes the musical quotations. The same is true for other aspects of *On Your Toes*: If an audience is familiar with vaudeville dance styles and with classical ballet, it can appreciate the stylistic contrasts between *Princess Zenobia* and *Slaughter on Tenth Avenue* (and the contrasting kinds of dance talent demonstrated by Junior and Morrosine). Because of this dependence on prior knowledge, "The Three B's" is a song that doesn't work for everyone. In other words, "The Three B's" may very well demonstrate the same kind of class distinctions that characterize so much of *On Your Toes*.

"The Three B's" is a song that expects the audience to *think* quite a bit (which had certainly not been the norm for prior musical comedies). Bit by bit, Rodgers and Hart began to pull their audience away from mindless entertainment by using intriguing rhyme schemes and word play, complex harmonies and musical forms, plot-enhancing dance, and storylines that challenged the audience. (Their crowning achievement would be *Pal Joey* [1940], to be discussed in Chapter 22, "New Achievements from Familiar Names.") Much of this trend, however, could still be laid at Kern's door, as Rodgers explained: "To me the greatest gratification allowed anyone is to be able to gather a large group of people under one roof, and through words and music, impel them to feel something deeply and strongly within themselves. This was Kern's mission and he accomplished it superbly." Despite the increased pressure to write for increasingly sophisticated audiences, however, Rodgers and Hart never forgot a fundamental objective in their shows: to be entertaining.

FURTHER READING

Abbott, George. *Mister Abbott*. New York: Random House, 1963.

Block, Geoffrey. *Enchanted Evenings: The Broadway Musical from* Show Boat *to* Sondheim. New York: Oxford University Press, 1997.

Gottfried, Martin. *Broadway Musicals*. New York: Abradale Press/Abrams, 1984.

Green, Stanley, ed. *Rodgers and Hammerstein Fact Book: A Record of Their Works Together and with Other Collaborators*. New York: The Lynn Farnol Group, 1980.

Hart, Dorothy, ed. *Thou Swell, Thou Witty: The Life and Lyrics of Lorenz Hart*. New York: Harper & Row, 1976.

Hyland, William G. *Richard Rodgers*. New Haven and London: Yale University Press, 1998.

Mordden, Ethan. *Make Believe: The Broadway Musical in the 1920s*. New York: Oxford University Press, 1997.

Nolan, Frederick. *Lorenz Hart: A Poet on Broadway*. New York: Oxford University Press, 1994.

Rodgers, Richard. *Musical Stages: An Autobiography*. New York: Random House, 1975. Reprinted New York: Da Capo Press, 1995.

Secrest, Meryle. *Somewhere for Me: A Biography of Richard Rodgers*. New York: Alfred A. Knopf, 2001.

Steven, Suskin. *Show Tunes: The Songs, Shows, and Careers of Broadway's Major Composers*. Revised and expanded 3rd edition. New York: Oxford University Press, 2000.

Taylor, Deems. *Some Enchanted Evenings: The Story of Rodgers and Hammerstein*. New York: Harper & Brothers, 1953. Reprinted Westport, Connecticut: Greenwood Press Publishers, 1972.

PLOT SUMMARY: *ON YOUR TOES*

In one sense, *On Your Toes* could be viewed as a show about class distinctions, but rather than overtly addressing social classes, *On Your Toes* depicts the snobbism that accompanies different forms of artistic entertainment. The first debate—between vaudeville and art music—opens the show: Lil and Phil Dolan disagree about the best path for their son, Junior, a **hoofer** (dancer). Should he join them on the vaudeville stage? His mother wants him to pursue the more "respectable" career of a music teacher. Junior himself unwittingly settles the argument—and exposes another class distinction—when Phil discovers that Junior has been dating a girl who's a member of a "number-two act." The Dolans receive *top* billing in vaudeville, and Junior shouldn't be caught dead consorting with lesser performers. Junior's fate is sealed; he must abandon the vaudeville circuit and train to become a music professor.

Some 15 years later, Junior is now in front of his music history class at Knickerbocker University. In "The Three B's" (**Musical Example 22**), his pupils reveal the same kind of confusions about historical composers that plague music students today! Two of Junior's students are promising composers, however; Miss Frankie Frayne is a songwriter, and Sidney Cohn is working on a jazz ballet score, *Slaughter on Tenth Avenue*. Here another class distinction is revealed: Junior values jazz more than Frankie's Tin Pan Alley style. But Frankie makes a deal with her teacher: if he helps her with her current song, she'll enlist the help of Peggy Porterfield, a wealthy society matron, to back Sidney's ballet.

Peggy supports the Russian Ballet, and the company has mixed reactions to *Slaughter*. Vera Baronova, the *prima ballerina* (the female star), is intrigued with the jazz ballet; she's miffed with her costar and unfaithful lover, Konstantine Morrosine, and Sidney's ballet calls for her to perform a striptease—an ideal way to punish Morrosine. The head of the ballet troupe, Sergei Alexandrovitch, is driven by yet another set of class distinctions; he feels a jazz ballet is not "elevated" enough.

Junior has begun to realize that he loves Frankie, but while he is at ballet rehearsals, he catches Vera's eye; she demonstrates the company's current ballet, *Princess Zenobia*, to him. He's able to follow the moves quickly, thanks to his old vaudeville dance training. On the ballet's opening night, a member of the chorus has been arrested, so Junior is immediately conscripted into putting on a costume and joining in.

In a panic, he starts to flub the part—but the audience thinks the humor is deliberate, and suddenly *Princess Zenobia* starts to enjoy much stronger ticket sales.

Although Junior loves Frankie, he needs be charming to Vera, since her support is needed to get Sidney's ballet to the stage. Frankie worries how deep Junior's feelings really are. A jealous Morrosine is also worried about Vera's interest in Junior. At last, rehearsals start for *Slaughter*, and Sergei discovers that Junior can dance the lead male role far better than Morrosine. Morrosine, who already thinks Junior has stolen

Vera's attention, is outraged at losing his position in the ballet company as well. His solution? Hire a hit man! Morrosine tells the gangster that everyone will be distracted during the ballet. The gunman positions himself in the front row of the audience, ready for his moment, and the ballet begins. A member of the ballet company hears about the scheme and hands Junior a note—during the ballet—explaining the danger. Junior realizes he needs to be a moving target, so he keeps dancing and dancing and dancing until at last the police arrive and Junior can collapse into Frankie's arms.

MUSICAL EXAMPLE 22

ON YOUR TOES
RICHARD RODGERS/LORENZ HART, 1936
"The Three B's"

Junior
1   Whom was this written by ?
Miss Wasservogel
By "Cesar Franck." [*pronounced "Caeser"*]
Junior
2   Pronounce it "Fronck." [*Plays a few bars of* Les Preludes] Name this for me, Joe McCall.
McCall
"We won't get home until morning."
Junior
You won't get home at all!
3   Now please name the Russians who love to use percussions:
Class
4   Tchaikovsky, Moszkowski, Mussorgsky, Stravinsky.
Junior
5   And what did Shostakovich write?
Sidney Cohn
"Lady Macbeth from Minsky."
Junior
6   Four masters I quote now, you tell me what they wrote now:
7   Puccini, Bellini, Von Suppe, von Bülow.
Cohn
8   Puccini wrote "Poor Butterfly."
Junior
That answer hits a new low!
9   [*spoken*: Who are the three B's of Music?]
Class
10   Bach, Beethoven and Brahms. Great examples of the charms of Orpheus,
Throw us right into the arms of Morpheus.
Junior
11   Johannes B., Ludwig van B. and Johann
Class
Be sure to sing their praise. You will never get the old diploma here
If they catch you whistling "La Paloma" here.
Junior
Two of them wrote symphonies, and one wrote psalms.
Class
Bach, Beethoven, and Herr Johannes Brahms.
12   Rossini, Bellini, Campanini, Tetrazzini, Cambini, Trentini, Martini, Paganini,
Stokowski, Godowsky, Levitski, Leschetitsky,
Wolf-Ferrari, Molinari, and the man who wrote "Sari."

Miss Wasservogel

13   There isn't one name ending in a "vitch."

Junior

You forgot Borrah Minnevitch!

Class

14   Bach, Beethoven and Brahms. Great examples of the charms of Orpheus,
Throw us right into the arms of Morpheus.

Junior

15   Johannes B., Ludwig van B. and Johann

Class

Be sure to sing their praise. You will never get the old diploma here
If they catch you whistling "La Paloma" here.
Two of them wrote symphonies, and one wrote psalms.
Bach, Beethoven, and Herr Johannes Brahms.

Chapter 18
Great Partnerships of the Early Book Musical: The Gershwins (1)

Like many other Broadway composers, **George Gershwin** (1898—1937) worked his way up through the Tin Pan Alley ranks. While attending an aunt's wedding, Gershwin had been thrilled by the orchestra's renditions of Jerome Kern's music; he immediately formed the ambition of learning to compose like Kern, since he felt Kern's show tunes were of a higher quality than the typical Tin Pan Alley song. Gershwin had started his musical career on the "Alley" in 1914, at the age of 15, when he left school to become a song plugger for Jerome H. Remick. The years at Remick's were invaluable for the young musician, but the job primarily cultivated his performance skills—not his writing abilities. In fact, when Gershwin submitted one of his tunes to Remick for consideration, they turned him down flat. Undaunted, he continued to write songs, often playing them for his listeners side by side with the works he was supposed to be playing from the Remick catalogue.

Gershwin was anxious to find an outlet for his compositional aspirations, and for a time it looked like he might find a place in Yiddish theater. Yiddish was a high German language spoken by many Jews in eastern Europe, and the language continued to be used in various pockets of New York and other cities. As immigrant populations swelled in size, an entire network of Yiddish theaters developed, running in tandem with the English-speaking theaters of Broadway (in addition to the vaudeville houses and the theaters catering to African American clientele). Gershwin attended many Yiddish performances at the National Theater in New York, and the impresario proposed a collaboration between Gershwin and another young composer, Sholom Secunda. Secunda balked, however; he had been trained at what would become Juilliard, and although Gershwin was a tremendous improviser on the piano, he didn't *read* music terribly well. Secunda therefore viewed Gershwin as somewhat primitive. Moreover, Secunda had already had a song published and he simply felt that Gershwin was not in his league.

Gershwin continued to play his tunes to sympathetic listeners, and the vaudeville star Sophie Tucker recommended one song to the publisher Harry von Tilzer (who had composed "[I Wants to Be] A Actor Lady" for *In Dahomey*—which, in 1916, led to Gershwin's first publication. Sigmund Romberg added another Gershwin song to *The Passing Show of 1916*, giving Gershwin his first Broadway credit. Remick's finally published one of Gershwin's pieces for piano in 1917. Gershwin's enthusiasm for song-plugging had long since faded; he felt, "Something was taking me away [from

Remick's]. As I look back, it's very clear that I wanted to be closer to production-music—the kind Jerome Kern was writing." Gershwin left Remick's to be the pianist at a vaudeville house, but quit the first evening after a disastrous debut. Soon, however, he was hired as a rehearsal pianist for a musical with tunes by Kern and Victor Herbert. This job went so well that Gershwin was kept on salary even after the show opened (when rehearsals had ended); members of the cast performed at Sunday evening concerts at the theater with Gershwin as accompanist. The show manager brought Gershwin to the attention of Max Dreyfus, who ran the publishing company T. B. Harms. Dreyfus examined the young composer's portfolio and then made an unusual offer: he would give Gershwin the rather handsome salary of $35 a week, and Gershwin's only duty was to compose songs. If Harms chose to publish any of them, he would get the customary royalties of three cents a copy. Gershwin was delighted to accept.

It was during this period that Gershwin approached Irving Berlin about a job. Berlin didn't read music, so he needed a musical secretary to transcribe his compositional ideas into notation. Berlin was very impressed with Gershwin's skill and offered him a job—but Berlin also advised the younger composer not to take the offer. "You've got more talent than an arranger needs," Berlin said, and Gershwin agreed that he should continue to try to forge ahead as a composer.

In 1919, the 20-year-old Gershwin got his first opportunity to be *the* composer for a Broadway production. Gershwin's real break, however, came early in the following year, when Al Jolson recorded a Gershwin song, propelling it into an enormous hit—both the recording and the sheet music sold more than a million copies. The income from this one tune allowed Gershwin to concentrate on writing complete Broadway shows instead of piecemeal interpolations.

Gershwin's reputation continued to grow with his scores to the *George White's Scandals* between 1920 and 1924. He worked with various lyricists for these revues, including his brother **Ira Gershwin** (1896–1983). Most of Gershwin's songs did well, but one contribution to the 1922 *Scandals* was *not* a hit; this was a short one-act opera called *Blue Monday*. Featuring African American characters (although performed by white singers in blackface), the story was tragic, similar in many ways to the stark *verismo* operas of Puccini and his peers. White pulled the opera after the first night's performance, arguing (correctly) not only that the piece was too long for a revue, but also that it depressed the audience.

Although *Blue Monday* bombed, its jazz-oriented score and subject matter made it an interesting antecedent to Gershwin's *Porgy and Bess* 13 years later. Moreover, throughout his later career, Gershwin suffered from what he called "composer's stomach" (which his friends called hypochondria), and he traced the first appearance of this indigestion to his nervousness over the mini-opera's debut.

By merging jazz with classical music, *Blue Monday* also set the stage for one of Gershwin's most famous compositions, *Rhapsody in Blue*, which premiered in 1924. This symphonic merger between popular and "art" music ensured Gershwin's lasting renown (and gave him a steady source of income for the next decade). It also demonstrated the increasingly pervasive effect jazz was having on American music (see the **Sidebar**: All Jazzed Up—New Sounds on the Musical Stage).

But what of George Gershwin's older brother Ira all this time? He worked as a photographer's darkroom assistant and as a receiving clerk; he even spent several months as the cashier for a traveling circus run by a cousin! Ira wrote sporadically, but he had been unable to earn a living as a writer. He had occasionally collaborated on lyrics for songs by George and by other composers, but for some time he chose to use the pseudonym Arthur Francis (the names of the other Gershwin siblings) so it would not appear that he was trying to climb on George's coattails.

The first joint effort of George and Ira's to reach Broadway was *Lady, Be Good!* in 1924. The show brought the brother-and-sister dance team, Fred and Adele Astaire, to full-fledged stardom, and their tap-dancing sparked a rage that lasted all through the 1920s. *Lady, Be Good!*, which included hits such as "Fascinating Rhythm," ran a very satisfying 330 performances, but the next collaboration of George and Ira had the shortest Broadway run of any work by George. Late in 1925, with another lyricist, Gershwin wrote the score for an operetta—a somewhat odd project, considering his rising fame as a composer of jazz-tinged popular tunes—but the operetta did surprisingly well.

George reunited with Ira for his next show, *Oh, Kay!* (1926), and they would continue to work together up to the end of George's life. Not all of their subsequent shows were hits, but nearly every production introduced at least one hit song. *Oh, Kay!* had "Someone to Watch Over Me," and although *Strike Up the Band* (1927) closed during its tryout tour, it included "The Man I Love" and of course its title song. *Funny Face* (1927) also featured a hit title song as well as "He Loves and She Loves," "My One and Only," and "'S Wonderful." Their next project was *Rosalie* (1928), but here George wrote only about half the score; the other tunes were by Sigmund Romberg. Romberg was hurriedly working on another operetta, and the Gershwins had agreed to help him finish *Rosalie*. Despite its hodgepodge nature, *Rosalie* worked—and in it the Gershwins found a place for "How Long Has This Been Going On?," a song they had dropped from *Funny Face*.

George and Ira hit a bit of a dry spell with their next two shows. The team's good fortune returned with a revised version of *Strike Up the Band*—the piece that had bombed so badly on tour in 1927 that they hadn't even bothered bringing it to New York. George S. Kaufman's original book

Ethel Merman stars in *Girl Crazy*.
Photofest.

was surprisingly bitter; it was a satire on war and the idiotic reasons for starting wars. Even with a Gershwin score and Red Nichols's jazz band, 1927 audiences hadn't liked the sardonic story about America battling Switzerland over imported cheese. Audiences had changed by 1930, especially after the stock market crash of the previous year; the lyricist Alan Jay Lerner later reminisced about the state of affairs:

> *In the United States by the end of 1930, 4.5 million wandered the streets in search of employment and filled makeshift soup kitchens across the country for nourishment to keep alive. By the end of that same year, 1,300 banks had failed, culminating with the collapse of the Bank of the United States with its 60 branches and 400,000 depositors. . . . Yet in that first year of the Depression, thirty-two musicals opened, only five less than the year before. . . . But the humour and subject matter of the best of the musical comedies immediately reflected the new and tragic circumstances of life. Gone for ever were the silly, skittish plots of the Flapper Age. Without losing any of its humour, comedy became deftly edged with satire, poking good-natured fun at politicians, government, the rich, business, and the human plight.*

Morrie Ryskind had overhauled Kaufman's original book, producing a story that was gentler and less cynical; the war was now over imported chocolate, and the battle took place in a dream of the hero. The Gershwins overhauled the music as well, keeping only seven songs of the original 15.

They reused a song from another show and also wrote 13 new tunes. Red Nichols's band was again the **pit orchestra**, performing in the "pit" just in front of the stage. This time, the strong book, the effective tunes, excellent performances, and a changed socioeconomic climate combined to establish *Strike Up the Band* as a hit at last—the first hit for the Gershwins in the 1930s.

Their next show, **Girl Crazy**, was also a hit, although it contradicts Lerner's assertion that "gone for ever were the silly, skittish plots of the Flapper Age" (see the **Plot Summary**). The simplistic storyline was counterbalanced by the many great tunes in the score as well as some strong performances. Ginger Rogers, for instance, sang "But Not for Me," "Could You Use Me?," and "Embraceable You." (Rogers had a little trouble with choreography for this last song, but Fred Astaire had stopped by to see a rehearsal. He took her out to the lobby to show her a few steps to use—thereby creating the partnership of Rogers and Astaire for the first time.) The Red Nichols jazz orchestra included Benny Goodman, Glenn Miller, Gene Krupa, Jack Teagarden, and Jimmy Dorsey—a phenomenal assembly of players.

One member of the cast made her debut in the show; Ethel Zimmerman was a stenographer who had been appearing at weddings, parties, and in small nightclubs. She dropped the first syllable of her last name to become Ethel Merman. Producer Vinton Freedley was impressed by her ability to project—without a microphone—all the way to the last row of seats. (Lerner recalled that Irving Berlin warned him, "If you ever write lyrics for Ethel Merman they had better be

---

Sidebar: All Jazzed Up—New Sounds on the Musical Stage

George Gershwin is often credited with introducing **jazz** onto the musical stage, but he did not do it alone. Nor, if the truth be told, does musical theater present "real" jazz, for at the heart of most jazz performance is **improvisation**. In improvisation, jazz musicians take a particular element of a tune—its melody or, very often, its harmonies—and ad lib new music that "fits" with the borrowed material. An improvisation measures a jazz musician's artistry—and the improvisation varies every time. When a jazz ensemble plays, performers take turns improvising on the same borrowed material, each person handling it in a unique fashion. Knowledgeable listeners appreciate the pressure that each soloist faces—to produce a compelling performance "on the spot"—and generally applaud after each soloist finishes. In this sense, jazz is not really "popular" music. As is true for classical music, the listener needs to possess a certain degree of understanding in order to appreciate the performance fully.

When composers borrow jazz elements for use in musical theater, they usually do not expect the stage performers to improvise. Instead, the composer adopts some other characteristic jazz techniques in order to give the stage tune a jazz "feel." Jazz numbers often use a **swing rhythm**—a compound subdivision sensation—and syncopation is also very common. Jazz performers also employ **blue notes**, in which certain pitches are performed just a bit lower or higher than would be considered "in tune," adding a subtle tension to the music. Instruments such as the saxophone or muted trumpet (or trombone) can give jazz numbers a distinctive timbre. When a musical theater number employs some or all of these devices, theater audiences (and critics) perceive the piece as being a "jazz" song.

Some early listeners resisted jazz style on Broadway; one critic complained, "There's nothing in the piece that is real music. Jazz, yes. Any amount of it, but jazz isn't music. Not by a long shot." Even some musicians adopted an "ignore it and it will go away" attitude; John Philip Sousa maintained that Beethoven would survive far longer than "this passing fancy," and, as Chapter 13, "The Princess Shows" relates, Kern probably doomed one of his shows by refusing to allow its tunes to be reworked in a jazz style. Nevertheless, Broadway audiences soon developed a taste for the jazz-tinged shows written by Gershwin and others, and this new style gradually pushed the old-fashioned operetta into the shade. Ironically, many jazz-style Broadway tunes have since become favorites of jazz musicians, including "I Got Rhythm"—which is so linked in people's minds with "jazz" that many listeners are surprised to learn that it originated in a Broadway musical!

good, because *everyone* is going to hear them.") Freedley took her over to Gershwin's apartment, where Gershwin played some of *Girl Crazy*'s tunes for her. Merman recalled,

> When he played "I Got Rhythm," he told me, "If there's anything about this you don't like, I'll be happy to change it." There was nothing about that song I didn't like. . . . I smiled and nodded, but I didn't say anything. I was too busy thinking how to phrase the music. Gershwin seemed puzzled at my silence. Finally he said again, "If there's anything about these songs you don't like, Miss Merman, I'll be happy to make changes." It wasn't that; it was only that I was flabbergasted. Through the fog that had wrapped itself around me, I heard myself say, "They'll do very nicely, Mr. Gershwin." There were those who thought my reply funny when it was repeated to them, as if I'd given the great Gershwin the old hauteur treatment. I was so drunk with the glory of it all that I could have said anything, but whatever I said, I meant it to be grateful and humble. That's for sure.

One could argue that Merman expressed her appreciation for the song by helping to make it one of the show's great hits as well as one of Gershwin's best-known tunes overall.

"I Got Rhythm" seems such a perfectly balanced tune that it's surprising to learn that Ira Gershwin wrestled with its lyrics for some time. The normal working process for the Gershwins was for George to write the tune first, and then Ira would craft poetry to fit the music. Ira later described the struggle he had with "I Got Rhythm":

> Filling in the 73 syllables of the refrain wasn't as simple as it sounds. For over two weeks I kept fooling around with various titles and with sets of double rhymes for the trios of short two-foot lines. I'd ad lib a dummy to show what I was at:

> Roly-Poly,
> Eating solely
> Ravioli,
> Better watch your diet or bust.
> Lunch or dinner,
> You're a sinner.
> Please get thinner.
> Losing all that fat is a must.

> Yet, no matter what series of double rhymes—even pretty good ones—I tried, the results were not quite satisfactory; they seemed at best to give a pleasant and jingly Mother Goose quality to a tune which should throw its weight around more. Getting nowhere, I then found myself not bothering with the rhyme scheme I'd considered necessary (aaab, cccb) and experimenting with non-rhyming lines like (dummy): "Just go forward; / Don't look backward; / And you'll soon be / Winding up ahead of the game." This approach felt stronger, and finally I arrived at the present refrain (the rhymed verse came later), with only "more—door" and "mind him—find him" the rhymes. Though there is nothing remarkable about all this, it was a bit daring for me who usually depended on rhyme insurance.

Ira also explained his deliberate choice to use the ungrammatical title:

> In some entertainment reviews and on some disc labels this song is called "I've Got Rhythm." I appreciate the correctors' efforts to formalize the title, but I'm sticking with the more direct "I Got Rhythm" for this tune. . . . In the title and refrain of this song (also in "I Got Plenty o' Nuthin'") "got" is heard in its most colloquial form—the one used for the present tense instead of "have," and the one going back to my childhood: e.g., "I got a toothache" didn't mean "I had a toothache," but only

George and Ira Gershwin at work.
Photofest.

"I have" one. Thumbing through many authorities on usage, style, and dialect, I find no discussion of "got" as a complete substitute for "have." This is somewhat surprising when one considers, say, how often and for how many years the spiritual "All o' God's Chillun Got Shoes" ("I got shoes, you got shoes") has been heard.

The resulting song falls into a fairly conventional verse-chorus form, with two appearances of the chorus. The opening verse is generally sung fairly slowly, in a bluesy style. Appropriately, therefore, Gershwin calls for a **blue note** on the words *sigh*, *song*, and *lot* (see the **Sidebar**: All Jazzed Up—New Sounds on the Musical Stage.)

The chorus itself is in song form—*a-a-b-a'*. The final *a* is a "prime" version, slightly longer than the first two *a*'s, because it contains an extra repetition of the final question, "Who could ask for anything more?" The catchy, syncopated rhythm heard on the word *rhythm* unifies the song; the rhythm is borrowed from "The Charleston," a song that initiated a dance craze that swept the country. ("The Charleston," composed by James P. Johnson, had been introduced in a 1923 African American musical called *Runnin' Wild*.) The second syllable of *rhythm* (like the syllable *-ton* in "Charleston") slightly anticipates the second beat of the bar, giving the rhythm the sensation of pushing ahead. The same **Charleston rhythm** is heard on *music*, *my man*, *daisies*, *pastures*, and so forth. The Gershwins capitalized on the danceable feeling of this rhythm by specifically labeling the interlude between the two choruses as a dance.

When the melody of the chorus returns, the lyrics heard in the first chorus are repeated as well. In order to make this exact repetition of words and music interesting, the singer in the role of Kate generally modifies the second chorus in the manner of a jazz improvisation (although a true improvisation is made up on the spot, while a theater performer would generally repeat the *same* modification at many performances). Ethel Merman described how she wowed her audiences:

As I went into the second chorus of "I Got Rhythm," I held a note for 16 bars while the orchestra played the melodic line—a big tooty thing—against the note I was holding. By the time I'd held that note for four bars the audience was applauding. They applauded through the whole chorus and I did several encores. It seemed to do something to them. Not because it was sweet or beautiful, but because it was exciting.

Needless to say, Merman's version of "I Got Rhythm" was a guaranteed showstopper.

Although the title *Girl Crazy* was applied to three movies—including a 1943 version starring Judy Garland and Mickey Rooney—the storyline was changed substantially in each film. *Girl Crazy* was revamped as the stage musical *Crazy for You* in 1992, but again the plot was changed, and only five songs were retained (the remainder

of the score was drawn from other popular tunes by the Gershwins).

The book was a much more important factor in the Gershwins' next show, *Of Thee I Sing* (1931)—in fact, *Of Thee I Sing* was the first Broadway musical to win a Pulitzer Prize for Drama, and it was the first musical to have the text of its book published separately. (See the **Sidebar**: The Role of the Book.) The libretto was written by Kaufman and Ryskind (who had each written one of the versions of *Strike Up the Band*). The Pulitzer committee named only Kaufman, Ryskind, and Ira Gershwin as the award recipients, omitting George Gershwin on the basis that he did not contribute to the actual story. The irony of this omission is that George's music is *very* important to the story—*Of Thee I Sing* was the most integrated show he had ever written, because the majority of the tunes were written *after* the general plot had been hashed out. Most of the songs are true "book songs"; they make sense only in connection with the storyline. Moreover, many of the songs are linked together into extended, coherent scenes, and recitative is used at times as well. In fact, although *Of Thee I Sing* was initially billed as a musical comedy, the vocal score designated it as the "Pulitzer Prize Operetta." It has much in common with the Gilbert and Sullivan operettas, not only in its integrated songs and occasional recitative, but also in its skillful satirical treatment of politics and the "American way of life." The Pulitzer Committee received much criticism for the exclusion of George, and many years later—in 1998—the committee awarded a special prize in honor of the 100th anniversary of Gershwin's birth.

The show's first tune, "Wintergreen for President," illustrates the multifaceted ways in which the Gershwins' score and text served the story. The tune is march-like, perfectly suited for a campaign parade. Its minor mode, however, hints that trouble's afoot. As the chorus enters, carrying placards that announce "VOTE FOR PROSPERITY AND SEE WHAT YOU GET," "WINTERGREEN—THE FLAVOR LASTS," and "A VOTE FOR WINTERGREEN IS A VOTE FOR WINTERGREEN," they start proclaiming their simple campaign slogan, "Wintergreen for President." The three words of the title represent 20 percent of the song's 15-word text, making the poetry—according to Ira Gershwin, who investigated the issue—"one of the shortest lyrics in all songdom."

Gradually, the song grows more and more chaotic (perhaps to resemble the typical presidential campaign). George Gershwin quotes phrases from John Philip Sousa's march "Stars and Stripes Forever", "Tammany" (a ragtime-era song that had been all the rage in 1905), "The Sidewalks of New York" (sometimes better known by its opening words, "East side, west side . . ."), "A Hot Time in the Old Town Tonight," and "Hail, Hail, the Gang's All Here." Technically, this last melody is the policemen's tune ("Tarantara! Tarantara!") from Gilbert and Sullivan's *The Pirates of Penzance*, but American audiences had long since learned the tune with newer (slightly ribald) words by D. A. Esrom.

The mishmash of popular tunes within this campaign march evokes the many political speeches in which the candidate strings together various clichés, all of which "sound good" but have no overall meaning. Moreover, the historian Deena Rosenberg argues that a subtle psychological message is imbedded in "Wintergreen for President":

> *"Wintergreen" is an appropriately hybrid tune. The music to the "Wintergreen for President" line, hummed without words, sounds like a Jewish prayer, and the rapid switching between minor and major in other parts of the refrain suggests Irish folk song. After all, doesn't Wintergreen love the Irish and the Jews?*

Oscar Hammerstein II called "Wintergreen for President" the perfect union of text with music, explaining that if you think of the words, the tune comes to mind, and if you hear the melody alone, the tune instantly makes you recall the lyrics.

Of Thee I Sing never loses track of this opening energy in the course of the show; the book and lyrics are humorous parodies of American life, while George Gershwin's score subtly lampoons many different musical styles. The beauty contest, the inauguration/wedding, and the impeachment proceedings are opportunities for operatic ensembles; Mary sings a mock-Viennese waltz in "I'm About to Be a Mother," while numbers like "Of Thee I Sing, Baby" reflect a clear jazz influence. (In a bit of insider humor, Gershwin quotes from his own symphonic work, *An American in Paris*, when the French Ambassador appears with his entourage.) Audiences responded enthusiastically to this unusual work, and the show played 441 performances—the longest run of any Gershwin show. The show also saved Irving Berlin's Music Box Theatre, which had been teetering financially from the impact of the Depression. Moreover, by demonstrating that musicals did not have to follow a boy-meets-girl formula to succeed, *Of Thee I Sing* encouraged other writers to tackle unconventional topics.

Reluctantly, the Gershwins agreed to write another show, *Pardon My English*, for Freedley and his coproducer, Alex A. Aarons. The Gershwins didn't like the book and audiences didn't either; it closed after 46 performances. Freedley fled the country for a time to elude his creditors (although he would return in 1934 to reestablish himself with Cole Porter's *Anything Goes*), while Aarons never produced another Broadway show. Fortunately for the Gershwins, however, their earnings from their previous successes—especially *Of Thee I Sing*—meant that the flop did not do them much damage.

Of Thee I Sing's popularity was not sufficient to ensure the success of a sequel, however. Although the same team of creators reunited for *Let 'Em Eat Cake* (1933), and although it featured many of the same performers, the sequel fizzled after 90 performances. *Of Thee I Sing* had poked fun at existing American rituals, but *Let 'Em Eat Cake* was a "what-if" depiction of Wintergreen as the leader of a fascist nation. Not only was this a harder topic to satirize, but it also came uncomfortably close to home, since the first Batista revolution was then taking place in nearby Cuba. Like the first version of *Strike Up the Band*, the subject matter was too uncomfortable for the audiences of its day.

It seemed for a time that the Gershwin magic had come to an end, but *Porgy and Bess* (the focus of Chapter 19, "Great Partnerships of the Early Book Musical. The Gershwins (2)")

Sidebar: The Role of the Book

"Rodgers and Hart and _____?" "Lerner and Loewe and _____?" Book writers of musicals never seem to get much attention, but they contribute an essential element to musical theater. George Abbott always argued that a strong book was primary; if it couldn't stand on its own, good songs were useless in saving a production. In many ways, the book is the skeleton upon which the rest of the show is built. Theater scholar Richard Kislan cites five dramatic elements within the book: **character**, **plot**, **situation**, **dialogue**, and **theme**. Collectively they determine the type of show that the audience will see.

The characters are, of course, the *people* in a show; the book writer helps to establish how believable they are (or aren't). The plot is comprised of the dramatic events that move the characters from one situation to the next, while the situations are the unstable moments within the plot that have to be resolved. The characters communicate by means of dialogue and songs; a good librettist can balance the two forms of communication. (Sometimes, a book writer does his job *too* well; many a lyricist has confessed to "lifting" effective dialogue from the book and using those lines as song lyrics!) Kislan points out that the song should be the focus of the scene; if the dialogue doesn't propel the performers forward to the song, then perhaps the property really shouldn't be a musical in the first place! The theme is probably the most elusive of the musical's elements, but it might be viewed as the "message" communicated by the musical. The theme is also the element that has received increasing attention over the years, as book writers have striven to "say something" in their shows; a traditional song-and-dance approach just is not enough of a "theme" to satisfy many contemporary writers.

Not all elements get equal amounts of emphasis in every show; in fact, it would be difficult to find two book musicals that use exactly the same balance of materials. Some characters remain more two-dimensional—or "stock"—than others. Plots can be fast paced or can proceed quite slowly. In the "sung-through" approach used by many recent musicals, dialogue vanishes altogether. One thing that *is* typical is that the book writer's billing usually comes third (if he or she is credited at all!), even though the librettist's work is usually the first that needs to be done during the musical's creation and often is the most important element in determining the production's success or failure.

was yet to come. Although this next Broadway collaboration would not reach "hit" status either, posterity would establish this work, their last show together, as one of the most interesting works—and perhaps the greatest—they would ever write.

FURTHER READING

Carnovale, Norbert. *George Gershwin: A Bio-Bibliography*. (Bio-Bibliographies in Music, Number 76; Donald L. Hixon, series advisor.) Westport, Connecticut: Greenwood Press, 2000.

Ewen, David. *A Journey to Greatness: The Life and Music of George Gershwin*. London: W. H. Allen, 1956.

Furia, Philip. *Ira Gershwin: The Art of the Lyricist*. New York: Oxford University Press, 1996.

Gershwin, Ira. *Lyrics on Several Occasions: A Selection of Stage & Screen Lyrics Written for Sundry Situations; and Now Arranged in Arbitrary Categories. To Which Have Been Added Many Informative Annotations & Disquisitions on Their Why & Wherefore, Their Whom-For, Their How; and Matters Associative*. New York: Alfred A. Knopf, 1959.

Gilbert, Steven E. *The Music of Gershwin*. New Haven and London: Yale University Press, 1995.

Hischak, Thomas S. *Word Crazy: Broadway Lyricists from Cohan to Sondheim*. New York: Praeger, 1991.

Jablonski, Edward. *Gershwin*. London: Simon & Schuster, 1988.

Kimball, Robert, ed. *The Complete Lyrics of Ira Gershwin*. London: Pavilion Books Ltd., 1993.

Kislan, Richard. *The Musical: A Look at the American Musical Theater*. New, revised, expanded edition. New York and London: Applause Books, 1995.

Lerner, Alan Jay. *The Musical Theatre: A Celebration*. New York: Da Capo Press, 1986.

Merman, Ethel. *Who Could Ask For Anything More, as told to Pete Martin*. New York: Doubleday, 1955.

Rosenberg, Deena. *Fascinating Rhythm: The Collaboration of George and Ira Gershwin*. New York: Dutton, 1991. Ann Arbor: University of Michigan Press, 1997.

Sandrow, Nahma. *Vagabond Stars: A World History of Yiddish Theater*. New York: Harper & Row, 1977.

Schwartz, Charles. *Gershwin: His Life and Music*. Indianapolis and New York: The Bobbs-Merrill Company, 1973.

PLOT SUMMARY: *GIRL CRAZY*

"Girl crazy" is the diagnosis, and Danny Churchill is the wealthy New York playboy who is suffering from the condition. The cure? Ship Danny out West—to the all-male town of Custerville, Arizona. Danny invites the cab driver Gieber Goldfarb to drive him the whole way (after inviting an entire Broadway chorus line to come join him). Other New York friends also show up, including Tess Harding and the man who loves her, Sam Mason. Danny is inspired to transform his hotel into a glamorous dude ranch, complete with a gambling casino. The casino entertainment comes in the form of Kate, a high-energy singer who is married to gambler Slick Fothergill.

Danny starts to pursue the local postmistress, Molly Gray. Meanwhile, Kate is not too happy to find that Slick seems to be pursuing other female interests too. After Kate catches him in a compromising situation, Slick manages to explain the situation, and the relieved Kate goes on to perform the exuberant "I've Got Rhythm" Fortunately for their marriage, Slick convinces Kate of his love for her—and Danny accomplishes the same thing with Molly, so the show ends with both couples happily united.

Chapter 19
Great Partnerships of the Early Book Musical: The Gershwins (2)

Even if the Gershwins had not written their many previous works together, their final stage collaboration, **Porgy and Bess**, would merit their place in musical theater history. This powerful drama has been the most discussed work of the Gershwins' entire theatrical output. One of the fundamental questions about *Porgy and Bess* is its genre; the evidence, as discussed in the **Sidebar**: Opera versus Musical, is mixed.

Whether one chooses to call *Porgy and Bess* an opera or a musical, there were precedents that helped to set the stage for a show about African Americans. One of the musical comedy antecedents, *In Dahomey* (1902), was discussed in Chapter 12, "Challenges to Operetta," and there were sporadic appearances of other black musical comedies. A few African American revues had also played on Broadway. (Hollywood produced its first African American film musical in 1929, when MGM released *Hallelujah*.)

There had been previous black operas as well, although not all of them made it to the stage. The great ragtime composer Scott Joplin had trouble getting either of his stage works performed professionally during his lifetime. *Four Saints in Three Acts* (1934) featured black performers, although the plot did not specifically call for African Americans. Donald Heywood presented his operetta *Africana* later that same year, although it folded after three performances.

With this spotty history for African American productions, it is surprising that George Gershwin believed that *Porgy*, a best-selling 1925 novel, could make an effective musical production. Nevertheless, Gershwin wrote to the novel's author, **DuBose Heyward** (1885–1940), with his belief that *Porgy* could "sing." Heyward was delighted, but then discovered that his wife Dorothy was secretly turning *Porgy* into a play script; Heyward felt her effort should take precedence. The Theatre Guild produced the play in 1927, and it did quite well, although one critic claimed, "It seems all bits and pieces, and nothing but. Or else nothing but the beginnings of the opera George Gershwin hopes to make of it." Evidently Gershwin had been talking *very* freely about his idea!

Five years later, Gershwin was still talking about it, so Heyward wrote and said, "I would be tremendously interested in working on the book with you. I have some new material that might be introduced, and once I got your ideas as to the general form suitable for the musical version, I am pretty sure that I could do you a satisfactory story." Gershwin's busy schedule led to some delays, and for a time

it looked like a musical version of *Porgy* would be written by Kern and Hammerstein for Al Jolson instead. However, they pulled out, and Gershwin and Heyward resumed their collaboration.

Gershwin and Heyward signed a contract with the Theatre Guild in October 1933. Heyward then applied himself in earnest to creating a libretto (see the **Plot Summary**). Called *Porgy and Bess* to distinguish it from the Theatre Guild's earlier play, the libretto owed a great deal to Dorothy's plot modifications. In particular, she changed the ending: In the novel, when Porgy returns to Catfish Row and learns that Bess is gone, he simply gives up. Dorothy's version sent Bess to New York with Sporting Life, while Porgy vows to go after her even though he'd have to travel by goat cart—giving a slightly more optimistic ending to the unhappy story.

Although Heyward was writing the libretto, the song lyrics were another matter. Heyward wrote to Gershwin, "As to the lyrics, I am not so sure until I know more definitely what you have in mind. Perhaps your brother Ira would want to do them. Or maybe we could do them together. . . ." In the end, Ira and Heyward worked jointly on some of the song lyrics and individually on others.

The opening song of *Porgy and Bess*, "Summertime," was given its words by Heyward. Clara's lullaby to her baby is a perfect example of a prop song; it is diegetic singing that the *other* residents of Catfish Row would regard as "singing" as well. Because it *is* a lullaby, it uses a simple structure: a strophic form of two verses with a short, melismatic coda on *Ah* sung by the chorus. Each strophe follows a show tune pattern of *a-b-a-c*. The gently floating quality of "Summertime" makes it seem deceptively easy. In reality, the tune is operatic; it requires a long series of very high notes from the soprano, who must avoid becoming shrill, since no infant would find a strident voice very soothing! The first actress to play Clara was Abbie Mitchell, a trained opera singer who was married to Will Marion Cook (composer of *In Dahomey*); a surviving rehearsal tape reveals that she sang the tune in a beautifully light, ethereal fashion.

"Summertime" is a tune that functions as a sort of *leitmotif* in *Porgy and Bess*; it appears four times during the story. It is heard again as the crap game grows more and more heated; the simultaneous shouts sung by the angry men create a polyphonic texture with the "Summertime" tune. Clara sings the lullaby again during the hurricane, and Bess sings it after the storm has taken the lives of the infant's

---

Sidebar: Opera versus Musical—The *Porgy and Bess* Debate

Is *Porgy and Bess* an opera? Or is it a musical? George Gershwin himself frequently called the work a "folk opera." This style label presents problems, since "real" **folk** music has no known author and is usually uncomplicated music. *Porgy and Bess*'s music is seldom simple; in fact, it often requires much expertise to perform, which supports an operatic label. A separate problem, some writers maintain, is that white composers shouldn't presume to "speak" for African Americans. Composer Virgil Thompson argued, "Folk-lore subjects recounted by an outsider are only valid as long as the folk in question is unable to speak for itself, which is certainly not true of the American Negro in 1935."

Whether or not *Porgy and Bess* should have been written in the first place, the question of its genre remains. Several aspects support the opera designation: not only are there sizable vocal demands in many of the songs, but the show is filled with extended passages of recitative. Heyward was opposed to the recitatives: "I feel more and more that all dialogue should be spoken. It is fast moving, and we will cut it to the bone, but this will give the opera speed and tempo." Gershwin won out, however, and the recitatives stayed in. Moreover, Gershwin wrote evocative recurring melodies, linking the story together like *leitmotifs* and creating a sense of wide-reaching connections between events. In addition, Gershwin did the majority of the **orchestrations** himself, meaning that not only did he write the melody and harmony for a song (or aria!), he decided which instruments should be featured during the tune. Many Broadway composers leave the orchestrations to another collaborator, whereas most opera composers create their own orchestrations. (Gershwin ended up calling for a large number of orchestral players, which added to the expense of every performance.)

At the same time, there are arguments for labeling *Porgy and Bess* a musical. One is that Gershwin chose to present the work on Broadway. It is true that Gershwin had had some early discussions with the Metropolitan Opera, but the Met doubted it could find sufficient African American singers to cast the production; it proposed a presentation of white singers in blackface. Gershwin hadn't liked that approach when his *Blue Monday* had briefly appeared in a 1922 revue, and he refused to go down that path again. On Broadway, *Porgy and Bess* did have

an all-black cast (except for the performers playing the few "white" roles), but the vocal training of the singers varied wildly. Some performers were the products of music conservatories, while others had to have their parts taught to them by rote. No opera impresario would have tolerated some of *Porgy and Bess*'s most unpolished singers, and musically, many numbers in *Porgy and Bess* are catchy, upbeat affairs that are indistinguishable from many products of Tin Pan Alley.

The show's subsequent history doesn't clarify the issue. Advocates for a "musical theater" designation cite the first revival of *Porgy and Bess*, produced by Cheryl Crawford in 1942. Crawford modified the show in several ways: She reduced the size of the chorus; she had the orchestrations reworked so a smaller orchestra could be employed; and, most drastically, she converted the recitatives to spoken dialogue, explaining, "When I had seen the 1935 production I had been critical of only one element, the recitatives, which, I felt, were out of keeping with the black milieu." In all, Crawford cut about 45 minutes from the show's running time—and increased the show's profits enormously. The revival ran for eight months (doubling the original run) and then toured 47 cities. With the recitatives gone, *Porgy and Bess* seemed much more in keeping with conventional musical theater works.

Later, however, *Porgy and Bess* (with recitatives restored) embarked on a four-year worldwide tour sponsored by the U.S. State Department. In this very successful production, *Porgy and Bess* was billed as an opera and was presented in opera houses; in fact, it was the first work by an American-born composer to appear at *La Scala*, Milan's premiere opera venue.

Another unspoken dimension of the debate pertains to elitism. For some people, classifying *Porgy and Bess* as an opera is a compliment of the highest order. Other people are offended by the idea that *Porgy and Bess* is "too good" to be a Broadway show. Still other people claim that *Porgy and Bess* is a crossover work—the kind of piece that can get people into unaccustomed venues (drawing operagoers to Broadway theaters and Broadway audiences to opera houses). In any event, *Porgy and Bess* continues to be a fascinating combination of classical music, jazz, ragtime, and popular song—a show that is well worth seeing and hearing no matter how it is labeled.

---

parents. One scholar suggests that this final appearance reflects a change in status for Bess; she "demonstrates her hard-won acceptance into the Catfish Row community by singing one of their songs."

The lyrical "aria" "Summertime" stands in marked contrast to "I Got Plenty o' Nuttin'," Porgy's happy assessment of his life now that Bess is staying with him. This tune seems far removed from opera; interestingly, it was one of the few numbers in *Porgy and Bess* in which Gershwin wrote the melody *before* the lyrics were written, which had been his customary practice for musical comedies. Gershwin had tried to create a tune that would break up the mood between

two more serious numbers, and he demonstrated his idea on the keyboard to Heyward and Ira Gershwin. Ira suggested a "dummy" lyric: "I got plenty o' nuttin'"—and immediately followed it up with "And nuttin's plenty for me." Heyward liked the spirit of those lines and asked if he could complete the poetry, since he had never tried writing words to a pre-existing tune before. Heyward mailed back his draft about two weeks later, and after a little more polishing by Ira, it was ready to put into the show.

"I Got Plenty o' Nuttin'" is called a "Banjo Song" in the score, and it certainly contains the energy and texture of a typical banjo accompaniment. There is a clear simple-duple meter to the "boom-chick" pattern played by the orchestra, allowing the syncopation in Porgy's melody to be prominent. "I Got Plenty of Nuttin'" is very similar to many early Tin Pan Alley tunes, and the song also has much in common with Gershwin's earlier "I Got Rhythm." Besides the ungrammatical title, there is a similar contour to the opening melody in both tunes: both open with an ascending phrase, much in the manner of a question, which is answered by a reciprocal descending phrase. And, like "I Got Rhythm," "I Got Plenty o' Nuttin'" uses a song-form refrain of *a-a-b-a'*.

There *are* differences between the two numbers: "I Got Rhythm" immediately repeated its refrain, but "I Got Plenty o' Nuttin'" interrupts the repetition by inserting new commentary from the chorus. However, the interjection of the chorus transforms the structure of "I Got Plenty o' Nuttin'" into a ternary form of *A-B-A'*, with the first *A* corresponding to Porgy's first refrain, *B* representing the brief choral passage, and the final *A'* as the second refrain. (The "prime" is a result of the hummed choral accompaniment and the slightly extended call-and-response melody at the end.)

The diverse vocal requirements in *Porgy and Bess* demonstrate the considerable demands Gershwin put on his singers. The role of Bess was in good hands; the 20-year-old Anne Wiggins Brown, a voice student at Juilliard, had won the part easily. For Porgy, Gershwin had been led to Todd Duncan, a voice teacher and head of the music department at Howard University in Washington, D.C. Duncan's initial reaction upon being offered the role was fairly unenthusiastic, nor was he very impressed when he heard Gershwin play the opening phrases of the score in progress:

> [George] and Ira stood there with their awful, rotten, bad voices and sang the whole score.
>
> When [George] started the opening music, I said to myself: "All this chopsticks—it sounds awful." I looked at my wife and said quietly, "This stinks." They went on . . . with those awful voices. He just kept playing; they kept singing. He turned around and grinned. The more they played, the more beautiful I thought the music was. By the time twenty minutes or a half hour had passed I just thought I was in heaven. These beautiful melodies in this new idiom—it was something I had never heard. I just couldn't get enough of it.
>
> He got into the second act and he turned around to me and said, "This is your great aria. This is going to make you famous." I said, "Yes?" He said, "Listen hard." He started off—ump-pah ump-pah. And I just thought "Aria?" It was the banjo song, "I Got Plenty o' Nuttin'"—the song I've sung all over the world for nearly forty years. And to think that man knew that was the song I would sing all over the world. It was a little ditty, but so infectious and so beautiful. Well, they finally finished, and when he ended with "I'm On My Way," I was crying. I was weeping.

The expensive production and the perplexing genre of *Porgy and Bess* meant that the show struggled to make a profit on Broadway, and it closed after 124 performances. For a musical theater work, this was a disappointing run (although it did last longer than several of Gershwin's other shows); for an opera, this would be considered a phenomenal number of performances. The show did not recoup its expenses, but it did go on a brief tour after its 15 weeks in New York. The tour took the cast to the National Theatre in Washington, D.C. This was Duncan's hometown, and he knew that the National was a segregated theater, inaccessible to African Americans. Duncan announced that he would not perform at a theater he could not attend, and Brown declared she would support Duncan in his boycott. The theater manager, S. E. Cochran, offered to allow blacks to attend the Wednesday and Saturday matinees. Duncan said no. Cochran then suggested that African Americans could attend *every* performance—in the second balcony. Duncan again said no, even though the Musicians' Union was threatening him with a $10,000 fine and a year's suspension. Duncan wanted African Americans to be able to purchase any seat in the house, and at last Cochran yielded. The National Theatre was completely desegregated for the first time in its history, and even though blacks and whites were commingled in every row, Cochran was astonished to find that not a single white patron asked for a refund. In the years since, many African Americans have been unhappy with the depiction of their race in *Porgy and Bess*, but the show did help in the long struggle toward equal treatment.

Porgy (Todd Duncan) and Bess (Anne Wiggins Brown).
Corbis/Bettmann.

Porgy and Bess had other roles to play as well. A Danish production of the show (the first translated version of *Porgy and Bess*) opened despite the Nazi occupation of Denmark. (The Nazis allowed the show to be performed as long as it went unadvertised.) The Danes had the last laugh, however; after the daily Nazi propaganda reports over the radio, the underground radio broadcasters would immediately play Sporting Life's number, "It Ain't Necessarily So"! Music from the show was heard in many other contexts around the world, and eventually much of the score would become as familiar as the best-selling pieces Gershwin ever wrote.

The eventual recognition of *Porgy and Bess*'s stature lay in the future, however; in 1935, the show did not stir up tremendous reaction. The Gershwins turned to Hollywood, where they wrote a number of tunes that proved they still had "it"—including "Let's Call the Whole Thing Off," "They Can't Take That Away From Me," and "Love Is Here to Stay." However, in early 1937, George began suffering from problems: headaches, dizziness, and some personality changes. Doctors could find nothing wrong, but George's condition worsened until he went into a coma. Emergency surgery discovered a particularly malignant tumor, reaching deep into the brain, and George died without regaining consciousness. His passing, at age 38, was met with shock and grief, and John O'Hara summed up the view of many by asserting, "George died on July 11, 1937, but I don't have to believe that if I don't want to."

Despite his sorrow, Ira Gershwin maintained a successful career for a number of years, working on Broadway shows with Kurt Weill and Arthur Schwartz, as well as Hollywood films with Jerome Kern and Howard Arlen. During George's lifetime, he had been the superstar of their partnership, but posterity has begun to recognize that Ira—who died in 1983—was one of the finest lyricists ever heard on Broadway. To this day, George is the "famous" Gershwin, but it is possible that he would have never attained many of his theatrical achievements had it not been for his lower profile brother Ira.

FURTHER READING

Alpert, Hollis. *The Life and Times of Porgy and Bess: The Story of an American Classic.* London: Nick Hern Books, 1990.

Block, Geoffrey. *Enchanted Evenings: The Broadway Musical from* Show Boat *to Sondheim.* New York: Oxford University Press, 1997.

Carnovale, Norbert. *George Gershwin: A Bio-Bibliography.* (Bio-Bibliographies in Music, Number 76; Donald L. Hixon, series advisor.) Westport, Connecticut: Greenwood Press, 2000.

Ewen, David. *A Journey to Greatness: The Life and Music of George Gershwin.* London: W. H. Allen, 1956.

Furia, Philip. *Ira Gershwin: The Art of the Lyricist.* New York: Oxford University Press, 1996.

Gershwin, Ira. *Lyrics on Several Occasions: A Selection of Stage & Screen Lyrics Written for Sundry Situations; and Now Arranged in Arbitrary Categories. To Which Have Been Added Many Informative Annotations & Disquisitions on Their Why & Wherefore, Their Whom-For, Their How; and Matters Associative.* New York: Alfred A. Knopf, 1959.

Gilbert, Steven E. *The Music of Gershwin.* New Haven and London: Yale University Press, 1995.

Hischak, Thomas S. *Word Crazy: Broadway Lyricists from Cohan to Sondheim.* New York: Praeger, 1991.

Jablonski, Edward. *Gershwin.* London: Simon & Schuster, 1988.

Kimball, Robert, ed. *The Complete Lyrics of Ira Gershwin.* London: Pavilion Books Ltd., 1993.

Rosenberg, Deena. *Fascinating Rhythm: The Collaboration of George and Ira Gershwin.* New York: Dutton, 1991. Ann Arbor: University of Michigan Press, 1997.

Schwartz, Charles. *Gershwin: His Life and Music.* Indianapolis and New York: The Bobbs-Merrill Company, 1973.

Starr, Lawrence. "Gershwin's 'Bess, You Is My Woman Now': The Sophistication and Subtlety of a Great Tune." *The Musical Quarterly* 72 (1986): 429–48.

———. "Toward a Reevaluation of Gershwin's *Porgy and Bess*." *American Music* 2, no. 2 (Summer 1984): 25–37.

Woll, Allen. *Black Musical Theatre from* Coontown *to* Dreamgirls. Baton Rouge: Louisiana State University Press, 1989.

PLOT SUMMARY: *PORGY AND BESS*

Porgy and Bess opens in Catfish Row, a tenement in Charleston, South Carolina. Clara rocks her baby and sings "Summertime." Meanwhile, a fight breaks out during a crap game and Crown stabs Robbins. Crown flees, abandoning his girlfriend Bess. Because of Bess's immoral life, the God-fearing women of Catfish Row reject her. Sporting Life, a drug dealer who peddles "happy dust," wants Bess to go with him to New York, but the crippled Porgy offers her the chance to share his small living quarters. Meanwhile, the residents of Catfish Row pool their meager resources to help Robbins's widow Serena to pay for the funeral.

In the second act, Clara is worried. Jake insists he needs to keep fishing to provide for their son, but it's time for the September storms. In comparison, Porgy rejoices in his simple existence—especially now that Bess has come into his life—by singing "I Got Plenty o' Nuttin'." Bess is grateful that he is completely able to ignore her sordid past, and the two of them fall in love. Porgy arranges for an unethical lawyer to "divorce" Bess from Crown (even though they had never been married). Soon afterward, the residents of Catfish Row are going to Kittiwah Island for a picnic. Porgy's disability makes him unable to go, but he urges Bess to enjoy herself without him. At the end of the picnic, however, Bess learns that the island has been Crown's hiding place. Crown forces Bess to stay with him, but in a few days, a delirious Bess makes her way back to Catfish Row, begging Porgy to forgive her. The emotions reach a climax as a violent hurricane blows along the coast, just as Crown reappears. Jake's fishing boat has capsized, so Clara thrusts her baby into Bess's arms and runs to try to rescue her husband; Crown goes too, after mocking Porgy about his inability to help.

The third act opens with the tenement dwellers mourning Clara and Jake, who both died in the storm. Bess gently croons "Summertime" to their orphaned infant. Crown is presumed drowned as well, but soon he sneaks into Catfish Row—where Porgy kills him. Porgy doesn't cooperate with the authorities, so he is jailed for contempt. Bess, despairing at the loss of both her lovers, finally agrees to travel north with Sporting Life. When Porgy is released, the tenement dwellers reluctantly tell Porgy the sad news of her departure. Porgy hitches up his small goat cart, vowing to travel to New York and find Bess. His optimism as he sings "Oh, Lawd, I'm On My Way" is a closing ray of hope in the bittersweet story.

Chapter 20
Great Solo Acts: Irving Berlin

Although **Irving Berlin** (1888–1989) gave the United States one of its favorite patriotic tunes—"God Bless America"—he was not actually born in America. Berlin, however, had an uncanny ability to write "for the moment": he had an excellent sense of the public's musical taste, and decade after decade, he wrote tunes that became enormous hits. One of his numbers, "White Christmas," held the record for 45 years as America's best-selling single song. Moreover, he wrote the tune that has since become one of the best-known "anthems" for musical theater, "There's No Business Like Show Business."

Berlin started life in Mogilyov, a small Russian village, where his birth name was Israel "Izzy" Baline. His family fled persecution and came to New York when Berlin was five years old, but his father died when Berlin was 13. Since Berlin felt he was a burden, he left home and survived on the streets, singing popular songs for pennies. Briefly, he sang in the chorus of a Broadway show; he also worked as a **boomer**. A boomer shares some characteristics with a song-plugger; it's a person who applauds wildly during the performance of songs (often shouting for encores at the end of the song).

Although he did not have a voice with good tone quality, he sang with great fervor and energy, and Berlin was hired to be a singing waiter at the Pelham Cafe. Employees of a rival cafe published a song, which stirred the competitive spirits of the Pelham Cafe's owner. Berlin struggled with rhyming lyrics for some time, but at last produced the words for a song called "Marie from Sunny Italy." (Another man wrote the melody.) They found a publisher, and on the printed sheet music, Izzy used his new professional name—Irving Berlin—for the first time. Although the song sold only a few copies, it was an important milestone for Berlin, alerting him to the potential profits to be found via Tin Pan Alley.

Berlin's rough-and-tumble upbringing meant he had never learned to read or write music. He had learned to pick out melodies on the black keys of a piano, but he was by no means proficient as a player. He therefore wrote only the lyrics for his earliest songs. One of these joint efforts was interpolated into a show in 1908, and thus a work (partly) by Berlin enjoyed its first appearance on Broadway.

Berlin's first experience with tune-writing came about inadvertently. He had offered some lyrics to a publisher who liked the poetry, and Berlin was told to step into the next room and sing the melody to the publishing firm's staff arranger, who would transcribe the tune. Berlin didn't hesitate; he improvised a melody on the spot, and the published song went on to enjoy a modest success. It would be another couple of years, though, before Berlin would try producing a melody again.

Berlin also continued to broaden his understanding of musical theater. He had already learned how to write songs in various styles—ballads, African American songs, ragtime-influenced numbers, and a wide variety of novelty songs, or dialect songs, which depicted (or satirized) Jewish, Italian, Irish, and German ethnicities; dialect songs had been a predominant feature of vaudeville. Often, he mixed approaches within a single song, giving his music some of its unique flair.

Berlin began writing the melody for his songs with increasing frequency. Still restricted primarily to the piano's black keys, Berlin had discovered an enormously useful tool: the transposing piano. This instrument allowed the performer to change keys by means of a lever underneath the keyboard. Now Berlin could test various harmonies for his songs simply and easily, and his songs could incorporate a richer range of chords. Berlin would play a finished version to a transcriber, who would transfer Berlin's piece into musical notation. (George Gershwin once applied for the job of Berlin's transcriber.) Berlin liked being solely responsible for his songs; he told an interviewer, "Writing both words and music I can compose them together and make them fit. I sacrifice one for the other. If I have a melody I want to use, I plug away at the lyrics until I make them fit the best parts of my music and vice versa." He also argued that his approach was *better* than collaboration, explaining that the partners "either are forced to fit some one's words to their music or some one's music to their words. Latitude—which begets novelty—is denied them, and in consequence both lyrics and melody suffer."

In 1911, Berlin wrote the tune that first made him famous: "Alexander's Ragtime Band." The tune got off to a slow start, but various vaudeville performers began to feature it in their acts, and audiences grew increasingly enthusiastic. By the summer of 1911, "Alexander's Ragtime Band" had grown to be one of the biggest hits ever seen in vaudeville; the trade magazine *Variety* called it "the musical sensation of the decade." The stage performances were soon followed by various commercial recordings, which set records of their own. Sales of "Alexander's Ragtime Band" had topped a million copies by November.

Berlin also created an instrumental version of "Alexander's Ragtime Band" that featured one of his trademarks, the **quodlibet**, a type of non-imitative polyphony in which two familiar melodies are played simultaneously, and Berlin was very fond of this device. In his keyboard arrangement of "Alexander's Ragtime Band," he presented the song's chorus, followed by a polyphonic blend of Stephen Foster's "Old Folks at Home" ("Swanee River")—played by the pianist's left hand—with "Dixie" in the right hand. Berlin delighted in finding pre-existing tunes that worked together.

Gradually, Berlin built a larger presence in musical theater. He contributed four songs to the *Ziegfeld Follies of 1911*. The following year, he had a song featured in a competing revue, and another song by Berlin was interpolated into a show by George M. Cohan. Berlin also composed selected songs for several Lew Fields shows. He still wrote Tin Pan Alley tunes too, but in 1912, he wrote for himself. He had lost his new bride to a typhoid epidemic and he used music to express his sorrow. The bittersweet ballad "When I Lost You" went on to sell a million copies.

In 1914, Berlin wrote the songs for his first complete Broadway show, *Watch Your Step*, including one of his signature quodlibets. *Watch Your Step* featured the dancers Vernon and Irene Castle (appearing together for the last time); another credit on the program read, "Plot, if any, by Harry B. Smith." Audiences didn't care about the shaky storyline; the singing and dancing pushed *Watch Your Step* into becoming the biggest hit of the season, and Berlin's Broadway career was off and running.

By 1915, Berlin was secure enough as a songwriter that he felt able to offer a series of tips for aspiring composers. Berlin's rules, paraphrased, read as follows:

1. The melody should be within the range of most singers.
2. The title should be attention-getting and repeated within the body of the song.
3. The song should be "sexless": able to be sung by men and women.
4. The song requires "heart interest."
5. And at the same time, it should be "original in idea, words, and music."
6. Stick to nature . . . not nature in a visionary, abstract way, but nature as demonstrated in homely, concrete, everyday manifestations.
7. Sprinkle the lyrics with "open vowels" so that it will be euphonious.
8. Make the song as simple as possible.
9. The song writer must look upon his work as business, that is, to make a success of it, he must work and *work*, and then WORK.

No one adhered more closely to the ninth rule than Berlin himself; he had developed the habit of staying up until dawn, perfecting song after song. After *Watch Your Step*, he prepared Broadway shows on an almost yearly basis.

Early in 1918, the 30-year-old Berlin (a recently naturalized American citizen) was startled to find that he had been drafted into the United States Army. As a man accustomed to composing all night, Berlin found the 5:00 A.M. reveille to be a terrible shock. Once again, his real-life experiences led to a heartfelt composition; this time the result was "Oh! How I Hate to Get Up in the Morning," which sold a million and a half copies. His commanding officer requested that Berlin come up with a way to raise the $35,000 needed to build a community house (a building which could accommodate soldiers' visitors). Berlin created the revue *Yip, Yip,*

Yaphank and decided to stage it not on the army base but on Broadway itself. In between satires of chorus girls and leading Broadway stars, Berlin interspersed military drills and precision marching; he himself sang "Oh! How I Hate to Get Up in the Morning." After a month-long run, *Yip! Yip! Yaphank* had more than doubled its fund-raising goal, and almost $150,000 was raised by the time the show completed a brief tour. (Ironically, the war ended in November, and the community house was never built.)

Released from military service, Berlin was quickly hard at work writing for shows, revues, and his own publishing company. He also built a small jewel of a theater (1,010 seats) called the Music Box and wrote successful revues for this new venue. Berlin's personal life became busier in 1924, when he met Ellin Mackay. Ellin's father Clarence was bitterly opposed to his daughter's involvement with a Jewish immigrant songwriter (even though he himself was an Irish Catholic—another cultural group subjected to much prejudice in the United States). Mackay once publicly vowed that a marriage would take place "only over my dead body." The press delighted in publicizing the bad blood between the two men.

At last, Berlin and Ellin decided to elope, marrying in 1926. Ellin's father never fully forgave his daughter, although he did send her a letter of condolence when her second child died. However, a sort of truce was formed after the Wall Street Crash of 1929; Mackay had the unfortunate distinction of being the person to suffer the greatest individual financial loss. Despite various attempts at reconciliation, the relationship between Mackay and his daughter and son-in-law remained strained up to the time of his death.

Berlin soon fell back into his compositional routine, writing "Blue Skies" in 1927 for Belle Baker, who snuck it into a Rodgers and Hart show (despite a no-interpolations clause in their contract!). Berlin also began to write for Hollywood films, although most of his movies did poorly. To rebuild his reputation, Berlin decided to write his own satirical show. He teamed up with librettist **Moss Hart** (1904–1961), and together they devised a storyline about former millionaires reduced to eating at automats (a curious crossover between vending machines and cafeterias). The two biggest hits were "Let's Have Another Cup of Coffee" and "Soft Lights and Sweet Music," and Berlin proved—to audiences and to himself—that he could still write popular songs.

Berlin maintained a partnership with Hart for his next Broadway venture, although he had to work hard to sell Hart on the idea of doing a revue, a genre that was distinctly losing steam now that Ziegfeld had died. Hart did like Berlin's idea that *As Thousands Cheer* would use a newspaper motif for its skits (see the **Plot Summary**). As Berlin later remarked, "There are some persons, you know, who need no distortion to caricature, and the same is true of much of the world's news. It is satire in itself and has only to be photographically reproduced to be the most gorgeous kind of irony."

Berlin was not thinking ironically, however, when he drafted "Supper Time" (**Musical Example 23**), one of *As Thousands Cheer*'s most powerful numbers. Instead, the song makes a subtle but wrenching antiracist statement.

The anguished woman who sings this song is stunned to learn she is now a widow, thanks to a lynch mob. She finds herself frozen, wondering how she will find the strength to prepare her children's supper; moreover, she can't think what she will say to them to explain their father's absence. And how can she remind them to say their prayers before eating, when God could allow something like this to happen? The singer in this case is African American, but in truth she could be any woman of any background, faced with the responsibility of being strong for her family when her own heart is shattered. Her actions are simple and familiar: she is setting the table for supper—a process not dependent on race or color. It seems that Berlin wanted his audience members to break away from the old "us versus them" mentality and instead appreciate the common bonds of humanity we share.

There were those who felt that this type of serious social message had no place in "entertainment," and during the Philadelphia tryout tour, both Berlin and producer Sam H. Harris were under a lot of pressure to drop the number. The piece stayed in the show, but there were still some problems to work out. At the end of a show, the performers come back on stage for a series of **bows**; the orchestra continues to play, and the bows are generally modestly "choreographed" so that the whole cast comes forward for a first bow. Then the actors take bows individually or in small groups; the characters in the smallest roles bow first, and then they move backwards to form a long line that the subsequent actors join after bowing. The biggest stars are the last to bow, so that the applause will continue to grow louder and louder (in what musicians would call a **crescendo**, coming from the Italian verb "to increase"). Some of the white stars of *As Thousands Cheer* refused to share the stage during the bows with Ethel Waters (the singer of "Supper Time"), since she was black. Berlin calmly told the white actors that of course he would respect their feelings; in fact, he would eliminate the bows altogether. The white actors quickly decided that an integrated stage wasn't such a bad thing after all, and the bickering had stopped by the time *As Thousands Cheer* opened in New York on September 30, 1933.

Although its emotions run deep, "Supper Time" is a fairly simple song. It is in song form, with the *a-a-b-a* sections corresponding to **1**, **2**, **3**, and **4**. There is no verse, or vocal introduction, although the repetition of the last line of text at **5** might be a short vocal coda. The range is a little larger than many songs, making "Supper Time" slightly more demanding than many songs of its day. The question of the song's mode is a little more complicated, however; Berlin notated the tune in the major mode, but wrote a number of blue notes for the singer—on the first syllables of words such as *table*, *able*, *yellin'*, *tellin'*, and so forth—which makes the mode seem minor at times. Moreover, the pitch drops from the blue note to a slightly lower pitch on the second syllable in all the examples listed above, which gives each word a "weeping" quality. "Supper Time" resembles the **blues**, a twentieth-century vocal style that had a large influence on both jazz and rock. "Singing the blues" was a type of catharsis, although it is hard to imagine that *any* song could rid this widow of her inconsolable grief. The blues style was perfectly suited to the deep feelings expressed in the song, and Waters later remarked, "If one song can tell the whole tragic history of

Ethel Waters sings "Supper Time" in *As Thousands Cheer*.
Museum of the City of New York.

a race, 'Supper Time' was that song." And, of course, part of the continuing tragedy of "Supper Time" is that it hasn't become a dated "period" piece; on the contrary, hate crimes continue to be a dismaying curse of our modern, supposedly enlightened society.

Although "Supper Time" was a sobering number, it did not seem to undercut the audience's enthusiasm for the overall revue. In fact, the song proved to be a hit, and it became a signature tune for Ethel Waters in her later career. "Supper Time" was by no means the only hit in the show; "Easter Parade," based on an older Berlin melody, proved enormously popular, too. *As Thousands Cheer* ran for more than a year and was one of the Depression's few profitable shows.

As Thousands Cheer was not the last of the revues, but their appearances on Broadway had reduced to a mere trickle. A 1938 production, however, triumphed over poor reviews to establish a new long-run record on Broadway; the show was *Hellzapoppin'*, and the run was 1,404 performances. It was really more of a vaudeville show than a revue, for its producers (and stars) were a former vaudeville team who had never quite made it big; they stuck with the type of humor they knew from the old vaudeville circuit. The slapstick skits bordered on the raucous, as when a gorilla leaps into a box seat and drags away a woman. Much of the action took place in the house rather than on stage; for instance, a deliveryman kept wandering the aisles, carrying a houseplant and looking for a "Mrs. Jones." Each time he reappeared the plant had grown larger and larger, and even at the end of the show, as the audience exited, he was to be found in the lobby, next to a small tree, still searching for Mrs. Jones.

Meanwhile, Berlin found himself back in Hollywood, but this time, his efforts bore happier results. However, as Chapter 22, "New Achievements from Familiar Names" reflects, Irving Berlin had not seen the last of Broadway. The man who had contributed music to the *Ziegfeld Follies of 1911* would be back, big as ever, not only in the 1940s, but through 1962, still active in musical theater—an astonishingly lengthy compositional career.

FURTHER READING

Barrett, Mary Ellin. *Irving Berlin: A Daughter's Memoir*. New York: Simon & Schuster, 1994.

Bergreen, Laurence. *As Thousands Cheer: The Life of Irving Berlin*. New York: Penguin Books, 1990.

Freedland, Michael. *Irving Berlin*. New York: Stein & Day, 1974.

Hamm, Charles. *Irving Berlin: Songs from the Melting Pot: The Formative Years, 1907–1914*. New York: Oxford University Press, 1997.

Sharaff, Irene. *Broadway & Hollywood: Costumes Designed by Irene Sharaff*. New York: Van Nostrand Reinhold, 1976.

Waters, Ethel. *His Eye Is on the Sparrow*. Garden City, New York: Doubleday, 1951.

PLOT SUMMARY: *AS THOUSANDS CHEER*

Since *As Thousands Cheer* is a revue, it does not have a continuous storyline. However, the assorted vignettes are all unified: They represent the articles and sections of a daily newspaper, such as news stories, human interest features, weather reports, advice columns, and the comics. Overall, the revue's satirical "reports" are a fascinating overview of the concerns and values of readers in the 1930s.

The listing below presents the order of the "articles" in the revue's newspaper; each title was projected onto the theater's **proscenium** (the front wall that surrounds the stage) before each scene.

Act I

Prologue: The newsboys excitedly patter their way through the newsflash: not only did a dog bite a man, but the man bit the dog right back!

"Franklin D. Roosevelt Inaugurated Tomorrow": This lead article depicts the outgoing President Hoover and his First Lady as they "liberate" various mementos while packing to leave the White House; the President bids his Cabinet farewell with a Bronx cheer.

"Barbara Hutton to Wed Prince Mdivani": The odds concerning the heiress's wedding are discussed in the song "How's Chances?"

"Heat Wave Hits New York": This weather report features a sizzling musical discussion of the current tropical "Heat Wave."

"Joan Crawford to Divorce Douglas Fairbanks, Jr.": The two film stars argue over who should get top billing in their divorce announcement.

"*Majestic* Sails at Midnight": In an era before air travel was commonplace, the sailings of the great passenger ships were reported regularly. Here, America's European allies sing "Debts," one of Berlin's clever quodlibets, blending Berlin's original melody with the "Star-Spangled Banner."

"Lonely Heart Column": The plaintive ballad "Lonely Heart" is a letter addressed to an advice columnist called Miss Lonely Heart; the melancholy letter-writer seeks someone to love.

"World's Wealthiest Man Celebrates 94th Birthday": John D. Rockeller's children try to give him something special for his birthday: the Radio City Music Hall (but he doesn't want it, telling them to "Take it right back to whoever sold it to you").

"The Funnies": In one of the show's most delightful production numbers, a number of characters from the Sunday comic strips come to life on stage.

"'Green Pastures' Starts Third Road Season": With Broadway close at hand, New York newspapers usually give reports on the ups and downs of show business.

"Rotogravure Section": For many years, newspapers depicted the latest fashions on pages printed in a sepia-colored ink—so the costume designer dressed the entire cast in brown hues, ranging from white through umbers, siennas, taupes, and chocolate, as they sang "Easter Parade."

Act II

"Metropolitan Opera Opens in Old-Time Splendor": The Met's production of Verdi's *Rigoletto* is interrupted by a series of inane commercials.

"Unknown Negro Lynched by Frenzied Mob": An African American mother sings "Supper Time" (**Musical Example 23**), wondering how she will explain to her children that their father won't be coming home for supper ever again.

"Gandhi Goes on Hunger Strike": Although the title might imply that this, too, is a serious topic, Gandhi discovers (along with evangelist Aimee Semple McPherson) the power of advertising.

"Revolt in Cuba": The revolution provides an opportunity for vigorous Latin American dancing.

"Noël Coward, Noted Playwright, Returns to England": Coward's eccentricities are lampooned as a hotel staff reflects on their attempts to serve the desires of the British playwright.

"Society Wedding of the Year": Another lavish production number allows the chorus to sing "Our Wedding Day" (even though the audience may well have been shocked to learn that the bride and groom may have shared an address *before* the wedding).

"Prince of Wales Rumored Engaged": Readers of newspapers followed the matrimonial entanglements of foreign heads of states as avidly as those of Hollywood stars and the rich.

"Josephine Baker Still the Rage of Paris": A homesick expatriate singer living in Paris still has "Harlem on My Mind."

"Supreme Court Hands Down Important Decision": The "decision" stipulated that musicals could no longer

end with the customary reprises of the show's most popular songs—so Berlin wrote "Not For All the Rice in China" to give the cast a "new" song at the end of the revue.

MUSICAL EXAMPLE 23

As Thousands Cheer
Irving Berlin/Irving Berlin, 1933
"Supper Time"

1 Supper time, I should set the table, 'Cause it's supper time.
Somehow I'm not able, 'Cause that man o' mine Ain't comin' home no more.

2 Supper time—Kids will soon be yellin' For their supper time;
How'll I keep from tellin' that, that man o' mine Ain't comin' home no more?

3 How'll I keep explainin' When they ask me where he's gone?
How'll I keep from cryin' When I bring their supper on?
How can I remind them To pray at their humble board?
How can I be thankful When they start to thank the Lord? Lord!

4 Supper time, I should set the table 'Cause it's supper time;
Somehow I'm not able, 'Cause that man o' mine, Ain't comin' home no more,

5 Ain't coming home no more.

Chapter 21
Great Solo Acts: Cole Porter and Other Efforts in the 1930s

Cole Porter (1891–1964) was born only three years after Irving Berlin, and, like Berlin, Porter wrote both the words and the melodies for his songs. Nevertheless, the backgrounds of the two composers could not have been further apart: Porter's upbringing was privileged and exclusive, he never knew hunger or financial need, and his musical training was extensive. While Berlin got his start via Tin Pan Alley and continued to write popular songs all through his life, Porter never was involved in the Tin Pan Alley publishing world; he wrote his songs either for Broadway or Hollywood or for the entertainment of friends. Stylistically, Porter's songs were very different from Berlin's; Porter wrote witty and often suggestive lyrics, and his poetry often built to humorous climaxes. The result of this careful attention to the text, according to scholar Thomas Hischak, was that "Porter taught the audience to listen for lyrics." Porter's writing was sophisticated and worldly, his humor was often adult, and he frequently battled censors because of his references to taboo topics: sexual issues, drugs, and so forth.

In 1915, at the same time that Porter was studying harmony and counterpoint at Harvard University, he had two songs interpolated into Broadway productions. Neither show did well, but Porter was hired in 1916 to compose an entire score—although the show bombed, closing after two weeks. Porter traveled to Europe, served in the French Foreign Legion, and met the wealthy divorcée Linda Lee Thomas (whose ex-husband had the dubious distinction of being the first American to kill someone while driving an automobile). They soon married and began to live glamorously, hosting opulent parties not only at their elegant home in Paris, but also in a Venetian palazzo and a villa on the Riviera.

Despite his hedonistic lifestyle, Porter wrote songs almost constantly, some of which made it to Broadway revues. None of the revues made much of a splash, but Porter's luck changed when some of his songs were used in a 1928 musical comedy—or, as *Variety* magazine would put it, a **tuner**. Critics singled out Porter's contributions as the show's highlights; the *New Yorker* critic wrote, "When it came to Cole Porter's songs . . . I cared for no one's opinion but my own, an ecstatic one." The critic gave special praise to what he called "Let's Fall in Love," in reality titled "Let's Do It." The writer may have simply mistaken the title, or this may have been an attempt to "sanitize" one of the many innuendoes in Porter's lyrics. "Let's Do It" would be the first of Porter's songs with lasting appeal, but it was by no

means the last. It was during the following year, 1929, that "Cole Porter" first became a household name, when two of his shows—one in London and one in New York—each became hits.

Porter's next show, ***Anything Goes*** (1934), had traveled a somewhat convoluted path before reaching the stage. Originally titled *Bon Voyage*, and then called *Hard to Get*, the show was the brainchild of producer **Vinton Freedley** (1891–1969). As Chapter 18, "Great Partnerships of the Early Book Musical, The Gershwins (1)" relates, Freedley had fled the country and his creditors when *Pardon My English* (with a score by the Gershwins) had flopped in 1933. Freedley had ended up in the Pearl Islands in the Gulf of Panama, where he spent his days fishing and dreaming of a comeback. Having hit on the concept of a shipwrecked gambling ship, Freedley contracted with Guy Bolton and P. G. Wodehouse to write a libretto and with Porter to write a score. Freedley was quite pleased with the songs—but was appalled by the script when it arrived. Then fate intervened: the *USS Morro Castle* caught fire and foundered off the coast of New Jersey; 134 lives were lost. No one could present a musical comedy about a shipwreck after such a disaster, so Freedley needed a new book that could incorporate the existing sets, costumes, and songs.

Since Wodehouse was in England and Bolton was suffering from appendicitis, Freedley turned to the director, **Howard Lindsay** (1889–1968), who reluctantly agreed to rewrite the script if he was given a collaborator; eventually **Russel "Buck" Crouse** (1893–1966), a press agent for the Theatre Guild, was picked. Stories disagree about how Crouse was chosen (one tale credits a Ouija board), but the collaboration soon proved to be extremely fruitful. Not only did they produce an effective alternative storyline (see the **Plot Summary**), but they also co-wrote librettos for six more musicals (including *The Sound of Music* in 1959) as well as scripts for eight plays, winning a Pulitzer Prize in 1946.

It took time to produce the new script and rehearsals had already begun. They still had not written the last scene when they traveled to Boston for the tryout tour. Ethel Merman (playing Reno) swears that Lindsay and Crouse emerged from the men's room on the train, triumphantly announcing that they had just finished the final scene. As is typical of a tryout tour, frantic calls were made for changes to the script; the pace was exhausting. The 41-year-old Crouse kept plugging along, but the 45-year-old Lindsay did not. As their biographer Cornelia Otis Skinner reports,

[Howard] suddenly gave out, took to his bed and announced in all seriousness that he was dying. It was the first time that Buck had come up against his partner's hypochondria and for a time he was taken in. When Howard weakly asked him to send for his sister Rose, who lived in Boston, Russel called her in a panic. Rose was a no-nonsense person, like her mother, and she knew and loved her brother well. Over the telephone she sounded curiously unmoved by the news of his imminent demise and when she walked purposefully into the room, her opening remark was, "Howard, get out of bed!" Obediently he did.

Despite Lindsay's malingering, the script came together, and the Boston opening was a success. A remaining problem was getting Porter's songs on the air. Radio stations were reluctant to play "I Get a Kick Out of You"—except as an instrumental number—because it included the line "I get no kick from cocaine." Porter gave in and changed the line to "Some like perfume from Spain." Porter would battle the censors on many occasions, since, as Hischak puts it, "romance in a Porter song usually has its tactile aspects." But sometime lyrics needed to be changed because of current events, as when the tragedy of the Lindbergh baby kidnapping unfolded. In "I Get a Kick Out of You," Porter had originally written:

I wouldn't care / For those nights in the air / That the fair / Mrs. Lindbergh went through . . .

The revised lyric reads:

Flying too high / With some guy in the sky / Is my idea of nothing to do . . .

Anything Goes soon opened in New York at the Alvin Theatre—a venue that Freedley had co-owned before the stock market crash; now he had to rent it. The critics were exuberant in their assessments of the new **song-and-dance show**; reviewer Walter Winchell outdid himself by writing, "Porter's bitter and pungent patter at the Alvin is a positive panic. The fooling and the fun were fervently fondled by the first fans." Those enthusiastic fans supported a 420-performance run of the show.

The strong cast contributed greatly to the success of *Anything Goes*. In particular, Freedley had wanted to use the powerhouse singer he had discovered four years earlier, Ethel Merman. This would be Merman's first Porter show; some critics argue that she grew to be the ideal Porter singer. Certainly, Porter gave Merman excellent material to sing; as Reno, she was responsible for "I Get a Kick Out of You," "Blow, Gabriel, Blow," as well as the title song, "Anything Goes" (**Musical Example 24**). "Anything Goes" does not really contribute to the development of the plot, but its lyrics certainly contribute to the humor of the show. The music supports the words in some subtle ways. For instance, the melody begins with an introductory verse addressing changes in society through time. The first portion of this verse (**1**), discussing the Puritan era, is set in the minor mode. When Reno begins to compare the past with the present day at (**2**), the same melody is now set in the *major* mode. The difference is minute, but it helps the listener to realize that times *have* changed (and so has the mode).

After the verse, "Anything Goes" proceeds through a straightforward song form (**3** through **6**) for its chorus; the melody of the chorus is repeated at **7** and at **8**. However, Porter changes his rhyme scheme in the *b* section (**5**) of the song form, and the music reinforces that alteration. **Figure 21–1** shows

Ethel Merman wows them in "Anything Goes."
Getty Images Inc. - Hulton Archive Photos.

thirst *worst*	**ONE-RHYME**
thirsting *bursting*	**TWO-RHYME**
first of all *worst* of all	**THREE-RHYME**
first of the lot *worst* of the lot	**FOUR-RHYME**

Figure 21–1

examples of several kinds of rhymes, as suggested by composer Stephen Citron. During the *a* sections of the song form (**3**, **4**, and **6**), Porter uses primarily a series of alternating **two-rhymes** and **one-rhymes**: *stock*ing / *shock*ing, *knows* / *goes*. At *b*, however, Porter switches to a long series of **three-rhymes**; moreover, each one ends with the word *today* in the first chorus. The second chorus uses the words *you like* at this point, and the third verse employs *you got*.

The contrast in the rhyme scheme puts a little extra focus on this section of the song form, and Porter employs a subtle musical device to support the rhymes as well: the majority of the *b*-section words are sung on a single pitch, but the first syllable of each three-rhyme is sung on a successively higher pitch. Each new pitch is only a **half-step** higher (the half-step is the smallest scale increment customarily employed in western music). This gradual ascent is graphically represented in **Figure 21–2**. As historian Mark Steyn remarks, the ascent "gives the song forward propulsion; that's why it seems to be getting *funnier*." Porter had a special knack for interweaving the music and the words in complementary and novel ways. In the following years, Porter would produce a number of Broadway shows (and film scores) before suffering a terrible injury that would undermine his self-confidence. As Chapter 23, "A Cole Porter Renaissance and the Rise of Recognition," relates, however, his greatest stage work, *Kiss Me, Kate*, was yet to come.

The financial tribulations of the 1930s had a distinct impact on the output of Broadway musicals, but the theatrical shortage was not unique to the United States; musical theater in England also suffered during the decade. The situation was not completely dire; *Bitter-Sweet* (1929) and other hits of the late 1920s were still playing, and *Cavalcade* opened in 1931. *Cavalcade*—like the extravaganzas of the nineteenth century and like the enormous musicals to come in the 1980s—was conceived on a massive scale, requiring a backstage crew of over 300 people. It ran for more than a year, selling more than £300,000 worth of tickets. Its wide-ranging story depicted people from both the upper and lower English classes, and English theater historian Sheridan Morley thinks it is no coincidence that when the television series *Upstairs Downstairs* was filmed some 40 years later, many of its principal characters were given the same names as leading roles in *Cavalcade*.

Cavalcade was atypical, however. Most hit shows in London during the early 1930s had been imported from America or were written for England by American composers, such as Rodgers and Hart's *Ever Green*. The British composer Ivor Novello, who had written the enormous hit "Keep the Home Fires Burning" in 1914, was stung by this trend, so he countered with an almost annual series of musicals from the mid-1930s onward. Most of Novello's shows were reminiscent of the old operetta genre (which might have had something to do with his having seen *The Merry Widow* some 27 times!), and his old-fashioned approach added to the appeal of his works; audiences could escape from some of the pressures of the day while lost in his romantic stories.

In 1937, a new variation on the Cinderella story opened, called *Me and My Girl*. It was not an immediate hit, but before the show closed, a stroke of fortune intervened: a last-minute cancellation left a BBC radio unit with nothing to air, so they visited the theater to relay some of the show as a substitute live broadcast. This was the first time any portion of a **West End** show (London's theater district, equivalent to New York's Broadway) had been aired while being performed in front of a live audience. Radio listeners were intrigued by the cheers they heard during a song called "The Lambeth Walk," so of course they went and bought tickets to see for themselves what was going on. Soon "The Lambeth Walk" sparked a dance craze, and the number eventually became a favorite song of British soldiers. *Me and My Girl* was performed twice nightly (although, during the Second World War's blackout periods, it played twice a day instead), and racked up 1,646 performances.

The war curtailed most new English theatrical activity, however. Even the foreign imports had ceased; for obvious reasons, there was nothing new coming from continental Europe, and the precarious conditions of the bombing raids made American producers too nervous to bring Broadway works to London. British theaters gradually began to get back on their feet after the war ended, but America still had one tremendous surprise to unleash: *Oklahoma!* arrived in England in 1947, inaugurating a flood of blockbuster hits imported from the United States. It would be many years before the West End would produce any shows that could rival the impact of American works of the mid-twentieth century.

FURTHER READING

Block, Geoffrey. *Enchanted Evenings: The Broadway Musical from* Show Boat *to Sondheim*. New York: Oxford University Press, 1997.

Brahms, Caryl, and Ned Sherrin. *Song By Song: The Lives and Work of 14 Great Lyric Writers*. Egerton, Bolton, U.K.: Ross Anderson Publications, 1984.

Citron, Stephen. *The Musical From the Inside Out*. Chicago: Ivan R. Dee, 1992.

Figure 21–2

The world has gone <u>mad today</u> And good's <u>bad</u> <u>today</u>, And black's <u>white</u> <u>today</u>, And day's <u>night</u> <u>today</u> . . .

Eells, George. *The Life That Late He Led: A Biography of Cole Porter*. New York: G. P. Putnam's Sons, 1967.

Gill, Brendan. *Cole: A Biographical Essay*. Edited by Robert Kimball. London: Michael Joseph, 1971.

Green, Stanley. *Ring Bells, Sing Songs: Broadway Musicals of the 1930s*. New Rochelle, New York: Arlington House, 1971.

Hischak, Thomas S. *Word Crazy: Broadway Lyricists from Cohan to Sondheim*. New York: Praeger, 1991.

Kimball, Robert, ed. *The Complete Lyrics of Cole Porter*. London: Hamish Hamilton, 1983.

Morley, Sheridan. *Spread a Little Happiness: The First Hundred Years of the British Musical*. New York: Thames & Hudson, 1987.

Skinner, Cornelia Otis. *Life with Lindsay & Crouse*. Boston: Houghton Mifflin, 1976.

Steyn, Mark. *Broadway Babies Say Goodnight: Musicals Then and Now*. New York: Routledge, 1999.

PLOT SUMMARY: *ANYTHING GOES*

The "emergency" replacement plot for *Anything Goes* did a brilliant job of incorporating the materials prepared for the original version, and the resulting storyline is an energetic farce. Like a nineteenth-century melodrama, *Anything Goes* is full of people in disguise, an unwelcome engagement, and myriad twists and turns before the "right" couples are united at the end.

The hero is Billy Crocker, a somewhat incompetent employee of the business tycoon Elisha J. Whitney. Whitney is sailing from New York to England, as is Reno Sweeney, a nightclub singer. Billy has given his heart to a mysterious young woman he met in a taxi; he doesn't know that she is the heiress Hope Harcourt or that she is sailing on the same ship with her fiancé, Sir Evelyn Oakleigh. One passenger who is *not* on board is Snake Eyes Johnson, Public Enemy Number One, who missed the boat. He was to have sailed with "The Reverend" Moon-Face Mooney and Snake Eyes's girlfriend, Miss Bonnie Latour. (Moon is Public Enemy Number 13, but wants to move up in the rankings.)

Billy is just about to leave the ship when he spots his former taxi companion (and her fiancé). He makes a snap decision; he stays on board as a stowaway, and Moon offers Billy the empty berth in his cabin. The one drawback to Moon's cabin is that it is directly across the hall from Whitney's cabin—who thinks Billy is back in New York, handling his business affairs. Moon steals Whitney's glasses, but Billy still has a lot of dodging to do, and he spends much of the show in various disguises.

Billy proceeds to woo Hope vigorously, but he doesn't know that Hope is marrying Sir Evelyn in order to save her family firm. Billy asks Reno for help: Will she try to lure Sir Evelyn away from his fiancée? Her first effort—to create a situation in which it would appear that Sir Evelyn has compromised her—goes awry, but she continues her pursuit. Soon, she is able to report that she's gotten Sir Evelyn to kiss her. At this rate, she may well end up a "Lady"—especially since this is an era in which "Anything Goes" (**Musical Example 24**). Meanwhile, Billy loses his disguise, but the captain and passengers believe that he is Snake Eyes Johnson, and Billy is startled to find that they're treating him like a celebrity rather than a criminal. At last Billy admits that he's not Snake Eyes Johnson after all, nor is Moon really a reverend. The captain throws both Billy and Moon in the brig.

When the ship arrives in England, the wedding party makes its way to the Oakleigh estate—but the proceedings are interrupted by Moon, Billy, and Reno, disguised in Chinese attire. Moon and Billy are "Plum Blossom's" parents, and they claim that Sir Evelyn violated their daughter and needs to do the right thing by her now. They think that Sir Evelyn will break off his engagement with Hope, but Sir Evelyn's Uncle Oakleigh offers a financial settlement instead, which Moon quickly accepts (to the disgust of his co-conspirators).

Billy then makes a discovery: it turns out that Hope's family business is *not* in trouble; they've been misled by the scheming Uncle Oakleigh. If the merger goes through, Whitney's business will be hurt, so Billy tells him the whole story. Whitney makes a large cash offer to buy Hope's (solvent) company, which removes Sir Evelyn's incentive to marry her. Things end neatly for Billy and Hope and for Sir Evelyn and Reno; even Moon is able to swallow his dismay over being demoted from the Most Wanted list, thanks to the large check he still has from Uncle Oakleigh.

MUSICAL EXAMPLE 24

ANYTHING GOES
COLE PORTER/COLE PORTER, 1934

"Anything Goes"

Reno

1
Times have changed and we've often rewound the clock
Since the Puritans got a shock when they landed on Plymouth Rock.

2
If today any shock they would try to stem,
'Stead of landing on Plymouth Rock, Plymouth Rock would land on them.

3
In olden days a glimpse of stocking was looked upon as something shocking,
But now God knows, anything goes.

4
Good authors, too, who once knew better words now only use four-letter words
Writing prose, anything goes.

5   The world has gone mad today and good's bad today, and black's white today,
  And day's night today, when most guys today that women prize today, are just silly gigolos.

6   So though I'm not a great romancer I know that I'm bound to answer
        When you propose, anything goes!

7   When mothers pack and leave poor father because they decide they'd rather
       Be tennis pros, anything goes.
   When Missus Ned McLean, God bless her, can get Russian Reds to "yes" her,
      Then I suppose anything goes.
    If driving fast cars you like, if low bars you like, if old hymns you like,
    Or bare limbs you like, if Mae West you like, or me undressed you like
        Why, nobody would oppose.
    When ev'ry night the set that's smart is indulging in nudist parties
       In studios, anything goes.

8   When you heard that Lady Mendl, standing up, now does a hand-spring landing up
      On her toes, anything goes.
   When Sam Goldwyn can with great conviction instruct Anna Sten in diction,
      Then Anna shows anything goes.
     Just think of those shocks you got and those knocks you got
 And those blues you got from that news you got, and those pains you got (if any brains you got)
    From those little radios. So Missus R., with all her trimmin's,
   Can broadcast a bed for Simmons 'cause Franklin knows anything goes.

A Greater Maturity

Chapter 22
New Achievements from Familiar Names: Rodgers and Hart, Irving Berlin

As the years elapsed during the first half of the twentieth century, musical theater works developed an increasing maturity and coherence. It was an exciting time for theater; not only did new names appear in the credits, but some new partnerships formed as well. As if rising to the challenge, though, several of the older theatrical veterans responded with their finest works, including Rodgers and Hart with their controversial *Pal Joey* (1940) and Irving Berlin with his charming *Annie Get Your Gun* (1946). These two shows reflect the wide range of musicals; one show is a cynical look at three-dimensional people leading somewhat sordid lives, the other is a more traditional tribute to an idealized American "can-do" frontier spirit—the belief that perseverance can overcome any obstacle. The contrast between the two productions demonstrates that Broadway was ready to accept a diversity of worldviews.

Or was it? *Pal Joey* met with some distinctly chilly criticism—but the musical held on tenaciously to survive an 11-month run of 374 performances (and a three-month tour). Certainly, it was helped by the established reputation of Rodgers and Hart, who had few rivals in the mid-1930s; their 1937 hit *Babes in Arms* had produced no fewer than five songs that became **standards**—tunes that belong to the standard popular repertory—including "I Wish I Were in Love Again," "Johnny One Note," "The Lady Is a Tramp," "My Funny Valentine," and "Where or When." In another show the same year, Rodgers and Hart persuaded George M. Cohan to make his first appearance on stage in ten years, and it was the only time Cohan would appear in a show he had not written himself. (Dorothy Hart, Hart's sister, relates, "At the climax of the show, George M. Cohan, as FDR, pleaded for a third term for

Roosevelt. And every night, the speech drew boos from the orchestra and cheers from the balcony.")

Rodgers and Hart continued their amazing productivity in 1938 with two more successful shows, but a 1939 effort wasn't as big a hit, and their first show of 1940, *Higher and Higher*, was even more disappointing. Rodgers himself called it a disaster, explaining, "Perhaps we should have waited for [our original star], but at the time it seemed best to have the play rewritten to fit someone else." Rodgers pointed out the folly of this approach, saying, "It had taken me years to learn that a show can be altered, songs can be added or dropped, and actors can be replaced, but once the basic structure of the production is set, it is suicide to try to change it." Ruefully, Rodgers added, "If [the show] is remembered at all today it is probably not because of its cast or songs but because of a trained seal. This leads to another of Rodgers's Irrefutable Rules: If a trained seal steals your show, you don't have a show."

Before this setback, Rodgers had received a letter from **John O'Hara**, who had written a series of short stories for the *New Yorker* magazine. (O'Hara was the man who, as mentioned in Chapter 19, "Great Partnerships of the Early Book Musical: The Gershwins (2)," had reserved the right to disbelieve George Gershwin's death if he wanted to.) O'Hara's tales were "about a guy who is a master of ceremonies in cheap night clubs, and the pieces are in the form of letters from him to a successful band leader. Anyway, I got the idea that the pieces, or at least the character and the life in general, could be made into a book show, and I wonder if you and Larry would be interested in working on it with me." (O'Hara's reference to a **book show** means that he was proposing a musical with a plot, or book, rather than suggesting a revue.)

Rodgers was interested, and soon afterward Rodgers attended *The Time of Your Life* featuring a young man playing an aspiring entertainer. The actor was Gene Kelly, and Rodgers immediately wrote to O'Hara, telling him that he'd found their Joey (see the **Plot Summary**). The rest of the cast was strong too; Vivienne Segal handled the difficult role of Vera with aplomb. Jean Castro (playing the reporter) got some tips on the art of striptease from burlesque star Gypsy Rose Lee. Lee, whose biography would be the subject of *Gypsy* (Chapter 30, "Jule Styne and Frank Loesser"), had personal reasons for stopping by; her sister June Havoc was making her Broadway stage debut in *Pal Joey*.

The two nightclubs that function in the story allow dance to play a natural role in the plot; like diegetic songs (and the other terms often used, prop songs and source music), the dancing makes sense as "real" dances that people actually would see in nightclubs. The choreographer Robert Alton, however, took the reality a step further in his casting: he created a **character chorus line**, meaning that he mixed the body types among *Pal Joey*'s dancers, to reinforce the message that these are "low-class joints." Normally, a producer or director choosing performers for a high-budget chorus line aspired to "match" the dancers so that they were all (for instance) tall and blonde, or short and brunette; the types of nightclubs in *Pal Joey* wouldn't be able to afford this type of matched line.

George Abbott was the director and producer of *Pal Joey* (and he also gave John O'Hara uncredited assistance with the book). Others had contributed to the storyline too; set designer Jo Mielziner suggested that the **curtain of Act I** (the scene that precedes the dropping of the curtain at the end of the act) could be a setting in which Joey envisions the glamorous nightclub that Vera is going to buy him. Abbott agreed to the expensive stage set ($10,000, or about one-tenth of the show's total budget) because he concurred that this scene would be an effective close to the first act. During the scene, Joey dances his way through a pantomimed vision of the future, and so the scene functions as a **dream ballet**. When *Oklahoma!* opened in 1943, its dream ballet was widely praised for its integration into the story—but *Pal Joey* had anticipated the device by three years and used it just as effectively.

Part of the reason that *Pal Joey*'s dream ballet received less attention may have been that *Pal Joey* simply was seen by far fewer people. Although *Pal Joey* had a better run than the two previous Rodgers and Hart shows combined, a myth arose that *Pal Joey* had been forced to close because of a widely quoted last line from a fairly severe critique by Brooks Atkinson in the *New York Times*:

> *If it is possible to make an entertaining musical comedy out of an odious story, "Pal Joey" is it. . . . Rodgers and Hart have written the score with wit and skill. Robert Alton has directed the dances inventively. Scenery out of Jo Mielziner's sketchbook and costumes off the rack of John Koenig—all very high class. Some talented performers also act a book that is considerably more dramatic than most. "Pal Joey," which was put on at the Ethel Barrymore last evening, offers everything but a good time.*

> *Whether Joey is a punk or a heel is something worth more careful thinking than time permits. Perhaps he is only a rat infested with termites. A night club dancer and singer, promoted to master of ceremonies in a Chicago dive, he lies himself into an affair with a rich married woman and opens a gilt-edged club of his own with her money. Mr. O'Hara has drawn a pitiless portrait of his small-time braggart and also of the company he keeps. . . . But the story of "Pal Joey" keeps harking back to the drab and mirthless world of punk's progress. Although "Pal Joey" is expertly done, can you draw sweet water from a foul well?*

Reviews customarily appeared in the papers on the day following a show's **opening night**—its first public performance. After the first performance ended, the cast and creators of a show would hold a party, at a restaurant or some such location, that would last until the earliest editions of the next day's papers were released, when the reviews would be read aloud. In this way, the entire company would share in the joy of a positive review—or the misery of a negative one. (Colleagues recall that Hart burst into tears after hearing Atkinson's comments.) Atkinson's review wasn't *too* damaging, since *Pal Joey* had a perfectly satisfactory run for months afterwards. However, two things emerge very clearly from Atkinson's review: first, he credits *Pal Joey*'s creators with doing a very, very good job, and second, he *really* finds the characters unlikable and the situation unsavory. Not since *Don Giovanni* had theatergoers been faced with such an antihero in the lead role, and even Mozart's (and da Ponte's) Don revealed more charm than O'Hara's "rat infested with termites."

Not all the critics condemned *Pal Joey*; one called it a rarity—"a song-and-dance production with living, three-dimensional figures, talking and behaving like human beings." The numerous character songs help us to understand the perspectives of the individual personalities (even if we don't fully sympathize with them). Vera's priorities, for instant, become much clearer during "Bewitched, Bothered, and Bewildered" (**Musical Example 25**), which she sings in a tailor shop while Joey is being outfitted. This number is also a comedy song, structured as a series of short jokes; most of Hart's humor is in the same vein as Cole Porter's, for the laughs are derived from sexual innuendo and double entendres. Vera is singing about Joey's attributes, but she's certainly not discussing his character in this tribute; it's strictly his qualities as a lover that come in for her praise. Hart was very gleeful about getting certain lines past the censors; for instance, Hart's friend Joshua Logan recalls Hart's delight over the bridge of the first chorus (**4**) in which Vera calls Joey a laugh, and then remarks that "the laugh's on me."

In Vera's introductory verse at **1**, the melody of each phrase starts with a downward drop, as if symbolizing how she's fallen for this man. The first chorus at **2** is set in a clear-cut song form (with the *a-a-b-a* corresponding to **2**, **3**, **4**, and **5**). Each *a* phrase begins with a short joke, then concludes with the same text: "bewitched, bothered, and bewildered." As Cole Porter experienced with "I Get a Kick Out of You," Rodgers and Hart had some trouble getting "Bewitched" played on the radio, since censors felt some of the lyrics were simply too suggestive. Moreover, as late as 1957, when the movie was filmed, a number of the lines were changed to be less racy—and Vera even hummed through some phrases! (On the other hand, the film had Vera sing the song languidly in her boudoir as she was just awakening, presumably after a night of passion—a far more suggestive setting than a tailor shop.)

The second and third choruses (**6** and **7**) conform to the same song-form pattern with the same series of "three-rhymes" (i.e., *sing to him / spring to him / cling to him*), each followed by the reiterated "bewitched, bothered, and bewildered." Vera's constant return to this triple-B alliteration may well represent her current obsession with Joey. Certainly, she reveals a lot of her ruthless determination to have him; as Lehman Engel puts it, "Vera Simpson, through the medium of this song, figuratively undresses herself." Moreover, as Geoffrey Block observes, "Vera's ability to rhyme internally reflects her complexity and sophistication—or, as Sondheim would say, her education."

"Bewitched" comes to a close after the third chorus, but Rodgers and Hart planned for an encore. Encores are prompted by enthusiastic audience applause and occur only on demand, but a savvy theatrical writer can anticipate places where an encore will probably be desired. Usually, an encore repeats a previous chorus, perhaps with some improvisation, but if the creators expect that a certain tune will be encored on a regular basis, they might write new words for the encore itself. This sort of "prepared" encore appears at the end of "Bewitched," as Vera muses to herself in song, rather ironically, about how quickly Joey is learning to spend Mr. Simpson's money. The encore (**8**) begins with the melody of the opening verse (**1**), followed by one last *a* phrase at **9**.

Rodgers and Hart found another place to use "Bewitched" in *Pal Joey*; it occurs near the end of the musical, as a reprise—but with different words (**10**), since Vera is determined to end the affair. The reprise eliminates the verse completely, and consists merely of one complete chorus—but this is sufficient for Vera to get her message across; she's "bewitched, bothered, and bewildered no more."

Pal Joey's frank acknowledgment of an adulterous sexual relationship and a seamy nightclub environment attached a lasting stigma to the show. The producer had trouble funding a revival in 1952, since backers recalled the musical's squalid reputation. However, the revival got a much different reaction than it had 12 years earlier. Society had altered during the war years, and it was now much more tolerant of the sordid situation and Hart's racy lyrics. Even Brooks Atkinson liked the revival; he admitted that he hadn't cared for the original, but commented, "It is true that *Pal Joey* was a pioneer in the moving back of musical frontiers, for it tells an integrated story from a knowing point of view," and he felt, "*Pal Joey* renews confidence in the professionalism of the theatre." By running 542 performances, the revival not only outran the **first run** (the duration of the original production)—an unusual achievement in itself—but it played longer than the first run of *any* Rodgers and Hart production. Curiously, the New York Drama Critics named the 1952 *Pal Joey* the "best musical of the year," even though their constitution mandated that the award was to be given only to *new* shows.

Sadly, by the time *Pal Joey* earned its belated recognition in 1952, Rodgers and O'Hara were estranged, and Hart had died. There had been no new Rodgers and Hart show in 1941, the year following *Pal Joey*, and according to Rodgers, the reason "was Larry . . . who was compulsively bent on self-destruction and who no longer cared about his work." Hart would vanish; there were allusions to homosexual forays and drinking bouts. Rodgers took the heat for Hart's disappearances, since Hart often missed meetings. Rodgers was only 39 years old, so he began to think about a new collaborator. In late 1941, he met with Oscar Hammerstein II, who said, "I think you ought to keep working with Larry just so long as he is able to keep working with you. It would kill him if you walked away while he was still able to function. But if the time ever comes when he cannot function, call me. I'll be here."

As it turned out, Hart was able to "function" for one more collaboration with Rodgers: *By Jupiter*, which appeared in 1942. The show was tailored around their star hoofer of *On Your Toes*, Ray Bolger, who had just returned to Broadway after appearing as the Scarecrow in the 1939 MGM film *The Wizard of Oz*. Rodgers hoped the project would keep Hart sober, but this proved not to be the case; much of the score, book, and lyrics were written while Hart was hospitalized between binges. Rodgers resorted to renting an adjacent hospital room and bringing in a piano. *By Jupiter* had its New York premiere in June 1942 and played 427 performances—the longest first run of any Rodgers and Hart musical.

Joey (Gene Kelly), Linda (Leila Ernst), and Vera (Vivienne Segal) in *Pal Joey*.
Museum of the City of New York.

Shortly after the opening of *By Jupiter*, two of Rodgers and Hart's Theatre Guild friends, Theresa Helburn and Lawrence Langner, approached Rodgers about reworking an older play, *Green Grow the Lilacs*, into a musical. Rodgers was excited by the idea, but Hart was not, saying he wanted a break in Mexico. Rodgers, knowing this "vacation" would be yet another alcoholic binge, was surprisingly direct; telling Hart, "This show means a lot to me. . . . If you walk out on me now, I'm going to do it with someone else." Hart merely said, "You know, Dick, I've really never understood why you've put up with me all these years. It's been crazy. The best thing for you to do is forget about me." Thus ended a remarkably fruitful 24-year partnership, later featured in a highly fictionalized 1948 biographical film called *Words and Music*. Before Hart walked out, however, he warned Rodgers that he didn't think *Green Grow the Lilacs* would make a good musical, and it would be a mistake. Of course, as Chapter 25, "Rodgers and Hammerstein," relates, the resulting *Oklahoma!* was the biggest blockbuster that Broadway had ever seen—but Rodgers had no way of knowing that, and all he could do immediately after Hart's departure was weep.

In contrast, by serving as his own lyricist, Irving Berlin avoided many of the problems that had eventually severed the partnership of Rodgers and Hart. After *As Thousands Cheer*, he divided his time between New York and Hollywood. For the 1942 film *Holiday Inn*, Berlin reused some older tunes, but wrote some new songs too, including the blockbuster "White Christmas." In his customary not-so-modest way, Berlin called his long-time transcriber Helmy Kresa and said, "I want you to take down a song I wrote over the weekend. Not only is it the best song *I* ever wrote, it's the best song *anybody* ever wrote." Berlin would later have some statistics to support his claim; during the first ten years after "White Christmas" was released, it sold 3 million copies of sheet music and 14 million records.

After *Holiday Inn*, Berlin's thoughts turned to a possible contribution to the war effort. He had an idea for a new all-soldier revue, similar to his *Yip, Yip, Yaphank* during World War I. The resulting *This Is the Army*, which would benefit the Army Emergency Relief Fund, opened on July 4, 1942. Berlin's efforts proved worthwhile; the show earned 10 million dollars for the fund plus another $350,000 for relief agencies in Britain. During its tour, it was seen by 2.5 million soldiers all over the world, and Berlin was awarded the Medal of Merit. Berlin's cast of 300 soldiers included a number of African American performers—a move resisted by the army, since the armed forces were currently segregated. Berlin prevailed, and *This Is the Army* featured the only integrated company in uniform. *This Is the Army* was preserved for posterity by means of an **original cast album** of the show, featuring the hit songs sung by their original singers. Original cast albums would eventually become an important source of revenue for a show, as rival recording companies would bid on the rights to record the music—and from the perspective of history, these recordings are often an important lasting testimony to a show's strengths and weaknesses as well as performance practice.

In the meantime, the new team of Rodgers and Hammerstein had taken Broadway by storm, and by 1946, they were ready to try the role of producers. Dorothy Fields had the idea of casting Ethel Merman as the sharpshooter Annie Oakley. Fields would write the lyrics and cowrite the book with her

brother Herbert, and Rodgers and Hammerstein invited Jerome Kern to write the score. Rodgers wrote, "It would be one of the greatest honors of my life if you would consent to write the music for this show." Sadly, shortly after arriving in New York from California, Kern collapsed on the street and died.

Despite their grief over the great composer's death, the creative team was determined that the Annie Oakley project should go forward, and they offered the score to Berlin. Berlin hesitated at first, unsure why Rodgers and Hammerstein weren't writing the score themselves, and a little reluctant to commit himself to writing "integrated" songs for specific situations (see the **Plot Summary**). Moreover, he was unconvinced that he would be able to write (as he called it) "hillbilly stuff," although Hammerstein told him, "All you have to do is drop the g's. Instead of 'thinking,' write 'thinkin'." At last Rodgers and Hammerstein persuaded Berlin to take the libretto home and try his hand at a song or two. Within a week, Berlin had produced a half-dozen numbers, and *Annie Get Your Gun* was underway.

One of the show's lasting hits almost never made it to the stage. Berlin would play his latest songs to Rodgers and Hammerstein for their approval. After Berlin had introduced "There's No Business Like Show Business," he looked at the faces of the listeners and decided they looked unimpressed. So, in a play-through a few days later, he omitted the tune. Rodgers asked about the missing number, and Berlin explained that he had sensed that Rodgers wasn't happy with it. Startled, Rodgers told him, "My God, Irving, . . . don't ever pay any attention to the expression on my face. I love that song. I looked sour only because I was concentrating on where it should go." There was an anxious scramble back in Berlin's office to find the abandoned **lead sheet** (a short-hand version of sheet music, which includes the melody and the chords), but "There's No Business Like Show Business" made it back into the score safely, going on to be one of the cherished anthems of the musical theater industry.

Overall, *Annie Get Your Gun* was Irving Berlin's best musical score, due in part to the integration of its 19 songs into the plot; most of the tunes "work" only in the context of this particular story. Undoubtedly, Berlin felt challenged to submit only his finest work, since the songs needed to be acceptable to Rodgers and Hammerstein—far more perceptive listeners than most Broadway producers. (Nevertheless, the Native American stereotypes within *Annie Get Your Gun* can offend modern viewers, just as *Show Boat* uses regrettable terms for African Americans.)

Rodgers and Hammerstein were a bit more daring than many producers of the time. They took the risky step of *not* selling **benefits** to *Annie Get Your Gun*. A benefit was a performance for which some (or all) of the seats had been presold to a charity. The charity would then sell the tickets at a profit to people who supported the charity; the profit was a form of fund-raising for the charitable organization. The advantage, from the theatrical producer's perspective, was that benefits ensured that seats would be sold for the show ahead of time; sometimes benefit bookings could fill the first several weeks of a new show's run. But there were two big disadvantages: if a production proved to be a hit on its opening night, people reading the show's reviews would then go to the box office only to find that they often couldn't attend the show until six or eight weeks later, since the tickets would have been sold to charities. A show could lose some of its momentum, since some potential customers would elect not to wait that long. The second disadvantage, as Rodgers and Hammerstein explained, was that many people who bought benefit tickets were strictly supporting the charity, not the show itself.

> *The people who have bought tickets at a very high premium . . . are the cruelest audience an actor can encounter. Opening night sophisticates and critics are gleeful children compared with these scowling, sour-pussed donors to charity. . . . They didn't choose [the show] themselves. They didn't even pick out the night to go to the theatre. They are making a donation. They are benefactors. They don't have to applaud or laugh or show any appreciation of the company's efforts. . . .*
>
> *What an abnormal, stony-faced group like this can do to the morale of a theatrical company is incalculable. When the actors face a succession of such audiences four or five times a week for six weeks they begin to lose faith in their play and in themselves.*

Rodgers and Hammerstein's gamble proved to be successful. The show met with universally positive reports when it premiered on May 16, 1946, and ticket sales were brisk for months and months to come.

Nearly all the critics regarded the musical as a terrific star vehicle for Merman. It certainly was the biggest hit of her career, and the newspapers commented that when Merman returned to the cast after a vacation in 1948, the weekly box office receipts jumped from $11,528 to $35,582. Merman is sometimes credited with having performed in all the 1,147 performances of *Annie Get Your Gun*'s first run, which is not entirely accurate—she took the previously mentioned six-week vacation—but she *did* stay with the production until it closed, which is almost never the case today with stars in a long-running show. Moreover, no less a name than Mary Martin played Annie in the touring production; tours seldom featured performers of her stature. Although *Annie Get Your Gun* did not run as long as *Oklahoma!* on Broadway, it actually outran the Rodgers and Hammerstein hit in several foreign countries.

One of the biggest hits in *Annie Get Your Gun* had an astonishingly short gestation. During a play-through of the existing numbers shortly before the first rehearsal, Joshua Logan, the show's director, felt that a duet was needed between Annie and Frank in the second act. The problem was that Annie and Frank aren't speaking to each other in much of Act II, but Rodgers suggested that what was needed was some sort of quarreling song, or a **challenge song**. Instantly, Berlin excitedly adjourned the meeting, wanting to race home and work out his ideas. Just as Logan walked in through the door of his own apartment, the phone was ringing; it was Berlin, who wanted to sing the chorus of his new song to Logan. The song was "Anything You Can Do" (**Musical Example 26**), and Logan knew it was the perfect solution—but he couldn't believe the timetable. How had Berlin composed it so quickly? Berlin told Logan that he'd written it in the taxicab on his way home—a journey of perhaps 15 minutes! But, as Berlin explained, "I had to, didn't I? We go into rehearsal Monday."

Before Berlin had written "Anything You Can Do," *Annie Get Your Gun* lacked an **eleven o'clock number**. Most performances began at 8:30 P.M., so it was customary to have some sort of climactic number in the show around 11 P.M., just before the end of the show. "Anything You Can Do" proved to be the perfect tune; besides being a showstopper, it sustained the concept of the show, illustrating the competitiveness between Annie and Frank. The duet toys with a number of musicians' performance skills (as well as other assorted abilities), which seem to grow funnier and funnier as the song progresses.

The tune is structured in **theme and variations form**. Theme and variations form is similar to strophic form, for the same basic material, or theme, unifies the song, but the initial theme undergoes a series of modifications, or variations; the overall structure can be diagrammed as A-A'-A'' (etc.). The theme itself (*A*) is made up of an *a-a-b-a* song form. The first of the subsections, *a*, begins at **1** with Annie's blanket assertion that "*anything* Frank can do, *she* can do better." The second challenge appears at **2** (the second subsection *a* of the song form), in which Frank insists he is "greater" than Annie. The first *b* section (**3**) consists of rival "brags"—"I can shoot a partridge with a single cartridge"—although some of the abilities are of somewhat dubious value. The last *a* subsection of the theme appears at **4**, which is the first of the "musical" challenges; Frank claims, "Any note you can reach, I can go higher," and immediately the two combatants engage in a "pitch" battle.

The first variation (*A'*) begins at **5**. The second *a* subsection of this variation (**6**) is another musical contest, this time focused on dynamics: who can say things the softest? The last subsection *a* of this chorus (at **8**) allows the two performers to parade their ability to sing sustained pitches, thus varying the initial theme in a new way. (Holding out long notes requires good breath control and is one measure of a trained singer.) At the end of this particular debate, as Annie continues to sing her last note for an impressively long time, Frank concedes the point to her: "Yes, you can!"

The next variation, *A''* (**9**), continues the same basic pattern. The second subsection *a* (**10**) is a tempo contest (one of the funniest moments of the song). In the final contest, during the last *a* subsection (**12**), Frank challenges Annie to "sing sweeter," introducing a new musical element to the series of variations. Although Annie has "won" most of the contests, one could argue that Annie—as played by Ethel Merman—*can't* sing more lyrically than Frank! In any event, it is easy to see how this fun song created an effective showstopper—and eleven o'clock number—for *Annie Get Your Gun*.

Irving Berlin had only a few more shows up his sleeve; the first failed to break even, but the second, *Call Me Madam* (1950), was another triumphant star vehicle for Merman. A late addition, the quodlibet "You're Just in Love," enjoyed seven encores on the first night of its tryout tour. The early years of the 1950s continued to go well for Berlin, particularly in Hollywood, but the flow dried up by mid-decade. Berlin attempted one last Broadway production in 1962, but it, too, failed to recoup its expenses.

Berlin had a final Broadway contribution to make, however. In 1966, *Annie Get Your Gun* was revived (again with Merman) after some refreshing of the book and score. Tunes were cut, and a new tune was inserted—Annie and Frank's description of "An Old-Fashioned Wedding." Like "You're Just in Love," the new song was a delightful quodlibet illustrating

Annie (Ethel Merman) and Frank (Ray Middleton), stars of *Annie Get Your Gun*.
Corbis/Bettmann.

the two partners' differing visions of the ideal marriage ceremony. Afterwards, Berlin grew increasingly reclusive and less cooperative with those who wished to interview him, license his works, or simply celebrate his career. He seldom emerged from his New York mansion, even failing to attend his wife Ellin's funeral in 1988. Little more than a year later, at the age of 101, "the Last of the Troubadours" died quietly at home.

FURTHER READING

Abbott, George. *Mister Abbott*. New York: Random House, 1963.

Barrett, Mary Ellin. *Irving Berlin: A Daughter's Memoir*. New York: Simon & Schuster, 1994.

Bergreen, Laurence. *As Thousands Cheer: The Life of Irving Berlin*. New York: Penguin Books, 1990.

Block, Geoffrey. *Enchanted Evenings: The Broadway Musical from* Show Boat *to Sondheim*. New York: Oxford University Press, 1997.

Engel, Lehman. *Words with Music*. New York: Schirmer Books, 1972.

Fordin, Hugh. *Getting to Know Him: A Biography of Oscar Hammerstein II*. New York: Random House, 1977.

Forte, Allen. *The American Popular Ballad of the Golden Era, 1924–1950*. Princeton, New Jersey: Princeton University Press, 1995.

Gaver, Jack. *Curtain Calls*. New York: Dodd, Mead, 1949.

Hart, Dorothy, ed. *Thou Swell, Thou Witty: The Life and Lyrics of Lorenz Hart*. New York: Harper & Row, 1976.

Hart, Dorothy, and Robert Kimball, eds. *The Complete Lyrics of Lorenz Hart*. London: Hamish Hamilton, 1987.

Hyland, William G. *Richard Rodgers*. New Haven and London: Yale University Press, 1998.

Marx, Samuel, and Jan Clayton. *Rodgers and Hart: Bewitched, Bothered and Bedeviled*. London: W. H. Allen, 1977.

Nolan, Frederick. *Lorenz Hart: A Poet on Broadway*. New York: Oxford University Press, 1994.

Rodgers, Richard. *Musical Stages: An Autobiography*. New York: Da Capo Press, 1995.

Secrest, Meryle. *Somewhere for Me: A Biography of Richard Rodgers*. New York: Alfred A. Knopf, 2001.

Taylor, Deems. *Some Enchanted Evenings: The Story of Rodgers and Hammerstein.* New York: Harper & Brothers, 1953. Reprinted Westport, Connecticut: Greenwood Press, 1972.

PLOT SUMMARY: *PAL JOEY*

The sordid tale that shocked 1940s audiences opens with a slick song-and-dance man, Joey Evans, auditioning to be Master of Ceremonies at a sleazy nightclub. Mike Spears, the owner, figures the glib Joey is the sort he can use, and Gladys Bumps, the club's lead singer, shows Joey the ropes. Meanwhile, Joey uses his best pickup line, "I Could Write a Book (About You)," on a young woman he spots on the street. Linda English is flattered by his attention, but she's not really the type Joey is looking for—not only is she not wealthy, but she's currently so poor that she's sleeping on her brother's couch.

Joey meets Linda again when she visits the nightclub with a boyfriend, but Mike tells Joey to pay attention instead to a wealthy society woman, Vera Simpson (*Mrs.* Simpson). The world-wise Vera knows Joey's type too, and Joey knows she knows it, so he refuses to entertain her as Mike wishes, and Vera leaves in a huff at being ignored. Mike fires Joey, but Joey makes a bargain with him: if Vera's not back in a night or two, then Joey will leave the job and forgo all salary. Mike, with nothing to lose, agrees to the bet. (During this altercation, Joey never noticed that Linda has left the club too.)

Joey loses the bet, for Vera never shows up. He tries calling Linda, but she hangs up on him. He then phones Vera, telling her that she cost him his job, and she ends up paying for his apartment, buying him clothes, and even setting him up in a nightclub of his own. She muses to herself that she's "Bewitched, Bothered, and Bewildered" (**Musical Example 25**). She and Joey both know that their relationship is strictly physical, but he dreamily envisions the future nightclub.

Joey hires Gladys and other performers away from Mike to staff his new venture, and he meets with a reporter who is covering the nightclub's debut. Gladys persuades Joey to sign with an agent as well. Some time later, Linda arrives at the club with a C.O.D. package. While she's waiting for payment, she overhears Gladys and the agent discussing a scheme to blackmail Vera by threatening to tell Mr. Simpson about the love nest Vera maintains for Joey. Linda immediately tells Vera and Joey about the plot. Vera is suspicious at first that Linda may want Joey herself, but Linda is fully aware of Joey's shortcomings—and isn't interested. Vera thanks the younger woman for her warning and places a phone call to the police commissioner, who arrests the blackmailers when they show up. Vera knows that when things have gotten to this stage, it's time to call the affair off. Joey is disconsolate at first, but soon he's heard conning yet another young woman, telling her "I Could Write a Book."

PLOT SUMMARY: *ANNIE GET YOUR GUN*

Although it is a fictionalized story, *Annie Get Your Gun* is based on a real person, Annie Oakley, and the real "Wild West Show" she joined to show off her marksmanship. The plot, set during America's frontier era, opens in Cincinnati, Ohio. The advance man Charlie Davenport—the person who travels ahead of a troupe, arranging bookings and lodgings—tries to persuade hotel owner Mr. Wilson to board the company for free if the troupe's sharpshooter, Frank Butler, can beat any local champion. Annie Oakley strides on stage; she has some game to sell, and Mr. Wilson is impressed with her clean shooting. Here, also, is a woman who might win the bet for him, and Annie is happy to be his champion.

Before the shooting contest, Annie brags to a handsome stranger about the challenge. She's very attracted to him, but his dream woman is nothing at all like tomboyish Annie. She's startled to find that the stranger is Frank himself (but not so shaken up that she loses her shooting eye). After she wins the contest, Charlie wants to add her to Buffalo Bill's Wild West Show as Frank's partner. Frank refuses until Annie begs to be merely his assistant, and Charlie, Frank, and Buffalo Bill celebrate by observing "There's No Business Like Show Business." Only Dolly, Frank's former assistant, is unhappy.

All goes smoothly enough for a time, until Annie accidentally makes Frank feel upstaged. Dolly's also angry with Annie, for Annie had helped Winnie (Dolly's daughter) to marry Tommy, another member of the troupe. In a temper, Frank announces that he is joining Pawnee Bill's show, where he'll perform his old act with Dolly. The only bright spot is that Chief Sitting Bull—who had been featured in Pawnee Bill's show—is intrigued with Annie to the point that he joins Buffalo Bill's show as a financial backer (despite his long-standing personal rules to the contrary!).

Time passes, and the Wild West Show returns from a triumphal tour of Europe—triumphal in the sense that they were greatly admired, but disastrous financially. All they have to show for their efforts is a chest of glittering medals Annie has earned with her shooting. What is worse, they learn that Pawnee Bill's show is currently playing at New York's Madison Square Garden, where it is the toast of the town. Sitting Bull has an idea: Even though Pawnee Bill's show is getting the attention, Buffalo Bill's show has the better acts; the two shows should merge to create one great powerhouse. (Annie is delighted at the idea, as long as *she* gets to merge with Frank.) Pawnee Bill is surprisingly amenable to the proposal, but his willingness is explained when it turns out his finances are in equally poor shape. In fact, the only way to save the two shows is to sell off Annie's medals. She's willing, but she's proud of her success, and she wants Frank to see her wearing them first. When she and Frank are reunited, he seems to feel his previous tenderness for her; in fact, he wants to give her the three medals he's won as a gift. Annie opens her coat to display the vast array of medals she's already earned herself, and Frank feels upstaged all over again. Instantly, the merger is off, but a new shooting match is proposed: Annie versus Frank, with her chest of medals staked against his three medals.

Dolly arrives at the contest location early the next morning, intent on sabotaging Annie's guns. She's caught by Sitting Bull and Charlie, but after she leaves, they get to thinking: Frank's pride is the crux of the matter; he just can't tolerate losing to Annie. If she should win, there's simply no chance of a merger. They happily complete the sabotage that Dolly had not finished. Annie and Frank taunt each other at the start of the match, boasting "Anything You Can Do (I Can Do Better)" (**Musical Example 26**). But Annie's shooting is wildly off target—and Frank's cheerfulness and affection toward her increases accordingly. Annie asks for a replacement gun, and her score improves dramatically, but Chief Sitting Bull feels compelled to intervene. He hands her the first (sabotaged) weapon, telling her that she *can* get a man with a gun, if she uses *this* gun. The truth dawns on Annie, and she returns to missing the target as she had before—but she does so with a light heart now. She cheerfully delivers the medals to Frank after he wins the competition. It is agreed that the proceeds from the medals will fund a new combined Wild West show that will star the world's best sharp-shooting team: Mr. and Mrs. Frank Butler.

MUSICAL EXAMPLE 25

PAL JOEY
RICHARD RODGERS/LORENZ HART, 1940
"Bewitched, Bothered, and Bewildered"

Vera

1 He's a fool, and don't I know it—But a fool can have his charms;
I'm in love and don't I show it, like a babe in arms.
Men are not a new sensation; I've done pretty well I think.
But this half-pint imitation put me on the blink.

2 I'm wild again! Beguiled again! A simpering, whimpering child again—
Bewitched, bothered and bewildered am I.

3 Couldn't sleep, and wouldn't sleep, until I could sleep where I shouldn't sleep—
Bewitched, bothered and bewildered am I.

4 Lost my heart but what of it? My mistake, I agree.
He can laugh, but I love it because the laugh's on me—

5 A pill he is, but still he is all mine and I'll keep him until he is
Bewitched, bothered and bewildered like me.

6 Seen a lot—I mean a lot—But now I'm like sweet seventeen a lot—
Bewitched, bothered and bewildered am I.
I'll sing to him, each spring to him, and worship the trousers that cling to him—
Bewitched, bothered and bewildered am I.
When he talks, he is seeking words to get off his chest.
Horizontally speaking, he's at his very best.
Vexed again, perplexed again, thank God I can be oversexed again—
Bewitched, bothered and bewildered am I.

7 Sweet again, Petite again, And on my proverbial seat again—
Bewitched, bothered and bewildered am I.
What am I? Half shot am I. To think that he loves me so hot am I—
Bewitched, bothered and bewildered am I.
Though at first we said "No, sir." Now we're two little dears—
You might say we are closer than Roebuck is to Sears.
I'm dumb again and numb again, a rich, ready, ripe little plum again—
Bewitched, bothered and bewildered am I.

Encore

8 You know it is really quite funny just how quickly he learns
How to spend all that money that Mr. Simpson earns.

9 He's kept enough, He's slept enough, and yet, where it counts, he's adept enough—
Bewitched, bothered and bewildered am I.

Final Reprise

10 Wise at last, my eyes at last are cutting you down to your size at last—
Bewitched, bothered and bewildered no more.
Burned a lot, but learned a lot, And now you are broke, though you earned a lot—
Bewitched, bothered and bewildered no more.
Couldn't eat—was dyspeptic, Life was so hard to bear;
Now my heart's antiseptic, since he moved out of there.
Romance—finis; Your chance—finis; those ants that invaded my pants—finis—
Bewitched, bothered and bewildered no more.

MUSICAL EXAMPLE 26

ANNIE GET YOUR GUN
IRVING BERLIN/IRVING BERLIN, 1946
"Anything You Can Do"

1

Frank
No you can't.

Annie
Yes I can.

Annie
Anything you can do I can do better. I can do anything better than you.

Frank
No you can't.

Annie
Yes I can.

Frank
No you can't.

Annie
Yes I can, Yes, I can.

2

Annie
No you're not.

Frank
Yes I am.

Annie
Anything you can be, I can be greater, Sooner or later I'm greater than you.

Annie
No you're not.

Frank
Yes I am.

Annie
No you're not.

Frank
Yes I am, Yes I am!

3

I can shoot a partridge With a single cartridge.

Annie
I can hit a sparrow With a bow and arrow.

I can live on bread and cheese.

And only on that?

Yes.

So can a rat!

4

Frank
No you can't.

Annie
Yes I can.

I can sing anything higher than you.

Frank
No you can't.

Annie
Yes I can.

Any note you can reach, I can go higher.

Frank
No you can't.

Annie
Yes I can.

5

Frank
Fifty cents.

Annie
Forty cents.

Anything you can buy, I can buy cheaper. I can buy anything cheaper than you.

Frank
Thirty cents.

Annie
Twenty cents.

Frank
No you can't.

Annie
Yes I can.

Annie
Yes I can, Yes I can!

6

Anything you can say, I can say softer.

Annie
Anything you can say, I can say softer.

I can say anything softer than you.

Frank
No you can't.

Annie
Yes I can.

Annie
Yes I can, Yes I can!

7

Frank
No you can't.

I can drink my liquor Faster than a flicker.

Annie
I can do it quicker And get even sicker,

I can open any safe.

Without being caught?

Frank
No you can't.

Annie
Yes I can, Yes I can!

Sure.

That's what I thought—You crook!

Any note you can hold, I can hold longer.

I can hold any note longer than you.

8

Frank
No you can't.

Frank
No you can't.

Annie
Yes I can.

Annie
Yes I can.

Frank
No you can't. No you can't.

Frank
Yes, you can!

Annie
Yes I can. Yes I—can.

9

Frank
In my coat?

Annie
In your vest.

Anything you can wear, I can wear better. In what you wear I'd look better than you.

Frank
In my shoes?

Annie
In your hat.

Annie
Yes I can, Yes I can!

Frank
No you can't.

10

Anything you can say, I can say faster.

Annie
I can say anything faster than you.

Frank
No you can't.

Annie
Yes I can.

Frank
No you can't, No you can't.

Annie
Yes I can, Yes I can!

11

Frank
I can jump a hurdle.

Annie
I can wear a girdle.

I can knit a sweater.

I can fill it better.

I can do most anything.

Can you bake a pie?

No.

Neither can I.

12

Anything you can sing I can sing sweeter.

I can sing anything sweeter than you.

Frank
No you can't.

Annie
Yes I can.

Frank
No you can't.

Annie
Yes I can.

Frank
No, you can't, can't, can't.

Annie
Yes, I can, can, can!

Annie and Frank
Yes, I can! // No, you can't!

Chapter 23
A Cole Porter Renaissance and the Rise of Recognition

Born into a life of privilege, married to a beautiful (and rich) wife, author of several hit Broadway shows—it seemed that Cole Porter should be on top of the world. Fate had a hard knock in store for Porter, however, and afterward it would be years before he could overcome his physical suffering as well as his increasing lack of self-confidence to produce his masterpiece, *Kiss Me, Kate*. But it was well worth the wait, as its success in the newly established Tony Awards amply demonstrated.

Porter's next show after *Anything Goes* did poorly, so he went to Hollywood to write his first full film score, *Born to Dance* (1936), which included the memorable "I've Got You Under My Skin." He worked with many of the *Anything Goes* team on *Red, Hot and Blue!* (1936), and then returned to Hollywood for the film *Rosalie* (1937)—a galling experience. He had struggled through six versions of a title song before auditioning his preferred setting for Louis B. Mayer. Furious over Mayer's gruff rejection of the tune, Porter dashed off yet another version in three hours—which Mayer accepted and which eventually sold 500,000 copies of sheet music. Porter told Irving Berlin at one point that he had written the song "in hate" and he still hated it; Berlin replied, "Listen, kid, take my advice, never hate a song that has sold half a million copies."

In 1937, Porter spent a weekend at a friend's country estate. During a horseback excursion, Porter's mount shied at a clump of bushes and fell; Porter was unable to kick the stirrups free, so one leg was crushed under the animal. The horse, trying to rise, fell to the other side, pulverizing Porter's other leg. Porter had suffered devastating injuries, but Porter's wife and mother agreed that the recommended amputation of both legs would devastate his spirit, so they begged the doctors for an alternative. A noted bone specialist began working with Porter in an effort to save the crushed legs (which Porter christened "Josephine" and "Geraldine"), but years of agony lay ahead. Porter discovered that composition was almost as effective a sedative for his pain as were drugs, so he continued to work on songs. However, Porter's chronic pain may have affected his perceptions of the quality of his efforts. There were those who thought Cole Porter was through.

Porter rallied to some degree with his next Broadway score, *Leave It To Me* (1938), when he worked for the first time with the librettists **Samuel** (1899–1971) and **Bella** (1899–1990) **Spewack**, a husband-and-wife team. *Leave It To Me* introduced "My Heart Belongs to Daddy," sung by Mary Martin (making her Broadway debut), and the show also featured the longtime vaudeville star Sophie Tucker in *her* first

musical. Although *Leave It To Me* was no blockbuster, it ran a perfectly acceptable 291 performances.

For a while, Porter's shows ran well but began suffering from poor reviews much of the time. However, he still produced the occasional hit songs, especially for Hollywood films. The movie *Broadway Melody of 1940* re-introduced "Begin the Beguine," which had been first heard in an unsuccessful musical. For the film *Something to Shout About* (1942), he wrote "You'd Be So Nice to Come Home To"; it was especially timely in a nation full of couples separated by war. Porter's career continued to zigzag between the two coasts, but the magic didn't always happen. Even though the Broadway show *Something for the Boys* (1943) starred his cherished Ethel Merman, one reviewer noted, "If it doesn't come close to *Anything Goes*, it is because Mr. Porter isn't the composer he once was. For Miss Merman is no less a wow."

With these damning words, the critic voiced what had been Porter's secret fear—that he had lost his touch. The same thing happened with his next show, *Mexican Hayride* (1944); the *Morning Telegraph* called Porter's score "indifferent." A 1944 revue, *Seven Lively Arts*, closed fairly quickly, and Porter later called it his unhappiest experience in the theater. Nevertheless, one tune, "Ev'ry Time We Say Goodbye," did eventually emerge as a new Porter standard. Despite this dismaying trend, Hollywood was proceeding with a biographical film about Cole Porter called *Night and Day*. Starring a somewhat miscast Cary Grant as Porter, the 1946 movie was rather more fiction than biography, and Porter later delighted in watching the film in television reruns in order to laugh at its inanities. (In 2004, Porter's life was again the subject of a film: MGM's *De-Lovely*. Starring Kevin Kline as the composer.)

The critical reviews continued to sting; after the debut of *Around the World in Eighty Days* (1946), a commentator dryly remarked, "The Porter songs are not in the finest Porter tradition," and the show folded after a disappointing 74 performances. Porter's next film project did equally poorly. As a composer, things looked very bad for Porter. Although he was still quite comfortably wealthy, producers were passing him over as they looked for composers. Investors, too, shied away from projects with which he was affiliated; the word was that Porter was passé.

It was at this low ebb in 1947 that he was offered a new project, **Kiss Me, Kate**, which would use Shakespeare's *The Taming of the Shrew* as the basis for a musical. There had been less than a handful of previous attempts at Shakespearean adaptations (see the **Sidebar**), and only one

---

Sidebar: **Shakespeare on Broadway**

Musical theater librettists have looked to many sources for ideas, and the centuries-old plays of Shakespeare have often been a fruitful inspiration. *Kiss Me, Kate* was neither the first nor the last of these endeavors, but it is unusual in its interweaving of the unaltered Shakespearean plot and characters with a second, modern storyline. In most instances, the original Elizabethan play served as a framework for the new story; sometimes the characters are updated into a more contemporary setting, and sometimes they are left largely as Shakespeare conceived them, but are given new dialogue. The earliest versions tended to use Shakespearean comedies, but just as more serious topics began to be addressed in other musicals, some of the Shakespearean tragedies also were adapted. Not all these adaptations have been successful; some have been tremendous hits, while some never came close to reaching Broadway. The following is a list of many of the musicals whose books were dependent upon the Bard of Avon:

	Musical	**Shakespeare Play**
1906	*The Belle of Mayfair*	*Romeo and Juliet*
1938	*The Boys from Syracuse*	*The Comedy of Errors*
1939	*Swingin' the Dream*	*A Midsummer Night's Dream*
1948	*Kiss Me, Kate*	*The Taming of the Shrew*
1957	*West Side Story*	*Romeo and Juliet*
1968	*Love and Let Love*	*Twelfth Night*
1968	*Your Own Thing*	*Twelfth Night*
1968	*Catch My Soul*	*Othello*
1970	*Sensations*	*Romeo and Juliet*
1970	*Music Is*	*Twelfth Night*
1971	*Two Gentlemen of Verona*	*Two Gentlemen of Verona*
1972	*The Comedy of Errors*	*The Comedy of Errors*
1974	*Pop*	*King Lear*
1976	*Rockabye Hamlet*	*Hamlet*
1976	*Dreamstuff*	*The Tempest*
1981	*Oh, Brother!*	*The Comedy of Errors*
1981	*Wild, Wild Women*	*Romeo and Juliet*
1984	*Beach Blanket Tempest*	*The Tempest*
1986	*Twelfth Night*	*Twelfth Night*
1988	*Nightshriek*	*Macbeth*
1995	*Another Midsummer Night*	*A Midsummer Night's Dream*
1995	*Much Ado*	*Much Ado About Nothing*
1996	*Hello, Hamlet!*	*Hamlet*
1997	*Play on!*	*Twelfth Night*

---

of these had been successful. The idea for the project came from **Arnold Saint Subber** (1918–1994), a young stage manager who had been entertained by the genuine backstage bickering of two actors performing in *The Taming of the Shrew*. He shared the idea with **Lemuel Ayers** (1915–1955), a set and costume designer. Neither of them had ever produced a show before, so they took their concept to Bella Spewack—who hated that play. But, gradually, a storyline began to take shape in her mind, and the trio started discussing composers. Bella proposed Porter. Saint Subber and Ayers resisted—after all, Porter hadn't had a hit in three years—but Bella was adamant. Porter didn't care for the idea, convinced that it would fail, nor did he think that his style was suitable for such a project—so he turned it down. That the enterprise didn't die at that point was thanks to Bella. Shrewdly, she got Porter to tackle some of the songs before allowing him to refuse outright. Thanks to her persistence, and before he fully realized it, Porter had embarked on writing the whole show.

The producers had several counts working against them: not only was Porter's reputation somewhat tarnished, and their own reputations completely nonexistent, but they had no big names in the cast, and the Spewacks were known primarily as playwrights—not librettists. Moreover, there were those who thought Shakespeare's plays were jinxed, since they had a reputation for not selling well to audiences. Not surprisingly, the two producers had a terrible time trying to raise money. It took them the best part of a year to get commitments for the necessary $180,000 from 72 investors; they gave 24 **backers' auditions**, an extraordinary number for a Porter show. In a backers' audition, potential investors hear a summary of the storyline interspersed with the show's songs. Usually, a show's composer and lyricist performed the music, and Porter was diligent in attending the auditions, despite his physical suffering and despite the undoubted blow to his pride that so many auditions were required.

Porter continued to churn out tunes, writing 25 numbers in all, although his score was trimmed to 17 tunes by the time the show opened in 1948. Bella Spewack had worked with her husband Samuel to polish the libretto (see the **Plot Summary**), but the storyline never diverged much from her initial conception. At the Broadway opening, the critics were gratifyingly ecstatic. Robert Garland exclaimed, "If *Kiss Me, Kate* isn't the best musical-comedy I ever saw, I don't remember what the best musical-comedy I ever saw was called. It has everything. A show of shows that is literate without being highbrow, sophisticated without being smarty, seasoned without being soiled, and funny without being vulgar." Rather presciently, he added, "When I left the Century [Theatre], the excited congregation was crying 'Bravo' for Cole Porter and Lee Shubert [the theater owner] was in the box-office selling seats for next year's Christmas holidays." Indeed, with 1,077 performances to come, *Kiss Me, Kate* ran well past the following Christmas; even with competition like *Oklahoma!* and *Carousel, Kiss Me, Kate* proved to be the fourth-longest running musical of the 1940s.

Kiss Me, Kate paid off the expenses of its New York production in a surprisingly quick 16 weeks, and it went on to do quite well overseas. The Viennese production was the Volksoper theater's biggest hit in 58 years, and it was the first American musical ever to play in Poland, where it ran for more than 200 performances. But, once again, a Porter song had been banned from the airwaves; "Too Darn Hot" contained the lines, "I'd like to fool with my baby tonight, Break ev'ry rule with my baby tonight," which were considered simply too suggestive for general consumption. On the other hand, Columbia Records did quite well with its release of an original cast LP of *Kiss Me, Kate*; this was the first Broadway show by Porter to be released on long-playing record. Moreover, *Kiss Me, Kate* employed several African American performers in supporting roles, without recorded incident; the theater was making progress in its racial integration.

Unusually for Porter, the tunes were carefully woven into the storyline, providing *Kiss Me, Kate* with strong "dramatic integration" as well. Porter also took care to distinguish the kinds of tunes he wrote for the backstage situations as opposed to those that were sung as part of the Shakespearean play. One of the many "onstage" numbers is Lilli's (as Katherine) impassioned "I Hate Men" (**Musical Example 27**). This comedy song depends not only upon the lyrics for its humor, but also on its musical setting. She starts with a series of slow, emphatic notes at **1**, set in a somewhat hymnlike minor mode. Her second phrase at **2** is a bit faster. She sings even faster at **3**, almost at a patter song pace, and so the return to the solemn, quasi-religious refrain at **4** seems even funnier in contrast. Kate's next lines (**5**) return to the patter-like melody of **3**, interrupting this rapid delivery with a brief melisma at **6**.

"I Hate Men" is structured in strophic form, so the whole sequence—hymn-like passages, patter effects, and melisma—is repeated at **7**. Like "Bewitched, Bothered, and Bewildered" in *Pal Joey*, "I Hate Men" has a planned encore; it is simply a third strophe for the song. Unlike *Annie Get your Gun*, however, the producers sold benefit nights to *Kiss Me, Kate*, leading to one uncomfortable incident:

One benefit performance in February, 1949, drew the world's worst audience, according to the performers. Midway through the first act the leading lady . . . has a solo entitled "I Hate Men" which invariably gets encores. Porter wrote special encore lyrics and the show is routined to allow for encores. But after the first chorus nothing happened; the audience was as unresponsive as it had been from the start. [The] director Pembroke Davenport, exasperated but calm, turned around in the orchestra pit and addressed the assemblage: "Well, you're going to get an encore whether you want one or not." And they did. "But it didn't do

Kate (Patricia Morison) who "hates men" in *Kiss Me, Kate*.
Photofest.

any good," commented Davenport. "The only proof I had during the whole evening that those people out there in their seats were alive came at one point when I felt breathing down my neck and discovered that some of the people in the front row were leaning over to examine my score. Apparently they wanted to reassure themselves that I was interpreting it properly.

The frustration that Davenport and the stage performers felt because of the unresponsive audience underscores the special chemistry that often *does* arise during live performance—a different experience altogether from watching movies or other static, "fixed" presentations.

Despite *Kiss Me, Kate*, Porter still had some failures to come, and his next show lost money despite a sizable advance ticket sale. Ironically, Columbia Records (buoyed by the success of the *Kiss Me, Kate* LP) had recorded the show before its debut, and "From This Moment On"—which had been cut from the show before opening night—became a sizable hit. *Can-Can* (1953), on the other hand, became Porter's second-longest running show at 892 performances. *Silk Stockings*, which opened in 1955, proved to be Porter's last Broadway show. Although it enjoyed much less success than *Can-Can*, it got better reviews than Porter had seen for a long time and played for a comfortable 478 performances.

Over the following three years, Porter's right leg began responding less and less to treatment, and by 1958 it was determined that it must be amputated. With this loss, Porter began a private, reclusive existence; no one could interest him in returning to the piano and composition. His general health continued to decline, and he succumbed to the combined pressures of pneumonia, a bladder infection, and a kidney stone in 1964. He left behind an outstanding legacy of sophisticated musical standards, and his ASCAP peers eulogized him by saying, "Cole Porter's talent in the creation of beautiful and witty songs was recognized as unique throughout the world. His brilliant compositions in the field of musical theater made him an international legend in his lifetime." Although there have been subsequent theatrical composers who write their own music *and* lyrics, no one has yet captured the general public's ear as well or as consistently as Cole Porter.

Not only did *Kiss Me, Kate* enjoy a substantial run and positive reviews, but it also received flattering recognition from several (but not all) award organizations. Besides the venerable Pulitzer Prizes—awarded to many endeavors in literature, not just theater—various groups had arisen around midcentury to honor theatrical endeavors. One of the oldest was the **New York Drama Critics' Circle**. Originally, membership was restricted to the critics from New York's daily newspapers; the voting membership has expanded to include magazine critics and wire services as well, although the *New York Times* is not currently represented in the Circle. (New York's **Outer Critics Circle** is a similar award-granting organization, founded in 1950 and now numbering some 75 members, consisting of critics who review New York productions for out-of-town magazines and newspapers.) Drama critics are opinionated people, not known for their cooperation, and it wasn't easy to get them to convene as a group. However, a theatrical press agent, Helen Deutsch, knew that many of the New York critics were unhappy with the Pulitzer committee's selection of *Old Maid* as the year's best play in 1935. She reasoned that they might welcome the chance to express their contrary opinions. "It occurred to me," Deutsch later explained,

that the only really qualified voters for a best play award were the drama critics of the New York papers. I therefore wrote a letter to about twelve of the major critics. I asked them if they were willing to meet just once (I knew how difficult it was to get those boys together) to vote on the best play of the season. I was surprised at the enthusiasm and success of the first meeting. They decided to form the Critics' Circle and subsequently invited several others to join, swelling the ranks to seventeen.

Since the Drama Critics' Circle chose *Winterset* as the best play of 1935–36, and Deutsch was one of the investors in this play, there were charges that she had convened the new group merely to drum up an award for her play. Of course, many of the critics were offended by these rumors, since they took great pride in their unbiased judgment, and several reviewers wrote columns in self-defense.

The Drama Critics do not award many citations each year—at most, they recognize the Best New Play, Best Musical, Best Foreign Play, and perhaps give a Special Citation. The first musical to win an award was *Carousel*, in the 1945–46 voting season. This was a particularly contentious year; for the third time since its inception, the Circle failed to agree on a winner for Best Play, since some critics took the position that *no* play that year deserved their vote. After the 1945–46 debacle, John Chapman of the *Daily News* resigned in disgust, arguing that their sole purpose in existing as a body was to choose a "best" play, and they should never fail to do so, even if the slate of competitors was relatively poor. Eventually, the rules were changed so that the play with the most votes wins, and ties are permissible.

Chapman rejoined the group after this change in the voting rules, but there was still controversy to come: In 1949, the Circle cancelled its usual cocktail party to honor the winners, because the date fell on Easter Sunday. But one critic, George Jean Nathan, stirred up something of a hornet's nest by hinting that it was "humiliating" for the critics to have to mingle with actors. The producers of that year's winning play, *Death of a Salesman*, decided to host a celebratory party themselves. As Jack Gaver relates, the critics in attendance somehow managed to enjoy themselves despite the presence of many, many actors! Later on, the *Post* critic issued a sort of humorous apology for Nathan's comment, saying, "The critics don't really feel that way about actors. The melancholy truth is that most of them don't really like each other." Like many jokes, this explanation probably had more than a grain of truth to it.

The New York Drama Critics did not award the Best Musical citation to *Kiss Me, Kate*; the honor went to *South Pacific* instead. However, *Kiss Me, Kate* was recognized by *Billboard* magazine through its **Donaldson Awards**. *Billboard* established its awards in 1944, naming them for the magazine's founder, W. H. Donaldson. The selection process was the most democratic of all the American stage awards, since the entire theatrical profession voted on the Donaldsons. The Donaldsons, therefore, were particularly appreciated as tokens of peer recognition. Two *Kiss Me, Kate* participants were honored: Alfred Drake took the Best Actor award, and Lemuel Ayers was recognized for his scenic and costume designs. The history of the Donaldson Awards was relatively short-lived, for the service organization known as the American Theatre Wing began to offer their rival **Tony Awards** in 1947. *Billboard* decided to eliminate the Donaldson Awards in 1955, since the Tonys were officially sanctioned, while the Donaldsons were not.

Few awards in American theater are as widely recognized as the Tonys, although the origin of their nickname is less well known. They were named for Antoinette Perry, a long-standing and hard-working member of the American Theatre Wing. Although the Tony Awards are now the most famous activity of the Wing, its services had begun in 1917, when seven women decided to form a war relief organization. They were known at first as the "Stage Women's War Relief," and their services took several forms: they ran sewing workrooms, which eventually produced 1,863,645 articles; they collected clothing and food donations; they organized a canteen (a type of cafeteria with recreational facilities) on Broadway for servicemen; and they sponsored troupes of performers who traveled all over the world to entertain the armed forces. One branch of their endeavors was to use their oratory skills to sell Liberty Bonds, resulting in sales of $10 million. A men's branch was formed in 1920, and the two organizations devoted their energies to help the civilian population recover from the effects of World War I.

The pace of the relief efforts slowed somewhat in the following years, but in 1939 the original committee was reactivated and rechristened as the American Theatre Wing War Service. It was a branch of the British War Relief Society until the bombing of Pearl Harbor, when it became an independent unit. Antoinette Perry was the Wing's tireless secretary. Again, the Wing embarked on a number of enterprises to aid the war effort; it operated eight Stage Door Canteens in various cities. A film and a weekly radio program—both called *Stage Door Canteen*—helped them raise money to support plays as part of the entertainment for servicemen provided by the United Service Organizations (the USO). The Wing also sent actors to entertain at various hospitals.

Once again, the Wing continued its efforts after the war had ended, founding a theatrical school for veterans as part of the GI Bill of Rights. Known as the American Theatre Wing Professional Training School, it offered theater and dance classes, with teachers such as Ray Bolger. Some of the school's students were Tony Randall, William Warfield, Charlton Heston, and Gordon MacRae.

That same year, however, Antoinette Perry died at age 58, to the surprise and dismay of her fellow American Theatre Wing board members. During the Wing's fall board meeting, Brock Pemberton proposed that the Wing give annual "Tony" awards for distinguished theatrical achievement, along the lines of the Academy Awards in the motion picture industry. The idea was accepted enthusiastically, and the first awards were given the following year, in 1947. The winners received a scroll and a cigarette lighter or compact (depending on the awardee's gender); it wasn't until 1949—the year that *Kiss Me,*

Kate was eligible—that the now-traditional Tony medallion began to be distributed. The voting membership has changed somewhat over the years, but it now is comprised primarily of the boards of various theatrical associations: the American Theatre Wing, Actors' Equity Association, the Dramatists Guild, the Society of Stage Directors and Choreographers, the United Scenic Artists, the League of New York Theatres and Producers, and so forth. About 450 people currently vote on the awards, which are divided between spoken plays (sometimes called "straight" drama) and musicals.

Kiss Me, Kate did extremely well in the 1949 Tony Awards, for it won in five categories: not only did it take the Best Musical honor (the first time that this category had existed), but the achievements of the producers, the authors (librettists), the composer, and the costumes were all recognized as well. Interestingly, the 2000 revival of *Kiss Me, Kate* did equally well, winning Tony awards for the revival itself, director, actor in a musical, orchestrations, and costume designer.

Both the Tonys and the Donaldson Awards focused on Broadway productions, but off-Broadway shows enjoy recognition as well. In fact, the name of their award itself, the **Obie**, was derived from "off-Broadway." These awards, like the Donaldsons, are sponsored by a magazine. When the *Village Voice* was founded in 1955, the editors soon decided that the theatrical activities in their midst (Greenwich Village) should be recognized, and these prizes have been awarded annually to the present day. Yet another agency, the **Drama Desk**, celebrates "creative stage achievements wherever they were presented." The Drama Desk was established in 1949 to address issues of concern to the theatrical community, and by 1955 it had decided to create its own awards. Its "constituency" is not only Broadway itself, but off-Broadway, off-off-Broadway, and legitimate not-for-profit theaters.

Awards are always gratifying for their recipients, but can have other benefits as well—many a show has enjoyed a healthy box office boost when named as an award recipient. Ironically, though, due to the timing of many awards ceremonies, many winning shows close before the awards presentations take place, so the potential boost is to no avail. Regardless of the box office impact, however, awards remain an important record of both individual and collective theatrical achievement.

FURTHER READING

Atkinson, Brooks. *Broadway.* Revised Edition. New York: Limelight Editions, 1974.

Block, Geoffrey. *Enchanted Evenings: The Broadway Musical from* Show Boat *to* Sondheim. New York: Oxford University Press, 1997.

Eells, George. *The Life That Late He Led: A Biography of Cole Porter.* New York: G. P. Putnam's Sons, 1967.

Gaver, Jack. *Curtain Calls.* New York: Dodd, Mead, 1949.

Gill, Brendan. *Cole: A Biographical Essay.* Edited by Robert Kimball. London: Michael Joseph, 1971.

Kimball, Robert, ed. *The Complete Lyrics of Cole Porter.* London: Hamish Hamilton, 1983.

Morrow, Lee Alan. *The Tony Award Book: Four Decades of Great American Theater*. New York: Abbeville Press, 1987.

Rosenberg, Bernard, and Ernest Harburg. *The Broadway Musical: Collaboration in Commerce and Art.* New York: New York University Press, 1993.

Schwartz, Charles. *Cole Porter: A Biography*. New York: The Dial Press, 1977.

Stevenson, Isabelle. *The Tony Award: A Complete Listing with a History of the American Theatre Wing*. New York: Arno Press, 1975.

Swain, Joseph P. *The Broadway Musical: A Critical and Musical Survey*. New York: Oxford University Press, 1990.

PLOT SUMMARY: *KISS ME, KATE*

Kiss Me, Kate's title comes from the last scene of Shakespeare's comedy *The Taming of the Shrew*, when Petruchio bids his newly cooperative wife Katherine to embrace him. Petruchio had wagered that he could bend the independent Kate to his will, and their power struggle is the source of most of the play's humor. The premise of *Kiss Me, Kate* is that *The Taming of the Shrew* has been adapted as a musical for a theatrical company headed by Fred Graham. Fred's ex-wife Lilli Vanessi plays Katherine; Lois Lane plays Bianca, Katherine's sister; and Bill Calhoun plays Lucentino, who loves Bianca.

The relationships are less tidy backstage. Since her divorce from Fred, Lilli has met the politician Harrison Howell, who is a backer of the new show. Fred, meanwhile, has grown interested in Lois. Lois, however, loves Bill, but is frustrated by his gambling. The story opens in Baltimore, where the last rehearsals of the new musical are underway. After rehearsal, Lois goes looking for Bill, who had missed the **curtain call** practice (in which the order of the bows at the end of the show is worked out). Lois learns that Bill has run up a $10,000 debt (*and* signed Fred's name to the I.O.U.!).

Lilli, meanwhile, engages in a verbal sparring match with Fred. Gradually, though, they stop sniping at each other and begin to reminisce about an old operetta in which they had appeared years before. They are interrupted by two mob-like heavies, who jabber at Fred about a $10,000 I.O.U. He's mystified by their visit, so they decide to give him a little more time to "remember," thinking this will intimidate him; they promise to return later. Fred's problems grow a little worse when Lilli receives a good-luck bouquet from him—he had

intended it for Lois, but it was misdelivered. Since it uses the same flowers that had been used in Lilli's wedding bouquet, she thinks it's a gesture toward reconciliation.

The story switches to the actors' portrayal of the Shakespearean adaptation. Bianca is wooed by multiple suitors, but Katherine makes it clear that she's not interested in Petruchio—or anyone else—in "I Hate Men" (**Musical Example 27**). But a problem develops: while Lilli was offstage between scenes, she found the card addressed to Lois within the bouquet. When she re-enters the stage as Katherine, she's in a rage and assaults Fred (playing Petruchio) in every way she can manage. When he gives her the spanking called for in the Shakespeare play, it's delivered with a nontheatrical intensity.

The explosion of onstage violence was not enough to let Lilli vent her outrage; she telephones Harrison to tell him she's quitting the theater and wants to marry him immediately. Fred desperately tries to stop her, for the show must go on, but she's too angry to listen. During the argument, the two gangsters reappear, still talking about a $10,000 debt. Fred has an idea; he decides to "confess" to the I.O.U., but tells the two bill collectors that he can't pay up until the show has earned the money through ticket sales, which may take most of the week. However, Fred lets them in on the secret that Lilli is walking out. If she leaves, Fred won't be able to raise the funds they want. Alarmed at this prospect, the gangsters decide to go "persuade" Lilli to stay with the show. Disguised as members of the chorus, they drag her onstage to force her through the marriage scene with Petruchio; the audience, knowing that Katherine is supposed to be an unwilling bride, thinks nothing is amiss.

Backstage, Harrison has arrived, and Fred gets him aside to tell him a series of believable half-truths. When Lilli complains about being kept prisoner, Harrison humors her but doesn't believe her—thereby adding to her vexation with Fred. Unexpectedly, the situation changes: thanks to a gangland power coup, the goons have lost their boss. The I.O.U. is now worthless, and Fred's free—and so is Lilli. She marches off to a taxi. The gangsters accidentally end up onstage, in front of the audience that has been waiting patiently; the two heavies leap into a spontaneous rendition of "Brush Up Your Shakespeare." At last the curtain rises, since Fred has decided to take the play through as far as he can, even without Lilli. To all the actors' surprise, however, Kate makes her expected entrance to deliver the "Women Are So Simple" speech, and both the onstage and backstage stories end with Lilli in Fred's arms.

MUSICAL EXAMPLE 27

KISS ME, KATE
COLE PORTER/COLE PORTER, 1948

"I Hate Men"
Lilli Vanessi (as Kate)

1 I hate men.
2 I can't abide 'em even now and then.
3 Than ever marry one of them, I'd rest a virgin rather,
For husbands are a boring lot and only give you bother.
Of course, I'm awf'lly glad that Mother had to marry Father,

4   But I hate men.

5   Of all the types I've ever met within our democracy,

I hate the most the athlete with his manner bold and brassy,

He may have hair upon his chest but, sister, so has Lassie.

6   Oh, I hate men!

7   I hate men,

Their worth upon this earth I dinna ken.

Avoid the trav'lling salesman though a tempting Tom he may be,

From China he will bring you jade and perfume from Araby,

But don't forget 'tis he who'll have the fun, and thee the baby,

Oh, I hate men.

If thou shouldst wed a businessman, be wary, oh, be wary.

He'll tell you he's detained in town on bus'ness necessary,

His bus'ness is the bus'ness which he gives his secretary,

Oh, I hate men!

Chapter 24
Politics and Social Commentary

Over the preceding centuries, many musical stage works had contained political undertones. The British government had come under fire in *The Beggar's Opera* (1728), while one of Mozart's operas was based on a play that had been banned in many countries for its inflammatory views. Even the light-hearted Gilbert and Sullivan operettas often lampooned British politics. Nevertheless, musical comedies and operettas in the early twentieth century had avoided controversial topics. As the century progressed, however, composers and lyricists began to address more serious social issues—sometimes with disastrous results for the success of their endeavors.

A rather spectacular incident of censorship occurred in 1937, when composer Marc Blitzstein tried to bring *The Cradle Will Rock* to the stage—only to find the theater doors barred because the American government feared the content of his anti-corporation musical. The show had been sponsored by the Federal Theatre Project, a branch of the Works Progress Administration (an agency devised to ease the devastating economic effects of the Great Depression). The Project's director wanted this WPA endeavor to support a "free, adult, uncensored theater" and had backed a number of musicals. However, just before the premiere of *The Cradle Will Rock*, government officials examined its subject matter and were alarmed at the extremely liberal story about an innocent man victimized by capitalism and ruthless big business. They hastily brought an injunction against the production, and both Actors' Equity and the Federation of Musicians, fearing the controversy, forbade their members to take part. When the audience and performers gathered at the theater, they were met with the news of the closure. Undaunted, everyone marched to another theater several blocks away. Blitzstein sat on stage at a piano, playing and singing the songs. Mindful of the order that they were *not* to appear on stage, several cast members and a few orchestral players purchased tickets and stood in their seats to sing or play at the appropriate moments. The lighting director followed the "action" with a single spotlight, and the notoriety kept the show going for some 19 performances before it transferred to another theater for a regular run.

Some years before, a European composer had gotten into big trouble with *his* government as well. **Kurt Weill** (1900–1950) had teamed up with playwright **Bertolt Brecht** (1898–1956) to create an updated adaptation of *The Beggar's Opera*. The resulting ***Die Dreigroschenoper (The Threepenny Opera)*** was a modification of a sardonic version by Elisabeth Hauptmann; Weill and Brecht's rendition was finished somewhat hurriedly for a new theater director in 1928—which, coincidentally, turned out to be *The Beggar's Opera*'s 200th anniversary.

The Threepenny Opera was set in the Victorian era (see the **Plot Summary**), allowing Weill and Brecht to ridicule the shoddy morals of the middle-class Berlin citizens (although the story takes place in England). Moreover, Brecht saw parallels between a London infested with plague and a Berlin infested with Nazis. *The Threepenny Opera* was a sensation and was performed over 10,000 times in various European cities during the next five years. Two movie versions—one German, one French—were filmed simultaneously in 1930 by G. W. Pabst (although he made substantial musical cuts, reducing the score to only 28–½ minutes). When the Nazis came to power in Germany in 1933, one of their first actions was to ban the show, as well as other artistic endeavors that they considered offensive. The Nazi Party opened an exhibit of this "decadent" art, and one room featured a recording of Weill's wife Lotte Lenya singing "Mack the Knife." Nazi officials had to shut down the room, however, since the public was not reacting with appropriate horror at the "degenerate" music; instead, they were enjoying it!

Despite the show's European success, *The Threepenny Opera* bombed when it made its American debut in 1933, closing after 12 performances. Part of the problem was a poor translation, but the actors and director had trouble understanding the bitterly sardonic tone of the story. Weill himself told Brecht that the too-literal translation was not geared for American theater. Critics were quick to condemn the effort, but the *New Yorker* critic did credit Weill's music with "a very new and fascinating rhythm."

Weill viewed the United States as his best haven after the Nazi regime made it clear he was not welcome to remain in Germany. He arrived in America in 1935 and fairly quickly recognized that his somewhat esoteric theatrical experiments simply would not work in the United States. Weill began to study American musical theater, and he soon learned that although commercial interests dominated the majority of new shows, there *were* several enterprises more concerned with artistry in theater. The Federal Theatre Project productions were one outlet, while the Theatre Guild had sponsored some of America's most influential playwrights (as well as launching Rodgers and Hart's Broadway career; see Chapter 17, "Great Partnerships of the Early Book Musical"). As the Theatre Guild grew more conservative, a spin-off organization broke free and formed the Group Theatre. Weill met one of the directors at a party and broached the idea of a show.

Out of this fortunate encounter came a whole series of unusual theatrical projects for Weill, most of which were not commercial successes but satisfied his thirst for experimentation. Weill also turned to Hollywood for a time, but although he was paid for his first film score, the producer rejected it in favor of a "more accessible" effort by another composer. During the same year, however, Weill and Lenya began the slow process of applying for American citizenship. (Although they filed their petition in August 1937, it took governmental bureaucracy until 1943 to complete the process.) Weill embraced his new adoptive homeland wholeheartedly, refusing to speak German, scolding editors when they referred to him as a "German" composer, and changing the preferred pronunciation of his name from the Germanic "Coort Vial" to an Americanized "Kert While."

In 1938, yet another spin-off group broke away from the Theatre Guild, calling their venture the Playwrights' Company. Their second production was *Knickerbocker Holiday* (1938), with a score by Kurt Weill. Not all the performers were singers, least of all Walter Huston, who was to star. Curious to know what Huston *could* do, Weill cabled the actor, who was at work on a film in California, asking, "What is the range of your voice?" Huston cabled back, "I have no range. Appearing tonight on Bing Crosby radio program. Will sing a song for you." After listening to the broadcast, Weill was undaunted by Huston's limited abilities, and wrote a "sentimental, romantic song" for him—the "September Song"—which proved to be a lasting hit.

During the following year, 1939, Weill met Moss Hart. Hart had written the books for a number of earlier musicals, working with composers such as Cole Porter and Richard Rodgers. Now Hart was anxious to write a story about a new experience he himself had undergone: Freudian psychoanalysis. Hart and Weill soon persuaded Ira Gershwin to write the lyrics; it would be Ira's first Broadway endeavor since the death of his brother George. The result, *Lady in the Dark* (1941), portrayed the troubled Liza Elliott. While exploring the source of her problems, Liza experiences a series of dreams. Interestingly, most of the singing appears during the dreams, so music helps to set these sequences apart from the real world. Like Marietta in *Naughty Marietta* (1910), Liza remembers part of an elusive childhood melody; she realizes the right man has come along when he is able to help her "finish" the tune. The critic Brooks Atkinson called Weill's music "the finest score written for the theatre in years."

Despite the success of *Lady in the Dark*, Weill continued to seek out new partnerships. His later works alternated between success and failure, and he even wrote a show that bordered on opera. *Love Life* (1948), a collaboration with Alan Jay Lerner, was clearly a musical, but it had a twist. It was not a cohesive story, but a series of scenes depicting different stages in a married couple's relationship. The twist was that the couple's lives spanned three centuries, so some of the events were set in the eighteenth century, others took place in the 1800s, and the final vignettes were modern. In essence, *Love Life* was a **concept musical**—a show in which the plot is not too important (and may even be nonexistent). Rather, the emphasis is placed on the ramifications of the central concept. In the case of *Love Life*, the couple is never in step with each other—the man has no time for his wife when he is a busy factory owner or a railroad magnate, while later, his wife has no time for their relationship when she is caught up in the fervor of the women's rights movement.

In 1949, Weill persuaded the Playwrights' Company to support *Lost in the Stars*, a "musical tragedy" about apartheid in South Africa and the sorrow of a father whose son is to be executed for a crime. To the relief of all concerned, this production proved to be profitable. Pleased by the critical and audience response, Weill decided to work on a musical adaptation of Mark Twain's *Huckleberry Finn*. But, with only five songs completed, Weill suffered a heart attack. He died two weeks later. It was not long before Weill's death that **Marc Blitzstein**—whose musical *The Cradle Will Rock* had run afoul of the authorities of its day—had turned his hand toward creating a better English translation of Weill's *Die Dreigroschenoper*. Weill had been delighted at the idea that his old score might find new life again, and he planned to collaborate on the new adaptation, but Weill was dead within a month. Blitzstein worked on *The Threepenny Opera* alone, and his new version was ready to be presented by 1952.

Here again, politics threatened to squash Blitzstein's theatrical aspirations, for McCarthy-era America was hot on the trail of known Communists. Therefore, Blitzstein found that his planned 1952 production in New York was suddenly cancelled: not only was Brecht known to be a Communist, but Blitzstein's own political leanings were suspect as well. Fortunately for Blitzstein, his protégé Leonard Bernstein was in charge of an arts festival that same year at Brandeis University. Bernstein conducted a **concert performance** (presented without stage sets) of *The Threepenny Opera*, with Weill's widow Lotte Lenya reprising the role of Jenny that she had sung in the 1928 Berlin production.

Blitzstein's new translation of *The Threepenny Opera* then opened at an off-Broadway theater in 1954. Although the styles in Weill's score—cabaret, early jazz, operatic satire—were fairly old-fashioned by this point, the show caught on like wildfire. The production had to close because of a previous booking in the theater, but something unexpected began to happen: people began demanding that the show re-open. In particular, Brooks Atkinson frequently included a plea for the return of *The Threepenny Opera* in his theatrical column. Finally, the show reopened in September 1955 after a gap of 15 months, and it went on to run for almost seven years and 2,611 performances. The production was seen by some 750,000 people—a remarkable feat for a theater that held 299 seats. Moreover, it was the first off-Broadway show to be preserved by a cast album, which itself sold some 500,000 copies.

The biggest musical hit from the show was the opening number, "The Ballad of Mack the Knife" (**Musical Example 28**), known as the "Moritat vom Mackie Messer" in the original German version. **Moritat** is derived from two German words: *Mord* ("murder") and *Tat* ("crime" or "deed"), and it was a type of ballad sung at German street fairs that described the misdeeds of legendary criminals. The inspiration for the song came somewhat inadvertently from the first man to play Macheath in 1928. Harald Paulsen, an operetta star and an idol of female audience members in Berlin, had come up with a costume for his role that included a flamboyant bright blue bow tie. Despite the complaints of others, Paulsen insisted on wearing the tie, insisting that he would rather quit the role than be parted from his costume. Brecht at last decided that he and Weill would write a Moritat that would relate the disgraceful deeds of this charming but oversweet gentleman; the outrageously cheerful tie would stand in marked contrast to Macheath's gruesome crimes. Brecht wrote the poetry that night; Weill then took the next night to write the tune. Accounts differ regarding the amount of collaboration on this tune. Brecht may have performed a sample melody while he read the poem to Weill, but Weill later told a friend that he heard the three main notes of the tune ebbing out of the Berlin traffic as he rode home on a streetcar.

In any event, after Weill played the completed melody of "Mack the Knife" for the cast, there was a quarrel over who would get to perform it. Paulsen wanted to sing it himself, as a form of self-introduction. The creators felt Paulsen's voice was too pleasant, however; they wanted a more sinister quality. Brecht and Weill added the role of a street singer to the story, who would seemingly accompany himself with a small barrel organ. In effect, the ballad singer functions as a **narrator**, explaining the background of the characters about to appear in the show.

Weill's haunting melody for "Mack the Knife" is marked "Blues-Tempo," and it opens with a simple duple-meter pattern of three pitches, repeated over and over with slight variations in the course of a verse. Like "Alkmoonac" or "I Am the Very Model," "Mack the Knife" is in strophic form, which is the typical structure for ballads. In order to keep the melody from seeming too monotonous, however, Weill continually modifies the accompaniment in subtle ways. In some productions, a second singer (and sometimes a third) joins in during the later verses. Somewhat surprisingly—given the grim subject matter—the song is in the major mode, but Weill may be suggesting that the ballad singer is not personally affected by the terrible anecdotes he is relating. In fact, some philosophers feel that the music helps to keep the listeners somewhat distanced from the story, allowing them to think about the events instead of expecting them to become emotionally involved. It may well be that Weill was trying to shock us when we realize how little we feel for the various victims of Macheath's crimes, reflecting the cynical, uncaring society he perceived in Berlin of the 1920s.

In the course of *The Threepenny Opera*, Weill uses "Mack the Knife" as a sort of *leitmotif* for Macheath, as Wagner had done in his music dramas in the previous century. "Mack the Knife" is played in the background on numerous occasions and even functions as a funeral march near the end of the show, when Macheath has been sentenced to death.

"Mack the Knife" achieved a significant life apart from Weill's musical: it has been recorded by dozens of singers and has sold tens of millions of recordings. Somewhat astonishingly, it was even used as an advertising theme for the McDonald's hamburger chain, in which the lyrics were modified to proclaim "Big Mac tonight!" Ironically, though, the song's tremendous popularity over the years has not propelled the show to equal popularity, nor, sadly, has the courageous Kurt Weill become a household name for the general public.

FURTHER READING

Aldrich, Richard Stoddard. *Gertrude Lawrence as Mrs. A: An Intimate Biography of the Great Star*. New York: Greystone Press, 1954.

Macheath faces death at the end of *The Threepenny Opera*.
Corbis/Bettmann.

Brecht, Bertolt. *Plays*. Volume I. London: Methuen & Co., Ltd., 1961.

Drew, David. *Kurt Weill: A Handbook*. London: Faber & Faber, 1987.

Hinton, Stephen, ed. *Kurt Weill:* The Threepenny Opera. Cambridge: Cambridge University Press, 1990.

Jarman, Douglas. *Kurt Weill: An Illustrated Biography*. London: Orbis Publishing, 1982.

Roth, Marc A. "Kurt Weill and Broadway Opera." In Loney, *Musical Theatre in America*; 267–272.

Sanders, Ronald. *The Days Grow Short: The Life and Music of Kurt Weill*. New York: Holt, Rinehart and Winston, 1980. London: Weidenfeld & Nicolson, 1980.

Schebera, Jürgen. *Kurt Weill: An Illustrated Life*. Translated by Caroline Murphy. New Haven and London: Yale University Press, 1995.

PLOT SUMMARY: *THE THREEPENNY OPERA*

Most of *The Threepenny Opera*'s characters are familiar names from *The Beggar's Opera*, but some of their roles have changed: Macheath is now the leader of the London underworld in the late nineteenth century, while Jonathan Jeremiah Peachum is the fence. The new version opens in a Soho street fair, with various beggars, criminals, and prostitutes milling around while a ballad singer relates Macheath's dreadful activities in a number called "The Ballad of Mack the Knife" (**Musical Example 28**). As before, Master Peachum and his wife are dismayed to learn that their daughter Polly has secretly married Macheath. Polly's father is determined to see Macheath hanged, even though Macheath is friendly with London's chief of police, Tiger Brown. But it is Macheath's fondness for women that proves to be his downfall; Mrs. Peachum bribes the prostitute Pirate Jenny to betray Macheath, one of her customers. Macheath is arrested and jailed. The police chief's daughter, Lucy, is outraged to hear that the man she believes to be *her* husband is also married to someone else. After the two "wives" vent their feelings in an angry duet, Polly's mother drags her away from the prison. Macheath then soothes Lucy's injured feelings by denying that he had married Polly, so Lucy agrees to help him escape.

Macheath is not on the loose for long; Peachum has galvanized Tiger Brown into action by threatening to lead the beggars of London in a public disturbance during the upcoming royal coronation. Once again, though, Macheath's taste for the ladies trips him up; he is betrayed by Pirate Jenny because she is upset to find him visiting a rival prostitute, Suky Tawdry. After his re-arrest, Macheath is sentenced to hang. But, suddenly, Macheath is pardoned—because of the civic celebrations for the coronation, convicted criminals are being granted amnesty. In fact, Macheath is elevated into the British peerage and given a castle. Peachum concludes the story by commenting, "Unfortunately, real life is very different, as we know. Messengers rarely arrive on horseback, if the downtrodden dare to resist."

MUSICAL EXAMPLE 28

THE THREEPENNY OPERA
KURT WEILL/BERTOLT BRECHT, 1928
TRANSLATION BY MARC BLITZSTEIN, (1954)
"The Ballad of Mack the Knife"

Ballad Singer
Oh, the shark has pretty teeth, dear, and he shows them, pearly white.
Just a jackknife has Macheath, dear, and he keeps it out of sight.
When the shark bites with his teeth, dear, scarlet billows start to spread.
Fancy gloves, though, wears Macheath, dear; there's not a trace of red.
On the sidewalk Sunday morning lies a body oozing life.
Someone sneaking round the corner. Is that someone Mack the Knife?
From a tugboat by the river a cement bag's dropping down.
The cement's just for the weight, dear. Bet you Mackie's back in town.
Louie Miller disappeared, dear, after drawing out his cash.
And Macheath spends like a sailor. Did our boy do something rash?
Sloppy Sadie was discovered with a knife wound up her thigh.
And Macheath strolls down on Dock Street, looking dreamy at the sky.
Suky Tawdry, Jenny Diver, Polly Peachum, Lucy Brown,
Oh, the line forms on the right, dear, now that Mackie's back in town.
There was rape down by the harbor. Little Susie caused a stir
Claiming that she'd been assaulted. Wonder what got into her?
Oh, the shark has pretty teeth, dear, and he shows them, pearly white.
Just a jackknife has Macheath, dear, and he keeps it out of sight.

Chapter 25
Rodgers and Hammerstein: Oklahoma!

If Richard Rodgers's musical theater career had ended when his 24-year partnership with Lorenz Hart drew to a close, he would have attained a firm place in Broadway history. And yet, if his *only* contribution to the stage had been his subsequent collaboration with Oscar Hammerstein II on *Oklahoma!* (1943), Rodgers's historical position would probably have been just about as secure. *Oklahoma!* has long been viewed as one of the most important achievements in twentieth-century musical theater, even though few of its innovations were actually "new"—most of its features can be found in earlier shows. Certainly, *Oklahoma!* had the advantage of being the "right show at the right time," but its success seems all the more remarkable because the show had so many factors working against it, and its eventual triumph took everyone—even its creators—by surprise.

The deck seemed stacked against *Oklahoma!* in a number of ways. Hart didn't think Lynn Riggs's original play, *Green Grow the Lilacs*, was a suitable subject for a musical, and this disagreement was the final wedge in breaking up Rodgers's and Hart's long-term partnership. Hammerstein had heard a similarly discouraging opinion from Jerome Kern. Although both Rodgers and Hammerstein were convinced that the play had the potential to be an effective musical show, it was unnerving for them to hear such negative views from partners they trusted.

The fact that *Oklahoma!* was to be written by a new, untried partnership was another count against it. Theresa Helburn and Lawrence Langner of the Theatre Guild had *thought* they were approaching the team of Rodgers and Hart. Since the Guild was struggling financially, it needed "name recognition" to win backers for the show. Rodgers's reputation was in good shape, but Hammerstein had suffered through a long string of bombs on Broadway and in London's West End; every show he'd written since 1932 had flopped.

To make matters worse, Hammerstein planned to write both the libretto *and* the lyrics himself.

Oklahoma! faced other obstacles. The original play had been unsuccessful back in 1931, which was not a promising basis for an adaptation, and the plot featured the onstage death of the story's villain (see the **Plot Summary**), an incident which didn't seem to be in keeping with the general tone of most musical shows. Since the Theatre Guild's financial coffers were so empty, the sets would have to be quite spartan. The choice of choreographer was also viewed as risky: Helburn hired **Agnes de Mille** (1905–1993) to design the dances, even though she had been fired from her two previous Broadway jobs. Moreover, De Mille was rocking the already-unsteady theatrical boat; instead of selecting an array of "matched" girls for the chorus line, de Mille wanted to hire real dancers, regardless of their personal attractiveness (see the **Sidebar**: The Rise of the Broadway Choreographer). And the outfits! Why, costume designer Miles White had studied a 1904–05 Montgomery Ward catalogue, and he had designed dresses that covered the chorus girls' legs completely! Certainly there had been many previous shows in which the chorus girls were dressed in chaste historical costumes, but to avoid showing off the dancers' legs was yet another risk taken by the creators of *Oklahoma!*

Needless to say, the producers had to work extremely hard to gather enough financial backing for the show they were calling *Away We Go!*, even though their goal was a quite modest $83,000. Rodgers and Hammerstein participated in dozens of backers' auditions clear up through the tryout in New Haven. New Haven proved to be an important stop, however, for at least two reasons. The first was that a famous quip about the show originated there, even though it has been attributed to two different people. The pessimistic gibe tersely

---

Sidebar: The Rise of the Broadway Choreographer

Back in 1936, George Balanchine had insisted on being listed as the "choreographer" rather than the "dance director" for *On Your Toes*. Balanchine's choreography went far beyond the conventional "step-turn-kick-turn" approach of the average chorus line. However, Balanchine's contributions were diegetic dances, since the dancing occurred in conventional dancing situations—the ballets of the story itself. Although Agnes de Mille incorporated some diegetic dancing in *Oklahoma!*, she also designed dances that illustrated the dreams within the mind of a character. De Mille believed that dance could set these dream scenes apart while making them believable; the performers' fluid dance moves evoked the airy, otherworldly atmosphere of the imagination.

This was not the first use of a dream ballet in a Broadway show, nor was de Mille the first to insist on dancers who would be distinct characters. Robert Alton had choreographed a dream ballet for *Pal Joey* three years earlier and had created a character chorus line representing a mix of body types. In de Mille's case, though, she simply wanted dancers who had the skills to perform her demanding choreography. She and Alton both owed much to the pioneering modern dance work of Ruth St. Denis and Ted Shawn (Chapter 12, "Challenges to Operetta"), but de Mille used a more wide-ranging dance vocabulary; she mixed classical dance (ballet) with popular dancing styles, blended with modern dance techniques as well as traditional folk or country dance. Moreover, de Mille pushed the dancers to express characters rather than merely being themselves, which meant that their dancing was closer to acting than ever before.

De Mille was also a force in integrating the dances into the drama. Hammerstein once observed, "There are few things in life of which I am certain, but I am sure of this one thing, that the song is the servant of the play, that it is wrong to write first what you think is an attractive song and then try to wedge it into a story." According to De Mille's later recollection of events, she helped Hammerstein to understand that dance could (and should) be treated the same way. After Laurey inhales the smelling salts (see the **Plot Summary**), Hammerstein envisioned a circus scene, with Aunt Eller driving a diamond-wheeled surrey, Curly as ringmaster, and Laurey as an acrobat. De Mille insisted that the situation was "all about sex." Knowing that Laurey would have seen the naughty postcards hung on the walls of Jud's smokehouse, de Mille felt she could bring the suggestive images to life as scantily clad French dancers (and thereby give *Oklahoma!* a bit more sex appeal). Other dancers depicted Jud, Curly, and Laurey and portrayed the possible consequences of Laurey's decision to go to the social with Jud. The resulting ballet is Laurey's nightmarish vision and brings the first act to an unusual close. Instead of the usual comic finale, Laurey, to her horror, imagines Curly's death. De Mille's choreography was a highly effective contributor to the dramatic story, and she helped to usher in an era of increased respect and regard for the potential of dance, both on Broadway and in Hollywood. Nevertheless, it would be quite a while before choreographers would earn financial rewards that reflected their important role in creative partnerships.

---

predicted the show as having "No Girls, No Gags, No Chance" (another version was remembered as "No Legs, No Jokes, No Chance").

The New Haven tryout was also the source of the show's eventual title. After one performance, Helburn mentioned to the creators that there should have been a song about the land itself. Hammerstein took that thought home with him and soon produced the lyrics for a new tune, "Oklahoma." With an added exclamation point, the song not only became a rousing eleven o'clock number, but gave the show its overall identity. Even though the Theatre Guild agreed to the title change, the tickets and advertisements had already been printed for Boston, the next and final stop of the tryout tour, and there was simply no money to print new materials. However, with the last-minute modifications made in New Haven, *Away We Go!* became a rousing success in Boston—so successful that Rodgers later joked that he would not do so much as open a can of tomatoes without taking it to Boston.

Despite this success on the road, *Oklahoma!* was by no means sold out when it opened on Broadway on March 31, 1943—at least, not for the first night of its run. Agnes deMille recalled hearing an audible sigh from the audience as "Oh, What a Beautiful Mornin'" drew to a close, and she knew at

that moment that the show was going to be a hit. *Oklahoma!* went on to play a record-breaking 2,212 performances. By July 1946, it had established the longest run ever for a Broadway musical and would hold that record for 15 years, until 1961. It was even awarded a special Pulitzer Prize for Drama in 1944. Tickets for the smash hit were notoriously hard to get; when Langner's wife Armina Marshall lost her Tibetan terrier named Chang, she contacted the newspapers, described her dog, and promised two tickets to *Oklahoma!* as a reward to anyone who found Chang. Chang was returned the following day. One of Hammerstein's employees, Peter Moën, told Hammerstein that his son was getting married and would love to have tickets to the show after the wedding reception had ended. Cheerfully, Hammerstein asked, "When's the wedding?" and Moën replied, "The day you can get the tickets."

Oklahoma! even enjoyed an original cast recording when other shows were having to go without. When Victor Herbert and his colleagues had formed ASCAP, they ensured that artists received royalty payments any time their works were played live. Recordings, however, were played without restriction, despite the Musician's Union's efforts to negotiate royalty payments from the leading record labels—Victor,

Columbia, and Decca. Finally, in August 1942, the union head, James Caesar Petrillo, ordered that no union musician could take part in any recording under any circumstances. All three record labels had a certain backlog of unreleased recordings to help them ride out the strike, but Decca specialized in up-to-date, popular tunes and shows, so it was particularly hurt by the "Petrillo Ban."

At last, in September 1943, Decca approached the Musician's Union and negotiated a truce; immediately, Decca rushed the singers and orchestra of *Oklahoma!* into the studio. Some tempos had to be adjusted, and some of the verses omitted, in order to fit the songs into the limited format of 78 rpm records (each side could hold only about five minutes of music), but Decca made a heroic effort to present plot information on the cover of the album so that the purchaser could come close to the actual theatrical experience. This well-packaged set of records helped *Oklahoma!* to become a nationwide phenomenon as well as a Broadway triumph. (It was more than a year before the other record labels agreed to the union's terms, so Decca enjoyed a monopoly on stage recordings for many months.)

Oklahoma!'s success is certainly due to many factors. Some people had initially believed World War II would be a "short" war; by 1943, when *Oklahoma!* premiered, the war was obviously not going to be a brief skirmish. For many viewers, *Oklahoma!* provided a temporary emotional escape; they could lose themselves in the nostalgia of this tale, set in America's heartland.

The music certainly played an important part in the show's success and many of the tunes illustrate the musical techniques that made *Oklahoma!*'s songs so effective. The second song in the show is "The Surrey with the Fringe on Top" (**Musical Example 29**), sung by Curly as he tries to convince Laurey to accompany him to the box social. Overall, "Surrey" is a type of **musical scene**, in which spoken dialogue is interwoven between sung portions. "Surrey" is actually a verse-chorus form, but listeners might perceive it as a strophic form, for the

first verse (**1**) seems like a brief vocal introduction. The first chorus starts at **2**, and it follows the pattern of a song form, with **2**, **3**, **4**, and **5** illustrating the conventional *a-a-b-a'* pattern. After this chorus, the verse tune returns at (**6**), but this time it is divided between Aunt Eller, Curly, and Laurey as they carry on a short "sung dialogue" about the surrey. The second chorus begins at **7**, and again it is followed by the verse (**8**)—but this time the characters *speak* their lines; it is only the orchestra that plays the verse's tune during this portion. Curly then sings a final chorus at **9**. (This was one of the tunes that had to be shortened in the cast recording; after the opening verse and chorus, Curly proceeds directly to the last chorus, eliminating not only the second chorus but the sung and spoken dialogues as well.)

Part of "Surrey"'s charm comes from a bit of **word-painting**. The *a* portions of each chorus are a long series of repeated notes, followed by an upward lift at the end of the line, perhaps depicting the upward flurries of the barnyard fowl disturbed by the passing carriage (see **Figure 25–1**). Or, as Richard Rodgers suggested, perhaps the long series of notes on the same pitch portray the drawn-out road in front of the travelers. Moreover, the simple duple meter might represent the clip-clop of the horse's hooves as he pulls the buggy along at a steady pace

"Surrey" puts the imagination to work in another sense, for the surrey is certainly not "real" in this scene. Gradually, though, Laurey begins to believe in its existence, and arguably, Curly may also be starting to believe in the image he's summoned up as he sings slowly in the third chorus about the serene late-night journey home. We might call this type of situation a "**vision song**," for during the course of the number, a character is carried away by his or her imagination into believing—at least briefly—that something imaginary is genuine. A vision song is an interesting logic puzzle for the audience, too, for if we believe that the character is imagining something, then we are acknowledging the "reality" of the character—and yet, of course, the character is *not* real; he or she is simply an actor on a stage. How can an imaginary character have something as genuine as an imagination? We—the audience—have to let ourselves "go" for a time to believe in this imaginative layering. This is one of the ways in which theater can play such a cathartic role; audiences who allow themselves to enter into an imaginary character's emotions can, literally, share that emotional experience. Rodgers tells us, "Oscar was so moved by this song that just listening to it made him cry. He once explained that he never cried at sadness in the theatre, only at naïve happiness, and the idea of two boneheaded young people looking forward to nothing more than a ride in a surrey struck an emotional chord that affected him deeply."

Oklahoma! reasserted musical theater's potential to be an artistic and dramatic achievement. It was not the first show to break theatrical conventions, but it did many unexpected

Richard Rodgers and Oscar Hammerstein II at an *Oklahoma!* rehearsal. *Photofest.*

| Chicks | and | ducks | and | geese | bet-ter | scur-ry |
| When | I | take | you | out | in the | sur-rey |

Figure 25–1

things differently: the solitary onstage character as the curtain came up; the first song beginning *off*stage; the dream ballet; the onstage death; even the new partnership, given Hammerstein's string of failures (as Hammerstein ruefully acknowledged in *Variety*; see **Behind-the-Scenes**). Moreover, Rodgers undertook a new compositional method. With Hart, Rodgers usually wrote the melodies, and then Hart would write lyrics to fit. For *Oklahoma!*, the two men had agreed to let Hammerstein write the *lyrics* first, and then Rodgers would create musical settings. None of these elements was unique to *Oklahoma!*, but the combination of these effects was staggering for its unsuspecting audience. In short, all the gambles paid off; it was years before all of *Oklahoma!*'s records were broken. Almost overnight, Rodgers and Hammerstein were a formidable team. The main problem for the new partners was: what next?

FURTHER READING

[Anon]. *Rodgers and Hammerstein.* Josef Weinberger Music Theatre Handbook 5. London: Josef Weinberger Ltd., 1992.

Bell, Marty. *Broadway Stories: A Backstage Journey through Musical Theatre.* New York: Limelight, 1993. Reprinted as *Backstage on Broadway: Musicals and their Makers.* London: Nick Hern Books, 1994.

De-Mille, Agnes. *Dance to the Piper.* Boston: Little, Brown, 1951. Paperback ed. New York: Bantom Pathfinder Editions, 1964.

———. *And Promenade Home.* London: Hamish Hamilton, 1959.

Easton, Carol. *No Intermission: The Life of Agnes de Mille.* New York: Little, Brown, 1996.

Engel, Lehman. *Words with Music.* New York: Schirmer Books, 1972.

Everett, William A., and Paul R. Laird, eds. *The Cambridge Companion to the Musical.* Cambridge: Cambridge University Press, 2002.

Feuer, Jane. *The Hollywood Musical.* 2nd ed. Bloomington and Indianapolis: Indiana University Press, 1993.

Fordin, Hugh. *Getting to Know Him: A Biography of Oscar Hammerstein II.* New York: Random House, 1977.

Goldstein, Richard M. "'I Enjoy Being a Girl': Women in the Plays of Rodgers and Hammerstein." *Popular Music and Society* 13, no. 1 (1989): 1–8.

Green, Stanley, ed. *Rodgers and Hammerstein Fact Book: A Record of Their Works Together and with Other Collaborators.* New York: The Lynn Farnol Group, Inc., 1980.

Hammerstein, Oscar, II. *Lyrics.* Milwaukee, Wisconsin: Hal Leonard Books, 1985.

Hyland, William G. *Richard Rodgers.* New Haven and London: Yale University Press, 1998.

Kislan, Richard. *Hoofing on Broadway: A History of Show Dancing.* New York: Prentice Hall, 1987.

———. *Nine Musical Plays of Rodgers and Hammerstein: A Critical Study in Content and Form.* Ph.D. dissertation, New York University, 1970.

Langner, Lawrence. *The Magic Curtain: The Story of a Life in Two Fields, Theatre and Invention, by the Founder of the Theatre Guild.* New York: E. P. Dutton, 1951. London: George G. Harrap and Co. Ltd., 1952.

Mordden, Ethan. *Beautiful Mornin': The Broadway Musical in the 1940s.* New York: Oxford University Press, 1999.

———. *Rodgers and Hammerstein.* New York: Abrams, 1992.

Nolan, Frederick. *The Sound of Their Music: The Story of Rodgers and Hammerstein.* New York: Walker & Company, 1978.

Riggs, Lynn. *Green Grow the Lilacs: A Play.* New York: Samuel French, 1931.

Rodgers, Richard. *Musical Stages: An Autobiography.* New York: Da Capo Press, 1995.

Secrest, Meryle. *Somewhere for Me: A Biography of Richard Rodgers.* New York: Alfred A. Knopf, 2001.

Taylor, Deems. *Some Enchanted Evenings: The Story of Rodgers and Hammerstein.* New York: Harper & Brothers, 1953. Reprinted Westport, Connecticut: Greenwood Press, 1972.

Wilk, Max. *OK! The Story of "Oklahoma!"* New York: Grove Press, 1993.

BEHIND-THE-SCENES: OSCAR HAMMERSTEIN HAS THE LAST WORD

Each year, the theatrical magazine *Variety* published a special holiday issue. Many show business people placed advertisements in this issue, trumpeting their recent accomplishments to the world; the somewhat immodest practice kept their names in front of their colleagues. How else could they ensure that people would continue to bring them ideas for new projects?

Given the overwhelming success of *Oklahoma!*, no one reading the January 4, 1944, issue was surprised to find an ad from the show's lyricist. Readers *were* startled by what the ad said, however (see **Figure 25–2**). Both Hammerstein's modesty and sense of humor were evident in this rueful acknowledgment of his many flops preceding *Oklahoma!* Hammerstein clearly was reassuring his theatrical colleagues that the enormous success of his first collaboration with Richard Rodgers would *not* be going to his head.

HOLIDAY GREETINGS
from
Oscar Hammerstein, 2nd.
Author of
Sunny River (6 weeks at The St. James)
Very Warm for May (7 weeks at The Alvin)
Three Sisters (7 weeks at The Drury Lane)
Ball at the Savoy (5 weeks at The Drury Lane)
Free for All (3 weeks at The Manhattan)

"I've Done It Before And I Can Do It Again!"

Figure 25–2

PLOT SUMMARY: *OKLAHOMA!*

For audiences accustomed to seeing a large-scale production number featuring the entire cast (and especially leggy chorus girls), the opening of *Oklahoma!* must have come as quite a surprise: Aunt Eller stands alone on stage, quietly churning butter. Then, offstage, "Oh, What a Beautiful Mornin'" begins, and it's a *solo* song rather than an ensemble number for the chorus. The cowboy Curly has come to Aunt Eller's farmhouse in the Oklahoma territory to ask Laurey, Eller's niece, to go with him to the box social that evening. Laurey has no interest in riding on the back of Curly's horse, but Curly enchants her with a description of "The Surrey with the Fringe on Top" (**Musical Example 29**). Laurey is outraged to hear Curly say that he invented the whole thing, so she agrees to go to the social with the farmhand Jud Fry. Since Curly actually *had* hired a comfortable surrey, he invites Aunt Eller to come with him.

Things are looking better for the love life of another cowhand, Will Parker. He won $50 in a steer-roping contest, so now he intends to propose to Ado Annie Carnes, since her father had said Will could marry her if he ever scraped together $50. Unfortunately, Will *spent* the entire $50 on gifts for his friends back home, so his matrimonial prospects are dim all over again. To make matters worse, while Will was gone, Ado Annie had been flirting with the peddler Ali Hakim, and she has made arrangements to go to the box social with Ali.

Aunt Eller's farmhouse is a convenient stop for freshening up before journeying on to the box social at the Skidmore ranch, so Laurey has to watch her neighbor Gertie Cummings flirt with Curly. Laurey finds herself alone with Curly, but neither of them is willing to admit his or her attraction to the other. Nevertheless, Curly makes a trip over

to the smokehouse, which Jud uses as his lodging. Curly tries to convince Jud that if Jud were to commit suicide, all the people of the neighborhood would weep and wail and regret treating Jud badly. Although Jud is temporarily entranced by this vision, he comes to his senses before actually hanging himself, and the two men proceed to quarrel over Laurey.

Ali shows his wares to Jud, but Jud wants a "little wonder"—a vicious, trick viewing device with a knife in it, and Ali doesn't sell that sort of thing. Ali does sell a bottle of smelling salts to Laurey. She sniffs the salts and begins to dream. She sees what her subconscious mind is fearing: Jud attacks and vanquishes Curly, and then carries her off. When she awakens, both men are waiting for her, but Jud grabs her arm. Fearful that he might hurt Curly, she does not resist, and Jud leads her away.

The second act opens with the rousing square dance "The Farmer and the Cowman." Meanwhile, Ali has an idea; he starts to buy Will's presents so that Will can once again have the $50 he needs to woo his bride. One of Will's purchases was a "little wonder." Ali doesn't want the dangerous device, but Jud buys it. Besides dancing, box socials feature an auction that is a type of dating ritual. The women of the community prepare box dinners, and when a man is the highest bidder for a particular picnic basket, he can share the meal with the woman who prepared it. Therefore, when Ado Annie's basket comes up for auction, Will excitedly bids his $50. Ali reluctantly bids $51, unable to think of any other way for the cowboy to keep his "bridal stake." Will eventually does claim his bride, but Ali finds himself married to Gertie Cummings before the show is over.

It looks as if Jud will win Laurey's basket, but Curly throws in his saddle, then his horse, and finally his gun. Jud then tries to get Curly to examine the "little wonder," but the

"The Farmer and the Cowman" production number.
Museum of the City of New York.

unsuspecting Curly is saved when Aunt Eller wants to dance. Jud later gets Laurey alone, but she struggles free and fires him. Curly comes looking for her, and Laurey is at last ready to accept his proposal of marriage. But Jud's not defeated yet. After the wedding, when friends of the newlyweds have come to interrupt their wedding night with a noisy serenade (sometimes known as a shivaree), Jud attacks Curly. In the ensuing struggle, Jud is killed by his own knife. The assembled friends serve as jurors at a remarkably speedy trial, determining that the death was caused in self-defense. Curly and Laurey celebrate *their* union while the territory residents also rejoice in the admission of "Oklahoma" into a larger "union."

MUSICAL EXAMPLE 29

OKLAHOMA!
RICHARD RODGERS/OSCAR HAMMERSTEIN II, 1943
"The Surrey with the Fringe on Top"

Curly

1 When I take you out tonight with me, Honey, here's the way it's going to be:
You will set behind a team of snow-white horses In the slickest gig you ever see!

2 Chicks and ducks and geese better scurry When I take you out in the surrey,
When I take you out in the surrey with the fringe on top.

3 Watch the fringe and see how it flutters When I drive them high-steppin' strutters—
Nosey-pokes'll peek through their shutters and their eyes will pop!

4 The wheels are yeller, the upholstery's brown, The dashboard's genuine leather,
With isinglass curtains y' c'n roll right down In case there's a change in the weather;

5 Two bright side lights winkin' and blinkin, Ain't no finer rig, I'm a-thinkin';
You c'n keep yer rig if you're thinkin' 'at I'd keer to swop
Fer that shiny little surrey with the fringe on the top!

Aunt Eller

6 Would y' say the fringe was made of silk?

Curly

Wouldn't have no other kind but silk.

Laurey

Has it really got a team of snow-white horses?

Curly

One's like snow—the other's more like milk.

7 All the world'll fly in a flurry When I take you out in the surrey,
When I take you out in the surrey with the fringe on top.
When we hit that road, hell fer leather, Cats and dogs'll dance in the heather,
Birds and frogs'll sing all together, and the toads will hop!
The wind'll whistle as we rattle along, The cows'll moo in the clover,
The river will ripple out a whispered song, And whisper it over and over:
Don't you wisht y'd go on forever?
Don't you wisht y'd go on forever and ud never stop
In that shiny little surrey with the fringe on the top?

8 *[dialogue]*

9 I can see the stars gittin' blurry When we ride back home in the surrey,
Ridin' slowly home in the surrey with the fringe on top.
I can feel the day gittin' older, feel a sleepy head near my shoulder,
Noddin', droopin' close to my shoulder, till it falls, kerplop!
The sun is swimmin' on the rim of the hill, The moon is takin' a header,
And jist as I'm thinkin' all the earth is still, A lark'll wake up in the medder . . .
Hush! You bird, my baby's a-sleepin'—Maybe got a dream worth a-keepin'.
Whoa! You team, and jist keep a-creepin' at a slow clip-clop;
Don't you hurry with the surrey with the fringe on the top.

Chapter 26
Rodgers and Hammerstein: Carousel and South Pacific

In 1943, Richard Rodgers and Oscar Hammerstein II launched *Oklahoma!*, one of the most successful shows ever seen on Broadway. Many people soon wondered what the two men would do next—and everyone had different ideas about the right answer to that question. Rodgers recalled,

> *One evening during the run of* Oklahoma! *I got a telephone call from Sam Goldwyn, who was at the show and was calling during intermission. He asked me to meet him at the theatre after the performance and go out for a drink. An hour later I took a taxi to the St. James just as the people were streaming out of the theatre. Sam was walking up the aisle, and when he saw me he danced over and planted a kiss on my cheek.*
>
> *"This is such a wonderful show!" he bubbled. "I just had to see you to give you some advice. You know what you should do next?"*
>
> *"What?"*
>
> *"Shoot yourself!"*

Needless to say, Rodgers did not comply with Goldwyn's extreme solution to the dilemma. But the problem was more than just deciding what material to work on next—the question was, *would* they continue to work together? Most Broadway partnerships of the day were temporary alliances; Rodgers's previous long-term collaboration with Lorenz Hart was highly unusual. In fact, after *Oklahoma!* was launched, Rodgers hoped that Hart might have sobered up enough to be able to team up again. Hammerstein, in contrast, had worked with more than a dozen different composers during his career. So, further collaboration between the two was by no means a sure thing, and both men had other projects that they wanted to complete before addressing the question of whether to unite once again.

Rodgers needed to work on a revival of *A Connecticut Yankee in King Arthur's Court*, a 1927 collaboration with Hart. Hart was enthusiastic, and together they created four new songs for the revival, including a hilarious showstopping number called "To Keep My Love Alive" in which the domineering queen dispatches a series of lovers when she tires of them. But Hart was able to stay on task for only a short time; shortly after the revival began its tryout tour, Hart's drinking became so bad that he was hospitalized. Then, a drunken binge on the day after the show opened led to a fatal case of pneumonia, and Hart died on November 22, 1943.

Hammerstein, in contrast, worked with a composer who had been dead for more than half a century! Hammerstein had written new lyrics for the familiar tunes of Georges Bizet's 1875 opera *Carmen*, calling the new version *Carmen Jones*. Hammerstein transformed the story's setting to a parachute factory in the American South during World War II. The adaptation worked remarkably well, and *Carmen Jones*, which opened a couple of weeks after *A Connecticut Yankee*, ran 502 performances.

With Hart's death, Rodgers and Hammerstein began to collaborate once more. One of their first joint endeavors was the establishment of a new publishing company so that they could control the publication of the music they wrote together. They called the new firm Williamson Music, for both men had fathers named William. They also developed another company, Surrey Enterprises, which they established in order to produce plays written by other authors.

The back-to-back successes of *Oklahoma!* and their first production venture made the team of Rodgers and Hammerstein a hot ticket, and they were soon approached by Twentieth Century Fox to write a score for a film musical. The movie was to be a remake of an older film, *State Fair*. Rodgers and Hammerstein agreed to do the score, but made an unusual demand: they wanted to stay in New York rather than move to California while working on the movie. The studio agreed, and all parties were happy with the results, as were audiences when the film was released in 1945.

Meanwhile, the genesis for their next musical, **Carousel**, came during a 1944 luncheon with Theresa Helburn and Lawrence Langner of the Theatre Guild. Helburn and Langner suggested that Rodgers and Hammerstein adapt a Hungarian play called *Liliom* as a musical. No, said the writers; they couldn't see themselves doing a story that was a fantasy, not to mention a fantasy that was set in Hungary. (Their days of writing a story set in Thailand, or "Siam," were yet to come!) Moreover, the play's author, Ferenc Molnár, was still alive *and* firmly opposed to a "musicalization" of his story; he'd turned down offers from Puccini and Gershwin. Molnár was quite frank with Puccini: "I prefer *Liliom* to be remembered as a play by Molnár rather than as the libretto of an opera by Puccini." The proposal sat in limbo for a while; then Helburn suggested setting the story in New Orleans. Hammerstein experimented with some dialogue using a Creole dialect, but soon gave up the idea. At last Rodgers suggested a New England setting in the late nineteenth century, a more familiar context for both the writers. Additional motivation came from the fact that Molnár had seen *Oklahoma!* and was surprisingly receptive to the idea that this new creative team might adapt his story.

Several *Oklahoma!* collaborators were reunited for the *Carousel* team: Rodgers and Hammerstein, of course, as well as Agnes de Mille as choreographer and Rouben Mamoulian as director. De Mille and Mamoulian had been less than compatible during *Oklahoma!*, and their working relationship didn't improve during *Carousel*. Their struggle peaked when it came to staging the dances. Like *Oklahoma!*, *Carousel* put an emphasis on dance, but *Carousel*'s choreography pantomimed events in the story, such as the first meeting of Billy and Julie, and a depiction of their daughter's childhood (see the **Plot Summary**). Since this latter dance portrayed scenes from Louise's unhappy life, de Mille's initial version ran an hour and 15 minutes! Mamoulian knew cuts needed to be ruthless, but he and de Mille argued over almost every gesture. By the time *Carousel* opened in 1945, the choreography was as much his as hers. The show's opening choreography, known as the "Carousel Waltz," was also painstakingly compressed to six and a half minutes. Like many of de Mille's freewheeling ideas, the waltz was more of a series of pantomimed gestures than a genuine dance (which Ethan Mordden calls "acting in tempo"), but this unexpected opening number had a tremendous impact on audiences. Once again, Rodgers and Hammerstein were working against the conventional expectations of musicals.

The choreography was not the only unusual feature of *Carousel*. As in *Oklahoma!*, the storyline featured an onstage death. This time, it was not a villain who died, but one of the starring characters, Billy Bigelow. Rodgers and Hammerstein had struggled to find a way to make audiences care about the unlikeable Billy, and their solution was to let Billy sing about his impending fatherhood in an extended soliloquy. Billy dreams aloud of all the things he will do with his son, and the audience shares his shock when he realizes that his future "boy Bill" might be a *girl*. Billy's appeal for Julie becomes a bit clearer—and his death therefore hits us harder than it would have without this insight into his character.

The question of Julie's feelings for this brusque, uneducated man is another challenge for *Carousel*, especially after the specter of spousal abuse has reared its ugly head. Rodgers and Hammerstein confront this issue in "What's the Use of Wond'rin'?" (**Musical Example 30**). In this character song, Julie earnestly explains to Carrie—and, we suspect, to herself—that "he's your feller, and you love him—that's all there is to that." Julie believes that she must stick with her man, come good or bad (even if "the endin' will be sad"). Because she loves him, she will take no steps to free herself from Billy's violence—a helpless attitude that pervades the thinking of many women in similar circumstances.

Julie's tune is set as a straightforward song form, in the customary *a-a-b-a* pattern, and the simple, syllabic text setting suits a woman of little education. After a brief dialogue between Julie and Billy, the women of the community echo a portion of Julie's song at **5**, as a vocal coda to the number. Although the song is skillfully written, it did not achieve the popularity of many other tunes by Rodgers and Hammerstein. Hammerstein later theorized that the ending of the song was to blame. He wrote,

I believe "What's the Use . . . " was severely handicapped because of the final word, "talk." The trouble with this word is the hard "k" sound at the end of it. The last two lines of the refrain are, "You're his girl and he's your feller, And all the rest is talk." This is exactly what I wanted the character to say. She is not a very well-educated girl, nor is she a subtle philosopher. . . . I realized that I was defying convention in ending with the word "talk," but I had a perverse desire to try it anyway. Now, every once in a while you should try to break rules, to test them and see if, indeed, they are breakable. Sometimes you succeed and this is the way the most exciting things in the theater are done. Sometimes you fail. This time a good and sound rule slapped me down. I will not break it again. I believe that this song might have been very successful outside of the play had I finished it on an open vowel instead of a hard consonant. Suppose, for instance, the last line had been: "You're his girl and he's your feller—that's all you need to know." The singer could have hit the "o" vowel and held it as long as she wanted to, eventually pulling applause on it. (There is nothing wrong with pulling applause. No matter how much an audience enjoys a song, it likes to be cued into applause. It likes to be given a punctuation which says, "There, now it's over and we've given you our all, and now is exactly the right time for you to show your appreciation.")*

Despite Hammerstein's willingness to blame the final "k," the song's subject matter may have been an inhibiting factor. Although feminism was not an overt societal movement in 1945, many women might have found it hard to subscribe to the song's viewpoint; Julie's subservient attitude is not for everyone. Moreover, although Julie wants to believe what she says, there is a forlorn quality to her lyrics. The song's major mode stands somewhat in opposition to this mood, as do the rather bouncy dotted rhythms of the *a* portions of the melody. At the same time, though, the simple melody is well suited to Julie's character, and the song certainly allows her to express the views that guide her choices in life. Rodgers and Hammerstein were sustaining the idea that songs could be written for characters rather than as potential hits, and that it didn't matter if a song was unsuccessful outside of the context of its show. (Not all the tunes of *Carousel* suffered the same fate as "What's the Use of Wond'rin'?"; the inspirational message of "You'll Never Walk Alone" has made it an anthem for many settings, from annual Jerry Lewis telethons and responses to natural disasters to AIDS Walk fundraisers. Moreover, a popular rendition in the late 1960s by the Liverpudlian rock band, Gerry and the Pacemakers, led to the song being sung at home games of the Liverpool Football Club. This tradition soon spread across England, Europe, and even to World Cup soccer tournaments. During *Carousel*'s 1992 London revival, local critics had to explain to their readers why a pivotal moment in Act II was heralded by what some might take to be a sporting song!)

The music of *Carousel* conveys a number of messages about the characters. It is no coincidence that Julie and Billy never sing together in the course of the show, for their relationship is too troubled for them to be able to create harmony with each other. In contrast, Carrie and Enoch's simple dreams of domestic bliss are beautifully expressed in their duets. Although audiences often would start to pack up their belongings as soon as they heard a reprise, Rodgers fought to include a repetition of "If I Loved You" near the end of the show; he knew that Billy and Julie needed to revisit this melody that had been so full of emotional possibilities.

With the inclusion of Louise's graduation and its underlying message of hope for the future, Rodgers and Hammerstein had changed Molnár's original story. (They were enormously relieved when Molnár told them, "What you have done . . . is so beautiful. And you know what I like best? The ending!" Rodgers felt this approval was "better than a rave notice in the *Times*.") Nevertheless, *Carousel* was a much darker and more somber show than their previous collaboration; Stephen Sondheim once remarked, "*Oklahoma!* is about a picnic; *Carousel* is about life and death." Many observers have regarded *Carousel* as Rodgers and Hammerstein's finest achievement together, and although it didn't enjoy quite the commercial success of *Oklahoma!*, it still ran for an impressive 890 performances, winning the Drama Critics, Circle Award for Best Musical and eight Donaldson Awards along the way.

Rodgers and Hammerstein were a gifted team, but they had their "off" moments, as they learned from *Allegro* in 1947. *Allegro*, like Kurt Weill's *Love Life*, is a concept musical. Among other things, it uses a group of singers to comment about the activities of the show's protagonist, in the manner of an ancient Greek chorus. An inexperienced Agnes de Mille tried to direct, but the production baffled many viewers. Even with 315 performances, its expensive set meant it closed at a loss.

Allegro's plot had been an original idea. Perhaps because of its failure, Rodgers and Hammerstein welcomed producer Joshua Logan's suggestion that they consider adapting James Michener's newly published *Tales of the South Pacific* for their next musical. Michener had based the stories on his own experiences while serving in the U.S. Navy in the Pacific theater during World War II. When Leland Hayward, the musical's coproducer, offered Michener $500 for the rights, Michener was struck by Rodgers and Hammerstein's anger over the reception of *Allegro*. He remarked, "Those fellows were so mad I was fairly confident that they could make a great musical out of the Bronx telephone directory." Therefore, Michener asked for a percentage rather than a flat fee. Rodgers and Hammerstein talked Michener down to 1 percent; they argued that Lynn Riggs's percentage from *Oklahoma!* had been 1.5 percent for what was already a successful play, while all Michener had to offer was a handful of short stories. (None of them knew that those stories would earn Michener a Pulitzer Prize in 1948; he certainly would have held out for a higher percentage had he been armed with that leverage!)

After **South Pacific** opened in April 1949, Rodgers and Hammerstein offered Michener the opportunity to purchase another percentage share for a fee of $4,500. Since Michener couldn't even scrape together $1,000 at that point, he declined. Rodgers and Hammerstein proposed that they lend him the money, however, which he could repay out of his royalties. The subsequent profits gave Michener financial independence for the rest of his life, enabling him to devote himself to writing full time.

Logan was less happy with the team. He had spent days at Hammerstein's farm in Doylestown, Pennsylvania, helping Hammerstein to interweave characters from various stories into a coherent plot. Hammerstein valued Logan's naval expertise as well as his many theatrical ideas for the show, but when Logan asked for credit as co-author of the book, Hammerstein refused. He claimed that sharing credit would penalize him, since he felt that people expected him to be the book's sole author. Moreover, Hammerstein insisted that the financial structure of his corporation with Rodgers made him unable to share copyright credit. Logan was dubious about that assertion but felt powerless to argue. Justice prevailed—to some extent—four days before rehearsals began, when the *New York Times* announced, "In recognition of the extraordinary contribution made by Joshua Logan in the preparation of the first script of *South Pacific*, Rodgers and Hammerstein announce that henceforth he will share credit for the book with Oscar Hammerstein II." Logan had to content himself with this acknowledgment, for they did not rewrite his contract to give him the customary percentage due to authors.

Despite this sour note, preparations for the new show ran fairly smoothly. At first, the plot centered on Michener's story "Fo' Dolla'" in which Lt. Joe Cable meets the Polynesian girl Liat (see the **Plot Summary**). The collaborators began to worry that this would seem too much like a Broadway version of Puccini's opera *Madama Butterfly*, which featured the tragic love affair of an American soldier and his Asian lover (and which would later inspire the plot of *Miss Saigon*). Hammerstein and Logan began to intertwine the plot of "Our Heroine" into the mix, which introduced the French planter Émile and the American Navy nurse Nellie. Unlike Rodgers and Hammerstein's earlier shows, where a serious storyline had been balanced by a humorous secondary story, both of *South Pacific*'s stories were serious. For comic relief, they used the wheeler-dealer Luther, who appeared in several of the other tales.

As the book of *South Pacific* came into focus, Rodgers and Hammerstein heard from a theatrical agent who represented the opera singer Ezio Pinza; the agent wondered if Rodgers and Hammerstein could use Pinza in some fashion. The collaborators quickly realized that Pinza would make an admirable Émile; the challenge was to find a singer to play Nellie who would not be overwhelmed by Pinza's deep bass voice. Their choice was Mary Martin, who had a deep, powerful voice of her own—but she was not an operatically trained singer, and she was initially panicked at the thought of sharing the stage with such a skillful performer. She jokingly asked the authors, "Why do you need *two* basses in the show?" Rodgers and Hammerstein promised her that she wouldn't sing *with* Pinza, she would sing in contrast to him. In fact, the marked difference between their voices would help to underscore that their characters came from very different backgrounds. Under these conditions, she agreed to take the role.

Commentators have remarked that Pinza seems to have been somewhat underused in the show, for he sings only two songs. This circumstance was carefully negotiated, however; as an opera singer, Pinza was accustomed to singing demanding roles, but only once or twice a week. The Broadway theatrical schedule expected him to appear in eight shows every week, and he was worried about straining his voice through overwork. By limiting his vocalizing to two songs each show, he ended up singing about the same amount of music each week that he would have sung during a week of an opera's run.

Rodgers, meanwhile, was regretting *South Pacific*'s exotic locale because he feared he would have to write for "native"-sounding instruments, such as the guitar and xylophone—tone colors he didn't particularly like. He then made a joyful discovery:

> *I found out that in this particular area of the Pacific there was no instrumental music of any kind and the nearest approach to it was simple percussion, such as drums made of hollow logs which could be beaten in a conventional way. . . . I realized I could use what is known as a legitimate orchestra. . . . I would also be allowed to do what I had always wanted to do by way of construction—give each character the sort of music that went with the particular character, rather than the locale in which we found him. . . . In the whole scene there are only two songs that could be considered "native." These are sung by a Tonkinese woman and here I made no attempt whatsoever to be authentic or realistic. The music is simply my impression of the woman and her surroundings in the same sense that a painter might give you the impression of a bowl of flowers rather than provide a photographic resemblance.*

One of these songs was the exotic "Bali Ha'i" (**Musical Example 31**). This song describes the seemingly magical island near the naval base where the Tonkinese (including Mary's daughter Liat) live. Only officers could visit, and Mary does her best to entice Lt. Cable by describing the exotic island with mysterious and hypnotic music. The short vocal introduction at **1** is an almost chant-like conjunct line, standing in marked contrast to the soaring disjunct leaps of the refrain, *a*, at **2**. Rodgers allows Mary to sing sustained pitches on "wrong" notes that ache to resolve to the expected pitch.

The disjunct refrain repeats at **3**, followed by a new tune, *b*, at **4**. This melody leaps upward in each phrase and then gently glides back down, somewhat like the rolling waves around the island. The refrain returns at **5**, with the three reiterations of "Bali Ha'i" at the end of **5** serving as a small coda-like section. Initially, the song ended here, having presented a conventional song form of *a-a-b-a'*. Moreover, this beautiful tune had been composed in an astonishingly short time: Hammerstein had labored for a week over the lyrics, and he took the words with him to a luncheon at Logan's apartment. He handed the lyrics to Rodgers, who looked them over, and then went to the piano in the next room and produced the melody—or at least a portion of it—within a few minutes. Rodgers later explained, "For months Oscar and I had been talking about a song for Bloody Mary that would evoke the exotic, mystical powers of a South Sea island. . . . Therefore, as soon as I read the words I could hear the music to go with them. If you know your trade, the actual writing should never take long."

"Bali Ha'i" did not remain a song form, however, because of the tight-knit collaboration between the show's creative artists. After "Bali Ha'i" was played for the set designer, Jo Mielziner, he returned to his studio and started sketching the island. Frustrated with the lack of mystery to his drawings, he dampened a brush and smeared the top of the island as if it were lost in a mist. When Hammerstein saw this drawing, he wrote another verse for the song, the poetry heard at **6**.

Nellie (Mary Martin) showers onstage in *South Pacific*.
Photofest.

Rodgers in turn wrote a new melodic line, *c*, for this section, more conjunct than the two earlier melodies. He concluded the song with another repetition of the *a'* melody heard at **5**, including its coda-like extension. With the new melodic section at **6**, the earlier song form was now transformed into a **rondo** form of *a-a-b-a'-c-a'*.

The partly tragic plot of *South Pacific* shouldn't have come as a surprise to audiences familiar with Rodgers and Hammerstein's work, but the decision to include no "mood-jarring" choreography was a bit more unexpected. There is some dancing in the Thanksgiving Follies scene (choreographed by Martin, a former "hoofer" herself), but nothing similar to the dream ballets of previous musicals. In fact, audiences might well have been beginning to "expect the unexpected" in Rodgers and Hammerstein shows, and *South Pacific* ran true to form. For instance, with the elimination of production dances, there was no need for traditional chorus girls. Another unexpected moment came when Nellie declared, "I'm Gonna Wash That Man Right Out of My Hair," for she then shampooed her hair onstage. Martin cut her hair quite short so that it would dry quickly enough for the rest of each performance, and fashion magazines soon were commenting on the array of turbans she wore in her daily life during the show's run.

The sets were carefully designed to create a seamless flow between scenes, much as a motion picture is constructed, so that no blackouts were necessary. (Mielziner had used this seamless technique once before, in *Allegro*; it was called **lap dissolve**, for the scenes overlapped each other with no darkening of the stage.) The lap dissolve puts considerable pressure on the skills of both the **flymen**, who operate the scenery that drops (or "flies") from a location high above the stage (known as the **fly floor**), and the **sliders**, the stagehands who slide scenery on and off the stage, occasionally assisted by treadmills.

South Pacific also surprised its audiences with its frank acknowledgment of racial prejudice, as expressed in Joe's "Carefully Taught," which in theater terms would be called a **message song**. Its creators disagreed as to their intent when writing the number. In his autobiography, Rodgers claimed,

> *The fact is that the song was never written as a "message" song. . . . It was included in* South Pacific *for the simple reason that Oscar and I felt it was needed in a particular spot for a Princeton-educated young WASP who, despite his background and upbringing, had fallen in love with a Polynesian girl. It was perfectly in keeping with the character and situation that, once having lost his heart, he would express his feelings about the superficiality of racial barriers. End of sermon.*

In an interview, Hammerstein agreed that the song expressed Joe's conflicted prejudices and his newfound love for Liat, but Hammerstein also declared that the lyrics *were* an overt protest against racial prejudice. Hammerstein's determination to make a statement may have resulted from a firsthand encounter with racism; Hammerstein's wife Dorothy had a sister (nicknamed "Doodie") who had married a half-Japanese executive, Jerry Watanabe. Watanabe was being held in a U.S. internment camp during the war, so Doodie and their daughter Jennifer moved in with the Hammersteins. As they enrolled Jennifer in a local school, they told the headmaster they didn't want the little girl hurt or teased by anyone. They were horrified by his response: "She'll have to pay the price for her antecedents"—a stance directly in opposition to the view expressed in *Carousel*, when the commencement speaker told Louise and her peers that they were responsible for neither their parents' successes nor their failures.

No matter what impulses led Rodgers and Hammerstein to compose this number, they stood by it staunchly once it was written. Michener reports that "experienced theatrical people" pressured him to tell Rodgers and Hammerstein that the show would be better off without such a controversial number; nevertheless, the song stayed in. When a touring production of *South Pacific* played in Atlanta in 1953 (where many residents still held to the merits of segregation and abhorred any hint of interracial relationships), members of the Georgia legislature tried to pass a law against entertainments that had "an underlying philosophy inspired by Moscow." (America was deeply enmeshed in the Cold War, and many people claimed to see "communistic sympathies" in anything they didn't like.) In response, Hammerstein told reporters that he questioned how well the legislators were representing the people of Georgia, remarking on his surprise that "anything kind and humane must necessarily originate in Moscow." When *South Pacific* was filmed in 1958, Rodgers and Hammerstein again insisted that the song remain as part of the show, despite considerable studio pressure to remove it.

Regardless of this controversy, *South Pacific* was another triumph for Rodgers and Hammerstein. It ran 1,925 performances in New York and was one of the few shows whose advance ticket sale actually increased during its run: there was an advance of $450,000 when it opened; nine months later, the advance was $700,000. *South Pacific* was also the year's big award winner; it edged out *Kiss Me, Kate* for the Drama Critics, Circle's best musical and won numerous Tony and Donaldson awards. In 1950, the Pulitzer Committee recognized *South Pacific* as the previous year's best drama, making it only the second musical to win this prize (after *Of Thee I Sing* in 1930) and the first time that a show's *composer* was awarded a Pulitzer Prize. Seen from a more modern perspective, *South Pacific*'s depiction of Pacific Islanders—especially in the form of Bloody Mary and Liat—might be viewed as simplistic and racist. Yet, at the time, it took a brave step toward refuting the need for racial prejudice, expressing a message that still has validity today. Many observers felt that *South Pacific* had ushered in a new era of serious, important stage musicals, and a question began to be asked: Was musical comedy dead?

FURTHER READING

Citron, Stephen. *The Musical From the Inside Out.* Chicago: Ivan R. Dee, 1992.

Easton, Carol. *No Intermission: The Life of Agnes de Mille.* New York: Little, Brown, 1996.

Flinn, Denny Martin. *Musical!: A Grand Tour.* New York: Schirmer Books, 1997.

Fordin, Hugh. *Getting to Know Him: A Biography of Oscar Hammerstein II*. New York: Random House, 1977.

Gaver, Jack. *Curtain Calls*. New York: Dodd, Mead, 1949.

Hammerstein, Oscar, II. *Lyrics*. Milwaukee: Hal Leonard Books, 1985.

Hyland, William G. *Richard Rodgers*. New Haven and London: Yale University Press, 1998.

Kislan, Richard. *Nine Musical Plays of Rodgers and Hammerstein: A Critical Study in Content and Form*. Ph.D. dissertation, New York University, 1970.

Laufe, Abe. *Broadway's Greatest Musicals*. New, illustrated, revised edition. New York: Funk & Wagnalls, 1977.

Martin, Mary. *My Heart Belongs*. New York: William Morrow, 1976. London: Q. H. Allen, 1977.

Mordden, Ethan. *Rodgers and Hammerstein*. New York: Abrams, Inc., 1992.

Nolan, Frederick. *The Sound of Their Music: The Story of Rodgers and Hammerstein*. New York: Walker & Company, 1978.

Rodgers, Richard. *Musical Stages: An Autobiography*. New York: Da Capo Press, 1995.

Secrest, Meryle. *Somewhere for Me: A Biography of Richard Rodgers*. New York: Alfred A. Knopf, 2001.

Steyn, Mark. *Broadway Babies Say Goodnight: Musicals Then and Now*. New York: Routledge, 1999.

Suskin, Steven. *Show Tunes: The Songs, Shows, and Careers of Broadway's Major Composers*. Revised and expanded 3rd ed. New York: Oxford University Press, 2000.

PLOT SUMMARY: *CAROUSEL*

Carousel's unusual opening is a pantomimed waltz depicting the meeting of the two lovers-to-be, Julie Jordan and Billy Bigelow, at the carnival carousel where Billy works. The carousel owner, Mrs. Mullin, is jealous of the attention her handsome barker is giving to Julie, a mill worker from a small New England town who is visiting the carnival with a coworker, Carrie Pipperidge. When Mrs. Mullin tries to interfere, Billy reacts angrily, so Mrs. Mullin fires him. Julie is horrified that Billy has lost his job on her account, so when he asks her to meet him, she readily agrees—even though she will miss her curfew at the dormitory where she stays with the other mill workers. Her boss, Mr. Bascombe, has no patience with what he regards as young women with loose morals, so Julie is soon out of a job as well.

Unlike Carrie, engaged to an upstanding fisherman named Enoch Snow, Julie has never shown interest in marriage. Billy is intrigued by this attitude and asks her if she would marry him; Julie replies that she would wed him only "If I Loved You." Soon enough, though, Julie and Billy become husband and wife. Their ensuing life together is far from happy-ever-after, for Billy has no luck finding a job. He grows surlier and surlier, finally striking Julie after picking a quarrel. People think even less of Billy after word gets around that he's a wife-beater, but they do nothing about it. Meanwhile, Carrie and Mr. Snow look forward to their own marriage.

Billy is feeling pressured on three fronts. He's been idling away the hours with a known troublemaker, Jigger Craigin, who has cooked up a scheme to rob the mill owner, and Jigger wants Billy's help. Also, Mrs. Mullin has offered Billy his old job back, and he is tempted by the thought of his carefree days as a barker—but Mrs. Mullin wants a bachelor; he must leave Julie to return to his former career. But Julie's news for Billy is the biggest pressure of all: she's going to have a baby. Billy is both thrilled and panicked by his impending fatherhood, and in the course of a dramatic "Soliloquy," he determines that he'll have to help Jigger with his plan, since he'll need money to raise a child.

The second act opens with the community busying itself with a clambake and treasure hunt. During the evening, Jigger has tricked the naïve Carrie into an embrace, and her fiancé Mr. Snow is outraged when he discovers them. Carrie is distraught, but Julie tries to be philosophical about relationships, asking Carrie, "What's the Use of Wond'rin'?" (**Musical Example 30**). At the start of the treasure hunt, Julie is hurt when Billy teams up with Jigger rather than her, and she's even more upset when she feels a hidden knife in his shirt. Billy shoves her aside and heads off with Jigger. They're not going to the treasure hunt, however; this is the night that they plan to rob the mill owner of his payroll.

Things go awry fairly quickly, for their knives are no match for Bascombe's gun. Jigger escapes, but Bascombe keeps his weapon pointed at Billy while waiting for the police. Billy can't face the horror of a life in prison, so he stabs himself. Julie arrives as his life ebbs away, and he tries to explain to her what he had wanted to accomplish. Julie tells him what she'd always been too shy to say—that she loves him—but it is too late; she is now a widow.

Julie feels lost, but knows that she must keep her head up for the sake of her unborn child. She's encouraged by her cousin Nettie Fowler, who insists, "You'll Never Walk Alone." Billy, in the meantime, meets the heavenly Starkeeper, who tells him that he can't enter heaven without more good deeds to his credit. Billy can attempt to redeem himself by returning to earth for one day; this will give him the chance to put right some of his misdeeds.

Heavenly time moves at a different pace than that of the earth, and Billy's child, Louise, is 15 years old and ready to graduate from school by the time Billy returns. Her life has been unhappy and lonely; in an extended dance, she depicts the miseries of a child who has been shunned all her life because her father was a criminal who committed suicide. Billy tries to tell her good things about her father; he's also brought her a gift of a star from heaven. But Louise is suspicious of this stranger and refuses the gift; frustrated, Billy hits her, just as he had hit her mother. Louise runs to Julie for comfort, and even though Julie can't hear Billy saying that he loves her, she finds the abandoned star and seems to understand his message.

During the graduation ceremony, it is as if the speaker is talking to Louise personally: "I can't tell you any sure way to happiness. All I know is you got to go out and find it fer yourselves. You can't lean on the success of your parents. That's their success. And don't be held back by their failures! Makes no difference what they did or didn't do. You just stand on yer own two feet." The wise old speaker bears an uncanny resemblance to the Starkeeper, and it is no surprise that the "magic" of *Carousel* occurs at this point. After listening to the speech, the girl sitting next to Louise reaches out to her with a hug, and, by sheer willpower, Billy helps his daughter to believe the doctor's message. In the process, Billy at last finds his own road to redemption.

PLOT SUMMARY: *SOUTH PACIFIC*

Although *South Pacific* is set against the backdrop of World War II's Pacific theater, the story is actually centered on two relationships and the role that prejudice plays in keeping people unhappy. The young nurse Nellie Forbush is stationed at a naval base on a South Pacific island, and she is increasingly attracted to Émile de Becque, a suave, older Frenchman who owns a local plantation. She's beginning to believe she wants to marry this man. Later, though, she discovers that he has been married before—to a Polynesian wife who bore him two children. Nellie had thought that the children were the offspring of a servant, and she is brought up short by the prejudice she feels against people of color; she simply can't conceive of becoming the stepmother to these mixed-race children.

A second troubled relationship develops after Lt. Joe Cable arrives at the base. He meets a native entrepreneur, Bloody Mary, and she immediately pegs Joe as the right man for her daughter Liat. Mary describes the lovely island of "Bali Ha'i" (**Musical Example 31**), hoping to lure the young Marine to her home. The enterprising sailor Luther Billis quickly volunteers to help Joe get to the island, since Luther knows that he can purchase native goods there cheaply. Mary's intuition is proved correct: Joe and Liat feel an immediate spark that is not hampered by the lack of a common language.

Joe's purpose for coming to the naval base is more complicated, however. The military commanders need to station a man on an island overlooking a channel used by the Japanese navy; this spy can radio back to them about the movements of the Japanese fleet. It will be a dangerous assignment, and Joe wants to meet with Émile de Becque, since Émile knows the islands well. In fact, Joe would like Émile to go with him on this hazardous mission. Émile refuses, however, because of the danger; he is on the brink of a new partnership with Nellie, and doesn't want to risk his life.

Matters come to a head on the night of the Thanksgiving Follies, which Nellie and the other nurses are presenting to the enlisted men. Bloody Mary is pressuring Joe to marry Liat, and he refuses, believing that he can't bring a wife of another race home to his family in the United States. Angrily, Mary tells Joe that she will therefore force Liat to marry an old wealthy planter who will beat her, and she drags her daughter away. Meanwhile, Nellie refuses Émile's proposal of marriage, saying that she can't overcome the prejudice that is born in her. In frustration, Émile turns to Joe, saying he doesn't believe that such feelings are born in people. Joe agrees with Émile; he exclaims that prejudice must be "Carefully Taught." Angry at himself for having been too weak to stand up against prejudice, he decides that he *will* marry Liat after his mission is over. Émile, on the other hand, feels he has lost everything, and he is now willing to go on the dangerous mission.

The two men are delivered safely to their hiding place and succeed in transmitting a great deal of valuable information. Nellie, while nursing wounded men, hears that the Frenchman is involved in the mission. The base commander allows her to listen in on the next radio broadcast, but they are all dismayed at Émile's report: Joe has been killed by enemy fire. Even as they listen, Émile is cut off.

Stunned, Nellie walks along the beach, cursing her stupid prejudice, only to encounter a distraught Bloody Mary and Liat. Liat absolutely refuses to marry the planter; she wants no one but Joe Cable. Nellie is heartsick and can only embrace Liat wordlessly. Nellie then comes to a decision; no one knows if Émile is alive or dead, and his children—no matter what their race—are alone. She goes to his home to care for them, and while singing a simple French tune with them, a fourth voice joins in: it is Émile, battered but safely returned.

MUSICAL EXAMPLE 30

CAROUSEL
RICHARD RODGERS/OSCAR HAMMERSTEIN II, 1945
"What's the Use of Wond'rin'?"

Julie

1   What's the use of wond'rin if he's good or If he's bad,
Or if you like the way he wears his hat? Oh, what's the use of wond'rin'
If he's good or if he's bad? He's your feller and you love him—
That's all there is to that.

2   Common sense may tell you That the endin' will be sad
And now's the time to break and run away.
But what's the use of wond'rin' If the endin' will be sad?
He's your feller, and you love him—There's nothin' more to say.

3   Somethin' made him the way that he is, Whether he's false or true,

4
And somethin' gave him the things that are his—One of those things is you.
So, when he wants your kisses, You will give them to the lad,
And anywhere he leads you you will walk.
And any time he needs you, You'll go runnin' there like mad.
You're his girl and he's your feller—And all the rest is talk.

[dialogue]

Girls
5
Common sense may tell you That the endin' will be sad
And now's the time to break and run away.
But what's the use of wond'rin' If the endin' will be sad?
He's your feller, and you love him—There's nothin' more to say.

MUSICAL EXAMPLE 31

SOUTH PACIFIC
RICHARD RODGERS/OSCAR HAMMERSTEIN II, 1949
"Bali Ha'i"

Bloody Mary
1
Mos' people live on a lonely island, Lost in de middle of a foggy sea.
Mos' people long for anudder island, One where dey know dey would lak to be.
2
Bali Ha'i may call you, Any night, any day.
In your heart, you'll hear it call you: "Come away, Come away."
3
Bali Ha'i will whisper On de wind of de sea;
"Here am I, your special island! Come to me, Come to me!"
4
Your own special hopes, Your own special dreams,
Bloom on de hillside And shine in de streams.
5
If you try, you'll find me Where de sky meets de sea,
"Here am I, your special island! Come to me, Come to me!"
Bali Ha'i, Bali Ha'i, Bali Ha'i.
6
Some day you'll see me, Floatin' in de sunshine,
My head stickin' out F'um a low-flyin' cloud.
You'll hear me call you, Singin' through de sunshine,
Sweet and clear as can be, "Come to me, Here am I, Come to me!"
7
If you try, you'll find me Where de sky meets de sea,
"Here am I, your special island! Come to me, Come to me!"
Bali Ha'i, Bali Ha'i, Bali Ha'i.

Chapter 27
Rodgers and Hammerstein: The King and I and The Sound of Music

For Rodgers and Hammerstein, the 1950s were framed by two blockbuster hits: *The King and I* (1951) and *The Sound of Music* (1959). The team continued to surprise audiences with various unexpected twists in their musicals, but Rodgers and Hammerstein were in for some surprises themselves. In the past, even when one of their shows was commercially unsuccessful, they still received praise from theatrical critics. In this decade, however, their financial successes did not always ensure equally positive critical reactions—and they experienced commercial failures more than once.

In the summer of 1950, both of their wives wanted them to read a novel, *Anna and the King of Siam*, by Margaret Landon. The novel had been based on Anna Leonowens's autobiography; in the 1860s, she had been governess to the children of King Mongkut of Siam (now Thailand). However, Rodgers and Hammerstein felt that the Siamese setting was too exotic for them. There the matter stood until actress Gertrude Lawrence saw a 1946 film version of Landon's novel. She hurriedly acquired the rights for a stage production, since she felt that Anna would be a perfect role for her—and (after Cole Porter turned her down) that Rodgers and Hammerstein would write the perfect score.

Rodgers and Hammerstein weren't so sure. Besides fearing they could not evoke the proper exotic atmosphere, they had never before written a star vehicle. And, to make things worse, Lawrence was not a very good singer. Rodgers recalled, "We felt that her vocal range was minimal and that she had never been able to overcome an unfortunate tendency to sing flat." However, Lawrence did have special gifts as an actress; she mesmerized audiences when she took the stage, despite her shortcomings as a vocal performer. Rodgers and Hammerstein arranged to view the film and at last got hooked on the idea. Drawn to the unusual characters and the nonformulaic storyline, they came away from the screening convinced they could make it work as a musical; the project was soon known as *The King and I*.

It took some time to decide on an actor to play the king. The role needed a forceful character, one who could counterbalance the dynamic Gertrude Lawrence. Rex Harrison, who had appeared in the film, was unavailable, and several other actors were considered before they settled on a relative unknown, Yul Brynner. At the time he was hired, Brynner (a former circus acrobat) was vainly fighting his receding hairline. Irene Sharaff, the costume designer, gradually coaxed him into shaving his head, and the striking result helped to make Brynner the "perfect" king in the eyes of many viewers.

With Brynner, however, Rodgers and Hammerstein were faced with another nonsinger. They had to craft his vocal lines so that he could "talk" through his songs while the orchestra played the melodies.

Hammerstein's libretto (see the **Plot Summary**) had little in common with the real events of Mrs. Leonowens's experiences in Siam (although apparently Mrs. Leonowens's published account took substantial liberties with the truth as well). Hammerstein developed the secondary plot of the star-crossed lovers, even allowing Anna to save Tuptim. He also placed Anna at the side of the dying king even though the real Mrs. Leonowens had left Siam before the king's demise. The invented ending made *The King and I* the fifth consecutive show by Rodgers and Hammerstein to present an onstage death.

This death of a principal, while becoming almost typical of Rodgers and Hammerstein, was still unconventional. *The King and I* had other unusual features too: all but four characters were Asians, and although there is a great deal of "chemistry" between Anna and the king, there is no overt display of love between these principals. *The King and I* also was atypical by being influenced by a movie—the adaptations of Disney animated films as stage shows (*Beauty and the Beast*, *The Lion King*) were yet to come.

The King and I reflected some unusual choices on the part of the creative team. Writing a star vehicle was in itself an unexpected step; moreover, they did not hesitate to present Anna as a flawed character. There was no chorus line in the show, and all the dancing in the show was diegetic—such as when Anna demonstrates the polka steps to the king and during the pantomime-ballet, "The Small House of Uncle Thomas," which the king's slaves perform for the entertainment of the foreign ambassadors.

Moreover, Rodgers's longtime **dance arranger**, Trude Rittman, composed the music for the ballet. Many listeners are unaware that most theatrical composers do not create every note that that audience hears in a show. Most Broadway composers use **orchestrators**, who choose the instruments that will play the melodic ideas; the process is called orchestration. Sometimes the orchestrator might compose a countermelody to underscore the main theme of a song, or interludes between phrases or verses. An orchestrator plays a tremendously important part in giving a show's music its tone or flavor. (The orchestrator for *The King and I* was one of Broadway's most sought-after artists, Robert Russell Bennett.) Another behind-the-scenes contributor to a show's score was the **dance arranger**, who usually created dance music for a musical by combining tunes sung elsewhere in the show, reworking them in the same way that an orchestrator does. However, when it came time to create the dance music for the great showpiece of the second act, "The Small House of Uncle Thomas," Rittman drew only some of its ballet arrangements from Rodgers's other songs for *The King and I*. Instead, she composed most of the dance music from scratch.

This unusual narrative ballet proved to be one of *The King and I*'s highlights. Choreographed by **Jerome Robbins**, (1918–1998) the dance featured both Asian and Western gestures. Sharaff designed exotic Thai-inspired costumes, and the ballet took place in a lavish stage set; the opulent display evoked the old term scenery show. The moral message of the dance, with its strong antislavery stance, also contributed to its power, and the psychological twist that this "play-within-a-play" mirrored Tuptim's own unhappy dilemma was yet another factor in the dance's effectiveness.

The songs played an important role in defining the characters, such as the bittersweet "Hello, Young Lovers" (**Musical Example 32**), in which the widowed Anna recollects those long-ago days when she first fell in love. Hammerstein struggled to find the words for Anna to express her memories, going through some seven drafts of the lyrics. After weeks of effort, he finally captured the nostalgic quality he wanted, and he sent the poem over to Rodgers. Hammerstein was crushed to hear Rodgers comment, four days later, that the lyric was "okay," and "worked just fine." Hammerstein generally kept any and all frustrations he may have felt well hidden, but this offhand remark drove him to telephone Joshua Logan, where he let off steam in a way Logan had never heard before—and never would again.

Despite the tension, "Hello, Young Lovers" is a beautiful and wistful expression of Anna's character. Stephen Citron calls it a "reflective love song," capitalizing on an audience's fondness for nostalgia. It's a fairly simple tune in song form (*a-a-b-a*), suitable for Lawrence's limited vocal abilities. During the introductory verse (**1**) in quadruple meter, the woodwinds and harp create gentle splashes of sound like drops of water. At **2**, when the song form begins, the meter changes to a softly swaying compound duple. It is easy to confuse compound subdivision with triple meter, and sometimes an examination of a composer's score is the only way to be sure which meter is intended. In fact, Rodgers used both meters during "Hello, Young Lovers"—when Anna thinks about Tuptim and Lun Tha, the subdivision is compound; when she remembers her husband, the meter is triple. Probably only one theatergoer in a thousand notices this metric alternation, but it subtly differentiates Anna from the unhappy Burmese couple to whom she sends her good wishes.

Despite an expensive and elaborate production, *The King and I*, which opened in 1951, returned a substantial profit for its investors. It won numerous Donaldson and Tony Awards, and its London run of 926 shows outdid the British production of *South Pacific*. Unfortunately, Englishwoman Gertrude Lawrence was not able to appear in the show when it opened in her native country, for she had succumbed to cancer on September 6, 1952. Her death came also before she was able

to appear in the movie version of *The King and I*, so Deborah Kerr acted the role of Anna in the Twentieth Century Fox film. Kerr's singing was dubbed by Marni Nixon (who would also sing Maria's songs for Natalie Wood in the film of *West Side Story*). The king was played by the inimitable Yul Brynner, however, giving audiences nationwide a sense of the stage actor's powerful command over the role.

After *The King and I*, Hammerstein waited while Rodgers worked on some independent projects. Neither man ever acknowledged a rift, but Hammerstein's private venting to Logan may have been an indication that some time apart was needed. Rodgers busied himself with a revival of *Pal Joey* (the revival that outshone the first production) and with an NBC television series called *Victory at Sea*. Hammerstein spent his time cooking up an original idea for a musical, *Me and Juliet*, but as he had with his previous original show, *Allegro*, he found that he just didn't seem to have the knack of inventing successful theater stories. Nevertheless, the team's reputation helped *Me and Juliet* achieve a profit. Moreover, the show reestablished their tight-knit working relationship, which would endure up to Hammerstein's death.

Although the New York mayor flatteringly declared the week of August 31, 1953, to be "Rodgers and Hammerstein Week," the partnership could not claim to have unerring theatrical instincts. They had held the rights to *Tevye's Daughters* and had decided that it didn't have the potential to be a good musical; Bock and Harnick would later transform the story into *Fiddler on the Roof* (1964). Similarly, they rejected a play called *Pygmalion*, which Lerner and Loewe would adapt as *My Fair Lady* (1956). (On the other hand, Lerner and Loewe missed the chance to write what would become *The Sound of Music*; Loewe couldn't see composing anything besides yodel music.) After meeting Meredith Willson, Rodgers and Hammerstein didn't think his ideas were workable; his material later became *The Music Man* (1956). And the next show which Rodgers and Hammerstein *did* decide to write themselves—*Pipe Dream* (1955)—would prove to be a critical and financial failure. Even with their biggest advance ever ($1.2 million), the show closed after seven months, incurring their greatest financial loss.

As a change of pace, Rodgers and Hammerstein agreed to adapt the tale of Cinderella for television. Julie Andrews, a hot star after playing Eliza in *My Fair Lady*, wanted to do some work on television, and the opportunity was irresistible for CBS. *Cinderella* was broadcast on March 31, 1957, 14 years to the day after the premiere of *Oklahoma!*. CBS reported that some 107 million people watched the show—more people than all the audiences at every performance combined at Rodgers and Hammerstein's stage shows. (A new television production of the charming show was made in 1997, featuring the pop star Brandy in the title role.)

Rodgers and Hammerstein had more success with their next stage show, *Flower Drum Song* (1958). Based on a novel by C.Y. Lee, the story depicted Chinese immigrants trying to adapt to life in America, and it addressed the age-old conflict between generations. In comparison to their earlier stage shows, *Flower Drum Song* was a fairly lighthearted story, and it ran 600 performances, breaking free from the dismal pattern of Rodgers and Hammerstein's two previous stage productions.

Even while the team was creating *Flower Drum Song*, negotiations were underway for what would be *The Sound of Music*. Like *The King and I*, a movie was an important part of the genesis of the show, and Rodgers and Hammerstein were again asked to write songs to suit a predetermined star—this time their old friend Mary Martin. Most Americans had not seen the movie, since it was a German-language film about the wartime adventures and escape of the von Trapp family (see the **Plot Summary**)—but Richard Halliday, Martin's husband, saw it and was instantly convinced this would be a perfect frame for his wife. He and director Leland Hayward devoted many months of effort toward obtaining permissions from Maria von Trapp and her stepchildren, who were scattered all over the globe.

Eventually, all members of the family had signed, and Halliday and Hayward asked for a libretto from Howard Lindsay and Russel Crouse (who together had salvaged a script for *Anything Goes* after the sinking of the *Morro Castle*). Lindsay and Crouse devised a plot that employed the repertory sung by the von Trapp family, but felt there was room for a new number or two—perhaps by Rodgers and Hammerstein. Rodgers and Hammerstein disagreed, however; they felt that either the show should feature authentic Austrian tunes exclusively or there should be an entirely new score. Since Rodgers and Hammerstein were willing to write that score, it was soon determined that this would be the format, even if it meant waiting a year for Rodgers and Hammerstein to become available.

Once the team set to work, Rodgers found that the task was not easy. He was anxious to avoid the sound of operetta, even though that genre was so "Viennese." Rodgers was also nervous about writing appropriate sacred music for the abbey. To help him, nuns and seminarians at Manhattanville College presented a complete concert of religious works ranging from medieval chants to twentieth century music. A friend of Martin's, Sister Gregory, asssited Rodgers by giving him a suitable Latin text and encouraging him to write "chant" of his own. The result was so pleasing that Rodgers and Hammerstein decided to surprise their audiences by beginning the show with a simple monophonic chant and then a choral hymn and alleluia sung by the nuns rather than opening with the customary orchestral overture.

Another song that delighted audiences was the show-stopper "Do-Re-Mi" (**Musical Example 33**). Martin recalled, "But oh, the music, the joy! I remember the first time I heard the song 'Do-Re-Mi' . . . I heard it with Dick playing the melody, Oscar singing the simple, beautiful, rhymed lyrics he had written. It was a revelation. Here,

I thought, is perfect communication, the perfect way to teach children the scale. It communicated so well that it turned out to be an international success." The song's purpose is to teach the children the traditional syllables for the pitches of the major scale. These syllables have been in use for hundreds of years, and "Do-Re-Mi" is a charming presentation of catchy mnemonics.

"Do-Re-Mi" is actually a musical scene, with the children learning to do more and more with their pitches as the song progresses. The song explores several simple melodies, all based on the do-re-mi pitches, and the melodies intertwine at one point to create nonimitative polyphony. After a vocal introduction at 1, Maria starts the famous "Doe, a deer" refrain (*a*) at 2, and the children echo her at 3. After a short dialogue, Maria presents the syllables in a new, more disjunct order (4), creating a *b* melody, which the children repeat at 5. Words replace the syllables at 6 and 7, but the *b* theme is used each time. The *a* melody returns at 8, while a new handbell-like tune, *c*, appears at 9. The *b* and *c* melodies overlap polyphonically at 10, and *a* returns once again at 11. During the brief coda at 12, Maria descends to a low "do"—a surprisingly low note for a woman to sing.

It is possible to argue that "Do-Re-Mi" simply represents a rondo form, as seen in **Figure 27–1**. No matter what form label is used, the song clearly represents a type often called the **charm song**; the appeal of Maria and the seven "stair-step" children stopped the show night after night. Maria accompanies the children with a guitar, and in preparing for the role, Martin took guitar instruction from the real Maria von Trapp, who had opened an Alpine ski resort in Stowe, Vermont. Von Trapp also taught Martin the correct way to cross herself in the Catholic fashion as well as the proper way to kneel. In addition, Martin ensured that one of her personal theatrical traditions was maintained in *The Sound of Music* (see **Behind-the-Scenes**: Bessie Mae Sue Ella Yaeger).

Overall, the score was one of Rodgers and Hammerstein's most ambitious projects. As biographer William G. Hyland notes, *The Sound of Music* calls for 47 musical episodes. In comparison, *Carousel* used 31, while Rodgers and Hart's *Pal Joey* needed only 19. The last song to be written for the show was "Edelweiss," a tender little homage to a native flower of Austria that has the effect of authentic Austrian folksong, much as "Ol' Man River" struck listeners as a genuine African American spiritual. In fact, just as some of the African American performers in *Show Boat* thought they recognized the latter tune from their childhood, one woman told Rodgers that she had known "Edelweiss" all her life—only in German. Unlike the team's usual procedure, Rodgers wrote the melody before Hammerstein had written the words. During the

	1	2	3	4	5	6	7	8	9	10	11	12
	intro	*a*	*a*	*b*	*b*	*b*	*b*	*a*	*c*	*b + c*	*a*	coda
or:	intro	*A* --------		*B* -------------------------------				*A*	*C* -------------		*A*	coda = **Rondo**

Figure 27–1

Captain Von Trapp (Theodore Bithel) drills Maria (Mary Martin) and the children in *The Sound of Music*.
Corbis/Bettmann.

tryout tour in Boston, it was determined that the captain should sing another song, but Hammerstein was ill and unable to come to Boston at the start of the tour, so Rodgers went ahead and drafted a theme. Meanwhile, the actor playing Captain von Trapp had learned to play the tune on the guitar. When Hammerstein finally arrived in Boston, he listened to the melody and was inspired to write words that suited the gentle tune; these proved to be the last lyrics he would ever write.

The Sound of Music was ready to open in 1959, and the promise of a show with the reunited talents of Rodgers, Hammerstein, and Martin led to a record-breaking advance of over $3.25 million. Many critics were somewhat aloof, regarding the show as overly sentimental and even hackneyed. Audiences couldn't have cared less about the critics' opinions, however, and although the show's 1,433-performance run did not challenge the longevity record of *Oklahoma!*, it was the big winner in that year's Tony Awards. The London production, on the other hand, set a new West End record for an American musical at 2,385 performances. A movie deal with Twentieth Century Fox was signed in 1960 for a then-impressive $1.8 million, but with the stipulation that the film could not be released until 1964 so as not to hurt ticket sales of the Broadway show and the touring productions. With debts of some $60 million, Twentieth Century Fox was close to bankruptcy, and its decision to make the $8 million film was somewhat of a gamble. However, *The Sound of Music* (1965) movie went on

to be one of Hollywood's all-time great moneymakers. The movie's soundtrack recording did equally well, becoming the best-selling LP ever. *The Sound of Music* was a major factor in putting Twentieth Century Fox back into the black; thereafter, studio head Darryl Zanuck always referred to the show as "the miracle movie."

Oscar Hammerstein did not live to see the full measure of *The Sound of Music*'s success, however; he died of cancer some nine months into the Broadway run, on August 23, 1960. On September 1, between 8:57 and 9:00 P.M., Broadway gave an unprecedented tribute to the beloved writer, turning off all lights and halting all traffic. Two trumpeters played taps for the assembled crowd of some 5,000 people; no other theatrical figure has ever been given such recognition by Broadway.

Rodgers and Hammerstein jointly created a legacy of musical shows that changed the nature of Broadway musicals completely, and some of their achievements are discussed in the *Sidebar*: Rodgers and Hammerstein as a Legacy. By the time of Hammerstein's passing, the old song-and-dance musical comedy had been left far behind, and it is no exaggeration to say that Broadway would never be the same again. Nor, as it turned out, would things ever be the same for Rodgers, either; as his daughter Mary noted, "My father never again found a compatible partner although he doggedly continued to grind out musicals (flawed and lacklustre work, for the most part) until his own death in 1979." Although the Rodgers and Hammerstein legacy lives on to the present day through films, recordings, and revivals of their stage shows, Broadway audiences began to turn their attention to the creations of other artists—and, as Chapter 28, "Lerner and Loewe" reveals, competitive teams had not stood still during Rodgers and Hammerstein's heyday.

FURTHE.R READING

Aldrich, Richard Stoddard. *Gertrude Lawrence as Mrs. A: An Intimate Biography of the Great Star*. New York: Greystone Press, 1954.

Brahms, Caryl, and Ned Sherrin. *Song By Song: The Lives and Work of 14 Great Lyric Writers*. Egerton, Bolton, U. K.: Ross Anderson Publications, 1984.

Citron, Stephen. *The Musical From the Inside Out*. Chicago: Ivan R. Dee, 1992.

———. *The Wordsmiths: Oscar Hammerstein 2nd and Alan Jay Lerner*. New York: Oxford University Press, 1995.

Goldstein, Richard M. "'I Enjoy Being a Girl': Women in the Plays of Rodgers and Hammerstein." *Popular Music and Society* 13, no. 1 (1989): 1–8.

Green, Stanley. *The Rodgers and Hammerstein Story*. London: W. H. Allen, 1963.

Hammerstein, Oscar, II. *Lyrics*. Milwaukee, Wisconsin: Hal Leonard Books, 1985.

Hyland, William G. *Richard Rodgers*. New Haven and London: Yale University Press, 1998.

Kislan, Richard. *Hoofing on Broadway: A History of Show Dancing*. New York: Prentice Hall, 1987.

———. *Nine Musical Plays of Rodgers and Hammerstein: A Critical Study in Content and Form*. Ph.D. dissertation, New York University, 1970.

Laufe, Abe. *Broadway's Greatest Musicals*. New, illustrated, revised edition. New York: Funk & Wagnalls, 1977.

Martin, Mary. *My Heart Belongs*. New York: William Morrow, 1976. London: Q. H. Allen, 1977.

Mordden, Ethan. *Coming Up Roses: The Broadway Musical in the 1950s*. New York: Oxford University Press, 1998.

———. *Rodgers and Hammerstein*. New York: Abrams, 1992.

Nolan, Frederick. *The Sound of Their Music: The Story of Rodgers and Hammerstein*. New York: Walker and Co., 1978

Rodgers, Richard. *Musical Stages: An Autobiography*. New York: Da Capo Press, 1995.

Sharaff, Irene. *Broadway & Hollywood: Costumes Designed by Irene Sharaff*. New York: Van Nostrand Reinhold Company, 1976.

BEHIND-THE-SCENES: BESSIE MAE SUE ELLA YAEGER

Mary Martin grew up in Texas, where her best friend was Bessie Mae Sue Ella Yaeger. Martin delighted in her friend's unusually extensive name and managed to incorporate bits of it into most of the movies and shows in which she appeared—sometimes her character might be named Bessie, or Mae, or Sue Ella; sometimes one of her fellow actors wound up with a portion of the name. Martin got the entire name into *South Pacific*, during the Thanksgiving Follies scene. The announcer would proclaim, "The barrel rolls will now be done by Lieutenant j.g. Bessie Mae Sue Ella Yaeger."

The theatrical world is famous for its superstitions, and Hammerstein—aware of Martin's tradition—was convinced that they needed to incorporate Yaeger's name into *The Sound of Music*, even though Bessie Mae Sue Ella just wasn't very "Austrian." At last, Hammerstein had an idea. All leading roles in shows have **understudies**—actors who have learned the stars' lines, and can step in if needed—and Martin's understudy was Renee Guerin. When not substituting, most understudies perform in the chorus or in minor roles; Guerin played a postulant during the wedding between Maria and Captain Trapp. Since Guerin was already getting credit in the program as Mary Martin's understudy, Hammerstein persuaded her to let the credit for the postulant's role go to "Sue Yaeger."

Mary Martin was delighted with the solution and sent flowers to her old friend on the show's opening night, along with a telegram that read, "You're now a postulant. No more barrel rolls." About two years later, however, the real Bessie Mae Sue Ella Yaeger begged Martin for help; it seemed that the Internal Revenue Service had picked up on her name in the program and determined that Yaeger was not paying the

---

Sidebar: Rodgers and Hammerstein as a Legacy

It is hard to imagine a time when the names "Rodgers and Hammerstein" will be forgotten, for the team established a host of conventions that defined the Broadway musical for subsequent generations. Not all of Rodgers and Hammerstein's practices are still sustained, but they have had a continued impact on nearly all shows produced to this day. Some of their procedures affected how theatrical shows are presented. Rodgers and Hammerstein worked toward a seamless flow between the spoken drama and the musical numbers, much in the manner that films depict their stories. They also helped open the door to dance as an important *dramatic* element. Rodgers and Hammerstein helped story-lines to change, too. They avoided the predictable, and they chose meaty, sometimes surprisingly dark stories for their plots. They did not shy away from serious social issues, tackling uncomfortable topics such as spousal abuse, racism, materialism, and even Western imperialism. The music in these stories was an important factor in bringing their characters to life; actors never sang simply because it was "time for a song."

The nature of the songs reflected the writers' attitudes as well. There is usually a thread of optimism to be found in the shows: *Oklahoma!*'s "Oh, What a Beautiful Mornin'" *Carousel*'s "June Is Bustin' Out All Over," *South Pacific*'s "A Cockeyed Optimist," and *The Sound of Music*'s "My Favorite Things." Hammerstein's lyrics were carefully crafted and emotionally expressive, and they were seldom written simply to be comic, unlike the lyrics of many earlier Broadway shows.

Rodgers and Hammerstein's endeavors were not path-breaking in all regards, however. Richard M. Goldstein has noted that their depiction of a woman's place was consistently conservative. Goldstein identifies four main roles for a female to play in their productions: she may be a chaste heroine whose destiny is to find her "dream" husband and to bear/raise his children; she may be a woman who surrenders to passion, either with comic consequences (Ado Annie in *Oklahoma!*) or with tragic results (Tuptim in *The King and I*); she could be an older character who dispenses good advice, urging the heroine to overcome obstacles; or she could be the heroine's rival for the love of the dream husband, usually singing much less than the other characters and inevitably losing out in the struggle for the hero.

Many (but not all) more recent musicals have moved away from the stereotyped and limited feminine roles displayed in Rodgers and Hammerstein's presentations. Modern shows hold tightly to most of Rodgers and Hammerstein's other innovations, however, striving for tight integration of dialogue and singing, using dance in dramatically effective ways, and being courageous in their choice of stories. Nevertheless, the breadth of Rodgers and Hammerstein's commercial and critical successes remain unmatched.

proper income tax for the salary she must be earning from the hit show. Martin recalled, "It took months, all of us working away, to unravel the whole story and get Bessie Mae out of the clutches of the computer and the Internal Revenue Service."

PLOT SUMMARY: *THE KING AND I*

A ship has just docked in Bangkok, where Englishwoman Anna Leonowens is to work as governess to the children of the King of Siam. As soon as she and her son Louis land, though, Anna learns that not everything is as she hoped; the Kralahome (the prime minister) informs her she is to live in the palace, even though her contract said she would have her own house. She wants to take the matter up with the King, only to find that she is not allowed to meet him—or her future pupils—for many weeks. Meanwhile, Lun Tha has escorted the beautiful Tuptim as a gift to the Siamese king from the prince of Burma. Sadly, though, Tuptim and Lun Tha have fallen in love during their journey.

Anna is at last introduced to the King, only to find that he is a cyclone of energy and she has no opportunity to speak to him at all. The King's chief wife, Lady Thiang, explains the King's exalted position to Anna; in Lady Thiang's view, for instance, Tuptim should be delighted to have become one of the King's possessions. Anna's not convinced; she muses about her sympathy for the unhappy couple in "Hello, Young Lovers" (**Musical Example 32**), but she is soon distracted by the myriad of royal children who are to become her students.

In a gradual way, Anna's instruction of these children starts to undermine the palace's status quo. The King wants his children to be well educated, but the more they learn about the wide world beyond Siam's borders, the more his position as absolute monarch is threatened. Matters come to a head when Anna presses the King on the issue of her house; when he calls her a servant, she is determined to leave Siam. Her departure would be disastrous for Lun Tha and Tuptim, for Anna has been helping the lovers to meet secretly. Moreover, Siam is threatened by an imperialist Britain, which regards the country as barbaric and in need of British stewardship. Lady Thiang pleads with Anna to stay and help the King with the delicate diplomatic measures needed to stave off this foreign encroachment

Anna recognizes the King's great need and agrees to do her best. She helps the King to come up with a lavish plan to host the English ambassador Sir Edward Ramsay when he visits, so the diplomat will see how civilized Siam is becoming. The King leads the court in praying to Buddha for success in their endeavor; in a subtle thank-you gesture to Anna, he promises Buddha to build Anna's bungalow.

The second act opens with the King's wives marveling at their new voluminous hoop skirts. Despite the inevitable gaffes, the diplomat's arrival goes smoothly enough. Trouble is brewing behind the scenes, though. Tuptim is making desperate plans to escape with Lun Tha, after narrating an entertainment which itself is a bit dangerous for her; it is a danced

pantomime of Harriet Beecher Stowe's antislavery novel, *Uncle Tom's Cabin*, which the Siamese call "The Small House of Uncle Thomas." Tuptim finds it hard to control her emotions as she recounts the sad tale of the slave separated from her lover. Nevertheless, the show goes well, and the King is happy that his guests have been entertained.

The King is much less happy, however, when he gets the news that Tuptim has escaped. He is soon distracted by a freewheeling conversation with Anna that climaxes when she asks him to dance, demonstrating the English polka. The mood is broken when the Kralahome announces that the runaway lovers have been stopped; Lun Tha was killed in the escape, and Tuptim has been captured. Anna tries to protect Tuptim from punishment, but the King won't listen to her; angrily, she accuses him of not understanding how the lovers felt, since he has never loved anyone himself—he has no heart. The King is furious with Anna, and he picks up a whip to punish Tuptim personally but finds he cannot beat the girl in front of Anna, and he storms out of the room. The Kralahome berates Anna for undermining the King's authority to the point that he can't even punish a traitor. Anna, meanwhile, has seen a side of the King that she can't condone or accept, and she resolves to leave Siam at last.

Anna is boarding a ship, but it seems the King *does* have a heart, and it is failing his body; he wishes to see Anna once again. Anna races to him, and just in time. The crown prince is there, and Anna realizes that the boy will need her help as he learns to rule his country; she orders that her bags be taken off the ship. The King talks with the prince about assuming the throne, and the prince begins to describe his first edict: he will forbid the traditional prostration in the King's presence in favor of a less humiliating form of bowing. As the prince talks, the King dies quietly, with Anna kneeling beside him.

PLOT SUMMARY: *THE SOUND OF MUSIC*

For those familiar with the 1965 Twentieth Century Fox film version of *The Sound of Music*, the opening of the stage musical comes as a bit of a surprise. Like *Oklahoma!*, the first singing heard in the show comes from offstage—but this singing is in Latin, it is a monophonic chant, and it is the *first* music heard in the show; there is no preceding overture. The chant summons the nuns of the Nonnberg Abbey to prayer, and soon they wonder: Where is Maria, one of the Abbey's postulants? (A postulant is a woman preparing for the life of a nun, but who has not yet taken her vows.) Maria is out in the adjacent hills, having forgotten the time. The Mother Superior, mistress of the Abbey, recognizing that Maria may not be well suited to a contemplative life in the church, sends Maria on a mission to help a widower with the upbringing of his seven children. Maria is reluctant to leave the abbey, but is obedient.

When Maria arrives at the von Trapp home, she realizes that Captain Georg von Trapp—a naval officer who is away from home—runs his household with military precision, dressing his children in uncomfortable uniforms. The children have rebelled by putting a long series of prior governesses to flight and at first it looks like they will have no trouble routing Maria as well. Then she discovers that they don't know how to sing and she distracts them from their mischievous ways by teaching them "Do-Re-Mi" (**Musical Example 36**). Moreover, Maria surprises the oldest daughter, Liesl, as she is trying to sneak back in out of the rain after meeting a boyfriend, Rolf. Liesl is startled to learn that Maria does not plan to tell Liesl's father of her misdeed, and she realizes that this new governess will be her friend—something the 16-year-old girl has long needed. Maria also comforts the younger children during a thunderstorm with the cheerful yodeling tune "The Lonely Goatherd."

Because the children have no playclothes, Maria resorts to making them rough-and-tumble outfits out of old curtains—which horrifies the captain when he returns to his home with a guest, Baroness Elsa von Schräder. The captain's friend Max Detweiler has already been teasing Elsa about wealth, so these recycled clothes seem even worse. The captain is starting to scold Maria when the beautiful singing of the children interrupts him. The captain had put music aside after the death of his wife, but their sweet song melts his heart, and soon he and his children are gathered in a rare embrace.

Since the captain is close to proposing to Elsa, he gives a party to introduce her. From the captain's perspective, the evening is not a success: his guests are polarized between loyalty to their Austrian homeland and affiliation with the Nazi forces that threaten to overtake Austria in 1938. After listening to the children sing, Max thinks the children would be a hit at an upcoming Music Festival. Meanwhile, the captain finds Maria teaching the traditional "Ländler" dance to young Kurt, and he cuts in to demonstrate the steps himself; he and Maria both sense that something special is happening. Since the captain and Elsa are virtually engaged, Maria sees no recourse but to flee, so she sneaks away while the captain argues with Max about the propriety of letting his children perform publicly. The Abbey is not the refuge Maria hoped it would be, however; the Mother Superior, singing, tells Maria that the convent is not a place to escape and that Maria must go back and face the situation in the von Trapp home.

The children are distraught over Maria's departure and refuse to sing, and the captain forbids them to speak of her.

They are even unhappier to hear that they will have a new mother, Elsa. The children are overjoyed when Maria returns, but when she learns of the captain's engagement, she says that she will stay only until he can make other arrangements for the children's care. Meanwhile, tension is growing in the household over Max's involvement with the Germans. Max's rationalization is that if the Germans gain power over Austria, he'd like to have some friends among them; Elsa agrees with Max. The captain most emphatically does not agree, and Elsa realizes that her fiancé is such a loyal Austrian that he is likely to become an outlaw if and when the Germans invade. She doesn't want to take the risk of marriage to such a man, and she breaks off the engagement. The captain and Maria are free to marry.

While they are on their honeymoon, the situation grows more tense at home, for despite the treaty terms resulting from the German surrender at the end of World War I, Germany has united with Austria in the maneuver known as the Anschluss. Max, while babysitting, helps the children to practice for the Music Festival and neatly sidesteps orders to fly the Nazi flag outside the von Trapp home. The newlyweds are horrified at the state of affairs when they return; not only does the captain not want his children to sing in the festival, but Rolf—using a Nazi salute—delivers a telegram that asks the captain to take up a commission in the German navy. Before the captain can make up his mind to flee with his family, a German admiral arrives to put further pressure on the captain to report for duty immediately. Fortunately, Maria has a copy of the festival program, and she convinces the admiral to give von Trapp more time, since the family must perform in two days.

After their festival performance, the von Trapps slip away one by one as the children sing "So Long, Farewell." The German soldiers who are guarding the hall assume that the family is backstage, awaiting the judges' results. When the von Trapps are named as the first-prize winners, and no one comes forward to accept the award, the guards run in pursuit. The family finds their way to the abbey, where they are hidden by the nuns. One soldier discovers them—but it is Rolf, and he finds that he cannot betray Liesl's family. After the coast is clear, the abbess allows the family to leave through the back gates, where they can "Climb Ev'ry Mountain" as they journey toward freedom in Switzerland.

MUSICAL EXAMPLE 32

THE KING AND I
RICHARD RODGERS/OSCAR HAMMERSTEIN II, 1951
"Hello, Young Lovers"

Anna

1   When I think of Tom I think about a night When the earth smelled of summer
And the sky was streaked with white, And the soft mist of England Was sleeping on a hill,
I remember this, and I always will.

There are new lovers now on the same silent hill Looking on the same blue sea,
And I know Tom and I are a part of them all, And they're all a part of Tom and me.

2 Hello, young lovers, whoever you are, I Hope your troubles are few.
All my good wishes go with you tonight. I've been in love like you.

3 Be brave, young lovers, and follow your star, Be brave and faithful and true,
Cling very close to each other tonight—I've been in love like you.

4 I know how it feels to have wings on your heels, And to fly down a street in a trance.
You fly down a street on the chance that you'll meet, And you meet—not really by chance.

5 Don't cry, young lovers, whatever you do, Don't cry because I'm alone;
All of my mem'ries are happy tonight, I've had a love of my own,

6 I've had love of my own, like yours, I've had a love of my own.

MUSICAL EXAMPLE 33

THE SOUND OF MUSIC
RICHARD RODGERS/OSCAR HAMMERSTEIN II, 1959
"Do-Re-Mi"

Maria

1 Let's start at the very beginning,
A very good place to start.
When you read, you begin with—
A, B, C.
When you sing you begin with do-re-mi.

Children
Do-re-mi?

Maria
Do-re-mi.
The first three notes just happen to be
Do-re-mi.

Children
Do-re-mi!

Maria
Do-re-mi-fa-so-la-ti

[Dialogue]

Maria

2 Doe—a deer, a female deer,
Ray—a drop of golden sun,
Me—a name I call myself,

Far—a long, long way to run,
Sew—a needle pulling thread,
La—a note to follow sew,
Tea—a drink with jam and bread—
That will bring us back to Do-oh-oh-oh!

Children and Maria

3 *Do—A deer, a female deer, Re—A drop of golden sun,*
   Mi—A name I call myself, Fa—A long long way to run,
   So—A needle pulling thread, La—A note to follow so,
   Ti—a drink with jam and bread, that will bring us back to Doe.
   Do-re-mi-fa-so-la-ti-do—So-Do!

[Dialogue]

Maria

4 So do la fa mi do re.

Children

So do la fa mi do re.

Maria

So do la ti do re do.

Children

So do la ti do re do.

[Dialogue]

Maria

5 So do la fa mi do re,
   So do la ti do re do.

Maria

6 When you know the notes to sing, you can sing most anything.

Maria and Children

7 When you know the notes to sing, you can sing most anything.
8 Doe—a deer, a female deer, Ray—a drop of golden sun,
   Me—a name I call myself, Far—a long long way to run,
   Sew—a needle pulling thread, La—a note to follow so,
   Tea—a drink with jam and bread—That will bring us back to Do.
9 Do re mi fa so la ti do, Do ti la so fa mi re do
   Do mi mi, Mi so so, Re fa fa, La ti ti [. . .]
10 When you know the notes to sing, you can sing most anything.
11 Doe—a deer, a female deer, Ray—a drop of golden sun,

Me—a name I call myself, Far—a long, long way to run,
Sew—a needle pulling thread, La—a note to follow so,
Tea—a drink with jam and bread, *that will bring us back to Do*.
Do ti la so fa mi re do.

12

Children
Do!

Chapter 28
Lerner and Loewe

After the era of Gilbert and Sullivan came to an end, exclusive creative partnerships became an anomaly in theatrical circles for many years. In the late 1930s, Richard Rodgers and Lorenz Hart excited much comment because of the longevity of their collaboration, but gradually, established teams became a more familiar feature of Broadway. Certainly Rodgers and Hammerstein were famous associates, but **Alan Jay Lerner** (1918–1986) and **Frederick Loewe** (1901–1988) established another widely recognized and successful team as well.

The two men did not have much in common. In 1905, in Berlin, Loewe's father Edmund had played Prince Danilo in Lehár's *The Merry Widow*, so the young Frederick grew up surrounded by professional musical activity. As an adult, Loewe described a career as a child prodigy, but historians have not been able to verify the majority of his claims. Even the details about his early life in the United States after his arrival in 1924 are sketchy. Loewe reportedly tried several careers—boxing, cowpunching, gold-prospecting, among others—then joined the Lambs (a New York theatrical club) in the mid-1930s. His friend Dennis King, star of *Rose-Marie* and *The Vagabond King*, sang one of Loewe's songs in a 1935 play, giving the composer his Broadway debut. Loewe also teamed up with Earle Crooker to write *Salute to Spring* (1937), which never came to New York, but which numbered Jerome Robbins among the dancers. Robbins choreographed Loewe and Crooker's next short-lived endeavor, an operetta. Loewe then concentrated on writing for the Lambs Club's annual shows, known as the *Gambols*.

In contrast to Loewe's European origins and diverse careers, American-born Lerner was raised in a life of comfortable privilege (his family owned the Lerner chain of dress stores). He co-edited his school yearbook with John F. Kennedy. Unlike many lyricists, Lerner was a fine pianist, studying music at Juilliard during the summers. He majored in literature at Harvard, where he contributed to the Hasty Pudding Club's annual musical theater productions. After he graduated in 1939, an eye injury prevented him from serving in World War II. Instead, he married his first wife (of eight) and began writing for a radio show. He also joined the Lambs Club, meeting Lorenz Hart and other theatrical luminaries. Various accounts exist of Lerner's first encounter with Loewe. Lerner himself recalled,

One day late in August of 1942, I was having lunch in the grill [of the Lambs Club] when a short, well-built, tightly strung man with a large head and hands and immensely dark circles under his eyes strode to a few feet from my table and stopped short. . . . His name was Frederick Loewe, Fritz to the membership . . . He came to my table and sat down.

"You're Lerner, aren't you?" he asked.
I could not deny it.
"You write lyrics, don't you?" he continued.
"I try," I replied.
"Well," he said, "would you like to write with me?"
I immediately said, "Yes." And we went to work.

Loewe needed a partner to help him update the songs he'd written for *Salute to Spring*, although the revised show closed in Detroit. Next, though, they agreed to write the music for *What's Up?*, a 1943 Broadway show, which ran for 63 performances. (Loewe later remarked, "*What's Up?* Obviously, nothing was. It was awful.") Undeterred, the duo tried again with *The Day Before Spring* (1945). Their reviews were better, as was the run, lasting 167 performances. Certainly, this five-month run could not be considered a full-fledged hit in an era of blockbusters such as *Oklahoma!* and *Carousel*, but Lerner and Loewe managed to sell the show to MGM Studios for $250,000 (although the film never was made).

Lerner and Loewe were fully aware of the innovations of Rodgers and Hammerstein—especially their integrated shows, which Lerner once described as "lyric theater." Lerner also liked fantasy and stories in which life triumphed

Frederick Loewe and Alan Jay Lerner in 1960.
Corbis/Bettmann.

164

over death, and all these influences are found in the next collaboration of Lerner and Loewe, *Brigadoon*. The plot origins are unclear, but Lerner recalled, "One day, . . . Fritz mentioned something about faith moving mountains. This started me thinking. For a while, I had a play about faith moving a mountain. From there we went to all sorts of miracles occurring through faith, and, eventually, faith moved a town." Lerner's fondness for a Scottish ambience is found in the show's title, which hints at the River Doon that runs through southwestern Scotland. Others have pointed out that the plot of *Brigadoon* (see the **Plot Summary**) bears quite a bit of resemblance to a German fantasy, *Germelshausen*, by Friedrich Gerstäcker. In fact, George Jean Nathan rebuked Lerner for "barefaced plagiarism," but Lerner argued that the parallels were no more than "unconscious coincidence."

For a while it seemed that the tale of Brigadoon would never be told on stage. The Theatre Guild turned it down because it didn't have an American locale. George Abbott and Rodgers and Hammerstein refused it as well. Billy Rose *was* interested, but offered the team a contract so onerous that they felt that it "negated Abraham Lincoln's Emancipation Proclamation that freed the slaves." At last Cheryl Crawford—who produced the successful 1942 revival of *Porgy and Bess*—agreed to take on the show.

It took a long time to raise the full production budget. Lerner recalled giving some 58 backers' auditions, the last one taking place a week after rehearsals had started. Agnes de Mille was their choreographer, and to give an authentic Scottish flavor to the dances, she hired folk dancer May Gadd and champion Scottish dancer James Jamieson to help her. De Mille exaggerated the traditional motions for theatrical purposes, so that small jumps sometimes became enormous arcs, but the Highland spirit of the dances was retained. (Not all of de Mille's specifications worked quite as she had intended, as Lerner learned; see **Behind-the-Scenes**: A Theatrical Façade?) Moreover, de Mille persuaded Lerner to let the dances carry a portion of the story, and the dramatic sword dance that concludes Act I was a particularly effective dramatic moment. Even critics who were tiring of the fad for ballets that had swept musical theater since the debut of *Oklahoma!* found little to complain about in de Mille's effective and colorful choreography (see the *Sidebar*: The Functions of Dance).

By the time *Brigadoon* was ready to open in 1947, it had accumulated a gratifying advance of $400,000. Both critics and audiences enjoyed the show, and the New York Drama Critics' Circle named *Brigadoon* the Best Play of 1947, making it the first musical ever to win this award. Tony Awards were distributed for the first time in 1947, and Agnes de Mille won for her choreography. (The category of Best Musical had

---

Sidebar: The Functions of Dance

Dance on the American stage has come a long way since the early 1800s, when choreographer Alexandre Placide evaluated solely physical appearance when choosing dancers. He was quoted as saying, "Give me . . . de pretty vimmens; I don't care, den, for de talent." Not much was expected of the "dancers" in chorus lines; their legs and smiles were much more highly valued than their skill.

Over time, however, many contributors left their mark on theatrical dance. Not only did Jack Cole use elements of ethnic dance, but he brought aspects of classical ballet, with its upright body and formal gestures, to the Broadway musical. Tap dance, in contrast, puts emphasis on the feet and the rhythm they can create; George Balanchine blended ballet and tap styles in his choreography for *On Your Toes* (1936). Jazz dancers isolated parts of the body, such as the shoulder, hip, or head, using movement in these **isolations** to establish rhythm and surprise. Agnes de Mille used innovations of modern dance in her *Oklahoma!* choreography, moving the entire body to the floor and into the air.

Dance historians see a "melting pot" effect in much of the choreography for twentieth-century stage musicals, with a mixture of gestures from many styles—ballet, modern dance, tap, jazz, ballroom, ethnic, social—in various combinations. At the same time, stage dance, or theater dance, could also play a dramatic role, and increasingly the dancers could become individual characters in the story. The first steps toward this individualization were fairly modest, as in the Princess Shows (where each chorus girl had "a dress of her own"), but by the time Jerome Robbins choreographed *West Side Story* in 1957, nearly every character was a dancer, and used dance—as well as speech and song—to communicate.

Richard Kislan has identified some seven functions in which dance can serve the needs of drama:

1. Dance may carry the plot forward, as when Tony and Maria of *West Side Story* meet and fall in love, all in the course of a single dance at the high school gym.
2. Dance may establish a mood (as when de Mille choreographed the joyful celebratory dances of *Brigadoon* or its somber and mournful "Funeral Dance").
3. Dance may embody key ideas of a musical, as is the case in "The Small House of Uncle Thomas" in *The King and I*, since the oppression of slavery mirrors the slave Tuptim's own oppression.
4. Dance may replace dialogue, and indeed, we need no words to know that Tony and Maria have fallen for each other during their "Dance at the Gym."
5. Dance may generate comedy—a well-known fact to minstrel show and vaudeville dancers.
6. Dance may extend a dramatic moment, in the sense that time might "stand still" for the duration of the dance.
7. The sheer spectacle of dance can be overwhelming.

A production number full of dancers still generates excitement, but this power was a lesson learned long ago by the creators of *The Black Crook* and other marvelous extravaganzas.

not yet been created, but the Composer award went to Kurt Weill.) The show also had a personal impact on Lerner; the actress playing Fiona, Marion Bell, became his second wife.

The Scottish flavor of *Brigadoon*'s dances was also evident in the majority of its songs, although one of the show's biggest hits—the duet "Almost Like Being in Love" (**Musical Example 34**)—reserves its Highland references for the verse, or vocal introduction (**1**), which has a lone mention of Loch Lomond. The remainder of the song, beginning with **2**, could be sung by any couple anywhere. Composer Frank Loesser felt this technique was simply practical. If all the "show-specific stuff" (in Loesser's term) was limited to the verse, the remaining song could stand on its own and could become a hit independently of the rest of the show. Whether Lerner and Loewe made this choice deliberately, the song's refrain could fit myriad situations—not just the blossoming affection between Tommy and Fiona.

After the opening, "Almost Like Being in Love" conforms to two repetitions of a song form, as seen in **Figure 28–1**. Tommy sings the first strophe alone, and then shares the lines of sections **6** through **9** with Fiona, sometimes alternating and sometimes harmonizing. The first two *a* sections of each strophe end with the same text, and a short pause after the first two words—"Why, it's—almost like being in love"—gives the phrase a sense of breathless excitement, which captures the emotion of the two new lovers. Lerner and Loewe's working method usually began with Lerner thinking up the title for a song needed at a particular juncture in the plot. Loewe, given the title, wrote music that suited its mood. Lerner then crafted poetry to fit Loewe's music, in much the same way that Rodgers and Hart had collaborated.

When *Brigadoon* was filmed by MGM in 1954, Gene Kelly choreographed instead of Agnes de Mille. This change in staffing was not particularly surprising, for choreographers did not yet have much clout—or copyright protection—on Broadway. Only in some situations did choreographers receive royalties from their endeavors. Directors had much the same problem, and it is probably for this reason that they joined with choreographers to form a new union, the **Society of Stage Directors and Choreographers** (SSD&C) in 1959. However, not until 1976 did they succeed in gaining United States copyright protection for choreography and pantomime; the law itself went into effect in 1978. At long last, artists could protect their designs for movement on the stage.

There were other changes in the film version as well. Cyd Charisse, a fine dancer, played Fiona—but Charisse was not a vocalist, so her "singing" was dubbed by Carol Richards. Fiona's vocal role was at times eliminated altogether, as was the case with "Almost Like Being in Love." In the film, the song has become a solo number for the love-struck Tommy, played by Kelly himself, and Tommy dances

to enliven the song in Fiona's absence. Because it is difficult to control the breath during the exertion of the choreography, dancers often do not sing much while dancing. Instead, the orchestra presents the melody; in this way, the same repetitive strophic form that was used in the stage musical is heard in the film.

Despite *Brigadoon*'s success, Lerner and Loewe had a falling-out and went their separate ways for a time. Lerner teamed up with Weill to create the concept musical *Love Life* (1948), featuring the unusual couple whose lives spanned three centuries. Next, Lerner headed to Hollywood, where he won an Academy Award for *An American in Paris*—the first Oscar ever given for the screenplay of a musical. In time, Lerner and Loewe put aside their differences and collaborated on *Paint Your Wagon* (1951). Afterwards, Lerner commented, "I didn't realize until many years later that practically every song in it is about loneliness." Even though Lerner himself produced the subsequent film of the same title, the movie has virtually nothing in common with the stage show beyond a similar Old West setting, some character names, and a few songs. The film does feature Clint Eastwood in a singing role, however.

After *Paint Your Wagon*, the partners separated once again, although they reunited briefly in 1952 to consider a proposal from Gabriel Pascal. Pascal, a producer, had persuaded the irascible George Bernard Shaw to give him the rights to *Pygmalion*. Wanting to make it into a musical, Pascal came to Lerner and Loewe (after approaching Rodgers and Hammerstein, Howard Dietz and Arthur Schwartz, Cole Porter, and others). After some initial interest, Lerner and Loewe got cold feet, so Pascal moved on to other writers.

The *Pygmalion* project languished until Pascal's death. When Lerner read Pascal's obituary, he thought about *Pygmalion* once more and started seeing possibilities where he had perceived only obstacles before. The problem now was: who held the performance rights? They discovered that the rights were part of Pascal's estate, that the estate executor was the Chase Bank, and that MGM Studios was after those same rights. MGM used the Chase Bank for its sizable deposits and threatened to withdraw those funds unless Chase decided in its favor. However, Pascal's estate executor was also the executor for Lerner's father's estate, which Lerner and Loewe hoped would work to their advantage. Since the situation was so tangled, Loewe talked Lerner into simply starting to write the show, letting the problem of the rights resolve itself through time.

In this way, the show that would be called **My Fair Lady** at last was underway. Shaw's play was a very "English" story (see the **Plot Summary**), and it was helped by the popularity of *The Boy Friend* (1953), a nostalgic salute to England's old Gaiety Girl musicals. (*The Boy Friend* ran 2,084 performances in London, and then introduced the young actress Julie Andrews to America.) Since Shaw was one of the most eloquent writers of the English language, Lerner was under a

2	3	4	5	6	7	8	9
a	a	b	a'	a	a	b	a'

Figure 28–1

Eliza (Julie Andrews) is upset with Professor Higgins (Rex Harrison) in *My Fair Lady*.
Corbis/Bettmann.

to *Pygmalion* had the most artistic merit, so they opted to appoint a literary agent to make the choice. Lerner and Loewe promptly hired the man to be *their* agent, so it came as little surprise that after his recommendation to the courts, the performance rights were awarded to Lerner and Loewe.

One remaining problem was a name for the show; the working title, *Liza*, was abandoned after they considered the problem of advertisements that would announce "Rex Harrison in *Liza*." No one was really happy with the alternative *My Fair Lady*—drawn from the children's song "London Bridge is Falling Down"—because it seemed to suggest an operetta, but when no better alternative was suggested, the revised title stayed. The writer Richard Traubner wonders if the title is a pun. One of the most exclusive neighborhoods in London is Mayfair, and in Eliza's cockney accent it would be pronounced *Myfair*. This is the central question of the show: Will she become a "Mayfair" lady by the end?

Like *Brigadoon*'s "Almost Like Being in Love," several of the songs in *My Fair Lady* can stand alone or can work in other contexts. Other tunes, however, are tightly integrated into the plot, needing the storyline to make sense. A radio audience, for instance, would hardly know what to make of a song like "The Rain in Spain." Another integrated tune is "Just You Wait" (**Musical Example 35**), in which Eliza furiously imagines ways to avenge herself for what she views as Professor Higgins's callous disregard for her feelings. "Just You Wait" easily could be regarded as a vision song, like "The Surrey with the Fringe on Top"; Eliza completely loses herself in the satisfying image of Higgins's suffering.

"Just You Wait," despite its lurid images of the many ways Higgins might die, is a comedy song as well as a vision song. Part of the humor is derived from the incongruous demises which Higgins might suffer, such as the idea that the King of England would order Higgins's execution simply "to celebrate the glory" of Eliza. The music intensifies the increasingly ludicrous scenarios; opening in the minor mode, the orchestra sounds a foreboding descending scale to announce the first of Eliza's dire threats at **1**. At **6**, when Eliza imagines herself as the toast of the English court, the mode changes to major, and her melodic line becomes more lyrical and elegant. The king issues his proclamation at **7** on a long series of repeated pitches, in a rather chantlike fashion. The mode returns to minor for the king's command at **9**. At **11**, when Eliza dreams of the firing squad that will spell the end of her tormentor, she returns to the martial melody of the opening—but this time the mode is major, reflecting her glee at this turn of events.

It could be argued that "Just You Wait," like "Do-Re-Mi," presents some rondo-like characteristics, which are apparent in the graph shown in **Figure 28–2**.

great deal of pressure to rise to Shaw's standards. The English actor playing Professor Higgins, Rex Harrison, owned a copy of *Pygmalion* published by Penguin Books, and during rehearsals, when he questioned the authenticity of a line, he would shout, "Where's my Penguin?" in order to check his script against Shaw's play. After a week, Lerner found a stuffed specimen of a genuine penguin at a taxidermist and arranged for the bird to be handed to Harrison the next time the actor called for his Penguin. The public script-consultation stopped, and the stuffed bird spent the remainder of the run in Harrison's dressing room.

Initially, Mary Martin considered the role of Eliza Doolittle, but after hearing five of the songs, she confided to her husband that she thought the partners had lost their talent (a comment he later repeated, somewhat tactlessly, to Lerner and Loewe). Eventually, the team settled on Julie Andrews. Despite *The Boy Friend*, she was comparatively inexperienced and probably would have been fired had it not been for director Moss Hart, who took her aside one weekend and drilled her relentlessly, hour after hour, until at last she *became* the character he wanted to see. As an Englishwoman with good diction, it was hard for her to master the uneducated Cockney accent and insouciant attitude needed for her role. She then had to tone *down* the accent for New York audiences when they couldn't understand her and intensify the accent all over again when *My Fair Lady* opened in London.

Meanwhile, the Chase Bank felt that it did not have the necessary expertise to decide which claimant for the rights

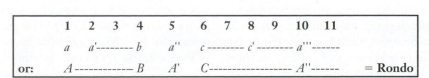

	1	2	3	4	5	6	7	8	9	10	11
	a	*a'*--------	*b*		*a''*	*c* --------	*c'* --------	*a'''*------			
or:	*A*-----------	*B*		*A'*	*C*-----------------	*A''*------			= **Rondo**		

Figure 28–2

Despite the repeated melodies, we hear Eliza's thoughts move sequentially through ever more gratifying deaths for Henry Higgins, and it is the progress to his climactic execution that matters.

My Fair Lady was a smash when it opened in 1956, and it continued to be a hit for six and a half years; its 2,717-performance run topped *Oklahoma!* by just over 500 shows. Even its tryout tour had been promising. Stuart Ostrow and Loesser went to see the show in Philadelphia, curious about the "competition." As the curtain came down, an envious Loesser turned to Ostrow and, making an extended pun on "The Rain in Spain," said, "The pain is plain and mainly in my brain; I think they've got it."

Loesser and Ostrow were not the only ones to foresee a hit; Columbia Records was so convinced that *My Fair Lady* would be a big success that it was the sole backer for the stage production—to the tune of $400,000—in exchange for the right to record the cast album. This was the first time a production had been supported by a single investor; it was a far cry from the 58 backers' auditions needed to finance *Brigadoon*. Columbia's faith was well merited, as it turned out. The record company rushed the entire cast into the studio on the first Sunday after the show's opening, and the album was released in an astonishingly short three days (albeit with errors in the title of at least one song). Sales of the album set new records, and it was undoubtedly an important factor in the show's very long run.

Lerner and Loewe deserve a lot of credit for *My Fair Lady*'s songs, for they had to accommodate the nonsinger Rex Harrison, just as Rodgers and Hammerstein had had to consider their stars' vocal limitations in *The King and I*. The rich orchestrations by Robert Russell Bennett were a helpful factor in filling the gap; the instruments could carry the melodies that the singer could not sing. Certainly, the fact that *My Fair Lady* was recorded some 60 times by 1970 indicated that audiences loved the music itself.

After *My Fair Lady*, Lerner found himself in Hollywood, under contract to write three films. Loewe joined Lerner on the third film, and the result, *Gigi*, took nine Oscars in the 1959 Academy Awards, more than any single film had ever won. Meanwhile, Lerner and Loewe had promised Moss Hart that the three of them would collaborate again. They eventually decided on the story of King Arthur and his Round Table; they called their stage version *Camelot*. By the end, both Lerner and Hart had ended up in the hospital, and Loewe was declaring he would never compose another note. (In truth, he had had a serious heart attack in 1959, so "taking it easy" was a medical necessity.)

Despite a weak book and illogical characters, *Camelot* had a lot going for it. Julie Andrews was cast as Guinevere, while Richard Burton—yet another untrained singer—played King Arthur, but Burton had a powerful stage presence that made up for much of his weakness as a vocalist. Newcomer Robert Goulet launched his career with his strong performance as Sir Lancelot. *Camelot* had so much going for it, in fact, that on its first night in Toronto it ran four and a half hours long—almost two hours overtime. The frenzied process of cutting the show hospitalized Lerner with a bleeding ulcer and Hart with a heart attack. Complicating matters was the elaborate stage scenery;

during the tryout tour, the sets alone needed eight baggage cars. Broadway insiders started calling the show "Costalot."

Despite the high costs and an inexplicable series of misfortunes, *Camelot* was at last ready to open on Broadway in 1960. (*My Fair Lady* was still playing at a nearby theater and would run for another two years.) The advance had reached $3 million, with one wag speculating that *Camelot* could be the first flop in history to run for two years. For a time, it looked like *Camelot* was indeed headed to failure. Critics found it overly long, with a weak storyline, and audiences seemed to agree. About three months after it opened, Hart talked his collaborators into taking the unusual step of revising a running show, but the alterations probably would not have been enough to save the production were it not for what Lerner referred to as "the miracle." On *My Fair Lady*'s fifth anniversary, its writers were invited to appear on the influential Ed Sullivan television show. Lerner and Loewe asked if Burton, Andrews, and Goulet could perform a 20-minute excerpt from *Camelot*, and Sullivan agreed. The new power of television was made crystal clear, for the next morning a long, long line stretched away from the box office. This boost pushed *Camelot* to 837 performances; its cast album stayed on the bestseller list for 60 weeks, while 2.5 million copies of the soundtrack sold after the film was released in 1967.

Camelot was linked in many people's minds with President John F. Kennedy, Lerner's old classmate. Jacqueline Kennedy said that her husband often played the album at bedtime. A line from *Camelot*'s title song—"one brief shining moment"—was all the more poignant after Kennedy's tragic assassination, and Lerner once admitted that he had never been able to watch *Camelot* again after Kennedy's death.

Camelot marked the end of Lerner and Loewe's glory days. Loewe, citing his damaged heart, retired from the theater, while Lerner, like Richard Rodgers, attempted various projects with new partners. Ironically, Rodgers *was* one of those partners for a time, but the two men were incompatible. At last the partnership broke up, with Rodgers complaining, "How dare that young man waste a year of my life?" Lerner saw some of his other collaborations reach the stage, but none became big hits. Even a stage version of *Gigi*, for which he lured Loewe out of retirement to create several new songs, closed after 103 performances. Despite this setback, Loewe was game for one last collaboration: a film based on the children's story *The Little Prince*. Although he and Lerner were proud of their score, they weren't happy with how it was performed, and they were not surprised by the film's failure. Loewe headed right back into a contented retirement, while Lerner resumed trying to create a successful show *without* Loewe.

Even with the tremendous talent of Leonard Bernstein, Lerner's next show bombed and, even worse, was accused of being racist. Lerner later compared *1600 Pennsylvania Avenue* to the *Titanic*; it vanished after seven performances. But this was a lengthy run in comparison with Lerner's final effort, *Dance a Little Closer* (1983). The show was written as a star vehicle for his eighth wife, but humorists renamed the show "Close a Little Quicker," for this last production survived only one performance—an ignominious ending to a career that had produced some of Broadway's most glittering works.

FURTHER READING

Easton, Carol. *No Intermission: The Life of Agnes de Mille.* New York: Little, Brown, 1996.

Green, Benny. *A Hymn to Him: The Lyrics of Alan Jay Lerner.* New York: Limelight Editions, 1987.

Green, Stanley. *The World of Musical Comedy.* Third edition, revised and enlarged. South Brunswick and New York: A. S. Barnes and Company, 1974.

Jablonski, Edward. *Alan Jay Lerner: A Biography.* New York: Henry Holt, 1966.

Kasha, Al, and Joel Hirschhorn. *Notes on Broadway: Conversations with the Great Songwriters.* Chicago: Contemporary Books, 1985.

Kislan, Richard. *Hoofing on Broadway: A History of Show Dancing.* New York: Prentice Hall, 1987.

Laufe, Abe. *Broadway's Greatest Musicals.* New, illustrated, revised edition. New York: Funk & Wagnalls, 1977.

Lees, Gene. *The Musical Worlds of Lerner & Loewe.* London: Robson Books, 1990.

Lerner, Alan Jay. *The Musical Theatre: A Celebration.* New York: Da Capo Press, 1986.

Mordden, Ethan. *Coming Up Roses: The Broadway Musical in the 1950s.* New York: Oxford University Press, 1998.

Ostrow, Stuart. *A Producer's Broadway Journey.* Westport, Connecticut: Praeger, 1999

Traubner, Richard. *Operetta: A Theatrical History.* Garden City, New York: Doubleday, 1983.

BEHIND-THE-SCENES: A THEATRICAL FAÇADE?

Audiences are aware that not all that takes place on stage is "real"; they understand that much of the theatrical presentation depends on make-believe. However, some of the things that even the creators of a show take to be real may involve dimensions of pretense, as Lerner discovered during the run of *Brigadoon.* In her quest for authenticity, de Mille had insisted on using two onstage bagpipers during the dramatic sword dance. Although bagpipe players were a rare commodity in 1947 New York, Crawford found two. Lerner says that all went well until one afternoon when one of the pipers came to Lerner and Loewe to inform them—since the other player was sick—that there would be no pipe music that evening. Lerner protested, "Can't you blow harder? No one can tell the difference between the sound of one bagpipes playing, or two." The piper insisted that he could not go on alone. When an exasperated Loewe asked, "Why not? You're getting paid enough!," the piper confessed, "I don't know how to play the bagpipes; I've been faking it and the other guy's been covering for me since opening night."

PLOT SUMMARY: *BRIGADOON*

What would happen if time could stand still? Two lost travelers, Tommy Albright and Jeff Douglass, find an answer to that question when distant singing leads them through the mist into the Scottish village of Brigadoon on market day. When they arrive, they are perplexed for many reasons: the village doesn't seem to be on their map, the townspeople are all dressed in quaint outfits (with no tourists in sight beyond Tommy and Jeff), and it seems odd that the vendors don't know what to make of their American currency. Soon, though, Fiona MacLaren and Meg Brockie take charge of the two wayfarers. Meg is man-hungry and gets Jeff aside for a private visit as soon as she can, but Fiona takes Tommy along to gather heather to use as decoration for her sister Jean's wedding to Charlie Dalrymple.

Not all the townspeople are celebrating, however. Harry Beaton is in love with Jean as well, so he is sick with jealousy and claims to hate the entire village. Tommy, meanwhile, is entranced with Brigadoon and with Fiona most of all. Tommy and Fiona remark to each other, "It's Almost Like Being in Love" (**Musical Example 34**), but this lighthearted mood dissolves when Tommy notices that Charlie has signed the MacLaren family Bible—and the date is May 24, 1746. Fiona won't say anything about this mystery, however, merely leading Tommy and Jeff to meet the schoolmaster, Mr. Lundie.

Mr. Lundie explains Brigadoon's peculiarities. In early 1746, the village had been threatened by a band of evildoers and wizards. The local minister, desperate to save his town, begged God to save the village by whisking it away from the marauders' path. God granted Mr. Forsythe's prayer, allowing the village to appear for only one day every 100 years; at night, while the townspeople slept, another 100 years would elapse. But, for this miracle to take place, Mr. Forsythe had to be willing to give up his own life. The minister loved his flock and agreed to the bargain. He died, and the miracle began: only two days have passed in the village, while 200 years have gone by in the outside world.

The wedding ceremony takes place, and then the dancing begins. Harry performs an intricate sword dance, and then asks Jean to join him. Before she can start to dance, however, he grabs her and kisses her. Charlie leaps to her defense, but Harry pulls a knife. Suddenly, though, Harry presents a greater threat: he runs away. One condition of the miracle is that all the townspeople must stay in their village. If even one person leaves, the miracle will be destroyed, and Brigadoon will vanish forever.

With this danger at hand, all the village men try to catch Harry. Jeff accidentally trips Harry, who falls onto rocks and is killed. Back in the village, the wedding festivities resume. Jeff cannot forget what just happened; he grows increasingly disturbed by this strange enchanted village, and he begins to urge Tommy to leave before night falls and they are doomed to stay in the village forever. Tommy has fallen in love with Fiona, but he is shaken by Jeff's fears and agrees to depart. He bids Fiona farewell, assuring her she has his heart, and the two men leave just as the mist begins to shroud the village once more.

Tommy tries to resume his busy New York life, but it is no use; he is constantly reminded of Brigadoon. He breaks off his engagement, knowing that his heart has been given elsewhere, and at last he decides to fly back to Scotland just to be where his love was, even if he can't see her again. Jeff agrees to go along, and they find their way to the remote spot where the village had first appeared to them. To their surprise, they hear the same sweet song that had rung through the forest the first time. They don't see the village itself, but a sleepy

Mr. Lundie appears, clad in his nightshirt. Tommy's great love for Fiona has become part of the miracle as well, so Mr. Lundie has been awakened to lead Tommy back to Brigadoon. As Mr. Lundie explains, "When ye love someone deeply anythin' is possible." A speechless Jeff watches the two men vanish into the mist, and the forest is silent once more.

PLOT SUMMARY: *MY FAIR LADY*

Derivatives of the Cinderella story had been absent from Broadway for a long time when *My Fair Lady* reached Broadway, but the musical proved that the old tale still could be entertaining. In this case, Cinderella is an impoverished flower seller named Eliza Doolittle. She splutters in indignation when a clumsy gentleman knocks her violets into the mud, but a bystander warns her that someone is writing down everything she says. She thinks he is a policeman, but he turns out to be Professor Henry Higgins, a scholar of language and dialects, who is fascinated by her mangled Cockney pronunciation. This conversation catches the attention of Colonel Pickering, who is knowledgeable about Indian dialects. The two men recognize their kindred interests and go off in each other's company; as they leave, Higgins absentmindedly hands Eliza all the change in his pockets—more money than she's ever seen before. She and her friends dream of ways to spend the windfall.

Armed with this fortune, Eliza goes to the Professor's house and asks him to give her elocution lessons so that she can get a respectable job in a flower shop. Boastfully, Higgins tells his new friend Pickering that he could improve Eliza's speech so much that she could pass as a lady at the upcoming Embassy Ball. Laughing, the Colonel proposes that they wager on it. Promptly, Higgins orders his housekeeper, Mrs. Pearce, to bathe and dress Eliza suitably.

Eliza's physical transformation is underway, but she is working far harder than Cinderella ever did; she finds it impossible to force her mouth to produce "proper" English. Her father arrives, accusing Higgins of having designs on his daughter. Higgins calmly offers to send her home, but that's not what Alfred Doolittle is after: he wants cash. Higgins is entertained at Doolittle's amoral willingness to sell his daughter and ends up giving him a whopping five pounds. Eliza is angry with everyone, and she dreams of ways Higgins might meet his comeuppance in "Just You Wait" (**Musical Example 35**).

At long last, an exhausted Eliza properly pronounces a phrase that has eluded her for weeks: "The Rain in Spain Stays Mainly in the Plain." Higgins, Pickering, and Eliza all whirl around the room in excitement. Higgins decides to take the "new" Eliza for a trial run at the Ascot races. Eliza looks lovely in her elegant clothes, but she still uses rude Cockney slang, now carefully enunciated. Despite these gaffes, the young Freddy Eynsford-Hill is completely smitten by her. Nevertheless, Pickering is appalled and wants to cancel the bet; Higgins, in contrast, is even more determined. At last, the night of the ball arrives, and all goes swimmingly—for a time. Then disaster looms: a guest at the ball is Zoltan Karpathy, himself an internationally famous expert on languages. He senses a mystery about Eliza and closes in on her as the act comes to a close.

When Higgins, Pickering, and Eliza return home in Act II, they are jubilant. Although Karpathy had declared that Eliza was indeed no lady, he felt that Eliza spoke English far *too* well to be a native Englishwoman; she must be a Hungarian princess! But as the elation settles down, Eliza worries, "What next?" Higgins ignores her frustration, casually suggesting that she could go get married or work in the flower shop that had initially motivated her education. Eliza is upset by his lack of concern, so she packs her things and leaves. On the doorstep she encounters Freddy, who would love to marry her, but he's too weak-willed to suit her. Going back to the flower market, she realizes that no one recognizes her. Only her father knows her, and he's focused on his own troubles. It seems that Higgins had told a philanthropist that Doolittle was the most original moralist he knew, and the millionaire left Doolittle a sizable bequest in his will—but now Doolittle's landlady insists on matrimony. Higgins, meanwhile, can't figure out Eliza and sings a "Hymn to Him" as a declaration of male superiority.

Eliza at last decides to go to Higgins's mother for advice. Eliza tells her the full story and Mrs. Higgins is appalled at her son's behavior—and she tells him so when he comes searching for Eliza. He and Eliza have yet another misunderstanding, and they both stomp away angrily. Back at his home, however, the Professor rather disconsolately starts to listen to a recording of Eliza's voice he had made during their lessons. As the recording plays, Eliza comes in, switches off the machine, and continues to speak the exercise herself. Higgins is too irascible to show his happiness at her return, but he growls at her, "Where the devil are my slippers?" and she knows that he wants her back in his life. Whether or not this is the typical prince of whom Cinderellas dream, Higgins is the grumpy prince whom Eliza wants.

MUSICAL EXAMPLE 34

BRIGADOON
FREDERICK LOEWE/ALAN JAY LERNER, 1947

"Almost Like Being in Love"

Tommy

1 Maybe the sun gave me the pow'r, for I could swim Loch Lomond and be home in half an hour.
Maybe the air gave me the drive, for I'm all aglow and alive!

2 What a day this has been! What a rare mood I'm in!

Why, it's almost like being in love!
3   There's a smile on my face for the whole human race!
Why, it's almost like being in love!
4   All the music of life seems to be like a bell that is ringing for me!
5   And from the way that I feel when that bell starts to peal,
I would swear I was falling, I could swear I was falling,
It's almost like being in love.
6   When we walked up the brae,

Fiona
Not a word did we say. It was almost like bein' in love.
7   But your arm link'd in mine made the world kind o' fine.

Tommy
It was almost like being in love!

Fiona
8   All the music of life seems to be

Tommy
Like a bell that is ringing for me!

Tommy and Fiona
9   And from the way that I feel when that bell starts to peal,

Fiona
I would swear I was fallin',

Tommy
I could swear I was falling.

Tommy and Fiona
It's almost like being in love.

MUSICAL EXAMPLE 35

My Fair Lady
FREDERICK LOEWE/ALAN JAY LERNER, 1956

"Just You Wait"

Liza
1   Just you wait, 'enry 'iggins, just you wait! You'll be sorry, but your tears'll be too late!
You'll be broke and I'll have money; Will I help you? Don't be funny!
Just you wait, 'enry 'iggins, just you wait!
2   Just you wait, 'enry 'iggins, till you're sick, and you scream to fetch a doctor double-quick!
I'll be off a second later, and go straight to the theatre!
3   Oh, ho ho, 'enry 'iggins, just you wait.
4   Ooooooooh, 'enry 'iggins! Just you wait until we're swimmin' in the sea!
Ooooooooh, 'enry 'iggins and you get a cramp a little ways from me!
When you yell you're gonna drown, I'll get dressed and go to town!
5   Oh, ho, ho, 'enry 'iggins! Oh, ho, ho, 'enry 'iggins! Just you wait!
6   One day I'll be famous! I'll be proper and prim!
Go to Saint James so often I will call it Saint Jim.
One evening the King will say, "Oh, Liza, old thing,
I want all of England your praises to sing.
7   Next week on the 20th of May, I proclaim Liza Doolittle Day!
8   All the people will celebrate the glory of you, And whatever you wish and want I gladly will do."
"Thanks a lot, King," says I, in a manner well-bred; "But all I want is 'enry 'iggins' 'ead!"
9   "Done!" says the King, "With a stroke. Guard, run and bring in the bloke!"
10   Then they'll march you, 'enry 'iggins, to the wall;
And the King will tell me: "Liza, sound the call."
As they raise their rifles higher, I'll shout, "Ready! Aim! Fire!"
11   Oh, ho, ho, 'enry 'iggins! Down you'll go, 'enry 'iggins! Just you wait!

New Faces of the 1940s and 1950s

Part Seven

Chapter 29
Leonard Bernstein

Although many musical theater composers have been classically trained musicians, very few have maintained their standing in the art music community at the same time that they compose for the stage. One of those few was **Leonard Bernstein** (1918–1990), who succeeded in writing musical theater master-works even as he became one of the most celebrated conductors in the classical music world.

During Bernstein's childhood, Bernstein's father was not enthusiastic about his son's interest in music—especially when he learned a prospective teacher charged three dollars an hour for lessons. Nevertheless, his father gave Bernstein a baby grand piano after his bar mitzvah. Bernstein went on to study music at Harvard, meeting some of classical music's luminaries along the way; several of them began urging Bernstein toward a career in conducting. In 1939, Bernstein organized a performance of Marc Blitzstein's *The Cradle Will Rock*, the show that—as Chapter 24, "Politics and Social Commentary" explains—had proved so problematic in 1937. Blitzstein himself attended and approved of the performance.

Back in New York, Blitzstein mentioned the student production to Adolph Green, who turned out to be an old friend of Bernstein's. Green had been working in New York with Betty Comden and Judy Holliday in a satirical comedy group called "The Revuers." The madcap players presented severely truncated classic novels in their act. An example was their version of *Gone With the Wind*:

Scarlett O' Hara's a spoiled pet,
She wants everything she can get.
The one thing she can't get is Rhett.
The end.

Green introduced his colleagues to Bernstein, who relished the energy of these new friends. In the fall, however, Bernstein began his serious conducting studies with Fritz Reiner. He also trained in the summers with Serge Koussevitzky at the Berkshire Festival at Tanglewood (an estate in Massachusetts).

In 1943, Bernstein was hired as assistant conductor of the New York Philharmonic, opening the door for Bernstein's big "break," which occurred later that year. The conductor was out of town, and the guest conductor fell ill. Without a rehearsal, Bernstein had to lead the New York Philharmonic in a concert that not only featured the premiere of a new work but was also broadcast nationally via radio. Bernstein triumphed, becoming a celebrity virtually overnight.

Besides conducting, Bernstein had been busy composing as well; his "Jeremiah" symphony got a lot of attention. Still, Bernstein was surprised when choreographer Jerome Robbins approached him with a commission for a ballet score. The ballet, *Fancy Free*, was a huge success—but then the set designer Oliver Smith urged the creators to turn it into a musical. Bernstein and Robbins set to work on what would become *On the Town*. However, as Bernstein took pains to point out afterwards, "There isn't a *note* of *Fancy Free* in *On the Town*. It was just the idea of ballet that struck people as a great idea for a show—three sailors with twenty-four hours' leave."

For help with the lyrics, Bernstein persuaded Robbins to work with his old friends Comden and Green. Some hitches delayed the writing: Bernstein needed nasal surgery for a deviated septum, so Green decided to have his troublesome tonsils removed at the same time in order to minimize the "down" time for the collaboration. As they recovered, Comden perched on a chair in their hospital room. Bernstein's sister Shirley remembered the raucous singing and laughter, and one nurse commented about Bernstein, "He may be God's gift to music, but I'd hate to tell you where he gives me a pain."

Since the majority of *On the Town*'s creators were Broadway novices, it was fortunate that George Abbott agreed to direct. Not only did he help them to raise the money needed to mount the show, but Abbott also used his solid theatrical instincts to insist on various cuts and insertions. After the debut in 1944, an Associated Press reporter called *On the*

172

Town one of those rare shows in which "a reviewer gets an opportunity to heave his hat into the stratosphere, send up rockets and in general start the sort of journalistic drooling over a musical comedy that puts an end to all adequate usage of superlatives."

When the creators had started *On the Town*, they agreed that it should be integrated, with the music, the dance, and the book all serving the needs of the story. As it turned out, it was integrated in the racial sense as well—for the first time, Broadway theatergoers saw black and white dancers hand in hand. Moreover, Robbins required the dancers to be as expressive as the actors in conveying both the mood and the plot. Bernstein's score was also a type of integration, blending classical devices with the syncopated rhythms and harmonies of jazz, supporting the exuberance of three sailors on shore leave. One tune—"New York, New York"—has attained the status of an unofficial anthem for the great metropolis. The production, which cost $150,000, grossed more than $2 million.

Nevertheless, Bernstein's mentor Koussevitzky gave his protégé a stern lecture, maintaining that a conductor with as much potential as Bernstein must not squander his talent. A chastened Bernstein proceeded to concentrate on conducting and art music composition for several years. In January 1949, however, his old friend Robbins called with an idea for a show based on Shakespeare's *Romeo and Juliet*. Their version would be updated to present-day New York and would depict the stress caused when a Jewish girl and a Catholic boy fall in love. Robbins wanted Arthur Laurents to do the book; Bernstein didn't know Laurents, but was agreeable. However, the show seemed to lose momentum even before it had really started, and the fledgling *East Side Story* was shelved.

Soon afterwards, Bernstein accepted the offer to write **incidental music** for *Peter Pan* (1950). Incidental music for a play is similar to the soundtrack of a motion picture: it enhances the stage action or mood with appropriate vocal or instrumental music. The same year, Robbins choreographed a ballet to accompany the score of Bernstein's second symphony, known as "The Age of Anxiety," and Bernstein also worked on his first opera, *Trouble in Tahiti*, in 1951, which premiered the following year.

Shortly after *Trouble in Tahiti*'s debut, Bernstein turned to writing the score for a second musical, based on an autobiographical novel by Ruth McKenney. Producers Robert Fryer and George Abbott wanted to turn McKenney's *My Sister Eileen* into a musical—*Wonderful Town*—but they had been dissatisfied with the score they had gotten from another composer and lyricist. So, with little more than a month to go before the show was due to open, they turned to Bernstein, Comden, and Green for help. Fired up by the challenge, the three collaborators produced a lively and entertaining score. Not only did the Tony Awards recognize their efforts, but *Wonderful Town* (1953) was named the Best Musical by both the Tonys and the New York Drama Critics' Circle. Sadly, though, despite several attempts, Bernstein, Comden, and Green would never be able to collaborate again.

Bernstein continued to be busy; he conducted, wrote the film score for *On the Waterfront*, and worked with Lillian Hellman on an operetta version of Voltaire's *Candide*. In part, *Candide* was their response to the divisive McCarthy-era politics. Bernstein himself had trouble with the State Department, which refused to renew his passport until he had undergone a hearing with a lawyer to support him—for a cost of $3,500. Hellman refused to testify in front of the House Un-American Activities Committee (but Jerome Robbins *did* testify, to the shock of many of his colleagues).

Bernstein's preparation of *Candide* was interrupted over and over again by other projects—television programs, various conducting gigs, a festival at the Hollywood Bowl, and a renewed attempt at getting *East Side Story* off the ground. In fact, while Bernstein was in California for the festival, he had a poolside meeting at a hotel with Laurents. During the meeting, Bernstein noticed a newspaper article reporting an incident of Los Angeles gang violence. Bernstein and Laurents realized that gang activity could be their story's modern equivalent of the hostility between the Montagues and the Capulets.

On Bernstein and Laurents's return to New York, they learned that the notorious tenements of New York's East Side had been demolished and that gang problems had moved west—and so their project was rechristened **West Side Story** (see the **Plot Summary**). They also brought a young Stephen Sondheim in to help with the lyrics when Bernstein became overwhelmed with the composition and orchestration. Sondheim had been reluctant to write lyrics, protesting, "I've never been that poor and I've never even *known* a Puerto Rican." Moreover, he wanted to launch his own career as a composer and didn't want to get pigeonholed as a lyricist. However, Oscar Hammerstein had pointed out that *West Side Story* would give Sondheim the chance to work with some of Broadway's brightest luminaries, and so Sondheim acquiesced. The writing went well, and the show was finished early in 1956.

Before *West Side Story* reached the stage, however, Bernstein's attention turned back to *Candide*. At last, they had found the right lyricist, Richard Wilbur, but Hellman was still struggling to find the right structure for the operetta's libretto, working her way through 14 different versions. *Candide* finally opened in December 1956, and many critics applauded the sharp-edged satire. Others condemned it resoundingly, and audiences found the story hard to follow; *Candide* flopped after 73 performances. Bit by bit, though, its cast album became a best seller. In 1973, Harold Prince and Hugh Wheeler adapted the show into a more compact "pocket" version, which became a hit—making *Candide* one of the few failures ever to experience a triumphant return to Broadway.

Although *Candide*'s initial failure was a blow to Bernstein's ego, he had recently been appointed as a joint principal conductor of the New York Philharmonic and would be directing the Philharmonic's "Young People's Concerts." But his ego suffered again when Cheryl Crawford, who had agreed to produce *West Side Story*, called a meeting in April 1957 to tell the creators that she was quitting. Crawford recalled the agony of

calling the writers and Jerry Robbins into my office to tell them. It was a miserable meeting, but at least I was able to soften the blow by telling them that Roger [Stevens, Crawford's production partner] wanted to continue. I will always remember their unbelieving angry faces as they walked out. Only Jerry stayed to shake my hand. I told Roger I was certain they would work harder than ever to prove me wrong.

They sure did.

After the shock of Crawford's resignation, Bernstein felt suicidal. Sondheim, in contrast, contacted Harold Prince and Prince's production partner Robert Griffith. Prince and Griffith agreed to listen to the score; intrigued, they agreed to coproduce the show with Stevens. But there were more difficulties to overcome: Robbins, who had the original idea for *West Side Story* and was directing the show, wanted someone else to do the choreography. At the time, however, Robbins's name was currently the biggest box office draw of all the collaborators, and Prince threatened to pull out unless Robbins choreographed. A compromise was reached by giving Robbins eight weeks of rehearsal rather than the typical four. Even so, Robbins was assisted in choreographing some of the dance numbers by Peter Gennaro.

Robbins had a tremendous impact on the tone of *West Side Story*. In a process similar to Constantin Stanislavsky's "method acting," Robbins required that the members of the two gangs avoid each other backstage; he wanted them to "become" the bitter enemies they portrayed on stage. Ironically, Lee Becker, who played "Anybody's" and is rejected by the Jets during the show, found herself ostracized during the lunch hour as well. Despite this unhappy isolation, Becker (later Lee Becker Theodore) was named as *West Side Story*'s **dance captain**, the person who trains replacements and monitors the dancing after the choreographer has left. Later, she used this expertise to help preserve the choreography of *West Side Story* and other shows by establishing an enterprise called the "American Dance Machine." In a rather surprising context, American television viewers of the early twenty-first century have been re-introduced to some of *West Side Story*'s choreography via a series of commercials for The Gap clothing chain; groups of dancers clad in Gap chino slacks perform some of Robbins's complex leaps and floor patterns, snapping their fingers in the rhythmic gesture so closely associated with the show. (The original dancers wore jeans, but not just any jeans, as Harold Prince discovered; see **Behind-the-Scenes**: Getting Your Money's Worth.)

In theatrical circles, the dancers who appear in chorus line after chorus line are called **gypsies**, partly because of their itinerant nature. *West Side Story* put special demands on the gypsies, for they had to be able to dance *and* sing, and it took quite a while to find performers who satisfied the producers on both counts. Because the dancing is so important to the story of *West Side Story*, the published book (containing only the dialogue) is one of the shortest ever for a Broadway show. As critic Brooks Atkinson observed, "The ballets convey the things that Mr. Laurents is inhibited from saying because the characters are so inarticulate. The hostility and the suspicion between the gangs, the glory of the nuptials, the terror of the rumble, the devastating climax—Mr. Robbins has found the patterns of movement that

express these parts of the story." The use of dance gestures to convey the feelings that the uneducated gang members don't have the words to say is an important achievement of *West Side Story*. In that same light, Sondheim has regretted the lyrics he wrote for Maria in "I Feel Pretty." He thinks that he made her poetry too "clever" for her character; the elaborate internal rhymes such as "It's alarming how charming I feel" are not the typical phraseology of a sheltered immigrant.

Not only do lyrics need to suit a character's vocabulary, but their pace needs to be within a performer's physical limits. Concerning "America" (**Musical Example 36**), Sondheim ruefully noted,

> *Thank God it's a spectacular dance because it wouldn't get a hand otherwise. It has 27 words to the square inch. I had this "wonderful" quatrain that went "I like to be in America / O. K. by me in America / Everything free in America / For a small fee in America." The "For a small fee" was my little zinger—except that the "For" is accented and the "sm" is impossible to say that fast, so it went "For a smafee in America." Nobody knew what it meant, and I learned my lesson: you have to consider an actor's tongue and teeth.*

(Sondheim recalled wrestling with *West Side Story*'s lyrics on other occasions; see the **Sidebar**: The Role of the Theater Lyric). In *West Side Story*'s opening number, the creators opted to drop the words altogether, allowing the mood of the number to be conveyed solely by dance, snapping fingers, and an occasional whistle. In "America," however, the chorus had to soldier on through the rapid-fire lyrics, even while dancing Robbins's energetic choreography.

Anita (Allyn McLerie) in "America" from *West Side Story*.
Photofest.

Sidebar: The Role of the Theater Lyric

Just as Irving Berlin articulated guidelines for composers aspiring to write popular songs, lyricist Sheldon Harnick enumerated four requirements for effective theater lyrics, arguing that they must:

1. continue the story's flow;
2. provide insight into the characters;
3. heighten the climactic moments; and
4. enrich the feeling of time and space.

Adherence to Harnick's first stipulation is a characteristic of an integrated show, while vision songs and other internalized numbers exemplify the second requirement. "Love songs" are almost an overused genre because of their effectiveness at achieving the third goal, while the language a character uses can be an important factor in making his context—the fourth requirement—believable.

Stephen Sondheim added two more items to Harnick's list, arguing that

5. the actor must have something to act, and
6. the actor must have something to do.

Sondheim's experience with *West Side Story* contributed to his belief in these additional requirements. During rehearsals, he learned how problematic his lyrics for "Maria" were. As Sondheim relates,

The first time Jerry Robbins heard "Maria," . . . he said, "Now what happens there?"

I said, "Well, you know, he is standing outside her house and, you know, he senses that she's going to appear on the balcony."

He said, "Yeah, but what is he doing?"

I said, "Oh, he's standing there and singing a song."

He said, "What is he doing?"

I said, "Well, he sings, 'Maria, Maria, I just met a girl named Maria and suddenly that name will never be the same to me.'"

He said, "And then what happens?"

I said, "Then he sings . . ."

"You mean," he said, "he just stands looking at the audience?"

I said, "Well, yes."

He said, "You stage it."

I knew exactly what he meant. He was being grumpy, but what he was saying was, "Give me something to play so the audience will be interested."

Robbins wanted twentieth-century musical theater (and Sondheim) to do more with solo songs: no longer could performers just stand and sing, as stars of the past often had done. Choreographers were knitting their dances ever more tightly into the story; lyricists had to make sure their poetry contributed to the drama as well.

Compounding the difficulty of "America" is the shifting accentuation of its **hemiola** rhythm. It is possible for a piece in triple meter to feel like it switches briefly to duple meter—or a piece in duple meter might begin to have a temporary "triple" feeling—and this effect is called hemiola. After a nostalgic vocal introduction at **1**—which Anita mocks at **2**—"America" is structured as a type of list song in alternation form. The *a* portions of this form (at **3**, **5**, **7**, and **9**) consist of almost constant shifts between the two metric feelings. The rapid changes in note groupings are evident in **Figure 29–1**. The hemiola rhythm of "America" is based on the *huapango* (or *huasteco*), a dance from the Huastec region of Mexico along the Gulf Coast. During certain sections of a huapango, dancers perform rapid feet movements called *zapateado*; these complex patterns are similar to those heard in "America." Moreover, Bernstein modeled the vocal introduction of "America" on the *seis*, a declamatory song characteristic of Puerto Rico. Although "America" does not pretend to depict authentic ethnic dance, it is certainly evocative of musical styles from Latin America (even though Bernstein had written the melody years before for an unpublished ballet).

Despite Robbins's efforts to separate the two gangs from each other, Bernstein wrote music that illustrated the ironic parallels between the Sharks and the Jets. The "Tonight (Quintet)" (**Musical Example 37**) is an example. The piece is called a quintet because it uses five different performers: Riff (backed by the rest of the Jets), Bernardo (supported by the Sharks), Anita, Tony, and Maria. At **1**, the Jets declare their intent to win that evening's upcoming rumble, while the Sharks (who are elsewhere on the stage) express identical sentiments—sung to the same melody—at **2**, ending at a slightly higher pitch as the tension rises. The two gangs trade off lines and melodies from **3** through **6**. Then, unaware of each other, the two gangs sing in unison at **7**—their attitudes are identical, which Bernstein underscores for us by having both gangs use the same tune. The two gangs think they are very different from each other, but their music betrays that they are actually all the same.

triple:	1	2	3	1	2	3
	I	like	to	be	in	A-
duple:	1	2	1	2	1	2
	mer-		i-		ca!	
triple:	1	2	3	1	2	3
	O.	K.	by	me	in	A-
duple:	1	2	1	2	1	2
	mer-		i-		ca!	

Figure 29–1

Anita makes her vocal entrance at **10**, using the same sequence of melodies heard at **1**, **2**, and **3**. She and the two gangs are identical in their excited anticipation of the evening.

At **11**, Tony introduces a new melody, although his tune is actually a reprise of an earlier song ("Tonight") he and Maria had sung on the fire escape outside her family's apartment. The "Tonight" theme is flowing and lyrical; its four lines (**11**, **12**, **13**, and **14**) conform to the customary a-a-b-a' of a song form. After Tony sings this reprise, the Jets enter at **15** with a reiteration of the same melodies sung in sections **1** through **3**.

Maria at last joins the quintet at **16**, but the texture changes from homophony to nonimitative polyphony. Maria sings the first *a* phrase of "Tonight" while Riff extracts a promise from Tony to come to the rumble, using a melody derived from the quintet's opening theme. As Maria presents the second *a* phrase of "Tonight" at **17**, the gangs and Anita take over Riff and Tony's melodies of **16**. At **18**, Tony joins with Maria on the *b* phrase of "Tonight" while the Jets and the Sharks argue about "who began it," and Anita dreamily sings a third theme anticipating her post-rumble date with Bernardo. The tripartite division is sustained at **19**, with Tony and Maria singing the final *a'* phrase of "Tonight" against the warring gangs (who sing in an unconscious unison) and the languid Anita who borrows phrases from each group for her own melody. All the forces unite on a final utterance of "Tonight" at **20**. Like the great ensemble finales of Mozart, the melody for each character is skillfully interwoven with the others, giving insight into the similarities of the characters at the same time that it distinguishes them.

It has been suggested that Bernstein was influenced by Aaron Copland's orchestral composition *El salón México* in writing "America." It is certainly possible to find hints of other composers in Bernstein's score for *West Side Story*. Scholars (Stephen Banfield, Geoffrey Block, Joan Peyser, and others) have found similarities between works by Beethoven and passages in "Cool" and "Somewhere," strains of Igor Stravinsky may be heard in the "Tonight (Quintet)," while an operatic tune by Benjamin Britten may have been a source for "Tonight." Moreover, Bernstein may also have been influenced by his friend Marc Blitzstein in the tune "Maria." Regardless of his sources of inspiration, Bernstein created one of the most powerful and impressive scores ever seen on Broadway. As Atkinson commented in his review of the New York premiere, "The subject is not beautiful. But what *West Side Story* draws out of it is beautiful."

Not everyone could perceive beauty in this tragic show. Some found it difficult to get past the incongruous image of dancing gangs; other listeners thought they heard raw language (although Sondheim and Laurents had carefully written lines such as "When the spit hits the fan.") Scheduled performances of *West Side Story* were cancelled in the Soviet Union and at the World's Fair in Brussels because State Department officials feared the gritty look at the sordid side of American life was *too* realistic.

At one point, Sondheim asked his mentor Hammerstein to sit in on a rehearsal. Although the style of *West Side Story* was markedly different from Hammerstein's own works, he was impressed by its power. However, he thought the scene on the fire escape was a bit empty and needed a song that "soared." This suggestion led the creators to expand the tender and hopeful "Tonight," one of the pre-existing melodies in the "Quintet." Rodgers, too, had a suggestion. Robbins reported,

> We had a death scene for Maria—she was going to commit suicide or something, as in Shakespeare. [Rodgers] said, "she's dead already, after all this happens to her." So the walls we hit were helpful in a way, sending us back for another look.

The end result was satisfying enough for audiences that *West Side Story* ran for 772 performances after its 1957 opening (and another 253 performances in 1960 when it returned to Broadway after a lengthy tour). The film was released in 1961, taking the Academy Award that year for Best Picture. Gradually but inexorably, *West Side Story* attained the status of one of musical theater's classics.

Bernstein accepted the post of conductor of the New York Philharmonic in 1958, prompting theater critic Brooks Atkinson to accuse him of abandoning Broadway and "capitulating to respectability." The fears proved to be well grounded, for it was years before Bernstein tackled a new stage project. He did not complete another full-fledged Broadway show until 1976, when the ill-fated *1600 Pennsylvania Avenue* premiered. He and collaborator Alan Jay Lerner received some negative feedback along the way—such as when their first producer, Arnold Saint Subber, resigned, shouting at Lerner, "It stinks, it stinks, it stinks!" But Bernstein and Lerner ignored any and all criticism, and Robbins, who refused to come in as a show doctor, commented, "Only two titans could have a failure like this." When another director did make a few changes, an actor shrugged, saying, "It was like changing chairs on the *Titanic*."

Bernstein refused to allow the show to be recorded, and subsequently he reused some of the tunes in later projects, including his final stage work. This was an opera entitled *A Quiet Place* (1983), which was crafted around his earlier opera, *Trouble in Tahiti*. It received mixed reactions at its debut, but after substantial revisions, it was taken to La Scala, the world's premier opera house in Italy, where it was a full-fledged success. However, this was to be Bernstein's last theatrical work of any kind, and he died in October 1990. His Broadway legacy was small in comparison to many other writers, but even if *West Side Story* had been his only show, his lasting place in the annals of musical theater would be assured.

FURTHER READING

Banfield, Stephen. *Sondheim's Broadway Musicals*. Ann Arbor: University of Michigan Press, 1993.

Burton, Humphrey. *Leonard Bernstein*. New York: Doubleday, 1994.

Burton, William Westbrook, ed. *Conversations About Bernstein*. New York: Oxford University Press, 1995.

Crawford, Cheryl. *One Naked Individual: My Fifty Years in the Theatre*. Indianapolis and New York: The Bobbs-Merrill Company, 1977.

Flinn, Denny Martin. *Musical!: A Grand Tour*. New York: Schirmer Books, 1997.

Guernsey, Otis L., Jr., ed. *Broadway Song & Story: Playwrights/Lyricists/Composers Discuss Their Hits*. New York: Dodd, Mead, 1985.

Henderson, Amy, and Dwight Blocker Bowers. *Red, Hot, and Blue: A Smithsonian Salute to the American Musical*. Washington: The National Portrait Gallery and The National Museum of American History, in association with the Smithsonian Institution Press, 1996.

Kasha, Al, and Joel Hirschhorn. *Notes on Broadway: Conversations with the Great Songwriters*. Chicago: Contemporary Books, 1985.

Kislan, Richard. *Hoofing on Broadway: A History of Show Dancing*. New York: Prentice Hall, 1987.

———. *The Musical: A Look at the American Musical Theater*. New, revised, expanded edition. New York and London: Applause Books, 1995.

Loney, Glenn, ed. *Musical Theatre in America: Papers and Proceedings of the Conference on the Musical Theatre in America*. (Contributions in Drama and Theatre Studies, Number 8). Westport, Connecticut: Greenwood Press, 1984.

Mandelbaum, Ken. *Not Since Carrie: Forty Years of Broadway Musical Flops*. New York: St. Martin's, 1991.

Mordden, Ethan. *Better Foot Forward: The History of American Musical Theatre*. New York: Grossman Publishers, 1976.

Peyser, Joan. *Bernstein: A Biography*. New York: Ballantine Books, 1987.

Prince, Hal. *Contradictions: Notes on Twenty-Six Years in the Theatre*. New York: Dodd, Mead, 1974.

Swain, Joseph P. *The Broadway Musical: A Critical and Musical Survey*. New York: Oxford University Press, 1990.

Theodore, Lee. "Preserving American Theatre Dance: The Work of the American Dance Machine." In Loney, *Musical Theatre in America*, 275–277.

Zadan, Craig. *Sondheim & Co.: The Authorized, Behind-the-Scenes Story of the Making of Stephen Sondheim's Musicals*. 2nd ed. New York: Harper & Row, 1986.

BEHIND-THE-SCENES: GETTING YOUR MONEY'S WORTH

Irene Sharaff was the costume designer for *West Side Story*, and it was her task to dress the young gang members in clothing that seemed "believable" to audiences of 1957. As producer, Harold Prince was anxious to keep costs down, so he found the expense of Sharaff's costumes irksome. He relates,

> I remember I didn't have much patience for the blue jeans Irene Sharaff "designed" for West Side at the cost of $75 a pair (today they would cost $200). I thought, How foolish to be wasting money when we can make a promotional arrangement with Levi Strauss to supply blue jeans for free for program credit. So I instructed the wardrobe mistress in New York to replace them as they wore out with Levi's. . . . A year later I looked at West Side and wondered, Why doesn't it look as beautiful as it used to? What's happened? What "happened"

> was that Sharaff's blue jeans were made of a special fabric, which was then dipped and dyed and beaten and dyed again and aged again, and so on, so our blue jeans were in forty subtly different shades of blue, vibrating, energetic, creating the effect of realism.

As Prince discovered, Sharaff's "fake" blue jeans seemed more real than genuine blue jeans—another instance of theatrical magic at work. Understandably, Prince titled his autobiography *Contradictions*.

PLOT SUMMARY: *WEST SIDE STORY*

In many urban areas today, conflicts between gangs are a regrettable but familiar occurrence. In 1957, however, the bitter struggles between a Puerto Rican gang (the Sharks) and a white gang (the Jets) shocked many viewers. The Jets want to organize a fight—a rumble—to protect their territory against a gang of "foreigners." The Jets decide to issue their challenge at the school dance that evening. Their former leader, Tony, has "retired" from fighting, believing that there is more to life than just the gang. However, his best friend Riff, the Jets' new leader, persuades Tony to go to the dance with them.

Tony's decision is fateful, for he sees Maria, the younger sister of Bernardo, leader of the Sharks. Maria has just come to America to marry Chino, and she is attending her first American dance. Tony and Maria are mesmerized by each other, and time seems to stop as they dance and then, gently, begin to kiss. Just then, Bernardo becomes aware of what his little sister is up to, and he angrily orders Tony to stay away from her. Riff interrupts the confrontation by delivering the challenge to rumble, and Bernardo agrees to meet Riff at the local drugstore after the dance to plan the details of the fight.

Tony finds his way to the fire escape outside Maria's apartment, where she sneaks out to meet him. Unaware of this secret meeting, Bernardo's girlfriend Anita tries to get him to look at the situation from Maria's perspective. Bernardo is too angry to share Anita's reasoning, and he leaves with the other Sharks for the war council at the drugstore. Anita and the other girlfriends argue about the merits and drawbacks of their new homeland in "America" (**Musical Example 36**).

The Jets are waiting at Doc's drugstore, where Riff tries to calm them down. When the Sharks arrive, tensions mount again until Tony talks them into letting the rumble be decided by a fistfight between the best man of each gang. Bernardo, thinking the Jets' combatant will be Tony, agrees; he's disappointed to learn that another Jet, Diesel, will be his opponent. The next day, Tony visits Maria at the bridal shop where she works; she's upset about the rumble and gets Tony to promise that he'll stop it.

As the sun sets, everyone starts to anticipate the night to come in "Tonight (Quintet)" (**Musical Example 37**). When the rumble starts, Bernardo mocks Tony, trying to goad him into fighting. Riff lunges forward on his friend's behalf, and Bernardo pulls a knife. Riff is armed too, so the fight has become very dangerous. Tony, not wanting Maria's brother to be hurt, calls out to his friend. While Riff is distracted, Bernardo lunges forward and kills him. In a fury, Tony grabs Riff's knife and kills Bernardo. Stunned, he stands staring at what he's done until the Jets drag him away.

Unaware of the events, Maria delights in her new love by singing "I Feel Pretty." The happy tune comes to an abrupt end when Chino comes to tell her about her brother's death. Maria worriedly asks about Tony, so Chino angrily tells her that it was Tony who killed Bernardo. Chino pulls out a gun and leaves to seek revenge. Tony creeps into Maria's room via the fire escape, however, and Maria is soon overwhelmed by her love for him. They huddle together, dreaming of a happier world.

The Jets are distracting themselves from their own fury and grief by lashing out at society in "Gee, Officer Krupke." Meanwhile, Anita wants to grieve with Maria, but is surprised to find Maria's door locked. Hurriedly, Tony and Maria arrange to meet at the drugstore later, and Tony slips away. It doesn't take Anita long to figure out what Maria's been up to, and she can't believe it. Maria brings Anita up short by asking her if she doesn't remember what it is like to be deeply in love. Chastened, Anita hugs Maria tightly—until the police arrive. They want to question Bernardo's sister. Maria realizes that she won't be able to get away to the drugstore, so she begs Anita to go in her place.

Anita soon regrets her attempt to help when she gets to the drugstore and is almost raped by the Jets, who are gleeful at finding an unprotected Puerto Rican right in their midst. Doc intervenes to save her, but Anita takes her revenge: she tells the Jets that Maria is dead—that Chino shot her in jealous rage. Tony is stunned and starts to run through Maria's neighborhood, begging for Chino to come kill him too. Hearing Tony's voice, Maria runs outside, and the two lovers run toward each other in joy. Chino also has heard Tony, however, and he shoots just as Tony reaches Maria; Tony crumples in her arms. Crazy with grief, Maria picks up the gun and threatens to kill all the gang members, Jets and Sharks, as long as there is still a bullet left for her. She cannot fire, however, and collapses in tears. The Jets gather around to pick up their fallen friend, but he is too heavy. Before they drop his body, however, several of the Sharks step forward to help shoulder the burden. They carry Tony away, with a grieving Maria following. No one had been able to stop the sad cycle of hate and violence until it was too late.

MUSICAL EXAMPLE 36

WEST SIDE STORY
LEONARD BERNSTEIN/STEPHEN SONDHEIM, 1957
"America"

Rosalia
1 Puerto Rico, You lovely island, Island of tropical breezes.
Always the pineapples growing, Always the coffee blossoms blowing.
Anita
2 Puerto Rico, You ugly island, Island of tropic diseases.
Always the hurricanes blowing, Always the population growing,
And the money owing, And the babies crying, And the bullets flying.
I like the island Manhattan. Smoke on your pipe and put that in!
Anita and Girls
3 I like to be in America! O.K. by me in America!
Everything free in America For a small fee in America!
Rosalia
4 I like the city of San Juan.
Anita
I know a boat you can get on.
Rosalia
Hundreds of flowers in full bloom.
Anita
Hundreds of people in each room!
Girls
5 Automobile in America, Chromium steel in America,
Wire-spoke wheel in America, Very big deal in America!
Rosalia
6 I'll drive a Buick through San Juan.
Anita
If there's a road you can drive on.
Rosalia
I'd give my cousins a free ride.

Anita
How you get all of them inside?

Girls
7 Immigrant goes to America, Many hellos in America,
Nobody knows in America Puerto Rico's in America!

Rosalia
8 I'll bring a TV to San Juan.

Anita
If there's a current to turn on!

Rosalia
I'll give them new washing machine.

Anita
What have they got there to keep clean?

Anita and Girls
9 I like the shores of America! Comfort is yours in America!
Knobs on the doors in America, Wall-to-wall floors in America!

Rosalia
10 When I will go back to San Juan

Anita
When you will shut up and get gone!

Rosalia
Everyone there will give big cheer!

Anita
Everyone there will have moved here!

MUSICAL EXAMPLE 37

West Side Story
Leonard Bernstein/Stephen Sondheim, 1957

"Tonight (Quintet)"

Riff and the Jets
1 The Jets are gonna have their day tonight.

Bernardo and the Sharks
2 The Sharks are gonna have their way tonight.

Riff and the Jets
3 The Puerto Ricans grumble: "Fair Fight." But if they start a rumble, We'll rumble 'em right!

Bernardo and the Sharks
4 We're going to hand 'em a surprise tonight.

Riff and the Jets
5 We're going to cut 'em down to size tonight.

Bernardo and the Sharks
6 We said, "O.K., no rumpus, no tricks." But just in case they jump us, We're ready to mix.

Sharks
Tonight!
7 We're gonna rock it tonight, we're gonna jazz it up and have us a ball!
They're gonna get it tonight; the more they turn it on, the harder they'll fall!

Riff and the Jets
8 Well, they began it!

Bernardo and the Sharks
Well, they began it!

Jets and Sharks
9 And we're the ones to stop 'em once and for all, tonight!

Anita
10 Anita's gonna get her kicks tonight. We'll have our private little mix tonight.
He'll walk in hot and tired, so what? Don't matter if he's tired, as long as he's hot tonight!

Tony

11   Tonight, tonight won't be just any night, Tonight there will be no morning star.
12   Tonight, tonight, I'll see my love tonight, and for us, stars will stop where they are.
13   Today, the minutes seem like hours, the hours go so slowly, and still the sky is light.
14   Oh moon, grow bright, and make this endless day endless night!

Riff and the Jets

15   I'm counting on you to be there tonight, when Diesel wins it fair and square tonight.
      That Puerto Rican punk'll go down, and when he's hollered "Uncle" we'll tear up the town!

Maria	**Riff**	**Tony**
16 Tonight, tonight	So I can count on you, boy?	All right
Won't be just any night,	We're gonna have us a ball.	All right
Tonight there will be no	Womb to Tomb!	Sperm to Worm!
morning star.	I'll see you there about eight.	Tonight.
Maria	**Sharks and Jets**	**Anita**
17 Tonight, tonight,	We're gonna rock it tonight!	Tonight
I'll see my love tonight	We're gonna jazz it tonight!	Tonight
And for us, stars will stop	They're gonna get it tonight,	Late tonight
Where they are.	Tonight!	We're gonna mix it tonight
Maria and Tony	**Sharks and Jets**	**Anita**
18 Today, the minutes	They began it, they began it,	Anita's gonna have her day,
Seem like hours,	They began it, and we're the ones	Anita's gonna have her day,
The hours go so slowly,	To stop 'em once and for all.	Bernardo's going to have his way
And still the sky is light.	We'll stop 'em once and for all.	Tonight.
Maria and Tony	**Sharks and Jets**	**Anita**
19 Oh moon, grow bright,	The Jets (Sharks) are gonna have their way	Tonight, tonight,
And make this endless day	The Jets (Sharks) are gonna have their day	This very night,
Endless night	We're gonna rock it tonight	We're gonna rock it tonight

All

20   Tonight!

Chapter 30
Jule Styne and Frank Loesser

In 1957, the collaboration of Arthur Laurents, Jerome Robbins, Leonard Bernstein, and Stephen Sondheim produced the landmark musical *West Side Story*. Two years later, **Gypsy** made its own enormous splash on the stage, generated by almost the same creative team with the sole exception of Bernstein. This time the composer was **Jule Styne** (1905–1994). The marked contrast between the two shows underscores the importance of music in setting the tone of a production. Like *West Side Story*, *Gypsy* is a powerful show, but it is a very different musical, challenging audiences in its own way.

Jule (pronounced "Joolie") Styne was no Broadway newcomer when he composed the score for *Gypsy*. Born in London (and christened Julius Kerwin Stein), he had emigrated to the United States as an eight-year-old child, when his family settled in Chicago. Styne quickly drew attention as a child piano prodigy, playing solo concerts (called *recitals*) and performing with the Chicago and Detroit symphony orchestras. Despite this early success in classical music circles, Styne was drawn to jazz and popular music—and to gambling, an addiction that would plague him for the rest of his life. He traveled to Hollywood, where he worked as an arranger and as a voice coach; Shirley Temple was one of his students. Styne began writing film scores too, but it was not until he met lyricist Sammy Cahn that he began to write songs. Their collaboration was particularly fruitful, producing "Let It Snow! Let It Snow! Let It Snow!" among other hits. Styne wrote the music for more than 50 movies, working primarily with Cahn or Frank Loesser; Frank Sinatra performed many of Styne's songs.

In 1947, Styne and Cahn contributed the score for a Broadway show, *High Button Shoes*; their previous stage effort had closed in Boston, never reaching New York. *High Button Shoes*, however, was a hit, running for 727 performances. This success lured Styne to New York, where he wrote music for more than two dozen shows over a 45-year span. One of his biggest hits was the song "Diamonds Are a Girl's Best Friend" for the show *Gentlemen Prefer Blondes* (1949), a number that helped Carol Channing rise to stardom; this show ran for an equally satisfying 740 performances. Styne worked with Betty Comden and Adolph Green for the first time in 1951, and the team collaborated on several additional shows over the years to come. Styne also was the producer of the successful 1952 revival of Rodgers and Hart's *Pal Joey*—the production that finally established *Pal Joey* as a recognized success.

Not all of Styne's efforts were hits, but he must have derived comfort from the fact that in 1954 his "Three Coins in a Fountain" won the Best Song Academy Award. Working again with Comden and Green (and choreographer Jerome

Robbins) in 1956, he wrote *Bells are Ringing*—and this time the team struck gold. *Bells are Ringing* ran for 924 performances, the longest run of any of the eight collaborations between the three writers. It made a star of Judy Holliday, Comden and Green's old friend from their days in The Revuers; one of the show's best-known tunes is "The Party's Over." Their experience was quite different after their next show, *Say, Darling* (1958), premiered. Although *Say, Darling* ran for almost ten months, it failed to earn back its full costs. Probably what hurt the show most was a prolonged newspaper strike in New York. Without daily advertisements in the papers, the box office business dropped off sharply, and *Say, Darling* was forced to close.

Styne had *almost* worked with Comden and Green for his next show, *Gypsy* (1959). Back in 1956, the flamboyant producer David Merrick read a chapter of Gypsy Rose Lee's autobiography in *Harper's Magazine*. He was so enthusiastic about its potential as a musical that he obtained the rights without having read the rest of her life story. Merrick got Styne, Comden, and Green working on the idea, but as 1957 wore on, Comden and Green had difficulty finding a way to tell Gypsy Rose Lee's story. When they were offered the chance to go to Hollywood to write a screenplay for *Auntie Mame*, they accepted. At first, they promised Styne that they'd continue to work on *Gypsy* in California, but they withdrew in late August. Styne, by that time, had moved on to the creation of *Say, Darling*, so *Gypsy* was set aside.

In mid-1958, Merrick joined with Leland Hayward to coproduce *Gypsy*, and they signed the inimitable Ethel Merman to play Gypsy Rose Lee's mother (see the **Plot Summary**). In fact, Merman was so enthusiastic about the role after reading Lee's autobiography that she threatened to shoot anyone who stood between her and the part—had playing Annie Oakley gone to her head? The new plan was for Laurents to write the book and Stephen Sondheim the lyrics and the score. Sondheim's own first show, *Saturday Night*, almost premiered in 1955, but the producer Lemuel Ayers had died unexpectedly of leukemia. With *Gypsy*, Sondheim was hoping at last to make his debut as a Broadway composer.

Fate—in the form of Merman—intervened. Merman was fresh from a relative flop, *Happy Hunting*. Its score had been written by Broadway newcomers, and Merman didn't want to take a chance with yet another novice. In her view, Sondheim had established his lyricist credentials in *West Side Story*, but as a composer, he was an unknown. Merman wanted a name she could trust, but Cole Porter and Irving Berlin said no, and George Gershwin was dead. Merman liked Styne's music, however, and insisted he would be the right choice. Sondheim, relegated to the role of lyricist, was tempted to bow out; once again, though, he talked it over with Oscar Hammerstein II. Hammerstein pointed out the advantages to Sondheim in writing for such an established star. Sondheim swallowed his pride and agreed to stay on.

Since time was fairly short, Styne played several trunk songs for Sondheim—but Sondheim wanted to start fresh, writing specifically for particular characters and moods, and working in tandem with Laurents to tie the songs into the libretto. Gradually, as the score developed, they re-examined Styne's trunk and ended up using four numbers, including "Everything's Coming Up Roses" (**Musical Example 38**), and "You'll Never Get Away From Me." Sondheim was unhappy to learn that the last tune had already been used in a television show, but this discovery came long after *Gypsy* had opened. Styne defended himself on the basis that the new version of the song "worked."

Producers Merrick and Hayward had their work cut out for them as well. Since the story centered around the real-life Gypsy Rose Lee and her family, Merrick and Hayward had to obtain releases from the people whose lives were to be depicted in the musical. Gypsy's younger sister, "Baby June," had launched a new career as June Havoc (having made her acting debut in *Pal Joey*), and she was reluctant to sign. She found the story vulgar and couldn't see how they could find her mother's behavior suitable for a musical, saying, "She's cheap. She eats out of tin cans." Havoc wanted all sorts of script changes, keeping her character as adorable as possible. The cast started rehearsals with no release from Havoc, and

The, "real" Gypsy Rose Lee chats with Mama rose (Ethel Merman).
Corbis/Bettmann.

when lawsuits loomed, Laurents simply changed the name to Baby Claire. During the tryout tour, Havoc came to see *Gypsy*; she didn't like being figuratively eliminated from the story, so at last she signed a release.

The beginning and the ending of the show were the remaining challenges. *Gypsy* began, as expected, with an overture (see the **Sidebar**: The Role of the Overture), but the orchestrators Robert Ginzler and Sid Ramin put together a swinging, jazzy big band feature that had much more to it than the usual string of choruses from the show's main songs. However, Robbins gave the arrangement a thumb's down. Frustrated, Styne and the conductor Milton Rosenstock insisted that they play it during the tryout tour. Styne arranged for one of the trumpet players, Dick Perry, to stand and blow as loudly as possible during the section that referred to the strippers. Rosenstock recalled, "When Dick got up and started riffing and blowing, he didn't get past three bars until the audience began applauding. They were still bravoing when I hit the cue of Merman's entrance." Despite this enthusiastic reaction, Robbins's response was the same: "I still don't like it"—but he agreed to let them retain it. The New York theater's pit was so deep that Styne wanted the orchestra members to sit on platforms, elevating them to increase their sound. Robbins conveniently "forgot" to arrange for the platforms until all the stagehands had left the theater. Styne's assistant ran out to purchase barstools, thereby raising the musicians about a foot and a half. At intermission, a surprised Robbins remarked that the orchestra was quite audible, and Styne revealed their last-minute innovation.

The show's ending also presented a problem. The story built to a natural climax at the point of Louise's debut as a stripper, but the show's creators wanted to bring the attention back to Rose afterwards. Although all the dancing in *Gypsy* was diegetic (very unlike *West Side Story*), Robbins thought that Rose's mental disintegration could be depicted by means of a "nightmare ballet." He worked on the idea for about a week, then abandoned it, telling the composer and lyricist that the burden was on them. At last Styne and Sondheim produced "Rose's Turn," a long solo number in which Rose sings bits of earlier melodies but with new, Rose-centered lyrics. She stops and starts as her emotional collapse takes hold of her, but she ends with a big finish, proclaiming, "Everything's coming up roses this time for me, for me, for me, for me, for me, for me!" The writers had found the means to depict a nervous breakdown through music, and "Rose's Turn" is one of *Gypsy*'s most powerful moments.

One section of "Rose's Turn" is based on "Momma's Talkin' Soft." Young June and Louise sang the tune as a countermelody while Rose mesmerized Herbie. The director wanted the girls to be observing the scene from a high perch. Unfortunately, one of the little girls was afraid of heights, and she started to cry every time she was placed on the elevated platform. Since no one could devise any other way to stage the number, the girls' song was cut altogether. Sondheim rationalized that the audience does not have to have heard the number earlier to appreciate its effectiveness in Rose's breakdown.

Incidentally, one of Rose's vocal lines is "I'm a woman with children." Styne was shocked by Sondheim's lyrics, exclaiming,

---

Sidebar: The Role of the Overture

For several centuries, overtures have prefaced many kinds of works. These orchestral features introduce the show to come, alerting the audience that it's time to sit down and listen, as well as building excitement. Overtures for most musicals usually employ excerpts from the songs that will be sung in the show. This type of "compilation" overture gives the audience a foretaste of the tunes to come, making the melodies somewhat familiar by the time the characters give voice to them in the show. If the song is then reprised later in the show, the audience may have had three hearings of the tune by the end of the show. This familiarity may help the sales of sheet music, but a composer needs to be careful that the listener does not grow bored with the melody. The orchestrator's skills may be especially helpful in this regard. In fact, many overtures are constructed entirely by the orchestrator rather than by the composer.

The orchestrator often relishes the freedom he or she has in an overture. During a song, the orchestrator needs to ensure that the instruments do not overshadow the singing voice of the actor. During the overture, however, the instruments themselves carry the melody. Phrases of the melody might be passed between different instruments, creating an exciting series of changing tone colors. The orchestrator might write a countermelody or use the song melody as the basis for imitative polyphony. Without the pressure of keeping words audible, the orchestrator can explore the full range of the orchestra's capabilities.

In the hands of a skilled orchestrator, an overture can become far more than just a medley of the show's tunes. Like many operatic overtures, some musical theater overtures have achieved a life of their own, played at concerts for the sheer pleasure of hearing the instruments. Styne's *Gypsy* overture, in particular, is regarded by many as one of musical theater's greatest overtures; although Styne *was* involved in writing the overture, he was helped by *Gypsy's* orchestrators, Sid Ramin and Robert Ginzler. Compare to Styne, these are unfamiliar names, yet orchestrators wield a great deal of power: they are largely responsible for a show's "first impression." By helping to craft the first thing the audience hears, they contribute to a show's success or failure. They are often the unsung heroes of Broadway.

"No man could sing this song." Styne was thinking of the potential secondary market for *Gypsy's* songs, while Sondheim was thinking merely of the character. Sondheim insisted to Styne that the song had to be "personalized" because "here's this lady who's trying to con the guy into handling her vaudeville act." Sondheim agreed to change the text later for the sheet music, but observed in a 1970s interview, "Today nobody has to worry about that sort of thing." Even though musical theater had long been aspiring toward integrated productions, the process of individualizing the songs to suit specific characters—and *only* those characters—was moving more slowly. Eventually, however, most "Tin Pan Alley" commercial considerations would be left almost entirely behind.

"Rose's Turn" is a highly individualized song—or, literally, a "star turn"—that is unlikely ever to work out of context. The references back to earlier tunes adds to its power, and a song that is reprised to great effect in "Rose's Turn" is the great closer of the first act, "Everything's Coming Up Roses." This trunk tune had been cut from Styne's first successful musical, *High Button Shoes*. Sondheim was proud of his title; he was trying to come up with a phrase that sounded familiar and yet was new. He felt he captured the spirit of "everything's gonna be great," but when he played the song for Robbins, he looked puzzled. "Everything's coming up Rose's *what*?" Robbins asked, confusing the song's title with the main character.

Throughout *Gypsy*, Styne and Sondheim used recurrent themes in the manner of Wagnerian *leitmotifs* to create continuity and, in Rose's case, to represent her obsessions. One prevalent melody was Rose's "I have a dream" theme, which made its first appearance in "Some People." This theme also functions as the vocal introduction (1) to "Everything's Coming Up Roses." After this introduction, the tune proceeds through what seems at first to be a conventional song form, with **2**, **3**, **4**, and **5** corresponding to the typical *a-a-b-a'* pattern. Surprisingly, though, Styne repeats the *b* theme at **6**, and concludes the song with an expanded version of *a* at **8**. The overall pattern would be diagrammed as *a-a-b-a'-b-a"*. Popular song composers might describe this as a non-standard song form, comprised of a song form chorus followed by a half chorus. A classical musician, however, might hear it as a **rounded binary form**. Diagrammed, a rounded binary form follows the pattern ‖: *a* :‖: *b a'* :‖, or, written out, *a-a-b-a'-b-a'*; this pattern is often used for the dance movements of classical symphonies and other works. However, few musical theater audiences would be expecting classical structures, so the nonstandard song form label is probably the better designation. No matter which label, the pattern is the same.

Rose is unstoppable during "Everything's Coming Up Roses," and Laurents called her a "gallant, joyous express train." Significantly, in the final line of the song form (and again at the end of **7**), Rose puts herself first: "Everything's coming up roses for me and for you." The whole song is an anthem to Rose's insensitivity; it doesn't matter to her in the slightest that Louise—and Herbie—are horrified at her new schemes. This portrayal was deliberate, according to Jule Styne: "Too many writers write self-pity. Audiences hate that in characters. In *Gypsy*, when Rose is deserted by her daughter, she's broke, the act's washed up, we could have had her sing about how miserable she is. Instead we turned the moment in on itself." Indeed, Rose has been fleshed out as such a monstrously ambitious mother in *Gypsy* that it is entirely convincing that this would be her response to the unexpected news of June's elopement. At the same time, the song is so well written that it seems to be Rose's *only* logical response, and Sondheim felt the constraints of writing lyrics that sustained her attitude. As he later put it,

> *there was very little to say in the lyric after the title was over, so I decided that I would give it its feeling by restricting myself to images of traveling, children, and show business, because the scene was in a railroad station and was about a mother pushing her child into show business. Now that may be of no interest except to someone doing a doctorate in 200 years on the use of traveling images in* Gypsy, *but the point is, it's there, and it informs the whole song.*

When *Gypsy* made its debut in 1959, the *Journal American* reviewer declared, "Anyone who doesn't think *Gypsy* is a fine, funny, satisfying evening in the theater needs oxygen, a nurse and a pint of blood." The respected Brooks Atkinson noted, "Since *Gypsy* has a literate theme, it has put everybody on his best behavior. Mr. Styne has written his most colorful score." Atkinson's review also declared, "Stephen Sondheim's lyrics are hackneyed." (Sondheim soon received a letter of apology from the critic, who explained that there had been a misprint; he had wanted to say *un*hackneyed rather than hackneyed.) Although *Gypsy* was nominated for Tony Awards in almost every category, it was running against *Fiorello!* (which would be the third musical to win a Pulitzer Prize) and the blockbuster *The Sound of Music*; *Gypsy* walked away with no awards at all. Audiences supported the show for 702 performances, however, and *Gypsy* is recognized as one of musical theater's great achievements.

Although *Gypsy* is generally held to be Jule Styne's greatest achievement as well, he did have one more success in store: *Funny Girl*. Before *Funny* Girl, however, came a show that was *not* a hit, *Subways Are for Sleeping*, which had been the focus of one of producer David Merrick's legendary publicity stunts: Merrick found seven men in the greater New York area who had the same names as seven of New York's leading theater critics. He wined and dined the "duplicates," and got their permission to "quote" their opinions about the show (which he thoughtfully wrote for them himself). "John Chapman," for instance, called it "the best musical of the century." Merrick and his press agent devised an advertisement containing the quotations; although a suspicious *New York Times* and *Post* killed the ad before it ran, the *Herald-Tribune* carried Merrick's advertisement in several early editions.

With *Funny Girl* in 1964, Styne had another hit on his hands. However, it took some effort to get it to the stage; its opening night was postponed five times, and the last scene went through 40 revisions—but eventually it ran 1,348 performances. *Funny Girl* was also one of the first Broadway shows to use individual microphones on the performers; it also made a star of Barbra Streisand. Oddly, it wasn't until the fairly mediocre *Hallelujah, Baby!* (1967) that a show by Styne won the Tony Award for Best Musical; Styne was as surprised as anyone. Although he had no more success with new shows, he had the comfort of several triumphant revivals of *Gypsy*, a show that seemed to many critics simply to get better with time—and which had been pretty strong from the start.

Jule Styne had been a musician nearly his whole life. **Frank Loesser**, on the other hand, tried his luck at multiple professions—as process server, restaurant inspector, office boy, waiter, hotel pianist, reporter for a small-town newspaper, knit-goods editor (!) for a journal, and press agent. He had been raised in a musical family, but one that favored the classics. Since Loesser's tastes leaned toward Tin Pan Alley, the family chose not to "waste" musical training on him. Consequently, Loesser's playing was mostly "by ear"; most of his early contributions to music were lyrics rather than melodies.

The first lyrics by Loesser heard on Broadway appeared in 1936 in an ill-fated revue—but they led to a six-month contract with Universal Studios. Loesser wrote lyrics for various composers, including Hoagy Carmichael, Burton Lane, and Jule Styne. In 1942, however, Loesser published a song for which he had written the music as well as the words— "Praise the Lord and Pass the Ammunition"—that raced into popularity, selling 2 million recordings and 1 million copies of its sheet music. (It might have done even better, but a backlash among clergymen slowed sales; they objected to linking the Lord's name with armaments.) While serving in World War II as an army private, Loesser continued to write songs, and their continued success encouraged him to think of himself as a composer.

Armed with this confidence, Loesser undertook his first Broadway score in 1948, *Where's Charley?* Based on a turn-of-the-century London farce, *Charley's Aunt*, Loesser's show was a star vehicle for Ray Bolger, who had come to Broadway prominence in Rodgers and Hart's *On Your Toes* in 1936 (Chapter 17, "Great Partnerships of the Early Book Musical"), but who was better known as *The Wizard of Oz*'s Scarecrow. Thanks also to George Abbott's book and directing abilities, Loesser's maiden effort was a major success, running 792 performances.

Loesser was anxious to collaborate again with the producers of *Where's Charley?*, **Cy Feuer** (b. 1911) and **Ernest Martin** (1919–1995), who had also been making their theatrical debut. They settled on an adaptation of a short story by Damon Runyon, "The Idyll of Miss Sarah Brown," with additional characters drawn from other Runyon short stories, especially "Pick the Winner." Loesser started working on the songs for ***Guys and Dolls*** (1950) while Jo Swerling, a Hollywood scriptwriter, drafted a libretto. Because of Swerling's film background, he shrewdly got a contractual promise that he would get first billing for the libretto—no matter whose version they used. Swerling's version treated the plot fairly seriously, which no one liked; everyone was much happier with a comic version (see the **Plot Summary**) by **Abe Burrows** (1910–1985)—but both men had to be credited with the book.

Since many of the songs were finished *before* the libretto, Burrows had to find places for them within his story. Burrows soon realized that Loesser had a natural theatrical instinct; much of the time Burrows's job consisted of simply building from one song to the next. One of the exceptions was the "Fugue for Tinhorns" (**Musical Example 39**). Loesser didn't really have a place in mind for this number, and initially the song wasn't even for the tinhorns; instead, it was called "Three Cornered Tune," and it was sung by Sarah, Nathan, and Sky. The writers placed the song, now speeded up and with new lyrics, right at the beginning, letting its "gangsterese" set the tone and mood for the show to come.

The "Fugue for Tinhorns" is not a genuine **fugue**; it is actually a canon, or round, because each person—Benny at **3** and Rusty at **4**—repeats Nicely-Nicely's melody *exactly* (as the Peachums had done in "Our Polly Is a Sad Slut!" discussed in Chapter 2). In contrast, in a fugue, each singer starts off with the same melody, but also sings some independent material. However, both structures—canon and fugue—emphasize the texture of imitative polyphony. The melody gets passed from singer to singer all through the trio, with each man starting the melody anew at various points. Nicely-Nicely sings it at **5**; Benny's got the main tune at **6**; Rusty takes over at **7**; Nicely-Nicely's got the lead again at **8**, followed by Benny again at **9**, and by Rusty at **10**. At **11**, the repetitive canonic melody stops, and each tinhorn sings a successively higher pitch to create a final coda flourish. (In the score, the orchestra is instructed to sustain the last chord until the onstage band of missionaries starts to play, so there is no break between one musical number and the next.)

With this involved imitative polyphony, Loesser presents theatergoers with a more complex musical structure than is customary on the musical theater stage. At the same time, he conveys a subtle message about the three gamblers: although each is promoting the virtues of different horses, they're all singing the same thing—their "picks" for the horserace are all equally good (or bad). Also, it is clear that none of them is listening to the others, which is a humorous reflection of real life itself.

Much of the score draws upon jazz and gospel traditions as well, and the show produced a number of hit songs, especially the showstopper "Sit Down, You're Rockin' the Boat." Loesser's music is not easy for singers, as several performers discovered during rehearsals (see **Behind-the-Scenes**: Think Before You Punch). The songs didn't always come easily to Loesser, either; during the tryout tour in Philadelphia, Jule Styne came to Loesser's hotel for a visit. He called up to Loesser's room, only to be told, "If you don't have any rhymes for 'mink,' don't come up."

The performers' sweat (and tears) paid off; John Chapman summed it up when he wrote,

The big trouble with Guys and Dolls *is that a performance of it lasts only one evening, when it ought to last about a week. I did not want to leave the theatre after the premiere last night and come back here and write a piece about the show. I wanted to hang around, on the chance that they would raise the curtain again and put on a few numbers they'd forgotten—or, at least, start* Guys and Dolls *all over again.*

Guys and Dolls swept the year's awards, winning the Tony, the Donaldson, and the New York Drama Critics' Circle Award for Best Musical. Besides a 1,200-performance run, the film rights were sold to the Samuel Goldwyn Studios for a record-breaking $1 million. Reportedly, the show was in line for the Pulitzer Prize as well, but the Trustees of Columbia University can veto the Pulitzer committee's recommendation. Because Abe Burrows had been blacklisted by the House's Un-American Activities Committee, the Trustees evidently exercised their veto power; no Pulitzer was awarded that year.

Frank Loesser was not finished making his mark on Broadway. It took him four years to write his next show, *The Most Happy Fella* (1956). Although it was billed as a musical, it was operatic in its scope, calling for recitative as well as various ensembles. Like George Gershwin's *Porgy and Bess*, it had a number of more traditional musical theater songs, including the popular "Standing on the Corner." Loesser was panicked to see newspaper reviews refer to the show as an opera, and he urged Stuart Ostrow to call the press "and tell 'em we're not an opera for God's sake; we're a . . . Loessercal!"

The Most Happy Fella was completely different in style from *Guys and Dolls*, and Loesser shifted gears again for his next musical, *Greenwillow* (1960). The show closed after a disappointing 95 performances—Loesser's first Broadway failure. But it was as if a completely different composer then wrote Loesser's *next* show, the frenetic comedy *How to Succeed in Business Without Really Trying* (1961). Loesser was reunited with his *Guys and Dolls* producers, Feuer and Martin, and librettist Burrows (although, once again, Burrows had been brought in to rewrite someone else's unsatisfactory script).

As with *Guys and Dolls*, critics were unanimous in their ecstatic reactions. Walter Kerr commented, "Not a sincere line is spoken in the new Abe Burrows–Frank Loesser musical, and what a relief it is. It is now clear that what has been killing musical comedy is sincerity. *How to Succeed* is crafty, conniving, sneaky, cynical, irreverent, impertinent, sly, malicious, and lovely, just lovely." Not only did it win the Best Musical prize from the New York Drama Critics' Circle and the Tonys, but it was honored as the year's best drama by the Pulitzer Committee. Its run was 1,417 performances.

How to Succeed was Loesser's final success; his next show closed in Detroit during its tryout tour. He left a musical unfinished at the time of his death; the completed portions were performed in 1985. Loesser's lasting influence was not solely dependent on his musicals, however; he established his own publishing company, the Frank Music Corporation, and he used it not only to circulate his own works but to promote the careers of up-and-coming composers. He helped to launch the team of Richard Adler and Jerry Ross (who would go on to write *The Pajama Game* and *Damn Yankees*), and he pushed Meredith Willson into crafting his first musical, *The Music Man*, out of Willson's boyhood memories of Iowa. Frank Loesser's own works, however, represented several possible directions for musical theater, and as Thomas Hischak has noted, "No generalization about them can be made. At times it seems that there must have been several Frank Loessers."

FURTHER READING

Banfield, Stephen. *Sondheim's Broadway Musicals*. Ann Arbor: University of Michigan Press, 1993.
Brahms, Caryl, and Ned Sherrin. *Song By Song: The Lives and Work of 14 Great Lyric Writers*. Egerton, Bolton, U.K.: Ross Anderson Publications, 1984.

Burrows, Abe. "The Making of *Guys and Dolls.*" *Atlantic Monthly* 245, no. 1 (January 1980): 40–52.

Byrnside, Ron. "'Guys and Dolls': A Musical Fable of Broadway." *Journal of American Culture* 19, no. 2 (Summer 1996): 25–33.

Gottfried, Martin. *Sondheim.* New York: Abrams, 1993.

Green, Stanley. *Encyclopaedia of the Musical Theatre.* New York: Dodd, Mead, 1976.

Guernsey, Otis L., Jr., ed. *Playwrights, Lyricists, Composers on Theater: The Inside Story of a Decade of Theater in Articles and Comments by Its Authors, Selected from Their Own Publication,* The Dramatists Guild Quarterly. New York: Dodd, Mead, 1974.

Hirsch, Foster. *Harold Prince and the American Musical Theatre.* Cambridge: Cambridge University Press, 1989.

Hischak, Thomas S. *Word Crazy: Broadway Lyricists from Cohan to Sondheim.* New York: Praeger, 1991.

Loesser, Susan. *A Most Remarkable Fellow: Frank Loesser and the Guys and Dolls in His Life.* New York: Donald I. Fine, 1993.

Mandelbaum, Ken. *Not Since Carrie: Forty Years of Broadway Musical Flops.* New York: St. Martin's, 1991.

Mordden, Ethan. *Better Foot Forward: The History of American Musical Theatre.* New York: Grossman Publishers, 1976.

Ostrow, Stuart. *A Producer's Broadway Journey.* Westport, Connecticut.: Praeger, 1999.

Runyon, Damon. *A Treasury of Damon Runyon.* Selected, with an Introduction, by Clark Kinnaird. New York: The Modern Library, 1958.

Taylor, Theodore. *Jule: The Story of Composer Jule Styne.* New York: Random House, 1979.

Zadan, Craig. *Sondheim & Co.: The Authorized, Behind-the-Scenes Story of the Making of Stephen Sondheim's Musicals.* 2nd ed. New York: Harper & Row, 1986.

BEHIND-THE-SCENES: THINK BEFORE YOU PUNCH

One of the numbers in *Guys and Dolls,* "The Oldest Established," is a mock alma mater anthem, sung while an actual crap game is enacted on stage. The song was added to the show during the tryout tour in Philadelphia, and choreographer Michael Kidd had to work out the number's staging during a rehearsal. The performers deliberately restricted their volume so they could listen to Kidd, and this quiet dynamic level made Loesser *very* unhappy. He wanted the song sung loudly and clearly every time. (This show had no amplification, so the volume was solely up to the performers.) Kidd and Martin tried to calm Loesser down, to no avail. At the top of his lungs, he compared Martin to Hitler, and shouted, "I'm the author and you're working for me." Panic-stricken, the cast on stage stopped any attempt at performing the choreography, and they bellowed the song as loudly as they could as Loesser backed away from the stage. As they continued to bellow, Loesser slipped into the lobby. Out of curiosity, the producers followed him, where they saw him purchase an ice cream cone that he happily consumed on his return to his hotel, with the performers still singing their hearts out back in the theater. Feuer and Martin realized that all Loesser wanted was to bring the actors' attention back to the music.

Loesser's tough-guy posturing backfired on another occasion. Isobel Bigley, playing Sarah, was learning the song "I'll Know." This number has a wide range, and Loesser did not like the sound of her break—the change in tone quality when a singer switches from the chest voice to the head voice. In fact, he grew so infuriated that without thinking, he jumped up onto the stage and socked her in the nose. Of course, Bigley burst into tears, and Loesser suddenly realized what he'd done. Bigley knew it too, and as Caryl Brahms and Ned Sherrin put it, "From that moment she had the upper hand—and an extremely expensive apologetic bracelet to decorate its wrist."

PLOT SUMMARY: *GYPSY*

Although *Gypsy* is named for Gypsy Rose Lee, the storyline centers on her mother, Rose, and the need for recognition. Rose is the quintessential stage mother, trying to make a vaudeville star of her daughter "Baby June." As the curtain rises, June is rehearsing "May We Entertain You"; she is taking part in a children's talent contest organized by Uncle Jocko. Unsurprisingly, the contest is rigged, but Rose figures out Jocko's scheme and threatens to expose him unless he names June as the winner.

In this aggressive way, Rose has been fostering June's career, but she is ambitious to reach the professional vaudeville circuits. Faced with additional publicity expenses, she tries to get her father to loan her the money. He refuses; angrily, she steals a plaque that's worth the amount she needs.

The vaudeville act is called "Baby June and the Newsboys," with June's sister Louise performing as one of the "boys." On the road, they meet Herbie, a candy salesman. Rose sees an opportunity: here is a man who *likes* children and here she is, a woman *with* children. Herbie would like to marry Rose, but she's more interested in promoting her daughter's career. Herbie compromises by becoming their agent.

Life is a struggle; the small troupe can afford only cheap hotel rooms, and breakfast might consist of leftover Chinese food. On Louise's birthday, Rose gives her a lamb. It is to be part of a new act—"Dainty June and her Farmboys"—but even so, Louise is delighted with the gift. But then there is a bigger surprise for them all: Herbie has managed to book them on vaudeville's Orpheum circuit.

Some time has passed. The Orpheum circuit booking failed to develop into anything bigger, but Rose is undeterred; she continues to force the not-so-young performers through the same tired routine. Herbie is disgruntled, for Rose had said she'd marry him if he got the act onto the Orpheum circuit—but now she's insisting that she wants to get June's name up in lights on Broadway first.

Rose arranges for the act to audition for a Broadway theater owner, T. T. Grantzinger. To everyone's amazement, he offers them a short contract—but it's because he sees actress potential in June. Rose refuses the contract because she has no interest in seeing June leave the act. June is in despair, knowing this could have been her big break. The act struggles on until Rose gets bad news: June has eloped with one of the "Farmboys." Rose is outraged at this betrayal, but Herbie tries to intervene. He urges her to retire and settle down with him as his wife, but Rose's gaze lights upon Louise. Why, she can make *Louise* into a star! She can create a whole new act centered on Louise. Louise is aghast at the prospect, but Rose describes her vision in "Everything's Coming Up Roses" (**Musical Example 38**).

Despite Rose's ambitions, the new act is just the old routine rehashed. By accident, the act is booked into a burlesque house (and burlesque, by this time, consists mainly of strip shows). Rose is ready to march out, but Louise is a realist: they are desperate for money, and they need the gig. When the booking ends, Rose at last agrees to marry Herbie. But just then, the burlesque star is arrested, and the "star spot" is vacant. Rose succumbs to show business fever all over again, pushing Louise forward as the replacement. Both Louise and Herbie are horrified, and it's the last straw for Herbie; he walks out because he's disgusted with how low Rose has fallen. But Rose's idea for Louise is to make the strip routine ladylike and demure; why, Louise can sing a song from the old act, now recast as "Let Me Entertain You." Amazingly, Rose is right for once: Louise finds that she has a knack for an effective striptease. Her new persona of "Gypsy Rose Lee" leads her to a long string of greater and greater triumphs, and at last Louise becomes the featured star at the great New York burlesque house, Minsky's.

Rose *should* be happy, but she's not. She can't control her daughter's life like she used to. Angrily, she asks why she put in so much effort over so many years. After venting her frustration at Louise, Rose wanders out onto the stage of an empty theater and begins to dream that it is *she*—Rose—who is the star. During "Rose's Turn," she draws upon the melodies that had driven her and the act through the years, as if she is slowly going mad. Louise, watching from the wings, realizes that her mother has simply always wanted to get some attention, much as Louise had wanted it as a child. She suddenly understands her mother and tenderly wraps her mink coat around Rose; they leave the stage together.

PLOT SUMMARY: *GUYS AND DOLLS*

Guys and Dolls doesn't begin with a song *or* a dance; it opens with "Runyonland." Various New Yorkers and tourists carry out their daily activities—many of which border on the illegal. Out of this riot of activity emerge three "tinhorns" (gamblers who aren't as wealthy as they pretend to be). Each tinhorn—Nicely-Nicely Johnson, Benny Southstreet, and Rusty Charlie—tries to pick a winner in the day's races during the "Fugue for Tinhorns" (**Musical Example 39**). The Salvation Army band marches into view, led by Miss Sarah Brown on cornet.

Nathan Detroit is in a dilemma. He finds locations for a crap game he runs for other gamblers, but the police have figured out most of his usual spots. He can't set up the game at the one remaining possibility—Biltmore's garage—because the garage owner wants a cash payment, and Nathan doesn't have the dough. What's worse, the high-roller Sky Masterson is in town, and Nathan just *knows* he'd get Sky to gamble if only they had a place to play. Nathan's working under a second pressure—he has been engaged to Miss Adelaide, a nightclub performer, for some 14 years, and she doesn't like his involvement with gambling. He goes to great lengths to keep her unaware of his shady dealings. Trying to raise the money he needs, Nathan bets Sky $1,000 that Sky can't get Sarah to travel to Havana with him the next day. Sky immediately promises Sarah to deliver a "dozen genuine sinners" in exchange for a dinner date. She's tempted, since the mission is at risk of being shut down, but she doesn't want to get involved with a gambler. When Sky kisses her, she slaps him—but it takes her a while!

For years, Miss Adelaide has invented a fictitious tale of marriage and kids to tell her mother, but she has found that the stress of no appointed wedding day brings out cold symptoms—and now Nathan's planning another crap game, too. Sarah, meanwhile, yields to Sky's deal, since she's been told that her branch of the mission will have to be closed. She rationalizes that it may be saved by the dozen sinners.

The police have grown suspicious: many known gamblers have gathered in the vicinity. The gamblers claim that they're holding a bachelor party for Nathan. Unfortunately for Nathan, Adelaide hears this cover-up story and is thrilled; she eagerly plans for them to get married the next evening, and Nathan sees no way out, so he agrees. But then the Salvation Army band comes by, and Sarah's not among them. Nathan realizes that Sky must have won the bet—and indeed he has. After showing Sarah around Havana, he starts plying her with milkshakes—laced with rum. They return to New York just in time for Sarah to discover that the crap game has been played in the mission during her absence!

Two unhappy women open the second act. Adelaide's come down with another cold, because Nathan has called off their wedding to visit a "sick aunt." Sarah is miserable, too, forgetting that Sky owes her a promise. Sky hasn't forgotten, however. Sky stakes his cash against his fellow gamblers' souls. One by one, after losing, they head to the mission. Adelaide spots Nathan and desperately begs him to come get married before the license expires at midnight. He refuses, saying he's going to a prayer meeting, and she is outraged at what seems to her to be such a feeble lie.

The mission starts to fill up with gamblers. Proving their sincerity, they confess to their sins, with Nicely-Nicely vividly relating his past in "Sit Down, You're Rockin' the Boat." Adelaide discovers that Nathan really *was* headed to a prayer meeting, and Sarah discovers that she loves Sky. A double wedding ensues, with Sky now playing the bass drum in Sarah's band. Oddly enough, as Adelaide happily contemplates her married state, Nathan has come down with a cold.

MUSICAL EXAMPLE 38

GYPSY

JULE STYNE/STEPHEN SONDHEIM, 1959

"Everything's Coming Up Roses"

Rose

1   I had a dream, A dream about you, Baby!
    It's gonna come true, Baby! They think that we're through, But, Baby.

2   You'll be swell, You'll be great, Gonna have the whole world on a plate!
    Starting here, Starting now, Honey, everything's coming up roses!

3   Clear the decks, Clear the tracks, You got nothing to do but relax.
    Blow a kiss, Take a bow, Honey, everything's coming up roses!

4   Now's your inning, Stand the world on its ear! Set it spinning, That'll be just the beginning!

5   Curtain up, Light the lights, You got nothing to hit but the heights!
    You'll be swell, You'll be great, I can tell, Just you wait!
    That lucky star I talk about is due. Honey, everything's coming up roses for me and for you!

6   You can do it, All you need is a hand. We can do it, Mama is gonna see to it!

7   Curtain up! Light the lights! We got nothing to hit but the heights!
    I can tell, Wait and see! There's the bell, Follow me!
    And nothing's gonna stop us 'til we're through!
    Honey, everything's coming up roses and daffodils,
    Everything's coming up sunshine and Santa Claus,
    Everything's gonna be bright lights and lollipops.
    Everything's coming up roses for me and for you.

MUSICAL EXAMPLE 39

GUYS AND DOLLS

FRANK LOESSER/FRANK LOESSER, 1950

"Fugue for Tinhorns"

Nicely-Nicely

1   I got the horse right here
    The name is Paul Revere
    And here's a guy that says if the weather's clear,

2   Can do, can do.
    This guy says the horse can do.
    If he says the horse can do, can do, can do,

	Benny	**Nicely-Nicely**
3	I'm picking Valentine 'cause on the morning line	Can do, can do,
	The guy has got him figured at five to nine	this guy says the horse can do

	Rusty	**Benny**	**Nicely-Nicely**
4	But look at Epitaph,	Has chance,	If he says
	he wins it by a half,	has chance,	the horse can do
	According to this here	This guy says the horse	can do,
	in the Telegraph	has chance	can do.
5	Big Threat,	If he says the horse	For Paul Revere I'll bite
	Big Threat,	has chance,	I hear his foot's all right,
	This guy calls the horse	has chance,	Of course it all depends
	Big Threat.	has chance.	if it rained last night.
6	If he calls the horse	I know it's Valentine	Likes mud,
	Big Threat,	The morning work looks fine	Likes mud,
	Big Threat,	Besides the Jockey's brother's a	This "X" means the horse
	Big Threat.	friend of mine.	likes mud
7	And just a minute, boys,	Needs race,	If that means the horse
	I got the feedbox noise.	needs race,	likes mud,

	It says the great-grandfather was Equipoise.	This guy says the horse needs race.	likes mud, likes mud.
8	Shows class, Shows class,	If he says the horse needs race,	I tell you Paul Revere; Now this is no bum steer
	This guy says the horse shows class.	needs race, needs race.	It's from a handicapper that's real sincere.
9	If he says the horse shows class,	I go for Valentine, 'cause on the mornin' line	Can do, Can do,
	shows class, shows class.	The guy has got him figured at five to nine.	This guy says the horse Can do
10	So make it Epitaph, he wins it by a half,	Has chance, has chance.	If he says the horse can do,
	According to this here in the Telegraph,	This guy says the horse has chance.	can do, can do.
11	Epitaph.		

Valentine!

All
I got the horse right here.

Paul Revere,

Chapter 31
Meredith Willson and Other Faces of the 1950s

For years, a writer raised in a small Iowa town struggles to tell—via a musical—the tale of his boyhood experiences; his hopes are dashed time and again as the enthusiasm of various producers waxes and wanes. But, when the show—his first Broadway effort—at last reaches the stage, it proves to be a blockbuster hit. A fantasy? No; the writer in this true story was the 55-year-old **Meredith Willson** (1902–1984), and his hard-won show was *The Music Man* (1957).

It was a long road to that debut. Willson studied at the Institute of Musical Art (later rechristened as Juilliard) at the same time as Richard Rodgers, but he left to play flute for John Philip Sousa. Willson also played in the New York Philharmonic until the 1929 stock market crash; then, on the West Coast, he worked for ABC and later NBC, writing radio and television themes, film scores, and even some art music.

All the while, Willson had entertained friends with tales from childhood, and he even wrote a book titled *And There I Stood With My Piccolo* (1948). His wife Rini urged him some "6,741 times" to turn his experiences into a musical, but only when various professionals began to advise the same thing did Willson treat the project more seriously. Willson was not immune to all this interest:

> So, one day, without giving the matter too much thought, I wrote ACT ONE, SCENE ONE on the empty paper, not, of course, to show these people that I could write a musical comedy but to show them I could not. And for the next six years I was way out in front.
>
> I looked at those fatal four words on the paper for some little time, that first day. . . . ACT ONE, SCENE ONE. So far so good. The fifth word was the sticker, though. Couldn't locate that fifth word. So I just sat there. Quite some time went by. Three years in fact.

At last Willson hit upon a story about a boys' band and an instrument-selling con man named Harold Hill (see the **Plot Summary**). The working title was *The Silver Triangle*, and Cy Feuer and Ernest Martin were delighted with his tale. Already committed to two upcoming productions, they begged Willson to wait for them. Willson was more than happy to do so, although their comments foreshadowed the biggest problems he would have in the coming months: They felt the show needed a different title, and they were worried that his subplot about a boy suffering from spastic paralysis would steal every scene.

Martin came up with the title *The Music Man* a couple of weeks later, but the plot alterations took *much* more effort. Martin came to California to help, but after six months, he headed back to New York. A few months later, Willson saw a short newspaper clipping that read, "Feuer and Martin have tabled *The Music Man* in order to concentrate on other plans." Feuer did try to interest other producers in the show, but to no avail. Meanwhile, Willson produced draft after draft (before computerized word-processing programs), changing Marian's character from a librarian to a school teacher and back again, trying to work convincingly from scene to scene and to write integrated, compelling songs.

When Willson had reached draft 32, he was surprised by an invitation from Feuer and Martin to write the songs for a *different* musical. Torn, Willson asked for three weeks to think about it. Just before calling Martin back, Willson had the idea of offering his show to producer **Kermit Bloomgarden**. Bloomgarden invited Willson and his wife to come to New York to audition *The Music Man* for him. The morning after the audition, Bloomgarden invited them to his office, where he uttered those words so dear to a writer's heart: "Meredith, may I have the privilege of producing your beautiful play?"

The Music Man was off and running. Bloomgarden, too, began nudging Willson to cut the subplot about the disabled boy. Willson wanted to emphasize that spastic paralysis handicaps the body, not the mind, but he knew Bloomgarden was right. The problem was what to put in the boy's place. Meanwhile, Bloomgarden assembled the rest of the creative team; the new collaborators were all intrigued by this offbeat show with its unusual tunes—and the music *was* unusual for Broadway. In the manner of Irving Berlin's quodlibets, Willson liked writing two tunes that could "partner" with each other in nonimitative polyphony. A famous example occurs in the first act, when the rapid-fire "Pick-a-Little, Talk-a-Little" is overlapped with "Goodnight, Ladies." *The Music Man* also introduced a generation of theatergoers (and later, moviegoers) to the rich harmonies of barbershop quartets. Although this uniquely American singing style has, to this day, devoted performers and equally loyal listeners, its participants tend to sing live rather than make recordings, so the style did not have a widespread familiarity. *The Music Man* is credited with the first appearance of barbershop harmony in a Broadway musical.

Even the opening scene of *The Music Man* is unconventional. The overture progresses directly into the "train" music. As the traveling salesmen deliver the lines of the first number, it is soon evident that they aren't speaking *or* singing; they are uttering their dialogue in rhythm with the clickety-clack of the train, which listeners today might identify as an ancestor of rap. (Willson referred to it as "speak-singing.") Rodgers and Hart had experimented with a similar technique in Hollywood, but the approach was new to Broadway.

Amaryllis's piano lesson launches another number in *The Music Man*. Amaryllis starts to play her "cross-hand" piece (in which the hands cross over each other), and to its gentle accompaniment, Marian sings "Goodnight, My Someone" (**Musical Example 40**). This sweet triple-meter ballad is a **want song**; Marian longs for a sweetheart just as much as—or perhaps even more than—Amaryllis. The song may sound familiar, however; it is essentially the same melody used in "Seventy-Six Trombones." The chief difference—besides a different rhythm—is that "Goodnight, My Someone" is fairly disjunct, while "Seventy-Six Trombones" makes the theme conjunct by "filling in" some of the gaps of "Goodnight," as shown in **Figure 31–1** (the letters represent the pitches from the C major scale). The relationship between the two songs was quite deliberate, as Willson explained,

Marian was lonesome and lovelorn underneath her stand-offishness. Wasn't Harold lonesome too, despite his flamboyance and girl-in-every-town behavior? Maybe it would be interesting if these two could subtly convey to the audience this characteristic they had in common by separate renderings of the same song—a march for him, a ballad waltz for her.

Even though the styles of the two numbers are very different, the shared melodic line is an effective way of showing the kindred spirit of the two lead characters. To clarify the relationship, Willson allowed the two tunes to be sung simultaneously in a second-act "double reprise."

"Goodnight, My Someone" is a graceful little song form, with *a-a-b-a* equaling sections **1**, **4**, **5**, and **6**. Nevertheless,

Willson employs some subtle devices to give the song musical interest. In particular, Willson repeats the melody of **1** at **2** and again at **3**, but each time the melody is sung at a higher level, in a technique called **sequence**. (In a sequence, melodies may also be repeated at successively lower pitches.) Then, at **5**, the *b* section, Willson changes key in an unexpected way. The starting key, or **tonic**, of the song is C major; we might expect a key change to take us to G (the **dominant**), five steps higher. Instead, Willson moves the *b* section to F major, the **subdominant**, only four steps away from C. Although this change is certainly not unprecedented, it gives the simple song richness and depth.

In all, it took more than six years and 40 drafts to bring the story and songs together in a show ready for Broadway. The audience at the 1957 premiere was certainly ready; *The Music Man* seemed to evoke a nostalgia for a simpler, sunlit past. Critics applauded as well; John Chapman regarded it as

one of the few great musical comedies of the last 26 years. It was 26 years ago that Of Thee I Sing *appeared and set a standard for fun and invention that has seldom been reached. Its equal arrived in 1950—*Guys and Dolls—*and I would say that* The Music Man *ranks with these two. This musical is put together so expertly and acted and sung and danced by so many enchanting people that it should be either twice as long or performed twice at each performance.*

Certainly, *The Music Man* stood in marked contrast to *West Side Story*, which had opened the same year; *The Music Man* won the Best Musical award from both the New York Drama Critics' and the Tonys.

Unfortunately for Meredith Willson, he established a standard with *The Music Man* that he never could attain again. The Theatre Guild produced his next musical, *The Unsinkable Molly Brown* (1960), but critics were disappointed. The show had plenty of energy, however, and a strong advance helped *Molly Brown* to profit, lasting 532 performances. Things went

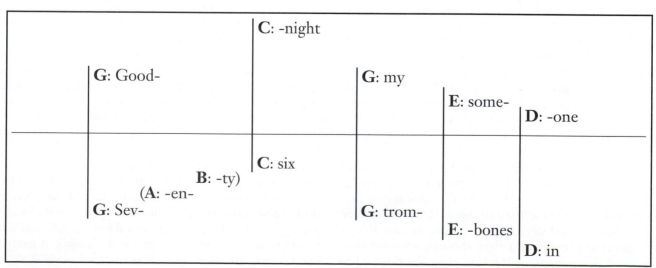

Figure 31–1

downhill from there; his next show stayed in the red, while Willson's last attempt closed in Los Angeles during its tryout tour. After a family tragedy, Willson retired and wrote no more. He passed away in Santa Monica, California, in 1984.

Some of the innovations of *The Music Man* stemmed from Meredith Willson's being a Broadway novice; unaware of all of musical theater's conventions, he was unfettered by tradition. **Mary Rodgers** (b. 1931), on the other hand, as the daughter of Richard Rodgers, had been in theatrical circles all her life. Coming to maturity in the heady atmosphere of Rodgers and Hammerstein's many successes (she was 12 years old when *Oklahoma!* premiered), it is not surprising that Mary Rodgers herself was drawn to a theatrical career; what *is* surprising is that *more* children of Broadway artists do not follow in their parents' footsteps. To be sure, younger generations may feel enormous pressure to live up to the standards implied by a family name. Moreover, success sometimes depends on luck, but much more of the time it reflects talent—and talent is not always a family legacy. In Mary Rodgers's case, however, a sizable degree of compositional flair seems to have been passed down from her father—and onward to her son Adam Guettel, a third generation of the Rodgers family to write stage musicals.

Mary Rodgers did not rely solely on observations of her father's work to develop her own craft. A number of resorts in the Poconos and Adirondack mountains hired lyricists and composers to write small shows for the entertainment of their summer guests—a new show every week. Many Broadway artists cultivated their writing skills in this fast-paced environment, and the shows were short, energetic, and often very funny. On occasion, a show written in these surroundings would later be the seed for a full-fledged Broadway production, and this was the case with Rodgers's *Once Upon a Mattress* (1959). Rodgers worked with lyricist **Marshall Barer** (1923–1998) on the one-act summer show at the Tamiment resort in the Poconos. Their goal was to tell the "true" story of the princess and the pea (see the **Plot Summary**). Like the old television cartoons *Fractured Fairy Tales*, which ostensibly were for children but contained many sly references to amuse adults, *Once Upon a Mattress* poked fun at the traditional story. Moreover, the "Quiz Show Scandals" had recently erupted into the nation's news. Americans had been shocked to learn that televised game shows such as *The $64,000 Question* were rigged. Rodgers and Barer capitalized on this awareness, inserting various quiz elements into the testing of the princesses. And, since Winnifred's eventual "win" was not entirely on the up-and-up (she had the Minstrel's secret help), the show mimicked real-life game shows in that way, too.

The title itself raised a few eyebrows. Although it's a reference to the traditional fairy-tale opening "Once upon a time . . . ," it is easy to read a suggestive double-entendre into the title. However, although *Once Upon a Mattress* is not free from allusions to sex (Lady Larken *is* pregnant, after all), the show in general is an innocent romp through puns and situational humor. In many ways, it evokes the old genre of burlesque, in the manner of *Evangeline* (1874) and other spoofs of literary tales.

Prince Dauntless (Joe Bora) and Fred (Carol Burnett) in *Once Upon a Mattress*. *Photofest.*

A typical pun occurs in the first production number, when the courtiers announce that the kingdom has an "Opening for a Princess" playing on the word *opening* as both a job vacancy and the opening number of the show. Winnifred's entrance, "Shy" (**Musical Example 41**), has a sly humor of its own. Most composers depicting a timid character would try to create a hesitant, tentative atmosphere. The music for "Shy," however, is brash and forceful, and the subtext is clear: Winnifred's not very shy at all. Not only has she swum the moat in her eagerness to arrive, but she wants to know the identity of the royal bachelor—and she wants to know *now*. Carol Burnett, who premiered the role, describes herself as "shy" at an almost ear-splitting volume; certainly the long, drawn-out syllables and the big-band setting are an ironic contradiction to her lyrics. As the song progresses, we realize that "shy" might mean something else altogether. Fred's character is a delightfully pungent contrast to the demure heroines of yore, and "Shy" captures her unexpected persona perfectly.

After the opening "hey, nonny, nonny" dialogue at (**1**), "Shy" follows a nonstandard pattern; although it initially follows a song form of *a-a-b-a'* (equaling **2**, **3**, **4**, and **5**), **6** introduces new material (*c*), followed by a call-and-response passage at **7** (*d*). Dance interrupts the song at **8**, and a small fragment of the *a* tune returns at **9**—leading directly to a vocal coda at **10**, with Fred still trying to discover the prince's identity. "Shy" resembles an old-fashioned song-and-dance number.

Besides introducing Carol Burnett to Broadway, *Once Upon a Mattress* featured Jane White as Queen Agravain. Ostensibly, this casting was color-blind—for White was an African American actress. However, the creators of the show asked White to wear "white face" makeup, because they were afraid audiences would be distracted by a mixed-race royal family. White agreed to their request, but was embarrassed to be seen by any of her friends. It would be many more years before Broadway was able to present minority actors playing Caucasian characters without attempting to disguise their race.

Ethan Mordden has quipped that *Once Upon a Mattress* was the only musical ever to "tour" Manhattan. The producers first opened the show off-Broadway in 1959. The show, directed by George Abbott, did so well that *Mattress* transferred to a Broadway theater—but soon *Mattress* had to shift to a third theater because of a previous booking. *Mattress* moved through two more theaters, but despite the upheaval, *Mattress* played 460 times. It continues to be a favorite show among smaller companies, with as many as 400 productions a year. Rodgers's score was nominated for a Tony, which meant she was competing against her father's *The Sound of Music*. (Styne's *Gypsy* was also part of the unenviable slate of competitors.)

Once Upon a Mattress was not Rodgers's sole theatrical effort, but it was her most successful Broadway show. She followed it up in 1963 with *Hot Spot*, which displayed several of the hallmarks of "a show in trouble." It underwent an extended **preview** period, postponing its opening at least four times. Since critics were supposed to wait until a show's official opening to write their reviews, the producers of *Hot Spot* were able to take advantage of the advance ticket sale without being subjected to critical lambasting. When the show at last *did* open, its premiere was on a Friday night—another hint of problems. Desperate producers often resorted to the ploy of a Friday-night opening with the belief that few people read the newspapers on Saturday morning and negative reviews might be overlooked. But the most telling hint of desperation was to be found on the printed program—or rather, *not* found, for both the director and choreographer refused to allow their names to be listed. *Hot Spot* lasted for only 43 performances. Before it closed, Rodgers had turned to Stephen Sondheim for help. Sondheim had been a protégé of her father's longstanding partner Hammerstein, and the two teenagers became good friends; they had even collaborated on a television musical in 1952, but had never been able to sell the show. Sondheim helped Rodgers craft a song for *Hot Spot*, but this could not save the troubled show.

Rodgers and Barer tried their hands at a revue—*The Mad Show*—in 1966. Sondheim wrote lyrics for a song called "The Boy From . . . ," spoofing a recent hit song, "The Girl from Ipanema." This satire was in keeping with the overall tone of the revue, which was inspired by the irreverent *Mad Magazine*. Sondheim opted to keep his identity a secret, using the pseudonym "Esteban Ria Nida"—a Spanish translation of his name. The hilarious number was revived in a 1976 revue devoted to Sondheim's works, called *Side by Side by Sondheim*, as well as in a revue of Rodgers's songs, called *Hello, Love*.

Next, Rodgers turned her hand to children's books, and in 1976 (followed by a remake in 2003) Walt Disney Studios made a feature film of her story *Freaky Friday*. Rodgers and her mother also wrote an advice column called "Of Two Minds" for *McCall's Magazine*. They prepared separate responses to letters from readers, and of course the generation gap separating the mother and daughter led them often to have sharply different viewpoints.

Along with several other composers, Rodgers contributed to the score of *Working*, a 1978 musical based on Studs Terkel's book about various American workers. Her most recent theatrical effort was a musical version of *Freaky Friday*, which was presented by Theatreworks/USA, a New York–based organization that sponsors children's and family musicals. Although she has never achieved the international fame of her father (few Broadway composers have), she was one of the first female composers to enjoy even a modest degree of Broadway success.

Mary Rodgers and **Richard Adler** (b. 1921) both had musicians for fathers, but Adler learned virtually nothing from his parent. Adler explained that not learning to read music or to play the piano was "an early act of rebellion against my father, who did both, magnificently." Adler majored in playwriting in college, but soon he found himself wanting to write melodies for his own lyrics. Using a toy xylophone, he laboriously composed his tunes. He was not the first to use this instrument for his creative activity; lyricist Bob Merrill, also a musical illiterate, had promoted their merits to Adler: they were portable on airplanes, and by assigning a number to each key, one could write down the series of numbers belonging to the notes of a tune and thereby preserve melodies without musical notation.

In 1950, Adler met **Jerry Ross** (1926–1955), who, like himself, enjoyed writing words and music for songs. Finding they had a good rapport, they teamed up, writing for assorted singers, occasional radio programs, the movies, and a revue. Their efforts eventually caught Frank Loesser's attention, who put them under contract to his new publishing company, Frank Music. Loesser's belief in the pair was justified; a 1953 song, "Rags to Riches," grew to be a huge hit, selling more than a million recordings (and copies of sheet music), and reaching the number one spot on the *Hit Parade*. (The *Hit Parade* was a weekly radio program that played the previous week's top-selling tunes, ranked in reverse order. It began broadcasting in 1935 and helped to spell the end of the old practice of song-plugging.)

Not long after the enormous splash of "Rags to Riches," codirectors George Abbott and Jerome Robbins started work on a new musical, *The Pajama Game* (1954). Loesser turned the project down but suggested that they listen to Adler and Ross. One of the songs that Adler and Ross submitted was a novelty number called "Steam Heat," which imitated the gurgling and hissing of a steam radiator. Not only did "Steam Heat" win them the job, but also a place was found for it in the show. Choreographer Bob Fosse designed one of his trademark dances for it, with the dancers in bowler hats using turned-in toes and bent bodies. (Fosse, like Adler and Ross, was also making his Broadway debut with *The Pajama Game*.) The second enormous hit from the show was "Hernando's

Hideaway"; it had little to do with the plot but added to the humor. The audience was alerted to the upcoming juxtaposition of comedy and mock-seriousness in the announcer's opening speech:

> *This is a very serious drama. It's kind of a problem play. It's about Capital and Labor. I wouldn't bother to make such a point of all this except that later on if you happen to see a lot of naked women being chased through the woods, I don't want you to get the wrong impression. This play is full of SYMBOLISM.*

Audiences delighted in the madcap humor of *The Pajama Game*, and after its 1954 opening, it was awarded that year's Tony for Best Musical. *The Pajama Game* went on to become the eighth musical in the history of Broadway to break the 1,000-performances mark, closing after 1,063 presentations.

The collaborators were anxious to work together again. Robbins bowed out, but the producers hired Abbott to direct, Fosse to choreograph, and Adler and Ross to write the songs. Their next product was *Damn Yankees* (1955)—and it also was a hit. No one expected this "baseball" story to succeed because baseball shows were believed to be jinxed. *Damn Yankees* surprised them all, winning the 1955 Tony for Best Musical and falling short of *The Pajama Game*'s run by only 44 performances.

The team of Adler and Ross seemed unbeatable—until November of 1955, when Ross succumbed to chronic bronchiectasis at the age of 29. It was soon evident that Adler could not succeed on his own or with new partners. He tried his hand at three more stage shows, but all three bordered on disastrous; his last effort closed after eight performances. Adler's theatrical career was not over, for he would work intermittently as a producer and a song composer. Among other events, he directed the famous party for John F. Kennedy at Madison Square Garden during which Marilyn Monroe crooned "Happy Birthday" to her good friend, the President. As a theatrical composer, however, Adler's career was finished; the door was open for other writers to become the new stars of Broadway.

FURTHER READING

Adler, Richard. *You Gotta Have Heart: An Autobiography.* New York: Donald I. Fine, 1990.

Banfield, Stephen. *Sondheim's Broadway Musicals.* Ann Arbor: University of Michigan Press, 1993.

Ewen, David. *Complete Book of the American Musical Theater.* New York: Henry Holt & Co., 1958.

Gottfried, Martin. *Broadway Musicals.* New York: Abradale Press, 1984.

Green, Stanley. *The World of Musical Comedy.* Third edition, revised and enlarged. New York: A. S. Barnes, 1974.

Kasha, Al, and Joel Hirschhorn. *Notes on Broadway: Conversations with the Great Songwriters.* Chicago: Contemporary Books, 1985.

Mandelbaum, Ken. *Not Since Carrie: Forty Years of Broadway Musical Flops.* New York: St. Martin's, 1991.

Mordden, Ethan. *Better Foot Forward: The History of American Musical Theatre.* New York: Grossman Publishers, 1976.

———. *Coming Up Roses: The Broadway Musical in the 1950s.* New York: Oxford University Press, 1998.

Prince, Hal. *Contradictions: Notes on Twenty-Six Years in the Theatre.* New York: Dodd, Mead, 1974.

Willson, Meredith. *But He Doesn't Know the Territory.* New York: G. P. Putnam's Sons, 1959.

PLOT SUMMARY: *THE MUSIC MAN*

The Music Man opens with a train carriage full of traveling salesmen, passing the time by playing cards and chatting about their profession in the newfangled world of 1912—and about that despicable musical-instrument seller Harold Hill, who gives other salesmen a bad name. The salesmen agree that Iowa, at least, is safe from Hill's double-dealings, since Iowans are too stiff-necked to fall for any con jobs. As the train pulls into the River City station, one card player stands up, declares that he thinks he should give Iowa a try, and debarks the train. In large letters, his suitcase reads "Professor Harold Hill."

Hill meets a former colleague, who warns Hill that the local librarian, Marian Paroo, is also the town's music teacher, and she won't fall for his sales tricks. But Hill, hearing the teacher is female, relaxes; he believes he can con her as he has conned so many women in the past. As he watches a pool table being delivered, Hill also figures out the way to grab the citizens' attention. Hill manages to start them worrying about the evils in their midst. Marian doesn't fall for his line, however, and goes home to give a lesson to her piano student, Amaryllis, arguing with her mother all the while about men like Hill.

Marian's young brother Winthrop has problems of his own. Embarrassed by his lisp, he's silent even when Amaryllis invites him to attend her birthday party. Amaryllis bursts into tears, explaining to Marian that she needs Winthrop to be her sweetheart so she can say goodnight to his name when the evening star rises. Marian reassures Amaryllis that all you have to do is leave a gap for that special person's name if you don't know it yet. As Amaryllis resumes playing her piano piece, Marian begins to sing "Goodnight, My Someone" (**Musical Example 40**) to herself.

Meanwhile, at the High School Hall, Mayor Shinn is offended when his wife's recitation is interrupted by a firecracker lit by Tommy Djilas. Four prominent members of the school board quickly start arguing until Hill grabs the audience's attention. Very quickly, he leads people to believe that the way to fight evil among young people is to involve them in a brass band. Hill makes some mistakes, however. For one thing, he doesn't know that the mayor bought the pool table. Moreover, after appointing Tommy to be the band's drum major, Hill selects a pretty girl to be the majorette alongside Tommy. Hill wins Tommy's loyalty, but he has chosen the mayor's daughter to consort with that young troublemaker. The mayor orders the school board members to find out Hill's credentials, but Hill distracts the incompatible men by discovering that they have the four voice types needed for a barbershop quartet. Before they realize it, they have stopped quarreling and have begun singing.

Because Hill can't play any instruments himself, who will teach the children how to play them? Hill plans to promote his "Think System," in which one "thinks" one's way to playing the right notes. His real ploy is to convince the townspeople also to buy uniforms for their offspring; once the kids look great, their parents won't care how they sound. Meanwhile, Hill hears all the gossip about Marian from the town ladies; they're shocked by the library's dirty books—written by Chaucer, Balzac, Rabelais, and the like. The school board members catch up to Hill again, but Hill soon starts them singing again. Like many parents, Mrs. Paroo orders a cornet for Winthrop, who is thrilled. Marian tries to warn her mother that Hill isn't what he seems, but Mrs. Paroo merely frets again about Marian's continuing unmarried state. Marian investigates Hill's background in the library's holdings. Finding the evidence she expected, she goes to the mayor—but they are interrupted by the arrival of the new instruments. To Marian's amazement, Winthrop is so thrilled by his bright cornet that he starts speaking excitedly. Marian realizes she can't betray the man who wrought this miracle, so she tears out the incriminating page.

Different styles of entertainment fill an evening at the gym, with barbershop harmony vying with young people's dancing. The mayor is still suspicious of Hill, and Marian is conflicted—should she pretend to believe in his "Think System"? Unexpectedly, she's no longer a social outcast, since Hill had persuaded the ladies of River City to read the books they had previously condemned. Hill keeps eluding the quartet by setting them off on more tunes. Winthrop chatters all the time about things he learned from Hill, although he doesn't seem to be learning the band's debut piece, *Minuet in G*.

Unexpectedly, Hill's previous misdeeds catch up to him. Charlie Cowell, a rival salesman, is tired of upset citizens when he visits a town after Hill's been there. Cowell's decided to warn the mayor about the charlatan Hill. Cowell makes the mistake, though, of asking Marian for directions; after learning why he's in town, she manages to flirt with him long enough that he has only enough time to run back to the train. When Hill asks Marian to the romantic rendezvous of the local footbridge, she agrees to go. Hill is shocked to realize that she knows everything about him—and he's even more surprised that she doesn't care because she's fallen in love with him. She kisses him, and Hill also realizes that he loves her, too. But there's bad news: Cowell missed the train, so he quickly spreads the word of Hill's duplicity. The mayor orders that Hill be arrested, but Marian speaks up, pointing out the many positive changes he has brought to their small town. The mayor is unimpressed, scornfully challenging those who support Hill to stand up. To his shock, he sees the townspeople rising one by one—including his own wife. To cap matters, the band makes its entrance, playing a barely recognizable *Minuet in G*. As Hill predicted, the proud parents don't care about the performance; they are in

raptures over the darling group of uniformed children. The mayor is forced to yield, and it is clear that Hill's traveling days are over; he now has reason to stay in River City.

PLOT SUMMARY: *ONCE UPON A MATTRESS*

As the curtain rises, a Minstrel steps forward and sings the story of the delicate princess who proved her royal blood by means of her sensitivity to a tiny pea placed under the 20 mattresses on her bed. The story is pantomimed behind him. The Minstrel then explains that although this account is the "prettiest" version of the tale, it's not exactly accurate, and he should know: it happened in his kingdom.

It seems that King Sextimus has been cursed; he will be mute "until the Mouse has devoured the Hawk." Repeated attempts to breed large mice and small hawks have been disastrous. Queen Agravain has been running the kingdom, and one of her decrees is that no one in the land may marry until her meek son Prince Dauntless is wed to a "true princess of royal blood," to be determined by a "royalty test" that she will administer herself. Of course, the citizens of the kingdom are eager for Dauntless to find a bride; Lady Larken is especially anxious, since she and her fiancé, Sir Harry, are in the family way. Sir Harry rides forth to comb the neighboring kingdoms in search of a suitable bride.

The courtiers rejoice when Harry returns with a most unusual candidate, Princess Winnifred, known as Fred, who swims the moat rather than be left outside. Although Fred proclaims herself to be "Shy" (**Musical Example 41**), Agravain takes one look at this newcomer and declares that Fred will be tested for "Sensitivity." Meanwhile, Lady Larken prepares a bedchamber for the guest; mistaking Fred for a servant, Larken shreds Fred's sopping dress into a mop and orders Fred to start scrubbing the floor. Sir Harry arrives and points out the mistake, so the humiliated Larken quarrels with him angrily.

After the argument, Larken is heartbroken, and she resolves to run away. Meanwhile, the Queen and the Wizard have hit upon a diabolical plan for their sensitivity test: they will secretly place a single pea on Fred's bed underneath 20 mattresses. When she can't detect the pea, this insensitivity will prove that she is not royal. To make doubly sure that Fred is too exhausted to feel *anything*, the Queen proclaims that there will be a ball that evening (with plenty of high-potency alcohol and wildly energetic dancing).

Despite the general exhaustion, there is much midnight activity in the castle. The Queen discovers Lady Larken attempting to sneak out of the castle. Larken is ordered to Fred's room, where Fred is trying to study for her royalty exam. Meanwhile, the King feels it's time to share the facts of life with his son; being mute, he must deliver his talk via pantomime. Wanting to help Fred survive her test, the Minstrel and the Jester flatter the Wizard into betraying the Queen's secret scheme.

In the meantime, Sir Harry and Lady Larken have reunited. Up in Fred's room, the Queen is using every trick she can to lull the princess into slumber—a hypnotic mirror, poppy incense, and even a little opium-laced milk. Fred goes to bed, relaxes—and then starts to toss. Twisting this way and that, it seems impossible for her to find a comfortable position. She finally sits up and tries counting sheep.

The new day arrives and the Queen is gloating in triumph. She announces to the assembled court that Fred is no true princess. Explaining that Fred *should* have been able to feel the pea if her blood was royal, Agravain notes that Fred's not even awake yet. But then, to everyone's surprise, a bedraggled Fred staggers in, still counting sheep one by one. She hasn't been able to sleep a wink because the bed was so uncomfortable. Angrily, Agravain tries to hustle Fred away, but Dauntless, for once in his life, stands up to his mother. The Queen is speechless at her son's rebellion, and suddenly the Jester realizes what has happened: the Mouse has at last devoured the Hawk. He cries, "The Queen can't talk!" and then an unfamiliar voice is heard, saying, "But *I* can! And I've got a *lot* to say!" It is the King, who has just regained his power of speech. He's now in charge again, and he's happy to sanction his son's marriage.

But what of Fred's insomnia? It seems that the Minstrel helped to make Fred's bed, and underneath her top mattress can be found his lute, a helmet, a couple of lobsters, and some old jousting gear. No one cares how Winnifred managed to stay awake, however, and the assembled courtiers remind us of the admonition sung by the Minstrel at the start of the show: "You can recognize a lady by her elegant air, but a genuine princess is exceedingly rare"—but Fred has fallen asleep at last and is snoring loudly.

MUSICAL EXAMPLE 40

THE MUSIC MAN
MEREDITH WILLSON/MEREDITH WILLSON, 1956

"Goodnight, My Someone"

Marian
1 Goodnight, my someone, goodnight, my love.
2 Sleep tight my someone, sleep tight, my love.
3 Our star is shining its brightest light for goodnight, my love, for goodnight.
4 Sweet dreams be yours, dear, if dreams there be; sweet dreams to carry you close to me.
I wish they may, and I wish they might. Now goodnight, my someone, goodnight.
5 True love can be whispered from heart to heart, when lovers are parted, they say.
But I must depend on a wish and a star, as long as my heart doesn't know who you are.
6 Sweet dreams be yours, dear, if dreams there be; sweet dreams to carry you close to me.

Marian and Amaryllis
I wish they may, and I wish they might. Now goodnight, my someone, goodnight.
Goodnight. Goodnight.

MUSICAL EXAMPLE 41

ONCE UPON A MATTRESS
MARY RODGERS/MARSHALL BARER, 1959

"Shy"

Winnifred
(*spoken*: Who's the lucky man?)
1 Hey, nonny, nonny, is it you?
Knight
Hey nonny, nonny, nonny, no!
Winnifred
Hey, nonny, nonny, is it you?
Knight
Hey nonny, nonny, nonny, no!
Winnifred
Hey, nonny, nonny, is it you, or you, or you, or you or?
Dauntless
Nonny, nonny, nonny, nonny, nonny, nonny, nonny,
Agravain
No, no, no!
Winnifred
Someone's being bashful. That's no way to be, not with me.
Can't you see that I am just as embarrassed as you? And I can understand your point of view:

2

I've always been shy, I'll confess it, I'm shy!
Can't you guess that this confident air is a mask that I wear 'cause I'm shy?

3

And you may be sure: way down deep I'm demure.
Though some people I know might deny it, at bottom I'm quiet and pure!

4

I'm aware that it's wrong to be meek as I am; my chances may pass me by.
I pretend to be strong, but as weak as I am, all I can do is try.

5

God knows I try! Though I'm frightened and shy
And despite the impression I give, I confess that I'm living a lie,
Because I'm actually terribly timid and horribly shy.

6

Though a lady may be dripping with glamour,
As often as not she will stumble and stammer when suddenly confronted with romance.
And she's likely to fall on her face when she's finally face to face with a pair of pants.
Quite often the lady's not as hard to please as she seems.
Quite often she'll settle for something less than the man of her dreams.

7

I'm going fishing for a mate.

Knights
She's goin' fishing for a mate.

Winnifred
I'm gonna look in every nook.

Knights
She's gonna look in every brook.

Winnifred
But how much longer must I wait with baited breath and hook?

8

[Interlude]

Oh, that was wonderful!

[Interlude]

9
10

And that is why, though I'm painfully shy, I'm insane to know
which sir? You, sir?

Knights
Not I, sir.

Winnifred
Then who, sir?
Where, sir? And when, sir? I couldn't be tenser,
So, let's get this done, man. Get on with the fun, man.

Winnifred   **Knights and Ladies**
I am one man   The lady's one man

All
Shy!

New Faces of the 1960s and 1970s

Chapter 32
New Names in Lights in the 1960s

No single team or individual would dominate Broadway during the decade of the 1960s, but several new names began to appear on theater marquees, and numerous experiments were conducted: darker, edgier stories—or no story at all, as in nonplot shows, the inclusion of rock and other musical styles, new technologies, new dramatic structures, and a variety of concept musicals. The audiences, too, were eclectic, embracing one experiment and rejecting the next. Some saw the new elements as tolling theater's death knell, while others welcomed the changes as a chance for theater to reinvent itself.

There were even individual composers who, arguably, reinvented themselves during this era. Cy Coleman had begun his career at the age of four, giving piano recitals in New York at age seven. He then came to fame with his studio recordings as a jazz pianist. With lyricist Carolyn Leigh, he wrote several hit songs, and the two soon started auditioning to write for Broadway. Eventually, they were hired to write *Wildcat* (1960), a star vehicle for television star Lucille Ball, and although she tired of the role before the show had earned back its investment, making it—financially speaking—a flop, her march-like anthem "Hey, Look Me Over" became a lasting hit. Coleman and Leigh also collaborated on *Little Me* (1962), showcasing television comedian Sid Caesar as seven different characters, but *Little Me* was never a New York success (although it did quite well in England). Revivals—first with James Coco and Victor Garber, sharing the role, and later with Martin Short—also failed quickly

Coleman's jazz background was evident in *Sweet Charity* (1966), written with Dorothy Fields. Like an increasing number of shows, *Sweet Charity* was inspired by a movie, the Fellini film *Nights of Cabiria*. Bob Fosse, the director, wanted to showcase his wife, Gwen Verdon, who had starred in Adler and Ross's *Damn Yankees* (1955). Verdon played a taxi dancer whose fiancé cannot reconcile himself to her unsavory background. (A taxi dancer was a woman who worked in nightclubs and other venues as a "dancer for hire"; patrons paid

taxi dancers to be their partners on the dance floor, and many taxi dancers had a reputation for being available for hire later in the evening as well.) Incidentally, *Sweet Charity* was the first book show to be performed at the Palace Theatre, New York's legendary vaudeville house.

With this show, Coleman at last attained his longed-for Broadway hit, and it is the only show by Coleman to have been filmed (as a 1969 movie starring Shirley MacLaine). *Sweet Charity* ran 608 performances, and its biggest song hits were "If My Friends Could See Me Now" and the seductive "Big Spender." Coleman and Fields worked together again on a show that flopped, and Fields died the next year. After her death, Coleman's partnerships—and successes—were varied. Although *I Love My Wife* (1977) ran well (872 performances), *On the Twentieth Century* (1978) excited twice as much critical admiration (and a Tony for Coleman). The French term for artwork that wins critical respect, but fails to become popular with the public, is *succès d'estime*. Kurt Gänzl suggests that *On the Twentieth Century* may simply have been too clever for its own good; it presented the complicated and hilarious behind-the-scenes maneuvers of actors and producers on board a passenger train. To listeners' surprise, Coleman had completely modified his style; instead of jazz, he wrote a lush, almost operatic score.

Coleman's next musical, *Home Again, Home Again* (1979) had an ironic title, for it closed on the road. He did much better with *Barnum* (1980), although he again made an unexpected change in style. *Barnum* was based on the circus personality P. T. Barnum, and the show's star was required to dance, juggle, and walk a tightrope while singing. The show ran 854 performances, and then, after a couple of disappointments, Coleman returned to Broadway with *City of Angels* (1989), a clever salute to the hard-boiled 1940s-era detective stories. Coleman had generated yet another hit.

Ever diverse, Coleman's next effort was a revue, *The Will Rogers Follies* (1991), again centered on the career of a real person. Audiences enjoyed the lighthearted celebration of an earlier era, and the show won that year's Tony for Best Musical. Coleman tried his hand at a **concept album** of *The Life* in 1995. This strategy—a studio recording of an as-yet unstaged show—was becoming an increasingly popular way of "selling" a show to prospective producers and investors, since it could replace backer's auditions. *The Life* reached the stage in 1997 for a run of 465 performances; it took a somber look at the lowlife characters who had inhabited Broadway's Times Square district during the 1980s. But this would be the final effort in a long and diverse career for Coleman.

Following Coleman's model, Jerry (Gerald) Herman maintained a "sine-wave" career, with some enormous successes intermingled with dismal failures. Like a number of others, Herman wrote both the music and lyrics for his songs, although he had come to music fairly late, having trained as a designer and architect. Some success with small revues encouraged him to turn his hand to a full-length show, *Milk and Honey* (1961), set in contemporary Israel. It caught on and gave the novice composer a 543-performance run for his first effort.

Ironically, even while *Milk and Honey* was still playing, Herman's second show closed, after only 13 off-Broadway performances. But it was Herman's second Broadway show that was his biggest triumph: playing 2,844 times, *Hello, Dolly!* (1964) set a new Broadway record and took the year's Tony for Best Musical. (The show also cost Herman more than $250,000, for he lost a plagiarism lawsuit that claimed the title song of *Hello, Dolly!* was derived from a 1940s tune called "Sunflower.") To be sure, *Hello, Dolly!*'s long run was aided by the shenanigans of its producer, David Merrick. He brought in a series of major stars to play the title role after Carol Channing had left the part, giving each one a splashy buildup (when Pearl Bailey took the role, he replaced the entire cast with African Americans). He also set the starting time a little later than that of surrounding theaters so that patrons unable to get tickets for nearby shows could still come see *Hello, Dolly!* and make an evening of it.

Herman had yet another powerhouse to unveil on Broadway: *Mame* made its debut in 1966. Angela Lansbury, who triumphed in the title role, was not the first choice for the part (nor the second or third)—in fact, some 40 actresses had auditioned after Mary Martin turned down the show. *Mame* achieved a 1,508-performance run, but it would be a long time before Herman had another hit. Nothing he wrote in the 1970s did particularly well. In 1983, though, he returned to the stage with *La Cage aux Folles*. Not only did the show play 1,761 times on Broadway, but it became a tremendous international success as well. This last triumph seems to have been enough for Herman; a number of compilation productions featuring his hit songs have been produced, but he has not created another Broadway show.

Like Jerry Herman, composer Charles Strouse began his Broadway career with a strong showing. In fact, his biggest successes all came as he was working with a new lyricist for the first time. His inaugural effort with Lee Adams was *Bye Bye Birdie* (1960), which not only produced the hit song "Put On a Happy Face," but won the Best Musical Tony Award; it ran for 607 performances. Their successive efforts did much

more poorly until they joined forces with the skilled craftsmen Comden and Green, producing *Applause* in 1970. Once again, Strouse had a Best Musical Tony to his credit.

Strouse then collaborated with Martin Charnin on *Annie* in 1977. Based on the comic strip *Little Orphan Annie*, the darling little girls of *Annie* endeared themselves to delighted audiences in much the same way that the ragged street urchins of *Oliver!* had charmed the London stage in 1960 (and the American stage in 1963). *Annie* was not the first show to be based on a comic strip. Earlier musicals had featured *Buster Brown*, *Little Nemo*, *Bringing Up Father*, *Li'l Abner*, *Superman*, and various characters of the *Peanuts* strip—but *Annie* was by far the most successful, running 2,377 performances.

Once again, though, a success by Strouse was still running while his next show opened and closed. He tried creating sequels to successes, but neither *Bring Back Birdie* (1981) nor *Annie 2* (1990) could hit the mark. His work with Alan Jay Lerner on what would be Lerner's last show, *Dance a Little Closer* (1983), did no better. Strouse saw many—but not all—of his subsequent shows make it to Broadway, but all of them have flopped to date. Nevertheless, with *Bye Bye Birdie*, *Applause*, and *Annie* on his resume, Strouse has had many reasons to be proud of his Broadway career.

It is not at all uncommon for a Broadway composer to enjoy a smash hit and then to strive fruitlessly for a follow-up success. Mitch Leigh, for instance, has never been able to repeat the triumph of his 1965 show *Man of La Mancha*, inspired by a television play that was based on the tales of *Don Quixote* by Cervantes. The success of *Man of La Mancha* took everyone by surprise, for the plot was dark and unsettling. Set in the era of the Spanish Inquisition, the novelist Cervantes is in prison for debt. Through the power of the imagination, Cervantes gets his fellow prisoners to see the world through the eyes of Don Quixote. Quixote sees beauty where others see ugliness, and even an unsavory serving wench, Aldonza, starts to believe in his vision, despite being beaten and raped by other characters. As the Don is dying, she encourages him to hold fast to what he had taught her, "The Impossible Dream."

Man of La Mancha first opened in a cramped off-Broadway theater, and patrons took so long clambering back to their seats after intermission that the show kept running past 11:30 p.m. (and costing overtime payments). So, the intermission was cut, and the continuous structure was retained when the show transferred to Broadway, where critics hailed it as an inspired artistic choice. In all, *Man of La Mancha* ran a staggering 2,328 performances.

Leigh was never able to capitalize on this breakthrough, however. His next show closed on the road in 1966 (and a 1989 revival attempt lasted only 44 performances). A 1970 effort survived only nine performances, while in 1976, *Home Sweet Homer*—even with Yul Brynner in the cast—folded the morning after its Broadway premiere. Perhaps to avoid that jinx, Leigh's next musical, *Saravà* (1979), played night after night of previews, postponing its premiere over and over again. Newspapers gave up waiting and came to review the show on whatever night they chose. Critics were mixed, but some came closing to raving, and it looked like *Saravà* might have a chance—but it finally folded at the end of the season without ever having made an official debut. And so it went; Leigh's two most recent compositional endeavors did little better than their predecessors. He had more success as a producer, but has never been able to regain the giddy triumph he had known with *Man of La Mancha*.

Another composer whose career started with a bang is Galt MacDermot (b. 1928), who was asked by New York actors Gerome Ragni (1942–1991) and James Rado (b. 1939, born James Radomski) to write the score for their brainchild, *Hair*. Their loose premise for the show was that a young man must decide what to do with his draft card in the Vietnam War era. There is no real plot beyond that question; instead, the singers—a group of hippies known as the Tribe—present their case for alternative lifestyles. In this sense, *Hair* is considered to be a **nonplot show**, for the characters stop to explore various ideas and experiences rather than depict a logically unfolding story. Whether the Tribe makes a case for refreshing personal freedom or for inconsiderate hedonism is up to the individual viewer to decide.

The creators themselves called *Hair* "An American Tribal Love-Rock Musical," and in one of those unexpected coincidences, Rado and Ragni shared a train one day with director Joseph Papp (1921–1991, born Yosl Papirofsky). Papp was involved with converting the Astor Library to the new Public Theater, and he expressed an interest in producing their property at the new venue—but on the condition that they get a composer. Ragni and Rado met MacDermot through a friend, and even though MacDermot had never written for the theater, he crafted a score for them in two weeks' time. *Hair* finally made its debut at the Public Theater in 1967. Then, after a short run at a discothèque, plans were made to take *Hair* to Broadway, and Tom O'Horgan (b. 1926) was hired as director.

The redesigned *Hair*, which opened at the Biltmore Theatre in 1968, was a substantially different show from the Public Theater version, with 13 new songs, new staging, revised scenes, and an almost entirely new cast. With the inclusion of so many new songs—and the deletion of only three—there was even less time to unfold the vestigial plot, such as it was. The earlier Papp production had clearly been an antiwar demonstration; by the time *Hair* reached Broadway, the focus was on the anti-Establishment attitude of the irreverent hippies—and on a notorious nude scene. Things were different backstage, too, with the management kindly providing "vitamin shots" (containing speed) to assist the actors in enlivening their performances. Absenteeism was frequent, and members of the Tribe were accustomed to taking on different roles with little prior notice.

Another aspect of freedom in *Hair* was in its musical score, which drew liberally from various styles of music—jazz, the blues, country, and especially **rock**. *Hair* is often cited as the first "rock" musical, although *Bye Bye Birdie* (1960) had contained some Elvis Presley-style rock-and-roll. *Hair*, on the other hand, had a plethora of pop-rock numbers, several of which became top-100 hits that year (in the tabulation maintained by *Billboard* magazine): "Good Morning Starshine" reached number 39, Three Dog Night's release of

A symbolic haircut in *Hair*.
Martha Swope.

"Easy to Be Hard" was 37, and the Fifth Dimension created a medley of two songs—"Aquarius" and "Let the Sunshine In"—which became the biggest hit of 1969. (This last hit came about merely by chance; one member of the Fifth Dimension left his wallet in a New York taxicab, and the next passenger was a producer of *Hair*. When they met to return the wallet, each invited the other to visit his current show—and after hearing the eerie opening of *Hair*, the group wanted to record it themselves.)

The title song of the show, "Hair," reached number 16 in 1969, in a version made by a wholesome family group, the Cowsills—a record which might never have received any airplay were it not for a wager. The Cowsills were booked to perform on a television show with Carl Reiner, who thought it would be entertaining to have them sing "Hair," since it was so contrary to their squeaky clean image. They prerecorded the song, since they would lip-sync during the television special, and they liked the result so much that they tried to persuade MGM to release the song. MGM kept refusing, but the family persuaded an MGM agent to take the song to a radio program director. The program director agreed to broadcast the single if he couldn't identify the performers. He was stumped, so he added the song to the station playlist, which forced MGM to make a general release of the song.

Hair drew sharply mixed reactions. Richard Rodgers attended the Broadway premiere and walked out at intermission. Others regarded *Hair* as the wake-up call Broadway had long needed; several critics named it the best musical of the year. The shock value of the nudity and the strong language is somewhat comparable to the revealing tights worn by the chorus dancers in *The Black Crook* just over a century before; certainly the moral outrage directed at *Hair* was reminiscent of the charges of lewdness and lasciviousness leveled at the earlier extravaganza. And, just as before, the notoriety of the show drew in additional viewers—for a run of 1,750 performances. In London, *Hair* did even better, playing 1,997 times. But Boston tried (unsuccessfully) to ban the show, and after the first night in Acapulco, the theater doors were barred and the cast threatened with arrest if they did not leave Mexico immediately. In Paris, though, some 5,000 French actors vied for the chance to play one of the 28 roles. In New York, about 10,000 people attended a second anniversary performance in Central Park.

MacDermot's newfound reputation as a "rock" composer meant that the New York Shakespeare Festival turned to him in 1971 for an updated score to support its open-air production of *Two Gentlemen of Verona*. The result was such a hit that the production was transferred to Broadway, where it ran for 627 performances. MacDermot and Ragni then tried their hands at another rock score in 1972, when *Dude* debuted. Insiders jokingly called it "Dud," and with good reason; it lasted for only 16 performances, costing investors just under $1 million. Later in 1972, MacDermot was ready with another Broadway show, *Via Galactica*. It did even worse than *Dude*, surviving only a week. Rado, meanwhile, had written the music and lyrics himself for an off-Broadway show the same year; his show managed to last for three weeks. With these efforts, though, the theatrical career for all three of *Hair*'s creators had essentially reached an end. The "youth" craze had drawn to a close, and their efforts seemed limited to that market.

The 1960s had just begun when *The Fantasticks* opened on May 3. A decade later, *The Fantasticks* was still playing, as it was when the 1970s, 1980s, and even the 1990s ended. In fact, *The Fantasticks* didn't close until January 13, 2002, after a run of 17,162 performances. *The Fantasticks* thereby established several records: not only was it the longest running show in American theatrical history, but it was the world's longest running musical *and* the world's longest running show of any sort to play continuously in its original theater. And yet, *The Fantasticks* is often discussed as a sort of footnote, for it was an *off*-Broadway show, playing in the tiny 150-seat Sullivan Street Playhouse in Greenwich Village. With that small capacity, it took a week of performances to equal a single night's audience at some of Broadway's larger houses. But a 42-year run—which outlasted nine U.S. presidents—is nothing to sneer at, and certainly the 44 original investors, who staked $16,500 to open the show, have been happy with the almost 10,000 percent return on their investment.

These astonishing figures almost didn't happen. After several mediocre reviews, the producer debated shutting down the production. At last, he loaned the show his life savings (some $3,300), and word-of-mouth built up a steady audience. It helped that several theatrical figures talked up the show, including Frank Loesser, Agnes de Mille, Bob Fosse, Jerome Robbins, and Anne Bancroft. By Christmas 1960, *The Fantasticks* had paid back all its backers, and from

that point on, in the words of one investor, it was "Katy bar the door." As early as 1961, the producer arranged for amateur and stock performance rights. Most shows wait to make those rights available only after the New York run ends, but it turned out to be a wise move, for *The Fantasticks* has been produced more than 11,000 times in 2,000 towns; it has even been performed at the White House. Moreover, many people who had been connected with the show elsewhere made a special effort to come see the "original" in New York.

Given this success, it is surprising to learn that the show's composer, Harvey Schmidt, can neither read nor write music; like Irving Berlin, he relies on an assistant to transcribe the tunes and harmonies he invents at the keyboard while playing by ear. He started collaborating with classmate Tom Jones while still in college in Texas, creating campus shows and the like. In 1959, they adapted an 1894 play called *Les Romanesques* into a one-act musical show for Barnard College; this was the basis of *The Fantasticks*. Reception was so positive that they expanded *The Fantasticks* to a full evening's entertainment. The simple—but not simplistic—story depicts two fathers who decide the best way to make their children, Matt and Luisa, fall in love is to build a wall separating them, reasoning that people always want what they can't have. Despite misunderstandings and quarrels, at last Matt and Luisa realize that they still love each other; the score's biggest hits were "Try to Remember" and "Soon It's Gonna Rain."

Schmidt and Jones made their Broadway debut three years later, when *110 in the Shade* opened in 1963. As before, their story was an adaptation of an earlier play, and the show enjoyed a solid run of 330 performances. Schmidt and Jones's next effort, *I Do! I Do!* (1966), did even better, running 560 times. A surprising feature of *I Do! I Do!* was that it had a two-person cast—but since the two were the legendary Mary Martin and Robert Preston, these larger-than-life actors more than sufficed. After this successful venture, Schmidt and Jones seemed to lose their touch, with most of their efforts closing before they reached Broadway. Nevertheless, the legacy of astounding records set by their first collaboration will be very, very hard to break.

Some unusual parallels existed between *Hair* and *1776*, a musical that debuted in 1969. For one thing, Broadway novices wrote both scores; for another, both shows conveyed an undercurrent of antiwar sentiment. Moreover, both turned into unexpected successes. *1776* was a particular surprise, since its libretto was by **Peter Stone** (1930–2003), whose only Broadway contributions were two previous failures. And its songs? They were by **Sherman Edwards** (1919–1981), a former high school history teacher who had become a songwriter (writing "See You in September" and "Wonderful, Wonderful"). To cap things off, the subject matter—the struggle to craft an acceptable Declaration of Independence—showed little promise; after all, generations of high school students already slept through American history courses as it was. But *1776* proved to be a **sleeper** of another sort, for it became the disregarded show that unexpectedly ran some 1,217 performances.

Most people thought Edwards was crazy for believing that the American Revolution would make a good musical, but as Gerald Bordman points out, "A great debate is always good theatre" (see the **Plot Summary**). Edwards had researched the subject for seven years, and only then—with the urging of Frank Loesser—did Edwards start to write songs for his show, spending another two and a half years on the task. When Stuart Ostrow agreed to produce, he persuaded Edwards to let Stone help with the libretto. Stone supported Edwards's vision of no chorus line or dancing, but tightened the drama of the debate to increase tension, taking some liberties with the chronology of events. He and Edwards chose to eliminate an intermission so that the anxiety rises continuously throughout the story.

One of the startling things about *1776* is that audiences *know* how the story ends, yet the authors still succeeded in making the tale suspenseful. Or, as critic Otis Guernsey put it, "When you entered the theater, you knew how it was going to turn out; after a half-hour, however, you weren't so sure." Part of the show's impact results from its depiction of curious historical details; many American citizens are unaware of the numerous compromises that were needed to create a declaration that was palatable to all the colonies. It is a melancholy discovery to learn that had Jefferson and Adams been successful in keeping a clause abolishing slavery in the final draft, America might have been spared the bitter history that led to its Civil War. But part of the tension is derived from a subtle theatrical device: a large calendar is displayed on stage. As each day passes, the custodian tears off another sheet. By July 3, it seems impossible that the quarreling constituents can reconcile by the next day, since their views are so sharply deadlocked. We know it must happen, but the breaking of the impasse still comes as a surprise.

Edwards, Stone, and Ostrow felt that there were parallels between the pressures of the Revolutionary era and the attitude of many Americans toward the Vietnam war, a timely issue for *1776*'s 1969 premiere. The antiwar sentiment comes through most clearly in "Momma, Look Sharp" (**Musical Example 42**), This forlorn lament is sung by a gravely wounded young soldier; in the first two sections of the song (**1** and **2**), he calls for his mother to come find him. Her voice is heard in a new melody at **3**, promising to comfort him. With some excitement, he describes the battle to her at **4**, but as he recalls how he was shot, he worries, "Am I done?" and he urges her to look sharp for him once more. Again at **5**, she sings her reassuring message, that she will close his sightless eyes and will bury him. The two characters are differentiated by two different melodies, with the young soldier's tunes contrasting with his mother's in an *a-a-b-a-b* pattern. But in truth, the boy's mother is simply a figment of his imagination; he has conjured her image to console him as he faces the loneliest task imaginable, that of dying. To create an archaic, folklike effect, Edwards sets the song in the *mixolydian* mode, an ancient scale with an odd, old-fashioned sound. The song is a heart-wrenching reminder of war's real cost.

1776 took a hard, unflinching look at several issues. The antislavery posturing of many northern colonists was pointedly questioned in "Molasses to Rum," while the self-protective outlook of some delegates was discussed in "Cool, Cool, Considerate Men." These antiwar, antiracist, and anticonservative numbers made many listeners uncomfortable, and when

1776 was invited to give a command performance at the White House, members of President Nixon's staff and others asked to have those three songs deleted. Ostrow refused, but it took the additional persuasion of Nixon's speechwriter before the White House agreed to have *1776* performed in its entirety. Afterwards, Ostrow could only marvel at the people who—after trying to censor the show—then publicly praised it for its patriotism.

There were many, however, who admired *1776* without ambivalence, which led not only to the show's lengthy run but also to a Best Musical Tony Award; *1776* was also named the New York Drama Critic's Best Musical. Unusually, almost the entire cast recreated their roles in the 1972 Columbia Pictures film; Betty Buckley, who played Martha Jefferson, was the only principal not to reprise her part. For Edwards, however, *1776* remained his only Broadway effort. Certainly his fine craftsmanship is a worthwhile legacy, and Denny Flinn is not alone in arguing that *1776* "should be required viewing for high school students." This powerful dramatization of a critical historical juncture helps us all to appreciate the remarkable achievement of ordinary, flawed men under extraordinary pressure.

FURTHER READING

Citron, Stephen. *The Musical From the Inside Out*. Chicago: Ivan R. Dee, 1992.

Davis, Lorrie, with Rachel Gallagher. *Letting Down My Hair*. New York: Arthur Fields Books, 1973.

Farber, Donald C., and Robert Viagas. *The Amazing Story of The Fantasticks, America's Longest Running Play*. New York: Carol Publishing Group, 1991.

Flinn, Denny Martin. *Musical!: A Grand Tour*. New York: Schirmer Books, 1997.

Green, Stanley. *The World of Musical Comedy*. Third edition, revised and enlarged. New York: A. S. Barnes, 1974.

Horn, Barbara Lee. *The Age of* Hair: *Evolution and Impact of Broadway's First Rock Musical*. (Contributions in Drama and Theatre Studies, 42.) New York: Greenwood Press, 1991.

Laufe, Abe. *Broadway's Greatest Musicals*. New, illustrated, revised edition. New York: Funk & Wagnalls, 1977.

Mandelbaum, Ken. *Not Since Carrie: Forty Years of Broadway Musical Flops*. New York: St. Martin's, 1991.

Mordden, Ethan. *Open a New Window: The Broadway Musical in the 1960s*. New York: Palgrave, 2001.

Ostrow, Stuart. *A Producer's Broadway Journey*. Westport, Connecticut: Praeger, 1999.

Richards, Stanley, ed. *Great Rock Musicals*. New York: Stein & Day, 1979.

PLOT SUMMARY: *1776*

During a stifling May in Philadelphia, in the year 1776, the only recourse is to wave a fan to cool off. Fans can't cool the hot tempers of the delegates to the Second Continental Congress, however. Their challenge? To determine the colonies' response to the burdens imposed by England. John Adams is impatient at the slow proceedings, complaining that nothing has been accomplished in a year. He, in turn, irritates the others with his constant urgings for independence. Adams is also under pressure from his wife Abigail, whose letters from Boston make her a visible presence. They argue about priorities; he wants her to rally women to manufacture saltpeter for the army, while Abigail says that women need dressmaker's pins. Nevertheless, the separated couple end by recalling their love for each other.

Adams goes to Benjamin Franklin for help. Franklin points out that people might be more receptive to the idea of independence if someone else proposed it. Franklin persuades Richard Henry Lee to talk to the Virginia legislature about such a proposal. A month later, the weather is still hot, Thomas Jefferson wants to go home, and General Washington is worried about his ill-equipped troops. But Lee returns, carrying a resolution for independence. Quickly seconded by Adams, John Hancock opens the floor to debate. John Dickinson wants no part of it, proposing that the motion be tabled indefinitely. The vote is close, but Stephen Hopkins casts the deciding vote to continue the discussion.

During the debate, it is clear that opinions are almost perfectly divided, to the point that an individual delegate can shift the balance. Dickinson moves that a decision for independence must be unanimous. Six colonies are in favor, six are against, and New York (as usual) elects to abstain. Hancock is left with the deciding vote; he opts for the unanimous decision. Adams then makes a motion himself: that further debate be postponed until a written document can be drafted, outlining the merits of independence. Once again, the Congress is split; this time Hancock's vote grants the postponement. Hancock orders Franklin, Lee, Adams, Roger Sherman, and Robert Livingston to form a "declaration committee," but Lee begs off, so Hancock appoints Jefferson instead—to Jefferson's dismay, for he still wants to go home. Moreover, Jefferson ends up with the quill in his hands to do the actual writing.

A week later, Jefferson has made no real progress, but Franklin and Adams have a surprise for him: they have sent for his wife Martha. Adams and Franklin return to the largely dysfunctional Congress; the conservative delegates are reluctant to take any action that might threaten their wealth, maintaining that they are "Cool, Cool, Considerate Men." Meanwhile, news from the military front is not good; Washington has lost the New York harbor to the British and fears Philadelphia will be next. We learn about the personal costs of the warfare in "Momma, Look Sharp" (**Musical Example 42**).

After Jefferson finishes his Declaration, a brief debate ensues about a symbolic bird for the fledgling country: Jefferson

advocates the dove, Franklin supports the turkey; at last they agree with Adams's choice, the eagle. The laborious project of rewriting the Declaration to suit all the delegates begins. Jefferson agrees to a series of minor changes, but when Dickinson wants him to delete the reference to King George III as a tyrant, Jefferson balks. Before the Congress can vote on the matter, Edward Rutledge of South Carolina raises another objection. Jefferson's draft calls for slavery to be abolished, but Rutledge argues that slavery is the foundation of the southern colonies' way of life, observing that Jefferson owns slaves himself. Jefferson retorts that he plans to free his slaves, but Rutledge regards him and the northern colonials as hypocrites, observing in "Molasses to Rum" that the north has gotten rich from its part in the slave trade. The southern delegates leave the chamber angrily.

Matters are at a crisis point. Adams begs the ailing Caesar Rodney to return from Delaware, knowing that Rodney's vote will tip the balance in that colony. Adams, like Jefferson, is staunch in his support of the antislavery clause, but Franklin tells him he must agree to delete it if he is to carry the South. Downcast, Adams is buoyed by a gift that arrives from his wife—two barrels of saltpeter—but he wonders why he feels no one shares his vision for the future. Washington continues to feel that Congress is unresponsive, but Hancock at last calls for a vote on the question of independence.

Each colony casts its vote. As expected, the northern and middle colonies support the resolution, although New York abstains and Pennsylvania has passed. When it comes time for South Carolina to vote, they ask again for the slavery clause to be stricken from the Declaration. Franklin turns to Adams, who turns to Jefferson—and Jefferson picks up a quill and strikes out the clause himself. With this concession, South Carolina, North Carolina, and Georgia are willing to vote in favor. At last, the issue comes down to Pennsylvania's vote. The Pennsylvania delegates are divided, so Hancock polls each of them. Franklin votes "yea" and Dickinson votes "no." James Wilson is now in an unenviable position. He usually follows Dickinson's lead, but realizing his name might be remembered as the man who prevented American independence, he nervously votes "yea" as well. Dickinson declares that he cannot sign the now-victorious Declaration, but he *will* enlist in the army and fight for the new country. In an eerie, spine-tingling close, the document appears above the stage and the Liberty Bell tolls over and over again as each delegate steps forward to sign the Declaration of Independence.

MUSICAL EXAMPLE 42
1776
SHERMAN EDWARDS/SHERMAN EDWARDS, 1969
"Momma, Look Sharp"
Boy

1 Momma, hey, Momma, come lookin' for me, I'm here on the meadow by the red maple tree.
Momma, hey, Momma, look sharp! Here I be. Hey! Hey! Momma, look sharp!

2 My eyes are wide open, My face to the sky, is that you I'm hearin' in the tall grass nearby?
Momma, come find me before I do die. Hey! Hey! Momma, look sharp!

Girl

3
Billy, darling Billy, I've come to where you lay,
And I'll hold you in the meadow while them soldiers march away.
I'll hold you in the meadow 'til the last light of day. Hey! Hey! Momma, look sharp!

Boy

4
Them soldiers, they fired. Oh, Ma! Did we run!
But then we turned 'round and the battle begun.
Then I went under, oh Ma! Am I done? Hey! Hey! Momma, look sharp!

Girl

5
I'll close your eyes, my Billy, those eyes that cannot see,
And I'll bury you, my Billy, beneath the maple tree.
And never again do you whisper to me, Hey! Hey! Momma, look sharp!

Chapter 33
Sondheim in the 1960s: Flash in the Pan?

Perhaps the finest new composer to emerge in the 1960s was **Stephen Sondheim** (b. 1930). Sondheim's name had already been seen on Broadway as a lyricist—first in *West Side Story* and then in *Gypsy*—but 1962 witnessed Sondheim's successful debut as a composer. As he would demonstrate in his very next show, Sondheim tried not to follow formulas—even at the risk of a flop. Viewers who enjoy one Sondheim production are often baffled by the next. Sondheim's ideas are complex and can be difficult to grasp during a single evening's performance. Moreover, as Gerald Bordman put it, "A Sondheim show is rarely comfortable or comforting." For these reasons, Sondheim's works are sometimes commercially unsuccessful, but for the viewer who teases out the multilayered meanings in a Sondheim show, the rewards can be rich.

Sondheim always had wanted to write for the stage. Fate was very kind to him when his mother settled in Doylestown, Pennsylvania, in 1942, near the country home of the Hammersteins. When Sondheim first met Oscar Hammerstein, the older man was still suffering through a series of failures. Hammerstein's fortune would change when he joined with Richard Rodgers to create *Oklahoma!*, but both before and after this new success, Sondheim found Hammerstein to be accessible and fatherly.

In 1946, Sondheim asked Hammerstein to look at a school show he'd written, asking his mentor, "Will you read it as if it was a musical that just crossed your desk as a producer? Pretend you don't know me." Sondheim had visions of being the first teenager to have a show presented on Broadway. The next day, Sondheim assured Hammerstein once more that he wanted a frank reaction. So, Hammerstein said bluntly, "It's the worst thing I've ever read in my life." Sondheim recalls,

> He must have seen my lower lip tremble or something, because he followed it up by saying, "I didn't say it wasn't talented. I said it was terrible. And if you want to know why it's terrible, I'll tell you." And he started with the first stage direction and he went through the piece for one afternoon, really treating it seriously—it was a seminar on [musical theater writing] . . . in the course of that afternoon he told me how to structure songs, how to build them, with a beginning, a development, and an ending. He taught me about character, how to introduce character, what relates a song to a character, stage techniques, and so forth. . . . At the risk of hyperbole, I dare say I learned more in that afternoon than most people learn about songwriting in a lifetime.

Hammerstein suggested that Sondheim work on a series of four complete musicals, writing the libretto, music, and lyrics

all himself but with Hammerstein's guidance. For the four shows, Hammerstein recommended that Sondheim should:

1. take an admired play and adapt it as a musical;
2. adapt an unsuccessful play that might be improved with music;
3. choose a literary source such as a novel or a short story, and let that be the basis for a show; and
4. write an entirely original show.

Even as Sondheim enrolled at Williams College in Massachusetts, he embarked on the ambitious composition project. His first musical was based on *Beggar on Horseback*; with the permission of the authors, George S. Kaufman and Marc Connelly, Sondheim tried out his show (titled *All That Glitters*) at Williams College during his sophomore year. (Hammerstein missed the production because he was in Boston for *South Pacific*'s tryout.) A school paper critic wanted tunes he "could whistle, and was disappointed that he didn't get them"—a complaint Sondheim would often hear in years to come. Nevertheless, *Variety* also sent a critic who felt that Sondheim had "great potential ability." Moreover, Broadcast Music Incorporated (BMI) published five of the songs, making Sondheim a published composer while still a teenager—no mean feat.

The next show was *High Tor*, but it went unperformed because Sondheim couldn't get permission from the play's author, Maxwell Anderson. For the third task, Sondheim chose *Mary Poppins*, but he never was able to complete the libretto to his satisfaction. By the time Sondheim graduated from college, he was ready to undertake the "original" project, titled *Climb High*. Its first act was 99 pages; by comparison, the *entire* libretto for *South Pacific* had been only 90 pages. During the same years that Sondheim crafted these shows, he also watched Rodgers and Hammerstein succeed with *South Pacific*, as well as flop with *Allegro*. Sondheim assisted Hammerstein as a "gofer" during the experimental *Allegro*, and it may have influenced several later concept musicals, including Sondheim's *Company* (1970).

When Sondheim graduated, he won Williams's Hutchinson Prize, a $3,000 stipend to support studies in music. Sondheim's choice of teacher came as a surprise to many, because the Princeton professor Milton Babbitt (later to write, "Who Cares If You Listen?") was a leader in the avant-garde world of nontonal music. Babbitt was trying to write a musical himself, and he and Sondheim also shared a fascination with mathematical relationships. They began each session by analyzing popular music; Babbitt particularly admired the harmonies in Kern's "All the Things You Are."

Richard Rodgers, Arthur Laurents, and Steven Sondheim.
AP Wide World Photos.

Sondheim studied with Babbitt for two years. At the same time, Sondheim continued to explore the theater, working as an apprentice at the Westport Playhouse and collaborating with Mary Rodgers on some projects. His first professional work was writing screenplays for a television series, *Topper*. By chance, Sondheim met producer Lemuel Ayers, who had the rights to produce a show about a group of kids living in Brooklyn who all invest in the stock market in 1928. Frank Loesser was busy, so Ayers asked Sondheim to write three trial songs for him. Sondheim won the chance to do the score for *Saturday Night*, but before Ayers could bring it to the stage, the unexpected happened: he died of leukemia. Sondheim's first opportunity to write a Broadway musical had come and gone; *Saturday Night* wasn't produced until 1997.

In 1955, Sondheim's friend **Burt Shevelove** (1915–1982) took Sondheim to an opening night party. During the party, Sondheim asked Arthur Laurents about his current project. Laurents replied, "I'm about to begin a musical of Romeo and Juliet with Leonard Bernstein and Jerry Robbins." Sondheim asked who was doing the lyrics, and Laurents, struck, replied, "I never thought of you, and I liked your lyrics very much" (adding rather tactlessly, "I didn't like your music very much"). Bernstein was enthusiastic about Sondheim's songs, but wanted to write the lyrics himself. However, when Bernstein took a careful look at all the *music* he needed to write for *West Side Story*, he offered Sondheim the position of colyricist.

Sondheim had mixed feelings. He wanted to work on Broadway, but not as a lyricist, explaining,

Lyric writing is, at best, a very limited art . . . It's largely a matter of sweat and time consumption. Once a basic idea for a lyric has been set, it's like working out a crossword puzzle. But composing music is genuinely creative. And it's much more fun.

The ever-practical Hammerstein said, "I think it will be very valuable for you to work with professionals of this caliber—they are first rate in their fields. The project sounds exciting and you will learn a great deal that I couldn't teach you because it's practical experience. So I think you ought to do it."

Although Bernstein appreciated Sondheim's musical understanding, they didn't always see eye to eye about the lyrics. Sondheim favored simple, direct language; Bernstein leaned toward flowery poetry. However, most of the final lyrics came from Sondheim, to the point that Bernstein offered him sole credit as lyricist. Sondheim was so pleased that he waved off the offer to increase his percentage of the gross accordingly—a carelessness he has often regretted. Sondheim also regretted some of his too-sophisticated lyrics for Maria and the lyrics that were impossible to sing during the fast-moving "America." But, as Hammerstein had promised, the experience was very valuable for Sondheim.

Next, Sondheim started work on a project with Shevelove; Shevelove felt the ancient comedies by the Roman writer Titus

Maccius Plautus (254–184 B.C.) would "musicalize" quite well. Robbins was intrigued at the idea of directing a lighthearted farce after the tragic *West Side Story*, but he decided to ask for a read-through of the script, using professional actors, before making a final decision. (This sort of reading—as pioneered by Robbins—is now called a **workshop**.) Robbins liked what he heard, but he was very much in demand after *West Side Story* and was just then signing a contract to direct *Gypsy*. Robbins asked Sondheim to write the words and music for *Gypsy*'s songs, but this plan was nixed by Ethel Merman, who would authorize Sondheim only as lyricist. Sondheim wanted to resign, but again he listened to Hammerstein, who noted that Sondheim could learn alot from writing for an established star. Since *Gypsy* had the financial backing it needed, Sondheim rationalized that at the worst, it would cost him six months of time. As he later remarked, "So instead of doing music and lyrics, I did just lyrics—and I haven't regretted it for one second."

Once *Gypsy* reached the stage, Sondheim resumed his ancient Roman project with Shevelove and with **Larry Gelbart** (b. 1928), the colibrettist. A wrinkle had developed in *A Funny Thing Happened on the Way to the Forum*: early on, David Merrick had bought an option to produce *Forum*. During *Gypsy*, however, Robbins spent a lot of money exploring a vaudeville concept that was eventually scrapped—along with many expensive costumes. Things grew so tense that Robbins swore never to work with Merrick again. Therefore, Robbins pulled out of *Forum*, since Merrick still held the rights.

Even after Merrick sold back the option (which was then sold to **Hal Prince**), Robbins didn't immediately rejoin the *Forum* project, so Prince turned to his former boss, **George Abbott**, who agreed to direct, while Jack Cole was hired as choreographer. It still took some 12 complete rewrites before *Forum* was prepared to start its tryouts; Sondheim's longtime mentor Hammerstein died in August 1960 before *Forum* was ready to debut. (Sondheim dedicated his score for *Forum* to Hammerstein's memory.)

Much of the delay came from honing the madcap farce to a sharply comic edge. The plot of *Forum* was original (see the **Plot Summary**), but Shevelove and Gelbart drew stock characters and situations from several of Plautus's surviving comedies, such as the shrewd slave, the empty-headed hero, the gullible old man, the alluring courtesan, the womanizing husband, and his ever-suspicious wife. *Forum* also spoofed modern styles, including vaudeville, burlesque, and musical comedy. *Forum* was a one-set musical, meaning there were no scene changes, and the characters wore the same costumes throughout. The audience focused instead on the characters' zany activities and increasingly funny dialogue.

Many people felt that farces weren't good material for musicals, because songs broke the comedic momentum. In the case of *Forum*, though, the songs allowed both the audience and the characters to catch their breath, even while building up additional humor. Most of the songs are tightly integrated into the plot, which limited their appeal as independent numbers. This was a choice Sondheim made knowingly (and the choice he would make all through his career); he cared—deeply—that his songs should develop a character or contribute to the drama, whether or not they became independent hits.

One song from the show, "Comedy Tonight" (**Musical Example 43**), did achieve hit status, becoming another anthem for Broadway along with tunes like Berlin's "There's No Business Like Show Business." However, "Comedy Tonight" was not yet in the show when *Forum* gave its triumphant **gypsy run-through**. All the cast members—gypsies (the chorus singers and dancers) and stars—would invite friends and family to attend the last rehearsal of the show before it left to start its out-of-town tryouts. Even though a gypsy run-through often was performed without costumes, stage sets, or even the orchestra, it took place in front of some of the most knowledgeable and experienced viewers who would watch the show. Audiences tended to be enthusiastic, but *Forum*'s gypsy run-through was exuberant.

Buoyed by that animated reaction, the cast and creators of *Forum* were hardly prepared for the reception they got on the road. As Hal Prince recalled,

> It opened a week later in New Haven and died. It died again (and worse) in Washington. A play designed for laughter played to silence for four weeks and all we had to keep the actors and creators going was the memory of the bare-stage run-through in New York.

At one matinee in Washington, only 50 people were in the audience. In desperation, the creators agreed to call in a show

Shenanigans in *A Funny Thing Happened on the Way to the Forum*.
Photofest.

doctor—an irony since Abbott had long been one of Broadway's leading show doctors. (Watching one listless audience, Abbott quipped, "I dunno. Maybe you had better call in George Abbott.") A fresh perspective was needed, so they turned to Robbins, who agreed to come.

The cast of a show often breathes a sigh of relief when a show doctor arrives, but Robbins came with a sizable amount of baggage. Although the year was 1962, memories of the bitter McCarthy era a decade before still burned. Robbins had outraged many performers by naming names when he was questioned by the House Un-American Activities Committee; one of those names was Madeline Lee. She was Jack Gilford's wife, and Gilford was cast in the role of Hysterium. To make matters worse, both Gilford and Zero Mostel (playing Pseudolus) had personally suffered from blacklisting. They were both professional enough to accept Robbins's last-minute direction but refused to socialize with him in activities outside the theater. Mostel said bluntly, "I can work with the man but I don't have to eat with him."

Despite this hostility, Robbins could identify an important flaw in the show. For the opening number, Sondheim had originally written an "Invocation" in which the characters prayed to the gods, asking their blessing on the show to come, but Abbott wanted something more hummable. Sondheim produced "Love Is in the Air," but Robbins felt that it didn't set the mood properly; he thought the "Invocation" had been a better approach. Rather than try to persuade Abbott to reinsert it, Sondheim recalls, "I wrote a [new] list song, 'Comedy Tonight,' saying 'This is what you're going to see.'" And indeed, "Comedy Tonight" is a litany of dozens of adjectives and nouns identifying all the things the viewers will (and will not) see in the course of the evening. Pseudolus adopts the role of "Prologus" in this song, explaining the background of the three central households that will figure in the show. He is joined by the Proteans—actors who specialize in quick costume and make-up changes so that they seem to portray dozens of characters—as well as most of *Forum*'s lead characters.

"Comedy Tonight" is in essence a strophic form, with each strophe consisting of an *a-a-b-a'* song form (represented by **1**, **2**, **3**, and **4**). Many of the strophes are interrupted by dialogue or orchestral interludes, as is the case in the second strophe (**5**). The third strophe (**6**) is left intact, but only one phrase is sung during the fourth strophe (**7**); the rest of the strophe is devoted to dialogue or slapstick stage business. A fifth stanza begins at **8**, but it, too, contains spoken dialogue. The final stanza (**9**) contains a long list of the character "types" (**10**) who will appear in the show, bringing the song to a climax.

As Jerome Kern did in "Ol' Man River," Sondheim lets a single rhythmic motive serve as the mainstay of the song. Interestingly, Sondheim reverses the pattern used by Kern; Kern's rhythm had been "long–long/short–long–short," whereas Sondheim delivers that same pattern in reverse ("short–long–short/long–long"), as shown in **Figure 33–1**. The mild syncopation of this rhythmic motif adds to the energy of the already upbeat song.

Robbins's timely suggestion—and Sondheim's brilliant solution to fill a need—turned the fortunes of *Forum* around. In 1962, it began a 967-performance run, delighting audiences

Long	*Long*	*Short*	*Long*	*Short*
Ol'	Man	Riv-	-er,	Dat
Ol'	man	riv-	-er,	He
Short	*Long*	*Short*	*Long*	*Long*
Some-	-thing	fa-	-mi-	-liar,
Some-	-thing	pe-	-cu-	-liar,

Figure 33–1

with its nonstop comedy; the illogic of the title (for no one even attempts to go to the forum) bothered no one. *Forum* won the year's Tony for Best Musical, and Tonys also went to Shevelove and Gelbart, Abbott, and Prince—but Sondheim was not even nominated. Moreover, when *Forum* was filmed in 1966 (with several of the stars reprising their roles), only five of the songs were retained.

In 1961, Sondheim commented, "I wouldn't mind putting my name to a flop if it has done something that hadn't been tried before." Sondheim got his opportunity to do just that—produce a flop—in 1964, when *Anyone Can Whistle* played only nine performances before closing, costing its investors (among whom were Irving Berlin, Frank Loesser, Richard Rodgers, and Jule Styne) their full $350,000 stake. The story, written by Arthur Laurents, conveyed the unpalatable messages that nonconformists are indistinguishable from lunatics, that corruption can go unpunished, and that giving up is sometimes the only way to loosen up. Besides being crippled by the difficult subject matter, Laurents later wondered if the show itself was simply jinxed, noting the string of misfortunes that dogged the tryout tour.

Regardless, there are historians who argue that the failure of *Anyone Can Whistle* was the making of Sondheim—that the experiment put him on the map. As Mark Steyn puts it, "Stephen Sondheim was a nobody until *Anyone Can Whistle*. All he'd done previously was write three solid hits, one after another. . . . But *Anyone Can Whistle* (1964) was his first cult flop." The show developed its following thanks to Goddard Lieberson of Columbia Records, who persevered in seeing that an original cast album of the show was made even though the show's quick closure released Columbia from the obligation to do so. After the album was released, *Anyone Can Whistle* proved to be one of the rare shows to have a hit recording even though the show flopped. Especially in its recorded form, Sondheim's score came under careful scrutiny, earning more and more admiration as time went by.

A couple of insightful critics did recognize the score's special qualities even at the premiere of *Anyone Can Whistle*; the New York *Morning Telegraph* argued, "If *Anyone Can Whistle* is a success, the American Musical Theater will have advanced itself and prepared the way for further freedom from now old and worn techniques and points of view. If it is not a success we sink back into the old formula method and must wait for the breakthrough." Norman Nadel was even more exuberant: "You have no idea how many breath-taking surprises are in store for you in the Arthur Laurents-Stephen Sondheim musical. At a time when even the good musicals look a little or a lot like something out of a recent season, it is exciting to encounter one so spectacularly original." This same process would unfold many times in Sondheim's subsequent career; several of his works met with initial resistance, only to be reassessed in later years and to have their achievement recognized belatedly.

Sondheim's next theatrical endeavor was quite a struggle. Before Hammerstein died, he asked Sondheim to promise to work with Rodgers on something. That project turned out to be *Do I Hear a Waltz?*, with Sondheim serving as a lyricist once again. Sadly, the collaboration was fraught with tension (Sondheim felt condescended to and ridiculed by the older composer), and Mary Rodgers acknowledged that the partnership of her father and her friend was "ghastly, for they were incompatible from every point of view."

Despite this unhappy atmosphere, the results were solidly crafted. The show itself was centered on some problematic premises, one being that the lead character possesses some unlikeable personality traits. When *Do I Hear a Waltz?* made its 1965 debut, Rodgers's name helped keep the show afloat for some time, but the show lost about half of its $450,000 investment. It was the shortest run Rodgers had seen for 20 years (although he would suffer even quicker closures in his shows to follow). The score was nominated for a Tony, but lost to *Fiddler on the Roof*. But the biggest cost may have been to Sondheim: He had just suffered back-to-back failures, and he would not bring another show to the Broadway stage for the rest of the decade. However, with *Company* in 1970 (Chapter 38, "Sondheim in the 1970s: The Endless Experiments,"), Sondheim would prove that Broadway "had seen nothing yet."

FURTHER READING

Banfield, Stephen. *Sondheim's Broadway Musicals*. Ann Arbor: University of Michigan Press, 1993.

Citron, Stephen. *Sondheim and Lloyd Webber: The New Musical*. Oxford: Oxford University Press, 2001.

Gottfried, Martin. *Broadway Musicals*. New York: Abradale Press/Abrams, 1984.

Green, Stanley. *The World of Musical Comedy*. Fourth edition, revised and enlarged. San Diego: A. S. Barnes & Company, 1980.

Ilson, Carol. *Harold Prince From* Pajama Game *to* Phantom of the Opera. Ann Arbor: U.M.I. Research Press, 1989.

Laufe, Abe. *Broadway's Greatest Musicals*. New, illustrated, revised edition. New York: Funk & Wagnalls, 1977.

Lewine, Richard. "Symposium: The Anatomy of a Theater Song." *The Dramatists Guild Quarterly* 14, no. 1 (1977): 8–19.

Mandelbaum, Ken. *Not Since Carrie: Forty Years of Broadway Musical Flops*. New York: St. Martin's, 1991.

Mordden, Ethan. *Open a New Window: The Broadway Musical in the 1960s*. New York: Palgrave, 2001.

Ostrow, Stuart. *A Producer's Broadway Journey*. Westport, Connecticut: Praeger, 1999.

Prince, Hal. *Contradictions: Notes on Twenty-Six Years in the Theatre*. New York: Dodd, Mead, 1974.

Sondheim, Stephen. "The Musical Theater: A Talk by Stephen Sondheim." *The Dramatists Guild Quarterly* 15, no. 3 (1978): 6–29.

Steyn, Mark. *Broadway Babies Say Goodnight: Musicals Then and Now*. New York: Routledge, 1999.

PLOT SUMMARY: *A FUNNY THING HAPPENED ON THE WAY TO THE FORUM*

The Roman slave Pseudolus begins by assuring us there will be "Comedy Tonight" (**Musical Example 43**). He identifies the owners of three adjacent homes; on one end is the empty house of Erronius, who is away searching for his children, stolen long ago by pirates. At the far end is Lycus's house (he sells female slaves), and in the center live Senex, Domina, and their son Hero, who own Pseudolus.

Lycus and Domina are headed to the country to visit Domina's mother and to take her a marble bust of Domina. They admonish their slave Hysterium to watch over the teenage Hero, who confides to Pseudolus that he is smitten with a beautiful girl who lives next door. Pseudolus warns Hero that she must certainly be a courtesan if she resides in Lycus's house, but Hero doesn't care. His difficulty is the purchase price, since Hero has nothing except a seashell collection, 20 minae, and of course Pseudolus. Pseudolus realizes that this might be his chance to realize his own dream and promises to find a way to unite Hero with his anonymous love if Hero will grant him his freedom in exchange.

Pseudolus's first ruse is to jingle the bag of 20 minae to sound like a great fortune. Lycus is ever-alert to the sound of money, and one by one he displays his wares. But none of the women is the one Hero wants. Hero then spots his beloved in an upstairs window, but Lycus tells him that the virgin is Philia, newly arrived from Crete, and she has already been purchased by the military captain Miles Gloriosus at a cost of 500 minae. Pseudolus doesn't drop a beat: he sympathetically hopes that the girl will still be alive by the time Miles claims her, since hasn't Lycus heard about that terrible plague in Crete? Lycus is panicked, for the plague could wipe out all his merchandise, so Pseudolus offers to keep Philia in their household until the captain arrives. Hero can't believe his good fortune.

Hysterium lives up to his name when the slave girl arrives at the house, and Pseudolus has to blackmail him—by threatening to reveal Hysterium's collection of erotic pottery—to keep him from heading straight to Domina with the news. Pseudolus then arranges for a boat on which the lovers can escape. But Philia has a moral streak; she is the property of Miles Gloriosus and insists on waiting for him. So Pseudolus decides he will mix a sleeping potion and give it to Philia. Lycus will be told she's dead, and Hero will take the "body" with him on the boat; she won't be awake to protest. But Pseudolus realizes he's an ingredient short; he needs a cup of mare's sweat, so he heads to the market.

Senex soon arrives, having dropped the marble bust and needing to have the nose repaired. Philia, thinking this must be Miles, greets him at the door, crying, "Take me!" Before a delighted Senex can oblige, Pseudolus returns home; trying to find a quick explanation for Philia, he suggests that she's a new maid. Senex happily plans to educate her about housework himself (although he will take her over to Erronius's vacant house for privacy during their lessons). Pseudolus, thinking fast, spills the smelly mare's sweat on Senex. Senex decides he will cleanse himself in Erronius's house, so Pseudolus browbeats Hysterium into standing guard outside, keeping Senex there at all costs.

The unexpected happens: Erronius returns from his long, fruitless search. Hysterium quickly declares that Erronius's house is now haunted, so he must walk seven times around Rome's seven hills to exorcise the ghosts. When Senex emerges from the house, he encounters Hero, and then Philia, and the father and son each wonder about the other's interest in the beautiful girl. But worse is to come: Captain Miles Gloriosus has arrived to claim Philia. Lycus is beside himself with anxiety, so Pseudolus offers to impersonate the slave dealer. The false Lycus tries to blandish Miles with other exotic slaves, but Miles is uninterested. Only one thing can save Pseudolus now—and that is the intermission.

Of course, the intermission has only delayed the inevitable. Pseudolus persuades Miles to wait in Senex's house (pretending it's Lycus's home) while waiting for Philia. Senex, too, back in Erronius's house, awaits Philia. Hysterium has finished making the sleeping potion for Pseudolus, but Pseudolus cannot get Philia to partake; she abstains from strong beverages. Pseudolus has a scheme, but needs a body, so he leaves to find one elsewhere.

Domina returns home to find out what Senex is up to, and Hysterium is anguished with fear that she'll discover even one of the many plots afoot. She adds to the complexity by dressing as a virgin to spy on her husband. Meanwhile, with somewhat tortured logic, Philia is trying to convince Hero that her submission to Miles will reveal her affection for Hero. Pseudolus returns, having failed to locate a corpse. He decides to dress up Hysterium as the deceased Philia to demonstrate to Miles that his bride is dead. Miles does the proper thing by grieving for the deceased girl and then wants to do more of the right thing by preparing her funeral pyre. Then Miles realizes two things: first, he had just been in Crete, where there was no plague, and second—the corpse isn't dead!

A mad chase ensues, with Erronius—just returned from the hills—joining in. He thinks Hysterium is his long-lost daughter, while Miles claims her (him) as his bride, and Senex believes her (him) to be the maid. In desperation, Hysterium yanks off his blond wig. Very soon, Pseudolus is revealed as author of the web of lies, so he must die by his own hand. Implying that he will take hemlock, he orders Hysterium to fetch the potion prepared earlier. Instead, Hysterium brings an aphrodisiac he had brewed for Senex. Fortunately for Pseudolus, the effects of the potion don't last *too* long.

The inevitable can be put off no longer, so Philia is handed over to Miles. A sorrowful Erronius mumbles about his poor lost children and a ring depicting a gaggle of geese. This brings Miles up short—what's this about geese? Is the ring anything like the ring *he* owns? It seems that Miles is Erronius's long-lost son. Now Philia asks: How many geese are in a gaggle? Does *her* ring represent the same thing? Since she is revealed to be the equally long-lost daughter, everyone realizes that it is out of the question for her to be Miles's bride—since she is his sister—and so Philia and Hero are joyfully reunited. Pseudolus wins his longed-for freedom, and all agree that it *has* been a "Comedy Tonight."

MUSICAL EXAMPLE 43

A FUNNY THING HAPPENED ON THE WAY TO THE FORUM
STEPHEN SONDHEIM/STEPHEN SONDHEIM, 1962

"Comedy Tonight"

Prologus

1   Something familiar, something peculiar, something for everyone, a comedy tonight!
2   Something appealing, something appalling, something for everyone, a comedy tonight!
3   Nothing with kings, nothing with crowns, bring on the lovers, liars and clowns!
4   Old situations, new complications, nothing portentous or polite.
Tragedy tomorrow, comedy tonight!
5   Something familiar, something peculiar, something for everyone, a comedy tonight!
Something appealing, something appalling, something for everyone, a comedy tonight!

[Interlude]

Proteans
Tragedy tomorrow, comedy tonight!

Prologus

6   Something convulsive, something repulsive, something for everyone,

Prologus and Proteans
A comedy tonight!
Prologus
Something esthetic,
Proteans
Something frenetic,
Prologus
Something for everyone,
Prologus and Proteans
A comedy tonight!
Proteans
Nothing with Gods, nothing with Fate,
Prologus
Weighty affairs will just have to wait.
Proteans
Nothing that's formal,
Prologus
Nothing that's normal,
Prologus and Proteans
No recitations to recite! Open up the curtain,

[Interlude]

Comedy tonight!

[Dialogue]

Prologus
7   Something for everyone, a comedy tonight.

[Dialogue]

Prologus
8   Something erratic, something dramatic, something for everyone, a comedy tonight!
Frenzy and frolic, strictly symbolic, something for everyone, a comedy tonight!

[Dialogue]

Anything you ask for . . . Comedy tonight!

[Dialogue]

Prologus and Proteans
9   Something familiar, something peculiar, something for everybody, comedy tonight!
Something that's gaudy, something's that's bawdy,
Prologus
Something for everybawdy,
Prologus and Proteans
Comedy tonight!
Miles
Nothing that's grim,
Domina
Nothing that's Greek.
Prologus
She plays "Medea" later this week!
Prologus and Proteans
Stunning surprises, cunning disguises, Hundreds of actors out of sight!
Erronius
10   Pantaloons and tunics,
Senex
Courtesans and eunuchs,
Domina
Funerals and chases,

Lycus
Baritones and basses,
Philia
Panderers,
Hero
Philanderers,
Hysterium
Cupidity,
Miles
Timidity,
Lycus
Mistakes,
Erronius
Fakes,
Philia
Rhymes,
Domina
Mimes,
Prologus
Tumblers, grumblers, fumblers, bumblers,
All
No royal curse, no Trojan horse, and a happy ending, of course!
Goodness and badness, man in his madness, this time, it all turns out all right!
All (except Prologus)
Tragedy tomorrow,
All
Comedy tonight!

[shouted]

One, Two, Three!

Chapter 34
New Partnerships: Bock and Harnick

Sheldon Harnick (b. 1924) started his career in musical theater by writing both the music and lyrics to his songs. **Jerry Bock** (Jerrold, b. 1928) did the same. By the time the two men met each other in 1956, however, each had drifted toward concentrating on his greatest strength; Bock had been composing tunes, while Harnick recalls taking Yip Harburg's advice: that he "could facilitate his career by writing with other composers." During their heyday, not only would they create a show that set a new Broadway long-run record, but another collaboration would also win the Pulitzer Prize for Drama.

Harnick used his writing ability to entertain the troops during his three years in the army and continued writing for entertainers while in college. When he made the move to New York, he soon was contributing numbers to various Broadway and off-Broadway productions—but Harnick was open to linking up with other composers. At one point, Harnick was asked to come help doctor a show, and although the show closed after 21 performances, a member of the cast, the actor Jack Cassidy, introduced Harnick to Jerry Bock.

Bock followed a somewhat different path to Broadway. He wrote for Camp Tamiment, the same Pennsylvania resort that later saw the birth of *Once Upon a Mattress*. With Larry Holofcener, Bock wrote a star vehicle for Sammy Davis, Jr., giving them their first moderate success on Broadway. It would also be their last success, for Bock met Harnick some three months later. As with Andrew Lloyd Webber and Tim Rice a decade afterwards, one of Bock and Harnick's earliest musicals was aimed at children, written for the puppeteer Bil Baird. Their first Broadway endeavor had only a short run, but it was their first collaboration with Joseph Stein, and it also brought them to the attention of Hal Prince.

Prince believed that Bock and Harnick were the right songwriters for his musical, *Fiorello!*, even though he made them prove themselves by writing several songs on speculation before he gave them the job. *Fiorello!* debuted in November 1959, a week after *The Sound of Music*. Although *Fiorello!* was only Bock and Harnick's second Broadway collaboration—while *The Sound of Music* was the venerable Rodgers and Hammerstein's final endeavor—the two shows tied for the Best Musical Tony. Moreover, the Pulitzer committee named *Fiorello!* the year's best drama—only the third time a musical had earned that designation.

Virtually the same creative team reassembled for *Tenderloin* (1960), yet *Tenderloin* failed to find an audience, even though Bock and Harnick's score is considered by some to be even better than *Fiorello!* Ken Mandelbaum called it "one of the finest scores of any unsuccessful musical," adding that it was "a classic example of a flop whose cast album leads people to believe that the show must have been sensational." Perhaps *Tenderloin*, also set in New York, felt too much like a *Fiorello!* derivative.

Undaunted, Prince worked with Bock and Harnick again on **She Loves Me**, this time making a debut as a director as well as producing. Their librettist was the novice **Joe Masteroff** (b. 1919), who based his libretto on the comedy *Illatszertár (Parfumerie)* by the Hungarian playwright Miklos Laszlo. Hollywood has turned to the play several times: *The Shop Around the Corner* (1940), *In the Good Old Summertime* (1949), and *You've Got Mail* (1998), with Tom Hanks and Meg Ryan. However, Masteroff's version is closest to the Hungarian original (see the **Plot Summary**).

Compared to most Broadway shows of its day, *She Loves Me* is an intimate musical, requiring only a small cast of seven principals plus a chorus to portray various customers and restaurant diners. The production was crammed full of music—more than two dozen tunes—and needed to have some 40 minutes cut before its 1963 opening. Harnick had never found it easy to write love songs, wryly observing, "No emotional content can be a fault in a love song." In *She Loves Me*, however, the music fully reflects the characters' exuberant emotions. All of the songs are tightly integrated into the storyline, although a few of them became independent hits. Even the overture is woven into the vocal score, featuring the orchestra only briefly before the characters begin to make their entrances.

Bock and Harnick's light touch is evident in Ilona's comedy song "A Trip to the Library" (**Musical Example 44**), describing the courageous journey she had taken the previous evening. The library was perhaps the most mysterious, exotic destination she could have possibly selected. The musical score reflects that exoticism, imitating the rhythm of a triple-meter Spanish bolero at **1**. Underscoring the humor, the bolero is a hushed, awestruck patter song, averaging six syllables of text per beat.

Ilona reaches a peak of panic at **2**, interrupting the bolero rhythm altogether. But it is her description at **3** of Paul's first words, "Pardon me," that pulls the meter of "A Trip to the Library" to a more comfortable (for Ilona) quadruple meter (even if some gentle ragtime rhythms are heard during the phrases *clearly respectable* and *thickly bespectacled*). Rhythm contributes to the humor of this narrative ballad at several points; Ilona hesitates before singing words such as *Ma'am* at **5**, reflecting her surprise at being treated—for once in her life—like a lady. During the vocal coda at **8**, Ilona replaces "someone I dimly recall" (Kodály) with "my optometrist Paul." "A Trip to the Library" is a charming illustration of a character song.

Most critics were delighted; John Chapman described *She Loves Me* as "so charming, so deft, so light, and so right that it makes all the other music-shows in the big Broadway shops look like clodhoppers." Norman Nadel regarded it as "that rare theatrical jewel, an intimate musical that affectionately enfolds an audience instead of shouting it down." Similarly, Howard Taubman maintained, "A bonbon of a musical has been put on display, and it should delight who knows how many a sweet tooth. *She Loves Me* has been assembled by confectioners. . . . They have found the right ingredients of sugar and raisins and nuts to add to their fluffy dough and have created a taste surprise."

Although several observers regard *She Loves Me* as Bock and Harnick's finest score, audience response did not measure up to the critical accolades. In later years, Prince remained unsure why the show had not been a hit. In retrospect, he still felt it was one of the finest shows he'd done, but he wondered if he had made two mistakes. He put the show in a small theater where even a sold-out house earned barely enough to meet expenses. Moreover, even though Julie Andrews was interested, Prince chose not to delay the opening of *She Loves Me* six months for her to become available. He believed that *She Loves Me* was an **ensemble** show, not dependent on individual stars. "What counts," he said, "is how good the show is." But the name Julie Andrews might have had just the draw that the box office needed. In any event, although Cassidy won a Best Supporting Actor Tony for his role as Kodály, *She Loves Me* closed after 302 performances, a relative failure by contemporary Broadway standards.

In marked contrast, Bock and Harnick's next project with Prince, ***Fiddler on the Roof***, established a new Broadway record—3,242 performances—taking the crown away from *Hello, Dolly!* Bock and Harnick were reunited with **Joseph Stein** (b. 1912), a librettist for their first show. They also worked with Jerome Robbins for the first (and only) time, for Robbins then retired from Broadway for 25 years.

The inspiration for *Fiddler on the Roof* came from the writer Sholem Aleichem, especially the tale of *Tevye's Daughters*. Most outsiders felt that the setting—a poor Jewish village in Czarist Russia shortly before the Revolution—held little promise (see the **Plot Summary**). According to Harnick, Robbins

> *was like the world's greatest district attorney, asking us question after question, probing—"What's the show about?"—and not being satisfied with the glib answers we were giving. We kept saying, "Well, it's about a dairy farmer and his daughters and trying to find husbands for them" . . . I don't know who finally made the discovery that the show was really about the disintegration of a whole way of life, but I do remember that it was a surprise to all of us. And once we found that out—which was pretty exciting—Robbins said, "Well, if it's a show about tradition and its dissolution, then the audience should be told what that tradition is." He wondered how we could do it succinctly. Then he suggested that we create a song that would be a tapestry against which the whole show would play. So we wrote "Tradition" because he insisted on it.*

In his staging of "Tradition," the opening production number, Robbins drew the villagers together into hora-like circular dances. When non-Jewish characters such as the village priest or constable were introduced during the number, they were never drawn into the circle itself, leaving the stage quickly. Robbins then mirrored the circular staging at the end of the show, but broke the circle apart as the villagers started their exodus away from Anatevka, visually demonstrating their disintegration.

Robbins's touch was felt through the whole show. Harnick also remembered,

> *Robbins would say again and again, "Well, if that's what the show is about, why isn't it in this scene? Why isn't it in that scene? Why don't we see it in this character, or that character?" And Jerry's only weapon, if we all ganged up on him and disagreed at a certain point, was to say, "Okay, do it your way. Get a different director"—which was maddening, and yet we had to trust him because he had a total vision. He drove everybody crazy because he had a vision that extended down to the littlest brushstroke in the scenery and the triangle part in the orchestra.*

Robbins was fully aware of the "concept musical" approach to the stage, and by unifying the story as an expression of the breakdown of tradition, he found a metaphor that would resonate with audiences everywhere. As alien as the portrayal of humble Jewish peasants was to urban New Yorkers, audiences

Golde and Tevye in *Fiddler on the Roof*
Getty Images Inc. - Hulton Archive Photo.

had no problem in sympathizing with a father whose children seemed determined to flout his values, and—especially at the time of *Fiddler*'s 1964 opening in the heart of the United States–Soviet Union Cold War era—audiences also related to Tevye's feeling that the outside world was falling apart.

The working title was originally *Tevye*, but stage designer Boris Aronson designed backdrops that were reminiscent of the painter Marc Chagall, who several times incorporated precariously balanced fiddlers in his paintings—inspiring the final title. Like Robbins's "Tradition" staging, Aronson's sets also portrayed curves and circles, so the framework surrounding the actors reflected the show's central theme. It could be argued that a similar circular motion is at work in "Do You Love Me?" (**Musical Example 45**), for Tevye keeps coming around, again and again, to the title's question: does Golde love him? The structure of the duet is a straightforward song form of *a-a-b-a'* (corresponding to **1**, **2**, **3**, and **4**). A brief vocal coda at **5** is the only time during the duet when the couple sing simultaneously, at first in unison, and then—perhaps symbolically—in harmony for the final phrase of text, "It's nice to know."

This simple, conversational duet was not easy to craft, according to Harnick, who said, "It took about a week of just wandering around every day trying to get another two lines and another two lines." *Fiddler* was already on its tryout tour, so Harnick at last handed over the dialogue he'd produced, telling Bock, "Do the best you can with it. I'll change anything if you can come up with a tune." To Harnick's relief, Bock found a way to set the text that seemed coherent to them both, so they showed it to Stein. Stein later said, "I remember Sheldon coming to my hotel room and reading the lyric of 'Do You Love Me?' He asked me what I thought of it. I could have hugged him. I think I did."

Harnick was initially somewhat blasé about the song, saying, "It was an assignment. It was something that had to be done, so we did it. We put it into rehearsal, and it worked, so that was a relief. And we went on to solve whatever the next problem was." But, watching the show two or three nights later, Harnick found himself crying after the number. Asking himself, "Why am I crying? Why am I crying?" he realized that the duet represented the kind of conversation he wished his own parents were capable of having. The seeming "authenticity" of the dialogue is part of the power of "Do You Love Me?" Thomas Hischak suggests that Tevye and Golde "are uncomfortable with abstract ideas; the humor comes from practical people trying to express the impractical notion of love." Richard Kislan considers "Do You Love Me?" to be a charm song, explaining, "Most successful charm songs feature an optimistic content that captivates us, makes us feel good and warm inside. Somewhere between romantic love and outright laughter lives an attitude of deep and secret smiles. The charm song liberates that smile."

At the same time, Bock and Harnick were demonstrating their customary ability to illuminate character in "Do You Love Me?" Like Poppea in Chapter 1, "The Birth of Staged Music," Tevye is doggedly persistent in asking over and over again until he gets the response he wants. Golde is impatient, busy with her daily labors, but she eventually gets caught up by memories of the past and softens enough to acknowledge

brusquely that she "supposes" she loves Tevye. With this expert depiction of a bickering couple's restrained expression of their deep feelings for each other, Tevye and Golde seem to us to be real people with real emotions.

Unlike *She Loves Me*, this time reviewers and audiences agreed, as did the New York Drama Critics' Circle and the American Theatre Wing when it came time to issue Best Musical Awards. Tonys also went to Bock, Harnick, Prince, Stein, Robbins (both for directing and for his choreography), Aronson, Patricia Zipprodt (for her costume designs), and to Zero Mostel and Maria Karnilova for their portrayals of Tevye and Golde. Some critics wondered if there was too much self-pity in the story. Other writers called *Fiddler* "one of the great works of the American musical theatre" and "an integrated achievement of uncommon quality." The London production ran 2,030 performances, and *Fiddler on the Roof* has gone on to be successful around the world. In Japan, an audience member was surprised that the show had been a success in America. Asked why, he explained, "Well, the story is so Japanese"—thereby proving Robbins's conviction that regard for tradition is a universal concern. Under Robbins's leadership, the creators of *Fiddler on the Roof* had crafted one of Broadway's finest shows.

Bock and Harnick switched gears entirely for their next presentation, *The Apple Tree* (1966). This set of three one-act musicals was an unusual project, spanning a time frame from the Biblical Garden of Eden to the present day. Their subsequent Broadway show, *The Rothschilds* (1970), was a difficult experience that led to the dissolution of Bock and Harnick's partnership. Since then, for the most part, their subsequent individual endeavors have been seen in venues other than Broadway. One more collaboration was in store, however: Bock and Harnick reunited to write an additional song, "Topsy-Turvy," for the 2004 Broadway revival of *Fiddler on the Roof*. The two men can look back with much pride at their impressive joint legacy: seven musicals in 12 years' time, along with multiple Tonys, their Drama Critics' Circle Award, and of course that rare Pulitzer Prize.

FURTHER READING

Alpert, Hollis. *Broadway: 125 Years of American Musical Theatre*. New York: Little, Brown, 1991.

Altman, Richard, with Mervyn Kaufman. *The Making of a Musical: Fiddler on the Roof*. New York: Crown, 1971.

Guernsey, Otis L., Jr., ed. *Broadway Song & Story: Playwrights/Lyricists/Composers Discuss Their Hits*. New York: Dodd, Mead, 1985.

Green, Stanley. *The World of Musical Comedy*. Third edition, revised and enlarged. New York: A. S. Barnes & Company, 1974.

Hischak, Thomas S. *Word Crazy: Broadway Lyricists from Cohan to Sondheim*. New York: Praeger, 1991.

Ilson, Carol. *Harold Prince From* Pajama Game *to* Phantom of the Opera. Ann Arbor: U.M.I. Research Press, 1989.

Kasha, Al, and Joel Hirschhorn. *Notes on Broadway: Conversations with the Great Songwriters*. Chicago: Contemporary Books, Inc., 1985.

Kislan, Richard. *The Musical: A Look at the American Musical Theater*. New, revised, expanded edition. New York and London: Applause Books, 1995.

Mandelbaum, Ken. *Not Since Carrie: Forty Years of Broadway Musical Flops*. New York: St. Martin's, 1991.

Mordden, Ethan. *Open a New Window: The Broadway Musical in the 1960s*. New York: Palgrave, 2001.

Prince, Hal. *Contradictions: Notes on Twenty-Six Years in the Theatre*. New York: Dodd, Mead, 1974.

PLOT SUMMARY: *SHE LOVES ME*

"Me" is Georg Nowack, an employee at Maraczek's parfumerie in Budapest, but who is "She"? Georg doesn't know; she is a pen pal. His fellow clerks are Ladislav Sipos, Ilona Ritter, and the suave Steve Kodály. Arpád the messenger boy notices that Ilona is wearing the same dress she wore the day before, indicating that she'd spent the night (again) with Kodály. Maraczek would like to see them sell some of the musical cigarette boxes he has overbought. Maraczek has no openings for clerks, but he creates one when Amalia Balash manages to sell one of the white-elephant boxes.

The seasons pass, with Georg happily writing to his unknown "dear friend." Things are less comfortable at work. He and Amalia have never gotten along, and now Ilona has quarreled with Kodály, too. Even Maraczek is grumpy; he seems particularly annoyed by Georg, who has no idea why his boss is irritated with him. Georg's long-awaited encounter with his pen pal is to take place that evening. He doesn't notice that Amalia is dressed up, but Ilona does, and she asks Amalia about her sweetheart. Amalia confesses she has never met him—they've simply been long-term pen pals.

No one is happy about Maraczek's sudden decision that the employees shall decorate for Christmas tonight. The decorating takes place with very little holiday spirit, and soon, goaded by Maraczek, Georg quits. Later that evening, Amalia sits at a small table in a café. Back at the parfumerie, Kodály woos Ilona, then drops her. Outraged, Ilona vows not to fall for Kodály again. Meanwhile, Sipos has to insist that Georg go to the restaurant for the planned rendezvous; Georg wants to chicken out.

A private detective arrives at the empty shop. Mrs. Maraczek, it turns out, is having an affair with an employee—but it is with Kodály, not Georg. Maraczek retreats into his office, realizing he had suspected the wrong clerk. Arpád—who had been in the stockroom—runs forward shouting, just as a shot rings out. Meanwhile, at the café, Sipos and Georg realize that Amalia must be the pen pal. Sipos orders Georg to go speak to her. Amalia is appalled, since she fears he will frighten away her date; at last she screams in frustration, so Georg leaves. She waits and waits, but her "dear friend" never arrives.

While Maraczek is hospitalized with a gunshot wound, he agrees to let Arpád be a sales clerk. Georg is rehired, but Amalia has called in sick. Georg goes to visit her, bringing her ice cream, and he leads her to believe that her pen pal is a stout older man. After he leaves, Amalia tries to write to her "dear friend," but she is continually interrupted by thoughts of Georg.

At the parfumerie, Ilona has good news, too. The night before, she had bravely made "A Trip to the Library" (**Musical Example 44**), where she met a *nice* man for once. The employees have no time to waste, however, for Christmas is coming. Finally, on Christmas Eve, Amalia has planned another rendezvous with her "dear friend." She and Georg are now cordial, and gradually the truth comes out: Georg is the dear friend and now they can truly celebrate Christmas.

PLOT SUMMARY: *FIDDLER ON THE ROOF*

What is a fiddler on the roof? He symbolizes the residents of the small Russian village of Anatevka in 1905, who try to sustain their Jewish traditions but run the risk of falling from their precarious balance because of the changing world all around them. The impoverished milkman Tevye has little time to worry about societal changes, for he and his wife Golde have five daughters, and three of them are of marriageable age. The eldest daughter, Tzeitel, warns her sisters about the prospects in store for them all, since their poor family is unable to provide them with dowries. But Yente, the local matchmaker, has been hard at work, and she has found a husband for Tzeitel: the butcher (and widower) Lazar Wolf.

Tevye, focused on his lame horse, ignores the news that Jews in distant villages have been evicted, but Perchik is appalled. Tevye takes pity on the penniless student, though, inviting him home for the Sabbath. Afterwards, Golde sends Tevye to see Lazar Wolf. Tevye thinks that Lazar Wolf wants Tevye's new milk cow, so a slightly disjointed conversation ensues. When the men straighten out the confusion, Tevye knows that this would be a good match for Tzeitel, even though he's not crazy about the man. As Tevye leaves the tavern, the constable pulls him aside, warning Tevye that he has been ordered to conduct some anti-Jewish demonstrations; he will try to keep them low-key. Tevye wonders why God sends him such good news and such bad tidings on the same day.

Perchik has been engaging Tevye's second daughter, Hodel, in political debate and daring her to learn current dance steps. But Tevye's preoccupied by Tzeitel right now; she says she loves her childhood playmate Motel. Tevye agrees to their marriage, but he now has a problem: How can he tell Golde that Tzeitel will marry a poor tailor rather than a wealthy butcher? Inspired, Tevye wakes Golde up in the night, telling her that he dreamed Golde's grandmother insisted that Tzeitel marry Motel—and that Lazar Wolf's first wife threatened to strangle the new bride. Golde, deeply superstitious, decides that if the spirits of their ancestors delivered these warnings, she and Tevye will have to comply.

At the wedding, Tevye and Golde remember when the bride and groom were only small children. Lazar Wolf is aggrieved over the broken engagement to Tzeitel, but the villagers' attention is soon drawn away to the spectacle of Perchik inciting Hodel to cross the customary barrier that separates the men and women. The two young rebels start to dance together in defiance of tradition. Tevye makes a choice; rather than making a bigger scene by separating the two, he condones their behavior by pulling Golde to the dance floor also. The newlyweds soon join in as well. This outrages some of the older villagers, but the remaining wedding guests are delighted, and the merriment increases—until a band of Russians burst in, smashing furniture and wedding gifts left and right. The threatened "anti-Jewish demonstration" has made its ugly appearance, and Perchik is beaten to the ground for resisting.

Perchik feels he will not be able to change events in the backwater of Anatevka, so he tells Hodel he must go to Kiev. She promises to consider herself engaged to him. They go to tell Tevye, but he will not give his permission for Hodel to marry a man who is so far away. The young people shock him by telling him that they don't want his permission, only his blessing. Reluctantly, he agrees to bless their union, since their love is so strong. He thinks about his own arranged marriage to Golde, remembering how his parents had assured him that he and his bride would grow to love each other. Curious to know if his parents' prediction has come true, he goes to Golde and asks her, "Do You Love Me?" (**Musical Example 45**). Golde is impatient, but at last admits that she does indeed love Tevye.

Although this realization is a comfort, it doesn't stop the escalating pressures of the outside world. One rumor is true: Perchik has been arrested and sent to Siberia. Hodel takes a bold step; she joins him there. The family's sorrow over her departure is partly allayed by the joy over Motel and Tzeitel's new arrival: a long-awaited sewing machine. It is now time for the third daughter, Chava, to shatter tradition even more; she tells her father that she loves Fyedka. To Tevye, this romance is unthinkable, for Fyedka is a Christian Russian. Tevye absolutely cannot condone their love. Chava marries Fyedka all the same, but Tevye holds firm: his little "Chavaleh" is now dead to him. But Tevye is about to lose even more; the pogroms that are driving Jews from their homes are coming too close to Anatevka, and Tevye and the other villagers realize it's time to go. For Tevye and Golde, the path will lead to America, where they have relatives. Chava and her husband have come to say goodbye, and although Tevye cannot bring himself to address Chava directly, he turns to Tzeitel and tells *her*, "God be with you." Tzeitel, realizing that Tevye is directing the blessing toward Chava, repeats her father's words to her sister. Tevye gestures for the fiddler to follow along; even in the new world, Tevye will uphold tradition as best he can.

MUSICAL EXAMPLE 44

SHE LOVES ME
JERRY BOCK/SHELDON HARNICK, 1963
"A Trip to the Library"

Ilona

1   And suddenly all of my confidence dribbled away with a pitiful plop.
My head was beginning to swim and my forehead was covered with cold perspiration.
I started to reach for a book and my hand automatic'lly came to a stop.
I don't know how long I stood frozen, a victim of panic and mortification.

2   Oh, how I wanted to flee, when a kindly voice, a gentle voice whispered,

3   "Pardon me."

4   And there was this dear, sweet, clearly respectable, thickly bespectacled man
Who stood by my side and quietly said to me,

5   "Ma'am.
Don't mean to intrude but I was just wondering
Are you in need of some help?" I said, "No . . . Yes, I am!"
The next thing I know I'm sipping hot choc'late and telling my troubles to Paul,
Whose tender brown eyes kept sending compassionate looks.
A trip to the library has made a new girl of me
For suddenly I can see the magic of books.

6   I have to admit in the back of my mind, I was praying he wouldn't get fresh.
And all of the while I was wondering why an illiterate girl should attract him.
Then all of a sudden he said that I couldn't go wrong with "The Way of All Flesh."
Of course, it's a novel but I didn't know or I certainly wouldn't have smacked him.
Well, he gave me a smile that I couldn't resist
And I knew at once how much I liked this optometrist.
You know what this dear, sweet, slightly bespectacled gentleman said to me next?
He said he could solve this problem of mine. I said, "How?"
He said if I'd like, he'd willingly read to me some of his favorite things.
I said, "When?" He said, "Now."
His novel approach seemed highly suspicious and possibly dangerous too.
I told myself wait, think, dare you go up to his flat?

What happens if things go wrong? It's obvious he's quite strong.
He read to me all night long. Now how about that?

7   It's hard to believe how truly domestic and happily hopeful I feel.
I picture my Paul there reading aloud as I cook.
As long as he's there to read, there's quite a good chance, indeed,
A chance that I'll never need to open a book!

8   Unlike someone else, someone I dimly recall,
I know he'll only have eyes for me, my optometrist, Paul.

MUSICAL EXAMPLE 45

FIDDLER ON THE ROOF
JERRY BOCK/SHELDON HARNICK, 1964
"Do You Love Me?"

Tevye

Golde

1   Do you love me?

Do I *what*?

Do you love me?

Do I love you?! With our daughters getting married,
and this trouble in the town,
You're upset, you're worn out, go inside,
Go lie down. Maybe it's indigestion.

Golde, I'm asking you a question.
2   Do you love me?

You're a fool!

I know—But do you love me?

Do I love you?

Well?

For twenty-five years I've washed your clothes,
cooked your meals, cleaned your house,
Given you children, milked the cow.
After twenty-five years, why talk about love right now?

3   Golde, the first time I met you
was on our wedding day. I was scared.

I was shy.

I was nervous.

So was I.

But my father and mother said we'd learn to
love each other, and now I'm asking, Golde,
Do you love me?

4

I'm your wife.

I know, But do you love me?

Do I love him?

Well?

For twenty-five years I've lived with him,
fought with him, starved with him,
Twenty-five years my bed is his.
If that's not love, what is?

Then you love me?

I suppose I do.

And I suppose I love you too.

Both

5   It doesn't change a thing, but even so, after twenty-five years it's nice to know.

Chapter 35
New Partnerships: Kander and Ebb

If you were to combine the steadfast partnership of Rodgers and Hammerstein with the quixotic interest in theatrical experimentation that characterizes Stephen Sondheim, you might create the team of **John Kander** (b. 1927) and **Fred Ebb** (b. 1932). Their shows have been anything but formulaic, and even with some offbeat and dark topics, Kander and Ebb have created a number of hit musicals. Like the works of Sondheim, their shows are never "easy," and also like Sondheim, they are expert at crafting music that serves the character and the situation. At the same time, they've also seen some of their tunes attain hit status. Yet, despite these commercial successes, their team has never attained the household-name familiarity enjoyed by Rodgers's two partnerships or even that of Lerner and Loewe.

Like more and more theater composers, Kander underwent considerable formal education in music, earning a master's degree in 1953. Much of his practical training came from stints as a pianist and as a dance-music arranger. The year 1962 was a big year for Kander; he composed for Broadway for the first time, and he met Ebb, who had also been building up a small array of Broadway experiences. Wasting no time, the two men sat right down and started writing songs; two numbers became hits after Sandy Stewart and Barbra Streisand released recordings. The new team was on its way.

Kander and Ebb's first joint Broadway effort debuted in 1965, featuring a young Liza Minnelli. They labored very hard to please Minnelli; Ebb recalled, "We worked our [tails] off—twenty songs for one situation. I had no ego. It was 'Which do you like?'" *Flora, the Red Menace* didn't last long, but the show was recorded just after its premiere, giving Kander and Ebb their first original cast album.

Hal Prince had produced *Flora*, and he next wanted the team to write the score for *Cabaret*. A bleak tale of decadence and despair set in Berlin between the two world wars, the subject matter of *Cabaret* did not seem to offer much promise (see the **Plot Summary**), but Kander and Ebb allowed themselves to be caught up in Prince's enthusiasm. Kander listened to as much German music of the era—when "gaiety border[ed] on hysteria," as one observer put it—as he could find. Kurt Weill had written *The Threepenny Opera* (1928) in those years, so it was perhaps inevitable that Kander would be accused of writing "watered-down Weill"—but Weill's widow, Lotte Lenya (who played Fräulein Schneider in *Cabaret*), defended Kander. She told him, "No, no, darling. It is not Weill. It is not Kurt. When I walk out on stage and sing those songs, it is *Berlin*."

The basis of *Cabaret* was Christopher Isherwood's autobiographical *Berlin Stories*, comprised of two novellas. After adaptation as a 1951 play titled *I Am a Camera*, the work had been turned into a 1955 film, which then led several people to see "musical potential" in the work. A bit of a race ensued, with Hal Prince winning the performance rights before anyone else. Various librettists were hard at work adapting the story, but Prince felt that the drawback to all their approaches was that they were creating star vehicles, and Prince didn't think that centering the entire musical on the cabaret singer Sally Bowles was the right way to go. He felt the right hook for the show would be to draw parallels between the troubled Berlin of the 1930s and the equally troubled world of the 1960s. Joe Masteroff had worked with Prince on *She Loves Me*; Prince trusted Masteroff to write a libretto with the spirit he wanted.

The process was by no means easy from that point. Some 15 songs appear in *Cabaret*, but Kander and Ebb wrote 47 songs along the way. Ebb explained, "The narrative kept shifting, and there were many more scenes that were seriously considered that were never done. Also, characters were being added. The whole [Schneider–Schultz] relationship came later, I think." Kander and Ebb's working method is different from most other songwriters; as Kander told an interviewer, "We work in the same room at the same time." Kander added that they had written one of *Cabaret*'s songs on the telephone, "but it was like being in the same room." Part of the frequent rewriting in the story stemmed from Prince's uncertainty about how explicit the parallels should be between the past and the present. He required the entire company of performers to read newspaper accounts of the tensions in the South as African Americans struggled for civil rights. Prince wanted to prove that the tolerance of fascism that led to legalized anti-Semitism in Germany *could* happen in the United States. The incorporation of the subplot of the timid love affair between Schneider and Schultz allowed the gentlest of characters to serve as the target of some of the show's most hateful gestures.

By the end, *Cabaret* became a three-layered musical. As in a traditional book musical, the characters sing about their feelings, such as their delight in the simple gift of a pineapple, and there are also diegetic numbers set in the Kit Kat Klub, since people sing and dance in "real" cabaret shows. In the course of the musical, however, it becomes clear that the cabaret songs *also* are commentaries upon the events of the book musical, adding a second layer of perception to the show. For example, the Master of Ceremonies sings "Willkommen" while Cliff's train is arriving in Berlin. As Schneider grows increasingly fearful about her engagement to a Jew, the Master of Ceremonies presents a cruel mockery of her dilemma in "If You Could See Her Through My Eyes," for he lets a gorilla represent the increasingly despised Jews. Of *course* a human couldn't truly love a gorilla, and the Emcee persuades us to believe that a person couldn't truly love a Jew, either—a disturbing insight into Nazi anti-Semitic mentality. (When Bob Fosse directed the 1972 film version of *Cabaret*, he eliminated the nondiegetic numbers—the book songs—so that almost all the singing took place only in the Kit Kat Klub. Nevertheless, the cabaret numbers continued to underscore the events unfolding in the drama.)

The third dimension to *Cabaret* was not in evidence until scenery designer Boris Aronson revealed his stage sets. Aronson clearly understood Prince's central concern that *Cabaret* should convey the uneasy similarity between those who sat watching—without protest—the Nazi party's rise to power and those who were passively watching the civil rights struggles of the present day. Aronson mounted a huge mirror above the stage, tilted not only to give a distorted reflection of the grotesque cabaret performances, but so that it reflected the real audience watching the musical. In this way, theatergoers became part of the story; they saw themselves in attendance at the sordid little Kit Kat Klub, thereby implicitly condoning the actions they saw taking place. Prince was delighted with the mirror, observing, "It cast an additional, uneasy metaphor over the evening."

A similar uneasy subtext is at work in "Tomorrow Belongs to Me" (**Musical Example 46**), sung in the nightclub just after Schneider and Schultz have gotten engaged and are dreaming of their future. A waiter begins singing the triple-meter song alone at **1**, and since he has no accompaniment, the texture is monophonic. Moreover, he is singing **a cappella**. The term means "in the chapel (or church) style," since it was long thought (erroneously) that early religious vocal music was sung without instrumental accompaniment. At **2**, the other waiters start to hum. Their accompaniment changes the texture to homophony—but the song is still a cappella, for it is only voices, not instruments, that are heard.

At **3**, which is the second verse of this strophic song, the male chorus stops its *hums* and *oohs* and switches to singing *four-part harmony*. This harmonization enriches the sound, making the song sound much like a sacred chorale. Because the harmonization merely supports the main melody, the texture is still homophonic, and the continued absence of instruments means the song is still a cappella.

Section **4** is yet another verse of the same strophic melody, but two things change: instruments gradually start to play (ending the a cappella section), and the voices divide up to create a different texture. The upper voices sing the main melody, starting at **4**, while at **5**, the lower voices (and soon the Master of Ceremonies) start to echo each line, creating imitative polyphony. All the voices join together briefly at **6**, but at **7** the instruments drop out and a short vocal coda of imitative polyphony begins, repeatedly echoing the title line of the song in successive voices, starting with the highest and ending with the lowest. The overall structure of the song is diagrammed in **Figure 35–1**.

As Figure 35–1 demonstrates, Kander uses skillful scoring to keep this strophic song interesting. The coda is particularly eerie, sounding like waves of voices marching forward with their message that, indeed, tomorrow belongs to them; they fervently believe in the coming "Reich of a thousand years" promised by Adolf Hitler. Ebb's deceptively simple and sentimental lyrics are transformed by their musical setting, and the song becomes a chilling foreshadowing of the world war to come. It is frightening to realize that the scrubbed and wholesome singers are eagerly anticipating the political and social upheavals that will later be known as the Holocaust.

The audience watches themselves watching *Cabaret*
Museum of the City of New York.

Section	Form	Texture and Medium
1	*a* (1)	monophony → homophony, sung a cappella
3	*a* (2)	homophony in four-part harmony, sung a cappella
4	*a* (3)	imitative polyphony with instrumental accompaniment
7	coda	imitative polyphony, sung a cappella

Figure 35–1

Despite the sobering context and unhappy resolution to the intertwining stories within *Cabaret*, the show was a solid success after its 1966 opening. In fact, tickets sold so briskly that Prince moved *Cabaret* to a larger theater not once but twice for a 1,166-performance run. *Cabaret* walked away with the New York Drama Critics' Circle Award and the Tony Award for Best Musical, while Tonys were also earned by Kander and Ebb, Harold Prince (both as producer and as director), Ronald Field (choreographer), Joel Grey (supporting actor), Peg Murray (supporting actress), Boris Aronson, and Patricia Zipprodt (costume designer).

Ironically enough, certain elements of *Cabaret* were criticized by some reviewers and singled out for praise by others. Richard Watts, Jr., wrote, "It is the glory of *Cabaret* that it can upset you while it gives theatrical satisfaction." Jill Haworth, playing Sally, came under the most critical fire, but in fairness, hers was the most difficult role. She was asked to represent a mediocre singer-dancer who is, at the same time, at the heart of the story. It is a very awkward line to tread: trying to depict a mesmerizing personality who is *not* a good performer. Minnelli, playing Sally in the film, faced the same problem; she seems too talented to be stuck in a backwater like the Kit Kat Klub. Nevertheless, Minnelli won an Oscar, one of eight Academy Awards given to the film. (By winning an Oscar for his direction, Fosse became the only person to win a Tony, an Emmy, and an Oscar in the same year; in 1973, he also won a Tony Award for *Pippin* and an Emmy for a Liza Minnelli television special.)

Prince did make a concession after *Cabaret* had opened. A public outcry grew over the line that claimed the gorilla "wouldn't look Jewish at all," so Prince had the Emcee say, "She isn't a *meeskite* [Yiddish for ugly person] at all." (Joel Grey, playing the Emcee, would conveniently "forget" the replacement line on occasion, especially when distinguished or influential visitors were in the audience.)

Post-*Cabaret* expectations were high for Kander and Ebb, so their next show came as a disappointment; it wasn't that *The Happy Time* (1968) was a *bad* show; it simply didn't have the hard-edged bite of *Cabaret*. Sadly, the show set a dismaying record by being the first to lose a million dollars. Their subsequent show, *Zorbá* (1968), also lost money, despite setting a new record of $15 for the most expensive seats. Like *Pal Joey* (1940), however, *Zorbá* was to come back even stronger in a revival, to the extent that it is now considered to be one of Kander and Ebb's successes. No such luck was in store for Kander and Ebb's next effort, which closed after a scant 36 performances.

The string of failures must have been daunting, but Kander and Ebb were back on Broadway in 1975 with a score for *Chicago*. The genesis of this show reached as far back as 1920, when a constitutional amendment made alcohol illegal, launching the Prohibition era. The not-too-surprising consequence of this legislation was the emergence of a huge secret system for obtaining liquor, often through speakeasies, where people like Helen Morgan had performed. It's been estimated that in 1929, there were between 35,000 and 100,000 speakeasies in New York City alone. The management of this illegal activity quickly became big business, and it soon became a focus of organized crime. Few cities were more infamous for their "mob" figures than Chicago, home of Al Capone.

Chicago, in 1920, was famed for other things as well. It was a major hub on the vaudeville circuit, the itinerant entertainment that still thrived in the United States. In 1919, there were some 900 vaudeville theaters operating around the country. This number would shrink to just one surviving hall by 1931—the rest would be done in by radio, the growing moving picture industry, and of course the Great Depression. Besides speakeasies and vaudeville, 1920s Chicago had another real-life factor to contribute to the 1975 stage musical. In 1924, a murderess named Beulah Annan was highlighted in a spectacular trial; two years later, in 1926, Maurine Dallas Watkins wrote a play based on the infamous case, which she titled *Chicago*. A film version was made in 1942, called *Roxie Hart*. Sometime during the 1950s, the actress and dancer Gwen Verdon saw the movie and thought, "This would make a great musical." So, she began to pester Watkins for permission to adapt the play.

Verdon, as it turned out, wasn't the only one with this idea. For years, Watkins had refused to allow a musical version. She had grown to hate reading the various requests and had arranged for the Theatre Guild to open her mail. If a letter was yet another petition, Theatre Guild personnel wrote "Roxie Hart Musical" on the envelope, and Watkins then tore it up without fear that she was destroying a royalty check or important correspondence. Watkins went to her grave in 1969, 43 years after writing the play, steadfastly refusing to allow its conversion to a musical. But the executors of her estate felt differently, and Verdon was at last successful in obtaining the rights for a musical adaptation.

Verdon took the play to her friend (and former husband) Bob Fosse. Fosse was intrigued by the *Chicago* idea as well, but stymied as to how to proceed with it. He turned to Kander and Ebb, having gotten to know them when he brought *Cabaret* to the screen. Eventually, Ebb had an inspiration: why not look to vaudeville, the entertainment style that had been so prevalent during the time in which the story is set? The other collaborators quickly agreed to the idea, and the show was at last on its way. There was one more incident, however, that affected the development of *Chicago*: During the very first week of rehearsals, Fosse was rushed to the hospital because of chest pains. It was determined that he needed open-heart surgery—much less routine in 1975 than it is today. Fosse's conception for *Chicago* grew much darker after this brush with death, accounting for much of the sardonic atmosphere that overlays the lighthearted vaudevillian structure (see the **Plot Summary**).

Modern viewers may not realize how prevalent the vaudeville references are in *Chicago*. Nearly every character in the musical is tied to a specific, historical vaudeville performer or style of performance. Velma is modeled on a Manhattan divorcée, Texas Guinan, who ran a number of notorious speakeasies; she was known for her raucous greeting to customers, "Hello, suckers!," which Velma uses to open the second act of *Chicago*. We also learn that Velma had been an acrobat with her sister. Vaudeville shows regularly offered such features—acrobatic routines as well as "sister acts."

Roxie adopts various vaudeville personas in the course of *Chicago*. Her vocal tribute to her ordinary husband is modeled on the queen of the torch-song, Helen Morgan, who used to sing while perched on a piano; Roxie often sits on a piano as well. Later, her lawyer, Billy Flynn, treats Roxie as an empty-headed ventriloquist's dummy. By itself, this is a funny image—the defendant merely a conduit for the slick lawyer's "razzle dazzle," but it is also a nod to the many ventriloquist acts that used to tour the vaudeville circuit. Roxie's "Me and My Baby" is a salute to Eddie Cantor; Roxie is often costumed to look like him, too, with pants that are a little too short, white socks, and a bow tie.

Billy makes his entrance by asking, "Is everybody here? Is everybody ready?" These questions imitated the bandleader Ted Lewis, who always started his performances that way. And, while Billy sings, he often takes part in an elaborate fan-dance in the style of vaudeville fan dancer Sally Rand. During Billy's description of his courtroom tricks, we see a satire of the many courtroom scenes that figured in vaudeville productions.

Other characters in *Chicago* were also recognizable tributes to bygone vaudeville stars. "Mama" Morton is modeled on one of vaudeville's biggest names, Sophie Tucker. Like Sophie, Mama is dressed luxuriously, and Mama's big number is just as racy as Tucker's suggestive tunes. The "sob sister" reporter Mary Sunshine imitates a long line of vaudevillian drag queens, especially Julian Eltinge and Bert Savoy. In the plaintive lament "Mr. Cellophane," Amos mimics the African American performer Bert Williams (costar of *In Dahomey*) in the process, who was famous for singing a self-deprecating number called "Nobody" while dressed in baggy clothes and white gloves.

Various vaudeville dance styles are demonstrated in "The Cell Block Tango" (**Musical Example 47**), which also functions as a comedy song. An announcer, like an old-time vaudevillian master of ceremonies, heralds the number, and the six "merry murderesses" start at **1** with an odd series of

one- and two-syllable words, eventually forming a regular ostinato-like pattern against a raucous tango background. The loose strophic form begins at **2**, followed by the first of six spoken interludes in which each prisoner describes the unfair circumstances that led to her jailing. (The other women sing the main chorus softly in the background.) The odd syllables of **1** grow more comprehensible as the interludes progress; each word is a reference to a particular woman's fateful crime.

Despite the very different moods of "The Cell Block Tango" and *Cabaret*'s "Tomorrow Belongs to Me," Kander and Ebb had the same challenge: how to keep a strophic form interesting. In "The Cell Block Tango," they adopted a variety of strategies. Sometimes the chorus is in the background, during the narratives; occasionally it reappears, as it does at **5**. Velma then leads the other girls in a passage of imitative polyphony at **7** (although their text is slightly different from hers). A brief contrasting interlude is sung at **8**, where the singers use the repeated word *bum* to build a pair of chords. At **9**, more imitative polyphony begins, and is sustained at **10**—but a key change adds a little more variety.

The song concludes with the six women reiterating the challenge they had repeated throughout the course of the song, telling us "I betcha you would have done the same!" All through *Chicago*, from the moment Velma invites us into the world of the speakeasy, the characters address us directly and try to make us complicit supporters of their immoral actions. In fact, at the end, Velma and Roxie make a special point of thanking us for our support, leaving us with a dilemma: *do* we support these murderesses? Should we applaud at the end? Are we endorsing *Chicago*'s violence and dishonesty?

Chicago makes us examine our society's mania for celebrating criminals—we cover car chases and sensational crimes in loving detail, perpetuating the "market" that brought Roxie into stardom. *Chicago* also opens the door to far more uncomfortable questions: does this thirst for invasive news coverage make crime more attractive? Do we foster an environment that encourages copycat criminals? Worst of all, are we gradually becoming desensitized to the horrors of domestic violence and murder?

Troubling questions aside, audiences flocked to see *Chicago*. During a nine-week stretch when Liza Minnelli filled in for an ailing Gwen Verdon, the theater announced that the only available tickets were **SRO** (**standing room only**), meaning that all the seats had been sold and that a few additional people would be allowed to stand in the back of the theater for a reduced price. (More stringent fire safety regulations have forced many theaters to discontinue the practice of selling SRO tickets.) *Chicago* amassed an 898-performance run, and a 1996 revival did even better; it broke the longevity record for Broadway revivals and is still running. A London revival is doing equally well. Although nominated for many Tony Awards, the original production of *Chicago* won none of them; it was closed out of the winner's circle by Hamlisch's *A Chorus Line* and Sondheim's *Pacific Overtures*.

Kander and Ebb went on in 1977 to write another star vehicle for their friend Liza Minnelli. The success of *The Act* was undercut when it was revealed that Minnelli increasingly relied on her prerecorded voice. Unlike the pop group Milli Vanilli scandal of the 1990s, in which the "singers" were lip-synching to the voices of others, Minnelli had recorded the original tapes herself—but Broadway audiences weren't paying ever-increasing ticket prices to hear "canned" (prerecorded) singing.

A bit of a gap then occurred in Kander and Ebb's theatrical output, but they were not inactive; instead, they followed the same siren call from Hollywood that had lured so many other Broadway composers to California. Their biggest hit was the title song for *New York, New York* (1977), but Kander wrote scores for several other successful films as well. Kander and Ebb had not given up on Broadway, but the changing economic atmosphere was evidenced by their 1981 effort, *Woman of the Year*, which closed in the red despite a run of 770 performances. Kander and Ebb's next show did no better, even though, as Ken Mandelbaum observed, "*The Rink* is one of those flops that collectors treasure."

Kander and Ebb's next choice for stage material was a musicalization of Manuel Puig's novel *Kiss of the Spider Woman*. The show won the Best Musical Tony; like Kander and Ebb's best shows, it addressed an unusual subject matter with a range of exotic musical numbers. Even with a run of 906 performances, *Kiss of the Spider Woman* did not earn back its full investment; inflation and increased production costs were taking their toll on Broadway shows.

Whether measured by "length of run" or the more pragmatic financial consideration of "did the show break even?," Kander and Ebb have not been able to mount another successful Broadway show despite some recent attempts. Nevertheless, Kander and Ebb's artistic achievements were recognized by the Kennedy Center in 1998; as honorees, they joined the ranks of some of theater's most significant songwriters, including Richard Rodgers, Alan Jay Lerner, Frederick Loewe, Leonard Bernstein, Jule Styne, and Stephen Sondheim. There is little question that Kander and Ebb's rich body of works has merited this recognition. Certainly, by examining many of the ominous and sinister qualities of mankind, they have helped a generation of theatergoers to confront the "dark."

FURTHER READING

Citron, Stephen. *The Musical From the Inside Out.* Chicago: Ivan R. Dee, 1992.

Garebian, Keith. *The Making of* Cabaret. Toronto: Mosaic Press, 1999.

Gottfried, Martin. *Broadway Musicals.* New York: Abradale Press/Abrams, Inc., 1984.

Guernsey, Otis L., Jr., ed. *Broadway Song & Story: Playwrights/Lyricists/Composers Discuss Their Hits.* New York: Dodd, Mead, 1985.

Green, Stanley. *The World of Musical Comedy.* Third edition, revised and enlarged. New York: A. S. Barnes & Company, 1974.

Hirsch, Foster. *Harold Prince and the American Musical Theatre.* Cambridge: Cambridge University Press, 1989.

Ilson, Carol. *Harold Prince From* Pajama Game *to* Phantom of the Opera. Ann Arbor: U.M.I. Research Press, 1989.

Kasha, Al, and Joel Hirschhorn. *Notes on Broadway: Conversations with the Great Songwriters.* Chicago: Contemporary Books, 1985.

Mandelbaum, Ken. *Not Since Carrie: Forty Years of Broadway Musical Flops.* New York: St. Martin's, 1991.

Miller, Scott. *Deconstructing Harold Hill: An Insider's Guide to Musical Theatre.* Portsmouth, New Hampshire: Heinemann, 2000.

———. *From* Assassins *to* West Side Story: *A Director's Guide to Musical Theatre.* Portsmouth, New Hampshire: Heinemann, 1996.

Mordden, Ethan. *Open a New Window: The Broadway Musical in the 1960s.* New York: Palgrave, 2001.

Prince, Hal. *Contradictions: Notes on Twenty-Six Years in the Theatre.* New York: Dodd, Mead, 1974.

PLOT SUMMARY: *CABARET*

Cabaret begins with a show-within-the-show: We are welcomed to the small Kit Kat Klub by the Master of Ceremonies. We can forget our troubles here, which might be desirable, for we are in Berlin just before the Nazi party comes into full power. There is an unspoken fear that life—which is none too good to begin with—is about to change for the worse. Like Mardi Gras revelers making the most of Carnival before the privations of the Lenten season begin, many German citizens are living desperate lives in an era of rampant inflation, moral decadence, and increasing violence.

Clifford Bradshaw, an American writer, is journeying to Berlin to seek his fortune; on the train, he meets Ernst Ludwig. Going through customs, Cliff realizes that Ernst hid an extra briefcase among Cliff's belongings. Ernst explains that he had purchased too many goods in Paris and didn't want to pay duty; as an apology, he offers to help Cliff find cheap lodging, and he promises to become Cliff's first English student.

Cliff moves into Fräulein Schneider's boarding house, which he shares with Fräulein Kost (a good-natured prostitute) and Herr Schultz, who manages a fruit shop and is shyly courting Schneider. Cliff is restless; he soon finds himself at the Kit Kat Klub. He is surprised to find an English girl as a mediocre lead performer, while Sally Bowles is equally intrigued to find another English-speaker in the club, but she hurriedly ends the conversation when her protector—a partner in the club—arrives.

During an English lesson, Ernst hints that Cliff could earn even more money if he'd be willing to make an occasional trip to Paris. Unexpectedly, Sally arrives; her protector had been suspicious of her interest in the American, so she's been kicked out of the relationship *and* her job at the club. She's hoping she can stay with Cliff for a while, and although Schneider is a little fretful, she's consoled by the extra rent. Back at the Kit Kat Klub, the Emcee notes that some people have even more than one roommate. Schneider is also distressed by all of Kost's male "visitors" but can't afford to evict a paying tenant. Thank heavens for Schultz, who always brings Schneider little presents, such as today's extravagant gift—a pineapple! At the club, the Aryan waiters are also pleased, proclaiming along with the Emcee that "Tomorrow Belongs to Me" (**Musical Example 46**).

Cliff's writing continues to go slowly, but it is in part due to his increasing love for Sally. She has become pregnant, however, and Cliff feels compelled to accept Ernst's offer of a trip to Paris, which will pay 75 marks. As if echoing Cliff's financial concerns, the Kit Kat Klub features "The Money Song." Back at the boarding house, Kost is surprised not to be scolded for the several sailors she's had in her room, but she quickly learns that Schneider's mind is elsewhere, having just agreed to marry Schultz. Sally immediately throws an engagement party, but there are some bumpy moments, such as when Schultz tries to be entertaining by singing a song full of Yiddish sayings. Ernst warns Schneider, that she would be making a mistake to marry a non-German husband (for Herr Schultz is Jewish). Ernst and the other guests join in a rousing chorus of "Tomorrow Belongs to Me."

As the second act begins, Schneider goes to the fruit shop to share her fears with Schultz. She doesn't want trouble, and if she has to keep living her life without love, she will. He tries to reassure her, but a brick comes crashing through his shop window, and they know what it signals. Meanwhile, the Emcee is tenderly singing to a gorilla in the Kit Kat Klub, explaining, "If You Could See Her Through My Eyes," that "she wouldn't look Jewish at all."

Cliff is looking for a job, since he realizes that his courier work supported the Nazi party. Sally's been offered her old job back, but Cliff is opposed. Their argument is interrupted by Schneider who has come to return their engagement gift. Schneider feels her life is centered in Berlin; she can't just run away. Cliff realizes that's what he and Sally *should* do, so he leaves to sell his typewriter for train fare, telling Sally to stay in the room. Sally, of course, leaves immediately, and he later finds her defiantly performing in the club, singing "Cabaret"—her tribute to the philosophy that we should grab everything we can out of the short life we're allotted. Even while she sings, Ernst has a gang of Nazi thugs beat Cliff for refusing to be a courier again.

Neither Cliff nor Sally is in good shape the next morning. Cliff is packing, but Sally tells him she's not going; moreover, she's had their child aborted. Cliff slaps her, but it doesn't help her to see the shallowness of her choice. She thinks of herself as a strange and extraordinary person, and this argument is all part of the drama in which she stars. Cliff leaves a train ticket for her, but she's not interested; her place is in the glittering, hard-edged world of the cabaret, where she now sings for a profusion of German military uniforms decked with swastikas.

PLOT SUMMARY: *CHICAGO*

An energetic, Charleston-era overture alerts us from the very beginning that the setting of *Chicago* is the late 1920s. As the curtain opens, Master of Ceremonies Velma Kelly invites us to join her in a visit to the Chicago speakeasy environment, where we will witness "a story of murder, greed, corruption, violence, exploitation, adultery, and treachery—all those things we all

hold near and dear to our hearts." Velma is addressing *us*—the audience—as if we're part of the real participants in the show.

The next scene depicts what happens when Fred Casely decides to end his affair with Roxie Hart. Pulling a gun, she shoots him—and then, when her husband Amos comes home, she tells him a sad story about this burglar she had to shoot. Roxie persuades Amos to tell the police that *he* shot the "burglar"; since Amos is nuts about Roxie, he goes along with the scheme, even though it will mean his own arrest. As Amos explains matters to the police, Roxie sings an affectionate tribute to her malleable husband. But, during the course of her song, the police identify the victim, and Amos realizes that this wasn't a burglar—this was the man who had sold them their furniture! Amos quickly figures out that Roxie and Fred must have been having an affair. He's no longer interested in taking the rap, and he tells the police all he knows. Roxie is arrested for murder.

Roxie is taken to the Cook County Jail, and "The Cell Block Tango" (**Musical Example 46**) introduces Roxie's cellmates. Each woman explains how she ended up in jail, although they all maintain that they're victims of circumstances rather than murderers. During their song-and-dance, we learn, among other things, that Velma had been part of a vaudeville acrobatic act with her sister. Velma had caught her sister in bed with Velma's husband, although Velma reports that she then blacked out and has no idea how her hands came to be so bloody.

We also meet the matron of the cell block, "Mama" Morton, who explains that the place can be quite tolerable. Mama has been helping to make Velma a media star and has been arranging vaudeville bookings for Velma after her expected acquittal. However, Roxie's appearance on the scene throws a monkey wrench in Velma's works: Roxie's crime is the new, hot topic with the press, and not only does Roxie steal Velma's limelight, but she grabs the attention of Velma's lawyer as well. Billy Flynn explains that he's not a lawyer for money; all he cares about is love—and, interestingly enough, all his clients are female. Billy's fee is $5,000, and Roxie quickly starts wheedling the cash out of Amos.

Billy preps Roxie for an interview with a reporter from the *Evening Star* named Mary Sunshine. She's just what Roxie needs, for Mary is perfectly willing to accept Roxie's now rather-twisted version of events. A press conference follows, with Roxie on Billy's lap so he can use her like a ventriloquist's dummy to tell her ever-changing tale about how Roxie and Fred "both reached for the gun."

Afterwards, Roxie rejoices in her newfound media stardom and begins to plan for a vaudeville career after her anticipated acquittal. Velma, on the other hand, is getting panicky—she's lost her publicity, her lawyer, and even her trial date, so she tries to persuade Roxie to team up with her in a new version of Velma's old sister act. Velma demonstrates a number of her old moves to Roxie, but Roxie wants no part of it—she thinks she's got it made on her own. But there's bad news: a new murderess has just captured Billy Flynn's attention.

At the start of the second act, Roxie hits on the idea of claiming to be pregnant, and this inspiration puts her right back in the center of attention. Roxie plays it to the hilt, while Velma is furious that *she* didn't think of the idea. One thing

Roxie *doesn't* count on is Amos's reaction—because even though the math doesn't quite work out, Amos is thrilled at the prospect of being a father. He proudly announces his paternity, only to find that nobody cares; the press ignores him. Sadly, he sings about being "Mr. Cellophane," since evidently everyone just looks right through him. Moreover, Billy wants Amos to divorce Roxie, thinking that this will increase public sympathy for the poor, persecuted mother-to-be.

Velma is growing increasingly desperate, and having gotten a little time alone with Billy Flynn, she shows him all the little acting tricks she has planned for her eventual trial. Roxie's been thinking she's smart enough to defend herself, but when another one of the Cook County Jail residents is found guilty (probably the only one of them who truly was innocent) and is sentenced to hang—the first woman to be executed in 47 years in Cook County—Roxie thinks better of

her decision, allowing Billy to "Razzle Dazzle" the jury himself. As Roxie's trial proceeds, Velma soon learns, to her horror, that Roxie is using all of Velma's proposed mannerisms in *her* trial: Billy has passed along Velma's ideas, even down to the kind of shoes she was planning to wear. Velma and the matron, Mama Morton, commiserate with each other, lamenting whatever happened to "Class"?

As we might expect in this cynical, jaded environment, Roxie wins an acquittal—but even before she can revel in her triumph in front of the press, news of an even more sensational crime in the next courtroom pulls away the attention of the reporters, and Roxie's fleeting celebrity is over. Amos begs her to come home, if only for the sake of the baby, and, surprised, she tells him there *is* no baby—so now there's no Amos, either. The only thing for Roxie to do is to team up with Velma in a second-rate vaudeville act.

MUSICAL EXAMPLE 46

CABARET
JOHN KANDER/FRED EBB, 1966
"Tomorrow Belongs to Me"

Solo Tenor

1   The sun on the meadow is summery warm, the stag in the forest runs free.

Solo Tenor	**Male Chorus**
2 But gather together to greet the storm,	Hum . . .
Tomorrow belongs to me.	Hum . . . Ooh . . .

All

3   The branch of the linden is leafy and green, the Rhine gives its gold to the sea.
But somewhere a glory awaits unseen, tomorrow belongs to me.

[Tenors]	**[Basses]**
4 Oh, fatherland, fatherland	Oh, fatherland, father,

[Tenors]	**[Basses and Master of Ceremonies]**
5 Show us the sign	oh, fatherland, fatherland
Your children have waited to see.	Show us the sign your children have
The morning will come when the	waited to see.

All

6   world is mine

Tenor Solo (and Tenors)	**Bass Solo (and Basses)**	**Master of Ceremonies**
7 Tomorrow belongs to me.	Tomorrow belongs, tomorrow belongs to me.	Tomorrow belongs to me.

MUSICAL EXAMPLE 47

CHICAGO
JOHN KANDER/FRED EBB, 1975
"The Cell Block Tango"

Master of Ceremonies
[spoken:] And now, the six merry murderesses of the Cook County Jail,
in their rendition of the Cell Block Tango!

	Liz	**Annie**	**June**	**Hunyak**	**Velma**	**Mona**
1	Pop	Six	Squish	Uh uh	Cicero	Lipschitz!
	Liz	**Annie**	**June**	**Hunyak**	**Velma**	**Mona**
	Pop	Six	Squish	Uh uh	Cicero	Lipschitz!

	Liz	**Annie**	**June**	**Hunyak**	**Velma**	**Mona**
	Pop	Six	Squish	Uh uh	Cicero	Lipschitz!

All

2

He had it coming, he had it coming, he only had himself to blame.

If you'd have been there, if you'd have seen it,

Velma

I betcha you would have done the same!

	Liz	**Annie**	**June**	**Hunyak**	**Velma**	**Mona**
	Pop	Six	Squish	Uh uh	Cicero	Lipschitz!

Liz **Girls (softly)**

3

[Liz's narrative] He had it coming, he had it coming,

He only had himself to blame.

If you'd have been there, if you'd have seen it,

I betcha you would have done the same! (etc.)

All

4

He had it coming, he had it coming, He only had himself to blame.

Annie **Girls (softly)**

[Annie's narrative] If you'd have been there, if you'd have seen it,

I betcha you would have done the same!

He had it coming, he had it coming,

He only had himself to blame.

If you'd have been there, if you'd have seen it,

I betcha you would have done the same! (etc.)

Liz, Annie, June, Mona **Velma and Hunyak (softly)**

5

He had it coming, he had it coming, Pop, Six, Squish, Uh uh,

He took a flower in its prime, Cicero, Lipschitz.

And then he used it and he abused it Pop, Six, Squish, Uh uh,

It was a murder but not a crime. Cicero, Lipschitz.

June **Girls (softly)**

[June's narrative] Pop, Six, Uh, Uh, Cicero, Lipschitz.

All

6

If you'd have been there, if you'd have seen it,

I betcha you would have done the same!

[Hunyak's narrative]

Velma **Girls (softly)**

[Velma's narrative] He had it coming, he had it coming,

He only had himself to blame.

If you'd have been there, if you'd have seen it,

I betcha you would have done the same!

He had it coming, he had it coming,

He took a flower in its prime,

And then he used it and he abused it

It was a murder but not a crime.

Velma **The Girls**

7

They had it coming, they had it coming, They had it coming, they had it coming,

They had it coming all along. They took a flower in its prime,

I didn't do it, but if I'd done it, And then they used it, and they abused it,

How could you tell me that I was wrong? It was a murder but not a crime.

Mona **Girls (softly)**

[Mona's narrative] He had it coming, he had it coming,

He only had himself to blame.

If you'd have been there, if you'd have seen it,

I betcha you would have done the same!

All

8

The dirty bum, bum, bum . . . the dirty bum, bum, bum . . .

Liz, Annie, Mona **Velma, June, Hunyak**

9

They had it comin',

they had it comin', They had it comin',

They had it comin' all along.   They had it comin', they had it comin'
'Cause if they used us   all along.
and they abused us,   'Cause if they used us
How could you tell us   and they abused us,
that we were wrong?   How could you tell us
                               that we were wrong?

All

10   He had it coming, he had it coming, he only had himself to blame.
If you'd have been there, if you'd have seen it,
I betcha you would have done the same!

[dialogue]

All

I betcha you would have done the same!

Chapter 36
New Partnerships: Andrew Lloyd Webber and Jim Rice

During the first two-thirds of the twentieth century, the United States had exported so many blockbuster hits that audiences were beginning to think that musical theater was a uniquely American phenomenon. In England, however, things were about to change, first because of a triumph by Lionel Bart and then by an onslaught of ever-increasing successes by **Andrew Lloyd Webber** (b. 1948). Lloyd Webber's shows in particular reawakened audiences' taste for spectacular extravaganzas—like *The Black Crook*—that had delighted theatergoers a century earlier. And the music itself? Lloyd Webber's productions revisited Italian opera's convention of continuous singing, blending this approach with distinctively twentieth-century musical styles. The resulting hybrid appalled many traditionalists, yet at the same time attracted brand new listeners who had rejected conventional musical theater as old hat. Morevoer, these megahits ushered in an era of commercialism that had not been seen since the days of *The Merry Widow*.

Like many American theatrical composers of the 1960s, Englishman Lionel Bart hit his stride early on, then failed to sustain that success when he tried to move away from the subject matter that had brought him to fame: working-class (and criminal) Londoners. The first of his shows hadn't enjoyed much attention, but *Fings Ain't Wot They Used T'Be* (1959) was so well received after a Theatre Workshop production at Stratford East that it transferred to London's West End, where it sustained a two-year run—right up to the premiere of Bart's *Oliver!* (1960). Based on Charles Dickens's novel *Oliver Twist*, *Oliver!* was set in Victorian London, populated by thieves, kidnappers, and—as the plot of the show revealed—murderers. Central to *Oliver!*'s success was the chorus of juvenile street urchins who sang and danced their way into the hearts of audiences at some 2,618 performances (setting a new West End record); in New York, *Oliver!* played 774 times, setting a new record for British imports. The 1968 Columbia film was a sizable hit as well, taking the Academy Award for Best Picture.

With *Oliver!*, however, Bart's career had already crested; although *Blitz!* (1962) presented an eye-dazzling exploding set, its stage designs cost a record-high £50,000, and, as Sheridan Morley observes, "Any show in which the sets attract all the attention is . . . a show in trouble." Still, Bart's tunes were admired, as was the music for his next show, *Maggie May* (1964) that borrowed from the new sound of the Beatles. Neither show transferred to Broadway, and Bart's next musical set a British loss record of £80,000. Bart was never able to create a new theatrical success. Nearly destitute,

he struggled with alcoholism for a number of years. He had long since sold his rights to *Oliver!*, but Cameron Mackintosh, producer of the 1994 revival, generously granted Bart a percentage of the royalties, allowing the older man to live out the remainder of his life in relative comfort.

Both of *Oliver!*'s records—in London and in New York—would be broken by the next British composer to make his name in theater. Like Stephen Sondheim, Andrew Lloyd Webber was born on March 22, although Sondheim was 18 years older. Lloyd Webber's father, William, taught at the Royal College of Music in London; his mother, Jean, was a well-known piano teacher; and his brother, Julian, was a serious cellist. After seeing *My Fair Lady*, Lloyd Webber got his entire family to build a toy theater with a revolving stage. Julian would move the characters while Lloyd Webber played the piano; at times Julian had to shine a flashlight as a spotlight. Lloyd Webber admitted that his "absolute idol was Richard Rodgers, at a time when everyone else's idol was Elvis Presley," and that these childhood shows convinced him, "If I were to be successful, it couldn't be anywhere but in the theater."

Like many budding theater composers, Lloyd Webber wrote school shows, none of which excited much attention. One positive note, though, was a 1965 letter from a discontented law student named **Tim Rice** (b. 1944), who had heard that Lloyd Webber was looking for a "with-it" lyricist. The two young men soon settled on their first project, which Rice described as "a bit of a ripoff of *Oliver!*; Victorian London, prostitutes with hearts of gold, all that." They managed to sell the rights to the show, but then discovered one of theater's harsh lessons: It is a long way between rights and an actual stage production.

Undaunted, the pair of writers had some pop songs recorded in 1967. Later that year, a family friend, Alan Doggett, asked them to write an end-of-term piece for Colet Court. This was the Junior School of St. Paul's Cathedral, where the young choirboys were educated. Rice ruefully confessed, "It was a big comedown for us after our ambitions to have a show produced in the West End—a small audience, a cast of 11-year-olds." Rice chose the Biblical tale of Joseph and his 11 brothers, and although the resulting *Joseph and the Amazing Technicolor Dreamcoat* uses modern language and musical styles, it followed the Book of Genesis account fairly closely. The 15-minute *Joseph* was ready for a 1968 presentation on a rainy Friday for some 60 parents. They were entertained, but not bowled over.

Joseph seemed poised to slip into oblivion, but William Lloyd Webber organized a performance to benefit a new drug-treatment center (an increasingly needed facility as the 1960s wore on). Lloyd Webber and Rice expanded the work somewhat, and Rice himself sang the role of the Pharaoh. The audience, some 2,000-strong, again consisted mainly of parents, including Derek Jewell. Jewell, the jazz and popular music critic for London's venerable *Sunday Times*, was startled by what he heard and wrote a **rave review** of the production, noting, "Throughout the twenty-minute duration it bristles with wonderfully singable tunes. It entertains. It communicates instantly, as all good pop should. And it is a considerable piece of barrier-breaking by its creators." (On the other hand, the *Times Literary Supplement* published a **pan** review, the antithesis of a rave.)

After some further expansion, Decca Records recorded the show (again with Rice as the Pharaoh), giving a wider audience a taste. Part of the novelty was the show's format: all the dialogue was sung, in the manner of Italian opera. Another innovation was *Joseph*'s diversity of musical styles. Much of the score was a bouncy pop-rock, but Lloyd Webber mimicked other styles in a technique called **pastiche**. The pastiche numbers ranged from a "surfer rock" sound to ragtime and a German oompah band. Later additions included a French café sound, a country-western number (sung, appropriately enough, by Levi), and even a Caribbean-tinged calypso. One of *Joseph*'s showstoppers was the 1950's rock-and-roll pastiche called "The Song of the King." From the Pharaoh's first words, the title's pun is evident: Not only does "The King" refer to the Pharaoh himself, but it also alludes to the twentieth-century "King," Elvis Presley, who is impersonated in this number. To underscore the joke, phrases from several well-known Elvis tunes are sprinkled through the lyrics, such as "don't be cruel" and "all shook up."

Even in this early show, there are instances of a device Lloyd Webber would use frequently in later works: the repeated use of a single tune to support rather different dramatic situations, creating in essence a "melody-only" reprise. Other features of Lloyd Webber's style are evident in *Joseph* as well, such as a penchant for sung-through presentations. Commentators struggled to find a genre label for the sung-through aspect of *Joseph*; the earliest version was often referred to as a pop **cantata**, thanks to its religious subject matter (many cantatas are sacred). Similarly, the later full-length version was sometimes called a pop **oratorio**, since the usual meaning of *oratorio* was a substantial continuously sung production centered on a religious topic. Others retained the one-size-fits-all label of "musical" because of the upbeat, simple tunes in their varied pop styles. England saw several versions of *Joseph* over the years, but the Broadway production didn't open until 1982—long after Lloyd Webber's later show, ***Jesus Christ Superstar***, had made its debut.

Lloyd Webber and Rice turned to a more conventional musical theater format for their next show, which was performed at another school—and it was an enormous flop. So, they turned their thoughts to a musical about the life of Jesus Christ, or rather, a view of Christ from the perspective of Judas Iscariot. They knew from the start that *Jesus Christ Superstar* ran the risk of being thought sacrilegious or even blasphemous.

The Pharaoh (Tom Carder) sings "The Song of the King" in *Joseph and the Amazing Technicolor Dreamcoat*. *Martha Swope.*

They asked the Dean of St. Paul's for his opinion; he advised them to do what they liked but warned them that they might be accused of anti-Semitism. Lloyd Webber also recalled talking with a vicar who had thought it would be a "fantastic idea," even when Lloyd Webber had argued against the notion. Ironically, Lloyd Webber believed that "it would be a terrible idea because it would never sell." But since Lloyd Webber and Rice were stuck for ideas, they plunged into the new project at last.

Lloyd Webber reported that the title song's fanfare-like refrain came to him while he was out shopping, and he had to scribble the melody on a paper napkin. Soon, Rice crafted the text for Judas's main question of Jesus: "Jesus Christ Superstar—do you think you're what they say you are?" This stance was the central tenet of the show; since Judas doesn't want to believe that Christ could be divine, he is willing to betray Jesus because he fears the increasing noisiness of Jesus's followers will get them all in trouble with the authorities (see the **Plot Summary**). Judas doesn't perceive Jesus's divinity until it is too late, and this presents a troubling question: Would any of us have been able to do any better?

Lloyd Webber and Rice were nervous enough about this rather daring perspective that they persuaded Brian Brolly of MCA-UK Records to let them record the tune as a single so that they could test the waters of listeners' response. The recording expenses for "Superstar" ran far over budget, leading others to dub the project "Brolly's Folly," but Brolly's faith proved to be justified. Although English sales were a disappointing 37,000 copies, the international reaction was much more enthusiastic. Now MCA wanted the writers to finish the rest of their show for a complete recording. MCA supported the project to the tune of £14,500—a fairly staggering expenditure for a relatively unknown pair of authors.

Lloyd Webber and Rice struggled to bring the album together. Much of the writing was unfinished, and they also had some trouble in finding the right voices—and in recording them once they were found. Murray Head, who, as Judas, had recorded the previous "Superstar" single, was filming another project, so it was hard to get him to the studio. Ian Gillen, singing the role of Jesus Christ, was a member of the rock group Deep Purple, so his busy performance schedule had to be accommodated. Their Pilate, Barry Dennen, was found in the London cast of *Hair*, while Yvonne Elliman, cast as Mary Magdalene, was found only by chance, when Lloyd Webber had gone to listen to another singer.

Perhaps because of the studio's time pressure, portions of earlier tunes can be found in the album. One melody came from their flop show; another was one of their 1967 pop songs. Brief passages from *Joseph* also made an appearance. Lloyd Webber's biographer Michael Walsh believes that some themes from other composers' works can also be found in the score, including bits of the Grieg Piano Concerto, Orff's *Carmina Burana*, and Prokofiev's *Alexander Nevsky*; Lloyd Webber himself admitted that he could hear echoes of the Mendelssohn Violin Concerto in "I Don't Know How to Love Him."

It was usually the case that recordings of musicals came *after* their stage premieres—and not always then, depending on the show's success and other factors. Recording a show as a concept album *before* it had reached the stage—as a means of interesting backers who might then support the show—was still far from the norm. In fact, when *Jesus Christ Superstar* was staged on Broadway, it was deemed ineligible for a Best Musical Tony because of its earlier incarnation as a recording. (By 1980, when *Evita* was in the running, the Tony committee had abandoned that particular prohibition.)

Jesus Christ Superstar was not the first show to be produced on stage after having been released as a concept album, but it was the first to attract much Broadway attention. *Shinbone Alley* (1957) had been preceded by a 1954 recording, but survived for only 49 performances. Later, songs inspired by the *Peanuts* comic strip characters were recorded in 1966. After its LP release, *You're a Good Man, Charlie Brown* played for 1,597 performances—but at an *off*-Broadway theater. Moreover, the rock group, The Who, created a concept album, *Tommy*, in 1969, but although the show was presented by the Metropolitan Opera (!) in a pair of performances in 1970, *Tommy* would not reach Broadway until 1993.

In their concept album, however, The Who had christened *Tommy* a **rock opera**; like *Joseph* and *Jesus Christ Superstar*, the dialogue is sung, but unlike *Joseph*, *Tommy* avoids pastiche, limiting itself instead to a mixture of rock, pop, and a few more theatrical tunes. Sales of *Tommy* had been wildly successful, so MCA promptly assigned the same genre label—rock opera—to the new *Jesus Christ Superstar*. As might be expected, some listeners resisted the label strenuously,

arguing that the designation of "opera" raised expectations that there would be trained voices rather than the pop-rock singers heard on the concept album (and also in the later stage productions). Others found the rock approach a welcome relief from the older musical comedy style that had pervaded Broadway for so long; they felt that the term *opera* was an appropriate recognition of the album's sung-through nature.

Two tunes from the *Jesus Christ Superstar* reflect the diversity to be found in the score. "Pilate's Dream" (**Musical Example 48**) was originally intended for Pilate's wife Procula, who, as recorded in the Bible in St. Matthew 27:19, had warned her husband not to harm the innocent Jesus. Lloyd Webber and Rice were so pleased with Barry Dennen's interpretation of the song that they rewrote the number for Pilate and eliminated Procula altogether. In this tune, Lloyd Webber's melody-only reprise technique is at work, for the melody appeared earlier in "Poor Jerusalem," sung by Jesus. Although the text is different in both settings, both men have an unhappy vision of the future in the course of their songs.

"Pilate's Dream" conforms to a textbook song form, with *a-a-b-a* conforming to **1**, **2**, **3**, and **4**. The gentle acoustic guitar in the background, supported by an electric bass, creates a dreamy, rock-ballad atmosphere, while the minor mode subtly underscores Pilate's ominous vision. Although there is a brief instrumental introduction, there is no coda. Instead, as Pilate reaches the final word of text, having foreseen a future in which he is to be demonized for his role in Jesus's death, the instruments freeze, letting the word *blame* resonate as if it had caught in Pilate's throat. The song is a beautiful evocation of the troubled atmosphere foreshadowing the doom that Pilate can do nothing to escape.

The controversial "King Herod's Song" stands in marked—even jarring—contrast. This text is based on the Biblical book of St. Luke 23:7–11 where Herod ends an encounter with Jesus by mocking him. However, Lloyd Webber's musical characterization of the king makes it clear that it is *Herod* who should be mocked as ludicrous, rather than Jesus Christ. The song is a verse-chorus, or alternation, form, with the *a* verses set in a moderato-tempo minor mode, switching to an exaggerated ragtime style in major mode for the *b* refrains, supported by an oompah accompaniment. Lloyd Webber and Rice were offended by the first Broadway production's depiction of Herod as a drag queen, but it is certainly the case that the music itself invites the listener to view Herod as a trivial, cardboard figure.

As with the single "Superstar," British sales of the *Jesus Christ Superstar* concept album after its 1970 release were modest. Once again, the American response was a different story, sending the album to number one on the *Billboard* charts, with sales of more than 3 million copies. A "touring production" presented an elaborate slide show of gothic religious paintings and architecture while the album was played. American stage producers began to woo the writers, but Robert Stigwood was shrewd enough to send a limousine for Lloyd Webber and Rice prior to his meeting with them. The two "twenty-somethings" were suitably impressed by this extravagant gesture, and they agreed to give Stigwood the production rights (as well as a ten-year contract, a decision they later rued bitterly).

Stigwood hired Tom O'Horgan, director of *Hair*, to direct the New York production. The briskly selling album helped ticket sales, but the box office also benefited from the storm of religious protest, much as viewers had flocked to see *The Black Crook* after hearing it denounced from the pulpit. By the time *Jesus Christ Superstar* opened in 1971, its million-dollar advance set a new Broadway record. The production was as controversial as its director, and even Lloyd Webber and Rice found it to be tasteless. Interviewer Guy Flatley was entertained by Lloyd Webber's response when asked about the New York staging: "A gurgling noise comes from somewhere inside Andrew and his mournful brown eyes roll heavenward . . . 'Let's just say that we don't think this production is the definitive one.'"

Even with fairly harsh criticism (one critic suggested, "You may want to attend simply to see how long a way a lot of bad taste can go"), *Jesus Christ Superstar* played for 711 performances. In England, however, where sales of the recordings had lagged behind, the success of its stage production took everyone by surprise. After opening in 1972, the London staging went on to present 3,358 performances—a West End record, surpassing the previous record-holder, *Oliver!*, by some 740 performances. The show was filmed twice; Lloyd Webber's own production company oversaw the 2000 film, so the results were more in keeping with his original vision for the show.

What next? Lloyd Webber and Rice tried setting *Peter Pan*, but it seemed terribly juvenile after a show about Christ, and they abandoned it. Rice also gave up on Lloyd Webber's next idea, a musical about the butler Jeeves, featured in P. G. Wodehouse's novels. Even the elderly Wodehouse warned that "it's been tried before and it's failed," and Lloyd Webber's staging flopped. Nevertheless, Lloyd Webber received some supportive comments from Richard Rodgers and Hal Prince. Prince's interest led Lloyd Webber to hope that he might collaborate with the director on a future show. Fired by this hope, Lloyd Webber reunited with Rice to work on Rice's pet project, *Evita*. Rice had been fascinated by a BBC radio documentary featuring Eva Perón, wife of the Argentine president. (Interestingly, Leonard Bernstein had said in the early 1970s that *he* was thinking of writing a show about Evita Perón, but nothing came of it.) Lloyd Webber and Rice decided to use the same procedures they had adopted for *Superstar*; they would draft the story, write tunes for the plot's high points, set text to those melodies, and then fill in the gaps with recitative. Also like *Superstar*, they would record the show first.

Because of the unusual source of inspiration—a radio broadcast—there was no clear preexisting plot for the show (beyond Eva Perón's biography), but Rice hit upon the device of a quasi-narrator, called Ché, who would explain Evita's maneuvering and at times challenge her directly (see the **Plot Summary**). The popularity of *Superstar* had been aided by the prior release of certain songs as singles; Lloyd Webber and Rice struggled to write something equivalent for *Evita*. Again, they went back to their pop-song years and

pulled out another tune; with new words, the song became an anthem-like refrain for Evita. Just before the concept album was finished, Lloyd Webber and Rice decided that the song's first line—"It's only your lover returning"—was a little pedestrian, so they called Julie Covington, the "voice" of Evita, back into the studio and had her dub a new opening phrase, "Don't Cry For Me Argentina." When released as a single, the song quickly skyrocketed to number one; the concept album did equally well despite its rather intimidating designation as an opera.

While still at work on the recording, Lloyd Webber and Rice signed with Hal Prince. Prince had a two-year stretch of commitments ahead of him, but at last the show was ready, and *Evita* premiered in 1978 in London. The critics were mixed, but Prince's inventive staging came in for praise. One of Prince's clever moments was found in a new tune for the show, which Prince had persuaded Lloyd Webber and Rice to write as a replacement for one of the concept album's tunes. The generals who are vying for control of Argentina are depicted in a row of rocking chairs. One by one, in the manner of the childhood game Musical Chairs, the rockers are removed until only Perón remains on the stage.

One frequent criticism came as a surprise: Lloyd Webber and Rice felt they were portraying the Argentine First Lady's greed and ruthlessness fairly explicitly, so they were startled to be accused of glorifying the dictator. Nevertheless, they deliberately accentuated the fascist nature of her leadership when *Evita* made its American debut. Anticipation had grown high by the time *Evita* reached Broadway in 1979, and *Evita* attained a new box office record of a $2.4 million advance. Critical reactions were again mixed, but Lloyd Webber and Rice won their first Tonys for the score and the book (even though the program listed no book writer!), while the overall show won the Best Musical Tony.

Some writers regard *Evita* as Lloyd Webber's finest score. Certainly, he plunged himself wholeheartedly into writing integrated, coherent numbers, and he used his orchestration skills to flavor the tunes with an Argentine ambiance. "Another Suitcase in Another Hall" (**Musical Example 49**), which also climbed high in the charts when released as a single shortly after "Don't Cry For Me Argentina," illustrates the mixture of Broadway and ethnic sounds. The scene opens with an instrumental prelude, mimicking the sounds of typical South American instruments, especially the harp. The subtle dissonance of this passage prepares the listener for the upheaval Evita is about to bring into the Mistress's life. At Evita's entrance at **1**, the accompaniment switches to a driving rock pattern, but with a strong emphasis on the weak beats of the meter, which itself creates an unsettling effect.

At **2**, the mood changes completely for the Mistress, who is supported again by harps, guitars, and other folklike instruments. Her melodic line and the accompaniment use syncopated rhythmic patterns, also evocative of South America. "Another Suitcase in Another Hall" is structured as a straightforward verse-chorus number, with the Mistress singing the verses (**2**, **4**, and **6**) and with the choruses (**3**, **5**, and **7**) sung by Ché and a small male chorus. The male voices also

The Mistress (Jane Ohringer) resigns herself to "Another Suitcase in Another Hall" in *Evita*.
Martha Swope.

Mandelbaum, Ken. *Not Since Carrie: Forty Years of Broadway Musical Flops*. New York: St. Martin's, 1991.

Mantle, Jonathan. *Fanfare: The Unauthorised Biography of Andrew Lloyd Webber*. New York: Viking Penguin, 1989.

McKnight, Gerald. *Andrew Lloyd Webber*. New York: St. Martin's, 1984.

Miller, Scott. *From* Assassins *to* West Side Story: *A Director's Guide to Musical Theatre*. Portsmouth, New Hampshire: Heinemann, 1996.

Mordden, Ethan. *Open a New Window: The Broadway Musical in the 1960s*. New York: Palgrave, 2001.

Nassour, Ellis, and Richard Broderick. *Rock Opera: The Creation of* Jesus Christ Superstar *from Record Album to Broadway Show and Motion Picture*. New York: Hawthorn Books, 1973.

Palmer, Robert. "The Pop Life: Writing Musicals Attuned to Rock Era." *The New York Times* (February 10, 1982): C 21.

Richmond, Keith. *The Musicals of Andrew Lloyd Webber*. London: Virgin, 1995.

Roper, David. *Bart!: The Unauthorized Life and Times, Ins and Outs, Ups and Downs of Lionel Bart*. London: Pavilion, 1994.

Walsh, Michael. *Andrew Lloyd Webber, His Life and Works: A Critical Biography*. Revised and enlarged edition. New York: Abrams, 1997.

contribute to the South American atmosphere by harmonizing in tight intervals in the manner of mariachi singers. It is surprising that this bittersweet number is set in the major mode, but it is an effective depiction of the helplessness felt by one of Evita's many victims, who attempts to be brave nonetheless.

The combination of effective staging, an evocative score, and a central character who aroused strong emotions (even if they were negative emotions) established *Evita* as a full-fledged success for the team of Lloyd Webber and Rice. Ironically, it also spelled the end of their partnership. They seem to have been gradually but inexorably drawn in separate directions, and differences in their attitudes were beginning to chafe. There would be a brief reunion in 1986 to create a short piece for the Queen of England's 60th birthday and a later collaboration to write a new song ("You Must Love Me") for the 1996 film version of *Evita*, so that they would be eligible for the Best Original Song Academy Award (which they won). But after *Evita* had reached the stage in the late 1970s, both men—still with much to offer to the theater—have been making those contributions in collaboration with new partners.

FURTHER READING

Bennetts, Leslie. "Lloyd Webber's 3d Broadway Show." *The New York Times Biographical Service* 13 (September 1982): 1210.

Braun, Michael, compiler. *Jesus Christ Superstar: The Authorized Version*. London: Pan Books, 1972.

PLOT SUMMARY: *JESUS CHRIST SUPERSTAR*

Judas, one of the 12 apostles of Jesus of Nazareth, is worried; when he had first joined Jesus's crusade, he felt that they could really do some good for their troubled land. Lately, though, people have started focusing not on their cause but on Jesus himself; why, some are even saying Jesus is the Messiah! It makes Judas nervous that the crowds are getting too big; he knows that the ruling Pharisees won't hesitate a moment to squelch Jesus and his followers if they become too high profile.

In Bethany, on Friday night, the apostles anxiously ask Jesus what's going on. Mary Magdalene, a former prostitute, sees that Jesus is stressed by all the agitation around him, so she tries to soothe him with some scented oil. Judas sneers at her efforts, telling Jesus that it's inappropriate to consort with a woman of her unsavory background. Jesus retorts angrily that only one whose slate is clean should throw stones. Mary again tries to calm Jesus, lulling him to sleep.

In the city of Jerusalem the following Sunday, the Pharisees and priests anxiously insist to Caiaphas, the head priest, that Jesus must die. Caiaphas agrees; he foresees their own destruction if this dangerous man is allowed to live. Outside, the crowd is excited at the sight of Jesus entering into Jerusalem. Furiously, Caiaphas orders Jesus to quiet the mob, but the crowd continues to roar. Simon views Jesus as the powerful leader who will rally the Jewish people to overthrow the Roman oppressors. Jesus softly replies that no one in Jerusalem understands the meaning of true power or glory.

The Roman governor of the region, Pontius Pilate, spends a restless night. In "Pilate's Dream" (**Musical Example 48**), he saw an amazing Galilean whom people seemed at first to hate, and then Pilate saw "thousands of millions crying for this man"—and blaming Pilate for his death. Jesus is busy elsewhere. He has found that the Temple in Jerusalem has not been kept holy; instead, its aisles are full of merchants and moneylenders. In a fury, he drives them out of the sanctuary, only to find himself exhausted by the demands of the crippled and poor who beg him for help. In anguish, he finally orders them to "heal yourselves!" Mary takes action; again soothing him, she gets him to rest. While he sleeps, she is puzzled over her own emotional response to him, musing, "I Don't Know How to Love Him." Although she's used to manipulating men, she finds that Jesus scares her; he's different, somehow.

Judas makes a momentous decision on Tuesday; he decides that he will stop Jesus before all of them are arrested as troublemakers. He goes to the Pharisees to betray what he knows of Jesus's planned activities; the priests are anxious to find a quiet opportunity to capture Jesus so that the arrest does not incite the crowds even further. The priests offer Judas 30 pieces of silver in payment for the information; Judas at first rejects the blood money, but the priests persuade him to take it, assuring him he can help the poor with the funds. Judas at last slowly names the Garden of Gethsemane as the best place to arrest Jesus; he and the apostles will be there on Thursday night.

On Thursday evening, Jesus and the apostles share a final meal, and Jesus is frustrated by their incomprehension of the events to come. When he insists that they will soon deny knowing him and will betray him, they're outraged—all of them except Judas, of course, who accuses Jesus of *wanting* him to commit the betrayal. Jesus simply urges him to hurry up and do it. Unaware of the impending disaster, the remaining apostles drift off to sleep in Gethsemane, leaving Jesus to pray on his own. Jesus reluctantly tells the Lord he is ready for his anointed duty.

Judas reappears with some armed guards; to identify the right man without waking the sleeping apostles, Judas kisses Jesus's cheek. Gradually, the apostles rouse themselves, but they can make only a feeble attempt at stopping the arrest. A crowd has gathered, and the people's mood is different; they seem more menacing and are almost gleeful about Jesus's troubles to come. After accusing Jesus of claiming to be the Son of God, the priests decide there's enough evidence against him for them to send him to Pilate for judgment. Meanwhile, the angry mob confronts Peter, accusing him of being one of Jesus's followers. Trying to save his own skin, Peter denies the charge over and over again—and Mary Magdalene is struck by the fact that his denial means Jesus's strange prediction has come true.

On Friday, Pilate is reluctant to get involved. He realizes that by rights, as a Galilean, Jesus falls under King Herod's jurisdiction, so Herod should be the one to question Jesus. Herod is delighted at first; as he announces in "King Herod's Song," he's wanted to see Jesus for a long time, hoping that Jesus will perform a miracle for him. Stoically, Jesus does not respond to the king's taunts, and Herod angrily orders that the prisoner should be returned to Pilate.

Judas is horrified at the treatment Jesus is receiving and goes to the priests to protest. They cut him off, and he realizes the enormity of his betrayal. Driven insane by guilt and panic, he hangs himself. During the trial, Pilate cannot find any real charge to bring against Jesus, but he decides that flogging Jesus might satisfy the bloodthirsty crowd that has begun to call for Jesus to be crucified. Since 40 lashes are said to kill a man, Pilate orders that Jesus be whipped 39 times, but the crowd is not appeased. They continue to shriek "crucify him!" and at last Pilate washes his hands of the matter: since Jesus won't defend himself, and the crowd wants him dead, then so be it.

When Pilate makes the fateful choice, Judas's voice is heard once more. He asks Jesus if all this sad story had been part of some great plan to become a "Superstar." But Jesus has no answer for Judas and the crowd; instead, now nailed to the cross, he prays during "The Crucifixion" for God to forgive these people, and finally, with his last breath, tells the Lord, "Father, into your hands I commend my spirit." No more words are heard, but the orchestra plays "John Nineteen: Forty-One," a reference to the Biblical verse that describes the waiting sepulchre near the spot where Jesus had been crucified.

PLOT SUMMARY: *EVITA*

In effect, *Evita* begins with its ending. A film is playing when suddenly the lights come on and an announcer's voice is heard. He tells the audience, "It is the sad duty of the Secretary of the Press to inform the people of Argentina that Eva Perón, spiritual leader of the nation, entered immortality at 20.25 hours today." The crowds start gathering for her funeral procession, but one observer, Ché, is unmoved by the weeping all around him. Disgustedly, he disparages the proceedings as a circus, and his disdain for the deceased woman is made clear as he leads us back through time to her early origins.

We learn that María Eva Duarte was born in the provinces, the illegitimate daughter of a local bureaucrat. At age 15, she is seduced by (or seduces) Agustín Magaldi, a second-rate singer. As his engagement in Junín comes to an end, she tells him what she wants in exchange for her virginity; she insists that he take her to Buenos Aires. Once in the big city, Eva quickly starts working her way into a position of minor prominence, as a model, a radio broadcaster, and a bit player in various films—even if her climb requires some sexual favors. Meanwhile, the Argentine government undergoes upheaval after upheaval, punctuated by military coups. The political shifts seem like a game of musical chairs, and Eva soon perceives that one Colonel Juan Perón is a likely candidate for coming out a winner. She quickly positions herself to meet him.

Intrigued by this brazen approach, Perón allows Eva to supplant his 16-year-old mistress. The mistress is resigned to her eviction, bravely telling herself that it's simply time for

"Another Suitcase in Another Hall" (**Musical Example 49**). Not everyone is complacent about Eva's increasingly powerful role; Perón's brother officers in the army resent her control over Perón, while the Argentine upper class refuses to accept a woman with such a shady past.

Now popularly known as Evita, the new Señora Perón has been a driving force behind her husband's 1946 campaign to become the president of Argentina. After his election, the couple stand "On the Balcony of the Casa Rosada"—the Argentine equivalent of the American White House—and greet the populace. The crowds soon shift their attention from the president to his first lady, and she basks in their attention, telling them, "Don't Cry For Me Argentina."

Indeed, one could only envy the 26-year-old's ensuing power. Having won over the common people, she wants to soar even higher. Anxious to widen Argentina's (and her own) influence around the world, she heads straight for Europe. After a gratifying reception in Spain, though, Evita finds that other European countries do not offer such enthusiastic hospitality; in fact, England virtually snubs her. She is enraged and resolves to undermine the Argentine upper classes, most of which have ties to Great Britain. Upon her return, she launches the Eva Perón Foundation. Her charity thrives, especially since she has cut off government subsidies to the preexisting charities that had been run by Argentine aristocrats. Admittedly, Evita's henchmen do occasionally resort to strong-arming contributions. Nevertheless, the Foundation promises an occasional prize lottery, so the people are excited about the possibility of sudden wealth—even if some of the Foundation's accounting methods would not stand up to close scrutiny. In fact, Evita is adored all the more by the Argentine people.

Ché is a lone dissenting voice, one who does *not* view the first lady as a living saint. (Most of Evita's other detractors have been forcibly silenced.) He challenges her activities, and she justifies herself on the grounds that she's done more good for the peasants than anyone else ever has. She argues that she would need centuries to accomplish more lasting changes—and she does not have centuries; in fact, she doesn't even have decades, even though she is only 33, for Evita has developed cancer. Perón is aware of the trouble he will face without her shrewd manipulations on his behalf.

For a time, Eva schemes to become vice-president, but Perón forces her to confront her own mortality. Increasingly feeble, she delivers a final broadcast to the ever-adoring populace, telling them, once again, "Don't Cry For Me Argentina." During her final hours, her wandering mind surveys images from her life (peppered by Che's furious denunciations), and her voice is heard again, insisting that she has no regrets.

MUSICAL EXAMPLE 48

JESUS CHRIST SUPERSTAR
ANDREW LLOYD WEBBER/TIM RICE, 1970

"Pilate's Dream"

Pilate

1
I dreamed I met a Galilean—a most amazing man.
He had that look you very rarely find, the haunting hunted kind.

2
I asked him to say what had happened, how it all began.
I asked again—he never said a word, as if he hadn't heard

3
And next the room was full of wild and angry men
They seemed to hate this man—they fell on him and then they disappeared again

4
Then I saw thousands of millions crying for this man
And then I heard them mentioning my name and leaving me the blame.

MUSICAL EXAMPLE 49

EVITA
ANDREW LLOYD WEBBER/TIM RICE, 1979

"Another Suitcase in Another Hall"

Evita

1
Hello and goodbye! I've just unemployed you. You can go back to school.
You had a good run; I'm sure he enjoyed you.
Don't act sad or surprised, let's be friends, civilized. Come on, little one!
Don't sit there like a dummy! The day you knew would arrive is here—you'll survive.
So move, funny face!
I like your conversation; you've a catchy turn of phrase . . .

Mistress

2   I don't expect my love affairs to last for long; never fool myself that my dreams will come true:
Being used to trouble I anticipate it, but all the same, I hate it, wouldn't you?

3   So what happens now?

Che

Another suitcase in another hall

                            Mistress

                          So what happens now?

Take your picture off another wall

                          Where am I going to?

You'll get by, you always have before

                          Where am I going to?

Mistress

4   Time and time again, I've said that I don't care; that I'm immune to gloom,
that I'm hard through and through:
But every time it matters all my words desert me; so anyone can hurt me and they do.

5   So what happens now?

Che

Another suitcase in another hall.

                            Mistress

                          So what happens now?

Take your picture off another wall

                          Where am I going to?

You'll get by, you always have before.

                          Where am I going to?

Mistress

6   Call in three months' time and I'll be fine, I know; Well, maybe not that fine, but I'll survive anyhow:
I won't recall the names and places of this sad occasion: but that's no consolation, here and now.

7   So what happens now?

Che

Another suitcase in another hall.

                            Mistress

                          So what happens now?

Take your picture off another wall

                          Where am I going to?

You'll get by, you always have before.

                          Where am I going to?

Don't ask anymore.

Chapter 37
Wunderkinder of the 1970s

As had been the case in the 1960s, the 1970s witnessed several new young composers whose careers both peaked and declined in the same decade. Several women enjoyed the theatrical limelight in the 1970s, although, like their male counterparts, they often found it difficult to sustain their careers. African American composers also contributed book musicals to the Great White Way, but it was seldom that an individual made significant contributions more than once or twice. However, the 1970s were a period of great experimentation, and some of those experiments would establish new theatrical records.

One of the first musicals to have been prerecorded as a concept album was *Shinbone Alley*, which had only a short run in 1957. One of the performances, however, enchanted a nine-year-old, Stephen Schwartz (b. 1948); his neighbor had written the score. Schwartz resolved to become a composer, and while still a student, he contributed a hit song to *Butterflies are Free* (1969). Also, during college, Schwartz presented a musical portraying Emperor Charlemagne's son Pepin, titled *Pippin Pippin*. This 1967 show led to an agent as well as a librettist—whose master's thesis was a theatrical adaptation of the final days in Jesus Christ's life. With songs by Schwartz, *Godspell* was born. Although *Godspell*'s "plot" addresses the same events depicted in *Jesus Christ Superstar*, the two shows were radically different. The ten actors who perform *Godspell* wear clownlike costumes, and the atmosphere is that of a circus.

After a tryout at the experimental theater LaMaMa, *Godspell* began an off-Broadway run in 1971. Even with a 1973 film release, ticket sales remained strong, and after 2,124 off-Broadway performances, the producers transferred the show to Broadway itself in 1976, where *Godspell* enjoyed 527 more performances. Meanwhile, Schwartz's agent had introduced him to her brother: Leonard Bernstein. Bernstein was working on a commission from the new John F. Kennedy Center for the Performing Arts in Washington, D.C. Bernstein had labored on his *Mass* for five years, and he was beginning to panic, so Schwartz assisted with the lyrics. Despite the title, *Mass* was a theatrical work, not intended for worship; it met with mixed reactions after its 1971 debut, but bit by bit, Schwartz's fame was increasing.

For some time, there had been talk of reviving his college musical. Producer Stuart Ostrow asked Roger O. Hirson to rewrite the book and hired Bob Fosse to be director/choreographer. Accounts differ as to how much cynicism Fosse added to the storyline. In any event, Fosse left his inimitable stamp on what he retitled *Pippin*. Fosse added the Leading Player, who functions as a puppet master, leading Pippin through his paces—until Pippin rebels. The scenes are short sketches, in the manner of vaudeville or minstrel show skits. When Pippin's grandmother sings, the words unfurl on a large scroll

so the audience can join in, in the style of an old-time sing-along. Straw hats, canes, and soft-shoe routines appear. At the same time, the white facepaint and costuming evokes the old commedia dell'arte traditions in which actors portray stock characters—young lovers, lecherous old men, shrewish housewives—and improvise their way through familiar dramatic situations.

Pippin got off to somewhat of a shaky start after its 1972 opening. Many people didn't comprehend the symbolism of some vignettes, while they understood all too well the political thrust of others. For example, many Buddhist monks had burned themselves to death as a protest against the ongoing Vietnam war, so Pippin's immolation scene at the end was recognized as a reference to this practice. To boost flagging ticket sales, Ostrow decided to start advertising the show on television—a novel approach for the time. Fosse, using techniques he had developed as a film director, created a dazzling commercial. Ticket sales skyrocketed, helping *Pippin* to a five-year run of some 1,944 performances. Ostrow was a bit chagrined at the long-term results of his television advertising, explaining,

> I have mixed emotions about having created the Pippin commercial . . . [I]t never occurred to me that it would change the way theatre was to be produced. From that moment on hucksters could sell shows as commodities so long as their spot had glitter and hype. Never mind producing a great show, produce a great commercial!

Indisputably, though, the power of television had become clear. Where earlier shows had depended on sheet music, pluggers, hit singles broadcast over the radio, cast albums, and newspaper advertising to promote their productions, television seemed to grab audiences' attention like no media before.

Schwartz had been unhappy with many of Fosse's directorial decisions, but it was hard to argue with such clear-cut success, and Schwartz would enjoy that type of success once more, when *The Magic Show* debuted in 1974. Since both *Godspell* and *Pippin* were still running, this new production gave Schwartz the distinction of being the first composer to have three musicals playing simultaneously on Broadway. *The Magic Show* was a vehicle for magician Doug Henning, who performed a beautifully choreographed series of illusions; the show lasted for 1,920 performances.

Although Schwartz's compositional style continued to advance and mature, he began to have trouble finding the right combination of libretto and collaborators. He was a leading contributor to a collaborative revue called *Working* (1978), along with Micki Grant, Craig Carnelia, Mary Rodgers, and James Taylor, but *Working* closed after 25 performances. Schwartz contributed to another revue, which had a better run—but off-Broadway. He wrote lyrics for *Rags* (1986), but despite the added expertise of Joseph Stein and Charles Strouse, *Rags* closed after four showings, with a loss of $5.5 million.

For the most part, Schwartz's stage endeavors in the 1990s continued to fail—with one large overseas exception. Schwartz wrote lyrics for the animated Disney films *Pocahontas* (1995) and *The Hunchback of Notre Dame* (1996), with music by Alan Menken. Not only did they win two Academy Awards for *Pocahontas*, but a German-language stage adaptation of *Hunchback* (1999) also set a new long-run record in Berlin. Schwartz wrote the words *and* music for two more animated features, *The Prince of Egypt* (for which he won another Oscar) and the made-for-TV *Gepetto*. Most recently, though, he has created another stage musical, *Wicked*, based on a novel by Gregory Maguire that looks at the Land of Oz from a different perspective entirely. *Wicked* opened in October 2003 and won three Tonys; it is a pleasure to see a composer of the 1970s making a rare comeback in the twenty-first century.

That same Land of Oz has inspired numerous stagings over the years, beginning with the wildly successful 1903 operetta *The Wizard of Oz*. In 1975, it was the source for another of Broadway's enormous hits, *The Wiz*. Part of the show's novelty was the race of its composer, for Charlie Smalls was a Juilliard-trained African American, but viewers were much more aware of the all-black cast—and the upbeat musical mix of pop, rock, and soul—than they were of the ethnicity of the creators. In fact, for many viewers, *The Wiz* made them aware of Broadway itself. As in the case of *Pippin*, an aggressive television advertising campaign was used as a primary marketing tool. The commercials attracted many young African American viewers who had never previously come to Broadway shows. Their support helped *The Wiz* achieve a run of 1,672 performances, and the show's popularity also led to a 1978 film version with Michael Jackson and Diana Ross. On Broadway, *The Wiz* won seven Tonys, including Best Musical. Smalls won a Tony for his score (he wrote both the words and music) and was working on songs for a show called *Miracles* when he suffered a burst appendix in Belgium. He was rushed to the hospital, but he suffered a heart attack during surgery, dying at age 43 and ending his chances to add further theatrical achievements to his name.

Marvin Hamlisch was born the same year (1944) as Charlie Smalls and, like Smalls, he attended Juilliard. They weren't true classmates, however, for Hamlisch was the youngest child ever to have studied at Juilliard; he was a somewhat reluctant piano student from the age of six. Hamlisch is also blessed with **perfect pitch** (which the British call absolute pitch), meaning he has the innate ability to determine the frequency of sounded notes. (Studies indicate that one person in 10,000 possesses this gift.) Unlike Smalls, however, Hamlisch served a fairly lengthy Broadway apprenticeship before being tapped to write his first score, but—again like Smalls—his first effort turned out to be a blockbuster.

Like numerous composers, Hamlisch worked as a rehearsal pianist and a dance music arranger; he had also worked for Kander and Ebb while they were writing a show for Hamlisch's high school classmate Liza Minnelli. Although these were valuable practical experiences, Hamlisch's reputation was built primarily on his pop songs and film scores; he has written for more than three dozen films. His name began exciting national attention when he made three trips to the winner's podium during the 1974 Academy Awards, taking two Oscars for *The Way We Were* and one for *The Sting*.

Meanwhile, two dancers were so disgusted by their involvement with a dreadful flop musical that they decided to assemble a company of gypsies who would "write, produce, direct, design, and choreograph their own shows." They reasoned that no one knew better than dancers what "worked" for dancers, and they also thought this project might attract one of the great dancer-turned-choreographer-turned-directors, Michael Bennett. Over several evenings, Bennett met with the group and tape-recorded their anecdotes about auditions, successes, failures, and the roads they had traveled to become hoofers. (Dancers have superstitions and traditions as well; see the **Sidebar**: Superstition and the Gypsy Robe.)

Bennett saw great potential in the gypsies' stories. He presented the idea for a concept musical showcasing those tales to Joseph Papp, whose New York Shakespeare Festival had supported many experimental shows (including *Hair*). Papp gave Bennett the go-ahead; Bennett engaged Hamlisch to write the music and then began to hold auditions. The "concept" of *A Chorus Line* is that it depicts a casting call for a new show, with various gypsies vying for a small number of chorus-line slots (see the **Plot Summary**). Each performer has undergone various struggles to get where he or she is, and the show teaches many viewers that a chorus line *is* comprised of individuals rather than a row of perfectly matched automatons. A paradox of *A Chorus Line* is that the "winning" dancers *lose* their individuality by the end of the show; as Stephen Banfield notes, "We cannot even tell who is who in their chorus line costumes." Another irony of *A Chorus Line* was that several of the gypsies whose actual life stories were used in the show failed to win spots in the cast, while other dancers who contributed anecdotes were given someone *else's* "biography" to perform. Denny Flinn dryly observed, "To audition for your own life story and not get cast was possibly the most frustrating aspect of the process."

Hamlisch, working with lyricist **Edward Kleban** (1939–1987), set the hoofers' various life experiences to music. (Curiously enough, Kleban's own life would later be depicted on stage in 2001, when *A Class Act* had a brief Broadway run.) Composer Sheldon Harnick observed,

> *[Hamlisch and Kleban] could have tried to write songs which might have had a chance in the commercial record market; or they could let Michael Bennett steer them in very specific directions toward songs that would probably be limited to their use in the show. . . . They made the decision right at the top not to worry about what songs might be recorded but instead to ask themselves what is the situation. What would these characters say? What's going to be effective on stage? How can we serve the* show?

One of the situational numbers is Mike's exuberant account of how he came to be a hoofer; after watching his sister take dance lessons, Mike realizes "I Can Do That" (**Musical Example 50**), which indeed he can, as he demonstrates in his

Sidebar: Superstition and the Gypsy Robe

The theatrical world is very superstitious, full of rituals and prohibitions. Many people are familiar with the habit of saying "break a leg" rather than "good luck." Does this fool the perverse theater gods into sending good fortune instead of bad? Some argue that theater curtains are called legs, and repeated curtain calls might "break" the cranking mechanism. Others note that the ancient Greeks stomped their feet instead of clapping; an audience that has broken its legs in applause is one appreciative audience! Some say the phrase is a corruption of "Baruch ata Adonai," the opening words of many Hebrew prayers (meaning "Blessed is the Lord, Our God"), and that actors in the Yiddish theater inspired non-Hebrew speakers to say a similar-sounding blessing before going on stage.

There are other things—besides saying "good luck"—that theatrical people won't do. Most of the prohibitions have origins in common sense; the strictures against mirrors or live flowers on stage are logical enough; mirrors can reflect stage lighting back into an audience's eyes, and fresh flowers wilt quickly under hot lights. Similarly, performers won't whistle backstage. This proscription originated in the days before radio headsets and microphones, when stagehands used whistles to prompt the **stage cues**, the signals to **fly** (drop or raise) a particular curtain, lighting bar, or backdrop. An ill-judged whistle could have brought something heavy down upon one's head.

A less rational tradition is the taboo against speaking aloud the title of Shakespeare's shortest tragedy, *Macbeth*. Actors are hard-pressed to explain their certainty that disaster will befall anyone who is unwise enough to say the title. The usual solution is to refer to *Macbeth* as "The Scottish Play." Actors believe there *are* remedies if they should slip and accidentally say the "M" word in their dressing room. For instance, after exiting the room, immediately, the offender turns around counterclockwise three times, breaks wind or spits, and then knocks on the door and asks for permission to re-enter. An alternative solution is to utter a line from *Hamlet*: "Angels and ministers of grace defend us."

Broadway's gypsies have also developed a superstition designed to bring *good* luck; they pass along the **gypsy robe**, a simple muslin garment that has been decorated with mementos and signatures from the dancers in previous shows. The hoofer with the longest Broadway résumé gets to wear the robe, and when the company of a new show has gathered in a ring, the "robed" gypsy runs around the circle three times (counterclockwise, of course), touching everyone's hand. Still wearing the robe, the gypsy visits the cast members in their dressing rooms. The completion of these rituals is supposed to bless the fledgling show, bringing it good luck, and the robe is kept until the next show opens on Broadway.

The gypsy robe tradition began in 1950, when Bill Bradley was dancing in the chorus of *Gentlemen Prefer Blondes*. One of the chorus girls had a hideously flamboyant dressing gown—pale pink, with white feathers—and Bradley talked her into letting him send it to one of his friends who was nervously awaiting the opening of *Call Me Madam*. Bradley's friend, appreciating the gag, added a large flower from Ethel Merman's costume to the robe, and sent it to a dancer about to appear in yet another show. The tradition has been maintained for more than 50 years, and when a gypsy robe is swallowed up by memorabilia, it is retired, and a new robe is inaugurated. The retired robes, stored by Actors' Equity, are treasured for their historic and cultural value; Equity has given robes to the Smithsonian Museum and the Museum of the City of New York, and displays robes at the Equity Audition Center.

Robes fill up with mementos fairly quickly; for instance, the robe that was used from March 1987 to November 1989 contains souvenirs from *Les Misérables*, *Starlight Express*, *Late Nite Comic*, *Cabaret*, *Teddy and Alice*, *The Phantom of the Opera*, *Mail*, *Chess*, *Carrie*, *Legs Diamond*, *Jerome Robbins' Broadway*, *Chu Chem*, *Dangerous Games*, *Meet Me in St. Louis*, *Threepenny Opera*, and *Prince of Central Park*. Obviously, this theatrical tradition does not always work, for although some of the shows "blessed" by the robe have gone on to be blockbusters, others have vanished from the stage in short order. But—as performers would shrug—that's show biz!

A gypsy robe loaded with memorabilia.
Carol Rosegg Photography.

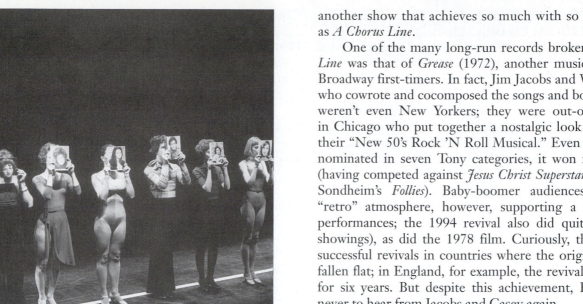

Resumes become faces in *A Chorus Line*.
Martha Swope.

rapid-fire tap-dance routine. The dance steps are interlaced between the phrases of a song form (**1, 2, 3,** and **4**), which is prolonged by not one but two coda-like extensions (**5** and **6**), each following another dance feature. Although the pride inherent in the song's title makes it immediately appealing, the number wouldn't make much sense apart from the context of this show, which is true of nearly all the songs. Many commentators have noted, somewhat disparagingly, that "What I Did for Love" is the only *non*integrated number in the show, and yet its success as a single was undoubtedly an important factor in *A Chorus Line*'s ultimate triumph.

And triumph it was. After appearing at Papp's off-Broadway Public Theater in 1975, *A Chorus Line* transferred to Broadway in July, beginning a record-breaking 6,137-performance run. It won nine Tony Awards, including Best Musical, and gave Hamlisch a Tony for his freshman effort as a Broadway composer (just as Charlie Smalls had won for *his* novice effort; even though both shows debuted in 1975, *The Wiz* was part of the 1974–75 season, while *A Chorus Line* belonged to the following theatrical "year"). Moreover, *A Chorus Line* was the fifth musical to win a Pulitzer Prize; it had been 14 years since *How to Succeed in Business Without Really Trying* had been given the same award.

Hamlisch's next "record" was less enviable; his subsequent seven contributions to Broadway and the West End all opened *and* closed before the phenomenal run of *A Chorus Line* had ended. Hamlisch portrayed his relationship with Carole Bayer Sager in *They're Playing Our Song* (1979); at 1,082 performances, it had a better run than their marriage. None of his other shows since have come close to that kind of run, however; his latest effort, *Imaginary Friends*, was designated a "play with music" and opened in late 2002 to mixed reviews; it closed in February 2003. It is hard to conceive that Hamlisch will ever be able to create

another show that achieves so much with so few resources as *A Chorus Line*.

One of the many long-run records broken by *A Chorus Line* was that of *Grease* (1972), another musical created by Broadway first-timers. In fact, Jim Jacobs and Warren Casey, who cowrote and cocomposed the songs and book for *Grease*, weren't even New Yorkers; they were out-of-work actors in Chicago who put together a nostalgic look at the past in their "New 50's Rock 'N Roll Musical." Even though it was nominated in seven Tony categories, it won none of them (having competed against *Jesus Christ Superstar* and Stephen Sondheim's *Follies*). Baby-boomer audiences adored the "retro" atmosphere, however, supporting a run of 3,388 performances; the 1994 revival also did quite well (1,505 showings), as did the 1978 film. Curiously, the film led to successful revivals in countries where the original show had fallen flat; in England, for example, the revival of *Grease* ran for six years. But despite this achievement, Broadway was never to hear from Jacobs and Casey again.

Grease spoke to baby boomers; Micki Grant's *Don't Bother Me, I Can't Cope* (1972) addressed pressures facing African Americans. Like Jacobs and Casey, Grant was a Broadway novice who hailed from Chicago, but there the similarities ended; she was a female African American composer (and actress; she was the first African American to be a soap opera contract performer). Musically, her revue-like show was different as well, mixing rock, gospel, calypso, and folk styles. *Don't Bother Me* remained on Broadway for 1,065 performances, earning Grant the Outer Circle Critics' Award for Best Musical and a Grammy Award for Best Score. Also unlike Jacobs and Casey, Grant was not finished after her initial success; she contributed half the songs to *Your Arms Too Short to Box with God* (1976), which ran 429 performances. No new show by Grant has done as well, but *Your Arms Too Short* has been revived twice, and Grant deserves much credit for her role as a pioneering black female composer.

Another composer who shared Grant's gender, if not her race, was Nancy Ford. (Also like Micki Grant, Ford has supported herself by means of soap operas, working for years as a staff writer for *As the World Turns* and other programs.) Ford, who routinely collaborates with lyricist Gretchen Cryer, began her career writing college shows. After graduation, Ford and Cryer saw a steady series of their works produced off-Broadway; their second show, *The Last Sweet Days of Isaac* (1970), ran a year and a half despite the pressures of a newspaper strike and later an actors' strike. Ford and Cryer have varied their musical style considerably; some shows sounded like "traditional" musicals, while the score to *Isaac* has been called "baroque rock." Ford and Cryer have never had a real Broadway success, but one of their off-Broadway shows, *I'm Getting My Act Together and Taking It on the Road* (1978), established a total run of 1,165 performances. After this achievement, however, Ford and Cryer, despite repeated efforts, have not been able to regain the limelight.

Elizabeth Swados, like Ford and Cryer, has seen many of her works performed in off-Broadway theaters, but she has also made it to Broadway on two occasions; both did poorly, but *Runaways* (1978) was admired for its innovation. Swados's career in New York began with LaMaMa Experimental Theater Club in 1970 and has been wide-ranging ever since. In addition to musicals, revues, and incidental music, she has written art music of many sorts. She has not turned her back on theatrical music, however, having written and directed shows for LaMaMa as recently as 2002.

Of all the women composers to be heard on stage in the 1970s, Carol Hall enjoyed the biggest initial stage success. Hall's early background was a little off the beaten track; born in Texas, Hall fell in love with musical theater after seeing a touring production of a show. Even though her parents were both musical (her mother played in the Abilene Symphony Orchestra, and her father owned Abilene's only music store), Hall knew she needed to learn her trade in New York. She joined the **BMI Musical Theatre Workshop**, led by Lehman Engel, which trained aspiring musical theater writers.

The workshop did not show immediate results, for marriage and motherhood intervened. Once the marriage broke up, Hall supported her child by writing for children's shows (including *Sesame Street*), singing in a café alongside coworker Kris Kristofferson, and composing songs. (Hall notes that her work has been recorded by singers ranging from Barbra Streisand to Big Bird.) In the early 1970s, her friend Pete Masterson mentioned he'd read an interesting article, so she read it too. Intrigued, she asked the writer's permission to adapt it for a musical show. In this way, *The Best Little Whorehouse in Texas* became perhaps the only Broadway show to be based on an article from *Playboy Magazine*.

The Best Little Whorehouse told the story of the Chicken Ranch, a real Texas brothel that had operated from the 1840s (sometimes accepting chickens as payment for its services) until 1973, when it fell victim to a crusade led by a Houston-based radio commentator. Hall wrote the words and music for the songs that captured the flavor of Texas twang and humor. Opening in 1978 at an off-Broadway theater, *The Best Little Whorehouse* transferred to Broadway and ran until 1983 for some 1,703 shows. Nominated for seven Tony Awards, *The Best Little Whorehouse* won two, for Best Actor and Best Actress. The same year the stage musical closed, the 1983 film premiered, starring Dolly Parton and Burt Reynolds.

For a time, Hall was riding high, but like many others, she has found it difficult to follow up on that early success in subsequent endeavors. She has written songs for several more musicals, including an unsuccessful sequel to *The Best Little Whorehouse*, and has been a lyricist for other writers as well. She continued to perform, even appearing in Ford and Cryer's *I'm Getting My Act Together and Taking It on the Road*. By default, however, Hall has become a member of an increasingly large club of composers whose initial triumphs have never been matched by their later efforts.

FURTHER READING

Banfield, Stephen. *Sondheim's Broadway Musicals*. Ann Arbor: University of Michigan Press, 1993.

Beddow, Margery. *Bob Fosse's Broadway*. Portsmouth, New Hampshire: Heinemann, 1996.

Citron, Stephen. *Sondheim and Lloyd Webber: The New Musical*. Oxford: Oxford University Press, 2001.

Doughtie, Katherine Shirek. "Rituals, Robes, and Hungry Ghosts." *Dramatics* (January 2001): 5–7.

Flinn, Denny Martin. *What They Did for Love: The Untold Story Behind the Making of* A Chorus Line. New York: Bantam Books, 1989.

Green, Stanley. *Broadway Musicals: Show by Show*. Third edition. Milwaukee, Wisconsin: Hal Leonard Publishing, 1990.

Kasha, Al, and Joel Hirschhorn. *Notes on Broadway: Conversations with the Great Songwriters*. Chicago: Contemporary Books, 1985.

Mandelbaum, Ken. A Chorus Line *and the Musicals of Michael Bennett*. New York: St. Martin's, 1989.

———. *Not Since Carrie: Forty Years of Broadway Musical Flops*. New York: St. Martin's, 1991.

Miller, Scott. *From* Assassins *to* West Side Story: *A Director's Guide to Musical Theatre*. Portsmouth, New Hampshire: Heinemann, 1996.

Ostrow, Stuart. *A Producer's Broadway Journey*. Westport, Connecticut: Praeger, 1999.

Richards, Stanley, ed. *Great Rock Musicals*. New York: Stein & Day, 1979.

Suskin, Steven. *More Opening Nights on Broadway: A Critical Quotebook of the Musical Theatre, 1965–1981*. New York: Schirmer Books, 1997.

———. *Show Tunes: The Songs, Shows, and Careers of Broadway's Major Composers*. Revised and expanded third edition. New York: Oxford University Press, 2000.

PLOT SUMMARY: *A CHORUS LINE*

On a bare stage, a line of dancers in rehearsal clothes has been auditioning for a show, each performer hoping to get a spot. The line has been weeded down to 17, but the director, Zach, needs only four men and four women. Now he wants to know something about the individuals standing on the stage, so a series of introductions begins to unfold. Mike had been a little kid, watching his sister go to dance class, when he realized "I Can Do That" (**Musical Example 50**). Bobby can talk about anything—and does. Sheila, Maggie, and Bebe all thought their lives would be like the ballet if they could learn to dance like ballerinas. Kristine is a good dancer, but—as her husband Al helps her explain—she's not a singer, which is a terrible disadvantage for a chorus line member.

Mark is so young that all he can really remember is puberty, while Connie kept waiting to grow tall enough to dance ballet. Diana started out as an actress, but she found that she could feel "Nothing" during the high school improvisation exercises. The formerly plain and flat-chested Val describes how plastic surgery equalized her chances during auditions. Paul, however, can't even talk about his background—and Cassie has a background that Zach already seems to know. She's back on Broadway, after their former relationship panned out along with her Hollywood aspirations. She returns to learning the audition's dance routine while Zach probes into Paul's past some more, learning that the young man has struggled to come to terms with his sexual preferences and his parents' views about his life.

Zach continues to assess how well the dancers can sublimate their individuality into a single, matched line; Cassie has to work hard to disguise her special flair. Suddenly, disaster strikes; Paul falls to the ground with torn cartilage. His career is over, and the other dancers all know they'll reach the same point someday. But for now, dancing is what they do—and the eight who are chosen for the line are overjoyed. The show closes with them in performance attire, glittering through their routine.

MUSICAL EXAMPLE 50

A Chorus Line
Marvin Hamlisch/Edward Kleban, 1975
"I Can Do That"

Mike

1   I'm watchin' Sis go pit-a-pat. Said, "I can do that. I can do that."

2   Knew ev'ry step right off the bat. Said, "I can do that. I can do that."

3   One morning Sis won't go to dance class. I grabbed her shoes and tights and all,
    but my foot's too small. So,

4   I stuff her shoes with extra socks, run seven blocks in nothin' flat.
    Hell, I can do that. I can do that!

(Dance)

5   I got to class and had it made and so I stayed the rest of my life.
    All thanks to Sis (now married and fat), I can do this.

(Dance)

6   . . . That I can do! I can do that!

Chapter 38
Sondheim in the 1970s: The Endless Experiments

After writing the hit *A Funny Thing Happened on the Way to the Forum* near the beginning of the 1960s, Stephen Sondheim pursued a series of innovations that left some viewers cold. Like many of his peers, he looked like a has-been by the end of the decade. Sondheim began to demonstrate his staying power at the start of the 1970s, however, followed by another success three years later. Interspersed among these hits, however, were a number of experimental shows that were not immediate successes. Sondheim's audience began to polarize between those who adored everything he wrote and those who simply couldn't understand him. Sondheim's chief Broadway collaborator in this period was director Hal Prince; together they delved ever deeper into musical theater's potential—thrilling some patrons, while leaving others behind.

Even their first "hit" in 1970 didn't satisfy everyone: *Company* was honed to a sharp edge, but like a brilliantly polished chrome chair, it simply wasn't as comfortable as an overstuffed recliner. Librettist **George Furth** (b. 1932) had written a series of short plays depicting various marriages; one actress would play all the wives. Furth's initial producer couldn't raise the money needed, so Furth asked Sondheim for advice—Sondheim told Furth to let Prince read his script. Prince's reaction was, "Why not make a musical out of it?" Sondheim felt the characters were unmusical—that they didn't "sing"—and Prince retorted, "That's what's interesting about it." This quirky perspective appealed to Sondheim.

The single-actress-in-multiple-roles idea was jettisoned fairly quickly, and instead, the show used a 35-year-old bachelor, Robert, as its pivot (see the **Plot Summary**). The name "Robert" was chosen with care, since it lent itself to a number of diminutives (Bob, Rob, Robby, Bobbie, Bubi, Rob-o, etc.); the other characters could each have a private name for him. Rather than trying to write a linear story, with a beginning, middle, climax, and ending, the writers decided to let *Company* be a nonplot concept musical, and the concept would be the examination of marriage. At the same time, *Company* conveys another theme, that "looking at it" is not the same as "living it." Robert observes his friends' often dysfunctional marriages, has ambivalent feelings about the kind of relationship he wants for himself (or even *if* he wants a relationship for himself), but by the end, he believes what the others have been telling him all along: that "alone is alone, not alive." (It is somewhat ironic that the first actor to play Robert, Dean Jones, left the show shortly after the premiere to attend to marital problems of his own.)

Scott Miller offers the intriguing notion that the seemingly random portrayal of couple after couple results from "swimming around inside Robert's head, reading his thoughts about his friends and therefore about marriage." Like *Pippin*, Robert may be imagining—or at least simply remembering—the events shown on stage. At the same time, Robert remains a cipher, almost a nonentity in the story; although he visits his friends, he doesn't seem to have any effect on them. We are as startled as Robert is when April decides to stay with him, for he simply hasn't been very persuasive as he asks her to stay. Even in the climactic moment of Act I when Robert proposes to Amy, her mind is still on Paul.

Company ends with a final focus on Robert. How does he really feel at the conclusion of the show? *Company* went through four different finales: first came "Multitude of Amys," because an early version of *Company* had Amy refusing to marry Paul, and Bobby deciding to propose to her at the end of the show. When Robert's proposal was moved forward to Act I, with Amy swallowing her fears about marriage to Paul, Sondheim wrote a different finale, "Marry Me a Little." This was literally a triumph of ambivalence, and the creators decided that Robert needed to have leaned one way or the other by the end.

The third finale candidate, "Happily Ever After," was a bitter critique of marriage. The subtextual message of the song was that Robert realizes he is lonely—but Prince felt the song was too harsh for audiences. Sondheim responded with "Being Alive" for Robert's closing number; it, too, conveys a subtle message. Early in the lyrics, Robert describes a partner as "someone to hold you too close"; by the end, he starts to beg, "Somebody, hold me too close." When Robert fails to appear at the final birthday party, his friends decide that he has gone in search of—or perhaps has found—that "somebody." Or has he? Prince theorized, "*Company* is about a fellow who stays exactly the same"—but if that is true, how can Robert come to the decision that he's ready for a partnership? Did the creators choose a believable ending for the nonlinear story after all?

Company poses other questions. Was Robert ever at the birthday party in the first place? Is each birthday party scene a return to the *same* event, or do the parties take place in successive years? Prince said, "I am certain they were one," even though the mood of each birthday scene varies. He suggests the changes of atmosphere reflect an increasing maturity; certainly

1	2	3	4	5	6	7	8	9	10	11	12	13	14
a	*b*	*c*	*d*	*a*	*c*	*d'*	*e*	*c*	*d*	*a*	*b/d*	*b/c*	*d"*

Figure 38–1

the recurring party, whether it is one event or many, gives the freewheeling show a sense of cohesion.

The birthday party is not the only motif used to hold the innovative musical together. The overture opens with a busy signal, representing the harried, frantic lives of all the characters. This repetitive *buzz-buzz-buzz* reappears in the score throughout the show, for of course everyone is busy. Moreover, set designer Boris Aronson built elevators on the stage that lent their own symbolism to the show. Besides evoking New York's high-rise apartments, the elevators could mirror the ups and downs of relationships as well as the sense that people in two different elevators will never be able to meet.

Dance, too, plays a role in depicting the show's outlook. Michael Bennett's choreography was astonishingly effective in expressing the lack of emotion in Robert and April's bedroom encounter. The dance is symbolic in other ways, such as a tap-dance routine in which each husband performs a short, four-beat tap step, and his wife then "replies" with another simple four-beat pattern. When Robert dances the brief tap routine, he is met by silence—a clear metaphor for his "wifeless" state.

Sondheim's music is also an important factor in bringing *Company*'s characters to life. Or, as Mari Cronin puts it, his music "captures twentieth-century anxieties. Just as he forces audiences to confront the reality of what he has to say verbally, he subjects them to the emotional equivalent musically." Emotional content is at the forefront of "Getting Married Today" (**Musical Example 51**); in fact, the song conveys conflicting emotions simultaneously, with rhythmic pace distinguishing each of the singers. The song is a fascinating blend of diegetic singing—for of course people often sing at weddings—and nondiegetic participation by Amy and Paul. The number opens with the *a* theme, a solemn, reverential prayer offered by Jenny at **1**; her tempo indication is **largo**, a very slow speed. (Jenny's contribution becomes *less* diegetic as the song goes on; "real" wedding singers usually don't describe the marriage as a "tragedy of life" or the bride as "totally insane, slipping down the drain.")

Paul enters at **2** with a new melody, *b*. Like Jenny's theme, Paul's melodic line is fairly disjunct, but while Jenny sings mainly sustained pitches, Paul's shorter notes give the effect of proceeding at a slightly faster pace, demonstrating his eagerness. But Paul's theme seems comparatively static once Amy makes her first entry at **3**, marked **presto** (*very fast*); her frenetic delivery of the *c* theme is a tour-de-force of patter-song technique. She concludes her hysterical fit with a new, slightly less frantic theme (*d*) at **4**. The *d* melody stresses the tonic and dominant notes of the key repeatedly, giving Amy's words particular emphasis. Undaunted, Jenny resumes her hymn at **5**; the changes of text are the only hint that she has heard anything Amy is saying. A four-part choir joins in, humming an accompaniment.

The spotlight is back on Amy and her patter-singing at **6**. Amy introduces a new note of hysteria at **8** with an ascending melody (*e*) that climbs upward over and over again as she demands, "Go! Can't you go?" Jenny's hymn (*a*), still accompanied by a humming chorus, laments Amy's mental decline at **11**. At **12**, Paul and Amy sing in nonimitative polyphony, with Paul resuming the *b* theme while Amy sings her *d* melody. In a subtle indication that this marriage might work after all, Paul joins Amy at **14** in what had been her *d* theme, with the two of them alternating lines, punctuated by interjected "Amens" from the guests. Overall, the nonstandard form follows the pattern shown in **Figure 38–1**. In an understated way, Sondheim might be expressing the compromise that marriage demands; only at the end are the voices dialoguing in a single, shared, coherent line. Moreover, the choice of melody for the ending is significant; it is not the artificial hymnlike tune, not Amy's mad patter, not Paul's disjunct leaps, but the most emphatic of all the themes, *d*. It is probably no accident that *d* has the clearest sense of tonality of any of the tunes in "Getting Married Today"; its stress of the key's tonic note gives us the impression that the melody (and the partnership) has found its correct resting place.

Other people in *Company* come into focus by means of their songs as well. Joanne's eleven o'clock number, "The Ladies Who Lunch," is a character song, for it sheds light on Joanne's personality and worldview—which, as we learn as the song progresses, is quite jaundiced. Yet, her cynicism is present primarily as subtext; on the surface, this song is merely a toast offered up to the society matrons of Joanne's social class. But as we hear Joanne detail their activities, we realize that these women are useless and pitiable—and that Joanne loathes herself as much as she does any of the others. Elaine Stritch, the first actress to play Joanne, had to work very hard while recording the song for the cast album; she had been in the studio for 14 hours by the time she began "The Ladies Who Lunch." The recording session was videotaped and commercially released, allowing viewers to share in her struggle to generate a satisfactory performance for the album.

Sondheim's careful control of language is evident throughout his songs. (The compositional *process* was not always well controlled, however; see **Behind-the-Scenes**: Good Electronics Make Good Neighbors.) In the poetry of "The Ladies Who Lunch," Sondheim stressed the letter *L*: "Here's to the ladies who lunch—Ev'rybody laugh. Lounging in their caftans and planning a brunch on their behalf." This reiterated *L* sound adds to the inebriated effect of Joanne's rant. Similarly, language distinguishes the characters in "Getting Married Today." Jenny uses archaic constructions such as "husband joined to wife." Paul is formal and sentimental: "Amy, I give you the rest of my life, To cherish and to keep you." In contrast, Amy's nonrhyming text is a stream-of-consciousness, since frantic Amy can hardly think straight: "A wedding? What's a wedding? It's a prehistoric ritual where everybody promises fidelity forever which is maybe the most horrifying word I ever heard, and which is followed by a honeymoon when suddenly he'll realize he's saddled with a nut and wanna kill me which he should."

Sondheim also wrestled with the challenge of making patter-singing doable and comprehensible. "Getting Married Today" originally opened with "Wait a sec, is everybody here?" His final version—"Pardon me, is everybody there?"—is just a bit easier to say. There is also a tendency for the ear to combine *sec* and *is* into a single word, *second*, and by the time the listener realizes that Amy did *not* say "Wait a second," she's already a line or two further ahead. This sort of unwitting elision between words is truly the bane of lyricists; an amusing example of a poorly handled structure appeared in a show called *Robert and Elizabeth* (1964). Lyricist Ronald Miller had asked his performer to sing "While earth contains us two," but the listener could not help but hear "While the earth contains a stew."

By the time *Company* premiered in 1970, the hard labor over tiny details paid off. Many writers cited *Company*'s excellent craftsmanship, even if there were particular aspects that left them cold. For several reviewers, the problem lay in the "company" itself. As Walter Kerr put it, "At root, I didn't take to Mr. Jones's married friends any more than he did." Or, in the words of Clive Barnes, "These people are just the kind of people you expend hours each day trying to escape from. They are, virtually without exception, trivial, shallow, worthless and horrid." (Barnes wrapped up his review with a self-deprecating observation: "But I stress that I really believe a lot of people are going to love it. Don't let me put you off. Between ourselves, I had reservations about *West Side Story*.") Barnes was right—a lot of people *did* love *Company*, allowing it to run 706 performances. *Company* won the New York Drama Critics' Circle Award and the Tony for Best Musical, and Sondheim was awarded two Tonys: one for the score, one for the lyrics.

Sondheim and Prince's next musical, *Follies* (1971), enjoyed a 522-performance run. This fascinating production depicted a rendezvous of former revue performers interspersed with flashbacks to their years of fame. The story inspired some of Sondheim's most evocative and haunting melodies, and gave him the chance to write pastiche numbers mimicking music of the past. The show was a remarkable and influential piece of theater—but despite its artistic achievement, Broadway accountants classify it as a flop since it lost money.

The next Prince-Sondheim collaboration proved to be a success. *A Little Night Music*, like a few predecessors, had been based on a movie: Ingmar Bergman's 1955 *Sommarnattens Leende* (*Smiles of a Summer Night*). Bergman told the collaborators, who included librettist Hugh Wheeler, that they could use anything from his film except for the title itself. Sondheim wanted to preserve the movie's old-world atmosphere, so he wrote music in the style of old dances—scherzos, minuets, polonaises, and especially waltzes. For this reason, the majority of the tunes are in triple or compound meter, and many people call the show Sondheim's "waltz musical." Sondheim himself, when turning the score over to orchestrator Jonathan Tunick, said, "This score should sound like perfume."

Somewhat to Sondheim's surprise, the score to *A Little Night Music* generated one of his few hit songs. "Send in the Clowns" was re-recorded a couple of years later, both by Frank Sinatra and by Judy Collins, and the song rocketed up the charts. Many people have enjoyed "Send in the Clowns" without understanding what the song means. The title is derived from the circus world: When things were not going well in the center ring, a manager would give the order to "send in the clowns!" to liven things up and distract the audience.

Desirée (Glynis Johns) sings "Send in the Clowns" in *A Little Night Music*.
Martha Swope.

Most critics admired *A Little Night Music* when it debuted in 1973, describing the show as "soft on the ears, easy on the eyes, and pleasant on the mind." Audiences, moreover supported the show through 601 performances, putting Prince back in the black. *A Little Night Music* also got the nod from the New York Drama Critics' Circle and won six Tonys, including Best Musical.

Sondheim's next musical was not a Broadway show at all. Instead, *The Frogs* (1974) was staged in the Yale swimming pool (!); chorus members included Meryl Streep, Christopher Durang, and Sigourney Weaver. (*The Frogs* had its first Broadway staging 30 years later.) It was back to Broadway, though—and back to Hal Prince—for *Pacific Overtures* (1976), a 120-year-survey of Japanese history using traditional forms of Japanese theater blended with Western theatrical styles. The problem was that Broadway audiences knew little about Japanese culture, and no one really understood what was happening. Critics were sharply divided; some appreciated what the writers attempted to do and felt they'd accomplished it, while others found the evening to be a bore. Baffled audiences meant the show lasted only 193 performances.

Prince, needing a hit, turned to other projects. Meanwhile, Sondheim saw a gothic horror play, *Sweeney Todd*, and tried to interest Prince in an adaptation; Prince's initial reaction was that the story "was a little on the campy side." As he thought about it more, though, Prince began to feel differently, concluding, "*Sweeney Todd* is a story about how society makes you impotent, and impotence leads to rage, and rage leads to murder—and, in fact, to the breaking down of society." Sondheim, more simply, felt the show was about obsession, although he also saw it as centered around revenge, noting that this "poses a problem for a lot of people who refuse to admit to themselves that they have a capacity for vengeance, but I think it's a universal trait." (See the **Plot Summary**.)

The story of **Sweeney Todd**, Sondheim's fifth show with Prince, stretched back to around 1820, when a French account was published in *Archives of the Police*. The first English version, "A Terrible Story of the Rue de la Harpe" appeared in *Tell-Tale Magazine* in 1825. Then, in 1846, *The People's Periodical and Family Library* published an 18-installment account of the gruesome tale titled "The String of Pearls, A Romance." Christopher Bond used this melodrama as the basis for his 1973 play, *Sweeney Todd (The Demon Barber of Fleet Street)*, and then Bond's play became the heart of Sondheim's musical adaptation. Both Sondheim and Bond acknowledge the importance of the other's work; Sondheim noted, "Bond humanized all the characters and gave the story motivation which had never existed before in the earlier versions of Sweeney Todd." Bond, on the other hand, said, "Until Steve performed his alchemical miracle on [the play], it remained a neat pastiche that worked well if performed with sufficient panache, but base metal nonetheless. But the transformation to pure gold was about to begin."

The show was expensive enough that it seemed it was created of pure gold. Prince and the production designer Eugene Lee found an abandoned factory in Rhode Island, purchased it, then reconstructed it onstage. The gritty, broken-glass ceiling and walls created a Victorian-era environment that "separated people from the sun," one of Prince's metaphors for the Industrial Revolution. The heavy backdrop dwarfed the characters, however, making it hard to keep them the focus of the show; some viewers have preferred later productions of *Sweeney Todd* that employed more austere stage sets.

Sondheim's score is seen as one of *Sweeney Todd*'s great strengths. The show opens with an archaic phrase—"Attend the tale of Sweeney Todd"—and it is set to one of the ancient church modes rather than a major or minor scale. Sondheim also quoted bits of the *Dies irae* ("Day of Wrath"), a Catholic chant sung during the funeral mass. Initially, Sondheim had thought to make *Sweeney Todd* a sung-through production, but it took him 20 minutes' worth of music to say what Bond's play had covered in five pages. Sondheim knew he needed help, so **Hugh Wheeler** (1912–1987) assisted with a libretto that used spoken dialogue to help move the story along.

Despite the spoken lines, there are those who still charge Sondheim with having written an opera. Sondheim resists that genre label strenuously, explaining,

> *I think an opera is something performed in an opera house in front of an opera audience by opera singers. I think the same piece performed in a Broadway house, in a West End house, by West End or Broadway singers, in front of a Broadway or West End audience is a show, meaning it's a musical. The approach is different, the audience's expectations are the major difference between operas and musicals. When an audience enters an opera house they are going for a specific kind of experience that's so much more related to a rock concert than it is to a musical. They are going to hear performers, which is what rock concerts are about—to hear that performer—they don't care if it's their fifth* Tosca *[an opera by Puccini] as long as it's the lady that they want to hear sing* Tosca.

Sondheim suggested another genre label at a later point, remarking that "*Sweeney Todd* is really an operetta, it requires operetta voices, that is to say the needs for the singers are slightly greater than the needs on Broadway but nowhere as great as the needs in grand opera. It's what I would call an operetta."

Sondheim's "operetta" comes complete with a waltz, "A Little Priest" (**Musical Example 52**). "A Little Priest" is somewhat of an anomaly in the story, for it is humorous—a macabre humor, to be sure, but still quite a change from the dark, brooding atmosphere that pervades the majority of the show. Arguably, though, *Sweeney Todd* needs this moment of comic relief, coming immediately after Sweeney's "Epiphany," when his mind turns inexorably to revenge and madness.

The essence of the humor in "A Little Priest" is its series of gleeful puns and demonic double entendres, as Sweeney and Mrs. Lovett try to outdo each other in imagining the people of various professions who might end up as pie ingredients. Sondheim uses at least six intertwining themes in a nonstandard form, as seen in **Figure 38–2**. The majority of the horrific duet is homophonic, but a short stretch of nonimitative

1	2	3	4	5	6	7	8	9	10	11	12	13
intro	*a*	*a*	*b*	*c*	*d*	*e*	*c*	*e*	*c*	*d*	*f*	*e*

Figure 38–2

polyphony appears at **3**. The climactic moment comes at **12**, when Sweeney realizes that what he *really* wants is to see "judge" on Mrs. Lovett's menu. Unfazed, Mrs. Lovett suggests that he might like to try "executioner" even more, and the song ends with one last awful pun, when the new partners-in-crime resolve to "serve anyone at all." The duet triumphs in its ability to disgust us with its references to cannibalism while making us laugh despite ourselves. Would we, too, have shopped at Mrs. Lovett's pie shop? The black humor continued behind the scenes too; Sondheim received an opening night telegram that read, "Bake a leg."

Sweeney and Mrs. Lovett are repellent, yet Mrs. Lovett, at least, is not unfamiliar. Foster Hirsch has observed, "As a bourgeoise with a criminal soul Mrs. Lovett is moral first cousin to the Peachums in *The Threepenny Opera*." Of course, Mrs. Lovett's "heritage" stretches back even further to *The Beggar's Opera*; she sustains that early ballad opera's sense of greedy opportunism when she recognizes a really horrid way to "make a buck." Sweeney, on the other hand, was a new sort of antihero for Broadway. The idea of a man who seeks revenge for the loss of his family is an old theme—in fact, it is possible to feel a reluctant admiration for Sweeney until madness unhinges his reason altogether—but the grisly means by which Sweeney disposes of corpses is what sets him apart.

Critics responded to the power of the drama and the music, many of them giving *Sweeney Todd* rave reviews after its 1979 premiere and awarding it the Drama Critics' Circle prize. Once again, the show took the majority of the year's Tony Awards. Sondheim and Prince's next (and final) collaboration, *Merrily We Roll Along* (1981), was much less successful, despite some beautiful songs and an intriguing "told-in-reverse"

storyline. With *Merrily*, the Sondheim–Prince string of six remarkably different shows over an 11-year stretch came to an end. Both men have continued to be busy—and to experiment—in the theater, but their efforts have been conducted in partnership with other people. Sondheim continued to craft unusual works, while Prince pursued his acquaintance with Lloyd Webber, thereby generating the biggest crowds ever witnessed in the theater. In turn, Broadway began to see its stages dominated not by "American" musicals but by a wave of foreign imports, some from England and others—to the surprise of many—from France.

FURTHER READING

Banfield, Stephen. *Sondheim's Broadway Musicals*. Ann Arbor: University of Michigan Press, 1993.

Berkowitz, Gerald. "The Metaphor of Paradox in Sondheim's *Company*." *Philological Papers* 25 (Feb. 1979): 94–100.

Bristow, Eugene K., and J. Kevin Butler. "*Company*, About Face! The Show That Revolutionized the American Musical." *American Music* 5 (Fall 1987): 241–254.

Citron, Stephen. *Sondheim and Lloyd Webber: The New Musical*. Oxford: Oxford University Press, 2001.

Cronin, Mari. "Sondheim: The Idealist" in *Stephen Sondheim: A Casebook*. Edited by Joanne Gordon. (Casebooks on Modern Dramatists, Volume 23; Garland Reference Library of the Humanities, Volume 1916.) New York and London: Garland Publishing, 1997, pp. 143–152.

Everett, William A., and Paul R. Laird, eds. *The Cambridge Companion to the Musical*. Cambridge: Cambridge University Press, 2002.

Gerould, Daniel. "A Toddography (including 'Sweeney Todd the Barber' by Robert Weston)" in *Melodrama*. Guest edited by Daniel Gerould. New York: New York Literary Forum, 1980, pp. 43–48

Gottfried, Martin. *Sondheim*. New York: Abrams, 1993.

Guernsey, Otis L., Jr., ed. *Broadway Song & Story: Playwrights/Lyricists/Composers Discuss Their Hits*. New York: Dodd, Mead, 1985.

———. *Playwrights, Lyricists, Composers on Theater: The Inside Story of a Decade of Theater in Articles and Comments by Its Authors, Selected from Their Own Publication*, The Dramatists Guild Quarterly. New York: Dodd, Mead, 1974.

Herbert, Trevor. "Sondheim's Technique." *Contemporary Music Review* 5 (1989): 199–214.

Hirsch, Foster. *Harold Prince and the American Musical Theatre*. Cambridge: Cambridge University Press, 1989.

Ilson, Carol. *Harold Prince From* Pajama Game *to* Phantom of the Opera. Ann Arbor, Michigan: U.M.I. Research Press, 1989.

Lewine, Richard. "Symposium: The Anatomy of a Theater Song." *The Dramatists Guild Quarterly* 14, no. 1 (1977): 8–19.

Mrs. Lovett (Angela Lansbury) and Sweeney (Len Cariou) envision "A Little Priest" in *Sweeney Todd*.

Photofest.

Mandelbaum, Ken. *Not Since Carrie: Forty Years of Broadway Musical Flops.* New York: St. Martin's, 1991.

Miller, Scott. *From Assassins to West Side Story: A Director's Guide to Musical Theatre.* Portsmouth, New Hampshire: Heinemann, 1996.

Mollin, Alfred. "Mayhem and Morality in *Sweeney Todd.*" *American Music* 9 (Winter 1991): 405–417.

Mordden, Ethan. *Better Foot Forward: The History of American Musical Theatre.* New York: Grossman Publishers (A Division of the Viking Press), 1976.

Ostrow, Stuart. *A Producer's Broadway Journey.* Westport, Connecticut: Praeger, 1999.

Prince, Hal. *Contradictions: Notes on Twenty-Six Years in the Theatre.* New York: Dodd, Mead, 1974.

Roberts, Terri. "Glynis Johns: Still Tearful in 'Clowns'." *The Sondheim Review* 5, no. 1 (Summer 1998): 16–17.

Sondheim, Stephen. "The Musical Theater: A Talk by Stephen Sondheim." *The Dramatists Guild Quarterly* 15, no. 3 (1978): 6–29.

Steyn, Mark. *Stephen Sondheim.* (Josef Weinberger Music Theatre Handbook 6.) London: Josef Weinberger, 1993.

BEHIND-THE-SCENES: GOOD ELECTRONICS MAKE GOOD NEIGHBORS

It was a wintry night in Manhattan when Stephen Sondheim finished composing "The Ladies Who Lunch." It was also three in the morning. Oblivious to the time, Sondheim sang Joanne's lyrics at the top of his voice, accompanying himself on the piano, testing how the lyrics and melody and harmony all fit together. His neighbor Katherine Hepburn awoke with a start. As the racket next door continued, she got madder and madder; finally, she opened her French doors and marched across the small snowy patio that separated their townhouses. She later reported, "I just stood there, and just stared with my nose up against the glass. And he just kept playing and singing—until he looked up and saw me and I can tell you this—*when he saw me, he stopped playing that piano.*"

An embarrassed Sondheim immediately went shopping for an electric piano and headphones. Hepburn probably regretted the piano purchase, however; Sondheim later learned that for several weeks she had been telling the director of her current show, *Coco*, that she needed to limit her rehearsal time because her sleep kept being interrupted by the young man next door. Now, with only silence emanating from Sondheim's townhouse, Hepburn lost her convenient excuse for shorter rehearsals.

PLOT SUMMARY: *COMPANY*

Five couples—all friends of Robert's—are gathered in his Manhattan apartment for a surprise party. Robert is turning 35 and is wondering if he should be married too. He starts to examine the partnerships of all these couples, trying to judge if any of these relationships might be a model for him.

Sarah and Harry are a quarrelsome pair, each with hang-ups: Sarah's got a problem with food, while Harry's got a problem with drink. During Robert's visit to their apartment, he's the referee as they take out their problems on each other. Sarah, a karate student, vents some of her frustration on Harry, whom she pins over and over again. He refuses to cry "Uncle," however, and in the background Joanne explains, "It's the Little Things You Do Together" that make "perfect relationships." Later, Robert asks Harry if he's ever sorry he got married; Harry replies that it's always a yes-and-no answer.

Susan and Peter have some shocking news for Robert: they're getting divorced. Things are even stranger at Jenny and David's apartment, for they're smoking marijuana. The conversation drifts toward the subject of marriage, and Robert, trying to prove that he's not against it, insists that he's *really* thinking about it and is dating three women as he explores the idea. His three female interests—April the flight attendant, Marta the nut, and Kathy who is from out of town—band together to express their shared frustration with Robert in three-part Andrews Sisters fashion.

The husbands aren't so concerned that Robert be in a solid relationship as they are hopeful to get a thrill from hearing about his various bachelor encounters. Robert has begun to dream of the perfect companion, a composite of all his female friends' best qualities. Meanwhile, Marta articulates the single person's desperate anxiety to meet people in the big, alien city without seeming too needy.

Paul and Amy, longtime partners, have decided to get married—but now that the day has arrived, Amy has cold feet. Frantically, she insists she's *not* "Getting Married Today" (**Musical Example 51**), and Paul, distraught, walks out. Impulsively, Robert proposes to Amy himself, and Amy is struck by the irony of the situation: she's afraid to get married, and Robert's afraid *not* to. Suddenly, she realizes that it's pouring outside and that Paul didn't take his raincoat. She goes tearing after him, but not without taking her bridal bouquet; the wedding is going to take place after all.

At the birthday party that opens the second act, Robert's friends describe their relationships with him, asking Robert, "What Would We Do Without You?" Near the end of the song, after the question has been asked yet again, Robert replies, "Just what you'd usually do," and without missing a beat, they snap back, "Right!" They console themselves with the idea that at least they are there for him, even if he has no one else. Robert is not quite as alone as they imagine, for even at that moment he is entertaining April for the evening. In "Tick Tock," a dancer simulates their nocturnal coupling, making it clear that they are having sex rather than making love. In the morning, during a rather stilted conversation, Robert suggests that April stay. No, she says, she is working a flight bound for "Barcelona," but suddenly she has a change of heart, and to Robert's dismay, she says she'll stay.

Things are not over with Robert's other relationships, either. He and Marta visit Susan and Peter. When Peter went to Mexico to file for divorce, he enjoyed the country so much that he called Susan and urged her to come join him. Now no longer married, they live together in deepest contentment, happier than they've ever been. Robert also goes with Larry and Joanne to a nightclub. Joanne drinks steadily, and while Larry is dancing, she mocks herself and other women in her situation, calling them "The Ladies Who Lunch." The alcohol has given her temporary courage, and she propositions the younger Robert, offering to "take care of him" in exchange for a relationship. Almost without thinking, Robert blurts out, "But who will I take care of?" and turns Joanne down.

At home, though, Robert realizes that he wants the feeling of "Being Alive," and he can only have that sensation if he allows himself to love "someone." The woman may not be perfect; there may be frustrations ahead, but he's ready to try commitment for the first time in his life. Meanwhile, his friends await him yet again at his birthday party. When he doesn't arrive, they slowly realize that he must have found someone else to be with at last, and saying "Happy Birthday" to the empty room, they depart.

PLOT SUMMARY: *SWEENEY TODD*

An ear-piercing factory whistle is heard, and various gravediggers and bystanders introduce us to the nineteenth-century "demon barber of Fleet Street." As the prologue ends, two men have arrived at the London docks. The younger, the sailor Anthony Hope, is in awe of the great city, but the older man, Sweeney Todd, views the metropolis as a black pit filled with the vermin known as society. They are accosted by a mad beggar woman offering her filthy body. Anthony cannot understand Sweeney's harsh response, but Sweeney tells Anthony the horrifying tale of "The Barber and His Wife." A powerful judge had desired Sweeney's beautiful wife, so he drummed up false charges against Sweeney and had him transported from England so that there would be no one to defend Lucy Todd. Anthony is horrified and asks what became of her. Sweeney tells him it was all a long time ago, then bids Anthony farewell.

Sweeney makes his way to Mrs. Lovett's shop on Fleet Street. He asks about her upstairs room, which she is trying to rent. She admits that no one wants it because of its unhappy past; she says the room once housed a barber and his wife, until Judge Turpin took a fancy to the wife and got rid of the husband. The judge, with his beadle's help, deceived Lucy by luring her to a masquerade ball at the judge's home. There he raped her and took away her child Johanna as his ward. Lucy killed herself.

As Mrs. Lovett tells the tale, she realizes that this is Sweeney himself. Sweeney is crushed, since the thought of returning to his family has buoyed him for 15 years, and now all that is left to him is revenge. Mrs. Lovett doesn't see how a powerless man could succeed in vengeance, but offers him the room; moreover, she still has his barber's tools, so he can earn a living.

Meanwhile, Johanna leans out a window, admiring the birds offered for sale by a street vendor. She is spotted by Anthony, and since she has grown to be as beautiful as her mother had been, he is instantly smitten. He asks a passing beggar about the girl's identity. The beggar woman warns him that the girl's guardian is dangerous. Nevertheless, Anthony buys a bird to please Johanna but is caught by the judge as he tries to deliver the gift. The judge warns Anthony away, but Anthony vows to rescue "Johanna."

Sweeney visits a street market where another barber is hawking "Pirelli's Miracle Elixir." Challenging Pirelli to prove his claims, Sweeney wins handily. Sweeney invites the assembled crowd to come to his shop to be shaved, and the beadle—one of the contest judges—wavers, then declines. Sweeney is frustrated, but Mrs. Lovett counsels him to "Wait."

Anthony comes to the shop and tells Sweeney about his intent to rescue Johanna. Sweeney does not react, but agrees that Anthony can hide Johanna in the shop after freeing her. The next visitor is Pirelli, who recognized Sweeney during the contest and has decided to blackmail him. Enraged, Sweeney strangles Pirelli, and then hides the body in his room. Unaware of what is happening upstairs, Mrs. Lovett feeds pies (and gin) to her young shop assistant, Tobias.

After chasing off Anthony, Judge Turpin is suddenly aware of how Johanna has matured and decides to marry her himself. Johanna is distraught, so when Anthony succeeds in climbing to her window, she quickly agrees to elope with him. Meanwhile, the beadle has persuaded the judge that he should look his best for his marriage, so the pair head off to Sweeney's shop, where Sweeney shaves the judge. But, just before Sweeney can take his revenge, Anthony bursts into the shop, speaking of his elopement plans before he realizes who is there. Sweeney is enraged, for the judge will never return. Mrs. Lovett, having learned what happened to Pirelli, is focused on a more immediate problem, however: what to do with the body? Suddenly, it dawns on her that here is a wonderful source of meat for her pies, and she and Sweeney begin to giggle over the varied ingredients he might be able to supply her, such as "A Little Priest" (**Musical Example 52**). Their course of madness has begun.

As the second act begins, the horror increases: Customers are now flocking to Mrs. Lovett's pie shop, wolfing down her wares. Sweeney, too, is doing well and has devised an elaborate trap door that sends victims straight from his barber chair down to Mrs. Lovett's basement. Anthony continues to search for Johanna and discovers that the judge had her committed to an asylum—but the beadle tries to arrest Anthony when he arrives to see her.

The crazy beggar woman is the only one who seems to recognize the monstrous nature of Mrs. Lovett's business, but no one listens to her. Mrs. Lovett starts dreaming of a seaside cottage, but Sweeney still dreams of vengeance. When Anthony tells him that he's found Johanna, Sweeney starts cooking up two schemes. He helps Anthony disguise himself as a wigmaker who can go to the asylum to buy hair from the inmates. But Sweeney also betrays this plan to the judge, hoping to lure Judge Turpin back to his barbershop by telling him Anthony will bring Johanna there.

Tobias, meanwhile, has grown to love Mrs. Lovett but mistrusts Sweeney. Tobias grows even more suspicious when he finds a purse belonging to Pirelli. Mrs. Lovett realizes that Tobias is a risk, so she leads him to the basement, telling him he can help her make the pies, then locks him in. Upstairs, she finds the beadle. He's come to her shop because there have been complaints about the smell, and he wants to inspect her basement. She fobs him off by claiming Todd has the key, and when Todd comes in, she urges the beadle to accept a free shave from Todd.

Tobias is having a rough time of it in the basement. Not only has he discovered a fingernail in a pie, but it is not long before the beadle's body comes hurtling down the chute. Anthony is having a hard time, too, dropping his gun during the rescue of Johanna. She manages to grab it, however, and shoots the asylum's warden, enabling their escape. Anthony brings Johanna, disguised as a sailor, to Sweeney's shop, but Sweeney's not there, so Johanna hides while Anthony goes in search of a coach. Sweeney, as it turns out, had gone to the basement to deal with Tobias, but the beggar woman has come into the barber shop, crying for the beadle. Sweeney needs to silence this madwoman, so he quickly cuts her throat.

The judge arrives, as Sweeney had hoped. He murders the judge; his revenge is complete. Headed down the stairs, he remembers that he still must deal with Tobias, so he goes back to his shop for his blade. There he sees Johanna, who had come out of her hiding place. Seeing only a young sailor, Sweeney prepares to kill Johanna when he is interrupted by Mrs. Lovett's screams. Judge Turpin was not quite dead as he came down the chute, so Sweeney races down to finish him off. Suddenly, as Sweeney and Mrs. Lovett drag the bodies to the furnace, Sweeney realizes that the old beggar woman was his long-lost wife. Now completely insane, Sweeney waltzes Mrs. Lovett around the room, then forces her into the furnace. Tobias, driven mad himself by these dreadful events, can only think of one thing: destroying the man who has murdered Mrs. Lovett. He picks up Sweeney's dropped blade and kills the man who killed so many others. When Anthony and Johanna arrive with the police, Tobias is found working away at the meat grinder. The Londoners all join in to finish "The Ballad of Sweeney Todd."

MUSICAL EXAMPLE 51

COMPANY
STEPHEN SONDHEIM/STEPHEN SONDHEIM, 1970
"Getting Married Today"

Jenny

1
Bless this day, pinnacle of life, husband joined to wife.
The heart leaps up to behold this golden day.

Paul

2
Today is for Amy, Amy, I give you the rest of my life.
To cherish and to keep you, to honor you forever,
Today is for Amy, my happily soon-to-be wife.

Amy

3
Pardon me, is everybody there? Because if everybody's there,
I want to thank you all for coming to the wedding. I'd appreciate your going even more,
I mean, you must have lots of better things to do and not a word of it to Paul.
Remember Paul? You know, the man I'm gonna marry, but I'm not
because I wouldn't ruin anyone as wonderful as he is; but I

4
Thank you for the gifts and the flowers. Thank you all, Now it's back to the showers
Don't tell Paul, But I'm not getting married today.

Jenny

5
Bless this day, tragedy of life, husband joined to wife.
The heart sinks down and feels dead this dreadful day.

Amy

6
Listen, everybody. Look, I don't know what you're waiting for—
A wedding? What's a wedding? It's a prehistoric ritual where everybody promises fidelity forever
which is maybe the most horrifying word I ever heard, and which is followed by a honeymoon
when suddenly he'll realize he's saddled with a nut and wanna kill me which he should, so listen,

7
Thanks a bunch, but I'm not getting married, go have lunch, 'cause I'm not getting married,
You've been grand, but I'm not getting married, don't just stand there, I'm not getting married,
And don't tell Paul, But I'm not getting married today!

8
Go! Can't you go? Why is nobody listening? Goodbye! Go and cry at another person's wake.
If you're quick, for a kick, you could pick up a christening,
But please, on my knees, there's a human life at stake.

9   Listen, everybody, I'm afraid you didn't hear, or do you want to see a crazy lady fall apart in front of you?
It isn't only Paul who may be ruining his life; you know, we'll both of us be losing our identities—
I telephoned my analyst about it and he said to see him Monday, but by Monday
I'll be floating in the Hudson with the other garbage.
10   I'm not well, so I'm not getting married.
You've been swell, but I'm not getting married. Clear the hall, 'cause I'm not getting married.
Thank you all, but I'm not getting married, and don't tell Paul, but I'm not getting married today.

Jenny
11   Bless this bride, totally insane, slipping down the drain
And bless this day in our hearts, as it starts to rain.

Paul	**Amy**
12 Today is for Amy,	Go! Can't you go? Look, you know I adore you all,
Amy, I give you the rest of my life,	But why watch me die like Eliza on the ice?
To cherish and to keep you,	Look, perhaps I'll collapse in the apse right before you all,
to honor you forever,	So take back the cake, burn the shoes and boil the rice.
13 Today is for Amy,	Look, I didn't want to have to tell you, but I may be
My happily soon-to-be wife.	coming down with hepatitis and I think I'm gonna faint,
	so if you wanna see me faint, I'll do it happily,
	but wouldn't it be funnier to go and watch a funeral?
My adorable wife	So thank you for the 27 dinner plates and 37 butter knives, and
	47 paper-weights and 57 candle-holders . . .

Paul
14   One more thing—

Amy
I'm not getting married . . .

Guests
Amen.

Softly said:
But I'm not getting married . . .
Amen.

With this ring
Still I'm not getting married . . .
Amen.

I thee wed.
See, I'm not getting married.
Amen.

Paul	**Amy**
Let us pray, And we are	Let us pray that we're not

Amy and Paul
getting married today!

MUSICAL EXAMPLE 52

Sweeney Todd
STEPHEN SONDHEIM/STEPHEN SONDHEIM, 1979

"A Little Priest"

[Dialogue]

Mrs. Lovett
1   Seems a downright shame.
Sweeney
Shame?
Mrs. Lovett
Seems an awful waste. Such a nice plump frame Wot's-'is-name has . . . had . . . has . . .
Nor it can't be traced. Business needs a lift . . . debts to be erased . . . think of it as thrift,

2

As a gift . . . If you get my drift . . . No? Seems an awful waste.
I mean, with the price of meat what it is, when you get it, if you get it . . .

Sweeney
Hah!

Mrs. Lovett
Good, you got it. Take, for instance, Mrs. Mooney and her pie shop.
Business never better, using only pussycats and toast.
Now a pussy's good for maybe 6 or 7 at the most.
And I'm sure they can't compare as far as taste . . .

3

Sweeney
Mrs. Lovett, what a charming notion,
Eminently practical and yet appropriate, as always.
Mrs. Lovett, how I did without you
All these years I'll never know!
How delectable!
How choice! How rare!

Mrs. Lovett
Well, it does seem a waste . . .
Think about it!
Lots of other gentlemen'll
Soon be coming for a shave, won't they?
Think of all of them pies . . .

4

For what's the sound of the world out there?

What, Mr. Todd, what, Mr. Todd, what is that sound?

Those crunching noises pervading the air?

Yes, Mr. Todd, yes, Mr. Todd, yes, all around . . .

It's man devouring man, my dear,

Sweeney and Mrs. Lovett
And who are we to deny it in here?

[Dialogue]

5

Sweeney
Is it really good?

Mrs. Lovett
It's priest. Have a little priest.

Sir, it's *too* good, at least. Then again, they don't commit
sins of the flesh, so it's pretty fresh.

Awful lot of fat.

Only where it sat.

Haven't you got poet or something like that?

No, you see, the trouble with poet is, how do you know
it's deceased? Try the priest.

[Dialogue]

Lawyer's rather nice.

If it's for a price.

Order something else, though, to follow,
since no one should swallow it twice.

Anything that's lean.

Well then, if you're British and loyal, you might enjoy
Royal Marine . . . Anyway, it's clean . . .
Though, of course, it tastes of wherever it's been . . .

6

Is that squire on the fire?

Mercy, no, sir, look closer, You'll notice it's grocer.

Looks thicker, more like vicar.

No, it has to be grocer, it's green.

7

The history of the world, my love . . .

Save a lot of graves, do a lot of relatives favors . . .

Is those below serving those up above.

Everybody shaves, so there should be plenty of flavors . . .

How gratifying for once to know

Sweeney and Mrs. Lovett
That those above will serve those down below!

[Dialogue]

8	**Sweeney** Maybe for a lark.	**Mrs. Lovett** Lovely bit of clerk.

Then again, there's sweep if you want it cheap
and you like it dark. Try the financier—Peak of his career.

That looks pretty rank.

Well, he drank. No, it's bank cashier.
Never really sold . . . maybe it was old.

Have you any beadle?

Next week, so I'm told. Beadle isn't bad till you smell it
and notice how well it's been greased. Stick to priest.

[Dialogue]

9   The history of the world, my sweet . . .

Oh, Mr. Todd, ooh, Mr. Todd. What does it tell?

Is who gets eaten and who gets to eat.

And, Mr. Todd, too, Mr. Todd, who gets to sell.

But fortunately, it's also clear

Sweeney and Mrs. Lovett
That ev'rybody goes down well with beer.

[Dialogue]

Mrs. Lovett
It's fop. Finest in the shop.
Or we have some shepherd's pie
peppered with actual shepherd on top.
And I've just begun. Here's the politician,
so oily it's served with a doily. Not one?

10

Sweeney
Put it on a bun. Well, you never know if it's going to run.

11   No, the clergy is really too coarse and too mealy.

Try the friar. Fried, it's drier.

Yes, and always arrives overdone.

Then actor. That's compacter.

12   I'll come again when you have judge on the menu . . .

[Dialogue]

13   Have charity toward the world my pet.

Yes, yes, I know, my love.

We'll take the customers that we can get.

High-born and low, my love.

We'll not discriminate great from small.
No, we'll serve anyone, meaning anyone,

Sweeney and Mrs. Lovett
And to anyone at all!

The Late Twentieth Century and Beyond

Part Nine

Chapter 39
Andrew Lloyd Webber without Tim Rice: Cats and Starlight Express

Only half jokingly, Mark Steyn once wrote, "This is how they divide history: BC—Before *Cats* and AD—Andrew Dominant." After an informal dissolution of his 14-year partnership with Tim Rice, Andrew Lloyd Webber, like his American peer Sondheim, had explored offbeat subject matter. Sondheim's experiments focused more on the ears and the mind; the majority of Lloyd Webber's works began to dazzle the eyes. In a society increasingly focused on the visual, Lloyd Webber's new shows found quick acceptance, setting new records on both sides of the Atlantic.

Just as *Evita* was reaching the stage, Lloyd Webber and Rice had been toying around with the idea of a song cycle. As in Wagner's "Ring" cycle, a cycle is a group of works linked by a shared poetic (or musical) idea, and the writers felt they could express a woman's problematic love life through a series of songs. Rice had a particular woman in mind; although married to Jane McIntosh, he had fallen for Elaine Paige, star of the London production of *Evita*. Rice's affair with Paige made Lloyd Webber and others uncomfortable, since Jane was well liked. Moreover, Rice's working pace was exasperatingly leisurely, so Lloyd Webber used this as an excuse to work with another lyricist, Don Black. The resulting song cycle, *Tell Me On a Sunday*, examined the adventures (and *mis*adventures) of an Englishwoman in America. It was developed into a television mini-musical, but Lloyd Webber also wanted to see it on the stage. The question was: How? It was too short to stand on its own, and some people felt it was too depressing as well.

Putting the problem aside for a time, Lloyd Webber and Rice talked about new ideas; Rice was eager to do a story about two chess players—one American, one Russian—who are rivals not only in chess but also for the same woman. Lloyd Webber wanted to depict the legendary feud between the opera composers Puccini and Leoncavallo, but he also had another idea: an adaptation of Billy Wilder's film *Sunset Boulevard*. Rice felt there was no way to improve on Wilder's movie, so he declined.

Stymied, Lloyd Webber began to work on something else altogether. When he was a child, Lloyd Webber's mother used to read T. S. Eliot's *Old Possum's Book of Practical Cats* (written for the poet's godchildren) to him. Reading them again as an adult, he thought they had potential as another song cycle; one plus was that his lyricist would always be at hand. Of course, he would have to reverse his usual compositional procedure, since the music had to conform to the constraints of the existing poetry.

The resulting cycle of songs, collectively called **Cats**, was performed at Lloyd Webber's country estate, Sydmonton, during the summer of 1980. He invited the poet's widow to attend—a lucky invitation, since Mrs. Eliot rhapsodized over the song settings and offered Lloyd Webber some snippets of poetry and correspondence from her husband's files. This offer was the seminal moment in turning *Cats* into a viable show, for some of the new poetry centered around Grizabella the Glamour Cat. Eliot had eliminated the lines, feeling that they were too sad for children, but they were exactly what Lloyd Webber needed to give the songs (and show) a pivot point (see the **Plot Summary**).

Lloyd Webber had already teamed up with up-and-coming producer **Cameron Mackintosh** (b. 1946), and Mackintosh wanted **Trevor Nunn** (b. 1940) to direct. Nunn was a surprising choice; director of the Royal Shakespeare Company, it would seem that Nunn was too highbrow to direct a musical, let alone a musical based on poetry for children. But Mackintosh's instincts were sound, for Nunn was intrigued. Nunn and **Richard Stilgoe** (b. 1943) began sorting through Mrs. Eliot's papers.

There was some worry about choreographer (and associate director) **Gillian Lynne**'s (b. 1926) contribution to this all-danced show, because Lynne was English, and everyone knew that the English just couldn't compete with the Americans when it came to exciting dance musicals. Would England have singers who danced well enough for Lynne and dancers who sang well enough for Lloyd Webber? Also, noted actress

Judi Dench had been hired as Grizabella. Could she carry a tune? No one was sure.

Even the show's venue, the New London Theatre, was seen as a risk; it was more frequently used for television shows and conferences. Ironically (given *Cats's* eventual triumph), the theater owners tried to wiggle out of the contract before the show opened, wanting to resume booking industrial trade shows. Understandably, backers were hesitant too, as Lloyd Webber himself acknowledged:

> I can give you the objections and they sound a convincing lot. Andrew Lloyd Webber without Robert Stigwood; without Tim Rice; working with a dead poet; with a whole load of songs about cats; asking us to believe that people dressed up as cats are going to work; working with Trevor Nunn from the Royal Shakespeare Company, who's never done a musical in his life; working in the New London, the theatre with the worst track record in London; asking us to believe that twenty English people can do a dance show when England had never been able to put together any kind of fashionable dance entertainment before. It was just a recipe for disaster.

In a curious echo of Sondheim, however, Lloyd Webber added, "But we knew in the rehearsal room that even if we lost everything, we'd attempted something that hadn't been done before."

Mackintosh took the desperate step of advertising in the newspapers for backers, offering shares at a minimum of £750. By this means he acquired some 220 small investors who provided the necessary capital. Mackintosh arranged for a London newspaper to photograph his own cat Bouncer making an investment in the show. With the necessary money in hand at last, one more problem remained. There was no tune that stood out as the potential hit song still expected of shows. Lloyd Webber thought of a melody he had written for his proposed Puccini show and had then put away, thinking it would suit his *Sunset Boulevard* adaptation. But, pulling it out and playing it for Nunn, they both believed that it could work as the theme for a plaintive number for Grizabella and her memories of a happier past.

The problem was that there was no existing Eliot poem that addressed that topic. Lloyd Webber asked Rice to craft lyrics, but Rice declined. So, Nunn reread all of Eliot's poetry twice in order to immerse himself in the poet's style and language, then set to work writing a poem himself. Suddenly, Dench injured her Achilles tendon only two weeks before the show was due to open, and she had to be replaced; Elaine Paige got the role. Nunn still wasn't happy with his poem; during the previews, he gave Paige some different lines to sing every night. And, with Paige on board, all at once Rice *was* interested in writing lyrics, since their personal relationship had not cooled. Rice submitted a new version, so now the problem was to decide which poem was better. Paige wanted to sing the poem written by her boyfriend, but could not object to singing lyrics by her director. Mackintosh, Nunn, and Lloyd Webber at last picked Nunn's submission, feeling that Rice's version made Grizabella too human, not feline.

In this way, "Memory" was added to the production; royalties from this one song alone have topped a million dollars. It has been recorded over 150 times, making it *the* most popular song written by Lloyd Webber. Fragments of the melody appear several times in the show before Grizabella's big feature. This **foreshadowing** functions in the same way that a reprise works; the melody becomes identified with a particular character or situation. Early on, the famous melody is set to the eight lines about Grizabella written by Eliot himself, thus linking Nunn's new text to the rest of Eliot's poems.

Cats was ready to make its debut in 1981. Critics were a bit baffled about what to make of this odd, nonplot, continuously danced production, and said so. Robert Cushman was the most succinct: "*Cats* isn't perfect. Don't miss it." Audiences complied and kept complying for some 8,949 performances. *Cats* closed on its 21st birthday in 2002, having broken the previous West End long-run record (held by *Jesus Christ Superstar*) in 1989. *Cats* did equally well in New York, opening in 1981, passing *A Chorus Line*'s Broadway long-run record in 1996, and closing in 2000, after 18 years and 7,485 performances. Lloyd Webber quipped, "Eighteen is a great age for a cat." It was a bittersweet moment for Broadway, however, to see the record for Broadway's longest running musical go to a British import; America's domination of musical theater was coming to an end.

Part of the Broadway success resulted from an aggressive and shrewd marketing campaign. Months before the opening, Mackintosh rented a huge billboard and painted it black, the solid color broken only by the two yellow cat's eyes (with dancers' silhouettes in the pupils) which was the show's emblem. Planes trailing banners flew overhead, and television commercials asked, "Isn't the curiosity killing you?" A new ministry was devised for a $200,000 **MTV video** in which a janitor sweeping a theater transforms himself into the glamorous Rum Tum Tugger. Through this novel advertising, 20 million households nationwide got a taste of the show, reaching many who were not traditional theatergoers.

Broadway audiences saw a different show than the production playing in London. The different theater layouts affected the stage designs of **John Napier** (b. 1944) to a marked degree. The biggest alteration came in the finale; in London, the staircase that Grizabella used to climb her way to the Heaviside layer emerged from the back of the theater; in New York's Winter Garden, the stairway needed to appear from above, and the roof had to be torn open in order to accommodate the mechanism.

There were musical changes as well: in London, during Growltiger's scene with his ladylove Griddlebone, he sang a ballad. In New York, however, a multitalented actor got the role. After seeing his abilities, Lloyd Webber and Nunn revived an idea they had scrapped in the London show; they presented "Growltiger's Last Stand" as an operatic satire, writing a Puccini-esque aria that soon became one of the Broadway production's high points. In general, Lloyd Webber found that "the basic caliber of the Broadway performers is so much higher," noting, "In London, there was a character we wanted to sing six crucial lines, but we had to go with a girl who couldn't sing at all, because she's one of the best dancers in London. Here, we were able to choose among three people in the last phases of auditions." The creators auditioned some 1,500 performers for the 26 slots in the Broadway show.

Not only were new songs added to the Broadway show to suit the skills of American performers, but Lloyd Webber rewrote some of the earlier songs. He needed to respond to the level of talent in New York, explaining, "Their skills are staggering. If you're suddenly given a whole lot of extra forces to use, it is imperative that you use them. . . . You can't see some of the performers we've seen here and not want to write for them." In both versions, however, Lloyd Webber sustained the sung-through technique that he employed in his earlier shows. Even though this continually sung approach was still out of the norm, he defended his choice on the basis that it avoided his pet peeve: "that awkward moment when you see the composer raising his baton and the orchestra lurching into life during the dialogue which indicates the impending approach of music." Without any dialogue at all—nor, in practical terms, any plot—*Cats* sustained its imaginary world of dancing-and-singing felines without interruption.

In the case of "Mungojerrie and Rumpleteazer" (**Musical Example 53**), although the words are largely the same, the London and New York musical settings are entirely different. The West End version is a duet for the two cats themselves, singing in unison from a first-person perspective. Their melody is largely conjunct, remaining on a single pitch for long stretches. The subdivision is a sing-song compound, and usually the meter is quadruple. The overall structure is strophic, with key changes to add interest. It is a setting that makes few vocal demands on its singers.

On Broadway, however, the number is sung from a third-person perspective (mirroring Eliot's poem); moreover, it is a modified alternation form of two radically different passages. Borrowing the poetic imagery—"knockabout clowns, quick-change comedians, tightrope walkers and acrobats"—the *a* melody at **1** resembles a showy circus promenade, set to a bouncy, disjunct melody. The opening contrasts with *b*'s frenzied patter at **2**; moreover, the duple meter switches to an asymmetrical grouping of *seven* beats. The driving pulse of this section stops at **3**; this **tag**, in the style of the opening, reflects the family's awareness of the probable identity of the household mischief-makers. The song continues to alternate between the "circus" theme and the manic patter section, while the two settings of "Mungojerrie and Rumpleteazer" illustrate the impact of compositional ideas on a song's mood.

Compared to the spectacle of *Cats*, and indeed to most musicals of the 1980s, Lloyd Webber's next show was a remarkably modest presentation. Mackintosh suggested that Lloyd Webber merge his earlier television drama/song-cycle with a classical composition, *Variations* (1977), written for his younger brother, the cellist Julian Lloyd Webber. With choreography, the *Variations* could serve as the second act of a two-act presentation; *Tell Me On a Sunday* would comprise the first act. The appropriately titled composite show, *Song and Dance*, opened in London in 1982 with the *Tell Me On a Sunday* soloist reprising her role. It was not long, however, before she was replaced by Sarah Brightman, Lloyd Webber's new vocal interest—and, as time would reveal, romantic interest as well.

Grizabella (Linda Balgord) is lost in "Memory" in *Cats*.
Museum of the City of New York.

With the opening of *Song and Dance*, Lloyd Webber attained a record never before held by a composer. ASCAP created a **Triple Play Award** to recognize Lloyd Webber's singular feat of having three Broadway musicals (*Evita*, *Cats*, and *Joseph and the Amazing Technicolor Dreamcoat*) playing at the same time as three West End shows (*Evita*, *Cats*, and *Song and Dance*). When *Song and Dance* eventually came to New York in 1985, with "Americanized" lyrics and new choreography, it earned Bernadette Peters her first Tony Award.

Lloyd Webber's projects continued to be wide-ranging. He wrote a *Requiem* for his father, who had died in 1982. Lloyd Webber, Rice, and Nunn worked on *Aspects of Love*, but they disagreed on the best focus for the show, and eventually Rice dropped out. Lloyd Webber was in the middle of a divorce, and his lawyers advised against releasing songs like "Married Man" (sung by Brightman) that were featured in the story. With these prohibitions, *Aspects of Love* lost steam, and Lloyd Webber put it aside.

His next stage venture was not designed for Brightman; instead, **Starlight Express** was a **gift show**, written for his two children, Imogen and Nicholas, using lyrics by Richard Stilgoe. The subject matter seemed far-fetched, based loosely on the English "Thomas the Tank Engine" character, comparable to "The Little Engine that Could" story familiar to American youngsters. There was also a slight Cinderella component to the tale as well (see the **Plot Summary**). Remarkably, Trevor Nunn came on board again for this production, and it was he who had the fateful idea of putting the actors on roller skates.

Nunn said later that he doesn't recall what led him to the idea (and added, "I can introduce you to a lot of people who wish I had been led almost anywhere else"), but he did remember the difficulties resulting from the decision; during the auditions, he and choreographer **Arlene Phillips** (b. 1943)

> *saw a ceaseless procession of people lurching out of control, heading straight for our table or at the pianist, unable to stop until they had become a crumpled heap on the floor. The first time we saw somebody skating with style and skill, we hugged each other. Then he opened his mouth. He was tone deaf.*

The idea of presenting a show on skates was not altogether a novel idea. Just as the "humans-as-felines" approach of *Cats* had been preceded by many actors in animal costumes—notably the Cowardly Lion in *The Wizard of Oz* and even the perennial dancing cow so beloved of vaudeville—actors on roller skates had appeared in America as early as 1868 in a pantomime show called *Humpty Dumpty*. The unique aspect of *Starlight Express* was in truth the elaborate set designed by John Napier. Its centerpiece was an enormous movable railroad trestle that changed positions to link sections of track. Napier removed 1,300 seats from the Apollo Victoria Theatre to make room for the twisting pathways (where skaters would attain speeds of nearly 40 miles per hour), spending £1.4 million on his theater modifications.

With this overwhelming stage set, Napier had created an exceedingly **heavy book**—the theatrical world's term for a technically complex show. The complicated sound, lighting, and stage effects all contributed to a sizable **nut**—Broadway's slang term for the weekly cost of running a show, taking into account the salaries, rents, and royalties. Hal Prince maintains that a show should target to pay for itself at 60 percent capacity; in other words, if weekly ticket sales filled at least sixth-tenths of the theater's seats, then the "nut" should be covered in a well-budgeted show.

As with many of Lloyd Webber's previous shows, many people felt he was nuts himself to mount such an expensive musical. But, once again his faith proved justified, for the London production of *Starlight Express* would be seen 7,406 times between its opening in 1984 and its closing in 2002. Critics were particularly tepid, but viewers didn't care, some regarding the show as the most intense theatrical experience they'd ever had. One especially loyal audience member—a postman from the county of Kent—saw the musical over 750 times, spending some £21,000 in the process. The creators "refreshed" the show in 1992, adding new songs, new choreography, new staging, and a revised plot.

The musical score of both the original and revised versions resembled Lloyd Webber's pastiche approach to *Joseph and the Amazing Technicolor Dreamcoat*. A mixture of styles is heard, including country-western, torch songs, techno-pop, rock, and even rap. The blues style is featured, appropriately enough, in "Poppa's Blues" (**Musical Example 54**), when Rusty has visited the old steamer Poppa for comfort. The blues originated during the early years of the twentieth century in the American South; it was an important ingredient when rock-and-roll emerged in the 1950s.

The blues style is itself a hybrid, using call-and-response from the African American field holler and chords derived from European harmonies. The style specializes in prominent out-of-tune blue notes, which have the psychological effect of creating additional tension. As a singer sings the blues, accompanying instruments play a simple chord sequence spanning 12 measures, giving rise to the term **12-bar blues**. Although performers can substitute alternate chords at will, the basic 12-measure sequence uses only three basic chords, played in a standardized order.

In addition to employing this standard chordal pattern, "Poppa's Blues" also satirizes the customary rhyme scheme of the blues. As Poppa explains in section **1** of the song, the usual poetic pattern of a blues verse is *a-a-b*. He observes at **2** that sometimes there is no real difference at all in the three lines of a verse. At **3**, the strophic form's third verse, Poppa again uses the *a-a-b* pattern and demonstrates the blues' penchant for suggestive lyrics. In addition to the chordal and poetic patterns of the typical blues, "Poppa's Blues" contains various other hallmarks of the blues style: interpolated comments from the singer and listeners, a harmonica (mouth organ) that seems to "respond" to the "call" in each line of the soloist, and ostinato-like patterns in the accompanying instruments.

Musicians enjoy the spoof nature of tunes like "Poppa's Blues," and even nonmusicians benefit from the mini-lesson contained in its lyrics. The spectacle, however, was *Starlight Express*'s chief claim to fame. On Broadway, that spectacle would prove to be the show's undoing. Although the tracks didn't wind all through the seats of the Gershwin Theater as they did in the Apollo Victoria, the stage modifications still cost $2.5 million, and the overall production costs exceeded $8 million—the most expensive show ever seen on Broadway. Even a run of 761 performances over almost two years was not sufficient to recoup these enormous expenses completely, so *Starlight Express* went on the books as a flop—Lloyd Webber's first Broadway failure. But the failure went almost unnoticed by many, for even before *Starlight Express* closed, Lloyd Webber had already opened his next blockbuster show, *The Phantom of the Opera*, proving that extravaganzas were alive and well.

FURTHER READING

Citron, Stephen. *Sondheim and Lloyd Webber: The New Musical.* Oxford: Oxford University Press, 2001.

Hanan, Stephen Mo. *A Cat's Diary: How the Broadway Production of* Cats *was Born.* (Art of Theater Series.) Hanover, New Hampshire: Smith and Kraus, 2001.

Jones, Garth. "Purr-fect Cats." *Harper's Bazaar* 115 (September 1982): 345, 216.

Kislan, Richard. *Hoofing on Broadway: A History of Show Dancing.* New York: Prentice Hall, 1987.

Mantle, Jonathan. *Fanfare: The Unauthorised Biography of Andrew Lloyd Webber.* New York: Viking Penguin, 1989.

McKnight, Gerald. *Andrew Lloyd Webber.* New York: St. Martin's, 1984.

Richmond, Keith. *The Musicals of Andrew Lloyd Webber*. London: Virgin, 1995.

Smith, Cecil. *Musical Comedy in America*. New York: Theatre Arts Books (Robert M. MacGregor), 1950.

Steyn, Mark. *Broadway Babies Say Goodnight: Musicals Then and Now*. New York: Routledge, 1999.

Wadsley, Pat. "Video: Marketing Broadway via MTV." *Theatre Crafts* 19 (February 1985): 14.

Walsh, Michael. *Andrew Lloyd Webber, His Life and Works: A Critical Biography*. New York: Abrams, 1989.

PLOT SUMMARY: *CATS*

As if we have shrunk to the size of ordinary alley cats, we see on the stage enormous discarded items—a spare tire, empty cans, and other assorted rubbish. The lights dim, and the bright eyes of dozens of cats can be seen hidden in the trash. As these "Jellicle" cats decide it's safe to emerge, they creep forward, then begin to exult in their freedom, explaining that every cat has a secret name, unknown to humans. The cats are excited by the upcoming Jellicle Ball, for the annual Jellicle choice will be made during the celebration, determining which cat will get to journey to the Heaviside Layer and there be reborn into another life. "Who will it be? Who will it be?" they wonder.

There are a number of possibilities. For instance, there is Jennyanydots, who forces the mice and cockroaches to study music, crocheting, tatting, and the like. "The Rum Tum Tugger" is the feline world's answer to Elvis Presley; he'd rather tangle your knitting than be cuddled. But suddenly, all the cats freeze; an outcast has appeared. It is old Grizabella, whose formerly sleek coat is tattered and torn, and even her eye is twisted. She is shunned by the other Jellicles and slinks away.

The presentations continue after Grizabella has gone. We meet "Bustopher Jones," a fine cat about town, a regular feature at the best men's clubs of London. "Mungojerrie and Rumpleteazer" (**Musical Example 53**), on the other hand, are housecats—but the terror of their particular household. They are a far cry from "Old Deuteronomy," who has seen perhaps 99 lives go by. The villagers will even erect a "road closed" sign, should beloved Old Deuteronomy wish to take a nap on the street pavement.

Now that Deuteronomy, the oldest cat, has arrived, it's time for a little entertainment, so a famous dogfight, which had ended only when the dreadful Rumpus Cat put them to flight, is re-enacted. The tale has just finished when the terrifying rumor sweeps through the assembled cats that Macavity is somewhere near; after hiding, they creep back out again when the rumor proves to be false. Their rejoicing resumes as the Jellicle Ball gets underway. Once again, Grizabella slinks by, and once again, she is chased off. Rejected by the others, the lonely cat dreams of a happier past.

When the second act begins, other cats remember the past too; after Old Deuteronomy recalls former happiness, and then "Gus: the Theatre Cat" steps forward to share his memories; among his many roles, he understudied Dick Whittington's cat, and—ah, yes!—once got to play Growltiger, a rough-mannered barge cat who was the Terror of the Thames. Gus wakes up from his reminiscing just in time to hear the others celebrate

the travels of "Skimbleshanks: The Railway Cat." Playfully, the cats construct a train out of items from the trash, then flee in fright once more when Macavity's diabolical laugh is heard echoing through the alley. The fiendish Macavity has spirited Old Deuteronomy away, and only the great feline magician, "Mr. Mistoffelees," can help; he drapes a scarf over one of the kittens and then, whisking it away, reveals the missing cat. Just in time, too, for daylight is coming, and it is time for Old Deuteronomy to name the feline who has been selected to go to the Heaviside Layer.

On the perimeter of the circle, Grizabella lets her "Memory" carry her back to happier times. She then starts to steal away, but one of the kittens comes and draws her back, soon joined by loving paws from the other cats. Grizabella is the chosen one, and the Jellicles watch as she ascends. Old Deuteronomy breaks the silence after her departure by explaining the proper and polite procedures for addressing cats. And, with these helpful protocol suggestions, the evening has come to an end.

PLOT SUMMARY: *STARLIGHT EXPRESS*

Many of us travel the same journey followed by Rusty in *Starlight Express*; he's a dilapidated steam train who has to learn to put faith in himself. Rusty is but one of many engines and carriages who are under the dominion of "Control," who speaks in a child's voice. The trains are very competitive, since the chief portion of their time is spent racing each other. Greaseball is a muscular diesel engine, and in one of the many rather adult allusions in *Starlight Express*, he assures us that we "gotta keep it going all night." Rusty is a pretty sorry sight in comparison, but he defiantly insists that he'll keep racing.

Various passenger coaches—Ashley, a smoking car; Buffy, the buffet; and Dinah, the dining car—tell him he's taking too big a risk. Another blow to his ego comes when Pearl, a passenger carriage, won't be his race partner any more. The freight cars argue that "Freight is great," but the coaches insist that carrying passengers is what it's all about. Even C. B. the caboose brags about himself. Suddenly, an eerie, distorted sound is heard: it is the ominous arrival of Electra, the electric train.

Every engine needs a coach for the race, and so Rusty gets penalized for being disconnected. Pearl tries to apologize; she's waiting for a special steam engine, since "nobody can do it like a steam train." She's heard the whistle she wants in her dreams. "The Race" begins, and Dinah realizes that Greaseball is cheating, but when she confronts him, he cuts her loose. Pearl agrees to be Greaseball's new partner, while Dinah joins Electra. Disconsolate over Pearl's rejection and his loss in the race, Rusty goes to listen to "Poppa's Blues" (**Musical Example 54**). Poppa tells Rusty that there are other coaches; why, look right over there at that old sleeper. Rusty is horrified, but "Belle the Sleeping Car" defends herself, insisting that she's just "down at wheel." Poppa also suggests that Rusty ask the "Starlight Express" for help; Rusty wonders if the Starlight is real.

The assorted engines and coaches taunt each other before the racing continues. Poppa won a spot in the next race, but has chosen Rusty to race in his stead. C. B. volunteers to be Rusty's partner—but it turns out that C. B. isn't the friendly caboose he pretends to be; it seems he crossed the river Kwai and now he's a "red caboose," wrecking trains left and right. Rusty, of course, doesn't fare too well with the double agent, who puts on the brakes whenever Rusty's not looking. When Pearl learns about this duplicity and realizes that Greaseball knew about the scheme, she refuses to race any further with him. C. B. mocks Rusty, claiming, "You're no engine." The assorted Rockies (the boxcars, of course, in a nod to the cinematic boxing champion Rocky) also tease Rusty, who protests angrily that he was cheated.

In despair, Rusty calls out to the Starlight Express for help, and to his amazement, the Starlight appears (sounding remarkably like Poppa). The Starlight teaches the battered steam train an important lesson, and suddenly Rusty understands, exulting, "I Am the Starlight"; he's had the power within him all along. Suddenly, things start to go Rusty's way: Dinah rebels and disconnects herself from Electra, and he flips a circuit when he loses. Greaseball and C. B. are involved in a pile-up. Rusty is triumphant at last, but he soon realizes there's more to life than racing. Pearl, meanwhile, sees Rusty through new eyes. Greaseball, apologizing to Dinah and others for his arrogance, is assured that he can be converted to steam. The assembled trains rebel against the dictates of Control at last, and Poppa exults that the days of steam will come again.

MUSICAL EXAMPLE 53

Cats
Andrew Lloyd Webber/T. S. Eliot, 1982
"Mungojerrie and Rumpleteazer"

Mungojerrie

1   Mungojerrie and Rumpleteazer were a notorious couple of cats.
As knockabout clowns, quick-change comedians, tightrope walkers and acrobats.
They had an extensive reputation, made their home in Victoria Grove.
That was merely their center of operation, for they were incurably given to rove.

2   If the area window was found ajar and the basement looked like a field of war,
If a tile or two came loose on the roof which presently ceased to be waterproof
If the drawers were pulled out from the bedroom chests and you couldn't find one of your winter vests
Or after the supper one of the girls suddenly missed her Woolworth pearls—

3   Then the family would say, "It's that horrible cat! It was Mungojerrie or Rumpleteazer!"
And most of the time, they left it at that.

4   Mungojerrie and Rumpleteazer had an unusual gift of the gab;
They were highly efficient cat burglars as well and remarkably smart at a smash and grab.
They made their home in Victoria Grove; they had no regular occupation.
They were plausible fellows who liked to engage a friendly policeman in conversation.

5   When the family assembled for Sunday dinner with their minds made up that they wouldn't get thinner on
Argentine joint, potatoes, and greens, then the cook would appear from behind the scenes
And say in a voice that was broken with sorrow, "I'm afraid you must wait and have dinner tomorrow.
The joint has gone from the oven like that!"

6   Then the family would say, "It's that horrible cat! It was Mungojerrie or Rumpleteazer!"
And most of the time, they left it at that.

7   Mungojerrie and Rumpleteazer had a wonderful way of working together
And some of the time you would say it was luck and some of the time you would say it was weather.
They'd go through the house like a hurricane and no sober person could take his oath
Was it Mungojerrie or Rumpleteazer? Or could you have sworn that it mightn't be both?

8   When you heard a dining room smash or up from the pantry there came a loud crash
Or down from the library came a loud "ping" from a vase which was commonly said to be Ming.

9   Then the family would say, "Now which was which cat?
It was Mungojerrie *and* Rumpleteazer, and *there's nothing at all to be done about that!*"

MUSICAL EXAMPLE 54

Starlight Express
Andrew Lloyd Webber/Richard Stilgoe, 1987
"Poppa's Blues"

1   Oh, the first line of a blues is always sung a second time.
I said the first line of a blues is always sung a second time.
So by the time you get to the third line you've had time to think of a rhyme.

2 Oh, there ain't no law that says third line got to be different at all.
I said there ain't no law that says third line got to be different at all.
No, there ain't no law that says third line got to be different at all.

3 Never borrow a mouth organ, not even from your best friend.
I said don't never borrow a mouth organ, not even from your best friend
You may survive the blowing, but the sucking's gonna get you in the end, oh, yeah.

Chapter 40
The Luxuriant Lloyd Webber

During the early 1980s, Andrew Lloyd Webber produced a series of concept musicals, each with its own twist. Yet, the diverse shows had aspects in common; for instance, they all had somewhat simple plots (and, in the case of *Cats*, barely any plot at all). Moreover, they emphasized visual appeal of various sorts, with dance playing an important role in all three. In the late 1980s and afterward, however, dance in Lloyd Webber's shows took a back seat, while the story lines became complex and increasingly adult. His new works demonstrated a sophisticated control of musical themes and characterization, but these shows also sustained the trend for the massive, ambitious productions seen in *Cats* and *Starlight Express*. Observers have suggested various genre terms to describe these ambitious undertakings—poperettas? mega-musicals?—but regardless of their label, they raised the theatrical stakes higher than ever before. Lloyd Webber was not solely responsible for the new breed of enormously expensive productions—after all, Hal Prince had been buying entire abandoned factories for stage sets in the 1970s—but Lloyd Webber was one of the first to ride the new wave successfully.

Perhaps the best-known example of the megashows is **The Phantom of the Opera**, which opened in London in 1986, in New York in 1988, and which is still running in both those cities to this day. The history of the show actually began in 1911, when the prolific Gaston Leroux published a gothic horror story called *Le Fantôme de l'Opéra*. Leroux paid careful attention to detail in his novel, which takes place in the Paris Opera House. The actual building covers three acres, is some 17 stories in height (measuring from its lowest basement), and indeed has a subterranean lake that helps to absorb the weight of the massive stage machinery (and is a convenient source of water in case of a theater fire).

Leroux's plot for *The Phantom of the Opera* was a far cry from the subsequent film adaptations. Of these, the earliest—a 1925 silent film starring Lon Chaney—was the closest to Leroux's original tale. The assorted movies usually emphasized the horror component, but in 1984, a rather comic stage version appeared in a London fringe theater. In this version, *Phantom* was a pseudo-musical, thanks to a string of opera excerpts by Verdi and others. The director wanted to cast Lloyd Webber's new wife, Sarah Brightman, in his show, so Lloyd Webber and Cameron Mackintosh viewed the production not only to see if it would be a good role for Brightman, but also to determine if the show had the potential to transfer to the West End. The campy mock-horror musical *The Rocky Horror Show* (1973), which spoofed science-fiction B movies, had been a London hit, and Lloyd Webber and Mackintosh wondered if *Phantom* might make a similar splash. They discussed the idea with *Rocky Horror*'s director, Jim Sharman

(who had also directed London's record-setting London *Jesus Christ Superstar*); Sharman felt the show was *too* comic, and, moreover, it needed new music by Lloyd Webber to be interesting.

When Lloyd Webber picked up a copy of Leroux's novel in a used-book shop, he realized that Leroux in truth had written a love story. (See the **Plot Summary**.) Wanting to write a romantic show about people (not cats or trains), Lloyd Webber was convinced that this would be excellent subject matter for his next musical; moreover, it would make a good vehicle for Brightman's wide-ranging soprano voice. Lloyd Webber initially felt that he could construct a score from segments of existing romantic operas, filling in any gaps with music of his own composition. The mixed approach soon proved to be unworkable, though, so Lloyd Webber set to work on an original score.

Lloyd Webber needed a lyricist, and since Rice—hard at work on *Chess* with musicians from ABBA, a Swedish rock group—was unavailable, Lloyd Webber wrote to the venerable Alan Jay Lerner. Somewhat to Lloyd Webber's surprise, Lerner was enthusiastic. When Lloyd Webber worried that the overblown story might not be the right choice, Lerner reassured him, saying, "Don't ask why, dear boy. It just works." Lerner drafted lyrics for the second-act "Masquerade," but then had to withdraw because of ill health; Lerner was already in the grip of the cancer that would kill him the following year, 1986. Lloyd Webber turned to Richard Stilgoe, his *Starlight Express* lyricist, who worked quickly enough that Lloyd Webber was able to present most of a first act at the 1985 summer gathering at Sydmonton.

The Sydmonton performance offered a number of surprises. Guests were suitably frightened by the collapsing chandelier, a special effect that set designer **Maria Bjørnson** (b. 1949) had incorporated into the Sydmonton chapel. One guest, Trevor Nunn, director of *Cats* and *Starlight Express*, encountered some surprises of his own. In several of *Phantom*'s tunes, he heard familiar melodies written for *Aspects of Love*—the chamber show he and Lloyd Webber had set aside in 1983. Now, hearing those same tunes with new lyrics, he knew that nothing would come of his contributions to *Aspects*. It would have been easy for him to be upset—and undoubtedly he was—but Nunn was fully aware of what Stephen Citron calls the "cardinal rule of showbiz: never, NEVER close a door on ANYONE. You can't know in which future production you will be working together."

In the case of *Phantom of the Opera*, however, Nunn's forbearance was for nothing; Lloyd Webber wanted Hal Prince, and Prince, having been accused of directing shows that were too emotionally cold, wanted to direct a romantic musical.

Prince went to Paris to explore the Opera House, built between 1861 and 1875. Prince's central metaphor for the show came from television, however; in a BBC documentary called *The Skin Horses*, handicapped people discussed their sexuality, and Prince realized that this very human urge was the dimension he wanted to bring forward in his production of *Phantom*.

For a time, though, it looked as though Prince would not direct *Phantom* after all. Mackintosh came to New York and invited Prince to lunch; during the meal, Mackintosh somewhat sheepishly admitted that he and Lloyd Webber thought Nunn should direct instead. Prince's response was to walk out of the restaurant. Back in England, though, the renewed collaboration between Lloyd Webber and Nunn wasn't going so well, and soon Mackintosh was on the telephone to Prince, re-inviting him to direct the show. Prince accepted; when "uninvited" previously, he had told his assistant to file his *Phantom* notes where they'd be handy, saying "they'll be back"—as indeed Lloyd Webber and Mackintosh now were.

A lyricist was still needed; Stilgoe was finding it easier to craft the show's libretto than the song lyrics. A year earlier, Mackintosh had been a judge for the Vivian Ellis Prize, sponsored by England's Performing Rights Society in order to support novice composers and lyricists. Mackintosh had been impressed by **Charles Hart** (b. 1961), a finalist (but *not* the winner, as Hart likes to point out), and suggested to Lloyd Webber that they give Hart a melody or two. Hart produced three alternative lyrics for one melody; one of the three became the aria for Christine's operatic debut. Hart won the job.

Although Lloyd Webber did not create a full concept album, he did see to it that the show's title song, "The Phantom of the Opera" (**Musical Example 55**), was released in January 1986, some nine months before the show premiered. It quickly climbed to number seven on the charts. As the rock-tinged single demonstrated, Lloyd Webber's score was a far cry from the operatic music that the title of the show might imply. Instead, the opening interweaves a driving rock beat with a chromatic motif. This descending and ascending motif is associated with the Phantom all through the show, in the manner of a Wagnerian leitmotif. The instrumentation evokes both the rock world—electric bass, drum machine—and the organ of the Phantom's subterranean lair. The form is a modified strophic, with Christine singing the first verse (**1**) and the Phantom taking the second verse (**2**). They begin to trade lines in the third and fourth verses (**3** and **5**), singing in unison in the second half of the verses. To give the strophic structure more variety, Lloyd Webber changes the key each time; the first verse is in d minor; the second verse is in g minor; the third verse shifts the key to e minor; and the fourth verse is in f minor.

The strophic pattern is modified because of the brief interruption at **4** by the distant voices of the chorus; they utter a refrain heard often in the show, when the characters refer to the Phantom—in effect, another leitmotif. Christine echoes the refrain herself at **6**, in the coda of the song; she then starts to sing a melismatic sequence on the syllable *Ah*, climbing higher and higher. Moreover, Lloyd Webber continues to change the key during the coda, from f minor to g minor and finally to a minor. In contrast to the song's predominant rock flavor, this melismatic coda sounds very operatic, and certainly the final note displays Brightman's virtuosic range; she sings a high E, four half-steps above high C.

The song illustrates a number of the show's salient features—its mixture of rock, pop, and operatic scoring, the use of characteristic "Phantom" motifs—but it also reflects the occasional awkward text setting that dogs the lyrics as well. In the choral refrain at **4**, the word *opera* is divided into two syllables rather than three. Admittedly, the word is often pronounced this way, but the stress is *always* on the first syllable: *OP-rah*. In the song, however, the second syllable of the word is placed on a higher pitch and is sustained for a longer duration. Higher pitches and longer notes both give extra emphasis to syllables, and so the word strikes the ear as *op-RAHHHH*. (Similar missettings occur elsewhere, such as when the first syllable of Christine's name is stressed.) Three lyricists are credited with the words for this particular song—Hart, Stilgoe, and Mike Batt—so the awkwardness may be a result of many cooks not being able to produce an entirely coherent broth.

The singers on the single (recorded before the show had been cast) were Brightman as Christine and Steve Harley (lead singer for the British rockers Cockney Rebel) as the Phantom. Neither Brightman nor Harley had a lock on those roles, however; auditions were held for both characters. To no one's surprise, Brightman won the part that had been written with her voice in mind, but the auditions were taken seriously because an understudy was also needed; the backup performer had to be able to handle the demanding range of the vocal part as well as be able to dance *en pointe* (on the tips of the toes) as a member of the ballet chorus. Although there was only a little dancing in *Phantom*, choreographer Gillian Lynne took care to make the ballet corps move in ways that were appropriate to the nineteenth-century setting.

To Harley's disappointment, however, the role of the Phantom went to Michael Crawford. Crawford and Brightman were taking voice lessons from the same teacher, and Lloyd Webber had overheard Crawford practicing when picking up Brightman after class. In contrast, the role of Raoul was proving harder to cast, but then Lynne remembered a young American, Steve Barton, who had impressed her in a previous show. Barton was performing on the continent, but Lynne called and suggested he fly over to London, offering him a bed in her flat to help keep his costs down. Intrigued by her offer, Barton made the trip, and halfway through his audition piece, Prince leaned over to Lynne and exclaimed, "That's it!"

Thanks to the success of the title song, interest in the new Lloyd Webber show was building dramatically. As in his earlier shows, the majority of the material is sung, although there are longer stretches of spoken dialogue than in any show except *Jeeves*. The impressive staging and hints of rock lured in a whole new generation of theatergoers. And the staging *was* impressive: besides the infamous chandelier, there were elephants, nooses suspended in midair, and thousands of "candles" lighting the lake. Most of these effects were computer-driven, and almost 100 trapdoors were built into the stage at Her Majesty's Theatre to accommodate the rise and fall of the lights and sets (and people).

Surprisingly, however, the sets themselves are fairly simple, almost economical. Much of the shadowy, brooding effect was achieved through **Andrew Bridge's** (b. 1952) lighting designs, which used only some 400 lighting fixtures, when 700 or 800 was the norm. Bridge was responding to Prince's desire for lots of shadows; Prince knew that viewers would wonder what illicit things were occurring in those darkened areas. Prince wanted the audience "to be contributors, to be collaborators, to use their imaginations to fill in the spaces we've deliberately left blank."

Despite the somewhat simple set designs, the other elaborate features meant that *Phantom* did not come cheaply; it cost some £2 million to mount the show in London (although this was only a quarter of the costs in New York). Eager audiences bought more than £1 million worth of tickets before the London opening. Word of mouth from overseas built the excitement to a fever pitch before the Broadway premiere in 1988, resulting in a mind-boggling $16 million advance, beating the previous record (set by *Les Misérables*) by some $4 million. Admittedly, the New York show had been more expensive to produce, since the theater had to be gutted to accommodate the stage machinery.

The New York show also struggled a bit in its casting. The creators wanted to use the London stars: Crawford, Brightman, and Barton. Actors' Equity, always anxious to preserve the rights of American actors, had no problem with American-born Barton, but they challenged Crawford and Brightman. Crawford argued that he was a star of international renown (capped by the fact he had been knighted by Queen Elizabeth II in 1987); he won his appeal. Prince, furious with Equity, went to bat for Brightman himself. Meeting with Equity's representatives, Prince allowed an implicit threat to hang over the discussion: without Brightman as Christine, Lloyd Webber would not bring *Phantom* to Broadway, and therefore *no* Equity actors would work. The union capitulated, especially after Lloyd Webber made the concession of promising to cast an "unknown American" in his next West End production.

Somewhat ironically, the Tony Awards named *The Phantom of the Opera* as the year's best musical. *Phantom* had also triumphed in England's **Olivier Awards**. The Olivier Awards, equivalent in stature to Broadway's Tonys, had been established in 1976 as "The Society of West End Theatre Awards." In 1984, however, renowned actor Sir Laurence Olivier agreed to let his name be given to the prizes, which are also known as Larrys. The Society of London Theatre currently awards the trophies, and an unusual feature of the review process is that selected members of the public serve as judges each year. It must have been particularly gratifying for Lloyd Webber to see his show win the 1986 Best Musical Olivier, since it was running against *Chess*, the candidate written by his ex-partner Tim Rice.

The Olivier Awards offer fewer categories than the Tonys, so although Bjørnson was nominated for her stage designs, there were no equivalent awards for composer or lyricist. (In America, Lloyd Webber's score had been nominated for a Tony, but lost to Sondheim's *Into the Woods*.) Crawford, however, took both the Larry and the Tony Awards as the Best Performance of an Actor in a Musical (although Brightman was not even nominated). On both sides of the Atlantic, reviewers had some harsh words for *Phantom*, but the show appeared to be critic-proof; the ongoing original productions plus the many successful international versions all attest to the musical's indisputable popular appeal.

In the summer of 1986, Lloyd Webber and Rice had reunited briefly to create *Cricket*, their tribute to the queen's 60th birthday. After a couple of subsequent performances, it was set aside. Or, rather, Rice set it aside; Lloyd Webber, on the other hand, began to raid from *Cricket*'s score freely when he returned once more to the long-deferred *Aspects of Love*. Rice was irked when he learned of this reuse, because the recycling eliminated any chance of later expanding *Cricket* into a full-length show.

This was not the only surprise about *Aspects of Love*. Lloyd Webber had also reunited with Nunn, who was the director. The rapprochement was remarkable considering the bitter struggle over *Phantom*. *Aspects of Love* opened in London in 1989 to mixed critical reactions but satisfactory ticket sales, running over three years for 1,325 performances. In New York, however, *Aspects of Love* did not fare so well. It opened in 1990 and was closed again after 377 performances, with a loss of $11 million (a new Broadway record). American audiences, never very permissive about sexual matters, found it hard to accept the freewheeling romantic partnerships depicted between a man, his wife, his mistress, his daughter, and his nephew. Ironically, though, *Aspects of Love* was nominated for six Tonys (winning none of them), while in London, *Aspects* failed to win even a single Olivier nomination.

Lloyd Webber and Brightman's marriage had hit a rough patch as well; they divorced in November 1990. Lloyd Webber married for a third time a few months later and returned to a long-deferred project: the musical adaptation of **Sunset Boulevard**, a 1950 film by Billy Wilder that had been awarded "Landmark" status by the Library of Congress's National Film Registry. Lloyd Webber began working with lyricist Amy Powers, but her inexperience led to a parting of the ways. Hurriedly, Lloyd Webber turned again to Don Black; bits of *Sunset Boulevard* were performed at Sydmonton in September 1991.

The hurriedly assembled Sydmonton presentation was not very satisfactory, so Lloyd Webber brought in yet another collaborator: **Christopher Hampton** (b. 1946), who won an Oscar for his *Dangerous Liaisons* screenplay. Hampton's adroit handling of that dark story suggested that he might be the perfect person to adapt Wilder's "film noir." Moreover, Hampton had already begun to create an opera libretto based on the movie for the English National Opera (the project had died when the rights proved unavailable). Although the plan was for Hampton to write the book and Black the lyrics, the two men worked closely together on both; the final program credits read "Book and Lyrics by Don Black and Christopher Hampton" (see the **Plot Summary**). Unusually,

Norma (Glenn Close) mesmerizes the audience "With One Look" in *Sunset Boulevard.*
Joan Marcus Photography.

a sizable portion of *Sunset Boulevard*—around 20 percent—consisted of spoken dialogue.

Meanwhile, Lloyd Webber was hard at work writing music that distinguished characters to a greater extent than ever before in his works. Norma, Cecil B. de Mille, and Max were given rich, expansive songs. A typical example is Norma's "With One Look" (**Musical Example 56**), her stirring defense of her abilities. Her disjunct melody sweeps through a broad range, in a solid quadruple meter. Sections **1** through **4** give the impression that the tune is a song form, but then the form is extended by two more repetitions of *a* at **5** and **6**, turning the structure into a ternary form. Norma launches into an impassioned declaration at **7**, the song's coda; she utters entire phrases on repeated pitches, gradually ascending to the last, defiant "I'll be me" that closes the song. This trumpetlike passage echoes Poppea's own militant avowal that she will fear no adversity 300 years earlier in *The Coronation of Poppea*.

The contrast between Norma and the younger characters was also expressed through the stage sets designed by **John Napier** (b. 1944). Norma's immense mansion is overwhelming; she is physically dwarfed by the massive staircase that runs up from the ground floor. It is staggering, therefore, to see her entire building rising upward, revealing Artie's cramped apartment below. Powerful hydraulics moved the set, controlled by the latest electronic valves. However, in rehearsal, the sets moved randomly, endangering both cast and stage crew. It turned out that the state-of-the-art electronic valves picked up cell phone signals, and the only solution was to tear out the valves and replace them with an earlier model—a remedy that forced the creators to delay the 1993 London opening of the £3 million show.

Even with *Sunset Boulevard*'s advanced musical craftsmanship, Lloyd Webber was still dismissed out of hand (and out of habit?) by some critics. Others, though, felt there were more attractive melodies in it than in any other of his musicals to date. Regardless of what the reviewers said, the public was anxious to purchase tickets, as was also the case in America when *Sunset Boulevard* reached New York in 1994. Glenn Close starred in the American production, first in its Los Angeles premiere and later in its Broadway debut. Nevertheless, Patti LuPone, who had created the role of Norma in the West End, maintained that she had been promised the Broadway role. She brought suit against Lloyd Webber because of the humiliation; the case was settled out of court for a rumored $2 million.

On the brighter side, *Sunset Boulevard* brought in favorable reviews from New York critics (see the **Sidebar**: The Frank Rich Fan Club), as well as a total of seven Tony Awards. But, even after a run of 977 performances, *Sunset Boulevard* closed at a loss in 1997; the West End production closed shortly afterward. Worse was to come: Lloyd Webber's next show, *By Jeeves* (1996)—a reworking of the 1975 *Jeeves*—closed in London after eight months. When *By Jeeves* arrived in New York in 2001, it lasted only two months, for a dismal 73 performances.

Lloyd Webber had better success with *Whistle Down the Wind* (1998) in England—but not in the United States. Based on a 1961 film in which English children mistake a transient for Jesus Christ, Lloyd Webber transferred the setting to the American South. English viewers had no problem with the revision, but *Whistle Down the Wind* struggled during its American tryout tour. The *Washington Post* observed, "Why set the show in the most musically rich state in America and then write a score that shows no influence of the blues, ragtime, or jazz?" *Whistle Down the Wind* closed in Washington, D. C.

Lloyd Webber's *The Beautiful Game* lasted a year in London after opening in September 2000. The show centered around football players in Northern Ireland struggling to play their sport against the backdrop of the "Troubles," the political upheavals of the late 1960s. No American production has been announced, but a new musical, *The Woman in White*, opened in London in 2004. In the meantime, his personal corporation, The Really Useful Company, has supported other writers by producing several stage shows, and hundreds of revivals and international productions are underway for Lloyd Webber's earlier works—including a production of *The Phantom of the Opera* at the venerable La Scala opera house in Milan.

Lloyd Webber turned 56 years old in 2004, so it is very likely that he will be contributing to the theater for many years to come. However, if he chose to rest on his laurels, he would have plenty of honors to sustain him: knighted in 1992, he was elevated to Baron in 1997. His net worth has been estimated at

Sidebar: The Frank Rich Fan Club

Things didn't start out so badly, judging by what Frank Rich wrote in *Time* magazine in 1978:

> Evita's *a cold and uninvolving show that does little to expand the traditional musical comedy format or our understanding of a bizarre historical figure. . . . Despite its synthetic Latinisms, flip dissonance and references to Lennon-McCartney songs, Webber's music is evocative and often catchy.*

By the time *Cats* came to America, Rich had been named the chief drama critic for the *New York Times*, but his own claws seemed to be sheathed. In fact, he almost purred:

> *It's a musical that transports the audience into a complete fantasy world that could only exist in the theater and yet, these days, only rarely does. Whatever the other failings and excesses, even banalities, of "Cats," it believes in purely theatrical magic, and on that faith it unquestionably delivers.*

Starlight Express didn't fare so well, however:

> *In a full-page program note, the composer Andrew Lloyd Webber modestly explains that he conceived his musical . . . as an entertainment "event" for children who love trains. Over two numbing hours later, you may find yourself wondering exactly whose children he had in mind. A confusing jamboree of piercing noise, routine roller-skating, misogyny and Orwellian special effects, "Starlight Express" is the perfect gift for the kid who has everything except parents.*

Song and Dance also came in for considerable bashing:

> *Empty material remains empty, no matter how talented those who perform it . . . The authors . . . don't bother to examine Emma—they merely exploit her. For all the time we spend with this woman, we learn little about her beyond her sexual activities. . . . As is this composer's wont, the better songs are reprised so often that one can never be quite sure whether they are here to stay or are simply refusing to leave.*

Although Rich didn't know a whole lot about music, he knew what he didn't like, as his review of the London production of *The Phantom of the Opera* made clear:

> *Mr. Lloyd Webber . . . undercuts himself. For every sumptuously melodic love song in this score, there is an insufferably smug opera parody that can't match its prototype (Meyerbeer? Salieri?), a thrown-in pop number that slows the action, or a jarring anachronistic descent into the vulgar synthesizer chords of "Starlight Express." Must a show that is sold out until 1988 . . . sell itself out quite so much?*

When *Phantom* reached Broadway a year and a half later, Rich's disdain for the score had not decreased:

> *With the exception of "Music of the Night"—which seems to express from its author's gut a desperate longing for acceptance—Mr. Lloyd Webber has again written a score so generic that most of the songs could be reordered and redistributed among the characters (indeed, among other Lloyd Webber musicals) without altering the show's story or meaning.*

Rich treated *Aspects of Love* no more kindly:

> *Andrew Lloyd Webber, the composer who is second to none when writing musicals about cats, roller-skating trains and falling chandeliers, has made an earnest but bizarre career decision. . . . He has written a musical about people.*
>
> *Whether* Aspects of Love *is a musical* for *people is another matter. . . . [It] generates about as much passion as a visit to the bank. . . . Mr. Lloyd Webber, as is his wont, rotates a few tunes throughout his show, some of them catchy and many of them left stranded in the musical foreplay.*

By the time *Sunset Boulevard* debuted, Lloyd Webber at last got a favorable review in the *New York Times*—because Rich had left his drama critic post several months earlier.

The venom in the past had certainly left its mark, however, so when Lloyd Webber jointly purchased a four-year-old racehorse in 1991 (for some $40,000), he immediately christened the gelding "Frank Rich." Lloyd Webber's wife clarified the reasoning behind the name: "That way if it falls we won't mind."

---

more than a billion dollars, and he has set theatrical records that will be very difficult to break. In addition to the New York and London long-run records of *Cats* and the Triple Play Award presented by ASCAP, Lloyd Webber enjoyed the remarkable achievement of having six different shows playing simultaneously in London during a stretch of 1991: *Cats, Starlight Express, The Phantom of the Opera, Aspects of Love*, a hit revival of *Joseph and the Amazing Technicolor Dreamcoat*, and a touring Kabuki-style interpretation of *Jesus Christ Superstar*. During the 1990s, more than half the tickets sold on Broadway were for Lloyd Webber productions. Lloyd Webber has established a legacy on both Broadway and the West End that may never be equaled, and he has reshaped the very definition of musical theater for millions of viewers.

FURTHER READING

Citron, Stephen. *Sondheim and Lloyd Webber: The New Musical.* Oxford: Oxford University Press, 2001.

Ilson, Carol. *Harold Prince From* Pajama Game *to* Phantom of the Opera. Ann Arbor, Michigan: U.M.I. Research Press, 1989.

Mantle, Jonathan. *Fanfare: The Unauthorised Biography of Andrew Lloyd Webber*. New York: Viking Penguin, 1989.

McKnight, Gerald. *Andrew Lloyd Webber*. New York: St. Martin's, 1984.

Perry, George. *The Complete* Phantom of the Opera. New York: Henry Holt and Company, 1991.

———. *Sunset Boulevard* from Movie to Musical. New York: Henry Holt and Company, 1993.

Richmond, Keith. *The Musicals of Andrew Lloyd Webber*. London: Virgin, 1995.

Smith, Cecil. *Musical Comedy in America*. New York: Theatre Arts Books (Robert M. MacGregor), 1950.

Steyn, Mark. *Broadway Babies Say Goodnight: Musicals Then and Now*. New York: Routledge, 1999.

Wadsley, Pat. "Video: Marketing Broadway via MTV." *Theatre Crafts* 19 (February 1985): 14.

Walsh, Michael. *Andrew Lloyd Webber, His Life and Works: A Critical Biography*. New York: Abrams, 1989.

PLOT SUMMARY: *THE PHANTOM OF THE OPERA*

"Sold!" a voice cries during an auction of various properties from an opera house. The auctioneer notes that Lot 666 was the very chandelier involved in the mysterious, long-ago case of the Phantom of the Opera. A mighty flash of light is seen, and suddenly the chandelier is high above the audience. The overture starts to play as we are transported back to Paris of 1861.

On the stage, the Opéra Populaire rehearses an extravaganza complete with elephants. Richard Firmin and Gilles André are the new managers, and they meet prima donna Carlotta Giudicelli, tenor Ubaldo Piangi, and two chorus members: Meg Giry, daughter of the ballet mistress Madame Giry, and Christine Daaé. André asks Carlotta to sing, but midway through her aria, a heavy backdrop crashes to the stage, and nervously the performers exclaim that the Phantom is responsible. Madame Giry comes to André and Firmin with a message from the Phantom, notifying them of his customary expectations: Box 5 shall always be left vacant, and his monthly salary of 20,000 francs must be paid as usual; moreover, payment is due *now*.

Startling as this news is, André and Firmin have a more immediate problem: Carlotta now refuses to sing that evening, and she has no understudy. Meg steps forward, saying, "Christine Daaé could sing it." It's odd that Christine cannot name her teacher, but they allow her to demonstrate the "Think of Me" aria, and as she sings, the set around her is transformed into that evening's performance, where the audience applauds loudly. One of the loudest bravas comes from the Vicomte Raoul de Chagny, a new patron; he has recognized Christine as a girl he had known when they were both children.

Back in her dressing room, Christine is congratulated by an unseen voice. This is her mysterious teacher, whom she thinks is the "Angel of Music" her dying father had promised would watch over her. Raoul arrives, wanting to take her to

supper, but when he leaves to get his hat, Christine's "angel"—the Phantom—summons her. She steps through the mirror and travels with "The Phantom of the Opera" (**Musical Example 55**) far below the opera house, across a lake illuminated by thousands of candles, to his chambers. When she sees a wax figure of herself dressed in a bridal gown, she faints. When she awakens the next morning, the Phantom is composing at a pipe organ. While the Phantom is distracted, she yanks the mask away from his face. They are both horrified, but as he calms down, he realizes he should return her to the opera house before the others come searching for her.

Backstage, a stagehand tells the chorus girls frightful tales about the Phantom and a mysterious noose known as the Punjab knot. Meanwhile, the managers are upset by a series of orders from the Phantom; he wants Christine to star and Carlotta to be given a nonsinging role. The managers refuse, but as Carlotta sings, she suddenly loses her voice and can only croak, toad-fashion. Even worse, the stagehand's body is found dangling from the Punjab knot. Pandemonium ensues, and Christine leads Raoul to the rooftop. But the Phantom sees their embrace, and later, when Christine takes the stage, the Phantom sends the chandelier crashing to the ground in front of her as a warning to obey his dictates.

Six months later, Christine and Raoul are engaged, but the betrothal is a secret, since Christine still fears the Phantom. Suddenly, during a New Year's Masquerade ball, the Phantom appears in a blood-red costume topped by a hideous skull mask. Jeering, he makes his announcement: he has written a new opera—*Don Juan Triumphant*—and it is now their duty to perform it, or else. Before he vanishes, he yanks the engagement ring off the chain where Christine had hidden it around her neck.

Raoul refuses to believe that the Phantom is supernatural and presses Madame Giry for information; she knows that long ago a skilled but deformed conjuror was enslaved by a Persian monarch. After he escaped, odd things began happening at the opera house. Now, the invisible Phantom is directing *Don Juan* from afar. Christine dreads the performance because Raoul sees this as the opportunity to capture the Phantom. During a visit to her father's grave, she hears her father's voice intermingled with the Phantom's—but Raoul has followed, and he sees the Phantom in the process of hypnotizing Christine. Raoul manages to break her trance, so the Phantom swears that he will be avenged on them both.

The night of the performance has arrived, and Piangi, playing Don Juan, steps off stage—and encounters the fatal Punjab noose. But a Don Juan re-emerges on stage; it is the Phantom, now wooing Christine himself. She is unmoved by his pleas to marry him, and she pulls away his cloak to reveal his identity to the audience. Howling in dismay, he vanishes, but not without Christine, pulling her down to the labyrinth below the stage. Raoul is the first to find them. Laughing, the Phantom strangles Raoul with the Punjab knot, but tells Christine that she can save Raoul if she agrees to renounce Raoul and to love the Phantom at last. She makes her choice: stepping forward, she kisses the Phantom without hesitation. The Phantom's thirst for vengeance is quenched, and in his first unselfish act, he lets Raoul and Christine leave. The crowd rushes in, but all that remains of the Phantom is his mask.

PLOT SUMMARY: *SUNSET BOULEVARD*

As the curtains open, a crowd of people stands around a swimming pool and a floating body. A young man steps forward, asking if we want to know what happened here on Sunset Boulevard. To learn the answer, we need to go back in time six months, to 1949 Los Angeles. The young man, Joe Gillis, is a struggling screenwriter in Hollywood. He's trying to shake off the repo men who are after his car because he's behind on the payments. At the studio, Joe meets dozens of old friends, all of whom have little to offer in terms of actual employment. Joe makes his way to Sheldrake's office, where he hears his latest script disparaged by Sheldrake's assistant, Betty Schaefer. Betty is aghast when she realizes Joe is present, and she anxiously apologizes. In fact, she thinks an old magazine story of Joe's—*Blind Windows*—has the potential to become a good script. He's not interested but agrees to meet her at Schwab's Drugstore on Thursday to talk—on the condition that she distract the repo men.

Despite Betty's efforts, the finance men are soon pursuing Joe along Sunset Boulevard. He veers into an empty garage. The repo men don't see his maneuver and race past; meanwhile, Joe sees that the garage is not completely empty; he shares it with a pristine and luxurious 1932 Isotta-Fraschini. A voice calls to him from the adjacent mansion, demanding to know why he is so late. Before Joe can answer, a butler ushers him in, asking if Joe needs help with the coffin. And in front of Joe's fascinated eyes, an overdressed, middle-aged woman embraces the dead body of a small chimpanzee, crooning to it that she will rejoin it when it's her time to "Surrender." The woman has mistaken Joe for a pet mortician, and she orders him out when she realizes her mistake. But he realizes that she had been an old-time silent film star, Norma Desmond, and he exclaims, "You used to be big." Offended, Norma tells him, "I *am* big—it's the pictures that got small," and soon she is lost in a reverie of nostalgia, recalling how she could mesmerize audiences "With One Look" (**Musical Example 56**).

Awakening from her daydream, she orders him to leave once again, but quickly calls him back. She wants him to look at a script she's written for her return to the screen. After wading through a portion of it, Joe tries to assure her that the awful script is a good effort for a beginner (even though her character, Salome, is only 16 years old). Norma wants Joe to revise it, and she won't take no for an answer; she orders the butler, Max, to make up the guestroom over the garage. Max, it seems, has already done so.

Joe keeps his appointment with Betty at Schwab's, where lots of film folks hang out. In the crowd, Joe runs into his friend Artie Green, who turns out to be Betty's fiancé. To Betty's disappointment, Joe doesn't want to work on a new script with her; he simply tells her she can do what she wants with it.

Back at Norma's home, Joe is startled to see that Max has brought in Joe's belongings from his apartment; moreover, Max scolds Joe for leaving without notice in the evening, explaining that Madame can become melancholy easily, and even suicidal. Max warns Joe that he must live by the house rules if he wishes to keep this job. The work begins, and a pattern develops: after editing all day, Joe views Norma's old movies with her in the evenings while she happily anticipates her comeback film.

At last, Norma is ready to send the script to Cecil B. de Mille. Joe wishes her luck, and she's startled: Isn't he staying? Seeing her genuine panic, Joe relents; he'll stay until there's news from Paramount. A few days later, the house is overrun by salesmen from a Beverly Hills men's clothiers. It is Norma's birthday surprise for Joe; she insists that he must look nice for the New Year's party she is planning. He had intended to go to Artie's annual party, but at last he relents, and the salesmen push him to choose the most expensive items, since "The Lady's Paying."

New Year's Eve arrives. After dancing with Norma, Joe asks when the other guests will arrive, and she merrily tells him that it's just the two of them. Joe panics at the realization that Norma is falling for him and leaves, going to Artie's party. There, Betty tells him that Sheldrake is interested in *Blind Windows*, but she's finding she can't write it alone; she needs Joe's help. She will have plenty of free time, because Artie's been called to Tennessee for a movie shoot. Joe makes a snap decision and calls Max to ask for his suitcases. To his horror, Joe learns that Norma has found his razor and cut her wrists. He dashes back to the mansion—and the curtain falls as she draws him to her on the couch.

Joe—now a "kept man"—is on hand when a call comes from Paramount. Because it was an assistant telephoning, Norma forces herself to wait three days before responding, and then decides to journey to Paramount in person. An old guard at the gate recognizes her, allowing her to pass through the gate without an appointment. She makes her way to a busy film shoot, where another oldtimer sees her and aims a spotlight at her. In a flash, she is transported back to her glory days. De Mille reminisces with her briefly, then eases her off the set; he sadly observes that she's never known the meaning of "Surrender."

Joe runs into Betty and promises to call her about the *Blind Windows* script. Elsewhere on the lot, Max makes an unpleasant discovery: Paramount called because they want to rent Norma's car. Norma, in blissful ignorance, believes she'll be filming soon and begins a vigorous health regimen to get in shape. During his free time, Joe sneaks out to work on script revisions with Betty. Norma grows suspicious, having found the *Blind Windows* script and Betty's name, but Joe fobs her off. That evening, at work in Betty's office, Joe and Betty realize that they've fallen in love—despite Norma, despite Artie.

As Joe arrives back at the mansion, Max is waiting for him in the dark, advising him to be careful. Joe says that the lies must stop, but Max insists that Norma must never know the truth. Joe gradually realizes that Max was formerly the film director Max von Mayerling, who had also been Norma's first husband. Max has devoted his life to preserving Norma's illusions, writing fan mail to her, and intercepting all unpleasantness. But events are spinning out of Max's control.

Norma, having found Betty's phone number, calls her up. Joe interrupts the phone call and invites Betty to come see for herself what's going on. When Betty arrives, Joe parades his pampered existence. Betty is horrified at seeing this side of Joe. It is as if Joe is doing all he can to drive her away, and he soon succeeds; she leaves in tears. Norma thanks Joe but can't understand where he's going with his typewriter. As she begins to clutch at him, he tells her the truth about the web of pretense Max has sustained for her. Telling her goodbye, he turns to leave. Angrily she insists, "No one ever leaves a star," and shoots him repeatedly. It is soon evident that she's suffered a complete mental breakdown, mouthing snatches of film dialogue and reprising earlier tunes. She mistakes the photographers' flashbulbs for movie cameras and lights, and descends the staircase, exclaiming that she's overwhelmed with happiness but ready for her close-up.

MUSICAL EXAMPLE 55

THE PHANTOM OF THE OPERA
ANDREW LLOYD WEBBER/CHARLES HART, 1986

"The Phantom of the Opera"

Christine

1   In sleep he sang to me, in dreams he came, that voice which calls to me and speaks my name.
And do I dream again? For now I find the phantom of the opera is there inside my mind.

Phantom

2   Sing once again with me our strange duet; my power over you grows stronger yet.
And though you turn from me to glance behind,
the phantom of the opera is there inside your mind.

Christine

3   Those who have seen your face draw back in fear. I am the mask you wear,

Phantom

It's me they hear.

Phantom	**Christine**
My spirit and your voice, in one combined;	Your spirit and my voice, in one combined;
The phantom of the opera is there	The phantom of the opera is there
inside your mind.	inside my mind.

Chorus

4   He's there, the phantom of the opera. Beware the phantom of the opera.

Phantom

5   In all your fantasies, you always knew that man and mystery

Christine

Were both in you.

Phantom	**Christine**
And in this labyrinth, where night is blind,	And in this labyrinth, where night is blind,
The phantom of the opera is there	The phantom of the opera is here
inside your mind.	inside my mind.

Phantom

[Sing, my Angel of Music.]

Christine

6   He's there, the phantom of the opera.
Ah! Ah! Ah! Ah! Ah! Ah! Ah! Ah!

MUSICAL EXAMPLE 56

SUNSET BOULEVARD
ANDREW LLOYD WEBBER/DON BLACK AND CHRISTOPHER HAMPTON, 1993

"With One Look"

Norma

1   With one look I can break your heart, with one look I play every part.
I can make your sad heart sing. With one look you'll know all you need to know.

2   With one smile, I'm the girl next door or the love you've hungered for.
     When I speak it's with my soul. I can play any role.

3   No words can tell the stories my eyes tell.
     Watch me when I frown, you can't write that down.
     You know I'm right, it's there in black and white.
     When I look your way, you'll hear what I say.

4   Yes, with one look I put words to shame, just one look sets the screen aflame.
     Silent music starts to play. One tear in my eye makes the whole world cry.

5   With one look they'll forgive the past, they'll rejoice I've returned at last
     To my people in the dark, still out there in the dark.

6   *[interlude]*

     Silent music starts to play. With one look you'll know all you need to know.

7   With one look I'll ignite a blaze, I'll return to my glory days.
     They'll say Norma's back at last.

8   This time I am staying, I'm staying for good,
     I'll be back where I was born to be. With one look I'll be me.

Chapter 41
The New Team in Town: Schönberg and Boublil

In 1972, a Frenchman was visiting New York when he was invited to attend the premiere of *Jesus Christ Superstar* because another guest had backed out. This chance opportunity had a profound impact on **Alain Boublil** (b. 1941), who went back to France determined to create something along the same lines for French consumption. His enthusiasm was infectious, and he quickly persuaded the composer **Claude-Michel Schönberg** (b. 1944) to join forces. In the years to come, Schönberg and Boublil would revitalize French musical theater, challenging not only the longstanding dominance of American musicals but also the new wave of British musicals created by Lloyd Webber himself.

Wanting an inherently "French" topic, Schönberg and Boublil decided to create a musical out of the most significant event in their nation's history. By 1973 they were ready to record *La révolution française*, following the concept-album method used by Lloyd Webber in several early musicals. The recording sold quite well, so the show was mounted in Paris that same year. The venue was a huge sports arena known as the *Palais des Sports*—reflecting Schönberg and Boublil's ambitious ability to "think big" from the very start of their joint career. The novel approach left a marked impression on the French public, who were curious to see what Schönberg and Boublil would come up with next.

It took some time to decide on the topic for their subsequent show, as Boublil noted: "We must have worked on half a dozen different ideas, before finally dropping them for one reason or another." They studied the musicals in New York and London; Schönberg recalled, "I remember an extraordinary black version of 'The Wizard of Oz' [*The Wiz*] and 'Pippin'." In London, meanwhile, Boublil viewed the *Oliver!* revival (staged by Cameron Mackintosh), and the character of the Artful Dodger—the young pickpocket—reminded him sharply of Gavroche, a Parisian street urchin who plays a significant role in the novel ***Les Misérables***. "It was like a blow to the solar plexus," Boublil said. "I started seeing all the characters of Victor Hugo's 'Les Misérables'—Valjean, Javert, Gavroche, Cosette, Marius and Éponine—in my mind's eye, laughing, crying and singing on stage" (see the **Plot Summary**).

Hugo, one of France's greatest authors, had died in 1885, leaving orders that his poetry should never be set to music. Since he didn't say anything about his *novels*, however, it seemed that these were fair game. Hugo published the epic *Les Misérables* in 1862, and its reception foreshadowed the treatment the musical would receive more than a century later: critics hated it, while the public devoured it. The Vatican put it on its list of banned books for a number of years, to no avail; it sold millions of copies. It has undergone a complete critical reappraisal and now is one of France's most cherished books.

Schönberg liked the idea of setting *Les Misérables*, pleased that it would allow them to celebrate their national heritage again. In fact, Schönberg decided to quit his job as a producer at a prestigious recording company to devote himself to composing music full time. As with their previous show, the team decided to prepare a concept album first. Released in early 1980, this album also did well, selling 260,000 copies, and a stage version was presented in September, once again at the *Palais des Sports*.

Although the show was seen by some 500,000 people, there did not seem to be much international interest in the show beyond a nibble from a small American opera company, which contemplated only a few performances. A couple of years later, however, a director, Peter Farago, fell in love with the concept album. Farago took it to Mackintosh's London office and persuaded the producer to listen to the recording. Mackintosh remembers, "It was an instant combustible decision. By the fourth track I was wildly excited and one November morning I called Alan Jay Lerner [then living in London] and asked to come round and see him. . . . Lerner thought it was a marvelous piece of work but, as he put it, 'it's not for me because I don't write about those sorts of people.' He did say: 'you must press on with this'."

Few of Mackintosh's initial collaborators were still on board by the end. Farago, of course, assumed he would be directing the show, but Mackintosh began quietly negotiating with Trevor Nunn. But would Nunn agree to do it? Mackintosh sent Nunn a tape of the concept album. Weeks went by, and finally Nunn confessed to Mackintosh: "I keep listening to the tape in my car and can't get the tunes out of my head. I'll do it." Nunn had a couple of conditions, however; he wanted **John Caird** (b. 1948) as his codirector, and he wanted the production to start out as a Royal Shakespeare Company endeavor. In turn, Mackintosh reserved the right to approve the hiring of all actors and musicians. Nunn agreed and was hired as director. At last, Farago was told about Nunn's hiring, but to sweeten the sting of dismissal, Farago was offered a financial settlement; with some degree of bitterness, he accepted.

Initially, Mackintosh teamed up with James Nederlander, who owned several Broadway theaters. Nederlander invited Mackintosh to bring his *Oliver!* revival overseas. During the process, Mackintosh discovered that his careful, meticulous working methods were incompatible with Nederlander's more cavalier approach. Again, delicate negotiations were undertaken (becoming less delicate and more acrimonious as time went by), and Nederlander eventually withdrew from the *Les Misérables* project.

Mackintosh invited poet **James Fenton** (b. 1949) to make the English adaptation, and Fenton, somewhat to Mackintosh's surprise, accepted. Fenton took Hugo's novel with him on a two-month journey through Borneo in 1983 in the company of Redmond O'Hanlon. As they struggled through the hazards of leeches, mosquitoes, killer ants, leaky dugout canoes, and head-hunters, Fenton tore off page after page of the paperback novel after reading them, thereby lightening his pack bit by bit. O'Hanlon later chronicled portions of their adventure in a bestseller, *Into the Heart of Borneo*.

During his labors, Fenton made some important structural suggestions for the musical. As Edward Behr observed, the original French version could have been titled "Scenes from *Les Misérables*," for it was in essence a *tableau*, the French term for a series of vignettes held together by a narrator. The arena production didn't attempt to portray the entire novel, because French audiences *knew* the story and would have been impatient with a page-by-page depiction. Non-French viewers needed more, however, and Fenton recommended that the show open with a prologue depicting Valjean's hard labor as a convict and the generosity shown to Valjean by the Bishop of Digné.

Nunn and Caird were less happy with some of Fenton's other contributions. His lyrics were polished, often quite esoteric—and at times unsingable. Moreover, Fenton was working very, very slowly, and Mackintosh began to realize that there was no chance that the show would be ready for the targeted October 1984 opening. Mackintosh knew something had to be done—and he did it. Fenton understood that Mackintosh was within his rights to fire him, but noted, "It was quite a painful experience just the same." Nevertheless, Fenton retained a percentage of the gross for his contributions, and this must have been a comfort, since he has earned upwards of £10 million to date from the show.

Mackintosh turned to **Herbert Kretzmer** (b. 1925). Hired on March 1, 1985, Kretzmer started working day and night, for Fenton's efforts had not extended much past the first act. As Kretzmer quickly discovered, it was not a simple matter of setting English words in place of the original French: "What I was engaged in can't in any way be called translation. A third of the work to be done consisted of a *form* of translation, a third was free adaptation, with completely new words to existing music, and a third of it involved writing completely new songs." Moreover, *all* the show's text had to be singable, because like the shows being written by Lloyd Webber, *Les Misérables* was to be a sung-through musical. (Ironically enough, *Les Misérables* is routinely mistaken for a Lloyd Webber musical.)

Schönberg, again in the manner as Lloyd Webber, unifies *Les Misérables* through the use of several reiterated melodies. The "Look Down" ostinato sung by the convicts at the opening is heard whenever Valjean encounters his nemesis Javert. Echoes of the tune are heard also in Thénardier's bitter "Dog Eats Dog," and also as the poor of Paris struggle through their own desperate existence. Valjean sings a powerful epiphany

during the Prologue, when he rebukes himself for stealing, then declares that he will justify the bishop's faith by putting an end to Valjean's existence and starting a new life. This tune is echoed in Javert's "Soliloquy," when Javert, too, puts an end to his previous existence—but his method proves to be suicide. Similarly, the melody of "Come to Me," sung by the dying Fantine, returns when Valjean himself is dying at the end of the show, intermixed with echoes of "Do You Hear the People Sing?" The Thénardiers repeat their "Master of the House" theme during "Beggars at the Feast." A stranger recycling occurs during Marius's "Empty Chairs at Empty Tables," for his melody comes from the bishop's assertion in the Prologue that he had just purchased Valjean's "soul for God." It is hard to see a connection between the scenes, but perhaps it concerns the issue of sacrifice; the bishop was willing to forego his "precious silver" to help Valjean to become an honest man, while Marius's comrades sacrificed their very lives in a rather fruitless effort to improve the lot of Paris's poor people.

There are also songs that stand alone in the show, such as Cosette's "Castle on a Cloud" (**Musical Example 57**). Delicate woodwinds and harplike instruments establish a childlike atmosphere. This accompaniment produces a music-box effect for Cosette's vision song. The structure of the young Cosette's brief escape from reality is a straightforward song form, but the musical setting supports the text in several subtle ways. The minor mode is well suited to Cosette's plaintive mood, and the unsubstantial nature of the fictional "castle on a cloud" is expressed by an asymmetrical meter during the *a* portions. These *a* sections (**1**, **2**, and **4**) constantly alternate between triple and duple meter, creating, in effect, a quintuple pulsation. The off-balance effect of this metric shifting and the bittersweet minor mode are both abandoned during the *b* section at **3**, however. Cosette reaches the climax of her vision: someone telling her "I love you"—words the abused waif never hears in real life. During this bridge, the mode shifts to major, and the meter moves to a stable quadruple. The closing *a*, with its return to the more uneasy triple-duple alternation and the minor mode, eases Cosette back into the misery of her day-to-day existence. This tiny "aria" for Cosette is followed by recitative expressing her sudden panic upon hearing the approach of Madame Thénardier. As in the musicals of Lloyd Webber, the line between musical theater and opera is increasingly blurred.

Kretzmer's (and before him, Fenton's) task was not easy, for Hugo's novel was some 1,200 pages in length. Unsurprisingly, *Les Mis* shaped up as a *long* show, lasting four hours in its first preview. Cutting and cutting, the creators brought it down to a still-hefty three-and-one-half hours for its 1985 London debut at the Barbican Theatre. Despite the cuts, *Les Misérables* met with many stinging criticisms. Its "rock opera" qualities came under particular attack, as did its treatment of the novel; Francis King believed that the show "stands in the same relation to the original as a singing telegram to an epic."

After the opening, Mackintosh was in agony—not just because of the harsh judgments, but because he had a mere 48 hours to make the decision whether or not to transfer *Les Mis* to a West End theater at the end of the ten-week Barbican run. Mackintosh had placed a £50,000 deposit on the Palace Theatre and had to choose whether to lose that nonrefundable

Bayard engraving of Cosette helps to advertise the Broadway production of *Les Misérables*
Museum of the City of New York.

amount or to risk a possibly greater financial loss by transferring the show, which would cost at least £300,000. Finally, he telephoned the Barbican, only to be told, "I'm amazed you managed to get through. The phones haven't stopped ringing. We've sold a record five thousand tickets already." Thanks to word-of-mouth praise, the production played to capacity crowds within three days, and the entire Barbican run sold out quickly. Just as had been the case with Hugo's novel, the initial negative reviews were gradually supplanted by much more favorable assessments, and Mackintosh breathed a sigh of relief, for he had decided to transfer the show.

But, by the time *Les Misérables* was ready to open at the Palace, trimmed to a length of just over three hours, the advance was only £300,000—much smaller than Mackintosh expected. Then, just as had been the case at the Barbican, the ticket sales took off, and the Palace began to sustain a nearly steady £2.5 million advance. The London production (which transferred to the Queen's Theatre in 2004) continues to run to the present day, having exceeded 7,500 performances, while the Broadway show racked up 6,680 performances during its run from 1987 to 2003 (winning some eight Tony Awards along the way and setting a record top ticket price of $50). Successful productions have been presented around the word, and cast members from many of the productions gathered for a glittering tenth-anniversary concert version of *Les Mis* at Royal Albert Hall.

At the opening night party after the Palace Theatre premiere, Schönberg and Boublil took a great deal of gleeful pleasure in telling Mackintosh that since it looked like they might have a future as professional writers, they were glad they had started work on a new show. They then refused to *tell* him anything about their latest idea for several months. Their working method depended on a careful working-out of the book, which would dictate the kinds of songs needed in particular situations. Like Lloyd Webber's collaborative process with Tim Rice, Schönberg generally wrote the music before Boublil crafted words to fit. Or, rather, Schönberg *crafted* the music at the piano; like Irving Berlin and others, Schönberg depended on someone else to transcribe his music into musical notation.

The inspiration for their secret project, **Miss Saigon**, had been a magazine photograph. The image captured the heart-wrenching moment when a Vietnamese mother, lips pressed tightly together to keep from weeping, bid farewell to her sobbing daughter; the child was boarding a plane to travel to the United States, where she would join the American father she'd never met. Schönberg was stunned by the photo: "The silence of this woman stunned by her grief was a shout of pain louder than any of the earth's laments. The child's tears were the final condemnation of all wars which shatter people who love each other."

For their libretto, Schönberg and Boublil were influenced by Puccini's opera *Madama Butterfly* (1904), the tragic tale of a Japanese geisha, Butterfly. She loves—and marries—an opportunistic American named Pinkerton. She waits for Pinkerton to come back, but when he does return, he brings an American wife with him, and they simply want to claim Pinkerton's son, the child born to Butterfly. In despair, Butterfly kills herself, wanting the child to go to America without impediment. Schönberg and Boublil updated the story to the Vietnam War era, but they made their American soldier a much more sympathetic victim of war's upheaval (see the **Plot Summary**). As with their earlier two musicals, there was

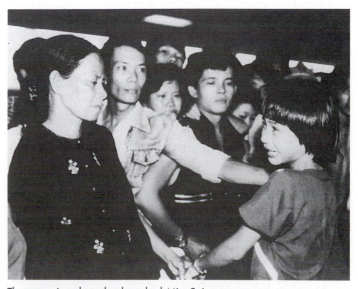

The magazine photo that launched *Miss Saigon*
France Soir Magazine.

a French connection: France had controlled Vietnam just prior to the American involvement.

Schönberg and Boublil auditioned the first act for Mackintosh in 1986. They played tapes of the score with Schönberg singing the lyrics (in French) and waited for Mackintosh's opinion. It wasn't quite the reaction they'd hoped for; Mackintosh was taken aback by the radical change in style and mood from *Les Misérables*, for *Miss Saigon* had a much harder edge and used more colloquial language. On their return flight to Paris, Schönberg recalls, "We were already resigned to Cameron saying no, and were practically reconciled to the fact." To their surprise and delight, Mackintosh called them two days later, saying he'd listened to the tapes repeatedly and was excited by the challenge.

While Schönberg and Boublil labored on the second act, Mackintosh tried to find a collaborator to assist with the lyrics. Boublil's own command of English was formidable, but Mackintosh and Boublil both knew that there would be moments when a native speaker was needed. Kretzmer was approached, but as he ruefully acknowledges, he talked them out of choosing him; his rationale was that they needed an American, whereas he was a British resident who had been born in South Africa. **Richard Maltby, Junior** (b. 1937) was an American writer who had worked with Lloyd Webber and Mackintosh on the U.S. production of *Song and Dance*, and Mackintosh felt Maltby would have the touch needed for the sometimes raw show. Maltby, however, never having heard of Schönberg and Boublil and being wary of a Vietnam war setting—still a highly emotional issue for many Americans—turned Mackintosh down.

For a time, Mackintosh was stymied. Gradually, though, the same tapes that had persuaded Mackintosh to undertake the production had their impact on Maltby. Maltby also saw a performance of *Les Misérables*, which gave him a much better appreciation for what Schönberg and Boublil were trying to accomplish. Finally, several months after their initial conversations, Maltby called Mackintosh to see if a writer had been hired; before he knew it, Maltby found himself hard at work with Boublil.

The creators planned to release a concept album, as they had done with their previous two shows. However, listening to the rough tapes of the recording sessions, Mackintosh decided that he didn't want to reveal the score in this way; moreover, the orchestrations didn't seem right for the show. So, Mackintosh cancelled the album (at a loss of £185,000) and fired the orchestrator as well. Moreover, just as the choice of director had been problematic in *Les Misérables*, the process was uncomfortable during *Miss Saigon*. This time, it was Nunn who assumed he would direct the show, but Mackintosh wasn't sure that Nunn was the right choice. Nunn had struggled with the American production of *Chess*, and *Miss Saigon* needed a director with a good understanding of American issues. Moreover, Nunn might be directing Lloyd Webber's *Aspects of Love*, set to debut the same year as *Miss Saigon*, and Mackintosh felt there was no way that Nunn could do justice to two separate shows.

Mackintosh wanted to offer the show to Michael Bennett (director of *A Chorus Line*), but Bennett was battling AIDS.

Jerome Robbins, in turn, decided that the project wasn't right for him. Mackintosh started negotiations with Jerry Zaks, but Zaks didn't want to live in London for a year or more. Finally, Mackintosh turned to the up-and-coming young director **Nicholas Hytner** (b. 1956). Hytner had been wooed to direct *Aspects of Love*, but Nunn had been named the director instead. With Nunn officially committed elsewhere, and with Hytner's availability, Mackintosh solved the problem of a director at last.

The expensive stage sets were another challenge. *Miss Saigon* was being mounted in the vast Theatre Royal, Drury Lane, which is London's largest theater (indeed, the largest commercial theater in Europe), and it would be all too easy to dwarf the actors. Set designer John Napier needed to bring the **trucks**—the movable platforms holding various sets—to the center of the stage in order to focus the audience's attention to the action. Computerized engines were required to propel the trucks along concealed rails. Ironically, *Miss Saigon*'s splashiest effect—the descent and ascent of the nearly full-scale helicopter chassis during the embassy evacuation—was one of the simpler stage sets to manage.

A split stage effect was needed for "I Still Believe" (**Musical Example 58**) in the first act. This duet opens as a solo for Kim; she awakens in Ho Chi Minh City after dreaming of Chris, singing of her memories of him at **1**; the gentle plucked-string effects and the *shakuhachi* (a Japanese bamboo flute) evoke her Asian environment. In the *b* section (**2**), Kim declares her faith that Chris will return. Then our eyes are drawn across the stage—and, symbolically, around the world—to Ellen, who watches her husband Chris while he sleeps. While the characters are distinguished by their voice types—Kim is a soprano, while Ellen is a slightly lower-pitched **mezzo-soprano**—the Western ambience of Ellen's world is also underscored by a change to an accompanying piano. However, the similarity between the women is demonstrated by Ellen's reiteration (at **3** and **4**) of the same *a* and *b* melodies just sung by Kim. Ellen then introduces a new theme, *c*, at **5**, as Chris stirs restlessly in his sleep; she tries to reassure him, unsure why he feels such tension. Ellen is joined by Kim at **6**, with Kim reprising the earlier *b* melody while Ellen sings the new *c* theme again. The two women continue to sing in nonimitative polyphony, unaware of each other, but joining together homophonically for the final line of the song, where they share an identical faith that their union with Chris will continue "until we die."

The casting took even more work than the stage sets. A mere 31 performers responded to the initial advertisement in the *Stage*, the British equivalent to the American *Backstage*, so Mackintosh's team put up ads in Chinese restaurants, Buddhist temples, and all the southeast Asian embassies. (The Vietnamese Embassy was careful to note that the show's title should be *Miss Ho Chi Minh City*.) The creators also journeyed to New York, Los Angeles, Hawaii, and then to the Philippines. The excitement grew in Manila after a number of actresses were tapped for roles, and when the creators returned to cast eight more male roles, the auditions were mobbed. One actor, 15th on the waiting list for an overbooked plane from a provincial town, told his fellow travelers why he was desperate to get to Manila—and another passenger gave him his seat.

Jonathan Pryce was cast in the pivotal role of the Engineer, as essential a character in establishing the mood of *Miss Saigon* as the part of the Master of Ceremonies in *Cabaret*. The ethnicity of the Engineer is described as Eurasian, so Pryce applied a cosmetic skin bronzing cream and initially taped his eyelids to reproduce the Asiatic fold, but otherwise played the part without extensive makeup. Pryce was well established as a dramatic actor, but few people were aware of his fine singing voice. Very soon, Pryce had put such a definitive stamp on the role that it was hard to conceive of any other interpretation—an issue that would come to the forefront when planning the Broadway production.

Miss Saigon finally premiered in 1989. It opened to largely favorable reviews, with sold-out performances for years ahead. The creators weren't content, however; in the spring of 1990, they made extensive revisions to the opening and final scenes. Moreover, they needed to simplify the stage sets, both for Broadway and for other productions. Kim's stage requirements were a typical problem; she needed three trucks—for her Dreamland cubicle, her shared Vietnamese hut after the Vietcong had come to power, and her room in Bangkok—and a considerable amount of backstage storage was needed for just these three small sets. As Mackintosh ruefully observed, "She's a penniless Vietnamese girl, and she's got more property than Donald Trump."

Concentrating on the technical issues facing the new productions, Mackintosh was unprepared for a political firestorm that arose around the American cast. Mackintosh wanted Pryce to reprise his outstanding performance, and he applied for the customary Equity waiver for a non-American Equity Association (AEA) actor. There should have been no problem, for it was a routine matter for the AEA to approve a recognized star, and Pryce had already received a Tony Award among other honors. To Mackintosh's dismay, a coalition of Asian AEA members protested Pryce's casting, arguing that an Asian—not Caucasian—actor should play the Eurasian Engineer. As one Chinese-American performer put it, "The time for actors of color to be playing 'their own' roles is certainly *now*. We cannot even begin to fight for *non-traditional* casting if audiences are not given permission to accept us enacting characters of our *own* colors." The American activists felt that the fact that British Equity had not challenged Pryce's casting was merely a sign that it had "not taken care of its own members."

Mackintosh was shocked and angry. As producer, he had the prerogative of hiring any actor he wished, but the protestors' position challenged that privilege. Moreover, there was a hysterical, hostile tone to much of the verbiage, and Mackintosh was worried that the entire backstage climate would be poisoned. He kept quiet, however, hoping that the AEA Council would rein in the belligerent faction. However, in 1990, the Council ruled against Pryce. The AEA president, Colleen Dewhurst (a Caucasian who herself had recently starred in *The Good Woman of Szechuan*), had tried to rationalize the decision by telling Mackintosh it didn't matter *who* played the Engineer, since the Broadway production had amassed an advance of some $25 million. Dewhurst, along with many others, clearly believed that Mackintosh would back down and sacrifice Pryce rather than lose that record-setting advance.

For Mackintosh, though, this was the last straw. Rather than begin arbitration proceedings—which he probably would have won—he placed a prominent notice in the *New York Times*, canceling *Miss Saigon* and observing that the AEA decision was "a disturbing violation of the principles of artistic integrity and freedom." Another storm broke out, with nearly all opinions supporting Mackintosh, and a week later, the AEA reversed itself and welcomed Pryce. This reversal was not sufficient for Mackintosh; he wanted a guarantee from AEA that the atmosphere would change—"that casting and pre-production would take place without intimidation, recriminations, innuendos or indirect pressures on Equity members." A formal agreement to this effect was hammered out, and auditions for the $10 million production—a new high for Broadway—began at last in October.

The controversy had at least one fringe benefit: the pre-opening ticket sales mounted to an eye-popping $31 million (achieved in part because the top ticket price set a new record at $100 a seat). Reaction to the show after its 1991 premiere was similar to the London reviews; some lamented the emphasis given to stage effects, but many others appreciated the heartfelt love story that underpinned the show. Pryce's important contribution was recognized by his Tony for Best Actor; *Miss Saigon* won three Tonys in all. Both the London and New York productions did well; the West End show closed after 4,246 performances, and the Broadway show played 4,092 times.

Schönberg and Boublil's fourth collaboration—and their second show to debut as an English-language production—opened *and* closed while both *Les Misérables* and *Miss Saigon* were still running. Although *Martin Guerre* (1996) won four Olivier Awards, including Best Musical, it was a troubled production, closing with a loss of some $8 million. Several attempts to salvage the show were made, both during the initial run (when it closed for a hiatus to be restaged and to have new songs interpolated) and again before it started its American tryout tour, but the show closed in Los Angeles.

In their program notes for the American touring production of *Martin Guerre*, Schönberg and Boublil indicated that they had started work on another show early in 1998, but found themselves pulled back to *Martin Guerre* over and over again, trying to complete what they felt were its unfinished aspects. Since the time that their revised *Martin Guerre* ended its American tryout, no new theatrical projects have been announced. Schönberg and Boublil are a theatrical team of considerable talent, however, and it is to be hoped that new works by them will soon find their way to the stage.

FURTHER READING

Behr, Edward. *The Complete Book of* Les Misérables.
    New York: Arcade Publishing, 1989.
Behr, Edward, and Mark Steyn. *The Story of* Miss Saigon.
    New York: Arcade Publishing, 1991.
Gänzl, Kurt. *The Musical: A Concise History*. Boston:
    Northeastern University Press, 1997.
Gottfried, Martin. *More Broadway Musicals Since 1980*.
    New York: Abrams, 1991.

Green, Stanley. *Broadway Musicals: Show by Show*. Third edition. Milwaukee, Wisconsin: Hal Leonard Publishing, 1990.

Miller, Scott. *From* Assassins *to West Side Story: A Director's Guide to Musical Theatre*. Portsmouth, New Hampshire: Heinemann, 1996.

Steyn, Mark. *Broadway Babies Say Goodnight: Musicals Then and Now*. New York: Routledge, 1999.

PLOT SUMMARY: *LES MISÉRABLES*

A group of convicts toils away, but Jean Valjean is being released after 19 long years. He's not a free man, as Inspector Javert is quick to explain: instead, he's merely on parole. Valjean is resentful, for as a parolee, Valjean finds that he is routinely robbed of payment for his labors and is shunned as a convict. Only the Bishop of Digné treats him with kindness, but Valjean is so embittered that he robs the bishop in the night. He is soon caught, but an astonishing thing happens: the bishop claims he had given the goods to Valjean; moreover, he presses enormous silver candlesticks into Valjean's hands also.

The bishop tells Valjean that he has bought his soul for God, and Valjean takes the gift as a new lease on life. He flees to a remote town, where, over the next eight years, he rises to become the mayor. One factory worker, Fantine, is especially unhappy; the foreman is relentless in trying to seduce her, and the other women are jealous that he pays her so much attention. A coworker grabs a note dropped by Fantine. It's a letter from the Thénardiers, innkeepers who are keeping Fantine's daughter Cosette. The coworkers gloat to learn that unmarried Fantine has a child, telling the foreman that they refuse to work with a woman of such obviously low morals. Angry that she won't submit to *him*, the foreman fires her.

Fantine is distraught; to support Cosette, she sells what she can—her locket, her hair—and finally her body. In time, she assaults an abusive customer, and both Javert and Valjean arrive during her arrest. Valjean decides she needs medical care, not prison, and sends her to the hospital. Javert does not recognize Valjean—mainly because he believes that a man who has been captured elsewhere is Valjean; that prisoner is about to stand trial. Can Valjean stand by and see another man imprisoned in his stead?

Of course he can't, so he reveals his identity at the man's trial, then flees to the hospital where Fantine is dying. Valjean promises to care for Cosette, just as Javert arrives. Javert refuses to believe that Valjean will return after retrieving Cosette, so Valjean uses force to escape. He hurries to the inn where Cosette, abused by the Thénardiers, dreams of a "Castle on a Cloud" (**Musical Example 57**). The innkeepers insist that Cosette has cost a lot; angrily Valjean throws them 1,500 francs and takes Cosette.

Ten years go by while Valjean lives quietly with Cosette in Paris, with Javert still searching for him. Elsewhere, the Thénardiers have ended up on the streets with the other unhappy Parisian beggars; only young Gavroche seems light-hearted. Meanwhile, students are rallying, knowing that when General Lamarque dies, the poor people will lose their best advocate. The students anticipate a rebellion, but one student, Marius, is distracted by a beautiful girl. He begs Éponine—daughter of the Thénardiers—to help him find the mysterious girl again. When the news of the general's passing arrives, the citizens prepare for battle, but even as the rebellion nears, Éponine leads Marius to Cosette's house. Cosette is overjoyed to see him when she comes out to the garden. Waiting outside the gate, Éponine recognizes her father among a gang of thieves who are about to rob Valjean's house; she screams to warn the occupants. The alarm makes Valjean worry that Javert is near, so he prepares to flee with Cosette.

The poor and the students have erected barricades in the streets. Marius begs Éponine to take a letter to Cosette. Because Éponine loves Marius herself, she agrees, handing the letter to Valjean. Meanwhile, Gavroche has caused an uproar. He has identified a spy among the revolutionaries: it is Javert. As Éponine tries to make her way back to the barricades, she is shot, and she dies in Marius's arms. Valjean is more successful in reaching the barricades, however; he has come to fight, but is there really to protect Marius, since he now knows that this is the boy Cosette loves. Valjean, assigned to guard Javert, recognizes that he has only been performing his sworn duty; he allows the inspector to escape.

The battle ceases at nightfall, and the students rest. Valjean prays that he will be able to protect Marius successfully. The fighting goes poorly the next day; Gavroche is killed early on, and the other rebels drop one by one. At last, Valjean appears to be the only fighter remaining, so he picks up the wounded Marius and escapes with him down into the sewers of Paris. Exhausted, Valjean faints. Thénardier lives in this foul environment, plundering bodies when he can. He steals a ring from Marius, but recognizes Valjean and runs away. When Valjean comes to, he picks Marius up again and quickly runs into Javert. Once again, Valjean begs Javert to let him take his burden to a doctor, promising that he will return—and Javert astonishes himself by agreeing. Javert is unable to believe that he has knowingly let a prisoner escape; maddened by his confusion, he at last leaps from a bridge.

Many lives were lost on the barricades; Marius grieves for his absent friends. But Marius has joy too; when he recuperates, he and Cosette will marry. Valjean trusts Marius with his secret—he is a wanted criminal—and he will leave after the wedding to spare Cosette disgrace. Two garishly dressed wedding guests have familiar faces: the Thénardiers have crashed the ceremony, intending to blackmail Marius because they think his father-in-law is a murderer. Why, Thénardier has a ring from the victim's body. Marius recognizes the ring as his own and now realizes that it was Valjean who had rescued him from the barricades. Marius and Cosette rush to Valjean's side; Valjean tells Cosette about her past while ghosts from the past gather around to lead him away from the miseries of this world.

PLOT SUMMARY: *MISS SAIGON*

The year is 1975, and the curtain rises on Dreamland, a seedy bar/brothel in Saigon, South Vietnam. It is run by the Engineer, who has a gimmick: each Friday, the hard-drinking American soldiers choose a "Miss Saigon" from among the bar girls; she is raffled off to spend the night with the winner. It is a sordid, desperate place, and Kim's innocent purity as she works her first night is a painful contrast.

A jaded embassy worker, Chris, has come to Dreamland with his friend John. Chris is immediately fascinated by Kim, who wears an *ao dai*, a modest traditional Vietnamese garment, unlike the other bikini-clad bar girls. Chris claps vigorously when her name is called in the Miss Saigon contest, but to no avail; provocative Gigi receives the most applause. For Gigi, though, the tinfoil crown is meaningless. Like the other bar girls, she hopes that one of the soldiers might be her ticket out of Vietnam; she dreams of what America must be like, so very far from her degrading life of prostitution.

Even the Engineer longs to get an American visa but has no luck trying to bribe John. John, however, does pay the Engineer for Kim, buying an evening with her for his buddy Chris. The Engineer orders Kim to go entertain Chris, urging them to go to Kim's room. Some time later, Chris is awake, wondering why something special happens *now*, when it's time for him to leave Saigon. Although he leaves for a while, he finds himself drawn back to Kim's room. She awakens, and they embrace again.

The next day, Chris asks John for all his accumulated leave so he can stay with Kim. John points out that Saigon is falling apart, and the Americans will be evacuating any day now, but he at last agrees to grant Chris one more day. Back in Kim's room, Chris finds several other Vietnamese girls, all singing a gentle tune. Chris asks what it means, and Kim tells him "It's what all the girls sing at weddings," adding "They didn't know what else to sing." Smiling (but nervous), Chris goes along with their ceremony until the door flies open and in comes Thuy, Kim's communist cousin. He had been betrothed to Kim before the destruction of their village, and now he wants to know why there is an American soldier in her bedroom. The two men brandish guns at each other until Thuy retreats, cursing Kim for dishonoring her family. Kim is in tears, and Chris can only hold her for comfort.

The scene changes to a time three years later. Saigon is now Ho Chi Minh City, and Thuy has risen to power; Thuy wants the Engineer to locate Kim. Kim is still waiting for Chris, telling herself "I Still Believe" (**Musical Example 58**) that Chris will return for her, but soon a voice from halfway around the world joins her. It is Ellen, whom Chris married after searching fruitlessly for Kim. Ellen knows that Chris hides some secrets, for at night he cries out another woman's name.

It does not take the Engineer long to find Kim, but Thuy finds that she is still resistant to marriage; she insists that she *has* a husband and a secret: her two-year-old son, Tam. But this revelation backfires; instead of giving up, Thuy threatens to kill the mixed-race child. In desperation, Kim pulls out Chris's revolver and shoots Thuy. Kim runs with Tam to the Engineer, who is upset that she might

have led pursuers to him. Then, discovering that Tam's father was a Marine, the Engineer realizes that here at last could be his ticket to America—he will become the young citizen's uncle. As the Engineer makes plans for them to leave Vietnam, Kim tenderly assures her small son, "I'd Give My Life For You."

In 1978, John is educating Americans about the hidden victims of war, the *Bui-Doi* (the "dust of life"). These mixed-race children are shunned by the Vietnamese *and* their American fathers. John has news for Chris: not only has Kim been found, but Chris has a son. John insists that Chris—and Ellen—should come to Bangkok, where Kim is a bar girl and the Engineer is a mere doorman for a Bangkok club. John meets Kim and starts to tell her about Chris's marriage, but she is so ecstatic at the thought of Chris's return that she has no ears for anything else John says. After John leaves, Kim shares her joy with the Engineer. He worries that Chris may abandon Kim when he learns about the child, so he leaves to find out where Chris is staying. Meanwhile, as Kim waits, she remembers the horrifying period three years before when she and Chris had been separated. She had fought to find a way inside the American Embassy. Chris, under orders not to leave the grounds, had tried phoning her over and over. When the Ambassador evacuated by helicopter, Chris was forced to go too, without locating Kim amid the uproar.

The Engineer arrives and tells Kim where Chris is staying, so she runs to the hotel—even as John is leading Chris to her abode. Kim finds only a strange American woman in the hotel room; she thinks this must be John's wife. Ellen soon realizes that she must be the one to tell Kim about Chris's marriage. Kim is disbelieving at first, and then insists that Ellen and Chris must take Tam. Ellen refuses, saying that she and Chris will help Kim, but a child's place is with his mother. At last Kim says that Chris must tell her himself that he refuses to take their son, and she runs home.

Chris and John return, having been unable to find Kim, and Ellen tells Chris he must choose between her and Kim. He assures Ellen that his life is now with her. Back at the nightclub, Kim fobs off the Engineer by saying Chris was delighted and will take them all back to the United States. The Engineer allows himself to dwell on "The American Dream," an America in which he will operate ever greater scams. Back in her room, Kim dresses Tam carefully as she sings to him. Kim explains to the uncomprehending child that she will watch him from above, but in order for Tam to find his place with his father, she must leave. When she hears footsteps approaching, she hands him a toy, then steps behind the bed curtain. The Engineer leads Chris, Ellen, and John into the small room, but moments later a shot rings out, and Kim collapses. Chris cradles her in his arms once more, but it is too late; she is gone.

MUSICAL EXAMPLE 57

LES MISÉRABLES

CLAUDE-MICHEL SCHÖNBERG/ALAIN BOUBLIL, 1980

"Castle on a Cloud"

Cosette

1   There is a castle on a cloud, I like to go there in my sleep.
Aren't any floors for me to sweep, not in my castle on a cloud.

2   There is a room that's full of toys, there are a hundred boys and girls,
Nobody shouts or talks too loud, not in my castle on a cloud.

3   There is a lady all in white, holds me and sings a lullaby.
She's nice to see and she's soft to touch; she says, "Cosette, I love you very much."

4   I know a place where no one's lost, I know a place where no one cries.
Crying at all is not allowed, not in my castle on a cloud.

MUSICAL EXAMPLE 58

MISS SAIGON

CLAUDE-MICHEL SCHÖNBERG/ALAIN BOUBLIL, 1989

"I Still Believe"

Kim

1   Last night I watched him sleeping, my body pressed to him.
And then he started speaking. The name I heard him speak . . . was Kim.
Yes, I know that this was years ago. But when moonlight fills my room
I know you are here. Still,

2   I still, I still believe you will return. I know you will.
My heart against all odds holds still. Yes, still. I still believe
I know as long as I can keep believing I'll live.
I'll live. Love cannot die. You will return. You will return. And I alone know why.

Ellen

3   Last night I watched you sleeping. Once more the nightmare came.
I heard you cry out something, a word that sounded like . . . a name.
And it hurts me more than I can bear, knowing part of you I'll never share, never know.

4   But still, I still believe the time will come when nothing keeps us apart.
My heart forever more holds still.

5   It's all over, I'm here. There is nothing to fear. Chris, what's haunting you?
Won't you let me inside what you so want to hide? I need you too.

Kim	**Ellen**
6 For still,	I will hold you all night, I will make it all right.
I still believe.	You are safe with me.
As long as I	And I wish you would tell what you don't want to tell.
can keep believing I'll live.	What your hell must be.
I'll live. You will return	You can sleep now.
And I know why	You can cry now. I'm your wife now
I'm yours	For life,

Kim and Ellen
Until we die.

Chapter 42
Somewhat in the Shadows

Cats, Starlight Express, Les Misérables, The Phantom of the Opera, Miss Saigon, Sunset Boulevard—Lloyd Webber and the team of Schönberg and Boublil were sending multiple block-busters to London and New York theaters during the 1980s and, in most cases, were seeing those shows stay on stage year after year. However, despite these powerhouses, there was still room for other shows in the same decade. Some writers produced their first hits in this period, while other authors changed directions—with varying degrees of success. To an increasing extent, however, the enormous financial burden of mounting a Broadway or West End show was determining the nature of many productions.

For a time, it looked as if there might be another Lloyd Webber–Rice musical in the early 1980s. In 1981, two years after *Evita*'s Broadway debut, Lloyd Webber said in an inter-view that his next major show would be "a full-length work based on a Russian chess game." This "chess" project had been a long-standing scheme of Rice's, so it looked like the old partnership would be back in business. Not long after-wards, however, Lloyd Webber was busy with *Cats*, and Rice had linked up with Stephen Oliver to create *Blondel* in 1983. *Blondel* did fine at first, both during its tryout tour and also at the Old Vic Theatre in London. After the 11-week Old Vic run, *Blondel* showed a profit in the ballpark of £70,000—a profit quickly eaten up by moving expenses when the show transferred to the more centrally located Aldwych Theatre. *Blondel* ran until 1984 but closed at a loss.

Rice resumed work on his chess project, but now he was collaborating with two composers (neither of whom could read music)—**Benny Andersson** (b. 1946) and **Björn Ulvaeus** (b. 1946)—the male members of the Swedish pop group ABBA. This was to be their theatrical debut, but what they lacked in experience they made up for in enthusiasm, and they agreed to begin the project with a concept album, the proce-dure that had been so beneficial when Rice had written *Jesus Christ Superstar* and *Evita* with Lloyd Webber. The album, ***Chess***, was ready by the end of 1984; in addition to using Mur-ray Head for the American (Head had "played" Judas in the *Jesus Christ Superstar* concept album), *Chess* employed Rice's girlfriend Elaine Paige as Florence (see the **Plot Summary**). Two singles from the album were big hits: "I Know Him So Well" and "One Night in Bangkok" (**Musical Example 59**).

The latter song, which became an international hit, is not truly representative of the rest of the score. Instead, its style is an unusual type of "**techno-rap**"—in which the American speaks his lines in rhythm against a driving musical background; the accompaniment is filled with a heavy rock backbeat, electric guitars, and synthesizers. During the interlude at **5**, a flute evokes Bangkok's Asian atmosphere. Near the beginning of the

interlude, the flute uses a technique called *flutter-tonguing*, pro-ducing a sound like a menacing growl—could there be tigers in this urban jungle? The unexpected musical style—so atypical of stage works—attracted many new listeners who had not been theatergoers in the past.

"One Night in Bangkok" is structured as a modified verse-chorus, or alternation form; the American's "rapped" verses are interspersed among a chorus of singing voices. The tune opens with two verses presented back to back at **1**; these *a* passages are followed by the first appearance of the chorus, singing the title refrain, *b*, at **2**. At **3**, it seems that the American is launch-ing into another *a* verse, but he soon is interrupted by inter-jections from the chorus, modifying the structure of this passage. The alternation of verses and chorus continues through the song.

The creators (who called themselves the "Three Knights") described the concept album as a work in progress, and a concert version of the continuously sung score toured a number of cities. There was no doubt that a stage production of *Chess* would soon follow, but there was a large question about who would direct. Sir Peter Hall indicated an interest, as did Trevor Nunn—an interesting development, since there had been an earlier contretemps regarding whose lyrics for "Memory" would be used in *Cats*. Rice leaned toward Nunn, but the Three Knights were also negotiating with the Shubert Organization as possible producers—and the Shuberts wanted Michael Bennett to direct. The deep pock-ets of the Shuberts wielded a great deal of influence, of course, and Bennett was hired by the spring of 1985.

Rewrites were necessary to make the earlier work-in-progress album suitable for the stage, and in late 1985, the creators decided to give the new theatrical version a tryout in Australia. The concept album singers performed the starring roles, but the touring production just didn't jell. Rice knew they needed Bennett's firm hand; he couldn't understand why Bennett was so slow in arriving, since a spring opening for *Chess* was planned. Bennett did order £1 million worth of equipment; his conception for the set was that a giant chess-board would be flanked by banks of 128 television monitors, symbolizing the inescapable media presence dogging the chess players and their entourages.

At the end of January—two weeks before rehearsals were to have begun—the creators were told Bennett was withdraw-ing from the show because of a heart problem. (In truth, though, Bennett had contracted AIDS and was beginning the long—and ultimately unsuccessful—fight for his life.) With the premiere of *Chess* scheduled in three and a half months, a new director was needed urgently—and Nunn was both interested and available. There was no time to make major

The start of a match in *Chess*.
Photofest.

changes to Bennett's concept; that could wait for a possible Broadway production. Nunn pulled things together rapidly, helping to squash the press rumors that inevitably swirled around an expensive show that had lost its director. Nunn's hurried work was successful, for the show caught on quickly after its 1986 opening, selling tickets for a year in advance. *Chess* went on to run for three years and some 1,209 performances in London.

Unfortunately, the West End stage production was never recorded, probably due to its use of the same singers who had been featured on the concept album. The stage show had made a number of changes: the American and the Russian both have names (Freddie Trumper and Anatoly Sergievsky), Florence has a surname (Vassy), and an American CIA agent was added. In the second act, Freddie is a news correspondent, covering the chess match in Bangkok (and antagonizing Anatoly). Many numbers were moved; "The Story of Chess" begins rather than ends the show, and more numbers are reprised.

New songs were added as well, and there is even a brief tongue-in-cheek insertion of "Money, Money, Money"—an old ABBA tune—serving as a seemingly inadvertent commentary on the action. The plot ends slightly differently, with Anatoly—still the champion—deciding to go back to the Soviet Union with Svetlana. Walter claims that this will enable the United States to exchange Anatoly for Florence's father—perhaps. At the end, Florence is left to wonder if her father is alive after all.

When plans began to be laid for a New York production, Nunn wanted to recraft the show according to his own (not Bennett's) conception. The plot and staging changed as well. Svetlana's role was expanded, and she was given some of the songs belonging to Florence in the earlier versions. Moreover, New York heard much more spoken dialogue. The

Broadway show opened with five-year-old Florence learning "The Story of Chess" from her father as the Hungarian rebellion against the Russians begins. The scene shifted to Bangkok, where the first chess match is held, so "One Night in Bangkok" was moved to the middle of the first act. Numerous new songs appeared throughout the score. The second act was set in Budapest two months after the first act, representing the second half of the Championship, with Anatoly and Freddie still as competitors.

Perhaps the most dramatic change was the ending. Anatoly is made to understand that if he were to lose the chess match, the KGB would see to it that Florence was reunited with her father. He wrestles with his conscience and his pride, but at last makes a deliberate error in the match, allowing Freddie to win. Anatoly and Florence bid a tearful farewell at the airport as he leaves to return to his family in the Soviet Union, but after his departure, Florence is handed an emotional bombshell; the aged man she had met was merely pretending to be her father. Anatoly's return to the USSR did benefit the United States, for he was traded for a captured CIA agent, but Florence gained nothing. She is now completely alone.

The duplicity of the ending may have contributed to the audience's dissatisfaction with the Broadway production; certainly Rice himself was very unhappy with many of the changes, including Richard Nelson's book with its spoken dialogue. Some of the underlying tension is evident in the libretto; a printed footnote stipulates, "Some lyrics in [the song] 'Endgame' have been changed without the authorisation of Tim Rice." Rice also wanted Paige to reprise her part as Florence. Without Nunn's support, however, there was little chance that Paige's petition for an Equity waver would be approved—and Nunn refused to support the waiver request. So, although Lloyd Webber had managed to bring Brightman to Broadway that same year, and Cameron Mackintosh would later succeed in bringing the *Miss Saigon* stars to New York, Rice had to withdraw Paige's petition—a galling surrender.

Thanks to a complicated financial deal, the Three Knights had to become 50 percent investors in Nunn's Broadway production of *Nicholas Nickleby* (a 12-hour adaptation of the Charles Dickens novel). When *Nicholas Nickleby* closed at a $1.5 million loss, the Three Knights owed half of the sum, putting them $750,000 in debt before *Chess* had even opened. Rice made a sizable personal investment of $3 million to help bring *Chess* to the New York stage, but after the show opened in 1988, its short run of 68 performances ensured that the entire investment of some $6 million was lost.

Like many writers of the 1930s and 1940s, Rice soon made his way to Hollywood, where he teamed up at the Disney Studios with Alan Menken, partnerless since the death of Howard Ashman in 1991. Ashman and Menken had triumphed with *Little Shop of Horrors* in 1982. Although this science-fiction/horror film spoof did not appear on Broadway, it played in the Orpheum, the queen of the off-Broadway theaters, where it amassed a 2,209-performance run. *Little Shop of Horrors* might have succeeded in one of Broadway's smaller houses, but the increasingly overwhelming expense of Broadway productions scared the creators away. The small-scale show (requiring merely a cast of nine) was an international success as well; in London, which has no real equivalent to off-Broadway, *Little*

Shop of Horrors played 817 performances—the best run ever of an off-Broadway show after transferring to the West End. Moreover, the musical was made into a 1986 film with Rick Moranis and Ellen Greene, thereby bringing the story full circle, back to the cinematic genre that had inspired it.

The team of Ashman and Menken diverged for a time, but reunited to write songs for the 1989 Disney animated film *The Little Mermaid*; they took home the Original Song Oscar for "Under the Sea," and Menken won the Original Score Oscar as well. In fact, as the **Sidebar:** "If I Can Make It There . . ." indicates, they were at the forefront of a new wave of Academy Awards earned by writers already known for their stage works. They again went to the 1991 winners' podium for their score for *Beauty and the Beast*. (When this film was adapted as a 1994 stage production, Ashman at last had a Broadway hit—albeit a posthumous success.) Ashman and Menken were working on *Aladdin* (1992) when Ashman succumbed to AIDS in 1991, leaving a substantial portion of the lyrics unfinished.

At this point, Tim Rice came on board; he too would earn an Oscar for his contributions to the *Aladdin* song "A Whole New World." There were more Academy Awards for Rice to come, but with different collaborators: first an Oscar with Elton John for *The Lion King* (1994) and then another Oscar after a brief reunion with Lloyd Webber to contribute a new tune to the film of *Evita* (1996). *The Lion*

Sidebar: "If I Can Make It There . . ."

The title song of the movie *New York, New York* expresses a widely held view of the American theatrical world when it declares, "If I can make it there, I'll make it anywhere—It's up to you, New York, New York." The song, which opens with the line "Start spreading the news," was made even more famous in a **cover** (a new recording of an existing song) by Frank Sinatra. The song's creators were John Kander and Fred Ebb, supplementing the 1940s-era tunes used in the 1977 Martin Scorsese film.

The bias that true success was "Big Apple" success held true for writers and composers too, and even Hollywood was drawn to those who had triumphed on Broadway. So, during the 1930s, 1940s, and 1950s, many prominent names were lured to California to write for the movies: Kern, Hammerstein II, Berlin, Rodgers, Loesser, Lerner, Loewe, and Styne—and many won Oscars for their cinematic efforts.

However, the next three decades were quite a dry spell for theatrical writers who were trying their hands at film compositions. No well-established theatrical figure made a trip to the Academy Award podium until 1989, when Ashman and Menken broke the long drought—but they then launched a remarkable stretch of successes, for over the next ten years, eight of the Original Song Oscars went to writers with clear-cut theatrical credentials:

1989   "Under the Sea" in *The Little Mermaid*, by Alan Menken and Howard Ashman

1990   "Sooner or Later (I Always Get My Man)" in *Dick Tracy*, by Stephen Sondheim
1991   "Beauty and the Beast" in *Beauty and the Beast*, by Alan Menken and Howard Ashman
1992   "A Whole New World" in *Aladdin*, by Alan Menken and Tim Rice
1994   "Can You Feel the Love Tonight?" in *The Lion King*, by Elton John and Tim Rice
1995   "Colors of the Wind" in *Pocahontas*, by Alan Menken and Stephen Schwartz
1996   "You Must Love Me" in *Evita*, by Andrew Lloyd Webber and Tim Rice
1998   "When You Believe" in *The Prince of Egypt*, by Stephen Schwartz

The fluidity of pairings in this list evokes the "old days" of Broadway, before the long-term team of Rodgers and Hart had begun to break the norm. More importantly, however, these Academy Awards demonstrated that theatrical writers were not an esoteric, isolated breed, capable of writing tunes to suit the taste of theater audiences only. Many observers had predicted in the 1980s that musical theater was dying, claiming it was becoming inbred and was failing to connect with wider audiences. These "crossover" successes in film scores, however, demonstrated that show musicians *could* write—and *were* writing—in ways that appealed to popular taste, giving hope to musical theater overall.

King found its way to the stage in 1997, with additional songs by John and Rice. Rather than trying to emulate the animated feature scene by scene—the approach followed by *Beauty and the Beast*—director-choreographer-designer Judith Taymor literally transformed the stage version of *The Lion King* through ingenious puppet designs, inventive choreography, and the additional atmospheric African musical scoring. *The Lion King* has settled in for an extended run both in New York and in London, even as it inspires dark rumors of "Disney domination" of Broadway.

Disney turned to John and Rice again; this time, Disney wanted a stage show from the very start. The subject was *Aida*, the story of an enslaved Nubian princess who falls for her Egyptian captor, the warrior Radames, thereby sparking a process of vengeance by Radames's fiancée, the Princess Amneris, leading to the tragic demise of the two lovers. The direct inspiration was Verdi's 1871 opera of the same title, although no lyrics or music were retained. John and Rice did not update the historical setting of *Aida*; their version sustains the ancient Egyptian world that had fascinated earlier operagoers.

Aida struggled to find a footing; it went through a fairly disastrous tryout in Atlanta in 1998, with the elaborate hydraulics for the central pyramid failing during nearly every performance. The show was withdrawn, the director and set designer were fired, and a new director, choreographer, and stage designer were brought on board. Meanwhile, John and Rice reworked their score, releasing it as a concept album in 1999, with various pop artists and groups singing the tunes. The new production was taken to Chicago for a tryout; except for a scary performance in which the tomb that imprisons Aida and Radames at the end of the show broke free and dropped eight feet to the stage, the show's machinery generally (but not always) functioned more reliably. The tryout went well enough that *Aida* transferred to Broadway in 2000. The critics were almost unanimous in their condemnation of most aspects of the show, but it didn't seem to matter; the public continued to flock to the box office until 2004.

Even with *Aida*'s poor reviews, many other composers would have been happy with the same kind of attendance at their shows of the 1980s and beyond; one such writer is William Finn. Like Sondheim, Finn seems often to have been drawn to topics that were interesting but not particularly "commercial." The parallels with Sondheim also include a degree from Williams College, followed by the Hutchinson Prize—and both men would collaborate with writer James Lapine and orchestrator Michael Starobin.

Even during his undergraduate years, Finn was drawn to offbeat subject matter, such as the trial and execution of the Soviet spies Julius and Ethel Rosenberg. Finn's best-known musicals chronicle the evolution of a Jewish family consisting of Marvin, Trina, and their son Jason. The first show, *In Trousers* (1979), explored Marvin's discovery that he is bisexual. The second piece in the series was *March of the Falsettos* (1981), when Marvin has divorced Trina and moved in with his new boyfriend Whizzer—yet wants to sustain a family life by sharing mealtimes with his son, his ex-wife, and his lover. Needless to say, these convoluted relationships drive all the

participants to the psychiatrist's couch; oddly, the same psychiatrist, Mendel, counsels all of them—and marries Trina.

After these first two shows, Finn undertook some different projects, none of which fared too well; *America* closed during its tryout, and while *Dangerous Games* was mounted on Broadway, it folded after four performances. *Romance* was staged off-Broadway at the Public Theater, but lasted only six showings. Almost a decade after the previous installment, Finn created *Falsettoland* (1990), the next chapter of the story. Set two years after *March of the Falsettos*, *Falsettoland* initially focuses on Jason's resistance to having a bar mitzvah, but everyone's attention is soon drawn to Whizzer, who has contracted AIDS and is dying. Jason at last resolves to hold his bar mitzvah in Whizzer's hospital room so that Jason can enter adult life just as Whizzer is departing from life. All of these shows had been produced off-Broadway by **Playwrights Horizons**, an organization founded in 1971 that is devoted to supporting new, experimental plays and musicals. In 1992, portions of the three "Falsetto" musicals were combined to create a sung-through Broadway production, *Falsettos*. Although *Falsettos* ran a mere 486 performances—a fairly short run in an era that mounted expensive shows with the hope they'd run forever—it received both the Best Book and Best Score Tony Awards.

People were puzzled by Finn's Tony acceptance speech, which was rambling and a bit incoherent. As it turned out, he was suffering from a brain tumor. Told at first that it was inoperable, Finn's tumor proved to be treatable by surgery, and his experiences then served as the basis for the musical, *A New Brain* (1998). Since that time, Finn has worked on another musical, *Muscle*, with James Lapine (who had written the book for *Falsettos*) and Ellen Fitzhugh; Finn was brought in after Sondheim pulled out in order to concentrate on *Passion*, originally intended to be partnered with *Muscle*. *Muscle*, addressing society's views about bodybuilding and body image, struggled in its workshop phase, and no further performances have been announced. Similarly, Finn's next endeavor, *The Royal Family*, has not been scheduled for a debut. However, his earlier works are enjoying frequent performances, and it is to be hoped that there will be more to come from the quixotic William Finn.

In comparison to William Finn's experimental topics, Maury Yeston's shows have seemed relatively mainstream. Yet he has been dogged by bad luck: more than once, another work based on the *same* subject has overshadowed his efforts. Yeston's compositional career started early—at the age of six—and his formal training led to a Ph.D. at Yale. Moreover, Yeston worked as a Yale theory professor for six years, later serving periodically as a guest professor. As a grad student, he wrote a musical based on *Alice in Wonderland*, produced in New Haven in 1970. Then Yeston had the idea that the Federico Fellini film *8¹/₂* would adapt well as a musical. He worked on the idea in the BMI Musical Theatre Workshop, the same workshop that supported early efforts by Alan Menken, Carol Hall, and others.

Yeston continued to work on the adaptation, which he called *Nine*, for some nine years. Finally, in 1982, Yeston, librettist Arthur Kopit, and director Tommy Tune felt *Nine* was ready to debut; their patience was rewarded when *Nine* won five Tonys, including Best Musical, along with a Best Score award for Yeston and Best Director award for Tune. *Nine* ran for 729 performances, with a revival in 2003. Steven Suskin regards its music as "Broadway's first intelligent score since *Sweeney Todd*."

As the 1980s progressed, Yeston wrote a show about various characters who *should* have been in the Old Testament but weren't. Originally titled *1-2-3-4-5* (1988), the show is better known by a later title, *In the Beginning: The Greatest Story Never Told*. In 1989, Yeston was asked to contribute seven additional songs to the struggling *Grand Hotel*, directed by his old friend Tune; Yeston was nominated for a Tony for his contribution; his efforts may have helped the show reach a 1,017-performance run.

Oddly enough, Yeston's next two musicals both ran into a problem—they competed with a blockbuster success of the same (or similar) title. The first was an adaptation of Leroux's *Le Fantôme de l'Opéra*. Yeston began work on his *Phantom* in 1983, but his deliberate pace meant that the show was still unfinished in 1986, when Lloyd Webber's megamusical premiered in London. Because Lloyd Webber's New York production has been running on Broadway since 1988, there is little chance that Yeston's version will reach Broadway while the British import is still playing. Nevertheless, Yeston's *Phantom* (1991) has been enjoying a modest success in a host of regional productions—and there are those who prefer it to the more famous Lloyd Webber show.

Similarly, Yeston's 1997 musical about the ill-fated passenger ship *Titanic* was hard-pressed to make a name for itself when audiences were distracted by the enormously successful James Cameron film released the same year. Even without this direct competition, Yeston's *Titanic* probably would have struggled due to its own hugely expensive staging. Nevertheless, *Titanic* stayed afloat for 804 performances, winning five Tonys (including Best Musical). Stuart Ostrow felt the scholarly score made the music a bit inaccessible, but he also believed that the triumphant song "There She Is" when the ship is seen for the first time "was a fanfare to begin the evening worthy of Aaron Copland."

Despite a second Tony for his *Titanic* score, Yeston has had difficulty making his way back to Broadway since that time. He has not been idle, having written *An American Cantata* (for some 2,000 voices) among other works. Yeston is sure to have a continuing impact on musical theater—even if he sends no more of his own works to the stage—for he has assumed the directorship of the BMI Musical Theatre Workshop and will be fostering many of the young theatrical writers of tomorrow.

At the same time that England was exporting the megamusicals of Andrew Lloyd Webber, who dominated the West End theaters as well, there were other homegrown British works continuing to reach the London stage. One unexpected success was by a compositional novice, Willy Russell. Russell, born in a Liverpool suburb, dreamed of becoming a writer. To help him avoid factory work, his mother suggested that he be a hairdresser. His daily exposure to the cares and concerns of the working-class women of Liverpool helped him with ideas for the writing he did in his spare time; he also studied drama (this time at his wife-to-be's suggestion) at the teacher's college.

Russell's "break" came when three of his one-act plays were presented at the 1972 Edinburgh Festival. This exposure led to

a pseudo-documentary about the Beatles; Russell invented a fifth character, Bert, for the band, and explored a number of fantasy situations. When *John, Paul, George, Ringo . . . and Bert* transferred to the West End in 1974, it quickly became an award-winning hit. Russell then focused on spoken drama, creating *Educating Rita* in 1980.

Three years later, in 1983, Russell tried his hand at two musicals, but only *Blood Brothers* was a success. It took *Blood Brothers* quite a while to catch on, for although laced with humor, the underlying story is tragic, portraying the slowly building dire consequences that result from the separation shortly after birth of twin boys, one raised in a life of privilege, the other in acute poverty. *Blood Brothers'* initial London run was a mere eight months, but there was such a flurry of ticket-buying when its closing was announced that the producers decided to launch a new production—but this second version folded on its tryout tour. A third touring production did better, making it to London in 1988, where it has been running ever since. A Broadway production opened in 1993, with a series of well-known singers—Stephanie Lawrence, Petula Clark, Carole King, Helen Reddy—playing the twins' mother.

Since 1983, however, Russell's attention has veered away from composition and returned to writing, producing successful stage plays such as *Shirley Valentine* as well as his first novel, *The Wrong Boy*. Russell spoke frankly about his struggle to write "hummable" songs for *Blood Brothers*, so it is likely that *Blood Brothers* will remain Russell's only well-known musical—but it must be no small satisfaction to see that one show rack up a run of more than 15 years to date.

Just as British productions *not* by Andrew Lloyd Webber were in the minority in the 1980s, hit shows featuring non-white performers also appeared only rarely on Broadway. The situation had not changed since the days of *In Dahomey* (1904); there had been occasional all-black revues, especially the periodic *Shuffle Along* and *Blackbirds* shows, but successful book musicals concerning African Americans appeared very infrequently. As important an achievement as many of the shows were, commercial success often eluded them, as was the case with Gershwin's *Porgy and Bess* (1935), Vernon Duke's *Cabin in the Sky* (1940), Weill's *Lost in the Stars* (1949), and other works.

After a couple of modest hits in the 1950s—*Mr. Wonderful* (1956) and *Jamaica* (1957)—the pace slowed down sharply in the 1960s. But African American–themed productions soon flowered. Besides *The Wiz* (1975), the decade's most successful show, other musicals racked up impressive runs: *Purlie* (1970) ran 688 times, *Raisin* (1973) ran 847, and *Bubbling Brown Sugar* (1976) played 766 times.

Ain't Misbehavin' (1978) also accrued a sizable count of 1,565 performances; it was not actually a book musical, but a **compilation show** (also called a **catalog show**), consisting of songs previously written or performed by Fats Waller. A catalog show draws from independent hits written by a particular individual or group and compiles them into a single theatrical event; the storylines of catalog shows range from very loosely connected songs (rather like revues) to fairly tightly knit librettos that manage to make the previously written tunes feel integrated into the story. Russell's *John, Paul, George, Ringo . . . and Bert* had been a catalog show, as is the current hit show *Mamma Mia!* (2001), which uses ABBA songs written in the 1970s. (*Mamma Mia!* was the first show to appear in the Winter Garden theater since the closing of the long-standing Broadway production of *Cats*.)

The success of *Ain't Misbehavin'* encouraged a string of imitators, such as *Eubie!* (1978), featuring Eubie Blake's songs; *Sophisticated Ladies* (1981), compiled from Duke Ellington tunes; and *Buddy* (1990), depicting Buddy Holly's life. The focus of most compilation shows is on songs and songwriters, but occasionally choreography is the focus; 1989 saw *Jerome Robbins' Broadway*, while the choreography of Bob Fosse was celebrated in *Fosse* (1999). Sometimes these productions generate new audiences, made up of people who were concertgoing fans of the featured person.

With the advent of the catalog show, African American book musicals were rarer than ever. An exception was *Dreamgirls*, which finally made it to Broadway in 1980 after careful crafting in four workshop productions and then a long tryout in Boston. The cautious approach was justified, for a workshop cost approximately $150,000, while the elaborate staging of the final version had production costs up to $3.5 million. Directed by Michael Bennett, composed by Henry Krieger, with a book and lyrics by Tom Eyen, *Dreamgirls* chronicled the rise, travails, and fall of a Motown-tinged "girl group," the Dreamettes, loosely modeled on the real-life group The Supremes. Like *A Chorus Line* (also directed by Bennett), *Dreamgirls* focuses as much on the backstage world encountered by the singers as it does on their on-stage triumphs. Krieger mixed a myriad of musical styles together to create the largely sung-through production, trying to evoke the broad spirit of not just Motown but the entire 1960s in his score. Whether or not listeners caught Krieger's references to James Brown, Bacharach and David, Fats Waller, or Chopin (to name a few), audiences loved *Dreamgirls*, supporting it through a 1,521-performance run.

No other show centered on African American characters did as well in the 1980s. *The Tap Dance Kid* (1983) played a very respectable 669 performances, while a South African import, *Sarafina!* (1988), also did well on Broadway, at 597 performances. In general, though, black shows were few and far between in the 1980s, and not only did they compete as always with the predominant Caucasian productions, but there was competition from things like cats, trains, and chandeliers as well.

FURTHER READING

Bennetts, Leslie. "*Chess*'s Backstage Drama." *Vanity Fair* (May 1988): 34–50.

Citron, Stephen. *Sondheim and Lloyd Webber: The New Musical*. Oxford: Oxford University Press, 2001.

Gottfried, Martin. *More Broadway Musicals Since 1980*. New York: Abrams, 1991.

Kislan, Richard. *The Musical: A Look at the American Musical Theater*. New, revised, expanded edition. New York and London: Applause Books, 1995.

Loney, Glenn. "Don't Cry for Andrew Lloyd Webber." *Opera News* 45 (April 4, 1981): 12–14.

Mandelbaum, Ken. *A Chorus Line and the Musicals of Michael Bennett*. New York: St. Martin's, 1989.

———. *Not Since Carrie: Forty Years of Broadway Musical Flops*. New York: St. Martin's, 1991.

Mordden, Ethan. *Better Foot Forward: The History of American Musical Theatre*. New York: Grossman Publishers (A Division of the Viking Press), 1976.

Morley, Sheridan. *Spread a Little Happiness: The First Hundred Years of the British Musical*. New York: Thames & Hudson, 1987.

Ostrow, Stuart. *A Producer's Broadway Journey*. Westport, Connecticut: Praeger, 1999.

Suskin, Steven. *Show Tunes: The Songs, Shows, and Careers of Broadway's Major Composers*. Revised and expanded third edition. New York: Oxford University Press, 2000.

Walsh, Michael. *Andrew Lloyd Webber, His Life and Works: A Critical Biography*. New York: Abrams, 1989.

PLOT SUMMARY: *CHESS*

Although the story of *Chess* went through various permutations in each stage version, the essential conflict driving the story was present in the concept album. Players and fans gather in a small Italian Alpine town for the World Chess Championship. The reigning champion is a brash and petulant American, who faces a Russian challenger. Molokov, the Russian's assistant, or "second," dismisses the American as a nut, but the Russian thinks that the American's behavior is carefully calculated.

The Arbiter insists that he will keep an eagle (and impartial) eye on the proceedings, while the diplomats comment about the delicate political balance. Many people are more-concerned with the many merchandizing opportunities. In an ongoing form of manipulation, the American makes a scene and storms out of the proceedings, leaving *his* second, Florence, to try to rationalize his insulting behavior. Back in their hotel, the American and Florence have it out; she won't stand for much more humiliation from him. She's a Hungarian-born British citizen, smuggled out of Budapest during the infamous 1956 uprising—ruthlessly quelled by the Soviets—and the fate of her father has always been a mystery. Although she is the American's second, she is on "Nobody's Side."

The first match of the championship goes poorly; in fact, they don't even finish the game, for the board is flung in the air. Florence meets with Molokov to try to salvage the situation, but he rattles her by implying he knows something about her father; it seems that Molokov is a KGB agent. Florence doesn't let herself be distracted, however, and suggests that they should arrange a secret meeting between the players to get the championship back on track. The American and Florence wait for the Russian, who is late. The American uses this as an excuse to march out, but Florence remains behind. When the Russian does arrive, he and Florence gradually realize that they are enjoying the conversation more than they should as opponents. When the American returns and discovers this budding romance, he throws a fit, but Florence smooths things over and gets the players to agree to resume the game.

As the match proceeds, the American plays badly, and he blames Florence. She retorts that she'll be leaving him after the match is over, no matter who wins. The American is furious, then terrified, at the thought of her departure. All his paranoia about the Soviets emerges, and he blames them for Florence's lack of sympathy. By accusing her of being a parasite, however, he pushes her too far, and she quits. The American's game falls apart completely, and the Russian is soon crowned as the new champion. But now the Russian wants to claim political asylum in the West—a blow to Russia's pride.

A year later, the next Championship is slated for Bangkok, where the Russian will be challenged by a new Soviet Union player. Bangkok's atmosphere is very different from the previous Championship, and the American comments on the exotic experience of "One Night in Bangkok" (**Musical Example 59**). Florence and the Russian have become lovers since his defection, but their relationship has its problems. After all, what is the American doing in Bangkok? They're not sure. Moreover, there's the little matter of the Russian's wife Svetlana; there are reports that the Russian's family is being punished for his defection. When Florence is alone, she wonders what hope there can be for their future together.

The Soviets are backing a new competitor to uphold their national pride, and so to rattle the Russian's concentration, they announce they're sending Svetlana to Bangkok in time for the match. The Russian and Florence argue about how much time they should spend together during the Championship.

The American, who shows up in the Russian's room, implies that the Russian's winning streak must end if he wants to spare Florence from learning some ugly information about her father—that he was a traitor rather than a hero. The Russian accuses the American of colluding with the Soviets. The American denies this charge, but Molokov's voice is heard, echoing the American. The American then tries to persuade Florence that if she comes back to him, he will share the information about her past. His attempts to manipulate the couple having been thwarted, the American indulges in a healthy bout of self-pity. Are parents responsible for their offspring's shortcomings? The American certainly thinks so.

The Russian shrugs off all the outside pressures and triumphs over his opponent. Both Florence and Svetlana realize that they have little hold on this man; he in turn resents their efforts to tie him down. By the end, no one is happy; Florence has lost the Russian, Svetlana knows she and her husband will not reconcile; Molokov is worried about his own fate now that the new protégé has failed; and the American wants revenge. Florence and the Russian still long for each other, yet they know love affairs are much like the limitless number of variations that can take place on the chessboard. Their musings lead them to contemplate the origins of the game many centuries before. Returning to the present, the Russian and Florence know that they are fools to pretend there's a happy ending in store. As the bittersweet tale comes to a close, the American approaches Florence, telling her he has some news for her. . . .

MUSICAL EXAMPLE 59

CHESS

BENNY ANDERSSON & BJÖRN ULVAEUS/TIM RICE, 1988

"One Night in Bangkok"

The American

1   Bangkok! Oriental setting and the city don't know what the city is getting,
The crème de la crème of the chess world in a show with everything but Yul Brynner.
Time flies—doesn't seem a minute since the Tirolean spa had the chess boys in it.
All change—don't you know that when you play at this level there's no ordinary venue.
It's Iceland—or the Philippines—or Hastings—or—or this place!

Chorus

2   One night in Bangkok and the world's your oyster, the bars are temples but the pearls ain't free.
You'll find a god in every golden cloister and if you're lucky then the god's a she.
I can feel an angel sliding up to me.

The American

3   One town's very like another when your head's down over your pieces, brother.

Chorus

It's a drag, it's a bore, it's really such a pity
To be looking at the board, not looking at the city.

The American

Whaddya mean? You've seen one crowded, polluted stinking town—

Chorus

Tea, girls—warm and sweet; warm, sweet, some are set up in the Somerset Maugham suite.

The American

Get Thai'd! You're talking to a tourist whose every move's among the purest.
I get my kicks above the waistline, sunshine.

Chorus

4   One night in Bangkok makes a hard man humble, not much between despair and ecstasy.
One night in Bangkok and the tough guys tumble, can't be too careful with your company.
I can feel the devil walking next to me.

5   *[interlude]*

The American

6   Siam's gonna be the witness to the ultimate test of cerebral fitness.
This grips me more than would a muddy old river or reclining Buddha.
And thank God I'm only watching the game—controlling it.
I don't see you guys rating the kind of mate I'm contemplating.
I'd let you watch, I would invite you but the queens we use would not excite you.
So you'd better go back to your bars, your temples, your massage parlours—

Chorus

7   One night in Bangkok and the world's your oyster, the bars are temples but the pearls ain't free.
You'll find a god in every golden cloister, a little flesh, a little history.
I can feel an angel sliding up to me.

8   One night in Bangkok makes a hard man humble, not much between despair and ecstasy.
One night in Bangkok and the tough guys tumble, can't be too careful with your company.
I can feel the devil walking next to me.

Chapter 43
Stephen Sondheim: Never a Formula

Mel Brooks—coauthor, composer, lyricist, and coproducer of *The Producers* (2000)—made repeated trips to the podium to accept his share of the record-breaking 12 Tony Awards won by his show in 2001. Brooks expressed his gratitude to many people, but one of the first he thanked was Sondheim—for *not* writing a show that year. Even though *The Producers* was one of Broadway's biggest commercial hits ever, Brooks knew that when it came to artistic achievement, no one could outdo Sondheim. Repeatedly during the 1980s and 1990s, Sondheim virtually reinvented himself as a composer and writer, creating a series of shows that were radically different from one another and that pushed musical theater to even greater heights.

A case in point was *Sunday in the Park with George* (1984), the first of Sondheim's three shows with librettist **James Lapine** (b. 1949). Searching for ideas for a project, they began to focus on a painting by Georges Seurat (1859–1891). Seurat is often labeled a pointillist or impressionist painter, although he described his technique as "divisionism" or "chromoluminarism." He daubed thousands and thousands of tiny dots of paint onto his canvases, choosing from 11 pure, unmixed colors. The viewer's eyes would "mix" the colors; the dots of paint create a shimmering effect, giving life to Seurat's paintings. Neither the public nor Seurat's fellow artists appreciated his achievement at the time; up to his death he had never sold a painting. Intriguingly, orchestrator Michael Starobin (b. 1956) used 11 instrumentalists, but he maintains this number was not a deliberate attempt to mirror Seurat's 11 hues; Starobin says, "I used eleven players because that's how many they told me I could have at the Booth Theater with its tiny pit."

The Seurat work that caught Sondheim and Lapine's attention was titled *Un dimanche d'été à l'île de la Grande Jatte* (A Sunday Afternoon on the Island of La Grande Jatte). They noticed that the people in the painting were looking in different directions, some facing out toward the viewer, others gazing beyond the edge of the painting, and Sondheim and Lapine began to speculate on the "stories" imbedded in the various figures. The first act culminates in a **tableau vivant**—a living painting—with the characters posed like the figures in Seurat's artwork.

Sondheim's diverse score often uses short, repeated motifs—like Seurat's daubs of paint?—that coalesce into melodies. Certainly, the result is a more challenging listening experience than the typical Broadway score; reactions ranged from dismay to delight. Frank Rich was very excited by the "audacious, haunting, and in its own personal way, touching work." In fact, the *Times* carried several highly favorable pieces about the show; this positive coverage helped the show achieve a 604–performance run (and led jealous competitors to dub the production *Sunday in the Times with George*).

George (Mandy Patinkin) and Dot (Bernadette Peters) explore "Color and Light" in *Sunday in the Park with George*.
Martha Swope.

Sunday in the Park with George took the Pulitzer Prize for Drama in 1985—only the sixth musical in history to do so. This recognition helped the show's producers to remain unfazed by the slight financial loss. Bernard Jacobs, an employee of the Shubert Organization, explained that they hadn't expected the show to make money, adding, "I don't regret a thing. 'Great' and 'popular' are two different words."

Sondheim and Lapine were pleased as well, and it was not long before they settled on a new subject: fairy tales. They felt fairy tales are not as benign as they seem, that many of them encourage attitudes of selfishness and greed that can have dangerous consequences. For ***Into the Woods***, Sondheim and Lapine chose several well-known stories and then invented a new tale about a baker and his wife; the purpose of these extra characters, Sondheim said, is to "go in and screw up everybody else's fairy story" (see the **Plot Summary**). All the ordinary resolutions of the various stories are achieved by the first act's end, at which point we would expect the characters to live "happily ever after." But, as Sondheim notes,

> *In order to get what they wanted, they each had to cheat a little, or lie a little, or huckster a little. . . . So when the second-act curtain goes up . . . , the story becomes one of how the characters have to band together and make amends for what they did. Among other things, the show is about community responsibility . . . you can't just go and chop down trees and tease princes and pretend that beans are worth more than they are. Everybody has to pay for that. So they all have to get together and get rid of the giant.*

Sondheim and Lapine's views have increasing resonance for people who have witnessed immense toxic cleanups, enormous tobacco-company settlements, and wholesale fraud in corporate accounting that inflated the value of "beans" far beyond than their actual worth. All of America's little financial swindles and small-scale environmental and health abuses have mounted up into sometimes overwhelming consequences, which need everyone's cooperation to overcome. The allegory of *Into the Woods* also demonstrates that it often doesn't matter "whose fault" it is; we *all* have to pay for it and must see to it that the problem is solved.

Partnered with this lesson is Sondheim and Lapine's belief that we also have to understand that we are interdependent on each other. In the second act, nearly half the characters lose partners and loved ones—Jack's Mother dies by accident, the Witch and Rapunzel's Prince see Rapunzel trampled to death, the Baker learns that he is left with a motherless son to raise, and Cinderella realizes that she cannot depend on her husband's fidelity. These surviving characters learn that they can no longer rely solely on one-on-one relationships to sustain them; they need to network with the larger group, for "no one is alone."

Some characters less more than others during *Into the Woods*, as the two Princes demonstrate in "Agony" (**Musical Example 60**) and in its reprise in the second act. Sondheim indicates that "Agony" should be played "a la Barcarolle." A **barcarole** is the kind of song traditionally sung by Venetian gondoliers; composers often imitated the musical style of these songs, usually writing compound duple meter pieces with a sing-song, repetitive accompaniment and a beautiful, fluid melody. The two Princes sing about love, but with an underlying purpose; just like the original gondoliers, the Princes try to outdo each other in their descriptions of each maiden's beauty and inaccessibility.

Cinderella's Prince initiates the swaying barcarole at **1**. His cry of "agony" at **2** is set on the highest pitch yet heard in the song. Not to be outdone, Rapunzel's Prince presents the

The Princes (Chuck Wagner and Robert Westenberg) recall their "Agony" in *Into the Woods*.
Martha Swope.

barcarole motif at **3**, but quotes Rapunzel's wordless melody at **4** before describing his own "agony" at **5**. Section **6**—a rhetorical question about princely attributes—quotes an ascending melody (and question) from earlier in the show. After determining that girls "must be mad" to run from their attentions, and briefly repeating Rapunzel's refrain, the two men sing of their mutual "agony" once more at **7**.

The resulting structure is a nonstandard form, but it is a highly effective characterization of two men whose attitudes toward women are identical—and limited—as seen by the melodies they share or borrow from other characters. "Agony" expands the succinct philosophy they expressed earlier: "the harder to get, the better to have." Moreover, "Agony" is reprised in the second act, essentially unchanged except for the maidens they now desire. Reprises are rare in Sondheim's shows; he maintains that if a character has grown and developed, the same old melody should no longer work. In the case of the "Agony (Reprise)," however, the repetition proves Sondheim's precise point: The two Princes have *not* grown since Act I. Even after marriage, the thrill of pursuit of unattainable maidens still holds the greater allure. Alone among the characters, the Princes don't change, so they don't experience the healing redemption of communal collaboration with the others. When Cinderella confronts her Prince with his unfaithfulness, his only defense is that "I was brought up to be charming, not sincere."

Sondheim uses music to link many other aspects of the story together. The five-note motif heard while the five magic beans are counted into Jack's hands is later expanded into the melody of the Witch's "Lament" for the deceased Rapunzel—a logical connection, since the beans had indirectly led to Rapunzel's demise. Similarly, Cinderella is the first character to sing in the musical, and she says, "I wish." Then, after the ensemble finishes the Finale, Cinderella's voice is heard once again, still singing, "I wish." We are left to wonder if the characters, even after having banded together to conquer the threatening giant, are doomed to repeat the same mistakes all over again.

Into the Woods made its Broadway debut in 1987 and ran 764 performances followed by a successful tour. Lapine and Sondheim each went home with a Tony for the book and score, but the show lost the Best Musical title to Andrew Lloyd Webber's *The Phantom of the Opera*. Reaction to *Into the Woods* was not uniform, but some critics immediately recognized the musical's excellence, calling it "the best show yet from the most creative minds in the musical theater today." Frank Rich suggested, "It may be just the tempting unthreatening show to lead new audiences to an artist who usually lures theatergoers far deeper and more dangerously into the woods."

Sondheim's path led viewers right back into those woods with his next show. Like *Urinetown* (2001), Sondheim's *Assassins* has a title guaranteed to alienate some viewers right from the start. As if that initial discomfort weren't enough, *Assassins* was similar to *Cabaret* and *Chicago* in that it reflected moral judgments and perspectives right back at the audience—do we as a society foster assassination by "rewarding" assassins? Do we give them unprecedented attention through media coverage? Does our national reluctance to limit the individual's right to bear arms mean that we must accept assassination as a natural consequence of that liberality? The show's librettist, John Weidman, wrote,

> *Thirteen people have tried to kill the President of the United States. Four have succeeded. These murderers and would-be murderers are generally dismissed as maniacs and misfits who have little in common with each other, and nothing in common with the rest of us.*
>
> Assassins *suggests otherwise.* Assassins *suggests that while these individuals are, to say the least, peculiar—taken as a group they are peculiarly* American. *And that behind the variety of motives which they articulated for their murderous outbursts, they share a common purpose: a desperate desire to reconcile intolerable feelings of impotence with an inflamed and malignant sense of entitlement.*
>
> *Why do these dreadful events happen* here, *with such horrifying frequency, and in such an appallingly similar fashion?* Assassins *suggests it is because we live in a country whose most cherished national myths . . . encourage us to believe that in America our dreams not only* can *come true, but* should *come true, and if they don't, someone or something is to blame.*

Many theatergoers do not expect to confront such unsettling ideas during an evening's entertainment.

The idea for *Assassins* was triggered by a play of the same name by Charles Gilbert. Sondheim was judging scripts for Stuart Ostrow's Musical Theatre Lab (taught by the producer at the University of Houston). Reading through the entries, Sondheim thought the title of Gilbert's play would be "a great idea for a musical." Sondheim remembers that when he shared the idea with Weidman, "His eyes lit up. And I said to him, 'You're having the same reaction I did—the word alone—I don't know what it is, but wouldn't it make a great musical?'" (see the **Plot Summary**).

Assassins opened in 1991 at the Playwrights Horizons Theater. Although tickets for the two-month run sold out quickly, the musical did not immediately transfer to Broadway, largely because of timing: the United States had just embarked on the Gulf War. Americans caught up in the flush of patriotic fervor would have been even more resistant than usual to a show that questioned some of the country's fundamental beliefs and practices. A decade later, a Broadway production had at long last been announced with an intended premiere date of November 29, 2001. After the tragic events of September 11, 2001, however, it was quickly determined that the darkly comic look at the tarnished side of the American dream was again inappropriate for the times. It was not until 2004 that *Assassins* at last made its Broadway debut; it had gained an additional song, "Something Just Broke."

Despite the long delay before its Broadway production, *Assassins* has attained a wide following and is performed in hundreds of smaller venues. It has held a particular appeal for younger viewers, those who have grown up in a climate (regrettably) of increased violence. Part of the attraction stems from *Assassins*'s outstanding score, which is very tuneful. Since the libretto of *Assassins* freely intermingles

1	2	3	4	5	6	7	8	9	10	11	12
a	*b*	*b*	*b'*	*c*	*d*	*c*	*e*	*d'*	*b*	*c*	*a*

Figure 43–1

characters from different eras, Sondheim makes liberal use of pastiche, letting the music help establish the appropriate time and place for each assassin. For instance, John Hinckley and Squeaky Fromme croon to their respective idols in a 1970s soft-pop style; Sondheim says that he listened to a lot of songs by the pop singer Karen Carpenter while writing the number.

In the same way, "The Ballad of Booth" (**Musical Example 61**) is set in a folk or bluegrass style, typical of the Appalachian mountains; one can imagine the news of Lincoln's assassination being passed from community to community. (Orchestrator Starobin admits, "I've gotten a lot of compliments on the banjo part. . . . And I'll be the first to admit, to create a banjo part for something like that you have to hire a great banjo player, put the chords in front of him and say, 'Give me a good bluegrass feel,' and he does just that.") Nevertheless, Sondheim's tune is surprisingly complex, consisting of multiple themes and constantly shifting meters—a far cry from the strophic form of "The Ballad of Mack the Knife" in Weill's *The Threepenny Opera*. As **Figure 43–1** reveals, the tune consists of five themes. Each theme conveys different kinds of material and contrasting moods. The Balladeer's opening *a* feels like a vocal introduction, but it returns at **12**, perhaps as a coda to demonstrate that the country *does* come "back where it belongs." The repetitive, narrative quality of the *b* theme, heard at **2**, **3**, and in fragmentary form at **4**, fits the "ballad" designation most closely. However, the second half of the *b* theme—beginning "Why did you do it, Johnny?"—asks a disturbing question, and perhaps this is why the *b* theme's meter constantly shifts between groups of six, four, seven, and five beats. At **5**, a new "cursing" theme (*c*) appears, used again for Booth's further damnation of Lincoln at **7**, as well as for the Balladeer's own denunciation of Booth at **11**. Booth introduces a sing-song theme, *d*, at **6**, like a school-yard taunt; the theme is expanded at **9**. Booth sings a melancholy, almost hymnlike theme (*e*) at **8**, but after rising to an impassioned peak that uses the most offensive word of the entire production, Booth's singing degenerates into the fairly self-pitying *d* melody.

The changing moods of the various themes used in this scene play upon our emotions in subtle but effective ways; Booth's point of view is treated seriously (a viewpoint which, historically, was shared by numerous people), yet we are repelled by his maudlin moments of self-pity and perhaps disturbed by the occasionally mocking tone of the Balladeer. Sondheim also manipulates the harmony, inserting unexpected minor mode passages, adding to the poignancy or alerting us that something is subtly wrong.

A number of writers point to *Assassins* as their favorite Sondheim show. It was awarded the London Critics' Circle Award for the Best New Musical when it was produced in

England in 1992 (helping to build the reputation of its theater, the Donmar Warehouse). *Assassins* still stands as Sondheim's most challenging show, but its uncomfortable stance may keep it out of the mainstream for years to come.

By this point, Sondheim's body of work had attracted the notice of various award-granting agencies. He rejected the first honor he was offered—the National Medal of Arts, in 1992—because he was disappointed by the political infighting taking place in the National Endowment for the Arts. He felt that the NEA was too much the puppet of overly conservative congressmen rather than standing for free artistic expression; he refused to feel like a hypocrite by accepting the award. (He did accept the prize in 1997.) Sondheim was also awarded the Kennedy Center Medal of Honor in 1993.

Sondheim reunited with Lapine for a third time in his next musical, *Passion* (1994), which was again a change of pace for Sondheim. Based on a film, *Passione d'Amore*, which itself was based on an incomplete novel, *Passion*'s music lived up to the show's title, being lush and romantic, but perhaps sounding more operatic than Broadway audiences expected. Unlike Sondheim's earlier romantic show, *A Little Night Music*, *Passion* was unleavened by humor. Sondheim and Lapine wrestled to make the show's central premise believable—that the handsome young soldier Giorgio would fall for the unhealthy, unattractive Fosca, who is obsessed with him. Even though critical and audience response was divided, *Passion* won the Best Musical Tony, along with three other Tonys (including a well-deserved Best Score Tony for Sondheim).

Since the closing of *Passion* early in 1995, Broadway has not seen another "new" Sondheim show except for *Assassins* and *The Frogs*, written 13 and 30 years earlier respectively. Numerous revivals and cabaret productions have appeared, as well as a long-delayed presentation of *Saturday Night* (1997) in London—the "first" Sondheim show that had derailed when its producer had died. A truly new show *is* in the works, featuring the escapades of the legendary crooks Addison and Wilson Mizner. However, *Bounce* has been delayed, first by an unsatisfactory workshop and then by legal battles over the rights. *Bounce* began a tryout tour in Chicago in 2003, followed by a run in Washington, D.C., but no Broadway debut has yet been announced.

Despite these travails, Sondheim continues to cast a long shadow across musical theater, as Mel Brooks indicated. His position in posterity is reflected by the fact that not one but two periodicals—*The Sondheim Society Newsletter* and *The Sondheim Review*—are devoted solely (as *The Sondheim Review* puts it) "to the Work of the Musical Theater's Foremost Composer and Lyricist." Even if Sondheim never writes another note or lyric, he will stand among America's finest musical theater writers.

FURTHER READING

Banfield, Stephen. *Sondheim's Broadway Musicals*. Ann Arbor: University of Michigan Press, 1993.

Citron, Stephen. *Sondheim and Lloyd Webber: The New Musical*. Oxford: Oxford University Press, 2001.

Flahaven, Sean Patrick. "Starobin Talks about *Sunday, Assassins*." *The Sondheim Review* 5, no. 2 (Fall 1998): 21–23.

Gordon, Joanne, ed. *Stephen Sondheim: A Casebook*. New York and London: Garland Publishing, 1997.

Gottfried, Martin. *Sondheim*. New York: Abrams, 1993.

Henderson, Amy, and Dwight Blocker Bowers. *Red, Hot, and Blue: A Smithsonian Salute to the American Musical*. Washington: The National Portrait Gallery and The National Museum of American History, in association with the Smithsonian Institution Press, 1996.

Mandelbaum, Ken. *Not Since Carrie: Forty Years of Broadway Musical Flops*. New York: St. Martin's, 1991.

McLaughlin, Robert L. "'No One is Alone': Society and Love in the Musicals of Stephen Sondheim." *The Journal of American Drama and Theatre* 3, no. 2 (1991): 27–41.

Miller, Scott. *Deconstructing Harold Hill: An Insider's Guide to Musical Theatre*. Portsmouth, New Hampshire: Heinemann, 2000.

———. *From* Assassins *to* West Side Story: *A Director's Guide to Musical Theatre*. Portsmouth, New Hampshire: Heinemann, 1996.

———. *Rebels with Applause: Broadway's Groundbreaking Musicals*. Portsmouth, New Hampshire: Heinemann, 2001.

Pike, John. "Michael Starobin: A New Dimension for *Assassins*." *Show Music* 7, no. 3 (Fall 1991): 13–17.

Secrest, Meryle. *Stephen Sondheim: A Life*. New York: Alfred A. Knopf, 1998.

Suskin, Steven. *Show Tunes: The Songs, Shows, and Careers of Broadway's Major Composers*. Revised and expanded third edition. New York: Oxford University Press, 2000.

Zadan, Craig. *Sondheim & Co.: The Authorized, Behind-the-Scenes Story of the Making of Stephen Sondheim's Musicals*. Second edition. New York: Harper & Row, 1986.

PLOT SUMMARY: *INTO THE WOODS*

"Once upon a time," begins the Narrator, "in a far-off kingdom lived a fair maiden, a sad young lad and a childless baker with his wife." These characters are Cinderella, who wishes to go to the King's Festival; Jack and his mother, who wish their cow Milky White would produce milk; and the Baker and his Wife, who wish for a child. The story portrays the fulfillment—and consequences—of those wishes.

Cinderella *can* go to the festival if she succeeds in picking a bucketful of lentils out of the fireplace ashes in two hours. Little Red Ridinghood visits the Baker to fill her basket before going to visit her grandmother. Meanwhile, Jack's Mother announces that they must sell the cow. The Baker and his Wife learn some startling news from the Witch next door: because the Baker's father had stolen greens from the

Witch's garden, she had claimed their child (Rapunzel, the Baker's sister) when she was born, and because his father had also stolen some special beans, the Witch placed a curse on his family tree—which is why the Baker and his Wife are barren. But the spell can be reversed, with four items: the cow as white as milk, the cape as red as blood, the hair as yellow as corn, and the slipper as pure as gold. The Baker's Wife wants to help search, but he refuses, arguing that the curse is on *his* house.

Although, with the help of birds, Cinderella completed her nearly impossible task, she is left behind when her family leaves for the festival, because she doesn't have the right attire. She weeps at her mother's grave, but her mother's ghost tells her to tell a nearby tree what it is she wants. Instantly, a silver gown and golden slippers drop into her arms. A disconsolate Jack shuffles through the forest with Milky White. Although Jack was told to accept no less than five pounds, a Mysterious Man scoffs, saying that Jack would be lucky to get a sack of beans for the skeletal animal. Elsewhere, Little Red Ridinghood meets a lascivious Wolf, and she's soon off on a detour.

The Baker is worried about the girl; the Witch just wants him to get the red cape. The Baker's Wife appears, bringing his scarf as an excuse. It's just as well, because the Baker is already getting the four ingredients confused. They spot Jack and the white cow, and although they have no money, they do have the stolen beans. They offer five beans in exchange for the cow, and Jack accepts. Afterwards, the Baker worries that they've cheated the boy, but his Wife maintains that the beans *might* be magical.

And what of the Baker's long-lost sister Rapunzel? The Witch keeps her in a tower with no doors. The Witch climbs the girl's hair to enter the tower. A hidden Prince watches and learns the secret of how to approach the sequestered beauty. The Baker rescues Little Red and her Grandmother, and in thanks for their release, the Baker gets the cape. Jack's Mother is considerably less happy; she throws the beans away in frustration. The Baker's Wife, headed home, sees Cinderella hiding from a Prince. Cinderella tries to explain, but is distracted by an enormous beanstalk growing in the distance. The Baker's Wife notices that Cinderella is wearing slippers "as pure as gold"—but Milky White has wandered off, so the Baker's Wife hurries to find her. By this point, the clock has reached the "First Midnight."

Jack, back from the beanstalk, is now laden with gold. Elsewhere, the Baker's Wife confesses to her husband that she's lost the cow. They split up to search, and the Baker's Wife discovers two Princes, discussing the "Agony" (**Musical Example 60**) of desiring elusive maidens. The Baker's Wife has a new objective: Rapunzel and her "hair as yellow as corn." When the Baker and his Wife are reunited, they have acquired three of the ingredients—the red cape, Milky White (found by the Mysterious Man), and a long hair yanked from Rapunzel. Their joy is short-lived, for Milky White suddenly keels over dead. The second midnight has passed, and after burying the cow and quarrelling, the Baker gives the last bean to his wife; he will look for another cow, while she tries to acquire one of Cinderella's golden shoes.

In the meantime, the Witch discovers that Rapunzel has been visited by a Prince. To forestall any future visits, she cuts off Rapunzel's hair and maroons her in a desert. The Prince, while escaping from the angry Witch, is blinded by thorns in a thicket. Red Ridinghood—now wearing a wolf-skin cape—meets Jack. Another trip up the beanstalk has resulted in a golden egg, but Little Red doesn't believe all his tales; she dares him to go get the golden harp he has described. Cinderella, who made another hurried departure from the second night of the Festival, has left a shoe behind (since the Prince had the forethought to spread tacky pitch on the stairs). The Baker's Wife tries to get Cinderella to accept the last bean in exchange for the other shoe, but Cinderella tosses the bean aside. However, as pursuit nears, Cinderella eagerly trades her shoe for the Wife's shoes, since they'll be better for running.

Soon, an enormous thud reverberates all through the woods; it was the sound of a Giant falling to the ground. Jack had escaped from him by chopping down the beanstalk. And, at last, the four ingredients have been obtained—except that the new cow isn't white, merely coated with flour. The Witch orders the couple to unearth Milky White; she restores the cow to life. The cow eats the other ingredients so that her milk will become a magic potion—but Milky White still can't produce milk, and they realize that the Witch, who cannot touch the ingredients, had handled Rapunzel's hair. The Mysterious Man suggests using corn silks instead. The Witch identifies the man as the Baker's long-lost father, but before father and son can speak, the older man dies, having at last broken the curse on his household.

With Milky White's magical milk, the Witch's former beauty is restored (at the cost of her powers). The Baker's Wife becomes pregnant, Jack and his cow are reunited, Cinderella marries her Prince, Rapunzel heals the wounded eyes of *her* prince with tears, and Cinderella's evil stepsisters are blinded by birds in punishment for their former cruelty. It seems that a happy (or deserved) ending comes to most of the kingdom's inhabitants—but they are unaware of a second giant beanstalk beginning to grow.

The Narrator tells us that the second act is also "Once upon a time—later" and that the people are happy, despite some small problems. But soon a big problem arises: another Giant is destroying their houses one by one, and the characters end up in the woods once again. Each Prince, it seems, has grown bored in his marriage and is suffering the "Agony" of having spotted a new woman to pursue—now a sleeping princess and a maiden in a casket surrounded by dwarves. Elsewhere, the characters learn that the Giant (widow of the slain Giant) wants revenge on Jack. Because she's nearsighted, the group tosses the Narrator to her when he's off guard. Trying to keep Jack's Mother quiet, the Steward inadvertently gives her a fatal blow. Rapunzel, in hysterics, runs into the Giant's path and is crushed.

With Rapunzel's death, the grieving Witch vows to deliver Jack to the Giant. The Baker and his Wife decide to protect Jack, so they hand the baby to Little Red and split up to search for him. The Baker's Wife encounters Cinderella's Prince, who quickly seduces her. Elsewhere, the Baker finds Cinderella grieving at the destroyed grave of her mother; he persuades her to come back with him for safety. After the amorous encounter, falling trees crush the Baker's Wife as the Giant passes by.

When the remaining people are gathered and realize how many have been killed, they start trying to assign the blame. The witch announces it is the "Last Midnight" and she is leaving; they're on their own. The Baker, panicked at raising a child alone, runs into the woods and encounters a specter of his father, who helps him understand that he can't evade responsibility. The Baker then devises a plan to slay the Giant. Cinderella stays to look after the baby, but when her Prince returns, she tells him his adultery has cost him his marriage. With everyone's combined effort, the plan works; the Giant is killed. Gradually, all the characters, living and dead, gather to share their own versions of the "moral of the story."

PLOT SUMMARY: *ASSASSINS*

The unlikely story opens in a shooting gallery, where the Proprietor offers guns to various passersby. He suggests that shooting a president can help people achieve their dreams. Leon Czolgosz wanders by, followed by John Hinckley, Charles Guiteau, Giuseppe Zangara, Samuel Byck, Squeaky Fromme, Sara Jane Moore, and the man whom the Proprietor recognizes as "our pioneer," John Wilkes Booth.

The customers all level their new guns at the targets positioned across the stage, but then an announcer's voice proclaims President Abraham Lincoln's arrival. A shot is heard—and a Balladeer begins to sing "The Ballad of Booth" (**Musical Example 61**), speculating on the reasons that might have driven Booth to the drastic act of assassination. Booth interrupts, claiming he had a political justification and denying that he was depressed over poor theatrical reviews or that he simply was insane. At last, though, realizing there is no escape, Booth raises his gun to his head, and another shot is heard. The Balladeer ends by cursing Booth, maintaining that Booth "paved the way for other madmen."

Many of the assassins-to-be are gathered in a bar, revealing their overwhelming frustrations. Booth is a cynical cheerleader, urging them to become masters of their fate. The scene changes to a 1933 political rally. A radio announcer narrates the events: the speech interrupted by gunfire; Roosevelt's waves afterwards; the realization that the Miami mayor had been hit. The shooter, Zangara, is taken into custody, and witnesses eagerly explain to reporters how they "saved Roosevelt." As Zangara sits in the electric chair, he claims his action created an equity between the rich and the poor. No one listens to him, however, and the lights dim and flicker as the sound of the electric chair in action closes the scene.

Anarchist Emma Goldman delivers an impassioned speech to a group of workers, among them Czolgosz. After her talk, he gets her alone and tells her that he loves her. Kindly, she tells him to channel his passion toward the fight for social justice. Elsewhere, Fromme and Moore meet on a park bench. Fromme, smoking marijuana, adores Charles Manson and is convinced he will make her his queen when he becomes king of a new order. Moore, maybe even less rationally, asserts that she works for the FBI (or used to), is a CPA, had five husbands and three children, and has amnesia. One thing the two women have in common is their distrust of the image of Colonel Sanders on Moore's bucket of chicken; they each pull out a gun and shoot the bucket to smithereens.

Czolgosz, examining a pistol, notes that "it takes a lot of men to make a gun"—miners, millworkers, gunsmiths—while Booth marvels, "and all you have to do is . . . move your little finger and—you can change the world." Guiteau sees many uses for guns: they can "remove a scoundrel, unite a party, preserve the Union, promote the sales of my book." Moore, in contrast, has little control over her firearm; she accidentally fires it. The Balladeer then relates how Czolgosz visits the Pan-American Exposition in Buffalo, New York, where President McKinley is greeting visitors. Czolgosz patiently waits in the long line, and when he at last reaches the front, he shoots the President at point-blank range.

Leaping forward in time, we witness a disheveled Byck, wearing a filthy Santa Claus outfit, tape-recording messages to Leonard Bernstein. Byck believes Bernstein could save the world if only he would write more love songs. But then Byck angrily accuses Bernstein of ignoring him, just like all the other celebrities to whom Byck has sent communications. Elsewhere, Hinckley and Fromme discuss the people they love, but Fromme feels superior; she *knows* Manson, whereas Hinckley has never even met Jodie Foster. Hinckley orders Fromme to leave, then comforts himself by singing to Jodie. Fromme sings the same tune to the "Charlie" she loves, and then mocks Hinckley for his inability to "kill" the photo of President Reagan that keeps reappearing on his wall.

Guiteau tries to give Moore some shooting tips, and then tries to kiss her, but she resists. Therefore, he assassinates President Garfield. Guiteau is sentenced to hang, and while performing a cakewalk on the steps leading to the gallows, he recites the poem he had written the morning of his execution.

Fromme and Moore are having a hard time. Not only has Moore brought along her nine-year-old son and the family dog to their intended assassination of President Gerald Ford,

but her clumsiness has led her to shoot the dog. Ford, too, who was perennially caricatured as clumsy during his presidency, collides with Moore and tries to help her collect her dropped bullets. Even at this close range, however, Moore misses her shot, while a defective gun thwarts Fromme's assassination attempt. Byck, meanwhile, is stirred to action; he intends to hijack a plane, which he will crash into the White House; he sees the killing of President Richard Nixon as the only way to solve America's problems.

A lamentation for all the victims is heard, while the various assassins defend themselves and their motivations. They start asking the Balladeer, "Where's my prize?" convinced that their actions must have earned them some reward. When the Balladeer tells them that all their assassinations "didn't mean a nickel," a rumble of discontent runs through the assembled group. Gradually, they begin to insist there must be something for those who are left behind by the American Dream.

The time has shifted to "November 22, 1963," when Lee Harvey Oswald is preparing to kill himself in the Texas School Book Depository. He is interrupted by the arrival of Booth, who startles Oswald by reciting all kinds of personal, intimate details about Oswald's life. Oswald is outraged when Booth suggests that Oswald's plan to commit suicide is childish and dumb. "So tell me what I *should* do!" Oswald shouts, and Booth quietly replies, "You should kill the President of the United States." Oswald is at first speechless, but the idea that his name will go down in posterity forever for such a bold act begins to appeal to him. Gradually, the other assassins enter and urge him onward, telling him, "Without you we're a bunch of freaks. With you we're a force of history." Voices of other assassins are heard too—those who shot Martin Luther King, Jr., Robert Kennedy, and George Wallace. They tempt Oswald with visions of his power: "You can close the New York Stock Exchange. Shut down the schools in Indonesia," and they encourage him to think of them as his family. With that, Oswald kneels at the window, points a rifle at the presidential motorcade passing below, and shoots.

As the assassins had predicted, the assassination of President John F. Kennedy has enormous repercussions. It is the kind of event that makes people remember exactly where they were and what they were doing when they heard the news, and various citizens share those accounts. The assassins are unmoved; they end the show by declaring again defiantly, "Everybody's Got the Right (to be Happy)."

MUSICAL EXAMPLE 60

INTO THE WOODS
STEPHEN SONDHEIM/STEPHEN SONDHEIM, 1987
"Agony"

Cinderella's Prince

1 Did I abuse her or show her disdain? Why does she run from me?
If I should lose her, how shall I regain the heart she has won from me?

2 Agony!
Beyond power of speech, when the one thing you want is the only thing out of your reach.

Rapunzel's Prince

3 High in her tower, she sits by the hour, maintaining her hair.
Blithe and becoming, and frequently humming a light-hearted air:

4 Aaahhh

5 Agony!
Far more painful than yours, when you know she would go with you, if there only were doors.

Both

Agony!
Oh, the torture they teach!

Rapunzel's Prince

What's as intriguing—

Cinderella's Prince

Or half so fatiguing—

Both

As what's out of reach?

Cinderella's Prince

6 Am I not sensitive, clever, well-mannered, considerate, passionate, charming,
As kind as I'm handsome, and heir to a throne?

Rapunzel's Prince

You are everything maidens could wish for!

Cinderella's Prince

Then why no—?

Rapunzel's Prince

Do I know?

Cinderella's Prince

The girl must be mad!

Rapunzel's Prince

You know nothing of madness
till you're climbing her hair and you see her up there as you're nearing her,
All the while hearing her: "Aaahhhh"

Both

7 Agony!

Cinderella's Prince

Misery!

Rapunzel's Prince

Woe!

Both

Though it's different for each.

Cinderella's Prince

Always ten steps behind—

Rapunzel's Prince

Always ten feet below—

Both

And she's just out of reach.
Agony
That can cut like a knife! I must have her to wife.

MUSICAL EXAMPLE 61

ASSASSINS
STEPHEN SONDHEIM/STEPHEN SONDHEIM, 1991
"The Ballad of Booth"

The Balladeer

1 Someone tell the story, someone sing the song.
Every now and then the country goes a little wrong.
Every now and then a madman's bound to come along.

2 Doesn't stop the story—Story's pretty strong. Doesn't change the song . . .
Johnny Booth was a handsome devil, got up in his rings and fancy silks.
Had him a temper but kept it level. Everybody called him Wilkes.
Why did you do it, Johnny? Nobody agrees.
You who had everything, what made you bring a nation to its knees?
Some say it was your voice had gone, some say it was booze.
They say you killed a country, John, because of bad reviews.

3 Johnny lived with a grace and glitter, kinda like the lives he lived on stage.
Died in a barn in pain and bitter, twenty-seven years of age.
Why did you do it, Johnny, throw it all away?
Why did you do it, boy, not just destroy the pride and joy of Illinois,
But all the U.S.A.?
Your brother made you jealous, John, you couldn't fill his shoes.
Was that the reason, tell us, John, along with bad reviews?

[dialogue]

4 They say your ship was sinkin', John . . .

[dialogue]

You'd started missing cues . . .

[dialogue]

They say it wasn't Lincoln, John.

[dialogue]

You'd merely had a slew of bad reviews.

[dialogue]

5 He said, "Damn you, Lincoln, you had your way,

Booth

Tell 'em, boy!

Balladeer

With blood you drew out of Blue and Gray!"

Booth

Tell it all! Tell them till they listen!

Balladeer

He said, "Damn you, Lincoln, and damn the day
You threw the 'U' out of U.S.A.!"
He said:

Booth

6 Hunt me down, smear my name, say I did it for the fame,
What I did was kill the man who killed my country.
Now the Southland will mend, now this bloody war can end,
Because someone slew the tyrant, just as Brutus slew the tyrant—

Balladeer

He said,

Balladeer and Booth

7 Damn you, Lincoln, you righteous whore!

Booth

Tell 'em! Tell 'em what he did!

Balladeer and Booth

You turned your spite into Civil War!

Booth

Tell 'em! Tell 'em the truth!

Balladeer

And more . . .

Booth

Tell 'em, boy! Tell 'em how it happened, how the end doesn't mean that it's over,

How surrender is not the end. Tell them:

8 How the country is not what it was, where there's blood in the clover,
How the nation can never again be the hope that it was.
How the bruises may never be healed, how the wounds are forever,
How we gave up the field but we still wouldn't yield,
How the Union can never recover
From that vulgar, high and mighty, niggerlover, never—!
Never. Never. Never. No, the country is not what it was . . .

9 . . . Damn my soul if you must, let my body turn to dust,
Let it mingle with the ashes of the country.
Let them curse me to Hell, leave it to history to tell:
What I did, I did well, and I did it for my country.
Let them cry, "Dirty traitor!" They will understand it later—
The country is not what it was . . .

Balladeer

10 Johnny Booth was a headstrong fellow, even he believed the things he said.
Some called him noble, some said yellow. What he was was off his head.
How could you do it, Johnny, calling it a cause?
You left a legacy of butchery and treason we took eagerly,
And thought you'd get applause.
But traitors just get jeers and boos, not visits to their graves,
While Lincoln, who got mixed reviews,
Because of you, John, now gets only raves.

11 Damn you, Johnny, you paved the way for other madmen to make us pay.
Lots of madmen have had their say—but only for a day.

12 Listen to the stories, hear it in the songs.
Angry men don't write the rules, and guns don't right the wrongs.
Hurts a while, but soon the country's back where it belongs,
And that's the truth. Still and all . . . Damn you, Booth!

Chapter 44
New Names of the 1990s and Beyond

"Half the theatres in New York are dark and with little prospect of future occupants," lamented Alan Jay Lerner in 1986. Eleven years later, Denny Flinn, while wrapping up his examination of musical theater, also felt "a great art form has passed." In fact, few artistic fields have been pronounced dead as often as musical theater—but like a phoenix, it rises again despite the passing of various writers, performers, directors, and producers. Consistently, there were (and are) dozens of aspiring creators hoping to fill the theaters anew. Their shows have used a wide variety of source material—novels, children's books, opera, film—while other works have been original ideas. In short, the 1990s saw an exciting diversity of approaches, and the breadth of offerings gave theatergoers a rich array of choices.

Lucy Simon's *The Secret Garden* (1991) put a women composer back on Broadway. Simon—sister of pop singer Carly Simon—worked with Marsha Norman to adapt the 1911 children's book written by Frances Hodgson Burnett. They also demonstrated that newcomers *can* succeed; neither writer had much prior experience with musical theater. Simon had written songs with her sister and had contributed to an off-Broadway revue in 1984. Otherwise, her theatrical experience was nonexistent. Norman, in contrast, had considerable theatrical exposure, winning the Pulitzer Prize for her play *'Night, Mother* in 1983, but she had never written a libretto for a musical before, let alone an adaptation.

Like Leroux's *Phantom of the Opera*, Burnett's novel has often been adapted, but the Simon and Norman production was one of the most successful versions. *The Secret Garden* opened on Broadway in 1991, running for 706 performances and garnering three Tony Awards. Daisy Eagan, who played Mary—the orphan who is sent to her uncle's lonely home in Yorkshire—won a Best Actress Tony; at age 11, she was the youngest actress ever to do so. Simon did not win for her score, but critics and audiences alike admired the music's contribution to the show's atmosphere. Simon has not made a theatrical contribution since *The Secret Garden*, but she has composed for television. Norman, though, was back on Broadway briefly in 1993 when Jule Styne's musical *The Red Shoes* played five performances; Norman wrote the book and lyrics. She, too, seems to have left musical theater behind since that point.

Despite the gender of its creators, *The Secret Garden* was a traditional book musical, using spoken dialogue and integrated songs to tell its story. *Bring in 'da Noise, Bring in 'da Funk*, in contrast, was quite a departure from nearly everything familiar. This was a dance show, and certainly it was a concept musical, like *A Chorus Line* or *Cats*. Its focus, however, was the entire history of African Americans told through dance. Earlier, when George C. Wolfe directed *Jelly's Last Jam* (a catalog show celebrating Jelly Roll Morton), he had been impressed with the dancer Savion Glover. When Glover and Wolfe agreed to collaborate, Wolfe asked him what kind of work he wanted to do. Glover replied, "I want to bring in 'da noise, I want to bring in 'da funk"—giving the show its title before even the tiniest thread of a storyline was conceived. Wolfe wanted to capitalize on Glover's ability to tap-dance—or, as Glover often distinguishes it, his ability to "hoof". He explains, "Hoofin' is dancin' from your waist down." Wolfe thinks that black Americans have "lost our original languages, so our languages live in different places in our bodies, and it comes out in all sorts of different kinds of rhythms, of the way we talk, speak, or move, so I think that tap is one of those manifestations of expressing a lost language in the body."

Gradually, working with writer Reg E. Gaines, they crafted a montage of episodes. Projected images of slave ships take us back in history to the dark era of human servitude. Other scenes include a 1739 slave uprising, lynching statistics in 1916, factory life, race riots, and, of course, the birth of jazz. The musical score reflected the changing world, drawing from jazz, gospel, hip hop, rap, and other styles.

This wide-ranging production required only a tiny cast: five dancers, a male narrator, a versatile female vocalist, and two on-stage drummers. A smash debut off-Broadway run encouraged a transfer to Broadway in 1996, where it ran for 1,135 performances, earning four Tony Awards. Some felt the historical aspects were unbalanced—one would never know that Martin Luther King, Jr. had existed, for instance—but all agreed that the dancing was outstanding. Encouraged, Wolfe undertook further celebrations of black history, including *Harlem Song*, which opened in 2002 at Harlem's Apollo Theater.

Dance also played a significant role in Jonathan Larson's *Rent*, which made its Broadway debut the same year as *Noise/Funk*. But in *Rent*, the choreography served the story but did not *tell* the story. *Rent* did have its own form of shock value in its depictions of nontraditional partnerships, strong language, and contemporary attitudes, but the biggest jolt of all came from the death of its creator just before the previews. **Jonathan Larson** (1960–1996) was in many respects a poster child for the American dream; after a long struggle, he created a show that not only made it to Broadway but walked away with many of theater's highest accolades. Only his premature demise didn't fit the success formula—but, in an ironic way, Larson's passing helped the show, since the musical addressed the death of young people.

The operas of Giacomo Puccini proved to be a fruitful source for more than one late twentieth-century musical. *Madama Butterfly* had contributed to *Miss Saigon*; *Rent* drew from *La Bohème* for inspiration. Larson and writer Billy Aronson saw parallels between people with the human immunodeficiency virus, living under the shadow of AIDS, and the tubercular Bohemian artists of Puccini's Parisian setting. However, Aronson envisioned a comedy, featuring yuppies, while Larson felt the topic should be serious. With this basic conflict, it was little wonder that people hearing the demonstration tape admired the three songs but felt the story didn't work. The men set the idea aside.

Later, Larson learned that his best friend had become HIV-positive, and suddenly he was afire once more to write the show. Larson attended some meetings of an AIDS support group with his friend, inspiring the musical's affirmation scenes. The anger of other friends with the disease also found its way into the story, giving it a gritty reality at times (see the **Plot Summary**). Although the three tunes written with Aronson were retained in the show, two of them went through substantial alterations. The third, however, remained largely untouched; this was the vision song "Santa Fe" (**Musical Example 62**).

"Santa Fe" is structured as a relaxed, moderato tempo verse-chorus form, set in a sing-song compound duple meter. The verses at **1** and **3** are conversational, combining free speaking, rhythmic speech, and singing. The choruses (**2** and **4**) are entirely sung, however, concluding with an extended melisma on *oh . . .*; their dream seems to inspire greater lyricism. Occasional "hesitations" are written into the rhythm, emphasizing the subsequent words, such as "Sunny Santa Fe would be—nice." A short coda quotes a 1967 pop hit, "Do You

Know the Way to San Jose?" changing the town in question to Santa Fe. This dream of a warmer, more relaxed existence, set to gentle, soothing music, is only a temporary respite from the hard-driving rock style that propels most of *Rent*'s tunes.

With persistence, Larson at last persuaded the New York Theatre Workshop to present the show in 1994, supported in part by a $45,000 Richard Rodgers Development Grant. After the workshop, the NYTW agreed to produce *Rent* in its newly renovated theater on East Fourth Street, but—as a nonprofit theater company—the NYTW did not have a big budget that could support its creative artists (even though they budgeted the show at $250,000—twice their normal costs). Therefore, Larson had to keep his job as a waiter even though he dearly wanted to quit and devote himself full time to writing.

And the show *needed* more writing; it had structural flaws and confusing aspects. Larson began to work with **Lynn Thomson**; she was a **dramaturg** (an advisor for playwrights), and she asked Larson to write a biography for each character, telling *Rent*'s story from various perspectives. The libretto improved, but the producers and director wanted even more alterations. Larson was tired of rewriting; he called his mentor Sondheim and shared his frustration. Sondheim pointed out that Larson had chosen to work with these people, saying, "You've chosen your collaborators, and now you have to learn to collaborate." Larson swallowed his pride and implemented many of the suggested changes.

Having quit the restaurant job, Larson was living hand-to-mouth (friends bought him groceries), but he was ecstatic that *Rent* was finally reaching the stage. A shadow loomed, however. Larson complained of chest pains, but was misdiagnosed twice: first food poisoning was blamed, and later the flu. In truth, Larson's aorta was weakening—a rare congenital condition for one so young—and at home after the final dress rehearsal, he was making tea when the aorta failed, leaving a foot-long tear. (The aneurysm, had it been diagnosed, need not have been fatal; early treatment is 80 to 90 percent successful.) Larson died on the day of *Rent*'s first preview. The performance was canceled, yet the cast presented a concert version (unstaged) of the show for the assembled family and friends. Performing under these emotional circumstances was very difficult, but it had a significant impact on the actors and their understanding of their characters; they were motivated to give their performances their very best effort.

Many shows go through drastic modifications during previews; there are even shows that close. So, Larson's absence—depriving *Rent* of its librettist, lyricist, and composer in one swoop—put great pressure on the remaining production staff, who had to play "a terrible game of second-guessing." An actor recalled, "I remember Michael [Greif, the director] saying that he had to say to himself, 'Okay, I know this is something I would push Jonathan for, but he wouldn't go for it, so I'm not going to do that.'" Primarily, the staff made cuts; the first act lost ten or more minutes of running time.

Meanwhile, a *New York Times* story appeared, focused on the untimely demise of *Rent*'s chief creator. Media attention grew quickly, and the press was out in force at the show's opening night in 1996—far more reporters than NYTW was accustomed to hosting. The reviews were glowing, especially

Angel (Wilson Jermaine Heredia), Collins (Jesse L. Martin), and Mark (Anthony Rapp) dream of "Santa Fe" in *Rent*.
Photofest.

Ben Brantley's article for the *New York Times*. Director Jim Nicola noted that the *Times*'s assessment is the

> *review that matters. I try to tell myself that all it is is a certain indication of how many seats are going to be filled or not. The biggest success ever in the past, the box office did six, seven, eight thousand dollars. The day of the* Times *review,* Rent *was close to forty thousand dollars. It was pandemonium down here.*

The tickets for the entire first month sold out in one day, and so the run was extended another month.

It was also time to decide where the show should play next. Some felt that a Broadway transfer would be selling out, that the show belonged in the more Bohemian world of off-Broadway. Others wanted to share *Rent* with as large an audience as possible, and clearly Broadway was the way to reach the most people. The question asked by everyone was, "What would Jonathan want?" Finally, the decision was made to take *Rent* to the Great White Way. Actor Adam Pascal (playing Roger) confessed,

> *I thought it was a bad idea, but with hindsight I was totally wrong. I was worried about the play losing artistic credibility and content. But it maintained everything. Downtown [home of the NYTW] was Jonathan's house, so there was a lot of pain and heartache in that run; I think when we moved uptown [to Broadway] we left a lot of the pain and heartache down there, where it needed to stay.*

The cast struggled to learn the stricter Broadway union rules; for instance, they were forbidden to move stage sets, so if a chair needed to be shifted, a tech had to be called to move it. There were new expenses, too; each performer had to have enough costumes for eight performances, a week's run. By April, however, *Rent* was ready to take its Broadway bow; once again, the response was overwhelming. Before the opening, the word came that *Rent* had been awarded a Pulitzer Prize; it was only the seventh musical ever to be awarded this recognition—and so far, it remains the last musical to win.

Regrettably, Larson didn't witness his show's triumph at the Tonys. *Rent* won Best Musical, Best Book, and Best Score, and Wilson Jermaine Heredia won as Best Actor in a Featured Role in a Musical. (Heredia was justifiably proud of that recognition, for he is *not* gay, and therefore felt that his portrayal of the transvestite Angel was an acknowledgment of his acting achievement.) In addition to numerous regional productions, the New York show, still running, has racked up more than 3,500 performances.

Even after his death, Larson has had another musical make it to the stage: his *tick, tick . . . BOOM!* was presented off-Broadway in 2001. This show, written while *Rent* was being developed, was an autobiographical depiction of a composer about to turn 30. The artist must decide whether to marry a long-term girlfriend and move to Cape Cod, to join the corporate rat-race like his roommate, or to keep waiting tables and trying to see his music produced on stage. Playwright David Auburn took the monologue form of Larson's original script and reworked it for three actors, and

the show enjoyed a modest success; there are those who prefer it to *Rent*. Unfortunately, these two works will remain the sole output of a talented writer whose early death was a great loss to the theatrical world.

Nevertheless, a new generation of composers started coming to the fore in the 1990s. Frank Wildhorn—born in 1958, just over a year before Larson—saw three of his shows playing on Broadway simultaneously in 1999, the first American in 22 years to do so. Unlike Larson, whose mentor was Sondheim, Wildhorn followed Lloyd Webber's path, writing popular works that often earned the disdain of critics. One of his producers quipped, "Nobody but the public loves his music," and Wildhorn learned to shrug off poor reviews, depending on the box office to prove his effectiveness as a writer.

In 1979, Wildhorn was attending the University of Southern California when the idea came for a musical based on Robert Louis Stevenson's short story, *The Strange Case of Dr. Jekyll and Mr. Hyde*. For years, he worked with Steve Cuden on a score, but after graduation, the writers went separate ways. Wildhorn met Leslie Bricusse in 1988, who soon replaced Cuden. (Bricusse had won an Academy Award for "Talk to the Animals" in the 1967 film *Dr. Doolittle*; he also had written for *Willie Wonka and the Chocolate Factory*, *Superman*, *The Return of the Pink Panther*, *Victor/Victoria*, *Home Alone*, *Scrooge*, and other films.) In 1990, Wildhorn persuaded RCA Records in London to make a concept album; the recording of *Jekyll & Hyde* was sung by Linda Eder (Wildhorn's wife) and Colm Wilkinson, the first Jean Valjean in *Les Misérables*. The album did well, selling 150,000 copies, and it led to a production in Houston. Local audiences loved it, but *Jekyll & Hyde* didn't transfer to Broadway.

Meanwhile, Wildhorn had other irons in the fire; with lyricist Nan Knighton, he recorded a concept album of *The Scarlet Pimpernel* in 1992. He and Bricusse kept tinkering with *Jekyll & Hyde*, though, and by 1994, they had made so many changes that they persuaded Atlantic Records to make an unprecedented *second* concept album. This double-CD set prompted a 1995 touring production—but once again, the show closed without reaching Broadway. However, the show was developing a fan-base of people who saw the show 10, 20, even 40 times—and the animated Internet discussions of these "Jekkies" kept interest in the show alive. Finally, in 1997, after further changes and legal battles, the show opened on Broadway, beating *The Scarlet Pimpernel* to New York by six months. Original cast recordings soon followed for both shows, resulting in a third recording of *Jekyll & Hyde* and a second *Scarlet Pimpernel*.

In 1998, Wildhorn also released a concept album of his next project, *The Civil War*. The show joined his other shows on Broadway in 1999, but failed to match their longevity; *The Civil War* closed after 61 performances. *The Scarlet Pimpernel* continued to be revised, even after its premiere; it closed after 772 performances and yet another recording, and *Jekyll & Hyde* finally went dark after 1,543 showings.

Wildhorn continues to pursue a myriad of projects, including a series of albums called *The Romantics*, written in collaboration with various lyricists. In 2004, Wildhorn took a new gothic horror show to Broadway, adapting Bram

Stoker's classic *Dracula* in collaboration with Don Black and Christopher Hampton, lyricists of *Sunset Boulevard*. Other endeavors include a dramatization of the life of sculptress Camille Claudel and an original show called *Havana*; Wildhorn has worked as a producer as well. It is likely the theatrical world will be hearing from Frank Wildhorn for many years to come.

Another composer of Larson and Wildhorn's generation, born in 1960, is Stephen Flaherty. Flaherty has worked almost exclusively with one lyricist, Lynn Ahrens, whom he met in the BMI Musical Theatre Workshop in 1982. Their first collaboration, *Lucky Stiff*, was presented at Playwrights Horizons in 1988 and enjoyed widespread presentations in various regional theaters in the United States and abroad. Two years later, Flaherty and Ahrens were back at Playwrights Horizons with *Once on This Island*; this time, the show made it to Broadway, where it ran for 469 performances and earned eight Tony nominations. Although it won none of them, the London show took the Olivier for Best Musical.

Their next show, *My Favorite Year* (1992) played only 36 performances, but was the first original musical ever to be presented at the Lincoln Center (previous musicals had all been revival productions). It was Flaherty and Ahrens's next show that put them on the map, however; the show was *Ragtime* (1998), based on E. L. Doctorow's novel depicting a tragic collision between pride and racial prejudice in New Rochelle, New York, at the start of the twentieth century. *Ragtime* depicted the intersections between three families: a family of upper-middle-class whites, an Eastern European Jewish immigrant and his young daughter, and an African American couple and their baby. *Ragtime* played 834 times and was nominated for 13 Tony Awards, winning four, including Best Score, Book, Orchestrations; and Best Actress in a Supporting Role (for Audra McDonald, whose character is killed by mob violence in Act I).

After *Ragtime*, Flaherty and Ahrens brought *Seussical* to Broadway in 2000, based on Dr. Seuss book characters; it did fairly well for a children's show. Flaherty and Ahrens also wrote for the animated film *Anastasia* (1997), while their most recent musical theater collaboration, set in 1964 Dublin, is *A Man of No Importance*. Just as *Ragtime* mixed theatrical music with ragtime-style tunes, *A Man of No Importance* blends traditional Irish music with the sounds of the emerging British rock-and-roll.

A number of other young composers, most of whom tend to write their own lyrics, have been coming to the fore recently. Some of them have built reputations in well-received off-Broadway productions; others have seen their works make the move to Broadway itself. Some newcomers have already won Tonys for their efforts. One characteristic that is shared by the diverse group is that they are all ambitious, legitimate musicians; the days of tinkling out tunes on a toy xylophone are long gone.

Adam Guettel's theatrical reputation is based primarily on *Floyd Collins* (1996), presented off-Broadway at Playwrights Horizons. He won an Obie for his portrait of a man who was trapped in a cave in 1925 and the media circus that developed around the efforts to rescue him. Guettel (son of

Mary Rodgers and grandson of Richard Rodgers) resisted becoming a composer (in what he calls rebellion) but found himself drawn to the field at last. His next work, staged off-Broadway under the title *Saturn Returns*, but recorded as *Myths and Hymns*, uses a wide palette of musical styles. He has been at work for some time on a third project, *A Light in the Piazza*—a show eagerly awaited by many of his fans.

In the early days of the twentieth century, it was not unusual for a composer to bring three or four shows to the stage in a single season. Currently, however, it is a long, slow (and expensive) process to see a musical develop into a stage production, so it was somewhat remarkable that composer/lyricist Michael John LaChiusa was able to bring two of his shows to Broadway in the same season: his *Marie Christine*—a modernized retelling of the Medea legend—opened in late 1999, while *The Wild Party*, a depiction of 1920s sexual excess, debuted in early 2000. The passionate, dissonant score of *Marie Christine* prompted more than one writer to accuse it of being an opera rather than a musical (a label LaChiusa resists), while the success of *The Wild Party* was hurt by the bankruptcy of one of the producers. (Moreover, another musical on the same topic, composed by Andrew Lippa, premiered a few months later; both shows undoubtedly were hurt by the confusion.) Nevertheless, LaChiusa received Tony nominations for both scores. LaChiusa has several other projects in various stages of development and is certain to continue broadening the horizons of theatergoers in years to come.

Jason Robert Brown, one of the youngest members of the new generation, had his *Songs for a New World* presented off-Broadway in 1995; the director was Daisy Prince, daughter of Hal Prince. Brown worked with Daisy's father in 1998, when *Parade* came to Broadway; the musical addressed the tragic miscarriage of justice in 1913 that led to the lynching death of Leo Frank, wrongfully accused of killing a young factory worker named Mary Phagan. The somewhat misleading title probably helped to limit the run to 84 performances, but Brown was rewarded with a Tony for his first Broadway score.

Another of Brown's creations opened off-Broadway in 2002, again directed by Daisy Prince. Titled *The Last Five Years*, the show requires only two singers. One is the aspiring actress Cathy, who describes their five-year relationship in reverse, starting with the present and working back to the past; Jamie, an author, proceeds chronologically through his version of their story, starting with their first encounter and moving forward to the breakup of their marriage. The two sing in duet only twice, once at the midway point of the show, during their wedding, and once again at the end, when the contrast between his sorrow over their failed marriage and her elation at meeting the man who might be "the one" is painfully sharp. Morevoer, we share in the agonies of the musical theater audition process during Cathy's "Climbing Uphill," which illustrates Cathy's thoughts during this pressure-filled experience. The novel structure of the show is surprisingly effective, and it will be intriguing to see what this unconventional composer produces for his next effort.

Brown is not the most recent composer to win a Tony for his initial Broadway effort. Mark Hollman won a 2002

Best Score Tony, while Greg Kotis took the 2002 Tony for Best Book, after *Urinetown* made its debut in 2001. The show spoofs a Big Brother-ish society in which bathroom access is tightly restricted because of a devastating water shortage. Despite the unfortunate timing of its intended opening—September 13, 2001, which had to be rescheduled—audiences have been drawn to the tongue-in-cheek humor of the show. The idea for the musical came when Kotis spent too much money during the first part of a trip to Europe; by the end of his visit, he was trying to eke out his remaining cash by waiting to use the restroom until he went to dinner, so he could use restaurant facilities for free rather than paying for Parisian public toilets (despite their fairly modest charge). Perhaps Kotis should undertake further journeys if his travels produce such quirky, offbeat fare in the future.

Guettel, LaChiusa, Brown, and Hollman are not alone; various other composers, such as Ricky Ian Gordon, Josh Rubins, Andrew Lippa, Matthew Sklar, Henry Krieger, and Jeanine Tesori are also hard at work on theatrical projects. Tony-winner Audra McDonald has helped the careers of several writers by singing their songs on her albums *Way Back to Paradise* and *How Glory Goes*. Funding is always a challenge, for instance, in Musical Theater Works, founded in 1983 to showcase aspiring composers and writers, closed its doors in 2004. Still, there are a number of other agencies and theaters anxious to promote new talent. Despite past fears, Broadway is not dead, or even dying; there is too much talent in the current generation of writers for the prognosis to be anything but hopeful.

FURTHER READING

Citron, Stephen. *Sondheim and Lloyd Webber: The New Musical.* Oxford: Oxford University Press, 2001.

Flinn, Denny Martin. *Musical!: A Grand Tour.* New York: Schirmer Books, 1997.

"Frank Wildhorn." *Contemporary Musicians*, Volume 31. Gale Group, 2001. Reproduced in Biography Resource Center. Farmington Hills, Michigan: The Gale Group, 2002.

"Jonathan Larson." *Encyclopedia of World Biography Supplement*, Vol. 18. Gale Research, 1998. Reproduced in Biography Resource Center. Farmington Hills, Michigan: The Gale Group, 2002.

Lerner, Alan Jay. *The Musical Theatre: A Celebration.* New York: Da Capo Press, 1986.

McDonnell, Evelyn, with Katherine Silberger, interviews and text. *Rent.* New York: Melcher Media, 1997.

Miller, Scott. *Deconstructing Harold Hill: An Insider's Guide to Musical Theatre.* Portsmouth, New Hampshire: Heinemann, 2000.

———. *Rebels with Applause: Broadway's Groundbreaking Musicals.* Portsmouth, New Hampshire: Heinemann, 2001.

Stearns, David Patrick. "The Smart Set." *American Theatre* 17, no. 2 (February 2000): 18–21, 76–78.

Suskin, Steven. *Show Tunes: The Songs, Shows, and Careers of Broadway's Major Composers.* Revised and expanded third edition. New York: Oxford University Press, 2000.

PLOT SUMMARY: *RENT*

It is Christmas Eve in New York's East Village in a loft apartment shared by aspiring filmmaker Mark and aspiring songwriter Roger. They get a call from their old friend Collins, but he's cut off (because he's being mugged, as it turns out). Benny calls next; he's a former roommate, but now he's their landlord. He had been letting them stay for free, but now he wants the rent. Worse, the power keeps going out, so they burn all sorts of paper to keep warm. Mark's ex-girlfriend phones; she needs help with her sound equipment for a performance that night, and Mark agrees to help. Meanwhile, Angel, a cross-dressing street musician, rescues the bruised Collins; they quickly discover not only that they are attracted to each other, but that both of them are HIV-positive. Soon, we learn that Roger is too—a legacy of his drug-addicted days, which ended when *his* HIV-positive girlfriend killed herself. Roger has become reclusive; he's trying to write one great song to stand as his monument after he has succumbed to the disease. His neighbor, Mimi, knocks; he resists her allure because he knows the signs of a junkie.

Joanne, Maureen's new love interest, is pressured by her parents not to embarrass their political ambitions. Meanwhile, Mark meets Collins's new friend Angel. Angel relates how he just acquired an easy $1,000: A woman hired him to play his drums, thinking it would force a neighbor's dog to bark itself to death. To his surprise, the Akita leapt off the balcony altogether. Benny comes by and wants Mark and Roger to stop Maureen's performance; if they do, he'll waive their rent. (Maureen is protesting Benny's plan to clear the homeless off of a vacant lot he owns.) Benny justifies his plans by explaining he's going to build a cyberstudio on the lot, which will raise the neighborhood property values. Mark still goes to help with the problematic equipment; he and Joanne compare notes about life with Maureen. Mark goes with Angel and Collins to an AIDS support meeting in order to film the group. Roger stays home, and when Mimi wants to go out, he puts her off; he doesn't want to discuss his health status.

After the meeting, Mark, Angel, and Collins go to the vacant lot and defend a homeless woman from the police. Mark films the encounter, which angers the woman. Hurt that their good deed is rejected, the three men dream of opening a restaurant in "Santa Fe" (**Musical Example 62**), far away from the physical misery of wintertime New York. Nevertheless, Collins and Angel are glad for their newfound love. Maureen and Joanne, however, are having some problems. Mark has talked Roger into coming out for the evening; spotting Mimi, Roger apologizes for rebuffing her earlier and invites her to dinner.

At the lot, Maureen presents her protest piece that features a cow who escapes Cyberland by taking a leap of faith over the moon. The friends all gather at the Life Café afterwards; Benny maintains that the Bohemian life is dead, but the others disagree. Leaving angrily, Benny recognizes Mimi, because they used to be an item. She shrugs him off, and then a beeper is heard; it's her timer reminding her to take her AIDS drugs. When Roger realizes that she, too, is HIV-positive, the major stumbling block to a relationship is gone. Outside, there's rioting because Benny padlocked the entrance to Roger and Mark's building. At the café, Joanne is tired of being Maureen's servant and tells her to pack; the party goes on, however.

After the friends break into their building, thanks to a blowtorch Angel and Collins have thoughtfully brought over, the next year races by. Mark's video footage of the rioting made the news and is bringing him job offers. Benny shows up, saying Mark and Roger can move back in. Roger is suspicious, even more so when Benny implies that Mimi "persuaded" him to be nice to Roger and Mark. Mimi's upset that Roger doesn't believe her, and she yields to an offer of drugs from her dealer.

By Valentine's Day, Roger struggles with jealousy over Mimi's prior relationship with Benny, whereas Angel and Collins are very happy. Maureen and Joanne's relationship is on and off again. By spring, Roger walks out on Mimi because he thinks she's been unfaithful. Collins is nursing Angel as he grows weaker. Soon, though, the couples are all shakily reunited. They practice safe sex with all its attendant frustrations, and by autumn, they are all separated again—but Collins and Angel have been divided by death. The friends gather for Angel's memorial service. Outside the church, Mark decides to start working for the gossip magazine *Buzzline*. He can't believe that things were so good last Christmas, and now they're falling apart. In fact, Roger has sold his guitar to buy a car so he can drive to Santa Fe. Anger

at Mark's departure leads to a fight, until Collins begs them to stop. Collins's sorrow prompts Maureen and Joanne to try to reconcile, but Mimi goes home with Benny.

Mark and Roger keep arguing; Roger accuses Mark of hiding behind his camera, while Mark suggests that Roger is leaving because he doesn't want to watch Mimi's health decline. Although Benny and Mark try to get Mimi to go to a rehab clinic, she runs away. Benny is able to help Collins, however, who can't afford Angel's funeral expenses; Collins realizes that Benny is no villain. As Mark starts his new job and Roger drives to Santa Fe, they both hate what they're doing. Mark abruptly quits his job so he can finish his own film, and Roger starts to hear the song he's been struggling to write for so long.

Christmas Eve has come again. Mark is ready to show a rough cut of his film, and Roger has come back to New York and gotten his guitar out of hock; he can't find Mimi, however. One by one, the friends reappear. Suddenly, Maureen and Joanne are heard calling from the sidewalk; they've found Mimi. She is delirious with illness, but tells Roger she loves him. He sings her the song he has written at last, but she stops breathing by the song's end. Suddenly she gasps; she tells them she saw a bright light and heard Angel telling her to go back and listen to Roger's song. The friends are overjoyed at her survival, and they reaffirm their determination to live "No Day But Today."

MUSICAL EXAMPLE 62

RENT
JONATHAN LARSON/JONATHAN LARSON, 1996
"Santa Fe"

Angel
New York City.
Mark
Uh huh.
Angel
Center of the Universe.
Collins
Sing it, girl.
Angel
Times are shitty, but I'm pretty sure they can't get worse.
Mark
I hear ya.
Angel
It's a comfort to know when you're singing the "Hit the Road Blues"
That anywhere else you can possibly go after New York would be
a pleasure cruise.
Collins
Now you're talkin'.
Well, I'm thwarted by a metaphysical puzzle, and I'm sick of grading papers, that I know.
I'm shouting in my sleep. I need a muzzle.
All this misery pays no salary, so
Let's open up a restaurant in Santa Fe. Sunny Santa Fe would be—nice.
Let's open up a restaurant in Santa Fe, And leave this to the roaches and mice.
All
Oh . . . Oh . . . Oh . . .

1

2

Angel

3

You teach?

Collins

I teach computer age philosophy, But my students would rather watch T.V.

Angel

Huh, America,

All

America.

Collins

You're a sensitive esthete, Brush the sauce onto the meat,

You can make the menu sparkle with rhyme.

You could drum a gentle drum, And I could seat guests as they come

Chatting not about Heidegger but wine.

4

Let's open up a restaurant in Santa Fe. Our labors would reap financial gain.

All

Gains, gains, gains.

Collins

Let's open up a restaurant in Santa Fe And save from devastation our brains.

Homeless

Save our brains.

All

We'll pack up all our junk and fly so far away, Devote ourselves to projects that sell.

We'll open up a restaurant in Santa Fe, Forget this cold Bohemian hell.

Oh . . . Oh . . . Oh . . .

Collins

5

Do you know the way to Santa Fe? You know, tumbleweeds, prairie dogs—Yeah!

Chapter 45
Whither Musical Theater?

Observers have wondered where theater is going next. The *Los Angeles Times* noted in 2000, "Nearly all of this season's new musicals are based on subject matter with immediate recognition, from literary classics to children's books to popular movies." Two years later, a *New York Times* headline proclaimed, "If It's a Musical, It Was Probably a Movie." Ties between Broadway and Hollywood have been strong for years, but recently the balance of power has shifted from the theater to the cinema.

The first half of the twentieth century was rife with musical films whose songs had first been heard on the stage; sometimes a show was filmed two or three times, although often with drastic changes to its book. For instance, none of the *Rose-Marie* films (1928, 1936, and 1954) had much at all to do with the plot of the 1924 stage show. The 1936 movie *Show Boat*, on the other hand, was much more faithful to the stage production, as was the case with most Rodgers and Hammerstein as well as Lerner and Loewe creations. Several of the fairly faithful stage-to-screen productions won Best Picture Oscars: *West Side Story*, *My Fair Lady*, *The Sound of Music*, and *Oliver!* Many Broadway writers then found their way to the West Coast studios; in fact, this was how many authors developed national reputations.

In turn, some of Hollywood's film musicals were transformed into stage productions, such as Rodgers and Hammerstein's *State Fair* and Lerner and Loewe's *Gigi*. Sometimes years elapsed; *42nd Street*, screened in 1933, began its Broadway run in 1980 (but then racked up some 3,486 performances; a 2001 revival is also doing well). Two of Disney's animated features have become long-running stage shows—*Beauty and the Beast* and *The Lion King*—but a successful film does not guarantee a profitable stage production. *Singin' in the Rain* came under critical fire when it was staged in 1985. *State Fair* lasted only 110 performances, *Gigi* endured for 103, while *Seven Brides for Seven Brothers* folded after five Broadway showings. Of course, many successful stage shows later fared poorly in the movie theaters; material that works in one format often loses its charm or effectiveness in another medium.

The number of movie musicals dropped in the latter twentieth century, so the fodder for direct stage adaptations was reduced. However, Broadway repeatedly borrowed plots from *non*musical films; some of the biggest successes of the 1950s and 1960s were *The King and I*, influenced by *Anna and the King*; *Sweet Charity*, based on the Fellini film *Nights of Cabiria*; *Cabaret*, which looked in part to the film *I Am a Camera*; and *Zorbá*, which followed the movie *Zorba the Greek*. The trend continued in the 1970s: Sondheim's *A Little Night Music* adapted Bergman's film *Smiles of a Summer Night*, while *Shenandoah* exemplified a growing trend; it kept the same title as its film basis, as did *42nd Street*, *Woman of the Year*, *The Goodbye Girl*, *Sunset Boulevard*, *Big*, *Footloose*, *High Society*, *Saturday Night Fever*, *The Full Monty*, *Sweet Smell of Success*, *Thoroughly Modern Millie*, *Hairspray*, and so forth.

Some films had only a little music, but then went on to be full-fledged stage musicals. One of the first film-inspired stage works, *Carnival*, had been based on *Lili*, which had one song and two dances. *Victor/Victoria* added many numbers not heard in the movie. Similarly, Mel Brooks's celebrated show *The Producers*—which won a record-setting 12 Tonys in 2001—came from a movie that had featured little singing except in the musical-within-the-movie *Springtime for Hitler*.

The Producers is, in many ways, a type of Valentine to Broadway, spoofing many of musical theater's traditions and landmark shows; it is filled with subtle allusions to previous musicals. Max Bialystock's big eleven o'clock number, "Betrayed," resembles the mental breakdown of "Rose's Turn" in *Gypsy*; he lets tunes from the show race through his mind, one after the other. And, of course, the subject matter itself is a tribute to the theater; Max and his accountant Leo Bloom determine that they can actually profit more from a flop show than from a hit, and so they are horrified to find that the show becomes a surprise success, thereby ruining their schemes.

Almost as prevalent as the current rage for movie-inspired shows are revivals of older shows. In 1995, the *New York Times* claimed, "Right now much of Broadway is a Museum of the American Musical staffed by busy curator-directors eager to put their stamp on every show they mount." For example, Broadway saw seven revivals of older shows in 2002—*The Flower Drum Song*, *The Boys from Syracuse*, *42nd Street*, *Cabaret*, *Chicago*, *Into the Woods*, and *Oklahoma!*—about a third of the 23 musicals playing on stage. In a sense, musical theater has become much like classical music; audiences willingly pay to hear the same Beethoven and Mozart symphonies played over and over again.

At the same time, 23 musicals on stage among Broadway's 37 theaters is a pleasing statistic. In their extensive study of the commercial aspects of Broadway musicals, Bernard Rosenberg and Ernest Harburg observed that there was a striking stability to the number of new musicals presented each year between the 1933–1934 and 1989–1990 seasons. On average, some 14 new shows opened each year, along with a handful of revivals; the total number of musicals has varied between 23 and 8. Even in the past few years, when many gloomy observers felt that musical theater was

Julie Taymor's elaborate puppetry of *The Lion King.*
Joan Marcus Photography.

dead, the actual number of newly opening productions has dropped only slightly (although the percentage of revivals *has* increased). We should remember that the trend toward long-running shows means that many other musicals are continuing to run even though they are not counted among a year's "new" shows. Ironically, as Rosenberg and Harburg note, the 1950s were a worse era for musical theater than the present day, even though America was experiencing a sizable economic boom at that time.

Why the current heavy reliance on film adaptations and on revivals? The primary reason seems to be economics. With Broadway shows now costing multiple millions of dollars, producers are anxious to present properties with a high likelihood of success. Audiences, when asked to spend upwards of a hundred dollars per seat—often months in advance—want to feel sure they'll enjoy the show. There is a comforting "known quantity" to shows based on films, and even more so in the case of revivals. Similarly, compilation or catalog shows bring together familiar songs; shows like *Mamma Mia!* even offer audiences a chance to sing along. (It is true, though, that this familiarity is no guarantee of success; even a 500-plus performance run is no longer a guarantee that a show will break even.) Because of this dependence on tried-and-true subject matter, it is a courageous producer nowadays who will mount an original production—and it is almost unheard of today to find a show supported by a single producer; most shows now list long strings of names who share production responsibility.

Under the circumstances, it is encouraging to see that original offerings still are making it to the Great White Way. It certainly seems to be the case that there *is* an audience for new shows with unusual, offbeat topics: the AIDS victims and nontraditional partners who populate *Rent*; the dance energy of *Bring in 'da Noise, Bring in 'da Funk*; the novelty of Siamese twins seen in *Side Show*; the simple shock value of a title like *Urinetown*; and even spectacle-driven shows along the lines of *Aida*.

Off-Broadway productions also enrich the theater world, as *The Fantasticks* ably demonstrated. Increasingly, though, there are producers who see no need to establish their shows in New York at all. Traditionalists may shudder, but the financial truth of the matter is that a show *can* profit by national and foreign tours as well as the sale of performance rights to amateur and stock companies (and even the sale of film rights). Nevertheless, New York retains its bragging rights as the "center" of the theatrical world, and it is still the dream destination of most American theatrical writers today.

Will Broadway continue to be the destination for American *audiences* in the years to come? As long as its theaters admit new productions—not just film adaptations, revivals, and catalog shows—musical theater should continue to thrive. True, adaptations and revivals can be important milestones in their own right; the inventive puppetry of *The Lion King*, for instance, transformed the story into a genuine theatrical experience, not just a re-enactment of the animated film. But musicals need to embrace new musical styles and social attitudes, which draw new audiences into the theaters (even as other viewers grow disenchanted and proclaim that musical theater has died). The theatrical doors need to remain open; if they do, the next generation of writers—and audiences—will be ready to enter. Their ideas are exciting and novel, and their abilities to write characters who "sing"— both literally and figuratively—will continue to enrich, delight, challenge, and entertain audiences of the future.

FURTHER READING

Citron, Stephen. *Sondheim and Lloyd Webber: The New Musical*. Oxford: Oxford University Press, 2001.

Henderson, Amy, and Dwight Blocker Bowers. *Red, Hot, and Blue: A Smithsonian Salute to the American Musical*. Washington: The National Portrait Gallery and

The National Museum of American History, in association with the Smithsonian Institution Press, 1996.

Marks, Peter. "If It's a Musical, It Was Probably a Movie." *New York Times* (April 14, 2002), Section 2, 1.

Pacheco, Patrick. "Start Spreading the New." *Los Angeles Times* (August 6, 2000): Calendar, 5, 72–73.

Rosenberg, Bernard, and Ernest Harburg. *The Broadway Musical: Collaboration in Commerce and Art*. New York: New York University Press, 1993.

Suskin, Steven. *Show Tunes: The Songs, Shows, and Careers of Broadway's Major Composers*. Revised and expanded third edition. New York: Oxford University Press, 2000.

GLOSSARY

A cappella – vocal music that has no instrumental accompaniment (Chapter 35)

Absolute pitch (= perfect pitch) – the innate ability to identify the frequency of sounded pitches (Chapter 37)

Accelerando – a gradual increase in the tempo (Chapter 6)

Accent – a note that is particularly stressed or emphasized (Chapter 8)

Accompaniment – music played (or sung) to support a featured melody (Chapter 1, 2)

Act – a large-scale subsection of a theatrical work, usually framed by the opening and closing of the main curtain (Chapter 3)

Actor's Equity Association (= Equity) – the American actors' union (Chapter 12)

Advance (= box office advance) – the income derived from ticket sales before a show has opened (Chapter 13)

Advance man – a person who travels ahead of a troupe, preparing for the troupe's arrival in a town (Chapter 8)

Allegro – a tempo term for a fast pace (Chapter 2)

Alternation form – a pattern related to verse-chorus form, but one in which the "chorus" has new words each time, resulting in a diagram of *a-b-a-b* and so on. (Chapter 13)

Alto – the term for a lower pitched female voice (or lower pitched castrato voice) (Chapter 1)

Andante – a tempo term for a walking pace (Chapter 2)

Andante con moto – walking pace "with motion" (Chapter 3)

Andante maestoso – a majestic walking pace (Chapter 2)

Antoinette Perry Awards – (see **Tony Awards**)

Aria – a number featuring a soloist, usually in an emotional moment; an aria is usually tuneful and memorable (Chapter 1)

Arioso – a singing style that is more tuneful than recitative, but not as rhythmically steady as an aria (Chapter 1)

Audition – a trial performance in which a prospective entertainer's capabilities are appraised (Chapter 11)

Authorized – a performance that has received its creators' (or their agents') approval and that pays the copyright owner(s) the proper royalty for the performance (Chapter 7)

ASCAP – the American Society of Composers, Authors, and Publishers; an agency that collects royalty fees from performers wishing to perform copyrighted works (Chapter 11)

Aside – a statement addressed directly to the audience rather than to another character (Chapter 9)

Backers' audition – a demonstration of a show's songs and plot to potential investors (Chapter 23)

Backlist – the older items of sheet music for sale in a publisher's catalog (Chapter 12)

Ballad – a song genre, often set in strophic form, and usually telling a narrative story of some sort (Chapter 2)

Ballad opera – an eighteenth-century satirical English genre with spoken dialogue and new poetry set to old tunes (Chapter 2)

Barcarole – a piece in compound duple meter with a lyrical melody, styled like a Venetian gondolier song (Chapter 43)

Baritone – a heavier, darker male voice than a tenor, but with a higher range than a bass (Chapter 3)

Baroque – the era of western art music spanning roughly 1600–1750 (Chapter 1)

Bass – the lowest male voice type (Chapter 2)

Beat (= pulse) – the steady background pulsation that occurs in most music (Chapter 1)

Bel canto opera – opera in which the emphasis is on the "beautiful singing" of the voice (Chapter 6)

Benefit – a performance of a show in which the seats are purchased by a charity or an agent for charities (Chapter 22)

Bill – an advertising flyer for a show (Chapter 5); the list of "turns" in a vaudeville show (Chapter 9)

Binary form (= two-part form) – a piece structured in two distinct and contrasting sections, which could be diagrammed as *a-b*. Once the *b* section begins, the *a* melody is not heard again (Chapter 2)

Blackface – the custom of using dark makeup to simulate (and exaggerate) African American facial features (Chapter 8)

Bit – a short, comic sketch, usually unrelated to anything else in a show (Chapter 12)

Blackout – a sudden and total reduction of the stage lights; also the term for "bits" in revues (Chapter 12)

Blue note – a deliberately out-of-tune note added to many jazz performances for expressive purposes (Chapter 18)

Blues – a musical style that laments some unfortunate situation, using swing rhythms and blue notes (Chapter 20)

BMI Musical Theatre Workshop – a training ground for writers, sponsored by Broadcast Music Incorporated (Chapter 37)

Book – the twentieth-century designation for the libretto, or sometimes only the spoken portion of a show (Chapter 13)

Book musical (= book show) – a show with a coherent story line as opposed to a revue (Chapter 14, 22)

Book show – a musical centered on a plot, featuring spoken dialogue interspersed with songs (Chapter 22)

Book song – a number that is tied into a show's plot, often carrying that plot further along (Chapter 16)

Boomer – a hired audience member who cheers wildly in order to stir up audience appreciation (Chapter 20)

Box office advance – (see **Advance**)

Bows (= curtain calls) – the performers' acknowledgment of audience applause at the end of a show (Chapter 20, 23)

Breeches role – a male character whose part is played by a female performer (Chapter 10)

Bridge (= release) – the *b* section of a song form (*a-a-b-a*) (Chapter 16)

Broadway show – a show presented in one of the main venues of the New York theater district (Chapter 10)

Buffo zarzuela – a Spanish genre modeled on Offenbach's opéra-bouffes (Chapter 5)

Burlesque – in its earliest form, a genre devoted to satirizing well-known works (Chapter 7, 9); later, a strip show

Burletta – a three-act comic opera with at least five songs that spoofed historical or legendary stories (Chapter 8)

Cakewalk – a feature of walkarounds in minstrel shows, derived from a southern plantation "challenge dance" in which couples strutted around in imitation of high-society manners; the best mimics won a cake (Chapter 8)

Call-and-response – a musical technique derived from African American slaves, who used to sing work songs featuring a soloist who would sing "calls" to which the other slaves would "respond" (Chapter 8)

Can-can – a risqué French dance in which the chorus line performs high kicks while lifting their skirts (Chapter 5)

Canon (= round) – a structure in which a melody is imitated exactly by a second performer, who starts to present the repetition of the melody before the first performer has reached the end of his or her presentation (Chapter 2)

Cantata – a genre that could be compared to a short opera, usually featuring only a small ensemble of singers (if not just a soloist) and usually unstaged; many cantatas are based on religious subject matter (Chapter 36)

Cast – the group of onstage performers used in a work (Chapter 1)

Castrati – male singers who were castrated at puberty to preserve their high-pitched vocal range (Chapter 1)

Catalog – the sheet music offered by a particular publisher (Chapter 12)

Catalog show (= compilation show) – a theatrical work devised by combining songs or dances previously created and presenting them as a single evening's entertainment, with or without a connective libretto (Chapter 42)

Challenge song – a song, usually comic, that depicts characters debating with each other over some issue (Chapter 22)

Character chorus line – a chorus line consisting of individualized people (Chapter 22)

Character song – a tune designed to reveal the personality of a particular role (Chapter 7)

Characterization – using the drama and music to highlight features of a particular character's personality (Chapter 1)

Charleston rhythm – a syncopated rhythm characteristic of the popular song and dance "The Charleston," consisting of two-note pairs in which the second note anticipates the beat slightly each time (Chapter 18)

Charm song – a number with cute or heartwarming lyrics, performers, and/or movements (Chapter 27, 34)

Chord – a group of three or more notes played simultaneously (Chapter 1)

Choreography – the planned dance steps and movements (Chapter 9)

Chorus – a group of singers (Chapter 1); the repetitive refrain of a verse-chorus form (Chapter 8)

Chorus girl – a female member of a chorus line (Chapter 9)

Chorus line – the nonfeatured performers of a production who sing and/or dance as a group (Chapter 9)

Chorus number – (see **Production number**)

Chromaticism – the use of notes outside the major or minor scale, usually to create tension or exoticism (Chapter 14)

Circuit – a series of geographical stops that touring performers make on a regular basis (Chapter 4)

Classic era – the era of western art music spanning roughly 1750–1815 (Chapter 3)

Coda (= postlude) – instrumental music played at the end of a song, giving the piece a sense of conclusion (Chapter 9)

Coloratura soprano – a high-pitched female voice with considerable flexibility (Chapter 11)

Comédie-ballet – a seventeenth-century French genre featuring humor, spectacle, singing, and dancing (Chapter 2)

Comedy song – a number whose primary purpose is to amuse (Chapter 13)

Comic opera – a Classic-era English genre, usually with spoken dialogue and specially composed music (Chapter 4)

Commedia dell'arte – groups of itinerant singer-actors who portrayed traditional characters in stock scenarios (Chapter 1)

Commission – a paid-in-advance contract to create an artwork (Chapter 2)

Company (= troupe) – a group of theatrical performers (Chapter 4, 7)

Compilation show – (see **Catalog show**)

Composer – the person who writes the music (Chapter 1)

Compound subdivision – a rhythmic device that divides each beat into three equal subpulses (Chapter 7)

Concept album – a recording made of a show before it has been staged (Chapter 32)

Concept musical – a show that is unified by a central idea rather than a linear plot (Chapter 24)

Concert performance – an unstaged presentation of a show with singing and dialogue only (Chapter 24)

Conjunct – a series of notes that are only slightly higher or lower than each other, as if the pitches were moving up or down the rungs of a ladder (Chapter 1)

Coon song – an old term for a song written in African American dialect or with black musical characteristics (Chapter 12)

Costuming – the attire worn by members of the cast in a production (Chapter 9)

Countermelody – a second tune designed to coordinate with a prior tune in nonimitative polyphony (Chapter 11)

Cover – a new recording of a song already released in a performance by someone else (Chapter 42)

Crescendo – a dynamics term indicating that the volume level increases gradually (Chapter 20)

Cue (= stage cue) – a theatrical signal; also a brief instrumental number that contributes to the mood (Chapter 9, 37)

Cue sheet – a list for the conductor of the cues needed from the orchestra by a particular vaudeville performer (Chapter 9)

Curtain calls – (see **Bows**)

Curtain of Act – the last scene before an act ends (Chapter 22)

Cycle – a set of pieces linked by a shared idea or musical motif (Chapter 6)

Dance arranger – the person who creates the music used for the dances in a show; often, the dance music is a type of aural "collage" compiled from melodies of songs in the musical, but sometimes the dance music is original (Chapter 27)

Dance captain – the member of the chorus line who trains new dancers to replace performers who have left the show and who keeps the performances polished after the choreographer has moved on to other projects (Chapter 29)

Dialect – text that tries to recreate the pronunciation habits of a particular ethnic or racial group; African Americans were the most frequently imitated, but other cultural groups were also targeted (Chapter 8)

Diegetic song (= prop song, source music) – a tune that is sung in an onstage situation that mirrors a real-life occasion in which singing genuinely takes place (Chapter 10)

Disjunct – a term describing a series of notes that seem to leap up or down between successive pitches (Chapter 1)

Dissemination – the process of making a show and its music familiar to potential audiences via sales of sheet music, radio and television broadcasts, and recordings (Chapter 13)

Dominant – a pitch or chord that is five steps higher than the tonic pitch or chord (Chapter 31)

Donaldson Awards – dramatic prizes issued annually between 1944 and 1955 by *Billboard Magazine* (Chapter 23)

Dotted note – a rhythmic technique for lengthening certain notes, creating a long–short grouping (Chapter 15)

Drama Desk Awards – awards issued by the New York Drama Desk agency for outstanding New York productions, both on and off Broadway (Chapter 23)

Dramaturg – a writing coach who works with a playwright (Chapter 44)

Dramma giocoso – a hybrid Italian genre, mixing characteristics of opera seria with opera buffa (Chapter 3)

Dream ballet – a theatrical device in which a character's dreams are portrayed by onstage dancers (Chapter 22)

Duo/duet – a piece featuring a pair of performers (Chapter 3)

Dummy lyric – a temporary poem that fits a melody with the proper rhythm and rhyme scheme (Chapter 15)

Duple meter – the organization of steady beats into a strong–weak–strong–weak pattern (Chapter 5)

Dynamic level – the volume at which music is performed (Chapter 3)

Eleven o'clock number – a rousing tune placed near the end of a show (Chapter 22)

Encore – to repeat a well-received number because of audience cheers; also, the repetition itself (Chapter 10)

Ensemble – a group of two or more performers; also a term for the kind of piece they perform (Chapter 3)

Ensemble finale – a concluding section of an act that incorporates multiple singers, each presenting separate material that blends together in nonimitative polyphony (Chapter 3)

Ensemble opera – an opera featuring many groups of singers rather than just soloists singing arias (Chapter 3)

Ensemble show – a work featuring the interworkings of the cast rather than focusing on a star (Chapter 34)

Extravaganza (= spectacle) – a lavish production emphasizing elaborate stage sets and mechanical marvels (Chapter 9)

Equity – (see **Actor's Equity Association**)

Falsetto – a technique of putting the male voice in an artificially high range (Chapter 1)

Fantasia (= olio) – the portion of a minstrel show in which individual performers displayed special abilities (Chapter 8)

Farce – a story with broad humor and often an improbable plot (Chapter 13)

Farce-comedy – a genre featuring specialty acts or turns of various performers, linking them with a loose plot (Chapter 9)

Fermata – a symbol that indicates that a note (or silence) should be sustained longer than usual (Chapter 3)

First run – the performances between a show's opening night and the closing down of the production (Chapter 22)

Fixer (= show doctor) – a person who is called in, just before the opening, to rescue a show in trouble (Chapter 17)

Flop – an unsuccessful show; usually indicating that it failed to recoup the expenses of mounting the production (Chapter 2)

Florentine Camerata – group of artists, writers, and musicians in late sixteenth-century Florence whose experiments with the *stile rappresentativo* led to the development of opera (Chapter 1)

Fly – to raise or lower a curtain, lighting bar, or backdrop (Chapter 37)

Fly floor – the area high above the stage from which some scenery drops or "flies" (Chapter 26)

Flymen – the stagehands who operate the scenery in the fly floor (Chapter 26)

Folk music – a style of music that is usually constructed in simple fashion, deals with issues affecting common people, and often has no known composer, having been passed down through oral tradition (Chapter 19)

Foreshadowing – the appearance of a melody, or hints of it, before its full-fledged presentation in a show (Chapter 39)

Form – the structure or pattern of repetition in a piece of music (Chapter 2)

Four-rhyme – a description for rhyming four-syllable words or phrases: "first of the lot/worst of the lot" (Chapter 21)

Fugue – a compositional technique and structure featuring imitative polyphony as well as independent tunes (Chapter 30)

Género chico – a Spanish genre with a great deal of spoken dialogue and not much singing (Chapter 5)

Genre – a category describing the type of musical presentation (Chapter 1)

Gesamtkunstwerk – "total art work"; Wagner's approach to theatrical works, in which all components—the music, libretto, costumes, stage sets, and so on—were unified to create a whole greater than the individual parts (Chapter 6)

Gift show – a show prepared in honor of someone (Chapter 39)

Grand Guignol – a French theater that specialized in gruesome productions; it lent its name to later shows that featured horrifying onstage violence (Chapter 13)

Great White Way – a nickname for the Broadway theater district (Chapter 10)

Guying – a comedian's habit of breaking away from the dramatic plot and telling jokes directly to the audience (Chapter 13)

Gypsy – a nickname for the itinerant dancers who audition for chorus line after chorus line (Chapter 29)

Gypsy robe – a garment decorated with Broadway memorabilia and passed along to the senior gypsy of the next Broadway show to open as part of a good-luck ritual (Chapter 37)

Gypsy run-through – a final rehearsal (without stage sets or costumes) before a show leaves on its tryout tour; usually presented in front of friends and families of the cast, including the chorus line gypsies (Chapter 33)

Half-step – the smallest possible distance between pitches in western music (Chapter 21)

Harmony – the technique of sounding different pitches together. Orchestral musicians create harmony together all the time; singers sing in harmony less often (Chapter 10)

Heavy book – a show whose staging demands are technically complex (Chapter 39)

Hemiola – the sensation of shifting from an established duple meter to the feeling of triple meter, or vice versa (Chapter 29)

Hit – a successful show, usually measured in financial terms (Chapter 2)

Homophony/homophonic – a texture in which a melody is supported by a subordinate accompaniment (Chapter 2)

Honky-tonk – an early twentieth-century popular style with a repetitive duple-meter accompaniment (Chapter 12)

Hoofer – slang term for a dancer (Chapter 17)

Hymn tune – the melody used for singing certain sacred texts; some hymn tunes came from stage melodies (Chapter 4)

Imitative polyphony – a texture in which one melody is used for successive, overlapping entrances, sounding much like a canon or round (Chapter 2)

Impresario – equivalent to the modern position of producer; the person who organizes the financing and staffing of a theatrical production, often retaining the power to make some of the creative decisions as well (Chapter 11)

Improvisation – a piece or section of music that is "ad libbed"—made up on the spot, during a performance—instead of having been composed ahead of time (Chapter 18)

Incidental music – music for a "straight" play; sometimes inserted songs and sometimes underscoring (Chapter 29)

Integrated – a designation for a show whose songs are appropriate specifically for the situation in which they are heard or for the characters who sing them (Chapter 13)

Interlude – instrumental music played in the middle of a song, without any singing (Chapter 9)

Intermezzo – comic genre performed during the intermissions of an opera seria (Chapter 3)

Interpolation – a song by another composer added to an original score (Chapter 10)

Introduction – instrumental music played at the start of a song, before the singing starts (Chapter 9)

Inversion – the technique of performing a series of pitches in the opposite direction from their initial presentation; for example, notes that ascend would invert to notes that descend (Chapter 16)

Isolations – a jazz dance technique singling out a part of the body, producing rhythmic effects or surprise (Chapter 29)

Jazz – a musical style originating in the twentieth century that emphasizes syncopation and improvisation (Chapter 18)

Jump tune (= rhythm song) – a piece that sustains a clear and prominent pulse, encouraging toe-tapping (Chapter 12)

Key – a set of specified pitches (usually a scale) that determine whether the key is major or minor (Chapter 6, 7)

Key change – (see **Modulation**)

Lap dissolve – a type of stage management in which the audience's attention is drawn to one section of the stage while the set is changed elsewhere on the stage, creating a sense of continuous flow in the story (Chapter 26)

Largo – a slow tempo (Chapter 38)

Lead sheet – written music containing the melody and symbols representing accompanying chords (Chapter 22)

Legs – theatrical slang for curtains (Chapter 37)

Leitmotif – "leading motive"; a short musical phrase associated with a particular character, object, or even idea (Chapter 6)

Librettist – the person who writes the poetry (or, in musical theater, the spoken dialogue) (Chapter 1)

Libretto – the poetry of an opera; later used to mean the spoken dialogue and general plot of musical theater (Chapter 1)

Lieto fine – a "happy ending," usually when applied to a story that traditionally does not end happily (Chapter 1)

Lighting – the science of aiming and diffusing light onto the stage to create various effects (Chapter 9)

List song – a type of comic song whose humor is derived from its long list of related items (Chapter 3)

Love nest ballad – a song in which a couple enjoy being alone with each other in a cozy environment (Chapter 15)

Lyrics – the poetry that serves as the words for a song (Chapter 13)

Lyrical singing – a performance style emphasizing a smooth, graceful approach with a beautiful vocal sound (Chapter 22)

Machinery – the stage equipment that produces much of the visual effect in a theatrical presentation (Chapter 1)

Major mode – the most common type of scale, often conveying an upbeat or positive mood (Chapter 7)

Masque – an English genre with masks, dancing, spoken dialogue, and new texts set to preexisting songs (Chapter 2)

Medium (= performance medium, performing forces) – the combination of instruments and voices needed for a particular work (Chapter 2)

Melisma – a passage of many notes all sung to a single syllable of text (Chapter 6)

Melismatic – a text setting in which a single syllable is sung to many different musical pitches (Chapter 6)

Melodrama – a genre in which the actors speak (or mime) between or during passages of instrumental music (Chapter 9)

Merchandizing – the selling of goods associated with a particular show, capitalizing on that show's popularity (Chapter 11)

Message song – a number that endeavors to win the audience over to a particular point of view (Chapter 26)

Meter (= time signature) – the grouping of beats in a piece of music (Chapter 5)

Metronome – a mechanical device that presents a steady pace for performers to follow (Chapter 2)

Mezzo-soprano – a female voice type that falls between the high-pitched soprano and the low-pitched alto (Chapter 41)

Minor mode – a less common type of scale, often used to convey a dark, somber mood (Chapter 7)

Minstrel show – a genre featuring performers in blackface (whether black or white themselves) who presented a variety of visual and musical entertainments, often satirizing the lifestyle of African Americans (Chapter 8)

Minstrel song – a song designed for performance in a minstrel show; usually upbeat, often humorous, and frequently mocking African American mannerisms and dialect (Chapter 8)

Mixed bill – an entertainment comprised of various sorts of presentations, like vaudeville (Chapter 12)

Mixolydian mode – an unusual scale rarely used in modern music except to produce an "ancient" effect (Chapter 32)

Mode – the kind of scale used in a piece; the mode helps to determine the mood of a piece (Chapter 7)

Modified verse-chorus form – a piece in which certain repetitions of the chorus are omitted (Chapter 10)

Modulation (= key change) – the technique of changing keys in the course of a single piece (Chapter 16)

Monophony/monophonic – a musical texture in which a melody is presented without any accompaniment (Chapter 2)

Moritat – a type of ballad sung at German street fairs, describing the misdeeds of legendary criminals (Chapter 24)

Motif – a short, melodic or rhythmic phrase, usually just long enough to be recognizable (Chapter 6)

MTV video – a filmed excerpt of a show intended to advertise that show (Chapter 39)

Music drama – a work written in accordance with Wagner's principle of *Gesamtkunstwerk* (Chapter 6)

Music hall – an English entertainment similar to vaudeville, but with greater emphasis on music (Chapter 9)

Musical comedy – a genre presented in modern costume with believable dialogue and popular tunes (Chapter 7, 9, 12)

Musical play – a genre label intended to underscore the integrated nature of a work's story and music (Chapter 12)

Musical quotation – the insertion of a recognizable motif from another familiar tune (Chapter 12)

Musical scene – a portion of a show in which the characters alternate between singing and speaking (Chapter 25)

Musical theater – a genre label for sung dramatic works, usually more commercial than opera (Chapter 1)

Narrator – a person who explains the current stage scene or its background to the audience (Chapter 24)

Nationalism – a spirit of patriotic pride conveyed in music (Chapter 6)

Neologism – a newly invented word, often used for comic effect (Chapter 7)

New York Drama Critics' Circle – reviewers from most of New York's newspapers, magazines, and wire services, who issue annual dramatic awards (Chapter 23)

New York Outer Critics' Circle – reviewers from out-of-town publications who evaluate Broadway productions and issue annual dramatic awards (Chapter 23)

Nonet – a piece featuring nine performers (Chapter 3)

Nonimitative polyphony – a texture in which two or more different melodies are heard simultaneously (Chapter 3)

Nonplot show – a production without a real story to guide the action (Chapter 32)

Nonstandard form – a form with clear-cut repetition that does not follow a standardized pattern (Chapter 3)

Note (= pitch) – a single musical sound (Chapter 1)

Nut – a Broadway slang term for the weekly costs of running a show (Chapter 39)

Obie Awards – awards presented by the *Village Voice* magazine to off-Broadway productions (Chapter 23)

Octave – the span from a scale's lowest note up to the point at which the scale begins to start over (Chapter 14)

Octet – a piece featuring eight performers (Chapter 3)

Off-Broadway – smaller theaters in New York situated outside of the main Broadway district (Chapter 10)

Off-Off-Broadway – an unconventional New York location used as a theatrical venue (Chapter 10)

Olio – (see **Fantasia**)

Olivier Award – known as a Larry, this is the British equivalent to the American Tony Award (Chapter 40)

One-rhyme – a description for rhyming single-syllable words: "thirst/worst" (Chapter 21)

Onomatopoeia – a word that imitates the type of sound produced by whatever is being discussed (Chapter 11)

Opening night (= premiere) – the first official performance of a show (Chapter 22)

Opera – strictly speaking, a genre term for an Italian-language theatrical presentation with continuous singing. The same genre label is often applied to works in other languages and works with spoken dialogue (Chapter 1)

Opéra-bouffe – a nineteenth-century French comic genre with an emphasis on social satire and dancing (Chapter 5)

Opera buffa – "comic opera"; an Italian genre, at its prime during the eighteenth century (Chapter 3)

Opéra-comique – a French genre presented at fairs, using preexisting music of two types: the *pièces/comédies en vaudeville* set their texts to folk songs; the *pièces à ariettes* employed Italian arias for the tunes (Chapter 2)

Opera house – a venue designed specifically for the performance of operas (Chapter 1)

Opera seria – "serious opera"; Italian genre of the eighteenth century (Chapter 3)

Operetta – a comic genre, usually in German or English, often featuring skilled singers in a fanciful plot (Chapter 5, 6, 7)

Option – a contract with a time limitation, often pertaining to performance or adaptation rights (Chapter 17)

Oratorio – a genre similar to opera, but usually based on a religious topic and performed unstaged (Chapter 36)

Orchestra – an ensemble of instrumentalists, usually performing accompanimental or introductory music (Chapter 1)

Orchestra seating – the "floor-level" seats for the audience; usually the largest block of seats in a theater (Chapter 13)

Orchestration – the process of assigning instruments to play various supportive roles in a tune (Chapter 19)

Orchestrator – the person who creates the orchestrations (Chapter 27)

Original cast album – a recording made with a show's initial performers (Chapter 22)

Original score – music composed for a specific show, not borrowed from a preexisting source (Chapter 9)

Ornamentation – a singer's embellishments of a melodic line, usually added to show off his or her virtuosity (Chapter 1)

Ostinato – a repetitive pattern (Chapter 15)

Outer Critics' Circle – (see **New York Outer Critics' Circle**)

Overture – introductory music played by the orchestra before the curtain rises at the start of the show (Chapter 2)

Pan – an extremely negative review (Chapter 36)

Pantomime – initially, a ballet depicting a mythological or imaginary story (Chapter 8); sometimes a play that is unspoken, acted solely by gestures accompanied by orchestral music (Chapter 9)

Papering the house – giving away free tickets so that a performance is well attended (Chapter 11)

Parlor song – a sentimental song intended for private entertainment; an ancestor of Tin Pan Alley songs (Chapter 8)

Pasticcio – a show that has a score made up of selections by multiple composers (Chapter 9)

Pastiche – a deliberate attempt to mimic an earlier or nontheatrical style of music (Chapter 36)

Patter song – a type of singing in which the text is delivered very rapidly for comic effect (Chapter 2, 3, 7)

Pentatonic scale – a set of notes consisting of five different pitches, often associated with Asian cultures (Chapter 7)

Perfect pitch – (see **Absolute pitch**)

Performance medium – (see **Medium**)

Performance practice – a modern concern for performing a piece of music in much the same way it was performed when first written (Chapter 1)

Performing forces – (see **Medium**)

Piracy – performing a show without permission and without paying proper royalties (Chapter 7)

Pit orchestra – the instrumental ensemble that sits in the depressed "pit" just in front of the stage (Chapter 18)

Pitch – (see **Note**)

Plantation song – a later type of minstrel song that moved away from dialect and mocking humor and more toward the sentimental nostalgia of parlor songs (Chapter 8)

Playwrights Horizons – a New York theatrical group supporting new, experimental plays and musicals (Chapter 42)

Pop song form – (see **Song form**)

Postlude – (see **Coda**)

Premiere – (see **Opening night**)

Preview – a rehearsal of a show in front of a paying audience (Chapter 31)

Presto – a tempo term meaning very fast (Chapter 38)

Prima donna – the leading woman in an opera (Chapter 1)

Primo uomo – the leading man in an opera (Chapter 1)

Princess Shows – a series of musicals written for New York's Princess Theater (Chapter 13)

Principle of Increasing Animation – an eighteenth-century desire to present ever-shorter, faster rhythmic values as a piece progresses (Chapter 2)

Producer – equivalent to the older term of impresario; the person who organizes the financing and staffing of a theatrical production, often retaining the power to make some of the creative decisions as well (Chapter 11)

Production number (= chorus number) – a piece featuring most or all of the cast (Chapter 9, 16, 25)

Program – a printed brochure naming a show's creative team and performers, along with a listing of the production's scenes and musical numbers (Chapter 14); a "story" associated with instrumental music (Chapter 13)

Programmatic – instrumental music that seeks to convey incidents in an associated storyline (Chapter 13)

Prop – a portable object used to support a scene (Chapter 7)

Prop song – (see **Diegetic song**)

Property – theatrical subject matter; the source on which a dramatic story is based (Chapter 13)

Proscenium – the front wall—facing the audience—that surrounds the stage (Chapter 20)

Pulse – (see **Beat**) – the steady background pulsation that occurs in most music (Chapter 1)

Quadruple meter – the organization of steady beats into a // strong–weak–not-as-strong–weak // strong–weak–not-as-strong–weak // pattern (Chapter 5)

Quartet – a piece featuring four performers (Chapter 3)

Querelle des Bouffons **(= War of the Buffoons)** – the mid-eighteenth-century debate between the merits of serious French opera and comic genres such as the Italian opera buffa (Chapter 3)

Quintet – a piece featuring five performers (Chapter 3)

Quodlibet – a polyphonic number constructed of two independent melodies performed simultaneously (Chapter 20)

Ragtime – a musical style heavily dependent on syncopation for its rhythmic energy and appeal (Chapter 12)

Range – the span of notes, from low to high, performed by a singer or an instrument (Chapter 14)

Rave – an extremely positive review (Chapter 36)

Recitative – a speechlike manner of singing, usually without any steady beat and with limited accompaniment (Chapter 1)

Recognition scene – an event in which a disguised or absent character is revealed or a key fact is disclosed (Chapter 14)

Refrain – a portion of a song that reappears with the same melody *and* words, such as the chorus in a verse–chorus form (Chapter 8)

Rehearsal pianist – a keyboardist who accompanies the singers (in lieu of the orchestra) during rehearsals (Chapter 13)

Release (see **Bridge**) – the *b* section of a song form (*a-a-b-a*) (Chapter 16)

Reprise – the repetition of a song later in the same show (Chapter 14)

Review – a critic's published evaluation of a new show (Chapter 36)

Revival – a new production of a show after the original production of a show has closed (Chapter 5)

Revue – a mixed-bill presentation in which a set cast of performers present the various entertainments; sometimes the skits are organized around a specific theme, such as a satirical re-examination of the previous year's events (Chapter 12)

Rhythm song – (see **Jump tune**)

Ritardando – a slowing down of the tempo (Chapter 6)

Road company – a troupe that takes a particular production on tour (Chapter 13)

Rock – a musical style characterized by distorted electric guitars, electric bass, and drum set, with a steady rhythm—usually in quadruple meter, with a heavy backbeat (Chapter 32)

Rock opera – a musical theater work using the musical style of rock, often in a sung-through format (Chapter 36)

Romantic Era/Romanticism – the musical era ranging from around 1815 to the end of the nineteenth century (Chapter 6)

Romanza – a love song that creates a romantic, lyrical atmosphere (Chapter 9)

Rondo form – a structure that can be diagrammed as *a-b-a-c-a* (Chapter 26)

Round – (see **Canon**)

Rounded binary form – a structure that can be diagrammed as *a-a-b-a'-b-a'* (Chapter 30)

Royalty – a payment for the privilege of performing a show (Chapter 7)

Run – the number of times a particular show is presented (Chapter 4)

Sainete – a short Spanish work intended for performance after a main work (Chapter 5)

SATB chorus – a vocal ensemble consisting of all four basic voice types: soprano, alto, tenor, bass (Chapter 8)

Savoy Operas – the Gilbert and Sullivan operettas presented at the Savoy Theatre; sometimes the label is applied to all of Gilbert and Sullivan's collaborative works or even to any other work performed at the Savoy Theatre (Chapter 7)

Savoyard – a member of the theatrical company that performed at the Savoy Theatre (Chapter 7)

Scale – a series of conjunct pitches, usually all belonging to a particular mode or key (Chapter 3)

Scene – a subsection of an act, sometimes distinguished by the arrival and departure of characters onstage (Chapter 3)

Scene change song – a number designed to be performed in front of the curtain while the stage scenery is changed behind the curtain, without interrupting the flow of the show (Chapter 16)

Scenery show – a production combining elaborate stage sets and effects with operetta characteristics (Chapter 10)

Score – the written music contributed by a composer (Chapter 1)

Season – the theatrical year, which ranges from June to May (Chapter 13)

Septet – a piece featuring seven performers (Chapter 3)

Sequence – the successive repetition of a musical motif at a higher or lower pitch level (Chapter 31)

Set (= stage set) – the onstage backdrops and furniture framing the performers in a particular scene (Chapter 9)

Sextet – a piece featuring six performers (Chapter 3)

Shadow show – a show in which puppets "acted" behind a semitransparent sheet in front of a bright light (Chapter 8)

Sheet music – the printed version of a song from a show (Chapter 12)

Show doctor – (see **Fixer**)

Show girl – (see **Chorus girl**)

Show tune form – a pattern diagrammed as *a-b-a-c* (Chapter 14)

Showstopper – a song, dance, or production number that is received so enthusiastically by an audience that their continued applause "stops" the show; sometimes the number must be encored before the show can resume (Chapter 13)

Sight gag – a visual display intended to amuse (Chapter 7)

Sight-read – to perform without prior rehearsal (Chapter 3)

Simple subdivision – a sensation that each beat of a piece of music can be divided into two equal half-pulses (Chapter 7)

Singing style – the vocal setting; initially, singing styles consisted of techniques like recitative and aria, but later expanded to include other approaches such as rock, jazz, and rap (Chapter 1)

Singspiel – a German-language genre with spoken dialogue. (Chapter 2)

Sleeper – an unpromising show that unexpectedly becomes a hit (Chapter 32)

Slider – a stagehand who propels scenery horizontally on and off the stage (Chapter 26)

Soliloquy – a speech (or song) by a character in the manner of someone musing his or her thoughts aloud (Chapter 3)

Solo – a piece featuring a single performer (Chapter 3)

Song-and-dance show – a common description of musical comedies in the first half of the twentieth century (Chapter 21)

Song form (= pop song form, 32-bar form) – a structure diagrammed as *a-a-b-a* (Chapter 16)

Song-plugger – a person who promotes the items in a publisher's catalog (Chapter 12)

Soprano – the highest singing voice of adult females (or castrated males) (Chapter 1)

Source music – (see **Diegetic song**)

Specialty act (= turn) – the featured number presented by each performer (or group) in a vaudeville show (Chapter 9)

Spectacle – (see **Extravaganza**)

Spinning wheel song – a compound duple tune in which a woman sings about her beloved (Chapter 9)

SRO – (see **Standing room only**)

Stage cue – (see **Cue**)

Stage set – (see **Set**)

Stagehand – a worker who moves scenery, pulls curtains, and assists in the mechanical operation of a show (Chapter 7, 26)

Standard – a song that has been a favorite for a long time (Chapter 22)

Standing room only (= SRO) – a situation in which a show that has sold all seats offers a few discounted "standing" locations (Chapter 35)

Star entrance – a deliberate attempt to build the audience's anticipation of the leading performer's first appearance on stage, resulting in applause that is not in response to the dramatic story or to any performed number (Chapter 13)

Star turn – a number designed to feature a leading performer's special abilities (Chapter 12)

Star vehicle – a show written to showcase the talents of a particular performer (Chapter 11)

Stile rappresentativo – "dramatic style"; a type of singing that followed the natural pacing of speech (Chapter 1)

Strophe – one presentation of *a* in a strophic form; sometimes called a verse (Chapter 4)

Strophic form – a pattern of repetition diagrammed as *a-a-a* and so on (Chapter 4)

Subdivision – the smaller increments of time equally dividing each beat of a piece of music (Chapter 7)

Subdominant – a pitch or chord that is four steps higher than the tonic pitch or chord (Chapter 31)

Subject – the main melodic theme of a fugue (Chapter 30)

Subtext – a situation where there is a deeper or double meaning to the words being sung or spoken (Chapter 7)

Succès d'estime – a show that is admired by critics but fails to become popular (Chapter 32)

Sung-through – a theatrical work where all (or nearly all) of the dialogue is sung (Chapter 6)

Swing rhythm – a rhythmic technique associated with jazz in which the first note in a pair is elongated and the second note shortened in a sing-song style, producing a compound meter effect (Chapter 18)

Syllabic – a text setting in which each syllable of the poetry is sung to a single note of music (Chapter 6)

Syncopation – a rhythmic device in which a stressed or accented note occurs on a weak beat or between beats (Chapter 8)

Tableau vivant – a staging in which the characters assume the poses of the figures in a famous artwork (Chapter 43)

Tag – an abrupt change in the music at the end of a section, much like a coda at the end of a piece (Chapter 39)

Take – a slang term for the money received from ticket sales (Chapter 7)

Techno-rap – a style with primarily spoken lyrics against a heavily synthesized electronic accompaniment (Chapter 42)

Tempo – the speed of a piece of music (Chapter 2)

Tenor – the label for the highest naturally occurring male voice type (Chapter 1)

Ternary form – a pattern diagrammed as *a-b-a* (Chapter 9)

Text expression – the desire to write music that is appropriate to the meaning of the poetry (Chapter 1)

Text setting – the relationship of notes to syllables in vocal music (Chapter 6)

Texture – the way in which melody (with or without accompaniment, etc.) is incorporated in a piece (Chapter 2, 3)

Theater – a venue for a seated audience to view a staged (or screened) presentation (Chapter 1)

Theme and variations form – a structure that can be diagrammed as *a-a'-a"* and so on (Chapter 22)

32-bar form – (see **Song form**)

Three-rhyme – a description for rhyming three-syllable words or phrases: "first of all/worst of all" (Chapter 21)

Through-composed – music written without any clear-cut repetition (Chapter 3)

Timbre (= tone color) – the unique sound of each instrument and voice type (Chapter 3)

Time signature – (see **Meter**)

Tin Pan Alley – an area of New York that published most popular songs in the first half of the twentieth century (Chapter 12)

Tonadilla – a short, comic Spanish work performed between acts of another work, like the Italian intermezzo (Chapter 5)

Tone color – (see **Timbre**) – the unique sound of each instrument and voice type (Chapter 3)

Tonic – the first note of a scale or the first key in a piece that later modulates (Chapter 31, 34)

Tony Awards – annual theatrical prizes for Broadway productions, presented by the American Theatre Wing (Chapter 23)

Trill – a rapid oscillation between two adjacent pitches; a type of ornamentation (Chapter 1)

Trio – a piece featuring three performers (Chapter 3)

Triple meter – the organization of steady beats into a strong-weak-weak–strong-weak-weak pattern (Chapter 5)

Triple Play Award – a special prize devised by ASCAP to congratulate creative artists with three Broadway works playing simultaneously with three works in London's West End (Chapter 39)

Troupe (= company) – a group of theatrical performers (Chapter 4, 7)

Truck – a movable platform holding components of a stage set (Chapter 41)

Trunk song – a older tune written by a composer which has not yet found a place within a show (Chapter 16)

Tryout tour – a preliminary trip to some out-of-town location, giving a new show a chance to play in front of paying audiences before facing New York critics (Chapter 11)

Tuner – *Variety*'s nickname for musicals (in contrast to "straight," or spoken, plays) (Chapter 21)

Turn – (see **Specialty act**)

12-bar blues – a structural pattern in many blues songs in which the performers follow a standardized series of chords for 12 bars, at which point the pattern repeats. The poetic rhyme scheme is often *a-a-b* in the 12-bar blues (Chapter 39)

Two-part form – (see **Binary form**)

Two-rhyme – a description for rhyming two-syllable words or phrases: "thirsting/bursting" (Chapter 21)

Two-tempo aria – a solo song with subsections in two contrasting tempos (Chapter 3)

Underscoring – instrumental music that is played during spoken dialogue, enhancing the mood of the scene, in the manner of the nineteenth-century melodrama or the modern film score (Chapter 16)

Understudy – an actor who learns the lines and movements (blocking) for a featured performer so there is a replacement on hand if the featured performer is unable to perform (Chapter 27)

Unison – two or more singers (or instruments) performing the same thing at the same time (Chapter 2)

Unstaged – a show presented in "concert" version, with the performers standing still to sing their parts rather than acting out their roles (Chapter 7)

Variety – (see **Vaudeville**)

Variety – a magazine devoted to the activities of American theater (Chapter 16)

Vaudeville – a type of stage entertainment consisting of many short, unconnected presentations ("turns") by a large array of performers depicting a wide variety of skills, many unrelated to music (Chapter 9)

Verismo – "realism"; a genre label for some late nineteenth-century Italian operas depicting real-life suffering (Chapter 6)

Verse – one presentation of *a* in a strophic form; each verse (each recurrence of *a*) has new text but repeats the same music (Chapter 4); the introductory, nonrecurring portion of many popular songs (Chapter 11); the portions of a song in verse-chorus form that contain new text to repetitive music (Chapter 8)

Verse-chorus form – a pattern diagrammed as *a-B-a-B-a-B* and so on, in which the *a* verses have differing text (but the same melody) each time, while the *B* choruses repeat the melody *and* words. Originally, an actual chorus of voices sang the chorus sections, while soloists sang the verses (Chapter 8)

Viennese operetta – an Austrian genre in which silly stories poked fun at current events; much of the singing was virtuosic, but the operettas put a great deal of emphasis on dancing as well (Chapter 6)

Virtuosa/virtuoso – a highly skilled performer (Chapter 1)

Vision song – a number in which a character sings about something imaginary in such a way that either the singer starts to believe that the vision is real or another character is drawn into believing in the vision (Chapter 25)

Vocal introduction – a sung prefatory passage that differs from the remainder of the song; often called the verse (Chapter 11)

Walk-around – a segment of a minstrel show featuring the entire cast in a choral tune with brief solo features for the individual performers, who competed for the audience's approval (Chapter 8)

Waltz – a dance in triple meter, notorious at first for the intimate contact between the dancers (Chapter 6)

Want song – a tune in which a character expresses an inner longing; something he or she "wants" (Chapter 31)

War of the Buffoons – (see *Querelle des Bouffons*)

West End – London's theater district, equivalent to New York's Broadway (Chapter 21)

Word-painting – a type of text expression in which the music tries to create a literal depiction of a particular word's meaning (Chapter 16)

Workshop – a trial presentation of a fledgling show in an informal atmosphere; sometimes used as a verb (Chapter 33)

Zarzuela – a Spanish theatrical genre whose characteristics have changed over the years; usually, a *zarzuela* contains spoken dialogue, some Spanish folk music, and a certain amount of choral singing (Chapter 5)

CREDITS

Chapter 10
pp. 53–54: G. Schirmer,   York 1891; © renewed by Reginald de Koven in 1919.

Chapter 11
p. 60: Score Published by M. Witmark & Sons, New York, c. 1910.

Chapter 12
pp. 67–68: Score Published by Thomas L. Riis, The Music and Scripts of In Dahomey; **p. 68**: Score Published by F. A. Mills [n.p.], 1901; all rights controlled by CBS Robbins Catalog.

Chapter 13
p. 74: The "Trio of Musical Fame" (Anonymous, but attributed to many to George S. Kaufman, NY Times; quoted in Davis, Lee. Bolton and Wodehouse and Kern: The Men Who Made Musical Comedy. New York: James H. Heineman, 1993. p. 171.

Chapter 14
p. 78: "Indian Love Call," by Rudolf Friml, Otto Harbach & Oscar Hammerstein II. © 1924 by Bambalina Music Publishing Company. Warner Bros. Inc. and Bill/Bob Publishing Co. in the United States. Copyright renewed. All rights on behalf of Bambalina Music Publishing Co. administered by Williamson Music. All rights on behalf of Bill/Bob Publishing Co. administered by The Songwriters Guild of America. International copyright secured. All rights reserved. Used by permission; **pp. 78–79**: Score Published © 1926 by B. Feldman, London.

Chapter 15
p. 83: © 1924 (renewed) Irving Casear Music Corp. (ASCAP) and WB Music Corp. (ASCAP). All rights administered by WB Music Corp. All rights reserved. Used by permission. Warner Bros. Publications U.S., Inc., Miami, FL 33014.

Chapter 16
pp. 89–90: ©1927 (renewed) PolyGram Int'l Publishing, Inc.

Chapter 17
pp. 95–96: © 1941 (renewed) Chappell & Co., Inc. (ASCAP). All rights reserved. Used by permission. Warner Bros. Publications U.S. Inc., Miami, FL 33014.

Chapter 20
p. 113: "Supper Time" by Irving Berlin. © 1933 by Irving Berlin. © Copyright Renewed. International Copyright Secured. All rights reserved. Reprinted by permission.

Chapter 21
pp. 115, 117: ©1934 (renewed) by WB Music Corp. (ASCAP). All rights reserved. Used by permission. Warner Bros. Publications U.S. Inc., Miami, FL.

Chapter 22
p. 120: (Dec. 26, 1940; Brooks Atkinson; New York Times); **p. 121**: (Revival Jan. 3, 1952; Brooks Atkinson; New York Times); **p. 126**: ©1941 and 1982 by Chappell & Co. Inc. NY; **p. 127**: "Anything You Can Do," by Irving Berlin. © 1946 by Irving Berlin. © Copyright Renewed. International Copyright Secured. All rights reserved. Reprinted by permission.

Chapter 23
p. 129: Quoted in Schwartz, Charles. Cole porter: A Biography. New York: The Dial Press, 1977, p. 228; Quoted in Suskin, Steven, Opening Night on Broadway, New York: Schirmer Books, 1990, p 625; **p. 130**: Quoted in Suskin, Steven, Opening Night on Broadway, New York: Schirmer Books, 1990, p. 369; **p. 134**: Quoted from "The Complete Lyrics of Cole Porter," edited by Robert Kimball. Published by Da Capo Press, 1992. © 1949 by Chappell & Co.

Chapter 24
p. 139: Published by Weill-Brecht Harms Co.; New York; English translation by Marc Bernstein.

Chapter 25
p. 145: "The Surrey with The Fringe On Top" Copyright ©1943 by Williamson Music, Inc. Copyright renewed. International copyright secured. All rights reserved. Used by permission.

Chapter 26
pp. 152–153: "What's the Use of Wond'rin," Copyright © 1945 by Williamson Music. Copyright renewed. International copyright secured. All rights reserved. Used by permission.; **p. 153**: "Bali Ha'I." Copyright © 1949 by Richard Rodgers and Oscar Hammerstein II. Copyright renewed. Williamson Music owner of publication and allied rights throughout the World. International copyright secured. All rights reserved. Used by permission.

Chapter 27
pp. 160–161: Copyright © 1951 by Richard Rodgers and Oscar Hammerstein II. Copyright renewed. Williamson Music owner of publication and allied rights throughout the world. International copyright secured. All rights reserved.; **pp. 161–163**: "Do-Re-Mi," by Richard Rodgers and Oscar Hammerstein II. Copyright © 1959 by Richard Rodgers and Oscar Hammerstein II. Copyright renewed. Williamson Music owner of publication and allied rights throughout the World. International copyright secured. All rights reserved. Used by permission.

Chapter 28
pp. 170–171: © 1947 (renewed 1975) by Allan Jay Lerner and Frederick Lowe. World rights assigned to Chappell & Co. and EMI U Catalog (Publishing) and Warner Bros. Publications U.S. (Print). All rights reserved. Used by permission. Warner Bros. Publications U.S. Inc., Miami, FL 33014; **p. 171**: © 1956 (renewed) Chappell & Co. (ASCAP). All rights reserved. Used by permission. Warner Bros. Publications U.S. Inc., Miami, FL 33014.

Chapter 29
p. 172: Quoted in Henderson, Amy, and Dwight Blocker Bowers. Red, Hot, and Blue: A Smithsonian Salute to the American Musical. Washington and London: The National Portrait Gallery and The National Museum of American History, in association with the Smithsonian Institution Press, 1996, p. 176; **p. 173**: Quoted in Burton, Humphrey. Leonard Bernstein. New York: Doubleday, 1994, p. 135; **p. 174**: Quoted in Suskin, Steven, Opening Night on Broadway, New York: Schirmer Books, 1990, p. 695; **pp. 178–180**: © G. Schirmer & Chappell & Co., NY.

Chapter 30
p. 183: Quoted in Zadan, Craig. Sondheim & Co.: The Authorized, behind-the-scenes story of the making of Stephen Sondheim's musicals. Second Edition. New York: Harper & Row, 1986, p. 51; **pp. 184–185**: Quoted in Suskin, Steven, Opening Night on Broadway, New York: Schirmer Books, 1990, p. 272; **p. 185**: Quoted in Suskin, Steven, Opening Night on Broadway, New York: Schirmer Books, 1990, p. 325; **p. 188**: © 1959 (renewed) Stratford Music Corporation (ASCAP) and Williamson Music, Inc. (ASCAP). All rights administered by Chappell & Co., Inc. All rights reserved. Used by permission. Warner Bros. Publications U.S. Inc., Miami, FL 33014; **pp. 188–189**: © 1950 Frank Music Corp.

Chapter 31
p. 191: Quoted in Suskin, Steven, Opening Night on Broadway, New York: Schirmer Books, 1990, p. 462; **p. 194**: From Adler, Richard, The Pajama Game (libretto), New York: Random House, 1954, p. 3; **p. 196**: © 1956 Frank Music Corp.; **p. 196–197**: © 1967 (renewed) Chappell & Co. (ASCAP). All rights reserved. Used by permission. Warner Bros. Publications U.S. Inc., Miami, LF 33014.

Chapter 32
pp. 203–204: © 1966, 1969 by Sherman Edwards. Reprinted by permission of 1776 Music, Inc.

Chapter 33
p. 209: Quoted in Zadan, Craig. Sondheim & Co.: The Authorized, behind-the-scenes story of the making of Stephen Sondheim's musicals. Second Edition. New York: Harper & Row, 1986, p. 94; Quoted in Suskin, Steven, Opening Night on Broadway, New York: Schirmer Books, 1990, p. 60; **pp. 211–212**: © 1962 (renewed) Burthen Music Company, Inc. (ASCAP). All rights administered by Chappell & Co. (ASCAP). All rights reserved. Used by permission. Warner Bros. Publications U.S. Inc., Miami, FL 33014.

Chapter 34
p. 214: Quoted in Suskin, Steven, Opening Night on Broadway, New York: Schirmer Books, 1990, p. 607–8; **p. 215**: Quoted in Suskin, Steven, Opening Night on Broadway, New York: Schirmer Books, 1990, p. 209; **pp. 217–218**: "A Trip to the Library," by Sheldon Harnick and Jerry Bock. Copyright © 1962 (Renewed 1990) Mayerling Productions Ltd. (Administered by R&H Music) and Jerry Bock Enterprises for the United States and Alley Music Corporation, Trio Music Company, and to Jerry Bock Enteprises for the world outside of the United States. Used by permission all rights reserved; **p. 218**: "Do You Love Me," from the musical "Fiddler on the Roof." Words by Sheldon Harnick, music by Jerry Bock. © 1964 (Renewed) Mayerling Productions Ltd. (Administered by R&H Music) and Jerry Bock Enterprises for the United States and Alley Music Corporation, Trio Music Company and to Jerry Bock Enterprises for the world outside of the United States. Used by permission. All rights reserved.

Chapter 35
p. 221: Quoted in Suskin, Steven, More Opening Night on Broadway, New York: Schirmer Books, 1997, p. 127; **p. 225**: © 1966 Alley Music Corporation and Trio Music Company, Inc. Copyright renewed. Used by permission. All rights reserved; **pp. 225–227**: © 1975 Unichappell Music Inc. (BMI) and Kander & Ebb, Inc. All rights administered by Unichappell Music Inc. All rights reserved. Used by permission. Warner Bros. Publications U.S. Inc., Miami, FL 33014.

Chapter 36
p. 229: Newspaper Review of Joseph and the Amazing Technicolor Dreamcoat (May 19, 1968; Derek Jewell, The Sunday Times, p. 57 - London); **p. 231**: Newspaper Interview with Andrew Lloyd Webber (Oct. 31, 1971; Guy Flatley, The New York Times, p. 34); Quoted in Suskin, Steven, More Opening Night on Broadway, New York: Schirmer Books, 1997, p. 491; **p. 234**: © 1970 – Leeds Music, London & NY; **pp. 234–235**: © 1979 Leeds Music Corporation.

Chapter 37
p. 241: Published by Wren Music Corp.

Chapter 38
p. 244: Quoted in Suskin, Steven, More Opening Night on Broadway, New York: Schirmer Books, 1997, p. 193; Quoted in Suskin, Steven, More Opening Night on Broadway, New York: Schirmer Books, 1997, p. 191; **p. 245**: Quoted in Suskin, Steven, More Opening Night on Broadway, New York: Schirmer Books, 1997, p. 535, 538; **pp. 249–250**: © 1970 - Range Road Music Inc. - Quartet Music Inc. and Rilting Music Inc. All rights administered by Herald Square Music Inc. Used by permission. All rights reserved; **pp. 250–252**: © 1973 (renewed) Revelation Music Publishing Corp. and Rilting Music, Inc. All rights reserved. Used by permission. Warner Bros. Publications U.S. Inc., Miami, FL 33014.

Chapter 39
p. 254: Quoted in Walsh, Michael. Andrew Lloyd Webber, His Life and Works: A Critical Biography. New York: Abrams, 1989, p. 125; **p. 258**: © 1980 The Really Useful Company, Ltd & Set Copyrights Ltd. (text); **pp. 258–259**: © 1987 The Really Useful Company, Ltd.

Chapter 40
p. 263: The Washington Post, Dec. 13, 1996, p. C-1; **p. 264**: Quoted in Walsh, Michael. Andrew Lloyd Webber, His Life and Works: A Critical Biography. New York: Abrams, 1989, p. 128, 165, 175, 204; New York Times, April 9, 1990, pg. C-11, 2; **p. 267**: © 1986 The Really Useful Group, Ltd.; **pp. 267–268**: © 1993 The Really Useful Group, Ltd.

Chapter 41
p. 276: © 1980 Editions Musicales / 1986 – Alain Boublil Music Ltd.; © 1987 / 1991 Alain Boublil Music Ltd; c/o Stephen Tenenbaum & Co, NY.

Chapter 42
p. 279: © 1977 United Artists Corporation. All rights controlled by EMI Unart Catalog Inc. (Publishing) and Warner Bros. Publications U.S. Inc. (Print). All rights reserved. Used by permission. Warner Bros. Publications U.S. Inc., Miami, FL 33014; **p. 283–284**: © 1984, 1986 – 3 Knights Ltd.

Chapter 43
p. 285: Quoted in Zadan, Craig. Sondheim & Co.: The Authorized, behind-the-scenes story of the making of Stephen Sondheim's musicals. Second Edition. New York: Harper & Row, 1986, p. 313; **p. 287**: Quoted in Citron, Stephen. Sondheim and Lloyd Webber: The New Musical. Oxford: Oxford University Press, 2001, p. 306; **pp. 291–292**: © 1988 Rilting Music, Inc. All rights administered by WB Music Corp. All rights reserved. Used by permission. Warner Brothers Publications U.S. Inc. Miami, FL 33014; **pp. 292–294**: © Rilting Music, Inc. All rights administered by WB Music Corp. All rights reserved. Used by permission. Warner Bros. Publications U.S. Inc., Miami, FL 33014.

Chapter 44
pp. 300–301: © 1996 – Finster & Lucy Music Ltd.

Chapter 45
p. 302: by Pacheco, Patrick. "Start Spreading the New." Los Angeles Times (August 6, 2000): Calendar, 5, 72–3; By Marks, Peter. "If It's a Musical, It Was Probably a Movie." The New York Times (April 14, 2002), Section 2, 1.

INDEX

A cappella, 220–21
Aarons, Alex A., 80, 102
ABBA, 260, 277, 278, 282
Abbott, George, 92, 102, 120, 165, 172–73, 184, 193–94, 207–8; Directs his first musical, 92; Impact of, 92
Absolute pitch. *See* Perfect pitch
Academy Awards: Broadway equivalent, 133; First musical screenplay to win, 166; Hamlisch wins three, 237; Record number of (*Gigi*), 168; Won by stage writers, 279
Accelerando. *See* Tempo
Accent, 40
Accompaniment, 1
Act, 12
Act, The (Kander and Ebb), 222
"Actor Lady, A" (Musical Example 15). See *In Dahomey*
Actor's Equity, 133, 136, 278; and Cohan, 65; and gypsy robes, 238; and *Miss Saigon*, 273; and *Phantom*, 262
Adam, Adolphe, 19
Adams, Lee, 199
Adler, Richard, 92, 185, 193–94, "Rags to Riches," 193. See also *Damn Yankees; The Pajama Game*
Adonis (Rice), 45
Advance man, 40
Advance ticket sales, 70, 132, 150, 165, 168, 193, 231, 262, 271, 273
Advertising, 32, 66, 87, 138; Effect of newspaper strike, 181; MTV video, 254; Newspaper, 236; Radio, 92, 236; Recording, 72; Television, 168, 174, 236, 237
AEA (American Equity Association). *See* Actor's Equity
Africana (Heywood), 104
"After the Ball." See *A Trip to Chinatown*
"Agony" (Musical Example 60). See *Into the Woods*
"Ah! Sweet Mystery of Life." See *Naughty Marietta*
Ahrens, Lynn, 298. See also *Anastasia; Lucky Stiff; A Man of No Importance; My Favorite Year; Once on This Island; Ragtime; Seussical*
Aida (John and Rice), 63, 280, 303
Aida (Verdi), 280
Ain't Misbehavin' (Waller), 62, 281–82
Aladdin (Ashman/Rice and Menken), 279; "Whole New World, A," 279
Aladdin II, 31
Aleichem, Sholem, 214
"Alexander's Ragtime Band." *See* Berlin
"Alice Blue Gown" (*Irene*), 72
Alice in Wonderland (Yeston), 280
"Alkmoonac, or the Death Song of the Cherokee Indians" (Musical Example 5). See *Tammany; or The Indian Chief*
All Quiet on the Western Front, 92
All That Glitters (Sondheim), 205
"All the Things You Are." *See* Kern
Allegro (Rodgers and Hammerstein), 148, 150, 205
"Almost Like Being in Love" (Musical Example 34). See *Brigadoon*
Alternation. *See* Form
Alto. *See* Voice type
Alton, Robert, 61, 120, 141
"Amazons' March" (Musical Example 10). See *The Black Crook*

America (Finn), 280
"America" (Musical Example 36). See *West Side Story*
American Company, The. *See* The Old American Company
American Dance Machine, 174
American in Paris, An. See Gershwin, George
American Theatre Wing, 133
Amplification, 186
Anastasia (Flaherty and Ahrens), 298
Anderson, John Murray, 61
Andersson, Benny, 277–79. See also *Chess; Mamma Mia!*
Andrews, Julie, 155, 166–68, 214
"Angels We Have Heard on High," 26
Anna and the King, 302
Annie (Strouse), 199
Annie 2 (Strouse), 199
Annie Dear, 58
Annie Get Your Gun (Berlin), 119, 122–24; "Anything You Can Do" (Musical Example 26), 123, 127–28; Death of Kern, 87; "Old-Fashioned Wedding, An," 123; Plot Summary, 125–26; "There's No Business Like Show Business," 109, 122, 207
Another Midsummer Night, 130
"Another Suitcase in Another Hall" (Musical Example 49). See *Evita*
Anya, 91
Anyone Can Whistle (Sondheim), 209
"Anything Goes" (Musical Example 24). See *Anything Goes*
Anything Goes (Porter), 102, 114–16, 129, 156; "Anything Goes" (Musical Example 24), 115–18; "Blow, Gabriel, Blow," 115; First title of (*Bon Voyage*), 114; "I Get a Kick Out of You," 115, 120; Plot Summary, 117; Second title of, 114
"Anything You Can Do" (Musical Example 26). See *Annie Get Your Gun*
Applause (Strouse), 199
"Aquarius." See *Hair*
"Are You Sleeping?," 26
Aria. *See* Singing style
Arioso. *See* Singing style
Arlen, Howard, 107
Aronson, Billy, 295–96
Aronson, Boris, 215, 220, 221, 243
Around the World in Eighty Days (Porter), 129
Artwork of the Future, 25
As Thousands Cheer (Berlin), 110–11, 122; "Easter Parade," 111; Plot Summary, 112–13; "Supper Time" (Musical Example 23), 110–11, 113
ASCAP, 57, 59, 132, 141, 255, 264
Ashman, Howard, 279. See also *Aladdin; Beauty and the Beast; The Little Mermaid; Little Shop of Horrors*
Ashton, Frederick, 61
Aside, 44
Aspects of Love (Lloyd Webber), 255, 260, 262, 264, 272
Assassins (Sondheim), 287–88; "Ballad of Booth, The" (Musical Example 61), 287–88, 292–94; Plot Summary, 290–91; "Something Just Broke," 287
Astaire, Adele, 61, 98
Astaire, Fred, 61, 93, 98, 99; Beginning of partnership with Rogers, 99

Atkinson, Brooks, 120, 121, 137, 174, 176, 184
Auburn, David, 297
Audience management, 34
Audition, 55, 190, 237, 255, 261, 298
Auntie Mame, 181
Austin, Frederic, 7
Authorized production, 33, 34
Away We Go! See *Oklahoma!*, Original title of (*Away We Go!*)
Ayers, Lemuel, 130, 133, 181, 206
Babbitt, Milton, 205-6
Babes in Arms (Rodgers and Hart), 119; "I Wish I Were in Love Again," 119; "Johnny One Note," 119; "Lady Is a Tramp, The," 119; "My Funny Valentine," 119; "Where or When," 119
Babes in Toyland (Herbert), 50–51, 56; "I Can't Do the Sum" (Musical Example 13), 51, 54, 71; "March of the Toys, The," 51; Plot Summary, 53; "Toyland," 51
Bach, Johann Sebastian, 93
Bacharach, Burt, 282
Backers' audition, 130, 140, 165, 168, 199
Backlist, 66
Backstage (magazine), 272
Bagpipes, inauthentic, 169
Bailey, Pearl, 199
Baird, Bil, 213
Baker, Belle, 110
Baker, Thomas, 43
Balanchine, George, 61, 93, 141, 165
"Bali Ha'i" (Musical Example 31). See *South Pacific*
Baline, Israel ("Izzy"). *See* Berlin
Ball at the Savoy, 143
Ball, Lucille, 198
Ballad, 6, 109, 110, 191, 213, 230, 254, 288; In America, 16; Moritat, 137; Strophic form, 138
"Ballad of Booth, The" (Musical Example 61). See *Assassins*
"Ballad of Mack the Knife, The (Moritat)" (Musical Example 28). See *The Threepenny Opera*
Ballad opera, 6–8, 16, 17–18, 19, 31, 38, 246
Ballet, 42–44, 46, 93–94, 141, 154–55, 165, 172, 173, 182, 261
Bancroft, Anne, 201
Banfield, Stephen, 176, 237
Banjo song, 105–6
Bara, Theda, 71
Barbershop. *See* Style
Barcarole, 286
Bardi di Vernio, Count Giovanni, 3
Barer, Marshall, 192–93
Baritone. *See* Voice type
Barnes, Clive, 244
Barnum (Coleman), 198
Baroque, 1
Barras, Charles, 43. See also *The Black Crook*
Bart, Lionel, 228. See also *Blitz!; Fings Ain't Wot They Used T'Be; Maggie May; Oliver!*
Barton, Steve, 261–62
Basili, Basilio, 21
Bass. *See* Voice type

Bastien und Bastienne (Mozart), 8–9, 11, 24; "Diggi, Daggi" (Musical Example 3), 8–9, 10, 43; Number of arias, 16; Plot Summary, 9–10
Batt, Mike, 261
Baum, L. Frank, 51
Beach Blanket Tempest, 130
Beat, 3, 20, 76
Beautiful Game, The (Lloyd Webber), 263
Becker, Lee, 174
Beethoven, Ludwig van, 13, 25, 93, 99, 176, 302
Beggar's Opera, The, 6–7, 16, 19, 31, 136, 246; American performances, 6, 16; "Our Polly Is a Sad Slut" (Musical Example 2), 7, 10, 185; Plot Summary, 9
Beggar's Wedding, The, 7
"Beggars at the Feast." See *Les Misérables*
"Begin the Beguine." See *Broadway Melody of 1940*
Begum, The (De Koven), 49
Behr, Edward, 270
"Being Alive." See *Company*
Bel canto, 24
Bell, Marion, 166
Belle of Mayfair, The, 130
Belle of New York, The (Kerker), 56
Bells are Ringing (Styne), 181; "Party's Over, The," 181
Benchley, Robert, 76
Benefit, 122, 131
Benefits: Disadvantages of, 122–23
Bennett, Michael, 237–39, 243, 272, 277–78, 282
Bennett, Robert Russell, 71, 154, 168
Bergman, Ingmar, *Smiles of a Summer Night*, 244, 302
Berkeley, Busby, 61
Berlin Stories, 219
Berlin, Irving, 109–12, 114, 209; "Alexander's Ragtime Band," 109; "Blue Skies," 110; Employed by Harry von Tilzer, 63, 66; Gives advice, 99, 129; "God Bless America," 109; Inability to read music, 201, 271; "Let's Have Another Cup of Coffee," 110; "Marie from Sunny Italy," 109; Music Box Theatre, 102; Offers job to Gershwin, 97; Quodlibets, 109, 190; Rules for composers, 110, 175; "Soft Lights and Sweet Music," 110; Turns down *Gypsy*, 181; "When I Lost You," 110; "White Christmas," 109, 122; Withdraws from *Sitting Pretty*, 72; Writes for Hollywood, 279. See also *Annie Get Your Gun; As Thousands Cheer; Call Me Madam; Cocoanuts; Music Box Revues; This Is the Army; Watch Your Step; Yip, Yip, Yaphank*
Bernstein, Leonard, 92, 137, 172–76, 206–7, 223, 231, 236, 291; "Age of Anxiety, The," 173; Conducts New York Philharmonic, 172–73, 176; Film score (*On the Waterfront*), 173; Influenced by other composers, 176; Mass, 236; Operas; *Trouble in Tahiti*, 173. See also *1600 Pennsylvania*

(Continued)

Avenue; Candide; Fancy Free; On the Town; On the Waterfront; Peter Pan; Quiet Place; Trouble in Tahiti; West Side Story; Wonderful Town

Bernstein, Shirley, 172

Best Little Whorehouse in Texas, The (Hall), 240

"Betrayed." See *The Producers*

Better Sort, The, 17

"Bewitched, Bothered, and Bewildered" (Musical Example 25). See *Pal Joey*

Bickwell, G., 43

Big, 302

"Big Spender." See *Sweet Charity*

Bigley, Isobel, 186

Bill, 20, 45

"Bill." See Princess Shows: *Oh, Lady! Lady!!; Show Boat*

Billboard, 132–33, 200, 230

Binary. See Form

Bit, 61

Bitter-Sweet (Coward), 75, 82, 116

Bizet, Georges, 19. See also *Carmen*

Bjørnson, Maria, 260, 262

Black Crook, Jr., The, 43

Black Crook, The, 42–44, 49, 165, 201, 228, 231; "Amazons' March" (Musical Example 10), 43–44, 48; Appearance of chorus girls, 61; Plot Summary, 47; "You Naughty, Naughty Men," 43

Black Rook, The, 43

Black, Don, 253, 262–63, 298

Blackbirds, 281

Blackbirds of 1928, 61

Blackface, 38, 40, 45, 85, 97, 105

Blackout, 61, 116, 150

Blake, Eubie. See *Eubie!*

Bland, James A., 40; "Carry Me Back to Old Virginny," 40; "O, Dem Golden Slippers," 40

Blitz! (Bart), 281

Blitzstein, Marc, 137, 172, 176, Translation of *The Threepenny Opera*, 137–38. See also *The Cradle Will Rock*

Block, Geoffrey, 121, 176

Blockheads, The, 17

Blondel (Oliver and Rice), 277

Blood Brothers (Russell), 281

Bloomgarden, Kermit, 190

Blossom Time (Romberg), 91

"Blow, Gabriel, Blow." See *Anything Goes*

Blue Monday (Gershwin), 97–98, 105

Blue note, 99, 101, 111, 256

"Blue Room." See *The Girl Friend*

"Blue Skies." See Berlin

Bluegrass. See Style

Blues. See Style

Blumenthal, George, 57

BMI, 59, 205

BMI Musical Theatre Workshop, 240, 280–81, 298

Bock, Jerry, 213–15. See also *Fiddler on the Roof; Fiorello!; The Rothschilds; She Loves Me; Tenderloin*

Bohème, La (Puccini), 25, 91, 295

Bohemian Girl, The, 49

Bolero, 213

Bolger, Ray, 61, 93, 121, 133, 184

Bolton, Guy, 69–72, 90, 114, Discusses plot integration, 71. See also *Anything Goes; Miss 1917; Sally;* Princess Shows: *Have a Heart; Leave It to Jane; Miss Springtime; Nobody Home; Oh, Boy!; Oh, Lady! Lady!!; Oh, My Dear; Sitting Pretty; Very Good Eddie*

Bon Voyage. See *Anything Goes*, First title of

Bond, Christopher, 245

Book, 69, 71, 76, 81–2, 92, 99, 101–2, 104, 114, 122, 137, 148, 181, 278; Brevity of *West Side Story*'s book, 174

Book musical, 75, 93, 219, 281, 295

Book show, 119, 198

Book song, 87, 101, 220

Book writer, 69, 71, 102

Boomer, 109

Bordman, Gerald, 72, 86, 201, 205

Born to Dance (Porter), 129; "I've Got You Under My Skin," 129

Borodin, Alexander, 91

Boublil, Alain, 269–73, Working method, 271. See also *Martin Guerre; Les Misérables; Miss Saigon; La révolution française*

Bounce (Sondheim), 288

Bows, 111, 134

Box office advance. See Advance ticket sales

Boy Friend, The, 166–67

"Boy From . . . , The." See *The Mad Show*

Boys from Syracuse, The (Rodgers and Hart), 92, 130, 302

Bradley, Bill, 238

Braham, John, 62

Brahms, Caryl, 186

Brahms, Johannes, 25, 93

Brandy, 155

Brantley, Ben, 297

Brecht, Bertolt, 136, 137–38

Breeches role, 49

Bricusse, Leslie, 297

Bridge, 86, 120

Bridge, Andrew, 262

Brigadoon (Loewe), 165–66; "Almost Like Being in Love" (Musical Example 34), 166, 167, 170–71; Backers' auditions for, 168; Inauthentic bagpipes, 169; Plot Summary, 169–70

Brightman, Sarah, 255, 260–62, 278

Bring Back Birdie (Strouse), 199

Bring in 'da Noise, Bring in 'da Funk, 295, 303

Britten, Benjamin, 176

Broadway, 50. See also Electrical lighting, Long-run record, Times Square, Top ticket price; African-American works, 40, 62, 63; Awards for, 133; Canteen for soldiers, 133; Changes in the 1920s, 75; Color-blind casting, 193; Competition from films, 157; Contributions of women, 56, 58; Dance integration, 93; Decrease of revues, 111; Effects of Depression, 87, 116; First LP release, 131; Foreign imports on, 56, 246, 254; Jazz style, 99; Lloyd Webber's record, 255; Merchandizing, 55; Musical anthems, 207; Oldest director, 92; Performers' skills, 254; Pulitzer-prize winners, 101; Racial integration, 61, 173; Record advance, 231, 262, 273; Record cost, 256, 273, 303; Record loss, 221, 262; Schedule of shows, 149; Schwartz's new record, 236; Smallest stage, 69; Ticket sales for Lloyd Webber shows, 264; Transfers from off-Broadway, 61, 62, 193, 199–200, 236, 239, 240, 295, 297; Tribute to Cohan, 65; Tribute to Hammerstein, 157; Union rules, 297; Use of interpolations, 52; Use of microphones, 184; Versus opera, 86, 105; Very short run, 199, 201, 209, 280; Wildhorn's record, 297

Broadway Melody of 1940 (Porter), "Begin the Beguine," 129

Broadway show, 50

Brolly, Brian, 229

Brooks, Mel, 288. See *The Producers*

Brower, Frank, 38

Brown, Anne Wiggins, 106

Brown, James, 282

Brown, Jason Robert, 298–99. See also *The Last Five Years; Parade; Songs for a New World*

"Brown October Ale" (Musical Example 12). See *Robin Hood*

Bruckner, Anton, 25

Bryan, Vincent, 63

Bryant's Minstrels, 39

Brynner, Yul, 154–55, 199

Bubbling Brown Sugar, 281

Buckley, Betty, 202

Buddy (Holly), 282

Buffo zarzuela, 22

Burlesque, 31, 35, 42, 44–45, 49, 56, 61, 64, 91, 93, 120, 187, 192, 207; Minsky's, 187

Burletta, 38

Burnand, Francis, 31

Burnett, Carol, 192–93

Burnett, Frances Hodgson, 295

Burrows, Abe, 184–85. See also *Guys and Dolls; How to Succeed in Business Without Really Trying*

Burton, Richard, 168, 184

Busenello, Giovanni Francesco, 2, 4

"But Not for Me." See *Girl Crazy*

By Jeeves (Lloyd Webber), 70, 263

By Jupiter (Rodgers and Hart), 121, 122

Bye Bye Birdie (Strouse), 199–200; "Put On a Happy Face," 199

Cabaret. See Style

Cabaret (Kander and Ebb), 219–21, 238, 273, 287, 302; "If You Could See Her Through My Eyes," 219; Plot Summary, 223–24; "Tomorrow Belongs to Me" (Musical Example 46), 220, 222, 225

Cabin in the Sky (Duke), 281

Caccini, Francesca, 2, 58. See *La Liberazione di Ruggiero dall'isola d'Alcina*

Caccini, Giulio, 2, 3

Caesar, Irving, 80–81

Caesar, Sid, 198

Cage aux Folles, La (Herman), 199

Cahill, Marie, 52, 57

Cahn, Sammy, 181; See also *High Button Shoes*

Caird, John, 269–70

Cakewalk, 39, 40, 291

Caldwell, Anne, 58; *Social Whirl, The*, 58

Call Me Madam (Berlin), 123, 238; "You're Just in Love," 123

Call-and-response, 39, 40, 106, 192, 256

Calypso. See Style

Camelot (Lerner and Loewe), 168

Cameron, James, 281

Campbell, Maurice, 88

"Camptown Races" (Musical Example 9). See Foster

"Can You Feel the Love Tonight?" See *The Lion King* (John and Rice)

Can-can, 20, 23, 44

Can-Can (Porter), 132

Candide (Bernstein), 173

Cannibal King, The, 62

Canon, 7, 185

Cantata, 229

"Carefully Taught." See *South Pacific*

Carmen (Bizet), 19, 91, 146

Carmen Jones, 91, 146

Carmichael, Hoagy, 184

Carnelia, Craig, 236

Carnival, 302

Carousel (Rodgers and Hammerstein), 131, 132, 146–48, 150, 164; "If I Loved You," 148; "June is Bustin' Out All Over," 158; Musical episodes in, 156; Plot Summary, 151–52; Sondheim's comments regarding, 148; "What's the Use of Wond'rin'?" (Musical Example 30), 147, 152–53; "You'll Never Walk Alone," 147

"Carousel Waltz." See De Mille

Carpenter, Karen, 287

Carrie, 238

Carroll, Earl, 61

"Carry Me Back to Old Virginny." See Bland

Caryll, Ivan, 58. See *The Pink Lady*

Casey, Warren, 239. See also *Grease*

Cassidy, Jack, 213–14

Cast, 2

Cast album. See Original cast album

Castle, Irene, 110

Castle, Vernon, 110

"Castle on a Cloud" (Musical Example 57). See *Les Misérables*

Castrato, 2, 3–4, 8, 12, 21

Castro, Jean, 120

Catalog, 66

Catalog show. See Compilation show

"Catalogue Aria, The" (Musical Example 4). See *Don Giovanni*

Catch My Soul, 130

Cats (Lloyd Webber), 253–56, 260, 264, 277, 282, 295; "Growltiger's Last Stand," 254; "Memory," 254, 277; "Mungojerrie and Rumpleteazer" (Musical Example 53), 255, 258; Plot Summary, 257

Cavalcade, 116

"Cell Block Tango" (Musical Example 47). See *Chicago*

Chagall, Marc, 215

Challenge song, 123

Chaney, Lon, 260

Channing, Carol, 181, 199

Chapman, John, 132, 185, 191, 214; Impersonated by Merrick, 184

Character, 102

Character chorus line, 120, 141

Character song, 34, 120, 147, 213, 243

Characterization, 3

Charisse, Cyd, 166

"Charleston, The," 101

Charleston rhythm, 101

Charley's Aunt, 184

Charm song, 156, 215

Charnin, Martin, 199

Chee-Chee (Rodgers and Hart), 92

Cherubini, Luigi, 22

Chess (Andersson/Ulvaeus), 238, 262, 272, 277–79; "Endgame," 278; "I Know Him So Well," 277; "One Night in Bangkok" (Musical Example 59), 277–78, 283–84; Plot Summary, 282–83; "Story of Chess, The," 278

Chicago (Kander and Ebb), 46, 221–22, 287, 302; "Cell Block Tango, The" (Musical Example 47), 222, 225–27; "Me and My Baby," 222; "Mr. Cellophane," 222; Plot Summary, 224–25

Children's Pinafore, The, 32

Chimes of Normandy, The. See *Les Cloches de Corneville*

Chocolate Soldier, The (Straus), 56

Chopin, Frédéric, 91, 282

Chord, 2, 46, 64, 93, 109, 122, 185, 222, 256, 264, 288

Choreographer, 141, 174. See also Alton; Balanchine; Michael Bennett; Berkeley; Cohan; Cole; De Mille; Field; Fosse; Kidd; Lynne; Phillips; Placide; Robbins; Tamaris; Taymor; The Society of Stage Directors and Choreographers; Tune

Choreography, 43–44, 165, 243, Compilation show of, 282; Copyright protection for, 166; Increasing respect for, 93; Integration of, 147; Omission of (*South Pacific*), 150; Preservation of, 174; Used in commercials, 174. See also Dream ballet

Chorus, 2, 39, 50

Chorus (refrain), 40

Chorus girl, 43, 50, 61, 110, 140, 150

Chorus line, 43–44, 61, 165; Costuming of, 62; Increasing skill of, 140–41; "Matched," 120, 237; Omission of, 154, 202. See also Gypsies

Chorus Line, A (Hamlisch), 222, 237–39, 254, 272, 282, 295; "I Can Do That" (Musical Example 50), 237, 241; Plot Summary, 240; "What I Did for Love," 239

Chorus number, 86
Christy Minstrels, 38–40
Christy, Edwin, 38
Chromaticism, 76, 261
Chu Chem, 238
Cinderella (Rodgers and Hammerstein), 155
Cinderella story, 72, 75, 116, 170, 255, 286
Cinderella the Younger, 31
Circuit, 17
Citron, Stephen, 116, 155, 260
City of Angels (Coleman), 198
Civil War, The (Wildhorn), 297
Clark, Petula, 281
Class Act, A, 237
Classic, 11, 13, 24, 26
"Cleopatterer" (Musical Example 17). See Princess Shows: *Leave It to Jane*
"Climbing Uphill." See *The Last Five Years*
Cloches de Corneville, Les, 21
Clorindy (Cook), 62
Close, Glenn, 263
Cobler's Opera, The, 7
"Cockeyed Optimist, A." See *South Pacific*
Coco, 247
Coco, James, 198
Cocoanuts (Berlin), 61
Coda, 43, 104, 150, 239, 261; Vocal, 111, 147, 149, 156, 185, 192, 213, 215, 220, 221, 261, 263, 288, 296
Cohan, George M., 63–65, 91, 92, 110, 119, "Over There," 64; "You're a Grand Old Flag," 64. See also *Little Johnny Jones*
Cole, Bob, 62–63
Cole, Jack, 61, 165, 207
Colegiales y soldados, 21
Coleman, Cy, 198–99. See also *Barnum; City of Angels; Home Again, Home Again; I Love My Wife; The Life; Little Me; On the Twentieth Century; Sweet Charity; Wildcat; The Will Rogers Follies*
Collins, Judy, 244
Coloratura. See Voice type
"Colors of the Wind." See *Pocahontas*
Comden, Betty, 172–73, 181, 199. See also *Bells are Ringing; On the Town; Say, Darling; Wonderful Town*
"Come to Me." See *Les Misérables*
Comédie en vaudeville. See Opéra-comique
Comédie-ballet, 6
Comedy of Errors, The. See Shakespeare
Comedy song, 70, 75, 120, 131, 167, 213, 222
"Comedy Tonight" (Musical Example 43). See *A Funny Thing Happened on the Way to the Forum*
Comic opera, 17, 31, 49
Commedia dell'arte, 2, 38, 236
Commission, 8, 90, 172, 236
Company, 32
Company (Sondheim), 46, 205, 242–44; "Being Alive," 242; "Getting Married Today" (Musical Example 51), 9, 243, 249–50; "Happily Ever After," 242; "Ladies Who Lunch, The," 243, 247; "Marry Me a Little," 242; "Multitude of Amys," 242; Plot Summary, 247–48; Problems with lyrics, 244
Compilation show, 62, 199, 281–82, 295, 303
Composer, See also Adler; Andersson; Arlen; Bach; Bacharach; Basili; Beethoven; Bernstein; Bizet; Blake; Bland; Bock; Borodin; Brahms; Bruckner; Francesca Caccini; Caldwell; Carmichael; Carnelia; Caryll; Casey; Chopin; Coleman; Cook; Copland; De Koven; Duke; Emmett; Flaherty; Ford; Franck; Friml; George Gershwin; Micki Grant; Grieg; Hamlisch; Charles K. Harris; Herbert; Herman; Hervé; Heywood; Hollman; Holofcener; Hubbell; Jim Jacobs; John; Joplin;

Kander; Kerker; Kern; Krieger; Lane; LeCocq; Mitch Leigh; Lehár; Leoncavallo; Liszt; Loewe; MacDermot; Mahler; Mendelssohn; Menken; Morton; Mozart; Monteverdi; Novello; Offenbach; Operti; Orff; Pepusch; Pergolesi; Pixérécourt; Prokofiev; Puccini; Rachmaninoff; Edward E. Rice; Rimsky-Korsakov; Mary Rodgers; Richard Rodgers; Romberg; Jerry Ross; Rossini; Schmidt; Schönberg; Schubert; Sullivan; Arthur Schwartz; Secunda; Shostakovich; Lucy Simon; Sklar; Solomon; Sousa; Stoller; Stothart; Straus; Strauss; Strouse; Styne; Sullivan; Suppé; Taylor; Tchaikovsky; Tesori; Thompson; Tierney; Ulvaeus; Verdi; Von Tilzer; Wagner; Waller; Andrew Lloyd Webber; Weill; Wildhorn; Youmans; *See also* Composer-Lyricist
Composer-Lyricist. See Bart; Berlin; Blitzstein; Brooks; Jason Robert Brown; Caldwell; Cohan; Sherman Edwards; Finn; Foster; Gordon; Adam Guettel; Carol Hall; Kummer; LaChiusa; Larson; Lippa; Loesser; Porter; Rubins; Willy Russell; Stephen Schwartz; Smalls; Sondheim; Swados; Willson; Yeston
Compound. See Subdivision
Comstock, F. Ray, 69–70, 72–73
Concept album, 199, 229–31, 236, 261, 269, 272, 277–78, 280, 297
Concept musical, 137, 148, 166, 198, 205, 214, 237, 242, 260, 295
Concert performance, 17, 137, 271, 277, 296
Conjunct, 56–57, 76, 149–50, 191, 255
Connecticut Yankee, A (Rodgers and Hart), 92, 146; "To Keep My Love Alive," 146
Cook, Will Marion, 45, 62–63, 104. See also *Clorindy; In Dahomey*
"Cool." See *West Side Story*
"Cool, Cool, Considerate Men." See *1776*
Coon song, 62
Copland, Aaron, 176, 281; *Salon México, El*, 176
Copyright, 33, 39, 43, 59, 66, 148, 166
Coronation of Poppea, The (Monteverdi), 2–3, 263; Castrati in, 4; Plot Summary, 4; "Tornerai?" (Musical Example 1), 2–3, 4–5
Così fan tutte (Mozart), 12–13, 24; Ensemble opera, 13
Costuming, 43, 44, 49, 62, 70; *West Side Story*, 177
"Could You Use Me?" See *Girl Crazy*
Countermelody, 56, 154, 182, 183
Countertenor. See Voice type
Country. See Style
Country western. See Style
Cover, 279
Covington, Julie, 231
Coward, Noël. See *Bitter-Sweet*
Cowsills, The, 200
Cox and Box (Sullivan), 31
Cradle Will Rock, The (Blitzstein), 33, 136–37, 172
Crawford, Cheryl, 105, 165, 169, 173–74
Crawford, Michael, 261–62
Crazy for You. See *Girl Crazy*
Crémieux, Hector, 20
Creole Show, The, 40
Crescendo. See Dynamic level
Cricket (Lloyd Webber and Rice), 262
Cronin, Mari, 243
Crooker, Earle, 164
Crosby, Bing, 137
Crouse, Russel, 114–15, 156. See also *Anything Goes; The Sound of Music*
Cryer, Gretchen, 239. See also *I'm Getting My Act Together and Taking It

on the Road; The Last Sweet Days of Isaac*
Cuden, Steve, 297
Cue, 46
Cue sheet, 46
Curtain call, 134
Curtain of Act I, 120
Cushman, Robert, 254
Cycle, 25, 34, 253

Da Ponte, Lorenzo, 11–12. See *Così fan tutte; Don Giovanni; The Marriage of Figaro*
Dafne, 1
Damn Yankees (Adler and Ross), 92, 185, 194, 198
Dance, 61–62, 81, 243; Functions of, 165
Dance a Little Closer (Strouse), 168, 199
Dance arranger, 154–55
Dance captain, 174
Dance director, 93
Dangerous Games (Finn), 238, 280
Darby's Return, 17
Daughter of the Regiment, The. See *La Fille du Régiment*
Davenport, Pembroke, 131
David, Hal, 282
Davis, Jessie, 49
Davis, Sammy, Jr., 213
Day Before Spring, The (Lerner and Loewe), 164
"De Blue Tail Fly." See Emmett
De Koven, Reginald, 49. See also *The Begum; Robin Hood*
De Mille, Agnes, 44, 140–41, 147–48, 165–66, 169, 201; Authenticity in *Brigadoon*, 165; "Carousel Waltz" (*Carousel*), 147; Dream ballet in *Oklahoma!*, 141; "Funeral Dance" for *Brigadoon*, 165; Modern dance in *Oklahoma!*, 165
Dearest Enemy, 75, 77
Death of a Salesman, 132
Dench, Judi, 253–54
Denishawn, 62
Dennen, Barry, 230
Desert Song, The (Romberg), 80, 81–82
Deutsch, Helen, 132
Dewhurst, Colleen, 273
Dialect, 40, 46, 62–63, 109, 146
Dialogue, 102
"Diamonds Are a Girl's Best Friend." See *Gentlemen Prefer Blondes*
Dick Tracy. See Sondheim: Academy Award
Dickens, Charles, 228
Diegetic, 49, 56, 76, 104, 120, 141, 182, 219, 243
Diegetic choreography, 141, 154
Dies irae, 245
Dietz, Howard, 166
"Diggi, Daggi" (Musical Example 3). See *Bastien und Bastienne* (Mozart)
Director. See Abbott; Michael Bennett; Caird; De Mille; Farago; Fosse; Frazee; Greif; Sir Peter Hall; Moss Hart; Heyward; Hytner; Lindsay; Logan; Mamoulian; Julian Mitchell; Nunn; O'Horgan; Papp; Daisy Prince; Harold Prince; Robbins; Sharman; Swados; Taymor; Tune; Wolfe; Zaks
Disappointment, The, 16–17
Disjunct, 56–57, 71, 76, 88, 149, 156, 191, 243, 255, 263
Dissemination, 72
"Dixie." See Emmett: "Dixie's Land"
"Dixie's Land." See Emmett
"Do You Hear the People Sing?" See *Les Misérables*
"Do You Know the Way to San José?," 296
"Do You Love Me?" (Musical Example 45). See *Fiddler on the Roof*
Doctor of Alcantara, The, 49

Doctorow, E. L., 298
"Dog Eats Dog." See *Les Misérables*
Dominant, 191, 243
Don Giovanni (Mozart), 11–12, 120; "Catalogue Aria, The" (Musical Example 4), 12, 14–15, 50; Plot Summary, 14
Don Juan, Legend of, 11
Donahue, Jack, 84
Donaldson Award, 132–33, 148, 150, 155, 185
Donizetti, Gaetano. See *La Fille du Régiment*
Donnelly, Dorothy, 58
Don't Bother Me, I Can't Cope (Grant), 239
"Don't Cry For Me Argentina." See *Evita*
"Do-Re-Mi" (Musical Example 33). See *The Sound of Music*
Dorsey, Jimmy, 99
Dotted notes, 81
D'Oyly Carte, Richard, 31–35; Carpet Quarrel, The, 35
Dr. Doolittle, "Talk to the Animals," 297
Dracula (Wildhorn), 298
Drake, Alfred, 133
Drama Critics' Circle, 150. See New York Drama Critics' Circle
Drama Desk, 133
Dramatists Guild, 133
Dramaturg, 296
Dramma giocoso, 11–12
Dream ballet, 44, 120, 141, 143, 150
Dream Girl, The (Herbert), 58
Dreamgirls (Krieger), 282
Dreamstuff, 130
Dreigroschenoper, Die. See *The Threepenny Opera* (Weill)
Dreyfus, Max, 80, 97
Dude (MacDermot), 201
Duet. See Ensemble number
Duke, Vernon. See *Cabin in the Sky*
Dummy lyric, 80, 100, 105
Dunbar, Paul Laurence, 62
Duncan, Todd, 106–7
Duo. See Ensemble number
Duple. See Meter
Durang, Christopher, 245
Dynamic level, 11; Crescendo, 111

Eagan, Daisy, 295
"Easter Parade." See *As Thousands Cheer*
Eastwood, Clint, 166
"Easy to Be Hard." See *Hair*
Ebb, Fred, 219–23, 237; "New York, New York," 223, 279; Working method with Kander, 219. See also *The Act; Cabaret; Chicago; Flora, the Red Menace; The Happy Time; Kiss of the Spider Woman; The Rink; Woman of the Year; Zorbá*
"Edelweiss." See *The Sound of Music*
Eder, Linda, 297
Edison, Thomas, 45
Educating Rita (Russell), 281
Edward VII, King of England, 56
Edwardes, George, 35, 56, 62
Edwards, Cliff, 84
Edwards, Sherman, 201–2; "See You in September," 201; "Wonderful, Wonderful," 201. See also *1776*
Edwin and Angelina, 17
8-1/2 (Fellini), 280
Electrical lighting, 34, 45, 50
Eleven o'clock number, 123, 141, 243, 302
Eliot, T. S., 253–55; *Old Possum's Book of Practical Cats*, 253
Eliot, Valerie, 253
Elizabeth II, Queen of England, 262
Elliman, Yvonne, 230
Ellington, Duke. See *Sophisticated Ladies*
Ellis, Mary, 75
Eltinge, Julian, 45, 222
"Embraceable You." See *Girl Crazy*
Emmett, Dan, 38–39; "De Blue Tail Fly," 39; "Dixie's Land," 39–40, 64, 110;

(Continued)
"Jimmy Crack Corn," 39; "Old Dan Tucker," 39
Emmy Award, 221
"Empty Chairs at Empty Tables." See *Les Misérables*
Encore, 17, 49, 57, 64, 101, 109, 121, 123, 131
"Endgame." See *Chess*
Engel, Lehman, 121, 240
English operetta. *See* Operetta: English
Enlightenment, Age of, 11
Ensemble number, 13; Duet, 13, 17, 26, 76, 123, 166, 215, 246, 255, 272, 298; Duo, 13; Nonet, 13; Octet, 13; Quartet, 13; Quintet, 13, 175, 176; Septet, 13; Sextet, 13; Trio, 13
Ensemble opera, 13
Ensemble show, 214
"Epiphany." See *Sweeney Todd*
Equity. *See* Actor's Equity
Esrom, D. A., 102
Eubie! (Blake), 282
Evangeline (Rice), 44–45, 49, 192; "My Heart" (Musical Example 11), 44–45, 48; Plot Summary, 47–48
Ever Green (Rodgers and Hart), 116
"Everything's Coming Up Roses" (Musical Example 38). See *Gypsy*
Evita (Lloyd Webber and Rice), 230, 231–32, 253, 255, 264, 277, 279; "Another Suitcase in Another Hall" (Musical Example 49), 231–32, 234–35; "Don't Cry For Me Argentina," 231; *Leitmotifs* in, 25; Plot Summary, 233–34; "You Must Love Me," 232, 279
"Ev'ry Time We Say Goodbye." See *Seven Lively Arts*
Extravaganza, 42–44, 49–50, 56, 116, 165, 228, 256; Burlesque spectacle, 42; Equestrian spectacle, 42; Fairy spectacle, 42; Military-nautical spectacle, 42; Romantic spectacle, 42
Eyen, Tom, 282

Falsetto, 4
Falsettoland (Finn), 280
Falsettos (Finn), 280
Fancy Free (Bernstein), 172
Fantasia, 39
Fantasticks, The (Schmidt and Jones), 201, 303; "Soon It's Gonna Rain," 201; "Try to Remember," 201
Fantôme de l'Opéra, Le, 260, 281
Farago, Peter, 269
Farce, 9, 35, 46, 50, 61, 69, 117, 184, 207
Farce-comedy, 46, 50, 61
Farinelli (Carlo Broschi), 21
Federal Theatre Project, 136
Federation of Musicians, 136
Fellini, Federico, *8-1/2*, 280
Fenton, James, 270
Ferber, Edna, 84–86
Fermata, 12, 50, 63
Feuer, Cy, 184–86, 190
Fiddler on the Roof (Bock and Harnick), 155, 209; "Do You Love Me?" (Musical Example 45), 215, 218; Original title of (*Tevye*), 215; Plot Summary, 216–17; "Tradition," 214–15
Field, Ronald, 221
Fields, Dorothy, 90, 122, 198
Fields, Herbert, 90–92
Fields, Lew, 52, 56, 90, 92, 110
"Fight Over Me." See *No, No, Nanette*
Fille de Madame Angot, La (LeCocq), 21, 22
Fille du Régiment, La (Donizetti), 19
Fings Ain't Wot They Used T'Be (Bart), 228
Finn, William, 280. See also *America; Dangerous Games; Falsettoland; Falsettos; In Trousers; March of the Falsettos; Muscle; A New Brain; Romance; The Royal Family*
Fiorello! (Bock and Harnick), 184, 213
Firefly (Friml), 76

First run, 121, 123
Fitch, Clyde, 63
Fitzhugh, Ellen, 280
Fixer, 92
Flaherty, Stephen, 298. See also *Anastasia; Lucky Stiff; A Man of No Importance; My Favorite Year; Once on This Island; Ragtime; Seussical*
Flatley, Guy, 231
Fledermaus, Die (Strauss, The Younger), 26; Plot Summary, 27–28; "Watch Duet, The" (Musical Example 7), 26, 28–30
Flinn, Denny, 202, 237, 295
Flop, 6, 42, 87, 102, 168, 181, 198, 205, 209, 213, 229–30, 237, 244, 256, 302
Flora, the Red Menace (Kander and Ebb), 219
Flora; or Hob in the Well, 16
Florentine Camerata, 1–3
Flower Drum Song (Rodgers and Hammerstein), 155–56, 302
Floyd Collins (Guettel), 298
Flutter-tonguing, 277
Fly (drop or raise), 238
Fly floor, 150
Flyman, 150
Fokine, Michel, 61
Folk. *See* Style
Folk music, 17, 21, 105
Follies (Sondheim), 239, 244
Footloose, 302
Ford, Nancy, 239. See also *I'm Getting My Act Together and Taking It on the Road; The Last Sweet Days of Isaac*
Foreshadowing, 220, 230, 254
Form, 8; Alternation, 71, 175, 255, 277; Binary, 8, 43; Nonstandard, 192; Rondo, 150, 156, 167; Rounded binary, 183; Show tune, 76; Song, 86–87, 101, 106, 111, 115–16, 120–21, 123, 142, 147, 149–50, 155, 166, 176, 183, 191, 192, 208, 215, 230, 239, 263, 270; Strophic, 17, 34, 38, 77, 104, 123, 131, 138, 142, 208, 220, 222, 255, 256, 261, 288; Ternary, 44, 57, 106, 263; Theme and variations, 123; Verse-chorus, 40, 50, 51, 56, 63, 64, 71, 76, 81, 86, 93, 101, 142, 230, 231, 277, 296
42nd Street, 302
Fosse, 282
Fosse, Bob, 193–94, 198, 201, 220–21, 222, 236, 282; Tony, Emmy, *and* Oscar, 221
Foster, Stephen, 39–40; "Camptown Races," 40–41, 57, 63; "My Old Kentucky Home," 40; "Old Folks at Home," 40, 109
Four Saints in Three Acts, 104
Four-rhyme, 116
Francis, Arthur. *See* Gershwin, Ira
Franck, César, 93–94
Frank Music Corporation, 193. *See* Loesser
Franklin, Benjamin, 17
Frazee, Harry, 80
Freaky Friday (Mary Rodgers), 193
Free for All, 143
Freedley, Vinton, 100, 114–15; Discovers Ethel Merman, 99; Financial disaster of *Pardon My English*, 102; Idea for *Anything Goes*, 114
Freischütz, Der, 24
Freud, Sigmund, 24, 137
Friml, Rudolf, 57, 76, 80. See also *The Firefly; Rose-Marie; Sometime; The Vagabond King*
Frogs, The (Sondheim), 245
Frohman, Charles K., 70
"From This Moment On." See *Kiss Me, Kate*
Fryer, Robert, 173
Fugue, 185
"Fugue for Tinhorns" (Musical Example 39). See *Guys and Dolls*

Full Monty, The, 302
Funny Face (Gershwin): "Funny Face," 98; "He Loves and She Loves," 98; "How Long Has This Been Going On?," 98; "My One and Only," 98; "'S Wonderful," 98
Funny Girl (Styne), 184
Funny Thing Happened on the Way to the Forum, A (Sondheim), 207–9, 242; "Comedy Tonight" (Musical Example 43), 207–8, 211–12; "Invocation," 208; Plot Summary, 209–10
Furth, George, 242

Gadd, May, 165
Gaiety Girl, A, 62, 166
Gaiety shows, 35, 62
Gaines, Reg E., 295
Galilei, Vincenzo, 3
Galop, 20, 27
"Galop infernal" (Musical Example 6). See *Orpheus in the Underworld*
Garber, Victor, 198
García, Manuel, 38
Gardella, Tess, 85
Garland, Judy, 101
Garland, Robert, 131
Garrick Gaieties, The (Rodgers and Hart), 61, 91–92
Gaver, Jack, 132
Gay, John, 6–7. See also *The Beggar's Opera*
Gelbart, Larry, 207–8
Genée, Richard, 26, 28
Género chico, 22
Gennaro, Peter, 174
Genre, 1
Gentlemen Prefer Blondes (Styne), 238; "Diamonds Are a Girl's Best Friend," 181
George White's Scandals (Gershwin), 61, 97
Gepetto (Schwartz), 237
German Reed, Thomas, 31
German Reeds, 31, 45
Germelshausen. See Gerstäcker, Friedrich
Gerry and the Pacemakers, 147
Gershwin, George, 71, 80, 88, 99, 97–103, 119, 146, 181; *American in Paris, An*, 102, 166; Employed by Remick's, 66; Higher billing than Ira, 91; Inspired by Kern, 73; "Let's Call the Whole Thing Off," 107; "Love Is Here to Stay," 107; Offered job by Berlin, 97, 109; *Rhapsody in Blue*, 98; "They Can't Take That Away From Me," 107. See also *An American in Paris; Blue Monday; Funny Face; George White's Scandals; Girl Crazy; Lady, Be Good!; Let 'Em Eat Cake; Of Thee I Sing; Oh, Kay!; Pardon My English; Porgy and Bess; Rosalie; Strike Up the Band*
Gershwin, Ira, 91, 97–103, Alias "Arthur Francis," 98; First musical after George's death, 137. See also *Blue Monday; Funny Face; Girl Crazy; Lady, Be Good!; Lady in the Dark; Let 'Em Eat Cake; Of Thee I Sing; Oh, Kay!; Pardon My English; Porgy and Bess; Rosalie; Strike Up the Band*
Gerstäcker, Friedrich, *Germelshausen*, 165
Gesamtkunstwerk, 25, 69
"Getting Married Today" (Musical Example 51). See *Company*
Geva, Tamara, 93
Gift show, 255
Gigi (Lerner and Loewe), 168, 302
Gilbert, Charles, 287
Gilbert, William, 6, 19, 21, 26, 31–35, 39, 49, 82, 101, 136, 164, Carpet Quarrel, The, 35. See also *H. M. S. Pinafore; Iolanthe; The Mikado; No Cards; Pirates of Penzance; Princess Ida; Ruddigore; The Sorceror; Thespis, or the Gods Grown Old; Trial By Jury*
Gilford, Jack, 208

Gillen, Ian, 230
Ginzler, Robert, 183
Girl Crazy (Gershwin), 99–101; "But Not for Me," 99; "Could You Use Me?," 99; "Embraceable You," 99; "I Got Rhythm," 99–101, 106; Plot Summary, 103; Revised as *Crazy for You*, 101
Girl Friend, The (Rodgers and Hart), 92; "Blue Room," 92
"Girl from Ipanema, The," 193
"Girl I Left Behind Me, The," 64
Girl in Pink Tights, The (Romberg), 44
Glover, Savion, 295
"God Bless America." See Berlin
Godspell (Schwartz), 236
Goldoni, Carlo, 11
Goldstein, Richard M., 158
Goldwyn, Sam, 146
Gone With the Wind, 172
"Good Morning Starshine." See *Hair*
"Good Morning, Carrie." See Von Tilzer
Goodbye Girl, The, 302
Goodman, Benny, 99
"Goodnight, Ladies." See *The Music Man*
"Goodnight, My Someone" (Musical Example 40). See *The Music Man*
Goodwin, John Cheever, 44–45
Gordon, Ricky Ian, 299
Gospel. *See* Style
Goulet, Robert, 168
Graham, Martha, 61
Grand Guignol, 69
Grand Hotel (Yeston), 281
Grande-Duchesse de Gérolstein, La (Offenbach), 20
Grant, Cary, 129
Grant, Micki, 236, 239. See also *Don't Bother Me, I Can't Cope; Your Arms Too Short to Box with God*
Grease (Jacobs and Casey), 239
Great Waltz, The, 91
Great White Way, 50, 236, 297, 303
Greek chorus, 148
Green Grow the Lilacs, 122, 140
Green, Adolf, 172–73, 181, 199. See also *Bells are Ringing; On the Town; Say, Darling; Wonderful Town*
Greene, Ellen, 279
Greene, Schuyler, 69, 73
Greenwich Village Follies, 61
Greenwillow (Loesser), 185
Greif, Michael, 296
Grey, Joel, 221
Grieg, Edvard, 91; Piano Concerto, 230
Griffith, Robert, 174
Group Theatre, 136
"Growltiger's Last Stand." See *Cats*
Gude, O. J., 50
Guernsey, Otis, 202
Guettel, Adam, 73, 192, 298–99. See also *Floyd Collins; A Light in the Piazza; Saturn Returns*
Guettel, Mary Rodgers. *See* Mary Rodgers
Guinan, Texas, 222
Guirard, Ernest, 22
Guying, 69
Guys and Dolls (Loesser), 184–85, 191; "Fugue for Tinhorns" (Musical Example 39), 7, 185, 188–89; Plot Summary, 187–88; "Sit Down, You're Rockin' the Boat," 185
Gypsies, 174, 207, 237, 238
Gypsy (Styne), 181, 193, 207; "Everything's Coming Up Roses" (Musical Example 38), 182, 183–84, 188; *Leitmotifs* in, 25, 183; "Momma's Talkin' Soft," 182; Overture, 183; Plot Summary, 186–87; "Rose's Turn," 182–83, 187, 302; "Some People," 183; Struggle over overture, 182; "You'll Never Get Away From Me," 182
Gypsy robe, 238
Gypsy run-through, 207

H. M. S. Pinafore (Gilbert and Sullivan), 32–33, 34
Haffner, Karl, 26, 28
"Hail, Hail, the Gang's All Here." See *Pirates of Penzance, The*
"Hair." See *Hair*
Hair (MacDermot), 200–201, 230, 231, 237; "Aquarius," 200; "Easy to Be Hard," 200; "Good Morning Starshine," 200; "Hair," 200; "Let the Sunshine In," 200
Hairspray, 302
Halévy, Ludovic, 20, 26
Half-step, 116
Hall, Carol, 240, 280. See also *The Best Little Whorehouse in Texas*
Hall, Sir Peter, 277
Hallelujah, 104
Hallelujah, Baby! (Styne), 184
Halliday, Richard, 156
Hamlet. See Shakespeare
Hamlisch, Marvin, 237–39. See also *A Chorus Line; Imaginary Friends; They're Playing Our Song*
Hammerstein, Arthur, 57, 75–76, 85
Hammerstein, Oscar, I, 56
Hammerstein, Oscar, II, 64–65, 88, 90, 121, 157–158, 193, 205; Advertisement in *Variety*, 143; As producer, 122–23; Asks Sondheim to work with Rodgers, 209; *Carmen Jones*, 146; Counsels Sondheim to do *Gypsy*, 182; Death of, 207; Influences Sondheim, 173; Last song written ("Edelweiss"), 157; Mentors Sondheim, 207; Refuses to produce *Brigadoon*, 165; Rejects property of *The Music Man*, 155; Rejects *Pygmalion* (later *My Fair Lady*), 155, 166; Rejects *Tevye's Daughters* (later *Fiddler on the Roof*), 155; Roles for women, 158; Suggestions for *West Side Story*, 176; Surrey Enterprises, 146; Williamson Music, 146; Withdraws from *Porgy*, 104; Writes for Hollywood, 279. See also (with Rodgers) *Allegro; Carousel; Cinderella; Flower Drum Song; The King and I; Me and Juliet; Oklahoma!; Pipe Dream; The Sound of Music; South Pacific; State Fair*; See also (with others) *Ball at the Savoy; Carmen Jones; The Desert Song; Free for All; Naughty Marietta; Rose-Marie; Show Boat; Sunny; Sunny River; Three Sisters; Very Warm for May*
Hampton, Christopher, 262, 298
Handel, George Frideric, 6. See also *Rinaldo*
Hanks, Tom, 213
"Happily Ever After." See *Company*
Happy Time, The (Kander and Ebb), 221
Harbach, Otto, 75, 80. See also *Roberta; Rose-Marie*
Harburg, Ernest, 302–3
Harburg, Yip, 213
Hard to Get. See *Anything Goes*, Second title of (*Hard to Get*)
Harlem Song, 295
Harley, Steve, 261
Harmony, 50, 147, 166, 215, 232; Four-part, 220, 243
Harnick, Sheldon, 155, 213–15, 237, Effective lyrics, 175. See also *Fiddler on the Roof; Fiorello!; The Rothschilds; She Loves Me; Tenderloin*
Harrigan, Edward, 64
Harris, Charles K., 64, 66, 87
Harris, Sam H., 64, 111
Harrison, Rex, 154, 167–68
Hart, Charles, 261
Hart, Dorothy, 119
Hart, Lorenz, 91, 90–94, 102, 110, 136, 140, 146, 164, 191, 279; Loses chance to present *Vagabond King*, 76; Lyrics following melodies, 143. See also *Babes in Arms; The Boys from Syracuse; By Jupiter; Chee-Chee; Connecticut*

Yankee; Ever Green; The Garrick Gaieties; The Girl Friend; Heads Up; Higher and Higher; Jumbo; On Your Toes; Pal Joey; Peggy-Ann; Poor Little Ritz Girl; Spring is Here
Hart, Moss, 110, 137, 167, 168
Hart, Tony, 64
Hatton, Anne Julia, 17. See also *Tammany; or The Indian Chief*
Hauptmann, Elisabeth, 136
Havana (Wildhorn), 298
Have a Heart. See Princess Shows
Havoc, June, 120, 182
Haworth, Jill, 221
Hay, Mary, 84
Hayward, Leland, 148, 156, 181–82
Heartz, Daniel, 11
Heavy book, 256
Helburn, Theresa, 91, 122, 140–41, 146
Hellman, Lillian, Struggles with *Candide* libretto, 173. See also *Candide*; Refuses to testify, 173
Hello, Dolly! (Herman), 6, 199, 214
Hello, Hamlet, 130
Hello, Love (Mary Rodgers), 193
"Hello, Young Lovers" (Musical Example 32). See *The King and I*
Hellzapoppin', 111
Hemiola, 175
Henning, Doug, 236
Hepburn, Katherine, 247
Herbert, Victor, 50–51, 58, 69, 73, 97, Founding of ASCAP, 59, 141; Musical continuity, 76; Resists interpolations, 52; Struggles with Emma Trentini, 57; Turns down the first Princess Show, 69. See also *Babes in Toyland; The Dream Girl; It Happened in Nordland; Naughty Marietta; Rose-Marie; Sweethearts*
Heredia, Wilson Jermaine, 297
Herman, Jerry, 199, Plagiarism suit ("Sunflower"), 199. See also *Cage aux Folles, La; Hello, Dolly!; Mame; Milk and Honey*
"Hernando's Hideaway." See *The Pajama Game*
Hervé, 19–20, 22, 26, 31
Heston, Charlton, 133
Heuberger, Richard, 55
Hewitt, James, 17–18. See *Tammany; or The Indian Chief*
"Hey, Look Her Over." See *Wildcat*
Heyward, Dorothy, 104
Heyward, DuBose, 104–6, Writes lyrics for "Summertime," 104. See also *Porgy and Bess*
Heywood, Donald. See *Africana*
Hicks, Charles, 40
High Button Shoes (Styne), 181, 183
High Society, 302
High Tor (Sondheim), 205
Higher and Higher (Rodgers and Hart), 119
Hip hop. See Style
Hirsch, Foster, 246
Hirson, Roger O., 236
Hischak, Thomas, 114, 185, 215
Hit, 6
Hitler, Adolf, 25, 56, 186, 220, 302
Hogarth, George, 31
Holliday, Judy, 172, 181
Hollingshead, John, 31, 35
Hollman, Mark, 299. See *Urinetown*
Holly, Buddy. See *Buddy*
Holmes, Oliver Wendell, 59
Holofcener, Larry, 213
Home Again, Home Again (Coleman), 198
Home Alone, 297
Home Sweet Homer (Leigh), 199
Homophony. See Texture
Honky-tonk, 63
Hooker, Brian, 76, 79
Hot Spot (Mary Rodgers), 193

"Hot Time in the Old Town Tonight, A," 101
House Un-American Activities Committee, 173, 185, 208
"How Long Has This Been Going On?" See *Funny Face; Rosalie*
How to Succeed in Business Without Really Trying (Loesser), 185, 239
Huapango, 175
Huasteco, 175
Hubbell, Raymond, 59
Hugo, Victor, 269–71
"Huguette Waltz." See *The Vagabond King*
Humpty Dumpty, 256
Hunchback of Notre Dame, The (Menken), 237
Hunter, Anne Home, 17
Huston, Walter, 137
Hyland, William G., 156
Hymn-tune, 17
Hytner, Nicholas, 272

I Am a Camera, 219, 302
"I Am the Very Model of a Modern Major-General" (Musical Example 8). See *The Pirates of Penzance*
"I Can Do That" (Musical Example 50). See *A Chorus Line*
"I Can't Do the Sum" (Musical Example 13). See *Babes in Toyland*
I Do! I Do! (Schmidt and Jones), 201
"I Don't Know How to Love Him." See *Jesus Christ Superstar*
"I Get a Kick Out of You." See *Anything Goes*
"I Got Plenty o' Nuttin'." See *Porgy and Bess*
"I Got Rhythm." See *Girl Crazy*
"I Hate Men" (Musical Example 27). See *Kiss Me, Kate*
"I Know Him So Well." See *Chess*
"I Love My Wife; But, Oh, You Kid," 71
"I Still Believe" (Musical Example 58). See *Miss Saigon*
"I Want to Be Happy." See *No, No, Nanette*
"(I Wants to Be) A Actor Lady" (Musical Example 15). See *In Dahomey*
"I Wish I Were in Love Again." See *Babes in Arms*
"If I Loved You." See *Carousel*
"If My Friends Could See Me Now." See *Sweet Charity*
"If You Could See Her Through My Eyes." See *Cabaret*
"I'm About to Be a Mother." See *Of Thee I Sing*
I'm Getting My Act Together and Taking It on the Road (Ford and Cryer), 239–40
"I'm Gonna Wash That Man Right Out of My Hair." See *South Pacific*
Imaginary Friends (Hamlisch), 239
Imitative polyphony. See Texture
"Impossible Dream." See *Man of La Mancha*
Impresario, 56, 97, 105. See also D'Oyly Carte; Edwardes; Oscar Hammerstein I; Hollingshead; See also Producer
Improvisation, 99, 101, 121
In Dahomey (Cook), 62–63, 64, 104, 222, 281; "(I Wants to Be) A Actor Lady" (von Tilzer) (Musical Example 15), 63, 67–68, 71, 97; Plot idea for, 62; Plot Summary, 66–67
In the Beginning: The Greatest Story Never Told (Yeston), 281
In the Good Old Summertime. See *She Loves Me*
In Trousers (Finn), 280
Incidental music, 173, 239
Incoronazione di Poppea, L'. See *The Coronation of Poppea*
"Indian Love Call" (Musical Example 18). See *Rose-Marie*
Indian Princess, The, 18

Integration: Dance, 141, 165, 174–75; Musical numbers, 69, 76–77, 82, 84, 87, 101, 122, 131, 158, 167, 173, 183, 207, 295; Poetry, 175; Racial, 46, 61, 111, 122, 131, 173
Interlude, 20, 40, 43, 57, 101, 222, 277
Intermezzo, 11, 24, 39
Intermission, lack of, 199, 202
Interpolation, 52, 69, 73, 76, 77, 97, 109, 110
Into the Woods (Sondheim), 262, 285–87, 302; "Agony" (Musical Example 60), 286–87, 291–92; "Lament," 287; Plot Summary, 289–90
Introduction: Instrumental, 20, 43, 56, 63, 230; Vocal, 57, 77, 93, 111, 142, 149, 156, 166, 175, 183, 288
Inversion, 86
"Invocation." See *A Funny Thing Happened on the Way to the Forum*
Iolanthe (Gilbert and Sullivan), 34
Irene, "Alice Blue Gown," 72
Isham, John William, 40
Isherwood, Christopher, 219
Isolations, 165
"It Ain't Necessarily So." See *Porgy and Bess*
It Happened in Nordland (Herbert), 52
"Italian Street Song" (Musical Example 14). See *Naughty Marietta*
"I've Got You Under My Skin." See *Born to Dance*

Jack, Sam T., 40
Jackson, Michael, 237
Jacobs, Bernard, 285
Jacobs, Jim, 239. See also *Grease*
Jamaica, 17, 281
Jamieson, James, 165
Janin, Jules, 20
Janney, Russell, 76, 91
Jazz. See Style
Jazz dance, 165
Jazz song, 99
Jekkies, 297
Jekyll & Hyde (Wildhorn), 297
Jelly's Last Jam, 295
Jerome Robbins' Broadway, 238, 282
Jesus Christ Superstar (Lloyd Webber and Rice), 229–31, 236, 239, 254, 260, 264, 269, 277; "I Don't Know How to Love Him," 230; "King Herod's Song," 230; "Pilate's Dream" (Musical Example 48), 230, 234; Plot Summary, 232–33; "Poor Jerusalem," 230
Jewell, Derek, 229
"Jimmy Crack Corn." See Emmett
John, Elton, 279–80. See also *Aida; The Lion King*
John, Paul, George, Ringo . . . and Bert (Russell), 281
"Johnny One Note." See *Babes in Arms*
Johnson, James P., 101
Johnson, James Weldon, 63
Jolson, Al, 97, 104
Jones, Tom, 201. See also *110 in the Shade; The Fantasticks; I Do! I Do!*
Joplin, Scott, 63, 104
Joseph and the Amazing Technicolor Dreamcoat (Lloyd Webber and Rice), 228–29, 230, 255, 256, 264; "Song of the King, The," 229
Joseph II, Emperor of Austria, 12
Jugar con fuego, 21
Jumbo (Rodgers and Hart), 92
Jump tune, 65
"June is Bustin' Out All Over." See *Carousel*
"Just You Wait" (Musical Example 35). See *My Fair Lady*

Kander, John, 219–23, 237; "New York, New York," 223, 279; Working method with Ebb, 219. See also *The Act; Cabaret; Chicago; Flora, the Red Menace; The Happy Time; Kiss of the*

(Continued)
Spider Woman; The Rink; Woman of the Year; Zorbá
Karnilova, Maria, 215
Kaufman, George S., 98–99, 101, 205
Keaton, Buster, 46, 47
"Keep the Home Fires Burning." *See Novello*
Keith, B. F., 45
Keller, Helen, 46
Kelly, Gene, 62, 120, 166
Kennedy, Jacqueline, 168
Kennedy, John F., 164, 168, 194
Kennick, T, 43
Kerker, Gustave. See *The Belle of New York*
Kern, Eva, 87
Kern, Jerome, 45, 62, 69, 73, 80, 84, 90, 94, 97, 107, 122, 140; "All the Things You Are," 205; Collaborates with Caldwell, 58; Hired to compose *Annie Get Your Gun*, 87; Princess Shows, 62, 69–72, 80; "They Didn't Believe Me," 69; Withdraws from *Porgy*, 104; Writes for Hollywood, 279. See also *Miss 1917; The Red Petticoat; Roberta; Sally; Show Boat; Sunny; Sweet Adeline*. See also Princess Shows: *Have a Heart; Leave It to Jane; Miss Springtime; Nobody Home; Oh, Boy!; Oh, Lady! Lady!!; Oh, My Dear; Sitting Pretty; Very Good Eddie*
Kerr, Deborah, 155
Kerr, Walter, 185, 244
Key, 25, 109
Key change, 88, 109, 191, 222, 255, 261
Kidd, Michael, 186
King and I, The (Rodgers and Hammerstein), 154–56, 158, 168, 302; "Hello, Young Lovers" (Musical Example 32), 155, 160–61; Plot Summary, 158–59; "Small House of Uncle Thomas, The," 154–55, 165
"King Herod's Song." See *Jesus Christ Superstar*
King Lear. See Shakespeare
King, Carole, 281
King, Dennis, 76, 164
King, Francis, 270
Kislan, Richard, 215
Kismet, 91
Kiss Me, Kate (Porter), 116, 129–32, 133, 150; "From This Moment On," 132; "I Hate Men" (Musical Example 27), 131–32, 134–35; Plot Summary, 134; "Too Darn Hot," 131
Kiss of the Spider Woman (Kander and Ebb), 223
Kleban, Edward, 237
Knickerbocker Holiday (Weill), 137; "September Song," 137
Knighton, Nan, 297
Kopit, Arthur, 280
Kotis, Greg, 299. See *Urinetown*
Kotzebue, August von, 42
Koussevitzky, Serge, 172–73
Kresa, Helmy, 122
Kretzmer, Herbert, 270, 272
Krieger, Henry, 282, 299. See *Dreamgirls*
Kristofferson, Kris, 240
Krupa, Gene, 99
Kummer, Clare, 58

LaChiusa, Michael John, 298–99. See also *Marie Christine; The Wild Party*
"Ladies Who Lunch, The." See *Company*
Lady in the Dark (Weill), 137
"Lady Is a Tramp, The." See *Babes in Arms*
Lady, Be Good! (Gershwin), 98; "Fascinating Rhythm," 98
LaMaMa Experimental Theatre Club, 236, 239
Lamb, Andrew, 80
"Lambeth Walk." See *Me and My Girl*
Lambs Club, 65, 164

"Lament." See *Into the Woods*
Landon, Margaret, *Anna and the King of Siam*, 154
Langner, Lawrence, 91, 122, 140–41, 146
Lansbury, Angela, 199
Lap dissolve, 150
Lapine, James, 280, 285–88
Largo. See Tempo
Larry Award. See Olivier Awards
Larson, Jonathan, 295–97, Premature death of, 296. See also *Rent; tick, tick . . . BOOM!*
Last Five Years, The (Brown), 298; "Climbing Uphill," 298
Last Sweet Days of Isaac, The (Ford and Cryer), 239
Laszlo, Miklos, 213
Late Nite Comic, 238
Laurents, Arthur, 173–74, 181–83, 207, 209; Chosen to write *West Side Story* book, 173. See also *Anyone Can Whistle; Gypsy; West Side Story*
Lawrence, Gertrude, 154–55
Lawrence, Stephanie, 281
Lead sheet, 122
League of New York Theatres and Producers, 133
Leave It to Jane. See Princess Shows
Leave It To Me (Porter), 129; "My Heart Belongs to Daddy," 129
Leavitt, Philip, 90
LeCocq, Charles, 19, 21. See also *La Fille de Madame Angot*
Lee, C. Y., 155
Lee, Eugene, 245
Lee, Gypsy Rose, 120, 181–82
Lee, Madeline, 208
Leg (curtain), 238
Leg drama, 44
Legs Diamond, 238
Lehár, Franz, 55–56. See also *The Merry Widow*
Leiber, Jerry: See *Smokey Joe's Café*
Leigh, Carolyn, 198. See also *Little Me; Wildcat*
Leigh, Mitch, 199–200. See also *Home Sweet Homer; Man of La Mancha; Saravà*
Leitmotif, 25, 34, 76
Lenya, Lotte, 136–37, 219
Leoncavallo, Ruggero, 253
Lerner, Alan Jay, 99, 102, 157, 164–69, 199, 219, 260, 269, 295; Kennedy Center Award, 223; Rejects property of *The Sound of Music*, 155; Writes for Hollywood, 279. See also *1600 Pennsylvania Avenue; An American in Paris; Brigadoon; Camelot; Dance a Little Closer; The Day Before Spring; Gigi; The Little Prince; Love Life; My Fair Lady; Paint Your Wagon; What's Up?*
Leroux, Gaston, 260, 295. See *Le Fantôme de l'Opéra*
Let 'Em Eat Cake (Gershwin), 102
"Let It Snow! Let It Snow! Let It Snow!" See Styne
"Let the Sunshine In." See *Hair*
"Let's Call the Whole Thing Off." See Gershwin, George
"Let's Do It." See Porter
"Let's Have Another Cup of Coffee." See Berlin
Lewis, Jerry, 147
Lewis, Ted, 222
Libby, Laura Jean, 63
Liberazione di Ruggiero dall'isola d'Alcina, La (Caccini), 2
Librettist, 1. *See also* Abbott; Barras; Black; Brecht; Bricusse; Burnand; Burrows; Busenello; Caldwell; Comden; Crémieux; Crouse; da Ponte; Donnelly; Dunbar; Eyen; Fenton; Dorothy Fields; Furth; Gaines; Gay; Gelbart; Genée; Gilbert; Goodwin; Green; Haffner; Halévy; Hammerstein II; Hampton;

Harbach; Moss Hart; Hatton; DuBose Heyward; Hellman; Hirson; Janney; Kaufman; Kopit; Kotis; Kretzmer; Kummer; Lapine; Larson; Laurents; Léon; Lindsay; Logan; MacDonough; Maltby; Mandel; Masteroff; Nelson; Norman; O'Hara; Ryskind; Schachtner; Shevelove; Shipp; Harry B. Smith; Sondheim; Bella and Samuel Spewack; Joseph Stein; Leo Stein; Stilgoe; Peter Stone; Striggio; Weidman; Wheeler; Wodehouse; Young; *See also* Book writer
Libretto, 1, 12, 16–17, 26, 49, 55–56, 58, 69, 84, 101, 104, 114, 130, 140, 146, 154, 156, 173, 182, 184, 201–2, 205, 219, 236, 245, 261–62, 271, 278, 295–296
Lieberson, Goddard, 209
Life, The (Coleman), 199
Light in the Piazza, A (Guettel), 298
Lightnin', 92
Lili, 302
Liliom. See Molnár
Lindbergh, Charles, 46
Lindsay, Howard, 114–15, 156. See also *Anything Goes; The Sound of Music*
Lion King, The (John and Rice), 154, 279–80, 302–3; "Can You Feel the Love Tonight?," 279
Lippa, Andrew, 298–99
List song, 12, 175, 208
Liszt, Franz, 22, 93
Little Johnny Jones (Cohan), 64–65, 75; Plot Summary, 67; "Yankee Doodle Boy" (Musical Example 16), 64–65, 68, 71, 76
Little Me (Coleman), 198
Little Mermaid, The (Ashman and Menken), 279; "Under the Sea," 279
Little Night Music, A (Sondheim), 244–45, 288, 302; "Send in the Clowns," 244
"Little Priest, A" (Musical Example 52). See *Sweeney Todd*
Little Prince, The (Lerner and Loewe), 168
Little Shop of Horrors (Ashman and Menken), 279
Liza. See *My Fair Lady*, Working title of
Lloyd Webber, Andrew, 213, 228–32, 253–56, 260–64, 269–70, 278, 281, 297; Country home (Sydmonton), 253, 260, 262; Discusses "chess" idea, 277; Knighted, 264; *Requiem*, 255; *Variations*, 255; Working method with Rice, 271. See also (with Rice) *Cricket; Evita; Jesus Christ Superstar; Joseph and the Amazing Technicolor Dreamcoat*; (with others) *Aspects of Love; The Beautiful Game; By Jeeves; Cats; The Phantom of the Opera; Song and Dance; Starlight Express; Sunset Boulevard; Tell Me on a Sunday; Whistle Down the Wind; The Woman in White*
Lloyd Webber, Imogen, 255
Lloyd Webber, Jean, 228
Lloyd Webber, Julian, 228
Lloyd Webber, Nicholas, 255
Lloyd Webber, William, 228–29
Loesser, Frank, 92, 166, 168, 181, 184–85, 193, 201–2, 206, 209; Dealings with performers, 186; Frank Music Corporation, 185; "Praise the Lord and Pass the Ammunition," 184; Writes for Hollywood, 279. See also *Greenwillow; Guys and Dolls; How to Succeed in Business Without Really Trying; The Most Happy Fella; Where's Charley?*
Loewe, Edmund, 164
Loewe, Frederick, 102, 157, 164–68, 219; Kennedy Center Award, 223; Rejects property of *The Sound of*

Music, 155; Writes for Hollywood, 279. See also *Brigadoon; Camelot; The Day Before Spring; Gigi; The Little Prince; My Fair Lady; Paint Your Wagon; Salute to Spring; What's Up?*
Logan, Joshua, 120, 123, 148–49, 155
"London Bridge is Falling Down," 167
London Company of Comedians. See The Old American Company
Longfellow, Henry Wadsworth, 44
Long-run record (Berlin), 237
Long-run record (Broadway), 45, 92, 111, 141, 168, 194, 199, 214, 228, 239, 254, 264
Long-run record (off-Broadway), 201
Long-run record (revival), 222
Long-run record (West End), 157, 228, 231, 254, 264, 279
"Look Down." See *Les Misérables*
L'Orfeo. See *Orfeo*
Lost in the Stars (Weill), 137, 281
Love and Let Love, 130
"Love for Sale." See *The Vagabond King*
"Love Is Here to Stay." See Gershwin, George
Love Life (Weill), 137, 148, 166
Love Song, The, 91
Love-nest ballad, 81
Lover's Opera, The, 7
Lucky Stiff (Flaherty and Ahrens), 298
LuPone, Patti, 263
Lynne, Gillian, 253, 261
Lyric theater, 164
Lyricist, 69. See Adams; Adler; Ahrens; Ashman; Barer; Black; Boublil; Bryan; Irving Caesar; Cahn; Casey; Charnin; Cryer; Cuden; Ebb; Herbert Fields; Ira Gershwin; Greene; Harnick; Charles Hart; Lorenz Hart; Hooker; Jim Jacobs; Jones; Kleban; Leiber; Carolyn Leigh; Lerner; Merrill; Powers; Rado; Ragni; Tim Rice; Jerry Ross; Wilbur; *See also* Composer-Lyricist; Librettist
Lyrics, 69, 104, 114

Macbeth. See Shakespeare
MacDermot, Galt, 200–201. See also *Dude; Hair; Via Galactica*
MacDonald, Will, 49
MacDonough, Glen, 51
Machinery, 2, 42, 280
"Mack the Knife." See *The Threepenny Opera*: "The Ballad of Mack the Knife"
Mackay, Clarence, 110
Mackay, Ellin, 110, 124
Mackintosh, Cameron, 228, 253–55, 260–61, 269–73, 279
MacLaine, Shirley, 198
MacRae, Gordon, 133
Mad Show, The (Mary Rodgers), 193; "Boy From . . . , The," 193
Madama Butterfly (Puccini), 25, 91, 93, 148, 271, 295
Maggie May (Bart), 228
Magic Flute, The (Mozart), 9
Magic Show, The (Schwartz), 236
Maguire, Gregory, 237
Mahler, Gustav, 25
Mail, 238
Major. See Mode
Maltby, Richard, Jr., 272
Mame (Herman), 199
Mamma Mia! (Andersson/Ulvaeus), 282, 303
Mamoulian, Rouben, 147
"Man I Love, The." See *Strike Up the Band*
Man of La Mancha (Leigh), 199–200; "Impossible Dream, The," 199
Man of No Importance, A (Flaherty and Ahrens), 298
Mandel, Frank, 80, 82
Mandelbaum, Ken, 213, 223
Marbury, Elisabeth, 69–70
March, 7, 20, 27, 43–44, 50, 51, 82, 101–2, 138, 191, 198

March of the Falsettos (Finn), 280
"March of the Toys, The." See *Babes in Toyland*
"Maria." See *West Side Story*
Marie Christine (LaChiusa), 298
"Marie from Sunny Italy." See Berlin
Marriage of Figaro, The (Mozart), 11
"Married Man." See *Song and Dance*
"Marry Me a Little." See *Company*
Marshall, Armina, 141
Martha, 49
Martin Guerre (Schönberg and Boublil), 273
Martin, Ernest, 184–86, 190
Martin, Mary, 123, 129, 148, 156–58, 167, 199, 201
Marx Brothers, 61
"Mary Had a Little Lamb," 45
Mary Poppins (Sondheim), 205
Masque, 6, 38
"Masquerade." See *The Phantom of the Opera*
Massine, 61
"Master of the House." See *Les Misérables*
Masteroff, Joe, 213, 219
Matthews, Charles, 38
Mayer, Louis B., 129
Maytime (Romberg), 58
McCarthy, Justin Huntly, 76
McDonald, Audra, 138, 298, 299
McIntosh, Jane, 253
McKenney, Ruth, *My Sister Eileen*, 173
Me and Juliet (Rodgers and Hammerstein), 155
"Me and My Baby." See *Chicago*
Me and My Girl, 116; "Lambeth Walk, The," 116
Medium, 8
Meet Me in St. Louis, 238
Meilhac, Henri, 26
Melisma, 26, 131, 296
Melismatic. See Text Setting
Melodrama, 42, 46, 49, 84, 245
Mélodrame, 42
"Memory." See *Cats*
Mendelssohn, Felix, Violin Concerto, 230
Menken, Alan, 279–80. See also *Aladdin; Beauty and the Beast; The Little Mermaid; Little Shop of Horrors*
Menuet. See Minuet
Merchandizing, 55
Merman, Ethel, 99–101, 114–15, 122–23, 129, 181–82, 207, 238; Performance of "I Got Rhythm," 101; Reacts to "I Got Rhythm," 99–100; Rejects Sondheim as *Gypsy* composer, 181
Merrick, David, 181–82, 184, 199, 207; Publicity stunt, 184
Merrill, Bob, 193
Merrily We Roll Along (Sondheim), 246
Merry Widow, The (Lehár), 55–57, 76, 81, 116, 164, 228; "Merry Widow Waltz, The," 55; "Silly, Silly Cavalier," 55
"Merry Widow Waltz, The." See *The Merry Widow*
Mesmer, Franz Anton, 8
Message song, 150
Meter, 20; Asymmetrical, 255, 270; Duple, 20, 26, 33, 34, 44, 56–57, 64, 77, 106, 138, 142, 155, 175, 255, 270, 286, 296; Quadruple, 20, 155, 213, 255, 263, 270; Triple, 20, 27, 33, 46, 56–57, 121, 155, 175, 191, 213, 220, 244, 270
Metronome, 9
Mexican Hayride (Porter), 129
Mezzo-soprano. See Voice type
Michener, James, 148, 150; *Tales of the South Pacific*, 148
Midsummer Night's Dream, A. See Shakespeare
Mielziner, Jo, 120, 149, 150
Mikado, The (Gilbert and Sullivan), 34–35; Inspires *The Begum*, 49;

"Miya sama, miya sama," 34; "Three Little Maids from School," 34
Milk and Honey (Herman), 199
Miller, Glenn, 99
Miller, Marilynn, 61, 72, 84, 93
Miller, Ronald, 244
Miller, Scott, 242
Milli Vanilli, 223
Minevitch, Borrah, 93
Minnelli, Liza, 219, 221–23, 237
Minor. See Mode
Minstrel show, 38–40, 42, 45, 49, 62, 165, 236
Minstrel song, 39–40
Minuet, 20, 244
Miracles (Smalls), 237
Miscegenation, 85, 150
Misérables, Les (Schönberg and Boublil), 24, 238, 262, 269–72, 277, 297; "Beggars at the Feast," 270; "Castle on a Cloud" (Musical Example 57), 270, 276; "Come to Me," 270; "Do You Hear the People Sing?," 270; "Dog Eats Dog," 270; "Empty Chairs at Empty Tables," 270; "Look Down," 270; "Master of the House," 270; Plot Summary, 274; "Soliloquy," 270
Miss 1917 (Kern), 71
Miss Saigon (Schönberg and Boublil), 25, 91, 148, 271–73, 277, 279, 295; "I Still Believe" (Musical Example 58), 272, 276; Inspired by photograph, 271; Plot Summary, 274–75
Miss Springtime. See Princess Shows
Mitchell, Abbie, 104
Mitchell, Julian, 51
Mixed bill, 61
Mixolydian. See Mode
"Miya sama, miya sama." See *The Mikado*
Mme. Pompadour, 58
Mode, 45; Major, 45, 56, 71, 76–77, 102, 111, 115, 138, 147, 156, 167, 191, 230, 232, 245, 270; Minor, 45, 56, 57, 71, 76–77, 101–2, 111, 115, 131, 167, 230, 245, 261, 270, 288; Mixolydian, 202
Moderato. See Tempo
Modern dance, 141, 165
Modulation, 88
Moën, Peter, 141
"Molasses to Rum." See *1776*
Molnár, Ferenc, *Liliom*, 146, 148
"Momma, Look Sharp" (Musical Example 42). See *1776*
"Momma's Talkin' Soft." See *Gypsy*
Monophony. See Texture
Monteverdi, Claudio, 2–3, 11. See also *The Coronation of Poppea; Orfeo*
Montgomery, David, 51, 58
Morality (hymn-tune), 17
Moranis, Rick, 279
Mordden, Ethan, 81, 86, 89, 147, 193
Morgan, Helen, 88, 221–22
Moritat, 25, 137
Morley, Sheridan, 116, 228
Morton, Jelly Roll. See *Jelly's Last Jam*
Most Happy Fella, The (Loesser): "Standing on the Corner," 185
Mostel, Zero, 208, 215
Motif, 25, 81, 86, 261, 285, 287
Mozart, Wolfgang Amadeus, 8–9, 11–13, 19, 22, 24, 26, 69, 136, 302. See also *Bastien und Bastienne; Così fan tutte; Don Giovanni; The Magic Flute; The Marriage of Figaro*
"Mr. Cellophane." See *Chicago*
Mr. Popple of Ippleton, 69
Mr. Wonderful, 281
MTV video, 254
Much Ado, 130
Much Ado About Nothing. See Shakespeare
"Multitude of Amys." See *Company*
"Mungojerrie and Rumpleteazer" (Musical Example 53). See *Cats*
Murray, Peg, 221
Muscle (Finn), 280

Music Box Revues (Berlin), 61
Music drama, 25, 75–76, 138
Music hall, 45
Music in My Heart, 91
Music Is, 130
Music Man, The (Willson), 155, 185, 190–92; "Goodnight, Ladies," 190; "Goodnight, My Someone" (Musical Example 40), 191, 196; Original title of (*The Silver Triangle*), 190; Overture, 190; "Pick-a-Little, Talk-a-Little," 190; Plot Summary, 194–95
"Music of the Night." See *The Phantom of the Opera*
Musical comedy, 44, 57, 62–65, 75, 80, 84, 93, 101, 136, 230; British, 35
Musical play, 64, 75–76
Musical quotation, 64, 93, 101, 296
Musical scene, 86, 142, 156
Musical theater, 105, 140
Musical Theater Works, 299
Musical Theatre Lab, 287
Musicians' Union, 33, 106, 142
My Fair Lady (Lerner and Loewe), 155, 166–68, 302; Inspires Lloyd Webber, 228; "Just You Wait" (Musical Example 35), 167–68, 171; Plot Summary, 170; "Rain in Spain, The," 167–68; Working title of (*Liza*), 167
"My Favorite Things." See *The Sound of Music*
My Favorite Year (Flaherty and Ahrens), 298
"My Funny Valentine." See *Babes in Arms*
"My Heart" (Musical Example 11). See *Evangeline*
"My Heart Belongs to Daddy." See *Leave It to Me*
My Maryland (Romberg), 58
"My Old Kentucky Home." See Foster
"My One and Only." See *Funny Face*
Myths and Hymns. See Saturn Returns

Nabucco (Verdi), 24
Nadel, Norman, 209, 214
Napier, John, 254, 256, 263, 272
Narrator, 138, 231, 270, 295
Nathan, George Jean, 91, 132, 165
Nation, Carrie, 46
Nationalism, 24–25
Naughty Marietta (Herbert), 56–58, 75–76, 137; "Ah! Sweet Mystery of Life," 76; "Italian Street Song" (Musical Example 14), 56–57, 60; Plot Summary, 58–59
Nazism, 6, 25, 107, 136, 160, 220
Nederlander, James, 269–70
Nelson, Richard, 278
Neologism, 34
New Brain, A (Finn), 280
New York Drama Critics' Circle, 121, 132, 148, 165, 173, 185, 191, 202, 215, 221, 244–46
"New York, New York." See Kander; Ebb; See also *On the Town*
New York Theatre Workshop, 296
Nicholas Nickleby, 279
Nichols, Red, 99
Nicola, Jim, 297
Night and Day. See Porter, Film about
Nights of Cabiria, 302
Nightshriek, 130
Nine (Yeston), 280–81
Nixon, Marni, 155
No Cards (Gilbert), 31
No, No, Nanette (Youmans), 77, 80–82; "Fight Over Me," 81; "I Want to Be Happy," 80; Plot Summary, 82–83; "Tea for Two" (Musical Example 20), 80–81, 83
"Nobody," 222
Nobody Home. See Princess Shows
Nonet. See Ensemble number
Nonimitative polyphony. See Texture
Nonplot show, 198, 200, 242, 254

Norman, Marsha, 295
Note, 2
Novello, Ivor, "Keep the Home Fires Burning," 116
Nunn, Trevor, 253–56, 260–62, 269–70, 272, 277–79
Nuove musiche, La, 1, 3
Nut, 256

"O, Dem Golden Slippers." See Bland
Obie, 133, 298
Octaroons, 40
Octave, 76, 87
Octet. See Ensemble number
O'Dea, James, 58
Of Thee I Sing (Gershwin), 101–3, 191; "I'm About to Be a Mother," 102; "Of Thee I Sing, Baby," 102; "Wintergreen for President," 101–2
"Of Thee I Sing, Baby." See *Of Thee I Sing*
Off-Broadway, 133, 199, 201, 279, 303; Awards for, 133; Definition, 50; First cast recording, 137; Revivals, 70. See also Broadway: Transfers from off-Broadway; Long-run record; Playwrights Horizons
Offenbach, Jacques, 19–22, 26, 91. See also *La Grande-Duchesse de Gérolstein; Orpheus in the Underworld*
Off-off-Broadway, 50; Awards for, 133
Oh, Boy! See Princess Shows
Oh, Brother!, 130
"Oh! How I Hate to Get Up in the Morning." See Berlin: *Yip, Yip, Yaphank*
Oh, Kay! (Gershwin), 98
Oh, Lady! Lady!! See Princess Shows
"Oh, London Is a Fine Town," 7
Oh, My Dear. See Princess Shows
"Oh, Promise Me." See *Robin Hood*
"Oh, What a Beautiful Mornin'." See *Oklahoma!*
O'Hanlon, Redmond, 270
O'Hara, John, 107, 119–21
O'Horgan, Tom, 200, 231
Oklahoma! (Rodgers and Hammerstein), 116, 122, 123, 131, 141, 140–43, 146–48, 155, 157–58, 164, 192, 205, 302; Dream ballet, 44, 120; "Oh, What a Beautiful Mornin'," 141, 158; Original title of, 140, 141; Performance record broken, 168; Plot Summary, 143–45; Sondheim's comments regarding, 148; "Surrey with the Fringe on Top" (Musical Example 29), 142, 145
"Ol' Man River" (Musical Example 21). See *Show Boat*
Old American Company, The, 16–17
"Old Dan Tucker." See Emmett
"Old Folks at Home." See Foster
"Old-Fashioned Wedding, An." See *Annie Get Your Gun*
Olio, 39, 45
Oliver! (Bart), 199, 228, 231, 269, 302; Best Picture Oscar, 228
Oliver Twist, 228
Oliver, George P., 42
Oliver, Stephen. See *Blondel*
Olivier Awards, 262, 273
On the Town (Bernstein), 172–73; "New York, New York," 173
On the Twentieth Century (Coleman), 198
On Your Toes (Rodgers and Hart), 92–94, 165, 184; Plot Summary, 94–95; "Questions and Answers," 94; "Three B's, The" (Musical Example 22), 91, 93–96
Once on This Island (Flaherty and Ahrens), 298
Once Upon a Mattress (Mary Rodgers), 192–93, 213; "Opening for a Princess," 192; Plot Summary, 195–96; "Shy" (Musical Example 41), 192, 196–97
110 in the Shade (Schmidt and Jones), 201

"One Night in Bangkok" (Musical Example 59). See *Chess*
One-rhyme, 116
One-set musical, 207
1-2-3-4-5. See *In the Beginning: The Greatest Story Never Told*
Onomatopoeia, 56
"Opening for a Princess." See *Once Upon a Mattress*
Opening night, 120
Opera, 1, 3, 21, 24, 33, 38, 39, 42, 86, 104–5, 231, 245, 270, 298
Opéra, 6
Opera buffa, 11–12
Opera houses, private, 2
Opera houses, public, 2
Opera seria, 11, 21, 24
Opéra-bouffe, 19–21, 31
Opéra-comique, 6, 19, 21; *Comédie en vaudeville*, 6; *Pièce à ariette*, 6; *Pièce en vaudeville*, 6
Operetta, 21, 22, 75, 86, 99, 101, 116, 167, 173, 245; American, 49–51, 55, 75, 80, 136; English, 31, 49; Viennese, 26, 55, 137, 156; Golden Age, 26; Silver Age, 26
Operti, Giuseppe, 43
O'Ramey, Georgia, 71
Oratorio, 229
Orchestra, 1, 2, 46, 51, 73, 136, 149, 167; Payment, 33
Orchestra seating, 69
Orchestration, 105, 154, 168, 272
Orchestrator, 71, 154–55, 183, 272, 285
Orfeo (Monteverdi), 1, 2
Orff, Carl, *Carmina Burana*, 230
Oriental America, 40
Original cast album, 72, 122, 131, 137, 141, 168, 209, 219, 236, 243
Original score, 45, 52, 260
Ornamentation, 3, 17
Orphée aux enfers. See *Orpheus in the Underworld*
Orpheus in the Underworld (Offenbach), 20, 26, 31, 44; "Galop infernal" (Musical Example 6), 20, 23; Plot Summary, 22–23
Orpheus, myth of, 1, 22
Osmond, Donny, 65
Ostinato, 81, 87, 222, 256, 270
Ostrow, Stuart, 168, 185, 202, 236, 281, 287
Othello. See Shakespeare
"Our Polly Is a Sad Slut!" (Musical Example 2). See *The Beggar's Opera*
Outer Critics Circle, 132
"Over There." See Cohan
Overture, 7, 11, 72, 156, 159, 183, 213, 224, 243; Role of, 183

Pabst, G. W., 136
Pacific Overtures (Sondheim), 222, 245
Paige, Elaine, 253–54, 277–78, 279
Paint Your Wagon (Lerner and Loewe), 166
Pajama Game, The (Adler and Ross), 92, 185, 193–94; "Hernando's Hideaway," 193; "Steam Heat," 193
Pal Joey (Rodgers and Hart), 92, 94, 119–21, 141, 155, 181–82, 221; "Bewitched, Bothered, and Bewildered" (Musical Example 25), 120–21, 126, 131; Musical episodes in, 156; Plot Summary, 125
Pan review, 229
Pantomime, 38
Papp, Joseph, 200, 237, 239
Parade (Brown), 298
Pardon My English (Gershwin), 102, 114
Parlor song, 39–40
Parton, Dolly, 240
"Party's Over, The." See *Bells are Ringing*
Pascal, Adam, 297
Pascal, Gabriel, 166
Passing Show, The, 61, 97
Passion (Sondheim), 280, 288
Pasticcio, 43

Pastiche, 229–30, 245, 256, 287
Pastor, Tony, 45
Patter song, 9, 12, 34, 71, 131, 213, 243–44, 255
Paulsen, Harald, 137
Pavlova, Anna, 61
Peggy-Ann (Rodgers and Hart), 75, 92
Pelham, Frank, 38
Pemberton, Brock, 133
Pepusch, Johann Christoph, 7
Perfect pitch, 237
Performance medium. See Medium
Performance practice, 3
Performing forces. See Medium
Pergolesi, Giovanni Battista, 11. See *La Serva Padrona*
Perón, Eva ("Evita"), 231
Perry, Antoinette ("Tony"), 133
Perry, Dick, 182
Peter Pan (Bernstein), 173, 231
Peters, Bernadette, 255
Petrillo, James Caesar, 142
Peyser, Joan, 262
Phantom (Yeston), 281
Phantom of the Opera, The (Lloyd Webber), 2, 238, 256, 260–62, 264, 281, 287; *Leitmotifs* in, 261; "Masquerade," 260; "Music of the Night," 264; "Phantom of the Opera, The" (Musical Example 55), 261, 267; Performed at La Scala, 263; Plot Summary, 265–66
"Phantom of the Opera, The" (Musical Example 55). See *The Phantom of the Opera*
Philip V, King of Spain, 21
Phillips, Arlene, 256
"Pick-a-Little, Talk-a-Little." See *The Music Man*
Pièce à ariette. See Opéra-comique
Pièces en vaudeville. See Opéra-comique
"Pilate's Dream" (Musical Example 48). See *Jesus Christ Superstar*
Pink Lady, The (Caryll), 56
Pinza, Ezio, 148
Pipe Dream (Rodgers and Hammerstein), 155
Pippin (Schwartz), 2, 221, 236–37, 242, 269; Television commercial for, 236
Pirated production, 33, 39, 43, 57
Pirates of Penzance, The (Gilbert and Sullivan), 33–34; "Hail, Hail, the Gang's All Here," 101; "I Am the Very Model of a Modern Major-General" (Musical Example 8), 9, 33–34, 36–37, 138; Plot Summary, 35–36; "Tarantara! Tarantara!," 101
Pit orchestra, 99
Pitch, 2, 123, 142, 149
Pixérécourt, René Charles Guilbert de, 42
Placide, Alexandre, 165
Plantation song, 40
Plautus, Titus Maccius, 207
Play On!, 130
Playwrights' Company, 137
Playwrights Horizons, 280, 287, 298
Plot, 102
Plugger. See Song-plugger
Pocahontas (Menken), 237; "Colors of the Wind," 279
Polka, 27, 44, 154
Polly, 7
Polonaise, 91
"Poor Butterfly," 93
"Poor Jerusalem." See *Jesus Christ Superstar*
Poor Little Ritz Girl (Rodgers and Hart), 90
Poor Soldier, The, 17
Pop. See Style
Pop (show title), 130
Pop song form. See Form: Song
Pope, Alexander, 7
"Poppa's Blues" (Musical Example 54). See *Starlight Express*
Pop-rock. See Style
Popular song form. See Form: Song

Porgy and Bess (Gershwin), 98, 103, 104–7, 165, 185, 281; "I Got Plenty o' Nuttin'," 105–6; "It Ain't Necessarily So," 107; Plot Summary, 107–8; "Summertime," 104–5; *Leitmotifs* in, 104, 105
Porter, Cole, 114–16, 129–32, 137, 166; *Anna and the King of Siam* project, 154; Biographical films, 129; Leg injury, 44, 129, 132, 246; "Let's Do It," 114; Turns down *Gypsy*, 181. See also *Anything Goes*; *Around the World in Eighty Days*; *Born to Dance*; *Broadway Melody of 1940*; *Can-Can*; *Kiss Me, Kate*; *Leave It To Me*; *Mexican Hayride*; *Red, Hot, and Blue!*; *Rosalie*; *Seven Lively Arts*; *Silk Stockings*; *Something for the Boys*; *Something to Shout About*
Porter, Linda Lee, 114, 129
Post, W. H., 76, 79
Postlude. See Coda
Powers, Amy, 262
"Praise the Lord and Pass the Ammunition." See Loesser
Presley, Elvis, 200, 228–29
Presto. See Tempo
Preston, Robert, 201
Preview, 193, 199, 254, 270, 295–96
Prima donna, 2, 57
Primo uomo, 2
Prince of Central Park, 238
Prince of Egypt, The (Schwartz), 237; "When You Believe," 279
Prince, Daisy, 298
Prince, Harold (Hal), 92, 173–74, 177, 207–8, 213, 215, 219–21, 231, 242, 244–46, 256, 260–62, 298; Mistakes in *She Loves Me*, 214. See also *Cabaret*; *Company*; *Evita*; *Fiddler on the Roof*; *Flora, the Red Menace*; *Follies*; *A Little Night Music*; *Merrily We Roll Along*; *Pacific Overtures*; *She Loves Me*; *Sweeney Todd*
Princess Ida (Gilbert and Sullivan), 34
Princess Shows, 82, 165; *Go to It!*, 73; *Have a Heart* (Kern), 70, 73; *Leave It to Jane* (Kern), 70–71, 73; "Cleopatterer" (Musical Example 17), 70–71, 74; Influence on Richard Rodgers, 73, 90; Plot Summary, 72–73; *Miss Springtime* (Kern), 73; *Nobody Home* (Kern), 69, 70, 73; *Oh, Boy!* (Kern), 70, 73; Tension over financial inequity, 72; *Oh, Lady! Lady!!* (Kern), 71–72, 73; "Bill," 71, 86; *Oh, My Dear*, 73; *Sally* (Kern), 72; *Sitting Pretty* (Kern), 72, 73; Use of *Gesamtkunstwerk*, 25; *Very Good Eddie* (Kern), 70, 73
Principle of increasing animation, 8
Producer, 56, 61, 91, 122, 273, 303. See also Aarons; Abbott; Anderson; Ayers; Bloomgarden; Brooks; Cohan; Comstock; Cheryl Crawford; Company; Lew Fields; Frazee; Freedley; Fryer; Griffith; Arthur Hammerstein; Oscar Hammerstein II; Charles K. Harris; Sam H. Harris; Hayward; Helburn; Janney; Langner; Mackintosh; Marbury; Ernest Martin; Merrick; Ostrow; Pascal; Harold Prince; Richard Rodgers; Rose; Saint Subber; Savage; J. J. Shubert; Stevens; Stigwood; George White; Ziegfeld; See also Impresario
Producers, The (Brooks), 285, 302; "Betrayed," 302
Production number, 43, 76, 165, 192, 214
Program, 72, 76
Programmatic, 72, 93
Prohibition, 88
Prokofiev, Sergei, *Alexander Nevsky*, 230
Prop song, 49, 50, 86, 104, 120
Property, 69, 303
Props, 32

Pryce, Jonathan, 273
Puccini, Giacomo, 24, 25, 59, 93, 97, 146, 148, 253–54, 295–96. See also *La Bohème*; *Madama Butterfly*, *Tosca*
Puig, Manuel, 223
Pulitzer Prize, 114, 132; *Chorus Line, A*, 239; *Fiorello!*, 184, 213; *How to Succeed in Business Without Really Trying*, 185; *Of Thee I Sing*, 101, 150; *Oklahoma!*, 141; *Old Maid*, 132; *Rent*, 297; *South Pacific*, 150; *Sunday in the Park with George*, 285; *Tales of the South Pacific*, 148; Veto of *Guys and Dolls*, 185
Purcell, Henry. See *Dido and Aeneas*
Purlie, 281
"Put On a Happy Face." See *Bye Bye Birdie*
Pygmalion. See Shaw

Quadrille, 27
Quadruple. See Meter
Quaker's Opera, The, 7
Quartet. See Ensemble number
Querelle des Bouffons. See The War of the Buffoons
"Questions and Answers." See *On Your Toes*
Quiet Place (Bernstein), 176
Quintet. See Ensemble number
Quiz Show Scandals, 192
Quodlibet, 109–10, 112, 123, 190

Rachmaninoff, Sergei, 91
Radio. See Advertising
Rado, James, 200–1
Ragni, Gerome, 200–1
Rags (Strouse), 193, 237
"Rags to Riches." See Adler; Ross
Ragtime. See Style
Ragtime (Flaherty and Ahrens), 298
"Rain in Spain, The." See *My Fair Lady*
Raisin, 281
Ramin, Sid, 183
Rand, Sally, 222
Randall, Tony, 133
Ransome, John W., 45
Rap. See Style
Rave review, 229
Recital, 181
Recitative. See Singing style
Recognition scene, 76
Reconciliation, The, 17
Recording, 72
Red Crook, The, 43
Red Petticoat, The (Kern), 58
Red Shoes, The (Styne), 295
Red, Hot and Blue! (Porter), 129
Reddy, Helen, 281
Refrain, 40, 56, 77, 82, 86–87, 93, 100, 102, 106, 131, 147, 149, 156, 166, 229, 261, 277, 286
Rehearsal pianist, 71, 73, 97, 237
Reiner, Carl, 200
Reiner, Fritz, 172
Release, 86
Remick, Jerome H., 66, 97
Rent (Larson), 25, 91, 295–97, 303; Plot Summary, 299–300; "Santa Fe" (Musical Example 62), 296, 300–301
Reprise, 77, 121, 148, 176, 183, 191, 202, 254, 264, 273, 278, 286; Melody only, 229–30
Resort, musical theater, 192, 213
Return of the Pink Panther, The, 297
Review, 120, 122
Revival, 20, 22, 43, 44, 85, 88, 92–93, 94, 105, 121, 133, 146, 155, 157, 165, 181, 184, 199, 221–22, 228, 239, 263–64, 269, 281, 288, 298, 302–3
Révolution française, La (Schönberg and Boublil), 269
Revue, 46, 61–62, 71, 75, 84–85, 88, 90–91, 93, 97, 105, 110–11, 114, 119, 122, 129, 193, 198–99, 236, 239, 281; African-American, 104

Revuers, The, 172
Reynolds, Burt, 240
Rhapsody in Blue. See Gershwin, George
Rhythm song, 65
Ria Nida, Esteban. *See* Sondheim, Stephen
Rice, Edward E., 62, Allows interpolations by Kern, 73; Opportunity for Cook, 62. See also *Adonis; Evangeline*
Rice, Thomas Dartmouth, 38
Rice, Tim, 213, 228–32, 253–54, 262, 279, 277–80; Working method with Lloyd Webber, 271. See also (with Lloyd Webber) *Cricket; Evita; Jesus Christ Superstar; Joseph and the Amazing Technicolor Dreamcoat;* (with others) *Aida; Aladdin; Blondel; Chess; The Lion King*
Rich, Frank, 285, 287; Reviews of Lloyd Webber's shows, 264
Richards, Carol, 166
Riggs, Lynn, 140, 148
Rigoletto (Verdi), 112
Rimsky-Korsakov, 90–91
Rinaldo (Handel), 7
Ring des Nibelungen, Der (Wagner), 25, 34, 253; "Wotan's Farewell," 25
Rink, The (Kander and Ebb), 223
Ritardando. *See* Tempo
Rittman, Trude, 154–55
Road company, 70
Robbins, Jerome, 164, 175–76, 194, 201, 207–8, 214–15, 272,; "Age of Anxiety, The," 173; Chorus dancers as individuals, 165, 174; Dance carrying plot forward, 165; House Unamerican Activities Committee testimony, 173, 208; Idea for *West Side Story* ("East Side Story"), 173; Symbolic dance in *The King and I,* 165. See also *Bells are Ringing; Fancy Free; Fiddler on the Roof; A Funny Thing Happened on the Way to the Forum; Gypsy; High Button Shoes; Jerome Robbins' Broadway; The King and I; On the Town; The Pajama Game; Salute to Spring; West Side Story*
Robert and Elizabeth, 244
Roberta (Kern), 87–88; "Smoke Gets in Your Eyes," 87–88
Robeson, Paul, 85
Robin Hood (De Koven), 49–50, 61; "Brown October Ale" (Musical Example 12), 49–51, 53–54, 76; Economical staging of, 49, 55; "Oh, Promise Me," 49; Plot Summary, 52–53
Rock. *See* Style
Rock opera, 230, 270
Rockabye Hamlet, 130
Rocky Horror Show, The, 260
Rodgers, Mary, 73, 157, 192–93, 206, 209, 236, 298. See also *Freaky Friday; Hello, Love; Hot Spot; The Mad Show; Once Upon a Mattress; Working*
Rodgers, Richard, 91, 90–94, 102, 110, 136–37, 157–58, 164, 190, 191–92, 209, 219, 231, 279, 298; Abortive partnership with Lerner, 168; As producer, 122–23; Dislikes *Hair,* 200; Idolized by Lloyd Webber, 228; Influenced by Kern, 73, 88; Kennedy Center Award, 223; Loses chance to present *Vagabond King,* 76; Refuses to produce *Brigadoon,* 165; Rejects property of *The Music Man,* 155; Rejects *Pygmalion* (later *My Fair Lady*), 155, 166; Rejects *Tevye's Daughters* (later *Fiddler on the Roof*), 155; Roles for women, 158; Suggestions for *West Side Story,* 176; Surrey Enterprises, 146; Unhappy collaboration with Sondheim, 209; Use of classics, 91; *Victory at Sea,* 155;

Williamson Music, 146; Writes for Hollywood, 146, 279. See also (with Hammerstein) *Allegro; Carousel; Cinderella; Flower Drum Song; The King and I; Me and Juliet; Oklahoma!; Pipe Dream; The Sound of Music; South Pacific; State Fair.* See also (with Hart) *Babes in Arms; The Boys from Syracuse; By Jupiter; Chee-Chee; Connecticut Yankee; Ever Green; The Garrick Gaieties; The Girl Friend; Heads Up; Higher and Higher; Jumbo; On Your Toes; Pal Joey; Peggy-Ann; Poor Little Ritz Girl; Spring is Here.* See also (with Sondheim) *Do I Hear a Waltz?*
Rogers, Ginger, 99; Beginning of partnership with Astaire, 99
Romance (Finn), 280
Romanticism, 24
Romanza, 44
Romberg, Sigmund, 58, 90, 97. See also *Blossom Time; The Desert Song; The Girl in Pink Tights; Maytime; My Maryland; Rosalie; The Student Prince*
Romeo and Juliet. See Shakespeare
Rondo. *See* Form
Ronger, Florimond. *See* Hervé
Rooney, Mickey, 101
Roosevelt, Alice, 72
Roosevelt, Theodore, 72
Rosalie (Gershwin), 98; "How Long Has This Been Going On?," 98
Rosalie (Porter), 129
Rosalie (Romberg), 98
Rose, Billy, 88, 92, 165
Rose-Marie (Friml), 75–77, 82, 84, 92, 164; Film versions, 302; "Indian Love Call" (Musical Example 18), 76, 77, 78; *Leitmotifs* in, 25, 76; Plot Summary, 77–78; "Rose-Marie," 76; "Totem Tom-Tom," 76
Rosenberg, Bernard, 302–3
Rosenberg, Deena, 102
Rosenfelt, Monroe, 66
Rosenstock, Milton, 182
"Rose's Turn." *See Gypsy*
Ross, Diana, 237
Ross, Jerry, 92, 185, 193–94, "Rags to Riches," 193. See also *Damn Yankees; The Pajama Game*
Rossini, Gioachino, 22
Round, 7, 185
Rounded binary. *See* Form
Rousseau, Jean Jacques, 8
"Row, Row, Row Your Boat," 7, 45
Roxie Hart, 221
Royal Family, The (Finn), 280
Royalties, 33, 43, 59, 80, 91, 97, 148, 166, 228, 254, 256
Rubins, Josh, 299
Ruddigore (Gilbert and Sullivan), 35
Run, 17
Runaways (Swados), 239
Runnin' Wild, "Charleston, The," 101
Runyon, Damon, 184
Russell, Lillian, 35, 45
Russell, Willy, 281. See also *Blood Brothers; Educating Rita; John, Paul, George, Ringo . . . and Bert; Shirley Valentine; The Wrong Boy*
Ruth, Babe, 46
Ryan, Meg, 213
Ryskind, Morrie, 99, 101

"'S Wonderful." *See Funny Face*
Sacred music, 156
Sager, Carole Bayer, 239
Sailor's Opera, The, 7
Sainetes, 21
Saint Subber, Arnold, 130, 176
Salisbury, Nate, 46
Sally (Kern), 72
Salute to Spring (Loewe), 164; Lerner helps revise, 164
Sant' Alessio, 2
"Santa Fe" (Musical Example 62). *See Rent*

Sarafina!, 282
Saravà (Leigh), 199
SATB chorus, 40
Saturday Night (Sondheim), 181, 206, 288
Saturday Night Fever, 302
Saturn Returns (Guettel), 298
Savage, Henry, 70
Savoy Operas, 34
Savoy, Bert, 222
Savoyard, 34
Say, Darling (Styne), 181
Scale, 167
Scarlet Pimpernel, The (Wildhorn), 297
Scene, 12
Scene change song, 85
Scenery show, 50, 155
Schachtner, Johann Andreas, 8
Schmidt, Harvey, 201. See also *110 in the Shade; The Fantasticks; I Do! I Do!*
Schönberg, Claude-Michel, 269–73; Working method, 271. See also *Martin Guerre; Les Misérables; Miss Saigon; La révolution française*
Schubert, Franz, 91
Schumann, Robert, 25
Schwartz, Arthur, 107, 166
Schwartz, Stephen, 236–37; Lyrics for Bernstein's *Mass,* 236. See also *Gepetto; Godspell; The Hunchback of Notre Dame; The Magic Show; Pippin; Pocahontas; The Prince of Egypt; Rags; Wicked; Working*
Score, 1, 8, 25, 42–43, 52, 66, 69, 73, 91, 155. *See also* Original score
Scorsese, Martin, 279
Scrooge, 297
Season, 70
Secret Garden, The (Simon), 295
Secunda, Sholom, 97
"See You in September." *See* Edwards
Segal, Vivienne, 120
Seis, 175
Sensations, 130
"September Song." *See Knickerbocker Holiday*
Septet. *See* Ensemble number
Sequence, melodic, 131, 176, 191, 261
Serva padrona, La (Pergolesi), 11, 39
Seurat, Georges, 285
Seussical (Flaherty and Ahrens), 298
Seven Brides for Seven Brothers, 302
Seven Lively Arts (Porter), 129; "Ev'ry Time We Say Goodbye," 129
1776 (Edwards), 201–3; "Cool, Cool, Considerate Men," 202; "Molasses to Rum," 202; "Momma, Look Sharp" (Musical Example 42), 203–4; Plot Summary, 202–3
Sextet. *See* Ensemble number
Shadow show, 38
Shakespeare, William, 16, 31, 92, 129–31, 176, 201; *Comedy of Errors, The,* 130; *Hamlet,* 91, 130, 238; *King Lear,* 130; *Macbeth,* 39, 93, 130, 238; *Midsummer Night's Dream, A,* 130; *Much Ado About Nothing,* 130; *Othello,* 130; *Romeo and Juliet,* 130, 173, 207; *Taming of the Shrew, The,* 129–30; *Tempest, The,* 16, 130; *Twelfth Night,* 130; *Two Gentlemen of Verona,* 130, 201
Sharaff, Irene, 154–55, 177; Costuming for *West Side Story,* 177
Sharman, Jim, 260
Shaw, George Bernard, *Pygmalion,* 155, 166–67
Shawn, Ted, 62, 141
She Loves Me (Bock and Harnick), 213–14; Films on same subject, 213; Plot Summary, 216; "Trip to the Library, A" (Musical Example 44), 213, 217–18
Sheet music, 66. *See also* Score
Shenandoah, 302
Sherrin, Ned, 186
Shevelove, Burt, 206–8

Shinbone Alley, 230, 236
"Shine On, Harvest Moon," 61
Shipp, Jesse, 62
Shirley Valentine (Russell), 281
Shop Around the Corner, The. See She Loves Me
Shop Girl, The, 35
Short, Martin, 198
Shostakovich, Dmitri, 93
Show Boat (Kern), 25, 73, 84–88, 122; Arrest of Helen Morgan, 88; "Bill," 71, 86; Film version of, 302; *Leitmotifs* in, 25, 86; "Ol' Man River" (Musical Example 21), 84–87, 89, 156, 208; Plot Summary, 88–89
Show doctor, 92, 176, 208
Show tune, 76, 104. *See* Form
Showgirl, 61
Showstopper, 71, 101, 123, 156, 185, 229
Shubert, J. J., 61
Shubert, Lee, 131
Shuffle Along, 61, 281
"Shy" (Musical Example 41). *See Once Upon a Mattress*
Side by Side by Sondheim, 193
Side Show, 303
"Sidewalks of New York, The," 101
Sight gag, 34
Sight-read, 11
Silk Stockings (Porter), 132
"Silly, Silly Cavalier." *See The Merry Widow*
Simon, Carly, 295
Simon, Lucy, 295. See also *The Secret Garden*
Simple. *See* Subdivision
Sinatra, Frank, 181, 244, 279
Singin' in the Rain, 302
Singing schools, 16
Singing style: Aria, 3, 6, 8, 12–13, 55, 105–6, 254, 261, 270; Arioso, 3; Recitative, 2–3, 6, 17, 24, 33, 38, 76–77, 101, 105, 185, 231, 270; *Stile rappresentativo,* 3
Singspiel, 6, 8–9, 38
"Sit Down, You're Rockin' the Boat." *See Guys and Dolls*
Sitting Pretty. See Princess Shows
Situation, 102
1600 Pennsylvania Avenue (Bernstein), 168, 176
Skinner, Cornelia Otis, 114
Sklar, Matthew, 299
Sleeper, 201
Slider, 150
"Small House of Uncle Thomas." *See The King and I*
Smalls, Charlie, 237, 239. See also *Miracles; The Wiz*
Smiles of a Summer Night. See Bergman
Smith, Harry Bache, 49, 110. See also *Robin Hood*
Smith, Oliver, 172
"Smoke Gets in Your Eyes." *See Roberta*
Smokey Joe's Café (Lieber and Stoller), 62
Sociedad Artística ("Artistic Society"), 21
Society of London Theatre. *See* Olivier Awards
Society of Stage Directors and Choreographers, 133, 166
Society of West End Theatre Awards, The. *See* Olivier Awards
"Soft Lights and Sweet Music." *See* Berlin
Soft-shoe, 81, 236
Soliloquy, 12, 67, 147, 151
"Soliloquy." *See Les Misérables*
Solo, 13
Solomon, Edward "Teddy," 35
"Some People." *See Gypsy*
"Someone to Watch Over Me." *See Oh, Kay!*
Something for the Boys (Porter), 129
"Something Just Broke." *See Assassins*
Something to Shout About (Porter): "You'd Be So Nice to Come Home To," 129

Sometime (Friml), 58
"Somewhere." See *West Side Story*
Sondheim Review, The, 288
Sondheim Society Newsletter, The, 288
Sondheim, Stephen, 92, 148, 174–75, 205–9, 219, 228, 242–46, 253–54, 280, 285–88, 296–97; Academy Award for "Sooner or Later" (*Dick Tracy*), 279; Composes too enthusiastically, 247; Effective lyrics, 175; Helps with *Hot Spot*, 193; Kennedy Center Award, 223; Mentored by Hammerstein, 173, 205; National Medal of Arts, 288; Opera vs. musical, 245; Promises Hammerstein to work with Rodgers, 209; Pseudonym (Esteban Ria Nida), 193; Pulls out of *Muscle*, 280; Unhappy with *West Side Story* lyrics, 174. See also *All That Glitters; Anyone Can Whistle; Assassins; Bounce; Climb High; Company; Do I Hear a Waltz?; Follies; The Frogs; A Funny Thing Happened on the Way to the Forum; Gypsy; High Tor; Into the Woods; A Little Night Music; Mary Poppins; Merrily We Roll Along; Pacific Overtures; Saturday Night; Side by Side by Sondheim; Sunday in the Park with George; Sweeney Todd; West Side Story*
Song and Dance (Lloyd Webber), 255, 264, 272; "Married Man," 255
Song cycle, 253, 255
Song form. See Form
Song of Norway, The, 91
Song of the King. See *Joseph and the Amazing Technicolor Dreamcoat*
"Song of the Vagabonds" (Musical Example 19). See *The Vagabond King*
Song-and-dance show, 24, 38–39, 42–43, 45, 102, 115, 120, 157, 192
Song-plugger, 66, 73, 97, 109, 236
Songs for a New World (Brown), 298
"Soon It's Gonna Rain." See *The Fantasticks*
"Sooner or Later (I Always Get My Man)." See Sondheim: Academy Award
Sophisticated Ladies (Ellington), 282
Soprano. See Voice type
Sorceror, The (Gilbert and Sullivan), 32
Soul. See Style
Sound of Music, The (Rodgers and Hammerstein), 114, 155, 156–58, 184, 191, 213, 302; "Do-Re-Mi" (Musical Example 33), 156, 161–63; "Edelweiss," 156; Musical episodes in, 156; "My Favorite Things," 158; Plot Summary, 159–60
Soundtrack recording, 157
Source music, 49, 76, 120
Sousa, John Philip, 50, 66, 99, 190; "Stars and Stripes Forever," 101
South Pacific (Rodgers and Hammerstein), 132, 148–50, 155, 158, 205; "Bali Ha'i" (Musical Example 31), 149–50, 153; "Carefully Taught," 150; "Cockeyed Optimist, A," 158; "I'm Gonna Wash That Man Right Out of My Hair," 150; Plot Summary, 152
Specialty act, 40, 45, 61–62
Spectacle. See Extravaganza
Spinning-wheel song, 44
Split stage, 272
Spoken dialogue, 6, 8, 16–17, 19, 21, 24, 38, 44, 69, 105, 142, 208, 245, 261, 263, 278, 295
Spousal abuse, 9, 147, 158
Spring is Here (Rodgers and Hart), 92
SRO. See Standing room only
St. Denis, Ruth, 61, 141
Stage (magazine), 272
Stage cue, 238
Stage lighting, 43
Stage set, 42–43, 51, 61, 81, 120, 137, 155, 207, 220, 245, 256, 260, 262,

272–73, 297; Problems with cell phones, 263
Stagehand, 32
"Standing on the Corner." See *Most Happy Fella, The*
Standing room only, 222
Stanislavsky, Constantin, 174
Star entrance, 72
Star turn, 63, 183
Star vehicle, 56–57, 63, 84, 123, 154, 168, 184, 198, 213, 222
Starlight Express (Lloyd Webber), 238, 255–56, 260, 264, 277; Plot Summary, 257–58; "Poppa's Blues" (Musical Example 54), 256, 258
Starobin, Michael, 280, 285, 287
"Stars and Stripes Forever." See Sousa
"Star-Spangled Banner, The," 64
State Fair (Rodgers and Hammerstein), 146, 302
"Steam Heat." See *The Pajama Game*
Stein, Joseph, 213–15, 237
Stein, Leo, 55
Steptoe, Andrew, 13
Stevens, Roger, 173–74
Stevenson, Robert Louis, *The Strange Case of Dr. Jekyll and Mr. Hyde*, 297
Stewart, Sandy, 219
Steyn, Mark, 92, 116, 209, 253
Stigwood, Robert, 230–31, 254
Stile rappresentativo. See Singing style
Stilgoe, Richard, 253, 255, 260–61
Stoker, Bram, *Dracula*, 298
Stoller, Mike: See *Smokey Joe's Café*
Stone, Fred, 51, 58
Stone, Peter, 201–2. See also *1776*
"Story of Chess, The." See *Chess*
Stothart, Herbert, 76
Straus, Oscar. See *The Chocolate Soldier*
Strauss, Johann (the Elder), 26–27, 91
Strauss, Johann (the Younger), 26–27, 91. See also *Die Fledermaus*
Stravinsky, Igor, 176
Streep, Meryl, 245
Streisand, Barbra, 184, 219, 240
Striggio, Alessandro, 1
Strike Up the Band (Gershwin), 98–99, 101; "Man I Love, The," 98; "Strike Up the Band," 98
Stritch, Elaine, 243
Strophe, 17
Strophic form. See Form
Strouse, Charles, 199. See also *Annie; Annie 2; Applause; Bring Back Birdie; Bye Bye Birdie; Dance a Little Closer; Rags*
Student Prince, The (Romberg), 58
Style: Barbershop, 190; Bluegrass, 287; Blues, 111, 200, 256, 263; Cabaret, 137, 219–20, 224, 288; Calypso, 229, 239; Country, 200; Country-western, 229, 256; Folk, 239, 287; Gospel, 185, 239, 295; Hip hop, 295; Jazz, 40, 61, 72, 80–82, 97–99, 101–2, 105, 111, 137, 173, 181, 185, 198, 200, 263, 295; Pop, 155, 223, 228–31, 237, 256, 261, 264, 280, 287, 296; Pop-rock, 200, 229–30; Ragtime, 40, 63, 73, 101, 104–5, 109, 213, 229–30, 263, 298; Rap, 191, 256, 277, 295; Rock, 4, 24, 31, 42, 111, 198, 200–1, 229–31, 237, 239, 245, 256, 260, 261, 277, 296, 298; Soul, 237; Techno-Rap, 277
Styne, Jule, 181–85, 209; Frank Loesser writes lyrics for, 184; Kennedy Center Award, 223; "Let It Snow! Let It Snow! Let It Snow!," 181; "Three Coins in a Fountain," 181; Writes for Hollywood, 279. See also *Bells are Ringing; Funny Girl; Gentlemen Prefer Blondes; Gypsy; Hallelujah, Baby!; High Button Shoes; The Red Shoes; Say, Darling; Subways Are for Sleeping*
Subdivision, 33; Compound, 33, 155, 244, 255, 296; Simple, 33, 56, 63, 106, 142

Subdominant, 191
Subways Are for Sleeping (Styne), 184
Succès d'estime, 198
Sullivan, Arthur, 6, 19, 21, 26, 31–35, 39, 49, 101, 136, 164; Carpet Quarrel, The, 35. See also *Cox and Box; H. M. S. Pinafore; Iolanthe; The Mikado; The Pirates of Penzance; Princess Ida; Ruddigore; The Sorceror; Thespis, or the Gods Grown Old; Trial By Jury*
Sullivan, Ed, 168
"Summertime." See *Porgy and Bess*
Sunday in the Park with George (Sondheim), 285
Sung-through, 24, 102, 229–30, 245, 255, 270, 277, 280, 282
Sunny (Kern), 77, 84
Sunny River, 143
Sunset Boulevard (Lloyd Webber), 253–54, 262–64, 277, 302; Plot Summary, 266–67; "With One Look" (Musical Example 56), 263, 267–68
Superman, 297
Superstition, 238
Suppé, Franz von, 26
"Supper Time" (Musical Example 23). See *As Thousands Cheer*
Surrey Enterprises. See Hammerstein, Oscar, II; Rodgers, Richard
"Surrey with the Fringe on Top, The" (Musical Example 29). See *Oklahoma!*
Suskin, Steven, 281
Swados, Elizabeth, 239
Sweeney Todd (Sondheim), 281; "Epiphany," 245; *Leitmotifs* in, 25; "Little Priest, A" (Musical Example 52), 245–46, 250–52; Plot Summary, 248–49
Sweet Adeline (Kern), 87
Sweet Charity (Coleman), 198, 302; "Big Spender," 198; "If My Friends Could See Me Now," 198
Sweet Smell of Success, The, 302
Sweethearts (Herbert), 59
Swerling, Jo, 184
Swift, Jonathan, 7
Swing rhythm, 99
Swingin' the Dream, 130
Syllabic. See Text setting
Syncopation, 40, 63, 80, 101, 106, 231

Tableau, 270
Tableau vivant, 285
Tacitus, 4
Take, 211
Tales of the South Pacific. See Michener
"Talk to the Animals." See *Dr. Doolittle*
Taming of the Shrew, The. See Shakespeare
Tamiris, Helen, 61
"Tammany," 101
Tammany Hall, 17
Tammany Society, 17
Tammany; or The Indian Chief, 17–18; "Alkmoonac" (Musical Example 5), 17–18, 138; Plot Summary, 18
Tap Dance Kid, The, 282
Tap-dance, 81, 165, 237, 243, 295
"Tarantara! Tarantara!" See *The Pirates of Penzance*
Taubman, Howard, 214
Taylor, James, 236
Taymor, Judith, 280
Tchaikovsky, Pyotr, 91
"Tea for Two" (Musical Example 20). See *No, No, Nanette*
Teagarden, Jack, 99
Techno-rap. See Style
Teddy and Alice, 238
Tell Me On a Sunday (Lloyd Webber), 253, 255
Tempest, The. See Shakespeare
Temple of Minerva, The, 17
Temple, Shirley, 181
Templeton, Fay, 45
Tempo, 8, 123; Accelerando, 26; Allegro, 9; Andante maestoso, 9; Largo, 243;

Moderato, 230, 296; Presto, 34, 243; Ritardando, 26
Tenderloin (Bock and Harnick), 213
Tenor. See Voice type
Ternary. See Form
Tesori, Jeanine, 299
Text expression, 3
Text setting, 26, 261; Melismatic, 26, 51, 56–57, 76, 104, 261; Syllabic, 26, 51, 56–57, 147
Texture: Homophony, 7, 8, 26, 50, 176, 220–21, 246, 272; Imitative polyphony, 7, 26, 183, 185, 220–22; Monophony, 7, 156, 159, 220–21; Nonimitative polyphony, 13, 26, 38, 56, 104, 109, 156, 176, 190, 243, 246, 272
The Threepenny Opera (Weill), 6
Theatre Guild, 91, 104, 114, 122, 136–37, 140–41, 146, 165, 191, 221
Theme, 102
Theme and variations. See Form
"There She Is." See *Titanic*
"There's No Business Like Show Business." See *Annie Get Your Gun*
Thespis, or The Gods Grown Old (Gilbert and Sullivan), 31
"They Can't Take That Away From Me." See Gershwin, George
"They Didn't Believe Me." See Kern
They're Playing Our Song (Hamlisch), 239
32-bar form. See Form: Song
This Is the Army (Berlin), 122; Original cast album, 122
Thompson, Lydia, 44
Thompson, Virgil, 105
Thomson, Lynn, 296
Thoroughly Modern Millie, 302
"Three B's, The (Musical Example 22)." See *On Your Toes*
"Three Coins in a Fountain." See Styne
"Three Little Maids from School." See *The Mikado*
Three Sisters, 143
Threepenny Opera, The (Weill), 136–38, 219, 238, 246; "Ballad of Mack the Knife, The (Moritat)" (Musical Example 28), 136–39, 288; *Leitmotifs* in, 25, 138; Plot Summary, 138–39
Three-rhyme, 116, 121
tick, tick . . . BOOM! (Larson), 297
Tierney, Harry, 58
Timbre, 11
Times Square, 65, 199
Tin Pan Alley, 61, 63, 66, 71, 80, 86, 91, 97, 105–6, 109–110, 114, 183–84
Titanic (Yeston), 281; "There She Is," 281
"To Keep My Love Alive." See *Connecticut Yankee*
Tommy (The Who), 230
"Tomorrow Belongs to Me" (Musical Example 46). See *Cabaret*
Tonadillas, 21
Tone color, 11
Tonic, 191, 243
"Tonight." See *West Side Story*
"Tonight (Quintet)" (Musical Example 37). See *West Side Story*
Tony Awards, 129, 133, 198, 214, 221, 255, 262, 273, 281, 298; *Aspects of Love* closed out of, 262; Best Musical, 133, 173, 184, 191, 194, 199, 202, 208, 213, 215, 221, 223, 231, 237, 239, 244–45, 262, 280–81, 288, 297, 302; *Chicago* closed out of, 222; First year of, 165; *Grease* closed out of, 239; *Gypsy* closed out of, 184; Ineligibility of concept albums, 230; Multiple, 133, 150, 155, 157, 185, 208, 215, 221, 231, 237, 239–40, 244–46, 263, 271, 273, 280–81, 285, 287–88, 295, 297, 298–99, 302; Nominated for, 193, 209, 281, 298; *Once on This Island* closed out of, 298
"Too Darn Hot." See *Kiss Me, Kate*
Top ticket price, 221, 271, 273

"Tornerai?" (Musical Example 1). See *The Coronation of Poppea*
Tosca (Puccini), 245
"Totem Tom-Tom." See *Rose-Marie*
Touring production, 43, 123, 150, 230, 240, 273, 277, 281, 297
"Toyland." See *Babes in Toyland*
"Tradition." See *Fiddler on the Roof*
Transformation scene, 42, 67
Traubner, Richard, 86, 167
Trentini, Emma, 56–57, 76
Trial by Jury (Gilbert and Sullivan), 31–32
Trill, 3, 17
Trilling, Lionel, 90
Trio. See Ensemble number
Trip to Chinatown, A (Harris), 62; "After the Ball," 66, 86, 89
Trip to Coontown, A, 62
"Trip to the Library, A" (Musical Example 44). See *She Loves Me*
Triple. See Meter
Triple Play Award, 255, 264
Trouble in Tahiti (Bernstein), 176
Troupe, 16
Trovatore, Il, 49
Trucks, 272–73
Trump, Donald, 273
Trunk song, 86, 182
"Try to Remember." See *The Fantasticks*
Tryout tour, 58, 80, 85, 98, 111, 114, 123, 141, 146, 157, 168, 182, 185–86, 192, 207, 209, 215, 263, 273, 277, 280–81, 288
Tucker, Sophie, 97, 129, 222
Tune, Tommy, 280, 281
Tuner, 114
Tunick, Jonathan, 244
Turn, 45
Twain, Mark, 92; *Huckleberry Finn*, 137
Twelfth Night. See Shakespeare
12-bar blues, 256
Two Gentlemen of Verona. See Shakespeare
Two-part form. See Form: Binary
Two-rhyme, 116

Ulvaeus, Björn, 277–79. See also *Chess; Mamma Mia!*
"Under the Sea." See *The Little Mermaid*
Underscoring, 86
Unison, 7, 175–76, 215, 255, 261
United Scenic Artists, 133
Unsinkable Molly Brown, The (Willson), 191
Urban, Joseph, 61
Urinetown (Hollman), 287, 299, 303

Vagabond King, The (Friml), 76–77, 91, 164; "Huguette Waltz," 77; "Love for Sale," 77; Plot Summary, 78; "Song of the Vagabonds" (Musical Example 19), 77, 79, 86
Valentino, Rudolf, 81
Variety, 87, 109, 114, 143, 205. See Vaudeville
Variety show, 45
Vaudeville, 45–46, 49–50, 61, 94, 207, 221, 236, 256; Circuit, 221; Dance styles, 94, 165; Dialect songs, 109;

Influence on *Chicago*, 222; Influence on *Very Good Eddie*, 70; Keaton's description of, 47; Similarity to *género chico*, 22; Similarity to minstrel show, 42
Verdi, Giuseppe, 24–27, 260. See also *Aida; Nabucco; Rigoletto*
Verdon, Gwen, 198, 221–22
Verismo, 25, 75, 97
Verse, 17, 56, 111, 115, 120, 142, 155, 166
Verse-chorus. See Form
Very Good Eddie. See Princess Shows
Very Warm for May, 143
Via Galactica (MacDermot), 201
Victor/Victoria, 297, 302
Viennese operetta. See Operetta: Viennese
Village Voice, 133
Virginia Minstrels, 38–39
Virtuoso/a, 3, 22
Vision song, 142, 167, 270, 296
Vittorio Emanuele, King of Italy, 24
Voice type: Alto, 4, 40; Baritone, 12; Bass, 8, 11–12, 40, 87, 148, 230; Coloratura soprano, 56; Countertenor, 4; Mezzo-soprano, 272; Soprano, 2, 3, 11–12, 40, 56, 75–76, 104, 260, 272; Tenor, 4, 12, 40, 49
Von Tilzer, Harry, 63, 66; "Good Morning, Carrie," 63. See also *In Dahomey*: "(I Wants to Be) A Actor Lady"
Von Trapp family, 156–57

Wagner, Richard, 22, 24–26, 34, 69, 76, 138. See also *Der Ring des Nibelungen*
Walk-around, 39–40
Walker, Aida Overton, 63
Walker, George, 62–63, 67
Waller, Fats, 281–82. See also *Ain't Misbehavin'*
Walsh, Michael, 230
Waltz, 20, 27, 44, 46, 55, 77, 82, 102, 147, 191, 209, 244–45; *Blue Danube, The*, 27; *Tales from the Vienna Woods*, 27; *Wine, Women, and Song!*, 27
Waltzes from Vienna, 91
Want song, 191
War of the Buffoons, The, 11
Warfield, William, 133
Washington, George, 17
"Watch Duet" (Musical Example 7). See *Die Fledermaus*
Watch Your Step (Berlin), 110
Waters, Ethel, 111
Watkins, Maurine Dallas, 221
Watts, Richard, Jr., 81, 221
"We Three Kings of Orient Are," 45
Weaver, Sigourney, 245
Webb, Clifton, 84
Weber, Joe, 56, 90
Weidman, John, 287
Weill, Kurt, 6, 107, 136–38, 219. See also *Knickerbocker Holiday; Lady in the Dark; Lost in the Stars; Love Life; The Threepenny Opera*
West End, 116; Domination by Lloyd Webber, 281; Imports from

America, 116; Lloyd Webber's record, 255; Oldest director, 92
West Side Story (Bernstein), 130, 173–76, 181, 191, 207, 244, 302; "America" (Musical Example 36), 174–75, 178–79, 207; Best Picture Oscar, 176; "Cool," 176; Dubbing in film, 155; "Dance at the Gym," 165; "I Feel Pretty," 174; "Maria," 176; Original title of (*East Side Story*), 173; Plot Summary, 177–78; "Somewhere," 176; "Tonight," 176; "Tonight (Quintet)" (Musical Example 37), 13, 175–76, 179–80
"What I Did for Love." See *A Chorus Line*
"What's the Use of Wond'rin'?" (Musical Example 30). See *Carousel*
What's Up? (Lerner and Loewe), 164
Wheeler, Hugh, 173, 244–45
"When I Lost You." See Berlin
"When Johnny Comes Marching Home," 45
"When You Believe." See *The Prince of Egypt*
"Where or When." See *Babes in Arms*
Where's Charley (Loesser), 184
Whistle Down the Wind (Lloyd Webber), 263
"White Christmas." See Berlin
White Crook, The, 43
White face, 193
White Fawn, The, 44
White Lilacs, 91
White, George. See *George White's Scandals*
White, Jane, 193
Whole Booke of Psalmes Faithfully Translated into English Metre, The, 16
"Whole New World, A." See *Aladdin*
Wicked (Schwartz), 51, 237
Wilbur, Richard, 173
Wild Party, The (LaChiusa), 298
Wild, Wild Women, 130
Wildcat (Coleman), 198; "Hey, Look Me Over," 198
Wilder, Billy, 253, 262
Wildhorn, Frank, 297–98; *Romantics, The* (albums), 297. See also *The Civil War; Dracula; Havana; Jekyll & Hyde; The Scarlet Pimpernel*
Wilkinson, Colm, 297
Will Rogers Follies, The (Coleman), 198
Williams, Bert, 61–63, 67, 205, 222
Williamson Music. See Hammerstein, Oscar, II; Rodgers, Richard
Willie Wonka and the Chocolate Factory, 297
Willson, Meredith, 185, 190–92. See also *The Music Man; The Unsinkable Molly Brown*
Winchell, Walter, 115
"Wintergreen for President." See *Of Thee I Sing*
"With One Look" (Musical Example 56). See *Sunset Boulevard*
Wiz, The (Smalls), 51, 237, 239, 269, 281
Wizard of Oz, The, 50–51, 58, 93, 121, 184, 237, 256

Wodehouse, P. G., 70, 90, 114, 231. See also *Anything Goes; Miss 1917; Princess Shows: Have a Heart; Leave It to Jane; Miss Springtime; Oh, Boy!; Oh, Lady! Lady!!; Oh, My Dear; Sitting Pretty*
Wolfe, George C., 295
Woman in White, The (Lloyd Webber), 263
Woman of the Year (Kander and Ebb), 223, 302
Wonderful Town (Bernstein), 173
"Wonderful, Wonderful." See Edwards
Wood, Natalie, 155
Word-painting, 87, 142
Words and Music, 122
Working, 181, 193, 236
Workshop, 207, 280, 282, 288, 296
"Wotan's Farewell." See *Der Ring des Nibelungen*
Wrong Boy, The (Russell), 281

Yaeger, Bessie Mae Sue Ella, 158
"Yankee Doodle," 16, 64
"Yankee Doodle Boy" (Musical Example 16). See *Little Johnny Jones*
Yeston, Maury, 280–81; *American Cantata, An*, 281. See also *Alice in Wonderland; Grand Hotel; In the Beginning: The Greatest Story Never Told; Nine; Phantom; Titanic*
Yiddish theater, 97
Yip, Yip, Yaphank (Berlin), 110, 122; "Oh! How I Hate to Get Up in the Morning," 110
"You Must Love Me." See *Evita*
"You Naughty, Naughty Men." See *The Black Crook*
"You'd Be So Nice to Come Home To." See *Something to Shout About*
"You'll Never Get Away From Me." See *Gypsy*
"You'll Never Walk Alone." See *Carousel*
Youmans, Vincent, 80; Collaborates with Caldwell, 58; Idolizes Kern's music, 73. See also *No, No, Nanette*
Young, Rida Johnson, 56, 58. See also *The Dream Girl; Maytime; Naughty Marietta; The Red Petticoat; Sometime*
Your Arms Too Short to Box with God (Grant), 239
Your Own Thing, 130
You're a Good Man, Charlie Brown, 230
"You're a Grand Old Flag." See Cohan
You've Got Mail. See *She Loves Me*

Zaks, Jerry, 272
Zapateado, 175
Zarzuela, 21–22
Ziegfeld, Florenz, 58, 61, 72, 85, 88, 110; *Follies*, 61, 70, 110, 112
Zimmerman, Ethel. See Merman, Ethel
Zipprodt, Patricia, 215, 221
Zorbá (Kander and Ebb), 221, 302
Zorba the Greek, 302